Prehistoric Lifeways

in the Great Basin Wetlands

Prehistoric Lifeways in the Great Basin Wetlands

Bioarchaeological Reconstruction and Interpretation

Edited by

Brian E. Hemphill

Clark Spencer Larsen

Foreword by

David Hurst Thomas

THE UNIVERSITY OF UTAH PRESS

Salt Lake City

LIBRARY OF CONGRESS CATALOGING-IN-PUBLICATION DATA

Prehistoric lifeways in the Great Basin wetlands : bioarchaeological
   reconstruction and interpretation / edited by Brian E. Hemphill,
   Clark Spencer Larsen : foreword by David Hurst Thomas.
      p.   cm.
   Includes bibliographical references and index.
   ISBN 0-87480-603-8 (alk. paper)
      1. Indians of North America—Great Basin—Antiquities. 2. Indians
   of North America—Anthropometry—Great Basin. 3. Human remains
   (Archaeology)—Great Basin. 4. Great Basin—Antiquities.
   I. Hemphill, Brian E. II. Larsen, Clark Spencer.
   E78.G67P74   1999
   979'.01—dc21   99-43317

In memory of
Carol J. Loveland and Christopher Raven
Esteemed colleagues, friends, and scholars
of the American Great Basin

Contents

Figures

Tables

Foreword

David Hurst Thomas

This volume brings forward a new perspective on the archaeology of the Intermountain West. The various authors describe their research on three newly discovered assemblages of ancient human remains from Nevada, Oregon, and Utah, the core region of the American Great Basin. These unprecedented finds have more than doubled the available sample of human remains from this vast and important region of the Americas. The skeletal assemblages were all excavated from wetland, lacustrine contexts. Each contributor explores some aspect of ancient lakeside adaptations of the Desert West and the papers reflect a healthy diversity of opinion.

Several authors discuss the relative merits of the so-called limnosedentary and limnomobile strategies in Great Basin wetland adaptations. Because considerable confusion still surrounds these two terms, I feel obliged to say something about their genesis.

Robert Heizer formally coined the term "limnosedentary" in a 1967 paper, but he had been developing the concept for decades. Having grown up in Lovelock, Nevada, Heizer was quite familiar with the massive array of wetland-related artifacts—fishing equipment, duck decoys, and other associated paraphernalia—excavated between 1914 and 1924 at Lovelock Cave. For three decades, Heizer directed his own excavations at Lovelock Cave and nearby sites in the Humboldt Sink. He was particularly impressed with the ecological potential of desert lakes and their margins.

Writing with L. K. Napton, Heizer argued that lacustrine resources "made possible" a residentially stable existence: "[I]t is obvious that the 'lacustrine biome' was far more productive of foods useful to man than was the vaunted Pinyon-Juniper zone of the upland or 'range' part of the Great Basin" (Heizer and Napton 1970:107). Not long thereafter, David B. Madsen (1982:207) extended Heizer's limnosedentary argument to the eastern Great Basin: "The Great Basin is characterized by rich riverine and lacustrine ecosystems, which form oases between areas of much more limited resources. . . . In some areas, such ecosystems were sufficiently sizable and productive to support large, stable populations throughout the year."

These investigators correctly emphasized the importance of a commonly overlooked aspect of Great Basin adaptations. But, I was conducting my own research in Great Basin lacustrine environments and several things bothered me about the limnosedentary argument as it was then phrased (see Thomas 1985):

- The normative emphasis on single-site archaeology (reflecting only cursory appreciation for other, nonlacustrine components in the overall settlement system);
- the lack of temporal focus and definition ("'limnosedentism' might well have lasted for only a few weeks or months at a time, and such episodes could have been separated by years, decades, or even centuries" [Thomas 1985:20]);
- emphasis on the alleged abundance and "high quality" of marsh resources (with only superficial concern for procurement, processing, and storage costs); and
- the failure to recognize the transitory nature of marsh and other wetland resources.

Attempting to broaden existing perceptions of lacustrine adaptations in the Great Basin, I coined the term "limnomobile" to open up the discussion about the residential and environmental stability implied in Heizer's initial definition of limnosedentism.

From the outset, the twin concepts were presented as "polar positions regarding the lakeside adaptation," to serve as heuristic devices to foster a broader discussion and to emphasize the variability and diversity evident in lacustrine adaptations. Even in the initial discussion of this dichotomy, I underscored "the bankruptcy of the extreme limnosedentary and limnomobile positions" (Thomas 1985:390), emphasizing instead the importance of studying the various fission-fusion strategies that once played out in these environments.

Although these distinctions have sometimes been distorted as "either/or polemics" (D. B. Madsen and Janetski 1990:1), the contributors to the present volume clearly appreciate the context within which these terms were presented and generally avoid the potholes of "either/or" thinking. In particular, the papers by Robert L. Kelly, Albert C. Oetting, and Steven R. Simms demonstrate the degree to which current models of various foraging strategies have transcended simple dichotomies of mobile/sedentary and good/bad places to live.

This volume concentrates on evidence obtained from the analysis of human skeletal remains, which is an extraordinary development that represents a significant departure from the formerly common practice of simply calling out a biological anthropologist to identify the bones after they were excavated. At best, a report prepared by this individual found its way into the publication as an appendix, without being integrated into the larger work. Not long ago, it was rare for archaeologists even to invite biological anthropologists to the site, much less to solicit advice about how best to expose and remove human remains from burial contexts.

The present volume shows how much a biological anthropologist can contribute as a key member of the excavation team. In many cases, biological anthropologists are skilled archaeological excavators in their own right, preferring to excavate personally the remains they would study. And very often, these bioarchaeologists undertake investigations that go far beyond the bones, as when mummified human tissue or human hair turns up in archaeological contexts. Furthermore, they found that, although it is possible to learn quite a bit about human diet from the study of these remains, they must also factor in the plant and animal remains recovered from the associated archaeological sites because this is another important source of information that can be used to cross-check and calibrate results obtained from human remains.

Over the years, various names have been proposed for an individual who did this work: osteoarchaeologist, human zooarchaeologist, biological archaeologist, and so forth. Here, we will follow Clark Spencer Larsen's self-description (1997) of "bioarchaeologist" to describe those who study the human biological component of the archaeological record. This volume highlights the importance of bioarchaeology, a relatively new discipline making important substantive and theoretical contributions to our understanding of the human past.

Although many archaeologists will find this volume a bit heavy on chemistry and biology, the central bioarchaeological concepts are not difficult to understand. The archaeological payoff is well worth the effort. Let me introduce briefly each of the major directions of inquiry.

One branch of bioarchaeology—paleopathology—studies the etiology and impact of ancient disease. The search for diseases of the past is hardly a new enterprise, but some disorders can now be placed in a more reliable biocultural matrix: for instance, the impact of anemia (and porotic hyperostosis, its skeletal manifestation) throughout the world. In this volume, Brian E. Hemphill proposes the use of osteoarthritis as reflecting patterns of mobility among ancient Great Basin populations in the Malheur Basin. Clark Spencer Larsen and Dale E. Hutchinson also find evidence of osteoarthritis and iron deficiency anemia, enabling them to situate the Stillwater Marsh skeletal series with other compatible North American foraging populations.

For years, ancient Great Basin subsistence practices were inferred mostly from food bones archaeologically excavated from domestic and refuse contexts. But determining the role of plant foods in ancient diets was largely a matter of guesswork since plant remains are only infrequently preserved in archaeological contexts.

Because researchers have established that stable carbon isotopes differentially reflect some kinds of plants, bioarchaeologists today can study past human diets by determining the ratios of carbon (and other) isotopes contained in human bone collagen. The first such "pathway," discovered in experiments with algae, spinach, and barley, converts atmospheric carbon dioxide into a compound with three carbon atoms. This C3 pathway is characteristic of sugar beets, radishes, peas, and wheat. A second pathway converts carbon dioxide from the air into a complex compound with four carbon atoms. This C4 pathway includes many plants from arid and semiarid regions, such as maize, sorghum, and millet—the cereal staples of the Americas and Africa. A third CAM pathway (an acronym for crassulacean acid metabolism) is found in succulents, such as cactus.

These findings proved to be critical to reconstructing past diets because human bone reflects the isotopic ratios of the various plants ingested by humans. Thus, by determining the ratios of carbon (and sometimes nitrogen) stable isotopes contained in bone collagen, bioarchaeologists can reconstruct the dietary importance of various kinds of plants and animals. In this volume, Joan Brenner Coltrain and Thomas W. Stafford, Jr., examine stable carbon isotope values in the Great Salt Lake wetlands skeletons, turning up (among other findings) intriguing sex-based differences in isotope levels (presumably reflecting significant dietary diversity).

Isotope studies depend heavily upon modern control samples. Margaret J. Schoeninger, for instance, has analyzed the isotopic composition for several Great Basin plant foods, including piñon pine; this botanical baseline enables her to explore its importance in ancient diets. Although stable carbon isotope analysis is just emerging from its developmental stage, it has already revolutionized the way in which archaeologists reconstruct prehistoric diets.

Another way to explore human diets is through the documentation of generalized stress responses in human hard tissue. Both the causes and the effects of malnutrition are complex and can rarely be traced precisely. So, instead, paleopathologists prefer to study the effects of stress, defined as any environmental factor that forces the individual or population out of equilibrium.

Stress has a behavioral impact that cannot be observed directly in archaeological skeletal samples. Instead past nutritional deficiencies can be inferred from the pattern and severity of the effects of stress on individuals as well as the distribution of that stress on the contemporary population. This approach views the degree of physiological disruption as dependent on both the severity of environmental stressors and the adequacy of host response.

A range of cultural factors—technological, social, and even ideological—can dampen the effect of stress on human populations. A particular nutritional constraint can, for instance, be overcome by (1) changes in technology that broaden (or intensify) the subsistence base, (2) social modifications that effectively distribute food to those in need, or (3) an ideology that rewards and reifies a sharing ethic. When insufficiently buffered, stress creates physiological havoc by disrupting growth, decreasing fertility and fecundity, triggering (or intensifying) disease, and, in some cases, causing death.

Numerous methods exist for evaluating the way in which environmental stress affects the growth, maintenance, and repair of the human skeleton. These techniques, when applied to skeletal remains from meaningful archaeological contexts, can be extraordinarily helpful for understanding the effects of nutritional stress among human populations in the past. Papers in this volume examine the evidence from Harris lines, bands of increased bone density, which are observable on X-rays of human long bones. They are often caused by a variety of nutritional (and other) stressors, especially severe episodes of dietary deprivation. Harris lines, which generally show up between birth and 18 years old, have been observed on dozens of archaeological samples, and are consistently associated with a shortened life-span.

Physiological stress is likewise reflected in dental hypoplasias, markers of growth arrest that are evident from gross examination and by looking at enamel in microscopic views. Not only does the presence of these enamel defects reflect a degree of physiological stress but also their size can be measured, allowing estimates of duration and/or severity of metabolic stress.

Greg C. Nelson argues that the frequency of such nonspecific indicators of physiological stress increases through time in the Malheur Lake wetlands population, perhaps in response to fluctuating environmental conditions.

Christopher B. Ruff explores evidence of mechanical forces on skeletal structure, noting particularly the robustness of the three Great Basin populations—Stillwater, Malheur, and Great Salt Lake—relative to other ancient North American populations studied by him. Jason R. Bright and the late Carol J. Loveland apply a similarly broad range of bioarchaeological techniques to the Great Salt Lake wetlands sample, documenting the degree of adaptive diversity in diet and behavior.

Today's technology also permits bioarchaeologists to analyze the past on an entirely different level. Calling upon the most recent developments in the field of genetic experimentation, so-called molecular archaeologists can now actually study the past at the level of the individual molecule. Molecular archaeology, and its counterpart, molecular biology, addresses the ultimate physiochemical organization of life, focusing particularly on the molecular basis of human inheritance. Although less than a decade old, molecular archaeology has already racked up some spectacular successes, providing unexpectedly precise answers to questions long explored through more conventional approaches. This volume exemplifies this research.

The bone recovered from the Great Salt Lake wetlands project provided nearly perfect conditions for a molecular approach to archaeology: large sample sizes, good preservation, and excellent dating (by AMS radiocarbon dating). The results, reported by Dennis O'Rourke, Ryan L. Parr, and Shawn W. Carlyle, reflect a mixed message. These authors discuss their difficulties in obtaining consistent results (which they believe is now a hallmark of ancient DNA research) and, not surprisingly, they push for even larger sample sizes. Still, O'Rourke and coworkers believe that their results confirm the early optimism regarding the potential for ancient DNA research. Frederika A. Kaestle, Joseph G. Lorenz, and David Glenn Smith have applied a molecular approach to the Stillwater Marsh sample of human remains. They frame several intriguing (and controversial) hypotheses to connect the ancient Stillwater population to surviving Native American populations.

The papers in this volume make it clear that fresh horizons of paleoenvironmental, behavioral, and bioarchaeological research condition the way in which American archaeologists view the past. And yet, the corridors of today's archaeological institutions echo with a strange new jargon: repatriation of patrimony, reburial of remains, and rights retained by concerned parties. In many ways, Americanist archaeology is today a profession under siege, and the ground rules governing the practice of modern archaeology are changing as rapidly as is the technology available to pursue such research.

Archaeologists have obvious motives for wishing to study human remains. We would like to understand Native American lifeways as part of the overall anthropological agenda: namely, to understand the diversity and variability of the human condition.

But today, many Native Americans oppose these scientific objectives. Many believe that archaeologists in particular have given science a bad name in the Indian world. They note with regret the remains of American Indians taken from the earth and deposited in museums. They accuse archaeologists of acting without respect, not to mention lack of reverence, toward these remains.

The sentiments have been clearly expressed by Scott Momaday (1996), Pulitzer Prize–winning Native American author:

> The violation of burial sites and the confiscation of human remains have been shameful and unprofessional. The boxes of human bones stacked in the Smithsonian Institution, often unidentified, virtually forgotten, are a sad reminder of this disrespect. . . . Indians have endured massacres, alcoholism, disease, poverty. The desecration of spiritual life has been no less an assault. Because the scientific scrutiny of human remains once interred in sacred ground is indelibly associated with this painful history, Native Americans will resist. They feel they must. At stake is their identity, their dignity and their spirit.

A century ago, this basic issue—esteem for the dead—underlay much of the resistance shown by native peoples to their forcible removal from their traditional lands. For instance, when federal troops forced Cherokee and Choctaw people to move from their southeastern U.S. homeland to Oklahoma, some families dug up and took the bones of their relatives along on the bitter "Trail of Tears." The ancestral bones were reburied after arrival in Oklahoma.

The Native American Graves Protection and Repatriation Act of 1990

(NAGPRA) reflects this concern with protecting Native American burial sites and returning certain sacred materials removed from Indian lands. NAGPRA covers five basic areas of concern:

- Protects Indian graves on federal and tribal lands;
- recognizes tribal authority over treatment of unmarked graves;
- prohibits the commercial selling of native remains;
- requires an inventory and (if requested by the tribal entity) repatriation of human remains held by the federal government and institutions that receive federal funding; and
- requires these same institutions to return inappropriately acquired sacred objects and other important communally owned property to native owners.

Most Indian people view this statute as an important initial step in reversing the transgression against Native Americans over the last 500 years and permitting the living to exercise traditional responsibilities toward the dead. The Native American community has become deeply involved in deciding what to do about the thousands of remains that resulted from the nineteenth-century practice of collecting Indian bones. NAGPRA also rocked the world of Americanist archaeology, forever changing the way we do business. Like it or not, all Americanist archaeologists must be aware of the legal and ethical implications for living people. For archaeologists, NAGPRA has become one of the major cultural resource management issues of the day.

At the most basic level, there is agreement: all archaeologists agree that the bones of known relatives should be returned to demonstrable descendants, no matter how concerned they are with preservation of scientific evidence. The disagreement comes over what is "demonstrable," and the specifics of the NAGPRA legislation are still being hammered out.

At issue here, of course, is our perception of human skeletal remains. The traditional archaeological perspective reflects long-standing social policy in this country, emphasizing the common heritage of the American citizenry. So viewed, the scientific community is responsible for understanding the human condition of all, including Indian peoples, ancient and living. By reburying skeletal remains, selected elements of the common heritage are being removed from the public domain.

Even today, a vocal minority of individuals view NAGPRA and the repatriation effort as the blatant destruction of archaeological collections. They urge archaeologists and biological anthropologists to stand up for their rights and duties as scientists. This argument holds that, as scientists, archaeologists and biological anthropologists are bound to an ethical system requiring honest reporting and preservation of the evidence. Repatriation and reburial efforts are viewed as censorship, undermining the ability of scientists to inspect the work of others for errors and misinterpretations—a procedure basic to all modern science.

Some believe that, 50 years from now, people will look back at NAGPRA and condemn the archaeological and museum community for its shortsightedness and for caving in to political and religious demands, allowing the destruction of irreplaceable scientific materials. They argue that human remains are vital scientific data and must remain in the public domain.

But many, perhaps most, in America's archaeological community seek to define a middle ground in the reburial and repatriation dispute. Passing judgment on anybody's values or beliefs is tricky business. But as long as people with very different religious beliefs and cultural backgrounds must coexist, some such assessment cannot be avoided. One of the key challenges for those charged with managing America's cultural resources is to find accommodations between the scientific and ethnic concerns.

Despite strong feelings on both sides of the repatriation issue, Indian groups and archaeologists are beginning to define common ground. This volume is an unambiguous statement that such conflicting aims can indeed be accommodated. Steven R. Simms and Anan W. Raymond discuss various repatriation issues relative to the three skeletal populations being considered in this volume. In fact, the three Great Basin wetlands projects reflect a newly emergent sense of cooperation that stands to facilitate similar research in other parts of the country (e.g., Dongoske 1996). Aside from the scientific merits of this substantive volume, this sense of cooperation, to me, is one of the most important and enduring contributions contained herein.

I

Bioarchaeological Perspectives on Precontact Lifeways in the Great Basin Wetlands

Brian E. Hemphill and Clark Spencer Larsen

Archaeological study of the aboriginal inhabitants of the Great Basin has a long history. Within only a few decades after Euramerican contact in the first half of the nineteenth century, the rich archaeological remains of this region of the Desert West began to play a key role in our understanding of the lifeways of precontact Native Americans. Yet, despite many archaeological excavations, skeletal analyses in this region have been few, which is unfortunate since skeletal analyses can provide important information about the ancestry and lifeways of past peoples. Until recently, skeletal remains recovered from the Great Basin have been either too few, too fragmentary, or too poorly documented to be of much use for serious scientific study. However, during the last decade this shortcoming has changed significantly for the better.

Abnormally high levels of precipitation and winter runoff over the course of several years during the early 1980s led to flooding of many wetland areas in the Great Basin of the western United States. The flooding peaked in 1985, and water levels began to decline, leading to erosion and exposure of many archaeological sites, artifacts, and human burials. Exposure of these antiquities to illegal collectors and other destructive processes prompted federal, state, and tribal authorities to solicit immediate documentation and analysis of the remains. Especially hit hard were three wetlands located in separate regions of the Great Basin—the Great Salt Lake wetlands of the eastern basin (Utah), the Stillwater Marsh wetlands of the Carson Sink in the western basin (Nevada), and the Malheur Lake wetlands of the northern basin (Oregon) (Figure 1.1).

Independent research teams conducted archaeological surveys of exposed sites in each of these wetlands areas. With permission from local Native American authorities, human remains were collected in the field and subjected to detailed

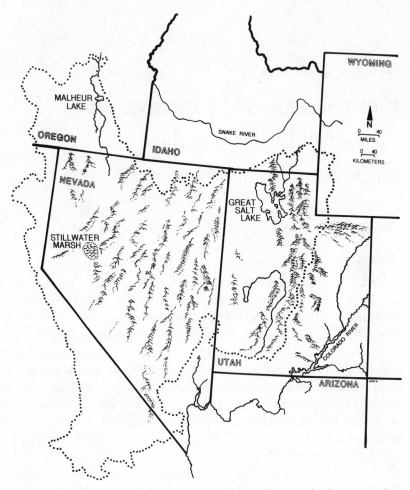

FIGURE I.I. The Great Basin of the western United States showing the three areas where skeletal remains were recovered. Boundaries of the Great Basin are depicted by dotted line.

analysis prior to repatriation. The human remains recovered as a result of these efforts more than doubled the number of known precontact human skeletal remains from this vast region of western North America. For some areas of the Great Basin, this is the first well-documented collection of remains even remotely representing a "population" sample (i.e., Stillwater Marsh). For the first time, relatively large samples of ancient human bones were available for study from scientifically excavated and well-provenienced archaeological contexts. Analyses of these remains provide a unique and previously impossible opportunity to gain new perspective on long-standing controversies in Great Basin prehistory.

UNIQUE INSIGHTS OFFERED BY BIOARCHAEOLOGY

Although much has been written on the lifeways of precontact populations of Great Basin wetlands environments, this reconstruction of lifeways has been based on archaeological remains, such as stone tools, plant remains, habitation structures, settlement patterns, and on the remains of animals dispatched as prey. Biological anthropologists have long been interested in fundamental issues raised by Great Basin archaeologists—that is, the nature of lifeways practiced by past peoples, the diets consumed by these populations, the types of adaptive strategies employed by a particular population, and the origins and history of living and past groups. Documentation of mobility and physical activity have been especially difficult for biological anthropologists, for mobility in particular represents only one factor behind the general activities that are reflected in human skeletal remains. Nevertheless, several recent breakthroughs in skeletal analysis permit insight into the types and intensities of mobility practiced by hunter-gatherers of Great Basin wetlands. In this regard, biomechanical analysis assesses differential strengthening of the long bones in order to understand the nature and intensities of stresses habitually encountered by individuals. When combined with theoretical developments in the issue of mobility, a careful analysis of the prevalence and velocity of osteoarthritic affliction among adult males and females permits a reconstruction of different types of mobility as well as an assessment of general levels of biomechanical stress and articular joint loading.

Some of the most compelling research in recent years in biological anthropology involves the reconstruction of past dietary patterns. Biological anthropologists have increasingly turned to analyses of stable carbon and nitrogen isotopes for information on the types of foods consumed by past populations. Not only do such analyses yield valuable insight into the dietary regime of a past population but also age and individual variation is potentially identified. In addition to the fund of data provided on diet, inferences can also be made regarding nutritional adequacy. A general lack of iron in the diet may be manifested by a classic skeletal syndrome known as porotic hyperostosis. General insufficiency of diet may lead, along with other factors, to nonspecific systemic stress. Such stresses may be indicated by the presence of linear enamel hypoplasia in the dentition. Infections may be manifested as periosteal reactions in the skeleton.

Recent advances in genetic research now make it possible to extract diagnostic protein and genetic material—DNA—from ancient tissues. The ability to extract this information from human bones recovered from archaeological contexts permits biological anthropologists to address questions concerning the ancestry of past populations in ways unthinkable just a few years ago. Comparisons of mitochondrial (mt) DNA lineages and protein-coding loci can now be used to address key questions concerning the biological history of the precontact populations of the Great Basin. These questions include not only the larger issues surrounding the peopling of the New World but also whether the appearance and distribution of Numic languages in the Great Basin was accompanied by population movements as well.

This volume serves to illustrate the variety and depth of contributions that bioarchaeologists are currently making in understanding the foraging strategies, diet, health, and population history of the precontact hunter-gatherers in the Great Basin of western North America. The chapters emphasize the diversity of stresses and adaptive strategies employed by individuals residing within each of these wetlands environments.

VOLUME ORGANIZATION

This book began as an effort to share information and address common research issues across the three regions of the Great Basin from which large skeletal collections became available during the last decade. As editors of the volume, we invited the members of research teams working in the Stillwater Marsh, the Great Salt Lake, and the Malheur Lake wetlands to present their research findings in a symposium entitled "Great Basin Bioarchaeology: Desert Wetlands Adaptations" at the annual meeting of the Society for American Archaeology held in Anaheim, California, in 1994. From the outset, we envisioned this project as a crucial step in establishing a bioarchaeological research agenda, which would inform our understanding of prehistoric native groups in the Great Basin. By bringing together the biological anthropologists and archaeologists working in each of the three areas, we felt that bioarchaeological investigations in the Great Basin could avoid several key problems that have plagued similar inquiry in other regions of the world. Specifically, we hoped to avoid the problems of (1) noncomparable analyses by separate research teams, (2) myopic interpretations based on studies of skeletal samples from a single ecological context, and (3) improper considerations of important research hypotheses due to a lack of communication between archaeologists and biological anthropologists.

The volume is organized into six parts. First, Simms and Raymond outline the difficulties and successes incurred when anthropologists and federal, state, and Native American authorities must agree on the appropriate way to deal with the sudden exposure, analysis, and subsequent reinterrment of precontact Native American human remains. The research was facilitated by the close cooperation of these various interests.

In the second part, the archaeological context and bioarchaeological studies for the Great Salt Lake region are presented. Simms sets the stage for bioarchaeology in the Great Salt Lake wetlands by highlighting the adaptive diversity and demographic flow among forager and farmer lifeways reflected by the variety of lithic and ceramic artifacts encountered in the Great Salt Lake wetlands. Coltrain and

Stafford explore dietary diversity among the inhabitants of the Great Salt Lake wetlands via stable isotopic analysis of human bone samples, presenting important temporal and spatial variability. O'Rourke and co-workers provide an assessment of four mtDNA markers among the precontact inhabitants of the Great Salt Lake wetlands and seek to address the issue of Anasazi incursions from the Southwest into the Great Basin and how such incursions may help explain the appearance and demise of the northern Fremont culture. Bright and Loveland conclude this part by evaluating the health status of precontact inhabitants of the Great Salt Lake wetlands through consideration of a broad array of skeletal pathological conditions.

The third part presents the bioarchaeology of the Stillwater Marsh. The archaeological context is presented by Kelly, who raises key issues about the various costs and benefits incurred by different foraging strategies employing various combinations of residential and logistical foraging to procure wetlands and upland resources. Schoeninger utilizes isotope analysis to determine the relative importance of upland versus marsh resources for providing the dietary staples relied upon by the precontact inhabitants of the Carson Sink. Kaestle and coworkers utilize albumin phenotypes and a characteristic 9 base pair (9 bp) deletion and other variation in mtDNA from both ancient and modern Native Americans to address the Numic expansion issue, long-debated among Great Basin archaeologists and anthropologists, with specific reference to the precontact inhabitants of the Stillwater Marsh wetlands. Larsen and Hutchinson then provide an assessment of dietary stress in the Stillwater Marsh wetlands through their examination of enamel defects (hypoplasias) in the permanent dentition, porotic hyperostosis in the cranium, and periosteal reactions on major skeletal elements. This chapter also provides an insight into levels of mechanical stresses experienced by Stillwater Marsh individuals through an assessment of osteoarthritis prevalence and pattern.

In the fourth part, the bioarchaeology of the Malheur Lake wetlands is presented. Oetting provides the archaeological context and contrasts two ethnographic models based on the Wada'tika Northern Paiute and the Klamath to evaluate the applicability of these ethnographic models for explaining Malheur wetlands use in the Harney Basin of southeastern Oregon. Nelson provides an assessment of physiological stresses encountered by the prehistoric inhabitants of the Malheur Lake wetlands through analysis of enamel defects and infectious periosteal reactions in skeletal remains. Nelson also seeks to explain changes in physiological stress resulting from changing environmental circumstances. Hemphill evaluates diversity of mobility patterns practiced by Great Basin wetlands inhabitants through a comparison of osteoarthritis prevalence and progression.

The fifth part addresses behavioral and activity diversity based on structural morphology. Ruff provides an alternative methodology to the osteoarthritis analyses presented for the three regions by undertaking an ambitious biomechanical study of long bones from the Stillwater Marsh, Great Salt Lake, and Malheur Lake wetlands in order to characterize levels and types of activities engaged in by precontact inhabitants. This broad-scale analysis reveals a commonality in activity and behavior across the three settings of the Great Basin, yet with some important differences.

Lastly, Bettinger presents a synthetic overview of Great Basin wetlands bioarchaeology, assessing the role of the study of human remains in the archaeology of this pivotal region of the American West. He takes special note of the general trends and specific variability in diet, population history, and activity patterns of the precontact inhabitants of the three Great Basin wetlands, underscoring the fact that our understanding of lifeways and adaptation is advanced by this new and rich bioarchaeological data set.

CONCLUSION

We regard this book as a beginning point for the broader consideration of human biology in reaching an understanding of prehistoric foraging adaptations and population history in the Great Basin. Collectively, the contributors show that while there are some features shared by populations from the three regions, there is a high degree of variability which is best understood in light of local factors, especially regarding diet, degree of mobility, and health and life-style in general. A basic finding that is beginning to emerge from this work is the indication of generally robust health among Great Basin populations, but in a harsh setting involving heavy physical demands and a high degree of mobility. The work is beginning to put flesh on the bones of native ancestors in this vast and important region. The findings presented in this volume make clear that a consideration of bioarchaeological lines of evidence provide a compelling picture of lifeways and population history of Great Basin native peoples in ways made possible only through study of their mortal remains.

Acknowledgements

First and foremost, we thank the Northwestern Band of the Shoshoni Nation, the Fallon-Shoshone Tribe, and the Burns Northern Paiute Tribal Council for granting permission to analyze human remains recovered from the Great Salt Lake, Stillwater Marsh, and Malheur Lake wetlands, respectively. Without their patience, concern, and cooperation, none of this research would have been possible. We extend our thanks to the contributors who stuck with us through the long process of transforming meeting presentations into book chapters. We thank M. Anne Katzenberg for helping out in the review process. The comments of two anonymous reviewers were extremely helpful in contributing to improving the organization and clarity of the book overall. Thanks are also extended to key funding agencies, especially the National Science Foundation (Simms, Kaestle, Kelly,

Larsen, Schoeninger, Ruff, O'Rourke), National Institutes of Health (Kaestle), Wenner-Gren Foundation (O'Rourke), State of Utah, State of Nevada, U.S. Bureau of Reclamation, Utah State University, University of Utah Research Committee (O'Rourke), Northern Illinois University Graduate School (Larsen), University of Wisconsin Alumni Research Foundation (Schoeninger), and U.S. Fish and Wildlife Service for financial and logistical support. A project like this is made possible only by working with a supportive editor and press. In this regard, we thank Jeff Grathwohl and the University of Utah Press for their help in the project, beginning with the proposal and concluding with the finished book.

2

No One Owns the Deceased!
The Treatment of Human Remains from
Three Great Basin Cases

Steven R. Simms and Anan W. Raymond

The human remains enabling the studies in this volume are from three cases: Stillwater Marsh, Nevada, Great Salt Lake, Utah, and the Malheur Lake, Oregon (See Figure 1.1). Each case is distinct not only in location but also in timing of the appearance of the human remains, the subsequent consultation process, the cast of players, and the resolutions pursued. Collectively, however, these remains are noteworthy from two very different anthropological vantages. From an educational vantage, they more than double the amount of prehistoric human skeletal remains known from the Great Basin and have greatly added to our understanding of ancient life. They appear at a time when significant advances in analytical capability are being achieved. From the very different vantage point of a reflexive anthropology struggling with its own cosmology, the human remains were brought into public view by the serendipity of climatic and geological forces at a time when a national conversation about cultural patrimony was taking place. Out of this combination of the natural and the cultural arises a potential to discuss some philosophical issues prompted by the three cases. In approaching these issues, we make several arguments: burials cannot be owned—by American Indians or anyone else; local solutions are more consistent with the principles of democratic process than national or state regulatory mandates (including NAGPRA—the Native American Graves Protection and Repatriation Act of 1990); we must concur with the result of local solutions regardless of whether we live in unenlightened times, but we must also seek solutions now that do not vitiate our options should we find ourselves in a more enlightened future.

With the passage of time, the distinctiveness of these and other individual cases of cultural patrimony will surely fade. What will be remembered are the decisions that resulted from this national conversation, whether those decisions were

cognizant that future political contexts and cultural constructions will surely devi-
ate from those of the present and whether the underlying issues of principle were
raised, acted upon, or sacrificed for the expedience of the present.

DIFFERENT CIRCUMSTANCES, DIFFERENT SOLUTIONS

Observers of the Great Basin, from John Frémont, to Mark Twain, to Wallace Stegner, have remarked on the unpredictability and fluctuation found in the
region's climate. True to its reputation, the Great Basin climate caused once-buried
human remains to be exposed at the surface in three cases, at different times, but
within the same decade.

Exposure and Discovery

Stillwater, Nevada, was first. Deep snowpack in the mountains of northern
and central Nevada and California's Sierra Nevada in 1983–85, coupled with valley
rainfall, swelled the Carson and Humboldt Rivers to their highest levels in
recorded history. Lacking an outlet to the sea, the rivers poured into the usually
dry Carson Sink. Stillwater Marsh, a 35,000-acre maze of islands, tules, and water,
lies at the southern margin of the Carson Sink. Water surged into the marsh transforming it into a vast but shallow lake. Wind-driven ice rafts and waves scoured
landforms and killed vegetation. In the summer of 1985 the high water began to recede. The emerging landscape revealed dozens of archaeological sites, each sec-
tioned horizontally by the flood. Human remains were scattered across the sites.

Great Salt Lake, Utah, was next. The 1980s turned out to be a wet decade. The
Stillwater floods were over, but in areas that historically supported lakes, waters
did not peak until 1987–88. In the spring of 1987, the Great Salt Lake reached its
highest level in recorded history. Fed by four moderate-sized rivers and a host of
streams emanating from the Wasatch Mountains, the eastern shores of the lake,
like Stillwater, constitute a mosaic of wetland habitats. There are slow moving
sloughs, ponds, tules, and stringers of slightly elevated ground on the natural levees bordering relict and active channels. Like Stillwater, the high ground was
planed by ice and waves; channels were filled in; vegetation was killed; and as the
lake receded, archaeological sites were exposed. Erosion continued as the ground
dried into a diffuse alkali dust that was soon blown into the mountains, causing
the ground surface to deflate, in some cases over 15 cm in two years. The surface
was scattered with human remains, and more appeared as deflation proceeded.

The effects of Great Basin climate on the land are predominately time-space
transgressive, and the floods of the 1980s were no exception. Malheur Lake, like
the Carson Sink and the Great Salt Lake, has no outlet to the sea. Above-average
precipitation caused Malheur Lake to rise to a historic record high and more than
double its surface area. Water inundated a vast network of islands and miles of

shoreline. Ice and wave erosion removed vegetation and topsoil. When the water finally began receding in 1988 and 1989, it revealed over 35 habitation sites, many containing human burials (Oetting 1990b).

Responses

The response in each case was as local as the climate, but shared a concern among all parties involved that something "right" should be done. Again, Stillwater Marsh, which is managed by the U.S. Fish and Wildlife Service (FWS), was in the lead. As soon as the water receded from the archaeological sites and burials in summer 1985, artifact collectors roamed the sites. Erosion and effervescence of the alkaline marsh soils damaged the burials and transformed archaeological contexts. There was a small uproar. Members of the local chapter of the Nevada Archaeological Association and archaeologists across the state expressed concern over the situation. The neighboring Fallon Paiute–Shoshoni tribe wanted their ancestors and heritage protected. The news media clamored for stories and pictures. The Nevada State Historic Preservation Office (SHPO) and Advisory Council on Historic Preservation looked to the FWS for a solution. With the help of the Nevada State Museum and SHPO, the FWS verbally enlisted the support of the Fallon tribe for collection, limited excavation, an unspecified level of analysis, and some sort of reinterment. The Nevada State Museum coordinated an extraordinary effort by professionals and volunteers to salvage the human remains (Tuohy, Dansie, and Haldeman 1987), while the FWS increased law enforcement and public education. By September 1986, over 4,000 human bones were collected from the surface of archaeological sites in Stillwater Marsh. The bones came from 144 relatively intact burials and 272 individuals whose remains had been scattered by the flood waters. These 416 individuals from Stillwater Marsh exceeded the total burials previously recovered in the state of Nevada (S. T. Brooks, Haldeman, and Brooks 1988). The bones were held in temporary curation by the Nevada State Museum.

Avocational archaeologists from the Utah Statewide Archaeological Society were the first to observe and record the human remains along the Great Salt Lake in the fall of 1987 and spring of 1988. They covered the exposed human remains with plastic and soil, and recorded their locations. In summer 1988 the Utah Division of State History organized several meetings of all possible participants, but consensus to recover the human remains was slower than at Stillwater and Malheur for two reasons. The closest American Indian tribal affiliations were the Ute, with headquarters in northeastern Utah, and the Northwestern Band of the Shoshoni Nation, at that time headquartered in Fort Hall, Idaho. Historic records indicate both had resided in the Great Salt Lake area. It seemed likely that consultation would ultimately be with the Shoshoni, but the proximity of the Ute demanded their inclusion. Also, while most of the human remains were found on State of Utah lands, federal lands managed by the U.S. Bureau of Reclamation and the FWS were also potentially involved and the extent of the problem was unknown. These factors required the coordination of several interested parties and led to systematic reconnaissance along much of the entire eastern shore of the Great Salt Lake in 1989 (Metcalfe and Shearin 1989; Russell et al. 1989; Simms et al. 1990). The recovery of human remains required further consultation and fund raising, and ultimately proceeded in 1990 via state funds, university field programs, and public programs (Simms et al. 1991). The U.S. Bureau of Reclamation conducted a survey in 1991 (Baker et al. 1992) and recovered the human remains in 1992 (Fawcett and Simms 1993). All of the remains were held in temporary curation by Utah State University. In all, a minimum number of 85 individuals were recovered.

Malheur Lake, Oregon, like Stillwater Marsh is managed by the FWS. The exposure of burials in the late spring of 1988 at Malheur came quickly on the heels of the experience at Stillwater, so response was prompt. However, the extreme isolation of the Malheur area afforded an atmosphere in which events transpired and decisions were made with far fewer exigencies than in the Stillwater Marsh and Great Salt Lake cases. The FWS turned to the Burns Paiute, whose ancestors once lived on the islands and shores of Malheur Lake (Whiting 1950). Consultation was achieved simply, and by a few people from each organization, although all decisions were subject to standard tribal and FWS protocol. The FWS and Burns Paiute formulated, in relatively relaxed settings, goals and procedures for the archaeological sites and burials with little participation by outside organizations. Verbal consultation quickly established a procedure where exposed burials were covered with plastic sheeting and soil while isolated human bone was collected. An October 1989 interim agreement allowed removal of 15 known burials and temporary curation at the Oregon State Museum of Anthropology. The parties agreed on a final memorandum of understanding in 1990 that called for removal and analysis of all burials as they eroded out of Malheur Lake through 1992. In all, archaeologists retrieved the remains of 50 individuals from 42 graves, as well as hundreds of scattered bones from sites in Malheur Lake (Hemphill 1992a, 1992b, 1992c).

Solutions

A consistent theme underlying all three cases was the goal of the archaeological community and the land managing agencies to include American Indian voices. In retrospect, there was never a question as to whether the remains would be repatriated, only a struggle with what this meant. The scientific value, and by extension, the long-term public and educational values were kept in view throughout the consultation process. The sacred quality, and by extension, the emotional import of the burials and bones drove the consultation process as well. This dualistic philosophy is consistent with an underlying assumption that the remains of the deceased cannot be owned by anyone.

In two of the cases, Stillwater Marsh and Great Salt Lake, repatriation into burial chambers was sought and achieved. In this way, the desire for an ethical interment of the remains was balanced with long-term public interests by holding open the possibility of future access. At Malheur, the burials were reinterred into graves in an isolated and protected plot of open ground with no possibility of future analysis.

At Stillwater Marsh the interested parties initially held, as one might expect, vastly different views on how human remains should be treated. A characterization of those views is familiar to many. On the one hand, there are those who believe the bones contain valuable information and should be analyzed and curated like other scientific data. On the other hand, there are those who believe that the bones are sacred and ancestral to the local tribes. Fortunately, the issue did not become as polarized as is often portrayed in today's popular press. There were many from both camps willing to listen to a supposed adversary and recognize the legitimacy of the opposing view.

Consultation over the Stillwater remains began in 1985. Verbal agreements and written interim agreements (which implemented various treatments of the burials) were eventually codified in the October 1988 "Memorandum of Understanding on Human Remains among the U. S. Fish and Wildlife Service, the Nevada State Historic Preservation Office, and the Fallon Paiute–Shoshoni Tribe" (MOU). Although the tribe and FWS were the primary negotiators, the Nevada SHPO, the Nevada Indian Commission, and professional archaeologists and anthropologists from other Nevada universities and institutions contributed significantly throughout the consultation process. The Nevada State Museum played a key role not only in salvage archaeology and as temporary curation facility but also as a champion of Nevada's cultural heritage.

The Stillwater MOU was negotiated and implemented before the advent of NAGPRA. The prevailing wisdom of the time was contained in the Archaeological Resources Protection Act (ARPA) and the Department of Interior Guidelines for the Disposition of Archaeological and Historical Human Remains (DOI 1982). Specifically, ARPA indicated that human remains are "archaeological resources." And, coming from federal land, the Stillwater bones were property of the federal government. Thus, the government had certain responsibilities for the treatment of the remains, including consulting with those who had an affinity with the remains. Although the government asserted sovereignty, the consulting parties and a whole community of Nevadans recognized that the Stillwater burials transcended mere "archaeological resources" and Department of Interior guidelines. The issue wasn't about ownership so much as it was about mutual respect and a sense for the common good.

The Stillwater MOU represents a compromise by consensus. The document asserts a philosophy that the appropriate treatment of human remains requires a responsible balance between respect for the deceased, respect for the feelings of the descendants of the deceased, and the interests of science. The MOU specifies criteria and procedures for recovery, curation, analysis, reporting, and reburial. It passively assumes a cultural relationship between the burials and the historical Paiute residents of the area, but makes no statement affirming or denying a genetic connection or a relationship presuming knowledge of historical continuity. The procedures that guided the recovery of remains from the 1983–85 flooding were encoded into the MOU, and they continue to guide the treatment of additional remains which have come to light and those which will surely come to light in the future. Remains are removed when more than 50 percent of the in situ elements are exposed. If remains do not meet this criteria, they are covered with plastic and earth and left in place. Artifacts spatially associated with the burials are treated as grave goods and are subject to reinterment, although the depositional conditions create an ambiguity in the archaeological contexts. Analyses include all observational techniques, but substance analyses are limited to skeletal elements recovered in a damaged or broken condition.

The Fallon Paiute–Shoshoni Tribe wanted the remains to be reinterred at their location of discovery, which was impractical because of erosion, the high water table, and the possibility of future flooding or vandalism. So the consulting parties decided on a single, mass grave. The dual recognition of the spiritual and the scientific values of the remains, as well as the likelihood that additional remains would come to light in the future, prescribed the construction of a burial chamber at the Stillwater National Wildlife Refuge. The chamber called for in the Stillwater MOU was a 12'×10'×30' underground structure of concrete. The interior was lined with shelves upon which rest 1'×1'×2' redwood caskets containing the human remains. The contents of the burial chamber are tagged and cataloged. After the remains and the documentation were placed inside, traditional Paiute ceremonies consecrated the burial chamber. Then, in November 1988, the double steel door was closed and a bulldozer pushed boulders and earth over the structure. Two locks secured the door—the key to one held by the FGWS and the other by the Fallon Paiute–Shoshoni Tribe.

The MOU calls for future access to the chamber to add more remains as fluctuating water levels at Stillwater Marsh continue to erode bones from archaeological sites. However, a recently scheduled reopening of the chamber in 1996 was canceled at the eleventh hour when the National Park Service informed the FWS that reinterring additional remains without exercising the NAGPRA process was inappropriate. The Stillwater MOU yielded in order to accommodate NAGPRA, and, a year later, the Fallon tribe and the FWS reopened the chamber and re-interred the additional human remains. It was somewhat disconcerting that a hard-earned process agreed to by the local community of Indians and archaeolo-gists was upset by a distant far-off agency and *post hoc* rule.

The Stillwater MOU also specifies a process for gaining access to the chamber to conduct additional research on the remains. Research proposals must submit to a scientific peer review process and, if successful, are then reviewed by the FWS and the tribe. The final decision on approval of proposals rests with the tribe. Since the signing of the MOU a couple of proposals for additional substance analysis were informally considered—trail balloons of a sort—but were not pursued.

The exposure of human remains at Malheur Lake came just as resolution was being achieved at Stillwater Marsh. Flushed with experience at Stillwater and seiz-ing continuity, the FWS pursued at Malheur a similar course for the treatment of human remains. But as mentioned earlier, the atmosphere of consultation and ul-timately the solution was different. Verbal and written agreements implemented in 1988 and 1989 were eventually finalized in a November 1990 Memorandum of Understanding on Human Remains among the FWS, the Oregon State Historic Preservation Office, and the Burns Paiute Tribe (Malheur MOU). As at Stillwater, the Malheur MOU identified the spiritual and the scientific value of prehistoric human remains. It specified similar procedures for the recovery of remains and their curation. Scientific analysis included detailed observational studies, CAT scans, and radiocarbon dating.

The Burns Paiute Tribe, like the Fallon Paiute–Shoshoni Tribe at Stillwater, wanted the remains reinterred at their location of discovery, which was similarly impractical. So a site safe from flooding and erosion was selected. Significantly different, however, the Malheur bones would be reinterred into individual graves in the ground at a site. The human remains were cataloged, labeled, wrapped in muslin, and placed in graves grouped according to the site from which they were recovered. After traditional Paiute ceremonies to consecrate the site and the re-interments, a map was made of each grave as to its contents and a single basalt boulder was placed at each one. At Malheur, there are no provisions for future ac-cess, only the interment of additional burials should the need arise.

As mentioned previously, the isolation of Malheur Lake colored the decisions over the human remains found there. The closest town and seat of Harney County is Burns—population 4,000 and 30 miles from Malheur Lake. Harney County sprawls over 10,000 square miles of sagebrush, yet only 7,100 people live there. The city of Portland, the populous Willamette Valley, the state capitol, most of the universities, the news media, as well as archaeologists and Indians are a six-hour drive and a world away. Consultation occurred chiefly among two FWS archaeol-ogists, a consulting physical anthropologist, and the Burns Paiute tribal staff, officials, and elders. Everybody embraced the spiritual and scientific importance of the burials. However, use of a burial chamber was discarded as an option for reinterment. Detailed scientific analyses of the remains was mandated, and after the bones served the needs of science, they would be reburied in the ground. A compromise was struck whereby the bones would give their information to the community and then the community would give the bones back to the earth.

The Great Salt Lake case took a decidedly different course, although the outcome, repatriation in a burial chamber with the possibility of future interment and study, was similar to the Stillwater Marsh case. Most of the remains were largely from state lands, with the smaller number from federal lands recovered several years after most of the collection had been made. Initially, consultation was similar to the Stillwater case, and there were various meetings of the interested parties and the usual diversity of perspectives, but there was a willingness to hear contrasting views. The ultimate course of consultation was set, however, by two factors: a special legislative bill to fund the initial recovery of the remains and a decision by the governor to appoint a task force, the Governor's Committee on Reburial, to write a law addressing American Indian graves and repatriation concerns. Thus, the Great Salt Lake case initiated the development of a Utah version of the federal Native American Graves Repatriation Act, which caused the consultation specific to the Great Salt Lake case to become embedded in what became a statewide issue involving all Utah tribes. Thus, a local situation not only drove the general statewide process but also in turn was influenced by nonlocal forces. This complicated process is described elsewhere (Simms 1993).

The State of Utah Native American Grave Protection and Repatriation Act was passed in 1992 and instituted a standing committee, the Native American Remains Review Committee (NARRC) under the aegis of the Utah Division of Indian Affairs. This committee continues to meet to develop regulations, most of which have not been subject to application or test. Legislative action leading to the construction of a burial chamber waited until 1993, and the chamber, planned as a statewide facility, was completed in 1996.

The remains were recovered, analyzed, and taken into temporary curation well prior to the passage of the state law. Instead of a memorandum of agreement as at Stillwater and Malheur, decisions about the Great Salt Lake case either took place in the meetings of the Governor's Committee on Reburial or were made informally via consultation between the Utah Division of State History, the principal investigator for the archaeological work, and the tribal council of the Northwestern Band of the Shoshoni. The decision to permit scientific analysis took the form of a legal memorandum negotiated by the principal investigator conducting the archaeology and voted on by the tribal council. The memorandum constituted permission for analyses to be included in grant proposals to funding agencies. It was signed only by the tribal council chair and tribal legal council. Observational analyses were permitted and a subsample of mostly fragmentary bone was segregated for substance analyses. The remains were placed under temporary curation at Utah State University.

As at Stillwater and Malheur, there was a strong desire for the remains to be reinterred close to the point of discovery. A consensus seeking a burial chamber was achieved by 1990, but subsequent debate and the complications of working across state agencies caused delays. These impediments were finally resolved when two state legislators became involved as advocates for the construction of a burial chamber in Salt Lake City, on lands administered by the Utah Division of State Parks. The goal was to have a burial chamber where remains from around the state could be repatriated, but the degree to which this approach would be successful remains unclear because, even though tribes were "consulted," they were not engaged in the decision-making process for the chamber. Tribes generally desire remains to be reinterred close to "home."

The Great Salt Lake case indicates the complications that can arise, despite the best of intentions, when the decision making becomes disengaged from those already working toward a local solution and becomes embedded in various levels of government. Perhaps on the positive side, the Great Salt Lake burials stimulated a broader discussion and led to a codified position for the state at large. But, more toward the negative side, after passage of the law, decision making was placed in the hands of the Native American Remains Review Committee under the Division of Indian Affairs and the construction of a burial chamber was placed with the Division of State Parks. None of the committee members, American Indian or otherwise, had any prior experience or involvement with the Great Salt Lake burial situation—that is, with the Governor's Committee on Reburial that drafted the law. Neither did the Division of State Parks have any such experience. By disengaging the process from the several years of groundwork laid between 1988 and 1992, the costs of instituting the regulatory apparatus increased, and after several large cost overruns, the burial chamber became so expensive that such places of interment may now be politically difficult as local solutions for other areas of the state. Finally, the nonlocal approach to the problem contributed greatly to why a situation that arose in 1988 was still not solved as this article went to press in the summer of 1999. The ancient bones remain in temporary curation.

A PHILOSOPHICAL UNITY? SOME UNSOLICITED ADVICE

The Native American Graves Protection and Repatriation Act did not apply to the three cases discussed here. Either they were resolved before enactment of the law (Stillwater or Malheur) or they occur on state lands free from the law (Great Salt Lake). The issues that we and our archaeological, tribal, and land-managing colleagues confronted then are not the same issues that vex land managers, archaeologists, and tribes today. NAGPRA is about determining the affiliation (ownership) of human remains, and then repatriating the remains to the affiliated. We were more interested in the pursuit of knowledge, respect for the deceased and those concerned with the deceased, and disposition of the remains in a way that all could embrace. The ultimate fallacy of NAGPRA, we believe, is its underlying assumption that archaeological human remains are "property."

"Burial sites are not fixed locations, and they cannot be abandoned or disrupted. No individual or group can 'own' the remains of another person" (Zimmerman 1988). "In a philosophical and spiritual sense this is surely so. In a legalistic and regulatory sense, however, ownership of the past has come of age. Bones, objects, and in some cases, perhaps even unpublished notes, photos, and maps are a potential commodity to virtually anyone who may become empowered by control over these things" (Simms 1993). This situation is unfortunate, and as either "side" in the reburial controversy ignores Zimmerman's basic tenet, the only thing likely to be served are the transient power interests of the present. The future, the very thing a fascination with the past is about, will be made irrelevant in today's decision making.

How so? If we simply reinter all American Indian remains does that not save us from having to deal with this issue in the future? We are surely being culturally sensitive if we accede to the spiritual wishes of American Indians specifically or the feelings among the general populace that human remains should be interred rather than stored. However, if archaeologists utilize regulatory ambiguity to force study, such as loosely interpreting the language of NAGPRA or state equivalents to conclude that study must be done to determine cultural affiliation (i.e., ownership), are we really fighting for the triumph of knowledge? If we argue that archaeologists are only serving science, are we being disingenuous? We suggest that all of the above positions are ethnocentric, shortsighted, and located in transient special interests.

The conclusion that American Indians should be the sole determinants regarding the treatment of the dead of their "race" is ethnocentric, if not racist. It amounts to the use of an arbitrarily defined racial category to allocate power and homogenizes the diversity that represents people labeled as American Indians. Perhaps more unfortunate in a practical sense, this position fails to take the future into account. We are not the first archaeologists of European descent to sometimes feel a bit awkward when studying the artifacts, bones, and culture of American Indians. The history of Indian-white relations has disenfranchised the American Indian, to say the least, but the granting of ownership will not absolve the sins of the past. Nor through ownership of bones do Indians gain continuity with the past or the cultural legitimacy that is their right. Rather, it is through the democratic process (consultation), the pursuit of knowledge, and basic morality that we achieve these goods. All human remains must be treated with the utmost respect. Reinterment is a basic moral principal that we cannot ignore, but we also cannot

ignore a similar obligation to America's past and to learn from it. The United
States is dedicated to the principal of *nation,* where citizens transcend parochial
angst and politically correct ethnicity by embracing democracy, knowledge, and
basic respect to mold a future *for all.*

As for the proponents of scientific ownership, the use of interpretive vagary
and bureaucratic gamesmanship to force analysis, perhaps against the wishes of the
"other side," is just a continuation of the regulatory manipulation that has characterized Indian/government relationships throughout U.S. history. A 1995 court
test of the Native American Graves Repatriation Act nudges the process even further toward division and the adversarial decision-making process characteristic of
the legal system. In a suit brought by a native Hawaiian organization, the court
found that cultural affiliation was not established and that it must be done before
the court would become involved in repatriation (Giesen and Gagne 1996). In one
sense, this finding was wise because it shifted the consultation out of the courts. In
another sense, some archaeologists are now arguing for the routine use of DNA
studies to resolve issues of cultural affiliation. No amount of evidence, be it archaeological, mythological, historical, or genetic, will ever determine the affiliation (cultural or biological) of human remains more than a few hundred years old.
The nature of these disciplines has always been to open new doors as others never
quite get closed. Surely, cultural affiliation must be part of the process and, regardless of the improbability of DNA studies resolving issues of affiliation, archaeologists who latch onto legalistic decisions to force more study may be doing more
harm than good. When either American Indians or archaeologists bring the consultation process into the legal system prematurely, consultation via consensus will
almost surely give way to embattlement among adversaries. Both parties end up
losing something and a pall of suspicion is cast over future negotiations. The only
beneficiaries in such a process are the attorneys. Should archaeologists give up the
pursuit of knowledge in the face of arbitrary and suspect tactics of some American
Indians? Of course not. Archaeologists may stand to lose more than American Indians would, however, if we jump into the legal mud pit with those who pursue
low-road tactics. The naïve assumption that archaeologists only have the good of
science at heart and thus should be granted special status with regard to the treatment of human remains flies in the face of public sensibilities and legislative action
of the past decade. It amounts to public suicide for the profession.

Despite the appearance that there are two "sides" in the reburial debate, this is
an illusion exposed by a common fault in each of the above polarized positions—
that the dead can be owned (or for the purposes of legal and regulatory expedience,
the dead should be treated as if they were owned). *Bogus!* Combine this realization
with an advocacy for local solutions and a way out of the contradictions becomes
apparent.

The local approach contrasts with the tendency to transfer solutions to attorneys and courts, boards of review, or committees (e.g., federal NAGPRA or state equivalents such as Utah's Native American Remains Review Committee—with the ignominious acronym, NARRC). Such parties are not intrinsically invested in the local solution (regardless of whether they are state or federal). Since they take on an official authority and stand in judgment, they tend to alienate participants, instill an adversarial climate, and force the process back toward an unproductive argument over ownership. The advocates of science will be trapped in a regulatory stereotype and so will the advocates for the spiritual value of the deceased. Such polemics are surely the misunderstanding evident in media coverage and public rhetoric today. A portrayal of adversaries may make for easily judged media images, but rarely brings consensus among parties who are closely affiliated with the local situation through *direct experience.* These parties include American Indians, land owners, members of the public, and, yes, even archaeologists with a demonstrated commitment to working in an area.

If no one owns the past, then collectively, we can only hold it in trust. Since we cannot know the cultural values that will be held in the future, we cannot decide for them. If no one owns the remains of dead people, then the knowledge about the past contained in human remains is as valuable as claims of their spirituality. If we simply rebury without study, and with no provision for access to those remains in the future, we have succumbed to ownership. If we simply study, we have done the same. The only way to avoid focusing the debate on ownership is through the combination of local solutions and the passage of time. Face-to-face consultation among parties with a commitment demonstrated through direct experience forms the basis for an agreement that may not satisfy everyone, but it holds the best chance to avoid speaking for those yet to be born and shutting them off from their past.

Responsibility to principles that transcend the special interests of the present and the convenience of government comes at a variety of costs: The cost of reinterment in contexts that can grant future access; the cost of scientific knowledge awaiting less volatile and hostile times; and the costs of restraining the power of appointed committees, boards, attorneys, and itinerant "advocates" over those more locally and directly invested in the outcome. In the Great Basin cases described here, the process determining the treatment of the remains fell squarely into many of the pitfalls we identify here. The solutions, however, show that it is possible to connect the past with the future while living in the present.

If consultation among interested parties toward a local solution produces a reburial solution, such as a burial chamber as happened in two of the three Great Basin cases, the future is not cut off. However, if the local solution also forbids some kinds of analysis or future access, then so be it. By considering the opinions of the present, the path toward greater understanding is left open and the advocates for the pursuit of public knowledge via scientific investigation stand a better chance of being heard. We should be advocates for this good. Whatever the local solution is with regard to scientific analysis in the present, the maintenance of a tie with the future by providing access to the remains ensures that future study in more enlightened times remains possible.

Acknowledgments

The achievements in the management and reinterment of human remains for these Great Basin cases would never have occurred without the interest and hard work of many individuals and their institutions. At Stillwater, we thank Amy Dansie and the Nevada State Museum; Alice Baldrica, Nevada State Historic Preservation Office; Ron Anglin and the U.S. Fish and Wildlife Service, and the Fallon Paiute–Shoshone Tribe, especially Richard Hicks and Alvin Moyle. At Malheur, Carla Burnside, U.S. Fish and Wildlife Service, was instrumental in the successful treatment of the human remains. We also thank the Burns Paiute Tribe, especially Minerva Soucie. At Great Salt Lake, the skeletons would have been lost to the flood without the effort of the Utah Statewide Archaeological Society, especially Mark Stuart. Many have worked toward a solution still in process. Thanks to Kevin Jones, and Wilson Martin, Utah Division of State History; David Madsen, Utah Geological Survey; Wil Numkena and Forrest Cuch, Utah Division of Indian Affairs; Eli Anderson and Rob Bishop, Utah State legislature; the Northwestern Band of the Shoshoni Nation, especially Mae Perry, Gloria Valdez, George Worley, Frank Timbimboo, and Leonard Alex. The opinions expressed here are the authors', both of whom are committed to the full inclusion of parties closest to particular cases of cultural patrimony.

3

Farmers, Foragers, and Adaptive Diversity
The Great Salt Lake Wetlands Project

Steven R. Simms

The Great Salt Lake wetlands project began in 1986 to explore adaptive diversity during the Fremont and Late Prehistoric periods. Previous application of the concept of adaptive diversity had directed methodological attention not only to behavioral variability but also to demographic fluidity among different lifeways as a behavioral feature of the Fremont historical sequence long known for the region (Simms 1986, 1990).

Adaptive diversity directs attention to behavioral dynamism, not as a substitute for the concept of culture nor as a denial of group identity. Since it is well established, however, that residence, affiliations, alliances, ideological perspectives, and identities—*behaviors*—do indeed change during the life histories of people, any perspective that can help us recognize this in the archaeological past can only add realism to our understanding. Archaeologists know that the realities of life are not adequately captured by the metaphor of the Fremont archaeological culture (nor the multitude of variants necessary to organize description). Yet other than reiterate that the Fremont were "variable," we have found few ways to break from the metaphors of boundedness when describing the dynamics of everyday life.

The Great Salt Lake Fremont is a natural case for exploring whether adaptive diversity is a useful device for deepening our knowledge because it has long been seen as a place where farming was of lesser importance than elsewhere in the Fremont culture area (e.g., Marwitt 1970; Jennings 1978). We now know that large, complex farming villages and full-time farmers were present in the Great Salt Lake Fremont (Simms and Stuart 1993, 1999) in addition to the previously understood, mixed forager-farming pattern. This study employs several lines of evidence to further this understanding by proposing and evaluating a model of adaptive diversity to help synthesize the archaeological evidence with the bioarchaeological evidence reported in detail elsewhere in this volume.

Beginning as a purely archaeological investigation, the Great Salt Lake wetlands project was presented an opportunity to incorporate powerful lines of evidence based on studies of human remains when flooding and subsequent regression of the Great Salt Lake in 1987 exposed hundreds of archaeological sites and dozens of human remains. This series of events led to an urgent management situation and eventually the recovery of a well-dated sample of human skeletal material representing a minimum of 85 individuals. Topics and analyses conducted on the Great Salt Lake human remains include dietary patterns using stable isotopes (Coltrain and Stafford, this volume) and osteological indicators (Bright and Loveland, this volume), activity patterns reflected in bone morphology (Ruff, this volume), osteological indicators of health and disease (Bright and Loveland, this volume), and population genetics using DNA extraction and polymerase chain reaction (PCR) amplification (O'Rourke et al., this volume). Analyses requiring manipulation of small amounts of bone were performed on bone fragments or small bones.

Primary descriptions of the archaeological fieldwork to remove the burials can be found in Simms, Loveland, and Stuart (1991) and Fawcett and Simms (1993). Descriptions of the consultation process are available in Simms 1993 and Simms and Raymond (this volume). An overview of the Great Salt Lake Fremont can be found in Simms and Stuart (1999), and a behaviorally oriented synthesis of the Fremont complex is available in D. B. Madsen and Simms (1998).

An important consideration when using the analyses in this volume is site formation processes, and these are described in this chapter. The depositional context of the remains is varied and often complicated by natural redeposition and/or secondary burial practices. Site formation processes also conditioned the character of the sample, which is distributed over a 65 km² area deposited over the past 1,500 years and exposed en masse by natural processes. The sample may approach being random, and as such may contrast with collections retrieved only from cemeteries or specific contexts within sites (structure floors, middens) because it likely includes burials that were difficult to locate with typical archaeological methods.

The archaeology of the Great Salt Lake and the eastern Great Basin/Plateau region suggests the presence of farmers and foragers in varying mixes during the Fremont period spanning the years from the time of Christ to about A.D. 1300 (D. B. Madsen and Simms 1998). A hypothesis of adaptive diversity and the movement of people among lifeways generates expectations for interpretation of the archaeological record and the evidence from the human remains, and I evaluate this relationship accordingly.

Concepts such as adaptive diversity result from thinking in terms of evolution and selection rather than adaptation and history (Zeanah and Simms 1999). A finding of adaptive diversity holds implications for how we frame questions and describe ancient history. I present two examples to illustrate the utility of this perspective: (1) the implications of adaptive diversity for bringing foragers and women into the questioning process using ceramic remains and (2) the relationship between the historical American Indians in the region and the ancient inhabitants as assessed via this behavioral approach, the findings of adaptive diversity, and a growing data set on population genetics.

SETTING AND PROJECT HISTORY

Perhaps most famous for its stark images of contrast between water and desert, the Great Salt Lake nevertheless supports vast tracts of ecologically varied wetland habitats along its eastern shores (Figure 3.1). Wetlands are best developed near the debouchments of the Bear, Ogden, Weber, and Jordan Rivers and a host of associated streams and springs along the nearby Wasatch Mountains rising to over 3,400 m asl. The influx of fresh water variously reduces the salinity of the lake depending on seasonal flow levels, wind patterns, lake elevation, and the arrangements among numerous stream channels guiding water into the lake. The considered "edge" of the lake is wide because the skilletlike configuration of the lake floor translates small fluctuations in water levels into large areal consequences. Wind from individual storms can raise lake levels along the eastern shores as much as 2 m (Atwood 1994). All of these factors conspire to form a dynamic mosaic of brackish to fresh water marshes and wetlands, with ponds and slow-moving streams bound by walls of bulrush and cattails. On slightly higher ground and along the natural levees flanking every stream channel, salt-grass meadows and greasewood plains predominate. These habitats support an abundance of wildlife including fish (suckers), a variety of small mammals, bison, and ungulates. The density of waterfowl in the region is of legendary proportions (e.g., Frémont [1845] 1988:148–49). Plant foods are also abundant and species yielding greens, shoots, roots, and seeds are available in various combinations from spring through fall.

The area has long been the focus of intensive human occupation. Archaeological investigation beginning in the nineteenth century documents hundreds of sites of many types. The Great Salt Lake wetlands project began in response to the fact that most archaeological investigation in the area is directed at the Fremont and that much of the investigation of either small Fremont sites and/or later periods is informal and unreported. To complement this record, the Late Prehistoric Orbit Inn site was excavated in 1986 and 1987 (Simms and Heath 1990). Findings at this site initiated the research perspectives applied to subsequent investigations, but the course of the project was fundamentally changed by the weather.

In 1983, the Great Salt Lake began a transgression resulting in a peak in lake levels in the spring of 1987 (Figure 3.2). Reaching an elevation of 1,283.8 m (4,211.8 ft), the lake perhaps exceeded the historically recorded maximum reached in the 1870s (the exact year and level is not known; see Mabey 1986). The lake soon receded; and by the fall of 1987, large areas of lake bed were exposed. Lake levels continued to decline for the next six years to approximately 1,280.2 m (4,200 ft). An area northwest of Ogden that would become the primary project study area expe-

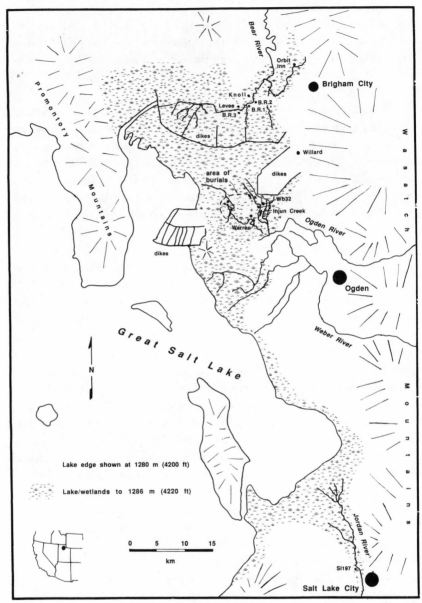

FIGURE 3.1. Map of Great Salt Lake wetlands showing surrounding sites and area of burial recovery and test excavations.

FIGURE 3.2. Aerial view in 1986 of flooding of the Great Salt Lake, looking southwest across inundated channels and oxbows of the Bear River. Promontory Mountains in background.

rienced the full brunt of prevailing northwesterly winds along a shoreline unprotected by the dikes that shielded other areas (Figure 3.1). Furthermore, this area comprises the floodplain of the Ogden River (at times in the past, that of both the Ogden and Weber Rivers), producing a shallow gradient and numerous meandering channels favored for occupation. Unlike some other areas along the eastern shores of the lake with different exposures and nearby dikes, the study area was subjected to a grading of the ground surface due to wave and ice action in water frequently less than a meter deep. Simultaneously, channels and ponds filled with sediments. The resulting landscape on regression of the lake was a flat, nearly featureless plain stripped of vegetation (Figure 3.3). Surface deflation ensued as wind removed the thin crust of alkali precipitates that blooms after each rainfall. These processes exposed numerous archaeological sites (Figure 3.3) and dozens of human remains (Figure 3.4).

A consultation process was initiated by the State of Utah (the primary landowner) with various American Indian groups prior to any removal of human remains. While the decision to begin removal of remains jeopardized by erosion and vandalism was made by November 1989, consultation regarding their disposition and analysis continued for several years (Simms 1993; Simms and Raymond, this volume).

The recovery of skeletons was accomplished primarily in 1990, but continued intermittently through 1992. Archaeological sites in the vicinity of the human remains were recorded and in some cases tested, but contractual arrangements limited the amount of attention given to the surrounding archaeology. Although other means were used to study the archaeology, they did not completely parallel the recovery of the burials.

FIGURE 3.3. a. Site 42Wb40 on natural levee (dark area) and sediment-filled stream channels on either side (light area). b. 42Wb48, a large, square pit house with antechamber exposed at the surface.

HUMAN REMAINS AND ARCHAEOLOGICAL CONTEXT

A minimum of 85 individuals was recovered, most were very fragmentary: 45 percent were represented by fewer than five elements, with only 20 percent consisting of more than half of the skeleton (Simms, Loveland, and Stuart 1991:24). The skeletons, many of which were directly dated using Accelerator Mass Spectroscopy radiocarbon dating (AMS ^{14}C) on extracted collagen, date between A.D. 400 and 1450, but most fall between A.D. 700 and 1300.

FIGURE 3.4. Samples (a–d) of human burials to illustrate range of conditions.

The archaeological context of the Great Salt Lake skeletons is provided by previous excavations in the area, by survey and testing of sites during the recovery of burials, and by unsystematic survey by avocationists over several decades. These investigations provide various levels of recording on nearly 500 archaeological sites located between the Wasatch Mountains and the historical low elevation of the Great Salt Lake (1,277.5 m, 4,191 feet, reached in 1963). The area of these investigations in relation to the smaller area of burial recovery reported here is shown in Figure 3.1.

Fifty sites were recorded during the recovery of burials. Eight were test excavated and 14 were tested using shovel scraping, a technique useful in this area where features are often visible near the ground surface (Fawcett and Simms 1993; Simms, Loveland, and Stuart 1991).

Burial Recovery Procedures

Most of the burials were located in 1987–88 by avocational archaeologists with the Utah Statewide Archaeological Society. Erosion had already begun, and vandalism was soon evident. In response, fieldworkers provided temporary protection with a thin covering of plastic and earth. Markers placed away from the remains at recorded distances and azimuths served to decoy vandals so the remains could be relocated. As the ground surface deflated in subsequent years, additional burials appeared.

Excavation began by removing the ubiquitous crust of alkali precipitate covering the ground to expose a fresh working surface. Thin layers were successively removed along one edge of the exposure to establish a profile. Subsequent excavation employed both horizontal and vertical planes in a search for stratigraphic information such as the presence of burial pits and/or evidence of erosion during previous transgressions of the Great Salt Lake. All sediment was screened by pushing the mud through ¼ in. mesh. Water screening was used in some cases, but generally did not aid processing (⅛ in. mesh was employed on small samples, but would not pass the clay balls common in these lake-bottom sediments). Each skeleton, or association of human bone, was exposed as completely as possible prior to removal. Sketch maps were made, often at different stratigraphic levels when present, and photographs taken. A sediment sample was retrieved from the abdominal area when this was evident (many remains being very scattered) to seek intestinal stones. One bone from each burial was removed without direct human contact and placed in virgin plastic bags to minimize contamination from human DNA. Subsequent curation met archival standards, and the remains are interred in a limited-access repository in Salt Lake City built specifically for American Indian remains (Simms and Raymond, this volume).

Site Formation Processes and Burial Characteristics

Site formation processes associated with a case such as the Great Salt Lake flooding are crucial for understanding the variety of conditions in which the skeletal remains were found. The surface planing that occurred during inundation and the deflation that began after regression of the lake waters exposed the remains at the surface, destroying levels of origins in virtually all cases. In many cases, the depth from ground surface to culturally sterile sediments was only a few centimeters, inhibiting the detection of burial pits. In some cases, bones were scattered by wave action, disarticulating what may have been relatively complete skeletons. It was stratigraphically demonstrated in several instances that previous fluctuations of the lake had exposed skeletons, only to rebury them. Stratigraphic and sedimentological evidence found with some of the burials was consistent with regional paleoclimatic evidence for comparable or higher lake transgressions during the seventeenth and nineteenth centuries (Simms and Stuart 1999).

Natural transport of individual bones among closely spaced burials often created a single locus of commingled human remains. However, in other instances, commingling resulted from human practices. In one case (burials 47 to 58), 11 individuals were found clustered in a circular area 4 m in diameter and resting on burned bulrush plants (the human remains were not burned). Several of the individuals appear to have been buried in a single event, but it is also clear that others were added later. In another case (burials 36 and 37), an infant was secondarily interred on the lap of a partial skeleton of an adult female who exhibited evidence of burning (the infant was not burned). A few cases appear to result from intentional commingling of one or two elements from several individuals. A practice that may produce such a pattern, but for which we have only sketchy documentation in the Great Basin, is token burial. Token burial is the practice of retrieving for reburial one or more bones of a deceased relative who was initially buried away from home (R. H. Brooks and Brooks 1990). Cut-marks are present on bones from two individuals and, in a third case, an ulna from a secondary burial (36 and 37) exhibited a borehole. Additional elements exhibit damage, which was determined to be postmortem and, in at least one case, can be linked to a twentieth-century relic hunter who left telltale broken wine bottles at his "digs."

Very few grave goods were found with the skeletons, but it is difficult to define associations in cases of extreme erosion when burials are scattered over an area in which the site density approaches 30 per square mile and the entire landscape yields artifacts. The low frequency of nonperishable grave goods is consistent with the Fremont pattern of interments with grave goods occurring in a minority of cases (e.g., Dodd 1982:104–6; Gunnerson 1969:157; Janetski and Talbot 1997: 315–20; D. B. Madsen and Lindsay 1977:77). A few of the Great Salt Lake burials contained grave goods, including a human ulna with a borehole and red ochre stain (burials 36 and 37), a fragment of deer antler (burials 12 and 13), a tubular bone bead and tiny shell pendant (burial 70), a large Utah-type metate (burial 47), a quartzite mortar (burial 32), and a burial (3) with a mano and freshwater clam shells (*Anodonta californiensis*). A few cases yielded red ochre nodules or ochre staining of human skeletal elements. Only one instance, the above-mentioned interment of 11 individuals, yielded numerous grave goods, including large ceramic sherds, fan-shaped arrangements of bone awls, an arrangement of 13 bone counters or gaming pieces, a carved bison horn, a Utah-type metate (these are found almost exclusively at Fremont residential bases), and a carved bone, duck-head effigy (Simms, Loveland, and Stuart 1991:51–52, Figures 13 and 14). Most of these items had been smeared or stained with red ochre.

Burial position and orientation was variable among the 27 individuals where this could be determined (Simms, Loveland, and Stuart 1991:25). Positions included flexed (reclining, resting on left side or resting on right side), extended, and unusual postures (Figure 3.4). Burials faced in all compass orientations, but in about half of the 27 cases where orientation could be determined, the head was located in a northerly quadrant (NW, N, NE).

Burial pits were detected in only a few instances, which, in many cases, can be attributed to previous erosion and reburial of remains, leaving only a few bones from each individual. However, even the complete or nearly complete skeletons were rarely associated with pits. In some cases, the sediments around the remains were unsorted, frosted sands suggestive of aeolian processes. C. S. Fowler (1992: 163) reports that Northern Paiute in the Stillwater area of western Nevada often buried the deceased in sand hills that flank the wetlands. Burial pits can easily become obscured if the sands are mobile. In other cases, water burial seems plausible and is known to the area, such as the case of the Shoshoni chief, Pocatello (B. D. Madsen 1986:112–13). If the deceased person were lowered into one of the slow-moving channels, the body would become covered with silts, a common sedimentary context among Great Salt Lake burials. Water burial may account for the position and sedimentary context of burial 61 (Figure 3.4a).

The Nature of the Burial Sample

The Great Salt Lake skeletal collection is a relatively large sample exposed by natural processes over a 65 km² area of dense human activity. As such it may approximate a random sample from the area of recovery over the last 1,500 years. The collection contrasts with existing samples of Fremont and Anasazi human skeletal material typically recovered from individual structures—and typically at large residential farming bases that represent the "strong" archaeological pattern of farmers that has received the bulk of archaeological attention (Plog 1984). The "weak" pattern common to foragers or farmers with some degree of residential mobility remains underrepresented in the Desert West (Plog 1984; Upham 1988; also see Upham 1994:118–19 and Gilman 1987:550–53). This bias extends to skeletal assemblages as well, and further enhances the scientific value of the Great Basin collections reported in this volume since all of them were exposed by natural processes across local landscapes.

One aspect of this bias is evident in the results of early attempts at stable carbon isotope analysis on Fremont and Anasazi skeletons to evaluate dietary composition. In a sample from museum collections containing human remains from large Fremont farming sites, stable carbon isotopes indicate a Fremont diet that was essentially as dependent on corn as were samples from Anasazi farming sites (Coltrain 1993). These are powerful results since they challenge the habit of stereotyping the Fremont as a people less reliant on farming than the Anasazi. Even though the homogenizing tendencies of archaeological description are countered by Coltrain's study, the samples were drawn only from the strong archaeological pattern of farmers. Thus, the results reported by Coltrain cannot address the weak archaeological pattern of foragers.

The Great Salt Lake skeletal sample complements existing collections because it is more likely to represent a full range of behavioral variability. This point is important when using the findings in the Great Salt Lake area to interpret lifeways found elsewhere in the Fremont area. What may seem unique to the Great Salt

Lake case in comparison to Fremont skeletons from elsewhere in the region may only be differences in the nature of the samples.

The Great Salt Lake sample is not however, free of bias. It is argued that the Great Salt Lake Fremont were more oriented toward foraging than other Fremont (Marwitt 1970; Jennings 1978). Although urbanization has destroyed most of the large sites associated with farming, requiring some interpretational temperance, there are examples that demonstrate the same reliance on farming as is known for other parts of the Fremont region (Marwitt 1970:145–148; Simms and Stuart 1999). Given that the skeletal sample is largely from wetland areas and not large farming sites, it too may be somewhat biased toward representing foraging or farmers with a more mobile behavioral pattern, despite the claim that the sample may approach randomness within the area of burial exposure.

To help control for this bias, a small sample of skeletal material from sites more consistent with farming were added to the wetland sample. The sample chosen included three individuals from museum collections representing the large Fremont farming bases of Willard and Warren (discussed in greater detail later). Also included were three individuals recovered during salvage excavations by the Utah Division of State History in 1993 at site 42Sl197, a substantial Fremont site near Salt Lake City. This site may or may not have been associated with farming (Schmitt, Simms, and Woodbury 1994). The locations of these sites are shown in Figure 3.1. A small sample of these human remains from other Fremont sites is included in some of the analyses reported elsewhere in this volume by Coltrain and Stafford.

To summarize, the Great Salt Lake skeletal sample may be biased toward representing foraging or intermittent farming due to its location in wetlands and the possible importance of foraged foods in the Great Salt Lake area. It thus complements existing samples from the eastern Basin/Plateau region as a whole, which tend to represent the more dominant pattern of farmers. However, due to its size and natural means of exposure, the Great Salt Lake sample is likely to be more random than most skeletal collections in the region and thus to represent a range of lifeways. It would be premature to compare the Great Salt Lake skeletal sample with other Fremont collections and conclude that the Great Salt Lake case was different from other Fremont without taking into account the differences in sample characteristics between the Great Salt Lake sample and most, if not all, other Fremont skeletal collections. Rather than creating an obstacle, the unique characteristics of the Great Salt Lake collection bestows exceptional scientific value on this collection.

Dating of the Human Remains

A small sample of bone was taken from whole bones or bone fragments from 57 individuals for AMS ^{14}C dating on extracted collagen. The samples were pre-

TABLE 3.1.

Direct AMS ^{14}C Dates on Human Skeletal Remains from the
Great Salt Lake Wetlands Project

Burial #	Site	Lab Sample #[a]	^{14}C Age[b]	Calibrated Range[c]	Comments
3	42Wb48	CAMS 4060	1020 ± 70	A.D. 888–1178	
Replicate of #3		CAMS 5327	960 ± 60	A.D. 983–1222	
6	4wWb48	CAMS 11110	1100 ± 60	A.D. 789–1029	
8	42Wb48	CAMS 8255	860 ± 80	A.D. 1016–1293	
11	42Wb184	CAMS 12283	790 ± 50	A.D. 1167–1296	
Different bone, #11		CAMS 11104	920 ± 60	A.D. 1010–1257	
14	42Wb185a	CAMS 12278	1430 ± 50	A.D. 547–678	In pit house
15	42Wb185a	CAMS 11119	1390 ± 60	A.D. 560–773	In pit house?
16	42Wb185c	CAMS 12285	920 ± 50	A.D. 1016–1245	In wickiup?
17	42Wb185c	CAMS 12282	1190 ± 60	A.D. 653–990	
20	42Wb269	CAMS 12277	900 ± 50	A.D. 1022–1257	
21	42Wb269	CAMS 11106	1130 ± 60	A.D. 778–1020	
22	42Wb269	CAMS 4059	1020 ± 70	A.D. 888–1178	
Different bone #22		CAMS 5312	770 ± 70	A.D. 1162–1386	
Different bone #22		CAMS 6909	910 ± 60	A.D. 1013–1275	
23	42Wb269	CAMS 5331	960 ± 50	A.D. 1011–1177	
Replicate of #23		CAMS 4915	960 ± 60	A.D. 983–1222	
26	42Wb269	CAMS 10214	730 ± 60	A.D. 1217–1393	
27	42Wb269	CAMS 12274	940 ± 60	A.D. 996–1230	
28	42Wb269	CAMS 5314	890 ± 60	A.D. 1019–1277	
29	42Wb269	CAMS 4917	870 ± 60	A.D. 1025–1283	
32	42Wb286	CAMS 4919	890 ± 60	A.D. 1019–1279	
33	42Wb304	CAMS 11108	1000 ± 60	A.D. 898–1179	
35	42Wb317	CAMS 5329	1010 ± 50	A.D. 900–1162/957–1167	
Replicate of #35		CAMS 5322	1020 ± 60	A.D. 893–1165/941–1164	
36	42Wb318	CAMS 12280	1500 ± 80	A.D. 411–672	
37	42Wb318	CAMS 11120	1110 ± 50	A.D. 818–1020	
Different bone #37		CAMS 10225	1230 ± 100	A.D. 640–1014	
40	42Wb319	CAMS 12279	870 ± 50	A.D. 1031–1279	
41	42Wb319	CAMS 8256	800 ± 70	A.D. 1046–1303	
43	42Wb320	CAMS 12284	540 ± 40	A.D. 1314–1442	
45	42Wb322	CAMS 5315	1150 ± 110	A.D. 662–1156	
47	42Wb324	CAMS 8254	1050 ± 70	A.D. 880–1162	
48	42Wb324	CAMS 5330	1010 ± 60	A.D. 895–1168/942–1172	#48–58
49	42Wb324	CAMS 5325	920 ± 60	A.D. 1010–1257	from 1 area,
51	42Wb324	CAMS 11115	1250 ± 60	A.D. 662–956	laid on
52	42Wb324	CAMS 10221	1330 ± 100	A.D. 547–956	burned
53	42Wb324	CAMS 4058	1260 ± 60	A.D. 659–945/659–893	bulrush
Replicate of #53		CAMS 4916	1110 ± 80	A.D. 727–1150/758–1050	
Triplicate of #53		CAMS 4920	1090 ± 80	A.D. 779–1156/775–1065	
55	42Wb324	CAMS 10363	980 ± 60	A.D. 972–1215	
Replicate of #55		CAMS 11113	1120 ± 80	A.D. 718–1037	

TABLE 3.1. (continued)
Direct AMS [14]C Dates on Human Skeletal Remains from the
Great Salt Lake Wetlands Project

Burial #	Site	Lab Sample #[a]	[14]C Age[b]	Calibrated Range[c]	Comments
56	42Wb324	CAMS 5328	1030 ± 70	A.D. 885–1168	
57	42Wb324	CAMS 5323	1350 ± 60	A.D. 608–786	
58	42Wb324	CAMS 5318	980 ± 50	A.D. 983–1180	
Replicate of #58		CAMS 5326	980 ± 60	A.D. 972–1215	
61	42Bo73	CAMS 4918	1090 ± 60	A.D. 819–1033	
62	42Bo73	CAMS 11112	1150 ± 60	A.D. 727–1014	
64	42Bo579	CAMS 10219	1630 ± 70	A.D. 252–602	
65	42Bo580	CAMS 5317	920 ± 60	A.D. 1010–1257	
66	42Bo580	CAMS 12269	980 ± 50	A.D. 983–1180	
68	42Bo599	CAMS 5324	1010 ± 50	A.D. 900–1162/<u>957–1167</u>	
69	42Bo599	CAMS 5316	780 ± 60	A.D. 1165–1303	
70	42Bo599	CAMS 5313	1130 ± 60	A.D. 778–1020	
73	42Wb144	CAMS 11117	1000 ± 60	A.D. 898–1179	
76	42Wb185	CAMS 12271	1170 ± 50	A.D. 726–990	
Replicate of #76		CAMS 11105	1040 ± 70	A.D. 883–1165	
77	42Bo700	CAMS 10360	1250 ± 70	A.D. 656–968	
78	42Wb32	CAMS 11107	1440 ± 70	A.D. 451–694	
79	42Wb32	CAMS 12275	1140 ± 50	A.D. 782–1012	
83	42Wb32	CAMS 12276	1050 ± 60	A.D. 885–1156	
84	42Wb32	CAMS 11116	1160 ± 60	A.D. 718–1011	
11349	Willard	CAMS 10220	1250 ± 50	A.D. 667–891	Willard
FS1/97	Willard	CAMS 10215	1220 ± 60	A.D. 670–974/<u>680–898</u>	sample
FS1/108	Willard	CAMS 11109	690 ± 60	A.D. 1237–1403	in mounds
Sample 1	Warren	CAMS 8349	1180 ± 60	A.D. 688–988/<u>754–990</u>	
Sample 3	42S1 197	CAMS 12281	1130 ± 40	A.D. 817–1007/<u>855–1007</u>	
Sample 4	42S1 197	CAMS 11114	1160 ± 60	A.D. 718–1011/<u>767–1011</u>	
Sample 5a	42S1 197	CAMS 10211	1380 ± 60	A.D. 570–776/<u>590–779</u>	

[a] Sample preparation by Joan Coltrain (University of Utah) in lab of and under direction of Thomas Stafford (University of Colorado). Dating at the Center For Accelerator Mass Spectrometry (CAMS), Lawrence Livermore National Laboratory, Palo Alto, California.

[b] All ^{14}C ages corrected for ^{13}C fractionation.

[c] Calibrations are to bidecadal dendrochronology data set to .05 interval (2 sigma) as per Stuiver and Reimer (1993: computer program). All samples except those underlined employed Method A (Stuiver and Reimer 1993). The underlined ages reflect use of Method B. This method produces a probability distribution compatible with the ^{14}C age and its Gaussian age distribution. In some cases this leads to a high probability the sample age lies within a range that is substantially narrower than the calibrated age ranges produced by Method A. Method B was applied to all samples, but only included in the table in cases where the p > .89 that the age was within the narrower range identified by method B. Rather than considering the underlined ages more accurate (when they are only more precise), they may be useful in assessing the likelihood of contemporaneity among some samples. The calibrated age range from method A (the nonunderlined ranges) should be employed for the greatest consistency among samples.

pared at the University of Colorado, Boulder, by Joan Coltrain and Thomas Stafford and dated at the Lawrence Livermore National Laboratory, Livermore, California. Fifty of the dates derive from the 85 individuals excavated in the Great Salt Lake wetlands, while the remaining 7 dates were obtained from the museum collections of individuals recovered from previously excavated Fremont sites in the area.

Direct dating is crucial to any significant analysis of the skeletons. The high site density (nearly 30 per square mile) and the nature of the site formation processes undermines the validity of any spatial associations between the human remains and archaeological sites for establishing the age and, by extension, the cultural affiliation of burials (Simms, Loveland, and Stuart 1991:26).

Table 3.1 lists the results of the ^{14}C dating according to burial number, which refers to identified individuals, some of which are from the same locus. Again, site formation processes indicate that individuals from the same locus need not be contemporaneous. Replicate samples were run on a few bones to check consistency, and different bones from the same burial locus were analyzed to evaluate the ages of commingled individuals. The numbers or names of sites spatially associated with the burials are provided, and where direct association with archaeological remains is known, it is noted. The bioarchaeological analyses of the Great Salt Lake skeletons reported in this volume use the burial numbers shown on Table 3.1.

Most of the remains date to A.D. 700–1300, yet the naturally exposed nature of the sample and the proposed tendency toward randomness imply that the period after A.D. 1300 should be represented as well. The rarity of remains after this time is consistent with the understanding that population density declined with the demise of Fremont farming. This aspect of the burial sample will be discussed in the section evaluating the model of adaptive diversity.

Archaeological Context

The Great Salt Lake wetlands have been known to be archaeologically rich since the nineteenth century (e.g., Maguire 1892), and several generations of avocationists have produced a wealth of unpublished information, some of it impressive in quality. The Great Salt Lake wetlands project revisited dozens of sites, examined private collections, and transferred much of this information to formal site forms and maps.

Surface survey provides a range of evidence that is primarily artifactual, but in some cases erosion exposes features as well. Evidence for a variety of structures, storage pits, and refuse areas can be combined with artifact tabulations to enable an evaluation of assemblage composition and diversity.

Past excavations provide information on nine sites: Willard (Maguire 1892; Judd 1926; Steward 1933; also see O. A. Kennedy 1930), Warren (Enger and Blair 1947; Hassell 1961; Manful 1938), the Knoll and Levee sites (Fry and Dalley 1979),

Bear River numbers 1 (Pendergast 1961), 2 (Aikens 1967), and 3 (W. F. Shields and Dalley 1978), Injun Creek (Aikens 1966), and Orbit Inn (Simms and Heath 1990). Their locations are shown in Figure 3.1. Sites referred to here using Smithsonian numbers (e.g., 42Bo48) are reported in Simms, Loveland, and Stuart (1991) and Fawcett and Simms (1993).

The sites include substantial residential farming bases, such as Willard, which are found located on a floodplain near the toe of an alluvial fan, a typical locus of Fremont agricultural sites along the eastern Great Basin rim (e.g., Evans Mound, Median Village, Pharo Village, Backhoe Village, Clear Creek, and various unreported sites that are lying under virtually every modern Utah town along Interstate Highway 15). At the Willard site, over 50 mounds contained superimposed pit structures and/or adobe surface structures (later destroyed by field leveling and dike construction). Superposition suggests pit houses evolved from round to square between A.D. 1125 and 1200 (see Dodd [1982:17–18, 37] regarding southwestern Utah; Fry and Dalley [1979] for the Great Salt Lake area; and Talbot [1997] for a thorough overview). Museum and private collections comprising hundreds of small side-notched and corner-notched projectile points, ground stone, slate knives, burials, corn, beans, squash, textiles, ornaments, and figurines attest to the size and diversity of the Willard assemblage. The nearby Warren site had 16 mounds (Manful 1938) containing houses "of the Willard type" (Enger and Blair 1947:142). Assemblage characteristics are broad, similar to the Willard site, and the site also yielded bison bone, corn, and "bushels" of fish bone (Manful 1938), figurine fragments, the large, Utah-type metates, a lignite bead necklace, and other trappings of a residentially stable occupation.

The Knoll site, and the late component of the Levee site, located along the lower Bear River, had round and square pit houses, but they were shallower than those at Willard. Radiocarbon dates on three square pit houses at the Levee site indicate a transition to square pit houses after A.D. 1100, with use possibly extending through the A.D. 1200s. No dates are available for Willard or Warren, but since both round and square forms were present, the occupations at least span this transition. Pit houses were also present at Bear River number 3 and at several sites in the area of burial recovery (42Wb48, 42Wb185a, 42Wb185c, and 42Wb324) and were found at lower elevations than ever before (1,282 m, 4,205–6 feet) (Figures 3.1 and 3.3). In contrast to Willard (and possibly Warren), where storage was in surface structures of adobe, storage at the other sites was limited to small, bowl-shaped subsurface pits. Although the assemblage is not as substantial as at the Willard and Warren sites, all of the pit house sites indicate considerable residential stability. The Great Salt Lake Fremont has long been portrayed as a foraging economy, but the presence of farming is supported by the site locations and the presence of corn remains at Willard, Warren, Bear River number 3, and Injun Creek (a site with no evidence for pit house architecture).

Other sites yielded circular mud-and-pole structures, indicative of less investment than pit houses. Included are the early component of the Levee site, Bear
River numbers 2 and 3, Injun Creek, 42Wb185c, and 42Wb32. At 42Wb32, three
such structures were superimposed, and three radiocarbon samples date them to
A.D. 1035–1155, the heart of the Fremont period (Fawcett and Simms 1993:119–20,
156–57). Like many of the pit house sites, storage is in small, bowl-shaped subsurface pits most suitable for short-term storage. An exception is Injun Creek,
where a larger, above-ground adobe storage structure was found. However, Injun
Creek is the only site in the area without a pit house that yielded corn remains. Assemblage diversity at most of these sites is again high, as would be expected at residential bases.

Higher mobility is indicated at Bear River number 1, a temporary camp with
no structures and a narrow assemblage composition. It was likely a stopover at the
location of a bison kill (Lupo and Schmitt 1997). The Orbit Inn site is a Late Prehistoric residential camp intermittently occupied from spring through fall for several weeks at a time and over many years. It had only insubstantial structures, but
did have distinct activity areas, 18 subsurface pits, sizable refuse deposits, and a
broad assemblage composition. Such structures reflecting brief use are also in evidence at several sites, some of which may be Fremont in age (e.g., 42Wb40,
42Wb144, 42Wb184 and 42Bo73). Subsurface pits abound across the study area,
and one site (42Wb317) had over 150 of them.

Lithic remains feature a high degree of tool-stone conservation, reflecting the
absence of tool stone in the wetlands. There was caching of primary and secondary
flakes (Cornell, Stuart, and Simms 1992); low flake weight; and frequent resharp-
ening of projectile points, producing tiny points with unusually high variation in
"notch height symmetry" (Simms and Whitesides 1993:175–78). As points are re-
sharpened, the ability to maintain equal notch height decreases. Of 203 side-
notched points assessed, 57 percent exhibit asymmetry in notch height on individual points from .4 cm to as much as 2.6 cm. Given the small size of these points
(< 1–4 cm), the degree of asymmetry and its frequency are striking and serve as an
indicator of conservation (Simms and Whitesides 1993:178).

The intensive use of tool stone appears to result not only from limited supply
but also from low residential mobility among many of the people much of the
time. There is a high frequency of bipolar reduction, suggesting low mobility and
tool-stone conservation, although biface reduction is evident at a minority of sites,
indicating logistic use (Elston 1988; Kelly 1988b, 1995b:23; Simms and Whitesides
1993).

There is a high variation among side-notched points, with many falling at the
boundaries of typological categories in terms of attributes. Such a case is particularly true for the "Fremont" side-notched points, which may be subject to too
much typological splitting in the absence of statistical analyses of variance. For in-

stance, measurements were taken of the notch height of over 100 Uinta and Bear River points. Notch height, defined only as "high" and "low," is the only attribute distinguishing the Uinta and Bear River point types (Holmer and Weder 1980:60). When their notch heights were plotted, the distribution formed a normal curve with absolutely no hint of the bimodality that should be expected if they are two distinct types. Furthermore, the variation in small side-notched points may also encompass the general subtype of the Desert side-notch points, a finding consistent with those reported by Ringe (1986:79–84) at the Wahmuza site in southeastern Idaho.

Study by Dean (1992) found significant overlap among ceramic types in attributes of temper, color, and wall thickness. Consistent with Dean, we found that when measurements typically used in the Basin/Plateau region to identify types *in collections of plainware ceramics* are plotted, the collection conventionally subdivided into several types (e.g., Great Salt Lake Gray, Promontory Gray, and Late Prehistoric Gray) and actually formed a single distribution, again suggesting the dangers of too much typological splitting (see Simms et al. 1993:149, Figure 44). Janetski (1994) uses dated occurrences of ceramics in Utah Valley to argue that a distinct Promontory type can be identified if the right sherds are present (typically rims) and shows that this type succeeded the Fremont types. These two conclusions may seem to be at odds, but an exploration of variability within Fremont ceramic collections and between Fremont and Late Prehistoric ceramics does not negate the cultural-historical sequence evident in ceramic types. Instead, it shows that Fremont ceramics can do more for us than merely describe the historical sequence (Simms, Ugan, and Bright 1997:790).

Virtually all of the ceramics in the region are plainwares, and body sherds are by far the most common found. These fragments can be difficult to type because of an absence of stylistic content or a paucity of rim sherds. Nevertheless, archaeologists often sort them into temporal categories on the basis of crudeness alone, a practice that obscures the search for anything other than the usual types.

Simms, Ugan, and Bright (1997) found a relationship between variation in investment and independent archaeological measures of residential mobility. Investment varies within culturally defined limits according to the intended use-life of the vessel, and we would expect these patterns to "cross-cut ceramic types and archaeological cultures because the behavior responsible for them may also cross-cut these categories" (Simms, Ugan, and Bright 1997:780). For instance, pottery with functional diversity and of higher quality is associated with the large residential farming bases (e.g., Willard), and pottery of lesser investment occurs at residential bases in locations suggestive of greater dependence on foraged foods or a mixed diet (e.g., the Levee site and 42Wb32). High variability among plainwares occurs at residential camps (e.g., the Orbit Inn), where ceramics reflecting diverse adaptive strategies were locally transported and/or manufactured over time. At a few small sites, we found high-quality plainware pottery similar to that found at farming bases, suggesting a logistic connection between them.

Simms, Ugan, and Bright (1977) also employed X-ray diffraction to test hypotheses about source proximity and expected variability in the use of sources with increasing mobility. Geological source does not vary solely by ceramic type or by period, but by locale. For instance, in plain, utilitarian ceramics in northern Utah, the temper often used to distinguish ceramic types, and by extension cultural affiliation, shows greater similarity across types from the same valley than do ceramics of the same type from two different valleys (Simms, Ugan, and Bright 1997).

Variability in ceramic quality can be found even at the height of Fremont farming times. This is clearly demonstrated at well-dated sites such as Levee and 42Wb32, the aforementioned site with the three superimposed circular pole-and-mud structures and three radiocarbon dates to A.D. 1035–1155. Although the site is clearly Fremont in age (pole-and-mud structures are different from pit houses), a significant portion of the ceramics from the superimposed structures blur the lines between types traditionally denoted as Fremont and Late Prehistoric simply on the basis of how crude they appeared (Fawcett and Simms 1993:119–20, 156–57).

The archaeological context provides a range of evidence that leads to expectations about adaptive diversity. These expectations are compared to the archaeological record and to the bioarchaeological analyses reported in greater detail elsewhere in this volume.

ADAPTIVE DIVERSITY

In the eastern Great Basin and the northern Colorado Plateau, the Fremont farmers are at once anomalous with the general prehistory of a region characterized by foraging societies, yet synchronous with the adjacent Southwest, a region best known for farming societies. This schism is apparent in early comparisons between the Fremont and the Southwest (e.g., Judd 1926; Morss 1931), a perception resulting in the term "northern periphery" applied to these anomalous farmers of the Basin/Plateau region (Steward 1933, 1936). The schism is also apparent in the knowledge that the society-building consequences of farming were never as fully expressed among the Fremont as in the Southwest.

True to its place among Great Basin foraging societies, the role of foraging is maintained in a Fremont literature that abounds with statements about foraging as providing part of a Fremont diet (Marwitt 1970) or the primary component of a Fremont diet (D. B. Madsen 1979, 1982) or as an option for a region intermittently risky for agriculture (Berry 1974). Jennings states the Fremont "was evidently a quite flexible or adaptable lifeway showing local diversity within a general model" (1978:155). His reference to diversity maintains the kinship with foragers so characteristic of Great Basin archaeology, and the "general model" he refers to is one of farming, acknowledging synchroneity and comparison with the Southwest.

Upham attempted to integrate the prehistories of the Basin/Plateau and the Southwest in response to the problem of what he calls the "two 'archaeologies' for the Desert West, one for nomads that is associated primarily with the Archaic and separate sequences for village agriculturists that are generally referred to as Formative, despite the fact that both gatherer/hunters and agriculturists were common features of the landscape" (Upham 1994:119–20; also see Upham 1988). Adaptive diversity directs attention to "a fundamental dynamic...which integrates the unique culture histories of different groups" (Upham 1994:116). The concept of adaptive diversity refers not only to variable expressions of culture but also to plasticity in behaviors within cultural groups and interactions among people with changeable lifeways through demographic fluidity, or "residential cycling." Adaptive diversity is not a polar concept to abandonment, migration, and population replacement, but helps give behavioral meaning to those terms.

Adaptive diversity directs attention to Fremont lifeways that were not only "flexible," to use Jennings's term, but also actually may have involved the presence of different adaptive systems in various mixes during the Fremont period (Simms 1986). People in these systems, through individual and small-group migration, interacted via the changing compositions of camp groups (C. S. Fowler 1982a, 1982b), such as residence changes through marriage in accordance with rules of exogamy, as well as via channels of trade and exchange.

It is important to not overstate the case made by Upham (1994) and to conclude that there was some sort of monolithic and synchronized relationship between periods of nucleation followed by periods when nuclear settlements were abandoned and everyone went foraging. This is a misunderstanding of the basic dynamic Upham was bringing to the analysis. Adaptive diversity is a process better expressed in terms of frequency shifts and involves individuals and small, related groups. As such, it enables us to look beyond the metaphors of ethnic groups acting in lockstep, with whole villages or entire "peoples" packing up on moving day and going somewhere. My challenge to these notions does not deny that such things can happen, but argues that the daily unfolding of life is far more interactive as well as mundane.

In a 1986 article, I built upon the awareness by Fremont scholars of variation in lifeways by introducing a behavioral cant to the modeling process, enabling the diversity to be seen as something individual people and their relations engaged in, perhaps more than once in their lives. At the same time, the evidence demanded a model that could acknowledge constancy in lifeways for some and the potential for interaction among peoples with contrasting lifeways, leading to a varying mix of adaptive strategies across the Fremont area and through time. There are three fundamental behaviors in the scheme: (1) full-time Fremont farmers with low residential mobility who supplemented their annual diet with some foraged foods and employed a logistic system; (2) Fremont farmers who may also have relied

Strategy 1: Farmers

- Residential bases located for farming.
- Long occupations with superposition or accretion of site.
- Pit house architecture, often in clusters. Possible "villages."
- Logistic system.
- Corn storage in winter and corn-based diet typical.

Strategy 2: The "variable" life

- Fremont farmers who switch settlement often to continue to farm or to adjust mix of farming and foraging. Leads to farming diet, or mixed diet.
- Variant A: Residential bases located for farming, but smaller and/or shorter spans of use. Hamlets or "rancherias," not villages. Corn-based diet.
- Variant B: Residential bases not located for farming, but in association with farming sites. Leads to mixed diet.
- Both variants exhibit less stability in material indicators such as architecture, ceramics, etc. than strategy 1.

Strategy 3: Foragers

- People who live in the Fremont area and period, but practice little or no farming.
- Lifeways within the range known for Great Basin Archaic foragers.
- Found in areas unsuitable for farming, and in hinterlands of farming spheres.
- Variable interaction with farmers. Possible demographic fluidity across cultural boundaries.

FIGURE 3.5. Three adaptive strategies during Fremont times and their attributes.

heavily on farming, but who switched agricultural settlement often by employing group fission and fusion to maintain a focus on farming or to adjust the mix of foraging and farming (this is the variable strategy traditionally envisioned by Fremont scholars); and (3) foragers who practiced little or no farming, but who could have variable relationships with farmers during their life history. The attributes of these strategies are shown in Figure 3.5.

There is some evidence for adaptive diversity. Study of strontium isotopes at Grasshopper Pueblo, Arizona, shows dietary differences "among individuals from the same site, and between communities," and "settlement of the site by diverse social groups of both local and nonlocal origin" (Price et al. 1994:315, 327). Whalen (1994) finds shifting residential mobility in the Late Prehistoric Jornada-Mogollon suggesting complex movements among peoples of different lifeways and the resulting changes of lifeways for individuals.

Ethnographic and ethnohistorical study establishes the fact of farmer-forager systems in numerous cases. The birth of this pattern should correspond to the beginnings of farming and pastoralism early in the Neolithic and be a continuing feature of these systems. It thus should be the rule rather than the exception. D. B. Madsen and I (1998) considered ethnographic analogies of farmers and foragers in relation to the Fremont evidence and developed a behavioral perspective on the Fremont cast as changing contexts of selection. These contexts of selection include (1) *behavioral options* that reflect an ever-present dynamic as new choices are presented; (2) *matrix modification* that highlights the impacts of people on others, as well as the impacts of human interaction with the resource base; (3) *symbiosis* among different adaptive strategies, which is a subset of matrix modification, that results from the spread of farming; and (4) *switching strategies,* highlighting the demographic fluidity that is variously stimulated by the other contexts. The four contexts of selection are not mutually exclusive, nor are they offered as a taxonomy for identifying sites or regions. Each context illustrates aspects of the Fremont archaeological record and shapes the questions asked of that record (D. B. Madsen and Simms 1998). As the contexts of selection change during Fremont history, the degree of adaptive diversity in any given place is expected to change and these expectations can be incorporated into a model of behavior for the Great Salt Lake case.

Adaptive diversity is one approach to connect behavioral changes over the life history of individuals with cultural patterning and to explain these changes in an evolutionary and selectionist context rather than an adaptationist and historical context (see Zeanah and Simms 1999).

A Model of Adaptive Diversity in the Great Salt Lake Wetlands

The Fremont presence in northern Utah begins between A.D. 400 and 500, and farming arrives in the Great Salt Lake area after A.D. 500, well after its appearance in central Utah around 100 B.C. (see D. B. Madsen and Simms 1998 for a review). Stable isotope data from the Great Salt Lake skeletons indicate a higher percentage of C4 plants in the diet between A.D. 650 and 750, with a peak after A.D. 900 (Coltrain and Stafford, this volume). Farming was thus an addition to an indigenous forager diet focused on the Great Salt Lake wetlands (D. B. Madsen 1982).

Barlow (1998:160–61) reports an analysis of the economic efficiency of farming and foraging among the Fremont and concludes that "corn farming with simple technology is economically comparable to collecting and processing a variety of eminently storable seeds and nuts," including several wetland resources. Farming is significantly more costly than the procurement of a large suite of large and small mammals, waterfowl, and the fish taken in the Great Basin.

The later addition of corn farming to the subsistence repertoire in the Great Salt Lake wetlands, the characterization of this area as the least dependent on farming (Marwitt 1970), and the high degree of variation in farmed vs. foraged foods in the diet (Coltrain and Stafford, this volume) suggest that farming was often less viable than foraging in the demographic context of the early Fremont, thus delaying its adoption by several centuries. Whether to farm was not only a decision made in the face of a new behavioral option but also subsequently became a constant decision about managing risk in the face of variations in farmed or foraged foods that were often storable but relatively inefficient. In a case such as the Great Salt Lake wetlands, farming should not only be late but there should also be variation in the diet throughout the farming period.

By the peak of the Fremont period in the A.D. 1000s and 1100s, the contexts of selection had changed. Matrix modification became more important and included increased population, colonization of available farming niches, and the effects of intensification—such as social constraints on mobility, territoriality and defense (D. B. Madsen and Simms 1998), and natural resource depletion (Janetski 1997). At the peak of the Fremont period, these factors should promote increased adaptive diversity. At the same time, the number of behavioral options should decrease as matrix modification limits opportunities. "Switching" among adaptive strategies and relationships of "symbiosis" between farmers and foragers identify contexts of selection that became more important during the Fremont peak (D. B. Madsen and Simms 1998). Adaptive diversity can be a feature of both switching and symbiosis, but the former would produce the most pronounced demographic fluidity.

A model of farmer-forager alternatives expected to be most pronounced near the peak of the Fremont period is schematically depicted in Figure 3.6. Farming is characterized by residential sites with substantial pit houses and facilities for long-term storage (more than a few months) and positioned on floodplains, often near alluvial fans for the purposes of farming. A logistic system is reflected by small, often specialized sites in the wetlands, but yielding high-quality Fremont ceramics just like those found at the farming bases. However, there are residential sites with pit structures, but not positioned for a reliance on farming and with subsurface pits indicative of short-term storage. This is the pattern of limited reliance on farming described decades ago as the Great Salt Lake variant of the Fremont (Marwitt 1970).

The forager system shows some of the same site distribution patterns, but with the farming portion removed. Far from nomadic, what we find are residential camps exemplified by the Orbit Inn site, a late fifteenth-century residential camp used for weeks at a time, but intermittently from late spring through fall (Simms and Heath 1990). This behavior was not just a Late Prehistoric pattern; the Injun Creek site also suggests residential stability, storage, and possibly some farming, with its many loci of occupation dating between the late A.D. 1200s and the 1600s. Evidence for a forager pattern during the Fremont period is found in the case of wickiups at 42Wb32 dating to the A.D. 1000s and 1100s, as well as in the early component of the Levee site and at Bear River numbers 2 and 3. In addition to resi-

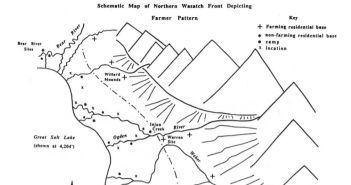

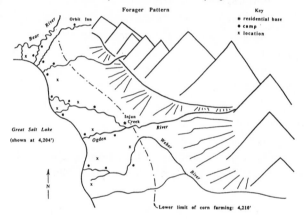

FIGURE 3.6. a. Oblique aerial depictions of farmer-forager settlement patterns, looking north along the Wasatch Front. b. Schematic depiction of farmer-forager systems when both elements are contemporary.

dential camps and bases, the forager system includes short-term camps and special purpose sites. Residential mobility is thus higher than in the farming system, but movement is tethered to a series of camps by short-term storage in subsurface pits.

Perhaps as early as A.D. 1150 in the Great Salt Lake wetlands (Coltrain and Stafford, this volume), and definitely by A.D. 1300 across the Fremont region, denouement (Janetski 1994:194; D. B. Madsen and Simms 1998) is signaled by a declining frequency of agriculture, changes in material culture, and lower population density. The Late Prehistoric transition was not, however, a unitary move from sedentism to nomadism, but was a frequency shift in residential stability, with some residential stability persisting into the centuries after the end of the Fremont period per se (Janetski 1994).

As decisions turned from farming, farmer-forager networks would contain smaller and smaller pockets of farmers. It would be the farmers who were under pressure to assimilate as their groups fissioned. Competition and interaction characterized the contexts of selection as adjustments were made in the distribution of a sizable regional population. Local impacts on game populations would likely continue and changes in hunting patterns would be expected (Lupo and Schmitt 1997). This is a time when long-term traditions in some types of artifact manufacture may be subject to rapid change, and a time when those individuals with broader interactions expressed in language and culture would benefit over those with fewer. Thus, the impetus for adaptive diversity is expected to continue to be strong during Fremont denouement.

Without the energy-intensifying effects of farming, absolute regional population must decline. A foraging system with reduced mobility would continue, but even though the wetlands may tether people during portions of the year, the amount of time spent outside of the wetlands would surely increase—as shown in other parts of the Great Basin with residential stability in wetlands, but without farming (e.g., Larsen and Kelly 1995).

For the end of the sixteenth century, the archaeological record is extremely sparse. Indeed, the post-A.D. 1600 archaeological record is so sparse in an area where it should be seen if it were present that it invites speculation of depopulation from European disease beginning in the seventeenth century (Simms 1990:7–8; Simms and Stuart 1999). The Great Salt Lake wetlands archaeological record supports a demographic anomaly at this time, but it unfortunately occurs when a transgression of the Great Salt Lake inundated the wetlands. Nevertheless, the hypothesis of disease-induced depopulation remains viable because the archaeological record fails to rebound after the lake level falls perhaps only a few decades later. The explanation for these changes remains unclear, but lake levels and climate may not be major factors behind the precipitous decline in the strength of the archeological record after A.D. 1600. It may be the introduction of the deadly novelty of

European disease in a densely populated locale in an otherwise sparsely populated region (see Simms and Stuart 1999).

Evaluating the Model: Archaeology and Bioarchaeology

The archaeological record supports the chronology long known for the Great Salt Lake area: a transition from a period featuring farming to one featuring foraging. Beyond this well-rehearsed culture history, the record also indicates variation in adaptive strategies *within* the Fremont period.

As shown in the previous section, a prediction of adaptive diversity is consistent with much of the archaeological evidence. Table 3.2 lists all radiocarbon dates taken from different types of archaeological sites in the study area and illustrates the extent of the chronological data that links the evidence for adaptive diversity with the Fremont period. Nevertheless, the archaeological record always begs for further support to test the hypothesis of adaptive diversity and tease apart a switching strategy from symbiosis. It is at this point that the bioarchaeological evidence reveals its priceless nature.

Several lines of bioarchaeological evidence are consistent with an expectation of adaptive diversity. There is high variation in stable carbon isotope values from Fremont-dated human remains, indicating that some people spent their lives consuming large amounts of corn while others ate very little (Coltrain and Stafford, this volume). Variation is even apparent in skeletons from the farming bases at Willard, Warren, and 42Sl197, where strong C_4 signatures co-occur with low C_4 values (Coltrain and Stafford, this volume). Stable carbon isotope values between these two opposites are also common, and given that these values accumulate over the life history of individuals, it remains possible that these people spent their life eating a mixed diet or experienced different periods when they ate mostly farmed or foraged foods. Thus, the stable carbon isotope evidence supports adaptive diversity, but by itself cannot tease apart the behavioral contexts of switching and symbiosis.

The biomechanical analysis of limb bones (Ruff, this volume) indicates that men tended to move greater distances, while women moved intermittently. This finding is consistent with an archaeological record of residential stability in the wetlands, of moves among base camps, with men being the primary participants in a logistic system that moved resources from around the wetlands as well as outside them, while women were more tethered to the wetlands. A similar pattern is reported for the Carson-Stillwater area of western Nevada (Larsen, Ruff, and Kelly 1995:121–22, 130–33; Zeanah 1996). The behavioral inferences from the biomechanical analysis are consistent across the Great Salt Lake skeletal sample. This observation compliments the stable isotope evidence by suggesting that the adaptive diversity occurred within a single overall pattern of life and that these varia-

TABLE 3.2.

Summary of Late Holocene Radiocarbon Dates from the Great Salt Lake Wetlands

Site	Elevation	^{14}C Age[a]	Lab #[b]	Calibrated Range[c]	Provenience
42Wb32	4210'	1010 ± 90	Beta64015	A.D. 880–1226	Pit above structure 1
		990 ± 70	Beta64016	A.D. 952–1220	Midden between floors of structures 1 & 2
		870 ± 60	Beta64017	A.D. 1025–1283	Structure 3
42Wb34	4210'	345 ± 170		A.D. 1296–1955 (A.D. 1421–1680 @ 1 sigma)	Injun Creek; Specific location unknown
				A.D. 1277–1471	
42Wb184	4210'	585 ± 90	Beta45881	A.D. 1287–1436	Hearth in structure?
42Wb185c	4208'	600 ± 60		A.D. 1292–1455	This and next sample from refuse
		560 ± 70		A.D. 789–1165	dumped in subsurface pit
		1060 ± 80	Beta45144	A.D. 1046–1099	Beam in pit house
		800 ± 70		A.D. 1114–1145	
				A.D. 1153–1003	
				A.D. 1307–1447	
42Wb317	4207'	540 ± 50	Beta45143	A.D. 870–1178	Beam in pit house
42Wb324	4208'	1040 ± 80		A.D. 686–1228	Bear River 1
42Bo55	4210'	1065 ± 120		A.D. 827–834	Bear River 2
42Bo57	4209'	995 ± 105		A.D. 863–1275	
42Bo98	4210'	1450 ± 110		A.D. 404–786	Bear River 3
42Bo109	4220'	640 ± 110		A.D. 1213–1454	Knoll
42Bo107	4210'	860 ± 110		A.D. 983–1308	Levee (late)
				A.D. 1360–1379	Dwelling 1 (square)
		810 ± 120		A.D. 1004–1403	Dwelling 2 (square)

TABLE 3.2. (continued)

Summary of Late Holocene Radiocarbon Dates from the Great Salt Lake Wetlands

Site	Elevation	^{14}C Age[a]	Lab #[b]	Calibrated Range[c]	Provenience
42Bo110		710 ± 100		A.D. 1162–1427	Dwelling 3 (square—later rounded)
		1170 ± 140		A.D. 627–1168	Levee (early) Dwelling 1 (wickiup)
		1250 ± 140		A.D. 547–1032	Dwelling 2 (wickiup)
42Bo120	4220'	300 ± 70	Beta25167	A.D. 1446–1683	Orbit Inn; all samples
		380 ± 60	Beta18265	A.D. 1430–1654	from hearth or pits
		420 ± 70	Beta17656	A.D. 1405–1647	
		440 ± 60	Beta18266	A.D. 1405–1635	
		570 ± 60	Beta25168	A.D. 1295–1444	
42Bo579	4205'	1690 ± 90		A.D. 134–592	Both dates from a subsurface pit
		930 ± 60	Beta45882	A.D. 1003–1250	Early date questionable
Camera Flats (Antelope Island)	4221'	1400 ± 75		A.D. 540–779	Minimum date on Late Holocene high stand of GSL

[a] This table includes previously published dates with updated calibrations for sites referenced in text, as well as Murchison (1989).

[b] Dates published for the first time include lab numbers.

[c] Calibrations are to bidecadal dendrochronology data set to .05 interval (2 sigma) as per Stuiver and Reimer (1993: computer program), unless otherwise noted.

tions are not expressed across two separate "cultures." Thus, residential cycling and the pattern of switching is supported, although demographic fluidity associated with symbiosis cannot be ruled out.

The molecular genetic analysis (O'Rourke, Parr, and Carlyle, this volume; Parr, Carlyle, and O'Rourke 1996) also indicates consistency across the sample. This, too, suggests actual behavioral linkage among these diverse adaptive strategies, thus supporting the hypothesis of adaptive diversity. The consistency is even more striking when the small size of the sample is considered relative to the 300-year span in which the majority of the samples occurred.

The bioarchaeological evidence cannot speak as directly to the issue of the Fremont–Late Prehistoric transition because the burial sample essentially terminates at A.D. 1300. However, it is possible to examine this transition in light of the drastic decline in human remains in this case since burials younger than the Fremont would be expected to occur if they were present. While it is conceivable that later burials have been destroyed by natural processes, leaving only the Fremont levels, the decline in burial representation is consistent with the culture historical sequence.

It is also possible that the decline in burial at A.D. 1300 results from an ethnic replacement that brought new burial customs. This factor alone is unlikely to account for the virtual absence of remains without speculating that this hypothesized new burial custom required the transport of the deceased out of the wetlands altogether. Parsimony, as well as the ethnographic record of burial in the Great Basin, demands that the decline in burials at A.D. 1300 be attributed to the loss of the intensifying effects of farming and changes in settlement patterns causing people to spend less time in the wetlands, thus decreasing the chances for interment there.

A.D. 1300 is the accepted date for the end of the Fremont period (Janetski 1994), but in terms of behavior the transition was likely underway before this time (Simms 1990; Coltrain 1997), with elements of continuity to at least A.D. 1500 (Janetski 1994). The archaeological context discussed previously supports some overlap in projectile points, ceramics, and settlement, without challenging the evidence that significant changes occur at the Fremont to Late Prehistoric transition.

Stable carbon isotope analysis yields some evidence for a decline in farming in the Great Salt Lake wetlands around A.D. 1150 (Coltrain 1997; Coltrain and Stafford, this volume). Forager diets predominate after this time, yet molecular genetic analysis indicates genetic continuity between the pre- and post-A.D. 1150 populations (O'Rourke, Parr, and Carlyle, this volume; Parr, Carlyle, and O'Rourke 1996). This evidence suggests that regardless of whether immigrants were in the area, changes in farming and material culture may have been underway by A.D. 1150. During these changes, the indigenous people persisted, perhaps as Fremont foragers at least to A.D. 1300, the date when the Great Salt Lake sample of human remains essentially ends.

IMPLICATIONS AND CONCLUSION

The concept of adaptive diversity directs attention to variability in behavior across space, and through time spans ranging from many generations to the life histories of individuals. This view implies variation in interactions among people. Interaction would produce gene flow across linguistic boundaries and could result from trade or warfare among well-bounded groups, low population density in tandem with the rules of exogamy, or the harsh realities of life when the availability of food, mates, and relatives required people to seize a variety of available opportunities—opportunities that may not have always been the most pleasant for people, but that were increased by the presence of farming centers.

The inevitable consequence of increased interaction of any sort is demographic fluidity—the actual movement of people among various groups over time. A tantalizing signal of demographic fluidity is found in the burial orientations in the Great Salt Lake skeletal sample (Simms, Loveland, and Stuart 1991:25). The multitude of positions in a sample spanning three centuries with no particular chronological pattern in those postures indicates that religious views on the matter of burial posture were diverse. This finding discounts a perspective that the Fremont buried their people in a particular way because of a singular "Fremont" religion.

The findings of adaptive diversity hold implications for general issues in the archaeology of the Desert West, and two examples are described here to illustrate the utility of the perspective. First, ceramic use by Great Basin foragers presents an opportunity to integrate the archaeology of foragers with the better-known farmers. Ceramics were likely a women's technology in the Desert West, leading to expectations about interactions among people relating to gender, rather than just culture. The second issue revolves around the relationship between peoples, migrations, and population genetics to suggest ways of framing the issue of continuity between contemporary American Indians and the ancient inhabitants of the region.

Ceramics, Gender, and Basin Plateau Foragers

The notion that ceramic use by foragers diffused from farmers is an old one (Baldwin 1945; Tuohy 1973; see Lyneis 1994:142–43). This idea can be expanded upon in two ways by modeling the circumstances of ceramic adoption in terms of contingent decision making and the larger demographic context in which such decisions are made.

As farming strategies spread, ceramics could be adopted by foragers when tethered to areas either by longer than usual periods of residence or through occupational redundancy (Lyneis 1994). Examples include Great Basin wetland habitats (based on springs, lakes, or streams) and areas of substantial pine-nut harvesting. While these settings can be found Basin-wide, Lyneis (1982) suggests we should also see the greatest frequency of ceramic use in parts of the region in greatest proximity to farmers—that is, east to west (Fremont proximity) and south to north (Anasazi proximity). Thus, we should expect increased ceramic use by foragers in wetland and pine-nutting areas, especially along the eastern, southeastern, and southwestern Great Basin rims.

The spread of ceramic use would also be conditioned by the degree of adaptive diversity. Ceramic use by Basin/Plateau foragers could conceivably have begun as soon as the use of ceramics by farmers appeared, perhaps by A.D. 400–500, but it would be infrequent until there was increased demographic fluidity. To reiterate, times of heightened demographic fluidity among farmers and foragers should have occurred during the demographic peak of farming between the A.D. 1000s and 1100s and have continued to be stimulated by the upheaval associated with the failures of farming from A.D. 1150 to at least A.D. 1300.

Rhode (1994) uses thermoluminescence dating to date ceramics from 14 sites in the southern and eastern Great Basin. He found brownware ceramics present as early as A.D. 800 (although they *may* date as early as A.D. 500 at Alta Toquima in central Nevada; see Grayson [1993:263]), but their presence is not well established until A.D. 1000, the period of increased adaptive diversity. It is well established that ceramic use by foragers persisted through the Fremont to Late Prehistoric transition, when adaptive diversity continued to be high.

This line of thinking can be further developed by an appeal to gender. Assuming women made ceramics in the ancient Desert West, ceramic use among foragers would create local industries and the spread of styles would be shaped by the mobility of women. A case in point: women's mobility would be low relative to that of men in day-to-day or month-to-month terms since women were tethered to bases and attended to stored foods while men pursued game and collected non-local raw materials and other resources worthy of transport. Over the life history of a woman, however, her mobility may have been considerable in response to marriage, divorce, and spousal death. Any of these events could cause women to move across the landscapes, lifeways, and cultural boundaries. During the height of Fremont adaptive diversity, foragers would increasingly have experienced fragmentation of groups and have cycled into the sphere of farming villages, often under conditions of greatly reduced status (Upham 1994:122–23, 139). The greatest impact of this behavior would have been on women and children. Conversely, women under residential conditions associated with the relative stability of intensive agriculture would have been less mobile if a matrilocal residence and land-tenure system is hypothesized, although villagers of low socioeconomic status were also subject to displacement due to the intrinsic variability in farming production (Upham 1994:123).

This scenario is consistent with the findings of Simms, Ugan, and Bright (1997), where the morphology of forager ceramics varies from those made by farmers. A recent study of ceramics across western Utah lends further support (Bright et al. 1998). The regional and subregional variability reflected in the traditional Fremont ceramic types surely occurs. There is, however, evidence that these types were produced with local materials, leading to variability in Fremont types across their distributions (Simms et al. 1997). This questions the habit of inferring whether ceramics are intrusive only on the basis of visual typing of sherds without determining if their materials fit a pattern of local production (contra Richens 1997:83). It remains possible that some long-distance movement of specialized vessels (painted and corrugated wares) occurred as well as the more common pattern of local manufacture (Richens 1997:83–84). However, in the Great Salt Lake area and Utah Valley (Simms, Ugan, and Bright 1997:786–87), highly distinctive sherds typed as Snake Valley Red-on-Buff and Sevier Gray, but which were manufactured locally in the Great Salt Lake area (Simms, Ugan, and Bright 1997:789) and were not intrusive. Finally, there would have been gradational rather than categorical differences among "types," but the gradation would be greater among foragers than among farmers. This distinction is supported by existing Great Basin ceramic studies (Dean 1992; Griset 1986; Lockett and Pippin 1990:71; Lyneis 1994; J. M. Mack 1990).

Adaptive Diversity, Peoples, and Migrations

The perspective taken here also holds implications for how we frame questions about, understand, and describe the relationship between the ancient Fremont archaeological culture and the historic, Numic-speaking inhabitants of the Basin/Plateau region. This is important not only to a scholarly interest in the past but also in terms of how archaeologists interact with American Indians descended from the ancients.

Archaeologists often portray the Fremont–to–Late-Prehistoric transition as a dying out of a culture, leading to the juxtaposition of population replacement *versus* in-situ development. Both of these views are cast as the product of an entity, an event, called the Numic Spread. The alternatives presented to account for this interpretation are, like the definition of the problem, typological and historical, sometimes with an adaptationist theme attached. There are those who opt for the recent arrival of Numic speakers to the region after Fremont denouement (e.g., Bettinger 1994; Janetski 1994) versus those who infer a long-term presence of Numic speakers in the region (e.g., Aikens 1994; Holmer 1994), but maintain the notion that *the* Numic are not *the* Fremont. The "mechanisms" and "causal factors" (Sutton and Rhode 1994) offered to account for this event are equally historicist and include a clash of adaptive strategies *cum* cultures (Bettinger and Baumhoff 1982) or a clash defined in the more familiar terms of warfare among cultures (Sutton 1991).

The perspective taken here in tandem with the bioarchaeological evidence suggests there may be less bounded ways of looking at the situation in order to get beyond the "we were always here" versus the "they (Numic speakers) arrived recently" polemics. For instance, the Uto-Aztecan language family (and Numic languages?) was in the Southwest for thousands of years, spreading from Mexico and across the Southwest with farming. The Fremont developed through the acculturation of an indigenous, Archaic population of unknown linguistic affiliation with the addition of an unknown number of farming immigrants, which implies, at a minimum, some relationship between the Fremont and historical Numa by virtue of a Uto-Aztecan connection. Conversely, those who argue for a recent, rapid spread beg the issue of whether the indigenous people were linguistically similar or different, since a recent-spread model presumes linguistic contrast without really indulging the issue of how much contrast allows a historical group to be related.

The behavioral context associated with the spread of farming across the Desert West and the consequences of intensification is one of connections and varying degrees of demographic fluidity among farmers and foragers. The context of the Numic Spread is thus the massive change that occurred during the last two millennia across much of western North America. A model of adaptive diversity predicts that interactions among people would peak at the height of farming's impact and continue to be high during the subsequent deintensification. It could be argued that depopulation from European-induced diseases only exacerbated demographic fluidity among people with diverse cultural genealogies.

The nascent field of molecular genetic analysis can assist in reformulating the question of relationships in less typological terms because genetic variation is best described as clines rather than in bounded terms. The purpose is not to substitute genetically defined types for cultural types, but to use the limited genetic findings to shape how we approach the behavior behind our cultural types and periods. The molecular genetic analysis on the Great Salt Lake skeletons is relevant to this issue even though the amount of work done is small and the findings more stimulating than conclusive.

Forty-seven individuals from the Great Salt Lake wetlands, dating between 550 and 1600 B.P., were screened for four mitochondrial DNA markers. They showed differences in two genetic markers that distinguish them from Athabascan populations (Parr, Carlyle, and O'Rourke 1996), thus failing to support the hypothesis that the Fremont were Athabascans who moved eastward onto the Plains in the Late Prehistoric period (Aikens 1966). This is significant to those who wish to claim the Fremont are decisively different from the historic Numic speakers of the region.

The Great Salt Lake series is also distinct from Anasazi skeletons from southeastern Utah (Parr, Carlyle, and O'Rourke 1996; O'Rourke, Parr, and Carlyle, this volume). On the one hand, this statement suggests that claims of Fremont ancestry by historical Southwestern cultures (such as the Hopi) are difficult to make. On the other hand, it would be dangerous to extend the Great Salt Lake data to the entire Fremont region (and from southeastern Utah to all Anasazi), lest we once again discount the potential for diversity in connections and interactions *within* our archaeological cultures, not just between them. The chances for admixture to the Fremont from the Southwest should increase considerably on the Colorado Plateau, where there is evidence of immigration in addition to indigenous development (D. B. Madsen and Simms 1998). In those parts of the Fremont region, affiliations with historical Southwestern cultures, such as the Hopi, may increase. This case is an example of how genetic analysis may help tease apart our understanding of the past as well as interpreting the claims of modern tribes.

Comparison of the Great Salt Lake samples with modern Paiute and Shoshoni samples from western Nevada (Lorenz and Smith 1994) shows marked differences. At first glance these differences are consistent with the model of a recent Numic spread and a distinctiveness from the Fremont. However, the Great Salt Lake samples are also different from late Archaic skeletons from western Nevada (O'Rourke, Parr, and Carlyle, this volume), suggesting that it is distance rather than linguistic affiliation that is producing this genetic pattern. If genetic analysis finds heterogeneity across the historical ranges of Numic languages and across the Fremont region, then the behavioral mechanics of the Fremont to Late Prehistoric transition and the Numic Spread would be far more textured than the image created by the polarized camps in the Numic Spread debate. The perspective represented by adaptive diversity shows that archaeological modeling can be moved toward greater behavioral realism.

The emerging picture of population genetics in western North America is one of heterogeneity and perhaps patchiness in affiliations (Kaestle, Lorenz, and Smith, this volume; O'Rourke, Parr, and Carlyle, this volume). This finding alone should temper the presumption of archaeologists that differences must be great and well bounded simply because we find there is archaeological and linguistic evidence of diversity (or because politics demand contrast and antagonism). The view taken here makes it appropriate to argue that physical elements of the Fremont past indeed survive today in the genetic variability being found across the Great Basin (e.g., Kaestle 1995; Kaestle, Lorenz, and Smith, this volume; Parr, Carlyle, and O'Rourke 1996; O'Rourke, Parr, and Carlyle, this volume; D. G. Smith, Bettinger, and Rolfs, 1995). The Fremont "people" and "the Numic Spread" still may be real in some abstract sense, but such metaphors hold less and less educa-

tional value for our discipline, the lay public, and American Indians because they
are unrealistic portrayals of history and people. As such, they disconnect *all* of us
from the past.

On a larger scale of problem, perhaps we need to apply more fully our
improved appreciation of the demographic robustness and intensity of pre-
Columbian America. It was likely more "cosmopolitan" than allowed for in archaeological or contemporary political cliché.

Acknowledgments

The Great Salt Lake Wetlands Project was supported by the National Science
Foundation (DBS 9223227 to S. R. Simms and D. H. O'Rourke), the State of
Utah, the U. S. Bureau of Reclamation, Utah State University, the University of
Utah, and the U.S. Fish and Wildlife Service. This project involved numerous
people and organizations. It meshed the talents of amateur archaeologists, professionals, students, and the public in numbers too great to extend individual thanks
despite the magnitude of many personal contributions. This project is the work of
members of the Utah Statewide Archaeological Society, the Utah State University
Archaeology Field Schools, the Utah Division of State History, a host of scientists
who donated time and expertise, and the good graces of the Northwestern Band of
the Shoshoni Nation, especially the tribal council of 1990–91. Thanks also to the
volume editors, and the various reviewers and editors. The inadequacies remain
mine. I do wish to dedicate this chapter to the memory of Carol Loveland, who
passed away in December 1995 and who was so much a part of this work.

4

Stable Carbon Isotopes and Great Salt Lake Wetlands Diet
Toward an Understanding of the Great Basin Formative

Joan Brenner Coltrain and Thomas W. Stafford, Jr.

Research on Great Basin wetlands has a lengthy history (for a review see C. S. Fowler and Fowler 1990). Generally characterized by a diverse fauna and dense stands of cattail (*Typha* sp.) and other edible hydrophytes, Great Basin wetlands have long been viewed as rich habitats in otherwise arid lowland settings. In the past few decades, researchers have been particularly interested in the seasonal use of wetland habitats. In this regard, recent studies have examined the relationship between mobility and the distribution, abundance, and productivity of wetland resources (Kelly 1985, 1990; D. B. Madsen 1979; Raven and Elston 1989; Zeanah et al. 1995), in keeping with the general perception that Great Basin wetlands offered a rich and diverse set of economic options likely important to prehistoric foragers. Such research has led to the recognition that wetland habitats are not uniformly attractive. Their role in foraging economies appears to vary with both the proximity and richness of other resource patches, uplands in particular, and the physical geography of specific marsh settings (e.g., Kelly 1985, 1990; Raven and Elston 1992; Rhode 1990a).

In the eastern Great Basin, debate over the importance of wetlands is complicated by the introduction of Fremont agricultural strategies (A.D. 400–1350). Understanding their impact on wetland exploitation is hampered by uncertainty surrounding the contribution of cultigens to Fremont diets. Rather than relatively heavy dependence on maize commonly associated with Formative economies, some researchers have argued that Fremont subsistence strategies were more diverse, characterized by a high degree of seasonal mobility in some settings and full-time foraging in others (Simms 1986; D. B. Madsen 1982). If so, wetlands may

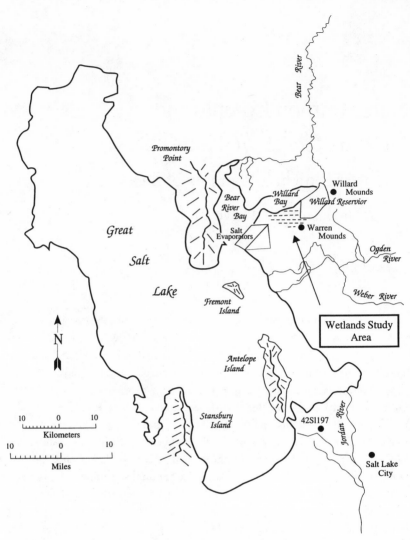

FIGURE 4.1. The Great Salt Lake wetlands study area and adjacent sites.

have continued to play an important role in Fremont economies after the adoption of cultigens.

In the decades following World War II and particularly since the 1970s, researchers have devoted increasing attention to Fremont subsistence (e.g., Berry 1974; D. B. Madsen and Lindsay 1977; Metcalfe 1984); yet, it has proven difficult to assess the importance of marsh resources using traditional methods. Macrofossil and palynological assemblages are inconclusive with respect to the composition of prehistoric diets. Although investigators can identify likely dietary elements, their relative caloric contribution is biased by differential transport, preservation,

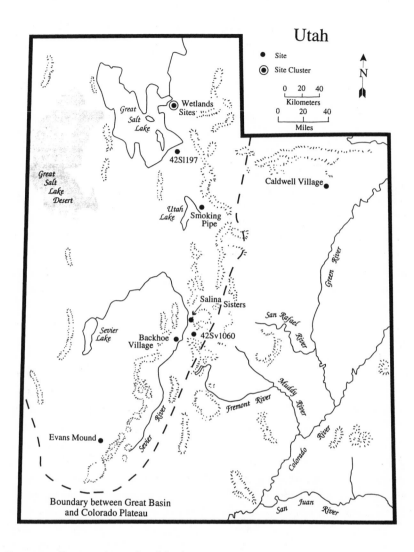

FIGURE 4.2. Fremont sites analyzed for diet.

and recovery of faunal bone, plant materials, and fossil pollens (e.g., Janetski 1990). Stable carbon isotope analysis of human skeletal remains yields an additional line of evidence for prehistoric diets. Recent recovery of the Great Salt Lake wetlands mortuary collection provided the opportunity to use this technique in a wetland setting (Figure 4.1). Previous research with Fremont burials from sites outside the wetlands supplied a comparative data set (Figure 4.2; see also Coltrain 1993), which allowed us to address two issues: (1) the influence of wetland environments on Fremont diets and, by extension, (2) Fremont economic diversity.

Research was initiated to investigate these topics by monitoring the stable carbon isotope ratios of bone collagen from a representative set of burials to assess the role of maize in wetland diets. However, recent controlled diet experiments (Ambrose and Norr 1993; Tieszen and Fagre 1993b) have raised a number of questions regarding this procedure. Initial results indicate that isotope ratios from the collagen fraction of whole bone may track the carbon isotope signature of dietary protein more closely than that of overall diet (Ambrose and Norr 1993; Tieszen and Fagre 1993b). This finding suggests that in some situations the percentage of maize in sampled diets cannot be reliably calculated from collagen isotope readings. The implications of our data for Fremont subsistence are discussed in light of this revision. Other contributions to this volume provide background on the Great Salt Lake wetlands project (Simms, this volume; see also Fawcett and Simms 1993; Simms, Loveland, and Stuart 1991), give circumstances surrounding recovery of the burial collection (Simms, this volume; see also Fawcett and Simms 1993; Simms, Loveland, and Stuart 1991), and discuss its osteological (Bright and Loveland, this volume) and genetic characteristics (O'Rourke, Parr, and Carlyle, this volume). The following section is a brief review of the Great Basin Formative and recent arguments regarding the role of native resources in Fremont diets.

THE GREAT BASIN FORMATIVE

Formative populations in the eastern Great Basin and on the northern Colorado Plateau are assigned to the Fremont archaeological culture (A.D. 400–1350) (Lindsay 1986; Talbot and Wilde 1989). It is thought that the Fremont cultural complex developed during the first half of the Christian era as individuals practicing mobile foraging strategies slowly added maize to a suite of native resources, becoming more dependent on cultigens over time (Jennings 1978). Village sites, for which the Fremont are best known, began to appear by ca. A.D. 400 (Talbot and Wilde 1989: Figure 2) and commonly consisted of pit houses or single-room surface dwellings, accompanied by surface and subterranean storage in association with maize and relatively well-made ceramics. After A.D. 700, these sites increased in frequency, reaching their maximum distribution between A.D. 1040 and 1190. At ca. A.D. 1190, pronounced habitational retraction took place; and by A.D. 1350, villages were no longer occupied. Populations in the study area were again reliant on mobile foraging strategies (see Talbot and Wilde 1989 for a review).

Land-use patterns clearly changed with the introduction and abandonment of cultigens, yet foraging appeared to remain important throughout the Fremont sequence. The abundance of native resources recovered from Fremont residential bases has led to ongoing debate over the importance of maize relative to wetland resources or wild foods in general. Berry (1974) has argued that the wild resource base was not productive enough to maintain even partial sedentism in the absence of maize agriculture. Others have contended that village sedentism was maintained by exploitation of resource-rich wetland habitats, whereas maize cultivation was a secondary strategy (D. B. Madsen 1979, 1982; D. B. Madsen and Lindsay 1977). To evaluate this argument, Janetski (1990) examined faunal assemblage diversity (see also Grayson 1984) and site location in the vicinity of Utah Lake with the premise that if both Fremont and subsequent forager (Late Prehistoric) economies were uniformly dependent on wetland resources, stability would be reflected in redundantly located, multicomponent sites, and faunal assemblages of similar richness and evenness. Hampered by a lack of uniformly collected data, results were inconclusive. Although site location tended to support D. B. Madsen's view, faunal assemblage diversity suggested that exploitation strategies changed at the Fremont/Late Prehistoric interface, indicating wetland resources were not utilized in the same way throughout the sequence.

A decade ago, the debate over Fremont subsistence was mitigated somewhat by Simms (1986; see also D. B. Madsen 1982), who proposed that the Fremont practiced a diverse set of economic strategies (see also Simms, this volume): (1) some individuals foraged logistically, supplementing maize yields with wild resources, but remained relatively sedentary at agricultural villages; (2) some Fremont practiced a more mixed strategy, abandoning smaller residential bases seasonally and/or during periods of shortfall, exhibiting greater mobility and dependency on wild resources than their logistical counterparts; and (3) some individuals were full-time foragers, highly mobile and largely dependent on wild resources.

A closer look at Fremont settlement patterns supports but fails to confirm Simms's model. In this regard, Fremont sites fall into three general categories (see D. B. Madsen 1989 for a review): (1) villages situated along perennial streams immediately below the piñon/juniper zone, at elevations that optimize the trade-off between growing season moisture and temperature requirements (Lindsay 1986); (2) temporary foraging and/or hunting camps often in piñon/juniper woodland or wetland settings; and (3) evidence for transitory occupation of caves and rock-shelters or their use as storage facilities.

Research on the Fremont has focused primarily on archaeologically visible residential bases, but ephemeral camps, rock-shelters, and caching sites are relevant features in many Fremont landscapes. Numerous surveys, beginning with Alice Hunt's work (1953) in the La Sal Mountains, illustrate the frequency of these campsites. Simms (1986) reports a foraging camp in the Sevier desert with two brush-and-pole structures, hearths, Fremont ceramics, and maize. S. J. Smith (1994) reports a similar site located in a shad scale vegetation zone ca. 30 miles southwest of the Great Salt Lake. Foraging/hunting camps are also common on the eastern margins of the Great Salt Lake (Aikens 1966, 1967; Fry and Dalley

1979; W. F. Shields and Dalley 1978). Some lack structures, but exhibit numerous subsurface storage pits and diverse assemblages of local fauna, indicating repeated temporary occupation.

Today, Simms's less polarized view (1986) of Fremont subsistence is widely accepted, yet it is a challenging hypothesis to test by traditional means. Full-time foraging, now recognized as a likely Fremont strategy, is the least visible archaeologically. Although correlations have been demonstrated between site type/sedentism and ceramic quality (Ugan and Simms 1994), it remains difficult to distinguish temporary camps resulting from the activity of full-time foragers from those left by farmers foraging logistically or during periods of shortfall (see also M. R. Schurr 1992). By extension, the exploitation of wetland habitats and their role in Fremont economies remain unclear.

MATERIALS AND METHODS

Stable carbon isotope biochemistry assists researchers in reconstructing economic strategies in conjunction with site structure, site distribution, and macrofossil counts. The technique uses isotope ratio mass spectrometry to monitor relative abundances of the stable isotopes of carbon ($^{13}C/^{12}C$) in human bone collagen or apatite. These abundances covary with the isotope signature of selected dietary elements and have been used in the past to estimate maize consumption (e.g., Decker and Tieszen 1989; Spielmann, Schoeninger, and Moore 1990). Maize belongs to a suite of tropical grasses that employs a C_4 (Slack-Hatch) photosynthetic pathway to metabolize atmospheric CO_2 (see Peisker and Henderson 1992 for a review). Most midlatitude native floras, including wetland vegetation, employ a C_3 (Calvin) pathway, discriminating heavily against $^{13}CO_2$ during photosynthesis (see O'Leary, Madhavan, and Paneth 1992 for a review). Enzymatic and physical properties of the C_4 pathway result in less discrimination, increasing the ratio of $^{13}C/^{12}C$ in C_4 plant tissues. Because discrimination against ^{13}C is tightly correlated with plant type, C_3 and C_4 plants have discrete stable carbon isotope means and ranges. These are passed up the food chain, from herbivores to omnivores and carnivores, leaving distinctive signatures in the bone tissue of consumers. A third pathway, Crassulacean acid metabolism (CAM), is restricted to succulents and, under certain conditions, may replicate C_4 isotope readings (see Griffiths 1992 for a review).

The ratio of $^{13}C/^{12}C$ in human skeletal remains is expressed in (delta) $\delta^{13}C$ notation as parts "per mil" (‰) difference from an internationally recognized standard. The standard, assigned a value of 0 ‰ (Craig 1957), is a Pee Dee Formation carbonate (PDB) enriched in ^{13}C relative to most naturally occurring carbon. Thus, carbon isotope readings from organic remains are negative values. The values of $\delta^{13}C$ are obtained with an isotope ratio mass spectrometer by comparing the ratio of $^{13}C/^{12}C$ in the sample against a standard and computed as follows:

Equation 1:

$$\delta^{13}C = \frac{Rsample - Rstandard}{Rstandard} \times 1000\ \permil$$

where $R = {}^{13}C/{}^{12}C$.

Prior to the publication of results from controlled diet experiments (Ambrose and Norr 1993; Tieszen and Fagre 1993b), $\delta^{13}C$ values were commonly thought to monitor the percentage of foods with a C_4 isotope signature in the diet of sampled individuals. This percentage was calculated as follows (modified from Schwarcz et al. 1985):

Equation 2:

$$\% C4 = \frac{|\delta_3| - |\delta s| - D_{dc}}{|\delta_3| - |\delta_4|} \times 100$$

where δ_3 = value for C_3 dietary component[1];

δ_4 = value for C_4 dietary component[2];

$D_{dc} = D_{diet} - D_{collagen}$ (+5 ‰ fractionation);

δ_s = value of bone collagen sample.

Recent experimental research indicates that the relationship between diet and bone collagen $\delta^{13}C$ is more complex than represented by Equation 2. Specifically, the fractionation offset between diet and collagen (D_{dc}) is not fixed at +5 ‰, but varies with the amount and isotope composition of dietary protein (Ambrose and Norr 1993; Tieszen and Fagre 1993b). In brief, if dietary protein carries a C_3 signal while the energy component of the diet (i.e, carbohydrates or lipids) comes from a C_4 food source, fractionation is less than 5 ‰. If the reverse holds, fractionation is greater than 5 ‰. Only in monotonic diets (i.e., all C_3 or C_4) is the 5 ‰ fractionation constant commonly used to reconstruct past diets likely to accurately represent diet-collagen spacing (Ambrose and Norr 1993:Table 4; Tieszen and Fagre 1993b:Table 5). If these results apply to human paleodiet, we may be underestimating the importance of maize in settings where animal protein derives primarily from browsers subsisting on C_3 forage and energy is supplied by maize. Conversely, in marine or Plains economies where protein is isotopically enriched relative to dietary energy (e.g., Chisholm, Nelson, and Schwarcz 1982; McGovern-Wilson and Quinn 1996; Tuross and Fogel 1994), we may be overestimating dependency on marine resources or bison, respectively.

Despite these complexities, it is clear that stable carbon isotope readings reflect long-term diets. Adult bone collagen turns over slowly. Researchers estimate mean residence time, or the average time for replacement of bone collagen carbon by an equivalent amount of carbon, at 30 years[3] (Stenhouse and Baxter 1977, 1979:333; see also Harkness and Walton 1972; and Libby et al. 1964). Thus, carbon isotope ratios provide a weighted average of adult dietary intake over approximately three decades.

TABLE 4.1.
Great Salt Lake Wetlands, Warren and Willard Mounds Stable Carbon Isotope Data

Burial & Site	Sex	Age	δ^{13}C ‰	Date B.P.	Calibrated Date	Calibrated 2σ Range	CAMS	Bone %N[a]	Collagen Yield[b]
3[c] 42Wb48	F	30–35	-18.4	1020 ± 50	A.D. 1017	A.D. 898–1159	4060	3.9	21.1
6 "		adult	-13.0	1100 ± 60	A.D. 973	A.D. 789–1029	11110	2.3	25.5
8 "		subadult	-17.6	860 ± 80	A.D. 1214	A.D. 1016–1293	8255	0.5	9.9
11 42Wb184	M	2–3	-17.2	790 ± 50	A.D. 1263	A.D. 1167–1296	12283	3.5	23.2
14 42Wb185a	M	45+	-14.8	1430 ± 50	A.D. 641	A.D. 547–678	12278	2.0	16.9
15	M	40–45	-18.4	1390 ± 60	A.D. 657	A.D. 560–773	11119	1.1	10.7
16 42Wb185c		adult	-15.5	920 ± 50	A.D. 1127	A.D. 1016–1245	12285	3.6	22.5
17 "		25–30	-12.8	1190 ± 60	A.D. 881	A.D. 683–990	12282	2.1	14.0
20 42Wb269		30+	-17.6	900 ± 50	A.D. 1165	A.D. 1022–1257	12277	2.5	18.2
21 "		adult	-18.8	1130 ± 60	A.D. 914	A.D. 778–1020	11106	0.9	11.8
22 "		12–17	-19.0	906 ± 34*	A.D. 1163	A.D. 1029–1224		1.8	10.1
23 "	M	20–30	-18.1	960 ± 39*	A.D. 1037	A.D. 1011–1177		3.2	17.8
26 "		7–8	-19.1	730 ± 60	A.D. 1286	A.D. 1217–1393	10214	2.7	16.9
27 "	F	17–25	-18.9	940 ± 60	A.D. 1115	A.D. 996–1230	12274	2.0	18.7
28 "	F	35+	-18.2	890 ± 60	A.D. 1168	A.D. 1019–1279	5314	3.7	19.2
29 "		6–7	-19.1	870 ± 60	A.D. 1195	A.D. 1025–1283	4917	3.4	12.3
32 42Wb286	F	35–40	-17.9	890 ± 60	A.D. 1168	A.D. 1019–1279	4919	3.5	19.8
33 42Wb304	M	Adult	-18.5	1000 ± 60	A.D. 1022	A.D. 898–1179	11108	2.9	16.9
35 42Wb317		1.5–3	-18.4	1014 ± 39*	A.D. 1018	A.D. 976–1155		1.0	6.6
36 42Wb318		2–4	-16.6	1500 ± 80	A.D. 596	A.D. 411–672	12280	1.0	6.6
37 "	F	adult	-18.1	1135 ± 46*	A.D. 918	A.D. 786–1011		0.8	3.3
40 42Wb319		9–12	-18.3	870 ± 50	A.D. 1195	A.D. 1031–1279	12279	2.0	20.0

Table 4.1. (continued)

Burial & Site	Age	Sex	$\delta^{13}C$ ‰	Date B.P.	Calibrated Date	Calibrated 2σ Range	CAMS	Bone %N[a]	Collagen Yield[b]
41	"	30–35		-18.3	800 ± 70	A.D. 1253	A.D. 1046–1303	8256	2.3	20.5
43	42Wb320	16–20	F	-17.2	540 ± 40	A.D. 1410	A.D. 1314–1442	12284	3.4	22.4
45	42Wb322	adult		-15.2	1150 ± 110	A.D. 891	A.D. 662–1156	5315	3.4	19.5
47	42Wb324	45+	M	-12.7	1050 ± 70	A.D. 1005	A.D. 880–1162	8254	3.3	19.2
48	"	10–12.5		-13.6	1010 ± 60	A.D. 1020	A.D. 895–1168	5330	2.8	19.0
49	"	25–30		-19.2	920 ± 60	A.D. 1127	A.D. 1010–1257	5325	2.0	16.3
51	"	9–10		-13.4	1250 ± 60	A.D. 779	A.D. 662–956	11115	2.1	16.3
52	"	12+		-14.8	1330 ± 100	A.D. 676	A.D. 547–956	10221	2.2	17.3
53	"	35–40	M	-10.8	1175 ± 42*	A.D. 884	A.D. 775–979		4.0	21.7
55	"	19–24	M	-10.0	1031 ± 49*	A.D. 1031	A.D. 895–1156		3.7	20.8
56	"	17–22	M	-11.3	1030 ± 70	A.D. 1014	A.D. 885–1168	5328	3.6	21.9
57	"	5–9		-13.5	1350 ± 60	A.D. 668	A.D. 608–786	5323	3.3	17.5
58	"	25–30	M	-10.2	980 ± 39*	A.D. 1028	A.D. 997–1165		3.8	19.2
61	42Bo73	40+	F	-15.1	1090 ± 60	A.D. 978	A.D. 857–1033	4918	2.1	18.8
62	"	Unk		-17.5	1150 ± 60	A.D. 891	A.D. 727–1014	11112	3.1	18.1
64	42Bo579	18–23	F	-17.0	1630 ± 70	A.D. 423	A.D. 252–602	10219	0.4	5.9
65	42Bo580	45+		-18.2	920 ± 60	A.D. 1127	A.D. 1010–1257	5317	0.8	14.4
66	"	subadult		-18.3	980 ± 50	A.D. 1028	A.D. 983–1180	12269	1.7	17.3
68	42Bo599	45+	F	-18.0	1010 ± 50	A.D. 1020	A.D. 900–1162	5324	3.4	19.2
69	"	1.5–3		-17.9	780 ± 60	A.D. 1275	A.D. 1165–1303	5316	1.0	12.0
70	"	5.5–8		-18.5	1130 ± 60	A.D. 914	A.D. 778–1020	5313	2.5	14.9
73	42Wb144	adult		-19.8	1000 ± 60	A.D. 1022	A.D. 898–1179	11117	2.4	19.2
76	42Wb185c	adult		-17.0	1170 ± 50	A.D. 886	A.D. 726–990	12271	3.0	21.3

TABLE 4.1. (continued)

Burial & Site	Age	Sex	δ¹³C ‰	Date B.P.	Calibrated Date	Calibrated 2σ Range	CAMS	Bone %N[a]	Collagen Yield[b]
77 42Bo700	50+	M	-14.4	1250 ± 70	A.D. 779	A.D. 656–968	10360	2.4	18.6
78 42Wb32	adult		-19.2	1440 ± 70	A.D. 635	A.D. 451–694	11107	1.0	14.5
79 "	adult		-15.4	1140 ± 50	A.D. 893	A.D. 782–1012	12273	1.7	13.1
83 "	45+	M	-10.2	1050 ± 60	A.D. 1005	A.D. 885–1156	12276	2.9	19.0
84 "	50+	F	-16.7	1160 ± 60	A.D. 888	A.D. 718–1011	11116	2.5	18.5
1[d] 42S1197 subadult		-15.8	1130 ± 40	A.D. 914		A.D. 817–1007	12281	3.5	19.5
2 "	adult		-13.2	1380 ± 60	A.D. 660	A.D. 570–776	10211	3.2	27.0
4a "	8		-16.2	1160 ± 60	A.D. 999	A.D. 718–1011	11114	3.7	22.9
W. Warren (21750)/15)	adult		-12.0	1180 ± 60	A.D. 883	A.D. 688–998	8349	3.3	21.9
Willard Mds (11349)	adult		-13.7	1250 ± 50	A.D. 779	A.D. 667–891	10220	3.1	19.6
Willard Mds[e] (Fs 1/97)	adult		-11.9	1220 ± 60	A.D. 789	A.D. 670–974	10215	1.4	9.2
Willard Mds[f] (Fs 1/108)	adult		-18.0	690 ± 60	A.D. 1295	A.D. 1237–1403	11109	1.9	10.3

[a] Percent nitrogen in whole bone by weight.
[b] Percent collagen in whole bone by weight.
[c] Burials recovered in the Great Salt Lake wetlands project (Simms, Loveland, and Stuart 1991).
[d] Burials salvaged by the Utah State Division of History, Antiquities Section, from a wetlands construction site at south end of the Great Salt Lake.
[e] 42Bo30.
[f] 42Bo76.

*Pooled mean date on two or more replicate readings. See Coltrain (1997: Table 4.3) for CAMS and further discussion of radiocarbon dates.

TABLE 4.2.

Stable Carbon Isotope Values ($\delta^{13}C$) for Human Remains from
Six Fremont Sites with a Subset of Calibrated Radiocarbon Dates

Site	Burial	$\delta^{13}C$ ‰	Site Mean $\delta^{13}C$ ‰
Evans Mound	Fs210.57	–7.6	
Evans Mound	Fs267.16	–10.2	
Evans Mound	Fs1276.83	–8.7	–8.8 ± 1.3
Backhoe Village	76As1.16.20	–7.4	
Backhoe Village	76As1.37.51	–7.6	–7.5 ± 0.1
Caldwell Village	3	–8.8	
Caldwell Village	2	–8.4	
Caldwell Village	4	–8.2	
Caldwell Village	6	–11.0	–9.1 ± 1.3
Salina Sisters	1	–8.4	
Salina Sisters	2	–8.0	–8.2 ± 0.3
Smoking Pipe	N/A	–9.2	
*42Sv1060	N/A	–9.5	

Site	Burial	Calibrated 2σ Range	Calibrated Date	CAMS
Salina Sisters	1	A.D. 869–1023	A.D. 973	12275
Salina Sisters	2	A.D. 890–1162	A.D. 1014	10213
Smoking Pipe	N/A	A.D. 778–1020	A.D. 914	10212

* Gooseberry Valley burial mound adjacent to two pit structures.

Procedures used to analyze samples in the previous study (i.e., Evans Mound, Backhoe Village, Caldwell Village, and 42Sv1060) are reported elsewhere (Coltrain 1993). The remainder of the collection was analyzed as follows. Approximately two grams of cortical bone were cleaned of exterior contaminants, then decalcified in 0.6 N HCl at 4°C. The collagen pseudomorph was rinsed to neutrality then treated with 5 percent KOH to remove organic contaminants and again rinsed to neutrality, then lyophilized and weighed to obtain collagen yields. Gelatin was extracted by heating approximately 200 mg of lyophilized, decalcified bone with 5 ml of H_2O (pH 3) for 24 hours at 120°C. After gelatinization, water-soluble and water-insoluble phases were separated by filtration and the water-soluble supernatant lyophilized. Eight to 10 mg of sample, 1 gr copper, 0.5 gr cupric oxide and 0.1 gr silver were loaded into 6 mm quartz tubes, combusted at 800°C for three hours, then cooled slowly. CO_2 was collected off-line by cryogenic distillation. One aliquot of CO_2 was reserved for stable isotope analysis. A second was graphited and the graphite forwarded to Lawrence Livermore National Laboratory, Livermore, California, for accelerator dating. CO_2 was analyzed for stable

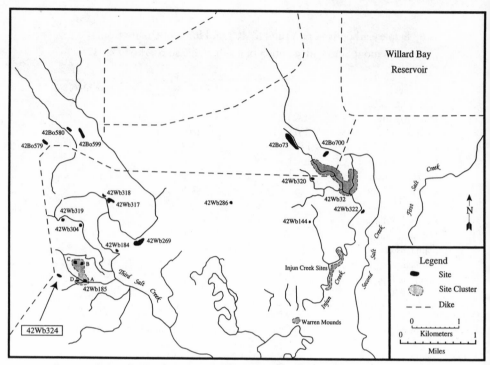

FIGURE 4.3. Great Salt Lake wetlands sites analyzed for diet.

isotopes, against a calibrated reference gas, on a Finnigan Delta S mass spectrometer in the Stable Isotope Research Facility for Environmental Research on the University of Utah campus. Chemical preservation of sampled burials was evaluated by whole-bone percent nitrogen (Stafford et al. 1990) and collagen yields (Ambrose 1990). All samples met designated preservation criteria (Table 4.1).

RESULTS

"Village" Burials

Burials from Fremont structural sites and residential middens outside the Great Salt Lake area are collectively categorized as "village" burials for purposes of discussion. Ten individuals from four residential settings (Figure 4.2) were previously analyzed for stable isotopes (Coltrain 1993), but not dated (Table 4.2). After completion of the earlier study, two individuals from Salina in central Utah (Billat and Billat 1988) and a third from the Smoking Pipe site (Forsyth 1984), along the Provo River (Figure 4.2), were added to the "village" data set. We directly dated the latter three burials and report ages of A.D. 914, A.D. 973, and A.D. 1014, respectively, with an A.D. 778–1162 range at the 95 percentile confidence interval (Table 4.2). All

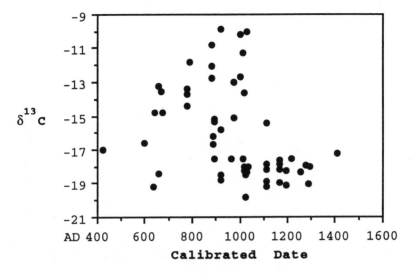

FIGURE 4.4. Great Salt Lake wetlands stable carbon isotope values graphed against calibrated radiocarbon dates.

"village" burials exhibit surprisingly positive ^{13}C values, ranging from –7.4 ‰ to –11 ‰ with a mean of –8.7 ± 1.1 ‰ (Table 4.2).

Great Salt Lake Area Burials

We obtained stable and radio-isotope readings for 53 individuals from 20 wetland sites (Figure 4.3) and 4 individuals from Warren and Willard Mounds (Judd 1917), Fremont residential bases adjacent to the wetlands (Figure 4.1). Individuals from the wetlands exhibit highly variable stable carbon isotope readings before A.D. 1150 and uniformly negative readings after (Table 4.1, Figure 4.4). Individuals from Warren and Willard Mounds that date before A.D. 1150 (n = 3) have ^{13}C values at the upper end of the wetland range. The remaining mound site burial (Fs 1/108) dates to A.D. 1295 and has a negative ^{13}C value typical of the post-A.D. 1150 wetland population. The Great Salt Lake burial collection dates from A.D. 423 to 1410. At the 95 percentile confidence interval, this spans a period from A.D. 252 to 1442.

The diets of the Great Salt Lake wetlands collection exhibit patterning relative to three monitored variables: radiocarbon age, gender, and age at death. The relationship between these variables and diet are examined in the following sections. Burials from mound sites are dated, but not sexed or aged reliably. Thus, they form part of the sample analyzed for temporal variation in diet, but are excluded from sex and age at death analysis. The majority of "village" burials are not dated, reliably sexed, or aged and are thus excluded from those analyses.

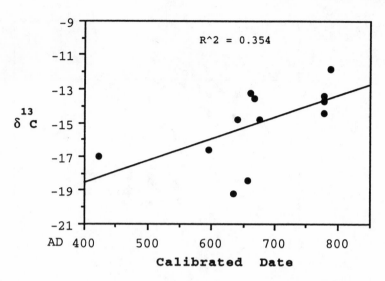

FIGURE 4.5. Period I: A.D. 400–850, Great Salt Lake wetlands stable carbon isotope values graphed against calibrated radiocarbon dates.

Temporal Variation in Great Salt Lake Diets

Between A.D. 400 and 850, designated Period I for discussion purposes, individuals from the Great Salt Lake wetlands and Warren and Willard Mounds became increasingly more dependent on C_4 resources, as is illustrated by a statistically significant increase in $\delta^{13}C$ over time (ANOVA, F = 5.484, p = 0.0412) (Figure 4.5). Period I isotope values exhibit a 7.3 ‰ range (–19.2 ‰ to –11.9 ‰) and a mean of –15.1 ± 2.2 ‰, (n = 12). During Period II (A.D. 850–1150), both the range of isotope values and variability within that range broaden (Figure 4.6). $\delta^{13}C$ varies between –19.8 ‰ and –10.0 ‰, (n = 32) with a 9.8 ‰ range and a mean of –15.7 ± 3.1 ‰. No temporal trend is present. In contrast, Period III (A.D. 1150–1400) $\delta^{13}C$ values are uniformly negative; within-group diversity is negligible (Figure 4.7). $\delta^{13}C$ varies from –19.1 ‰ to –17.20 ‰ with a mean of –18.1 ± 0.6 ‰ (n = 13). The range narrows to 1.9 ‰. Deviation from the mean exceeds by merely 0.1 ‰ the range of experimental uncertainty in stable isotope analysis, suggesting that, unlike earlier periods, individuals dating after A.D. 1150 practiced very similar subsistence strategies. Uniformly negative isotope values represent a statistically significant departure from preceding periods (two-tailed t-test; Period I vs. Period III: t = 5.339, p = 0.0002; Period II vs. Period III: t = 3.655, p = 0.0033).

Sexual Variation in Great Salt Lake Diets

Twenty-one individuals from the Great Salt Lake wetlands collection are reliably sexed (Table 4.1). Within this subset (Table 4.3, Figure 4.8), the mean male

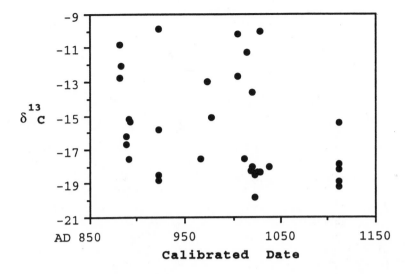

FIGURE 4.6. Period II: A.D. 840–1150, Great Salt Lake wetlands stable carbon isotope values graphed against calibrated radiocarbon dates.

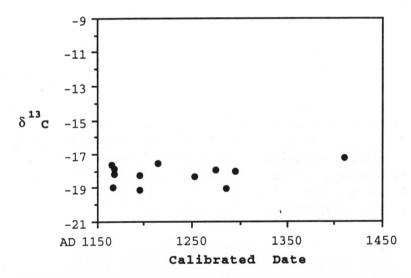

FIGURE 4.7. Period III: A.D. 1150–1400, Great Salt Lake wetlands stable carbon isotope values graphed against calibrated radiocarbon dates.

TABLE 4.3.
Stable Carbon Isotope Values ($\delta^{13}C$) for Sexed Great Salt Lake Wetlands Burials
by Burial Number and Site

Female			Male		
Burial	Site	$\delta^{13}C$ ‰	Burial	Site	$\delta^{13}C$ ‰
3	42Wb48	−18.4	14	42Wb185a	−14.8
27	42Wb269	−18.9	15	42Wb185a	−18.4
28	42Wb269	−18.2	23	42Wb269	−18.1
32	42Wb286	−17.9	33	42Wb304	−18.5
37	42Wb318	−18.1	47	42Wb324	−12.7
43	42Wb320	−17.2	53	42Wb324	−10.8
61	42Bo73	−15.1	55	42Wb324	−10.0
64	42Bo579	−17.0	56	42Wb324	−11.3
68	42Bo599	−18.0	58	42Wb324	−10.2
84	42Wb32	−16.7	77	42Bo700	−14.4
			83	42Wb32	−10.2

Mean $\delta^{13}C$

Female	Male
−17.5 ± 1.1 ‰	−13.6 ± 3.5 ‰
(n = 10)	(n = 11)

$\delta^{13}C$ (−13.6 ± 3.5 ‰ [n = 11]) is significantly more positive than the mean female reading (−17.5 ± 1.1 ‰ [n = 10]) (two-tailed t-test: t = 3.755, p = 0.0045). Male diets are also more varied. The standard deviation for male $\delta^{13}C$ is more than three times that of females and the range is more than double. Female $\delta^{13}C$ varies between −18.9 ‰ and −15.1 ‰, reflecting a 3.8 ‰ range, while male $\delta^{13}C$ has an 8.5 ‰ range (−18.5 ‰ to −10.0 ‰).

Great Salt Lake Diets and Age at Death

Forty-seven individuals from wetland sites have been assigned an age category (Simms, Loveland, and Stuart 1991). Their diets initially appear to be segregated by age at death (Table 4.4, Figure 4.9). Infants (0–5 years) exhibit the most negative $\delta^{13}C$ readings, whereas adults over 45 show the opposite trend. Visually the pattern is compelling; goodness of fit is high ($R^2 = 0.634$). However, the relationship between age category and mean $\delta^{13}C$ is not significant (Kruskal-Wallis 1-Way ANOVA, $X^2 = 3.649$, p = 0.601). Figure 4.9 error bars illustrate marked deviation

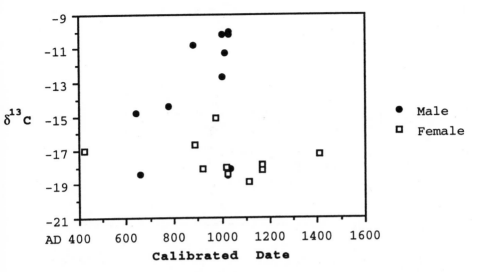

FIGURE 4.8. Female versus male stable carbon isotope values graphed against calibrated radiocarbon dates.

from the mean for all but one category, indicating mean differences are not significant relative to within-group diversity. When individual data points are plotted by category, it becomes clear that mean values are misleading (Figure 4.10). Here, R^2 drops to 0.033. Further, pair-wise comparisons (Mann-Whitney U) show no significant differences between means. In other words, age has no statistically significant effect on δ^{13}C. Nonetheless, it is difficult to ignore Age Category 1 (nursing infant/young child) readings. Within-group variation is slight and negative values

TABLE 4.4.
Mean Stable Carbon Isotope Values (δ^{13}C) for
Great Salt Lake Wetlands Age Categories

Age Category	Age Range	No.	Mean δ^{13}C ‰	General Category
1	0–5	4	−17.6 ± 0.7	Infant
2	6–11	7	−16.5 ± 2.8	Child
3	12–16	4	−17.4 ± 1.8	Subadult
4	17–25	5	−16.2 ± 3.2	Young Adult
5	26–44	20	−16.6 ± 2.9	Adult <45
6	45+	7	−15.0 ± 2.9	Adult >45

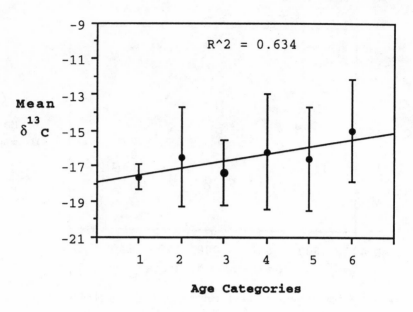

FIGURE 4.9. Mean stable carbon isotope values by age category.

are in accord with diets largely derived from nursing women whose $\delta^{13}C$ values appear uniformly low (Figure 4.8).

DISCUSSION
"Village" Diets

Macrofossil assemblages from "village" sites under study indicate that individuals residing at these sites consumed diets made up primarily of maize, native plants, deer, mountain sheep, antelope, and lagomorphs (Ambler 1966; Dodd 1982; Janetski 1997; Metcalfe 1984; Sharp 1989). Maize is a C_4 food, while representative prey species are browsers, subsisting primarily on C_3 forage (Zeveloff and Collett 1988). Thus, "village" diets (with $\delta^{13}C$ values between −11.0 ‰ and −7.4 ‰) appear to approximate a C_3 protein, C_4 energy regime. If Equation 2 is used to estimate C_4 consumption, mean intake of foods carrying a C_4 isotope signal varies between 70 percent and 85 percent. For reasons noted above, this range may represent a conservative estimate of the role of C_4 foods. Nonetheless, it places these diets within the isotope range of Anasazi burials sampled in other studies (Table 4.5; see also Coltrain 1993), suggesting that maize, perhaps supplemented by a small suite of native C_4 plants (Table 4.6), was on average the most abundant food in Fremont "village" diets. The role of wetland resources appears minimal by comparison. Backhoe Village and the Smoking Pipe site border riparian wetlands; yet,

FIGURE 4.10. Individual stable carbon isotope values by age category.

individuals sampled from these sites exhibit stable carbon isotope readings consistent with high maize diets.

Great Salt Lake Wetlands Diets

The most striking feature of wetland diets is their variation, both within the data set and in comparison to "village" diets, segregating individuals into three broad subsistence categories: (1) those who consumed high C_4 diets, indicated by the most positive stable carbon isotope values in the data set; (2) those who subsisted on high C_3 diets, indicated by the most negative values; and (3) individuals consuming mixed diets, apparent in intermediate $\delta^{13}C$ readings. In the following sections, we discuss wetland dietary regimes relative to these distinctions. We then address the implications of temporal and sex-based patterning. Finally, we consider the relationship between Great Salt Lake diets and "village" subsistence relative to issues raised in the introduction.

High C_4 Diets

Individuals from the Great Salt Lake wetlands with isotope ratios as positive as or more positive than ca. –13 ‰ consumed diets high in C_4 plant resources and/or isotopically enriched animal protein. They may have relied heavily on maize and native C_4 plants (Table 4.6). Alternatively, they may have regularily consumed bison grazing on C_4 grasses. The presence of bison in Great Salt Lake faunal assemblages (see Lupo and Schmitt 1997) and their feeding ecology make it

TABLE 4.5.

Stable Carbon Isotope Values ($\delta^{13}C$) for Human Remains from
Published Studies on Fremont and Anasazi Diet

Site/Location		No.	Cultural Affiliation[a]	Date[b]	$\delta^{13}C$ ‰	Reference
*42Sv1060	UT	1	Fremont		−9.5	1
Smoking Pipe	UT	1	Fremont	A.D. 778–1020[c]	−9.2	2
Grasshopper Pueblo	AZ	37		A.D.1275–1330	−9.2[d]	4
Caldwell Village	UT	4	Fremont		−9.1	1
Badger House MV	CO	6	PI		−8.9	3
Evans Mound	UT	3	Fremont		−8.8	1
Site 820 MV	CO	5	PII/III		−8.7	3
Grasshopper Pueblo	AZ	17		A.D.1330–1400	−8.6[d]	4
Two Raven House	CO	9	PII		−8.6	3
Pecos Pueblo	NM	8	Period VI	Post A.D. 1675	−8.5	6
Marcos Canyon	CO	4	PIII	A.D.1450–1550	−8.3	3
Unprovenienced	CO	1	Bskt Mkr III		−8.3	3
Badger House MV	CO	10	PII/III		−8.3	3
Salina Sisters	UT	2	Fremont	A.D. 869–1162[c]	−8.2	2
Pecos Pueblo	NM	9	Period IV	A.D.1550–1650	−7.8	6
Pecos Pueblo	NM	10	Period III	A.D.1450–1550	−7.7	6
Pecos Pueblo	NM	8	Period I	A.D.1300–1400	−7.7	6
Polly Secrest	UT	2	Fremont	A.D.1300	−7.7	7
Cedar Mesa	UT	4	Bskt Mkr II		−7.7	5
Pecos Pueblo	NM	11	Period V	A.D.1600–1675	−7.6	6
Backhoe Village	UT	2	Fremont		−7.5	1
Pecos Pueblo	NM	7	Period II	A.D.1400–1450	−7.5	6
Pecos Pueblo	NM	8	Black-on-white	A.D.1200–1300	−7.5	6
San Antonio Pueblo	NM	3	Late Anasazi	A.D.1300–1400	−7.4	7
Cedar Mesa	UT	3	PII/III		−7.3	5
Tijeras Pueblo	NM	5	Late Anasazi	A.D.1300–1400	−7.0	7

Abbreviations: MV = Mesa Verde

(1. Coltrain 1993), (2. Coltrain, this study), (3. Decker and Tieszen 1989), (4. Ezzo 1993), (5. Matson and Chisholm 1991), (6. Spielmann, Schoeninger, and Moore 1990), (7. Wooley 1988).

[a] Listed as cited in reference.

[b] Dates listed if cited in reference.

[c] calibrated 2σ range.

[d] $\delta^{13}C$ value obtained by averaging mean male and female readings as reported by author.

* Gooseberry Valley burial mound adjacent to two pit structures.

TABLE 4.6.
Native C$_4$ Taxa Exploited by Eastern Great Basin Ute, Paiute, and Gosiute

Genus and Species	Common Name	Remarks	Reference
Amaranthus spp.[1]	Amaranth	Cultivated	Chamberlin 1911
		Very Important	Palmer 1878
Atriplex canescens[5]	Saltbush	Used	Chamberlin 1911
			Palmer 1878
A. confertifolia[5]	Shad scale	Very Important	Chamberlin 1911
A. spp.[5]		Used	Chamberlin 1911
Carex spp.[4]	Sedge	Medicinal Use	Chamberlin 1911
Echinochloa crusgalli[2]	Barnyard grass	Used	Steward [1938] 1999
Eragostis oxylepis[3]	Love grass	Used	Steward [1938] 1999
Euphorbia albomarginata[5]	Spurge	Medicinal Use	Train et al. 1957
Sporobulus cryptandrus[1]	Sand dropseed	Much Used	Palmer 1878
Suaeda depressa[5]	Seepweed	Used	Chamberlin 1911
S. torreyana[1]	Seepweed	Medicinal Use	Train et al. 1957

(1. Downton 1975), (2. Cerling n.d.) (3. Raghavendra and Das 1978), (4. B. Smith and Epstein 1971), (5. Welki and Caldwell 1970).

more difficult to estimate the importance of maize in and around the wetlands than in other regions of the study area. Arguments in favor of high maize intake are dependent upon additional evidence for maize cultivation, while those that favor intake of isotopically enriched animal protein rely on the relative frequency of bison in wetland faunal assemblages and the isotopic signature of their forage.

Evidence for maize cultivation is less apparent around the Great Salt Lake than in other regions of the study area. Organic preservation is poor at wetland sites and maize is rarely recovered (Aikens 1966, 1967; Fry and Dalley 1979; W. F. Shields and Dalley 1978). To complicate the situation, pioneer settlement and subsequent urbanization have effectively destroyed residential sites east of the Great Salt Lake at elevations suitable for farming. Warren and Willard Mounds (Judd 1917) are the only recorded Fremont residential bases along the Wasatch Front. Located on grasslands between the Great Salt Lake and the Wasatch Mountains, they were heavily impacted at European contact and never formally investigated. The little that is known about them was published by Judd (1917, 1919, 1926) early in the century or is found in anecdotal accounts by pioneer settlers who commented on scatters of maize, ceramic sherds, lithics, and burned adobe on site (see Simms, Loveland, and Stuart 1991). In a brief report, Judd notes "[t]he mounds still visible at Willard have been much plowed over.... Of the dozen or more mounds noted twenty years ago...only one remained in the spring of 1915 in a comparatively undisturbed condition" (1917:119).

Despite the lack of well-documented evidence for maize cultivation, individuals from Warren and Willard Mounds dating to before A.D. 1150 exhibit isotope readings more positive than wetland averages indicating diets relatively higher in C_4 resources (see Table 4.1). Given their provenience, this difference may indicate higher than average maize consumption. Individuals residing at these bases or acquiring maize from them may be represented in the wetland mortuary collection, accounting for some or all high C_4 diets.

Alternatively, if C_4 grasses made up a significant portion of bison forage and some individuals derived 35 to 40 percent or more of their caloric intake from bison tissue, these individuals would exhibit $\delta^{13}C$ values more positive than –13 ‰. C_4 grasses are not common to the eastern Great Basin nor are bison common in Fremont faunal collections (Sharp 1989), but they were apparently attracted to grasslands northeast of the lake during the Fremont period (Harper 1967) and exploited by groups living in the Great Salt Lake area. Their representation in wetland faunal assemblages is not sufficient to indicate they were the primary prey species, but they undoubtedly made a contribution to wetland diets (Lupo and Schmitt 1997). Hence, intake of C_4 protein in excess of 35–40 percent of the total diet, although less probable than maize consumption, cannot be ruled out as an explanation for elevated wetland $\delta^{13}C$ readings.

High C_3 Diets

Isotope ratios as negative as or more negative than ca. –18 ‰ are indicative of hunter-gatherer diets dominated by native C_3 plants and prey species subsisting on C_3 forage. These diets may have been slightly enriched by low levels of C_4 intake in the form of either maize or seeds of native C_4 plants (Table 4.6). However, low levels of C_4 protein intake can be ruled out since they would have substantially enriched Great Salt Lake collagen $\delta^{13}C$ readings, producing stable carbon isotope ratios more positive than –18 ‰. Macrofossil and palynological studies at wetland sites indicate that individuals exhibiting $\delta^{13}C$ values in this range subsisted on diets of fish, waterfowl, wetland mammals, deer, lagomorphs (Janetski 1990) and a range of native C_3 plant species (D. B. Madsen and Lindsay 1977).

Mixed Diets

Great Salt Lake $\delta^{13}C$ readings in the midrange isotopically (i.e., > –18 ‰ but < –13 ‰) indicate mixed diets, comprised of energy (i.e., carbohydrates and lipids) from one isotope family of resources, supplemented by protein from the other. These are the least diagnostic values in the data set. For example, an individual with a wetland diet consisting of 80 to 85 percent C_4 plants, such as maize and amaranth or shad scale, in conjunction with 15 to 20 percent C_3 animal protein, would produce isotope ratios in the range of –15 ‰ to –17 ‰ based on experimental findings (Ambrose and Norr 1993:Table 5; Tieszen and Fagre 1993b:Table

5). If Equation 2 is used to calculate C_4 intake, the percentage of C_4 foods in this individual's diet is underestimated by almost 50 percent. Conversely, a diet consisting of 80 to 85 percent C_3 plants and 15 to 20 percent C_4 protein would produce $\delta^{13}C$ values in the −13 ‰ to −16 ‰ range (Ambrose and Norr 1993:Table 5; Tieszen and Fagre 1993b:Table 5). In this case, Equation 2 would overestimate the role of C_4 protein by ca. 30 percent. Based on these calculations, midrange $\delta^{13}C$ values indicate wetland diets dominated either by C_3 energy resources, such as native plants, augmented by approximately 15 to 20 percent C_4 animal protein or C_4 energy foods, such as maize and shad scale, supplemented by 15 to 20 percent C_3 protein in the form of fish, waterfowl, small mammals, artiodactyls, etc. The latter differs from "village" diets in that C_3 animal protein appears to play a more important role.

The Implications of Temporal Variation in Great Salt Lake Diets

The dietary diversity exhibited by individuals dating before A.D. 1150 indicates that a wide range of economic activities were taking place in and around the wetlands (see Simms 1986). Individuals apparently had differential access to maize or sources of animal protein. Some may have farmed, some foraged, and others traded foraged resources for cultigens. The growing importance of C_4 foods during Period I is in keeping with similar changes suggested by a marked increase in the number of Fremont residential bases across the study area. Between A.D. 700 and 800 (Talbot and Wilde 1989:Figure 2), the frequency of radiocarbon dates from residential sites increases more than tenfold, suggesting that populations were either growing, becoming more sedentary, or both as a consequence of increasing reliance on maize. Period II coincides with the apex of Fremont expansion (Talbot and Wilde 1989:Figures 2–4). Fremont sites are more numerous and were more intensely occupied than at any other time in Fremont history. This is mirrored in the temporal distribution of Great Salt Lake wetlands burials. More than half the collection dates to this period. The striking differences in diet they exhibit suggest that economic or social constraints on farming in the Great Salt Lake Basin may have been growing with the population.

The economic diversity evident in this setting was likely driven by competing subsistence strategies with relatively similar payoffs or socially mediated constraints on economic opportunity. Aboriginal farming, at the northwestern limit of its range, may have been risky, perhaps no more profitable on average than wetland foraging. Alternatively, sites suitable for farming may have been under the control of extended families excluding some individuals or family groups from access to cultigens other than through trade. In either setting, individuals were no doubt responsive to changing economic options, pursuing subsistence strategies contingent upon a broad suite of variables, such as kinship ties, group composition, amplitude of climatic fluctuation, availability of arable land, availability of bison, or the potential for elevated status associated with trade in animal protein or cultigens.

The dramatic reduction in C_4 intake after A.D. 1150 indicates that one set of resource options was eliminated. After ca. A.D. 1190, an equally striking reduction takes place in the frequency of radiocarbon dates from Fremont residential sites across the study area (Talbot and Wilde 1989:Figures 2, 5). These appear to be correlated events perhaps best explained by a shift from summer- to winter-dominated rainfall[4] (D. E. Newman 1988, 1994; see also Lindsay 1986 for a review), curtailing farming in some locations and precluding it in others. Archeomagnetic readings from the interior hearths of three wetland pit houses at the Levee site (Fry and Dalley 1979) indicate they were last fired at ca. A.D. 1150 (Shuey 1979:106). By A.D. 1190, most of the northern Colorado Plateau and northern and western Utah were no longer occupied by Fremont living in village settings (Talbot and Wilde 1989:Figure 7). The few residential bases that remained are clustered to the south, along the Great Basin/Colorado Plateau transition zone in the best watered regions of the study area. Thus, the abrupt reduction in reliance on C_4 resources around the Great Salt Lake appears to be one event in a series of similar responses to climatic change.

Implications of Sexual Variation in Great Salt Lake Diets

One of the most surprising outcomes of this study is the evidence for sex-based differences in the Great Salt Lake wetlands diet. On average, male diets were more varied and significantly higher in C_4 intake (+3.9 ‰) than female diets. Their standard deviation is more than three times that of females and their range more than double (Table 4.3, Figure 4.8). Although comparative studies are limited, this pattern is not common among North American Formative populations. M. R. Schurr (1992) reports no significant differences in male versus female diet among 40 Middle Mississippian burials (ca. A.D. 1300–1430) from an Ohio River site. At Grasshopper Pueblo, Ezzo (1993:Table 5.2) reports a slight but significant difference between female (−9.53 ± 1.25 ‰ [n = 18]) and male diets (−8.86 ± 0.76 ‰ [n = 19]) during the early phase of habitation (A.D. 1275–1330). However, the mean difference is less than 1.0 ‰ and significant only when outliers are deleted (Ezzo 1993:54).

While sex-based differences in Great Salt Lake wetlands diets are intriguing, there are three reasons to question their representativeness. First, analysis was based on 21 individuals, 10 females, and 11 males (Table 4.3), less than half the wetland collection. (Other burials were either too fragmentary to sex reliably or too young [Simms, Loveland, and Stuart 1991]). Second, sexed individuals are not evenly distributed across the temporal span of the study. All the sexed individuals that date to Period III are female (Figure 4.8). Since, as a group, Period III burials have extremely negative $\delta^{13}C$ values, it is reasonable to assume that were it possible

TABLE 4.7.
Stable Carbon Isotope Values ($\delta^{13}C$) for 42Wb324 Burials by Temporal Range

Burial	$\delta^{13}C$ ‰	Calibrated Date	Calibrated 2σ Range
51	−13.4	A.D. 779	A.D. 662–956
52	−14.8	A.D. 676	A.D. 547–956
53	−10.8	A.D. 884	A.D. 775–979
57	−13.5	A.D. 668	A.D. 608–786
Mean $\delta^{13}C$ = −13.1 ± 1.7 ‰			
47	−12.7	A.D. 1005	A.D. 880–1162
48	−13.6	A.D. 1020	A.D. 895–1168
55	−10.0	A.D. 1031	A.D. 895–1156
56	−11.3	A.D. 1014	A.D. 885–1168
58	−10.2	A.D. 1028	A.D. 997–1165
Mean $\delta^{13}C$ = −11.6 ± 1.6 ‰			
49	−19.2	A.D. 1127	A.D. 1010–1257

to sex the entire Period III collection, a subset of those individuals would be male and the mean male $\delta^{13}C$ value would decrease accordingly. Third, 5 of the 11 males analyzed for sexual differences in diet were recovered from 42Wb324 (see Figure 4.2), the only site in the Great Salt Lake wetlands with grave goods and multiple interments on a prepared ashy surface.[5] When calibrated at the 95 percentile confidence interval, radiocarbon dates from 42Wb324 burials segregate into three ranges roughly equivalent with Periods I, II and III (Table 4.7). Mean $\delta^{13}C$ for individuals falling in the first two time segments (n = 9) is significantly higher than the mean for remaining wetland Periods I and II burials (two-tailed t-test: t = −4.703, p = 0.0033). These individuals appear to represent a special case, distinguished by the co-occurrence of unusual funerary arrangements, the presence of grave goods, and diets high in C_4 resources. The first two features are commonly associated with elevated social status,[6] indicating a correlation between status and diets high in C_4 foods and suggesting that the diets of males from 42Wb324 were not representative of the male population as a whole. When these individuals are excluded from analysis, the mean male $\delta^{13}C$ value (−15.7 ± 3.3 ‰) is virtually identical to Periods I and II population means (Table 4.8), and male versus female diets are not statistically different (two-tailed t-test: t = −1.172, p = 0.294).

High-Status Male Diets

Excluding 42Wb324 male burials from the data set examined for sex-based differences in diet—assuming they are a special case—emphasizes the need to address their high C_4 diets and apparent high status relative to the remainder of the collection. Three patterns of consumption could account for these differences.

TABLE 4.8.

Mean δ^{13}C Values for Periods I and II Populations versus Males,
Excluding 42Wb324 Burials

Great Salt Lake	δ^{13}C
Period I Population Mean	-15.1 ± 2.2 ‰
Period II Population Mean	-15.7 ± 3.1 ‰
Mean Male Reading (Less 42Wb324 Male Burials)	-15.7 ± 3.3 ‰

Pattern 1: 42Wb324 males may have occupied farming bases east of the wetlands, consuming more maize than either females or nonresident males, acquiring status by virtue of their reliance on cultigens (see Bailey 1991). However, if maize was the staple food in some male diets, it is difficult to imagine a context in which co-resident females would have been largely restricted to wild foods. Females may have engaged in logistical foraging during the growing season, consuming slightly higher percentages of wild resources than males, especially if males provided the labor for crop cultivation. This scenario may explain the slightly depressed female δ^{13}C values reported by Ezzo (1993), but seems unlikely to account for the nearly 4 ‰ difference between mean male and female diets evident in the wetland collection. Further, maize grinding and meal preparation are commonly thought of as female activities and maize gruel is used as a weaning food. If above-average maize intake explains high-status male diets, this collection should include a subset of females with relatively similar diets. There *is* one adult from site 42Wb324 who has not been sexed (see Table 4.1, Burial 49); however, this individual dates to late in the sequence and has a δ^{13}C reading of -19.2 ‰, indicating a diet virtually absent of maize. Pattern 2: Alternatively, maize may have functioned as a ritual food consumed primarily by high-status males.[7] In some pre-Inkan settings, it appears to have been grown initially for ritual use (Hastorf and Johannessen 1993:119). Hastorf (1991:150–52) reports that a subset of males from a pre-Inkan population sampled for stable isotopes shows significantly higher C_4 intake than the remainder of the population. She attributes their elevated δ^{13}C readings to feasting and ritual consumption of maize beer. In a later study, she argues that consumption of maize beer accounts for 75 percent of the stable carbon isotope enrichment present in some pre-Inkan burials (Hastorf and Johannessen 1993). Pattern 3: Elevated male isotope values may indicate higher than average intake of isotopically enriched animal protein. High-status males may have had preferential access to dried bison meat, brought in from the Plains (see Spielmann, Schoeninger, and Moore 1990), where C_4 forage is prevalent (Tieszen 1994; see also Tieszen 1991). Alterna-

tively, some males may have engaged in logistical hunting, consuming large quantities of bison at kill sites outside the Great Basin before transporting meat back to residential bases, elevating both their status and $\delta^{13}C$ values through the acquisition of bison.

Great Salt Lake Diets versus Village Subsistence

Marked economic diversity evident among Fremont residing in the Great Salt Lake basin contrasts sharply with relatively uniform, high C_4 diets exhibited by individuals occupying village sites in other regions of the study area. Either sampled "village" burials are not representative of Fremont subsistence strategies outside the Great Salt Lake basin or such strategies were biased toward maize agriculture by high economic return rates and/or the storage potential of maize relative to foraged resources.

If, for example, average returns from farming exceeded returns from foraging, in the absence of extensive wetlands or in conjunction with reliable summer moisture, farming may have been favored by individuals with access to suitable locations, despite its attendant uncertainty, resulting in the characteristic Fremont village settlement pattern. The attractiveness of agriculture may have been further enhanced by maize's storage potential and status advantages accruing to individuals trading in maize or maize by-products.

A similar argument can be used as the basis for investigating dietary diversity among wetland populations. If mean agricultural yields were dampened by climatic uncertainty or if social constraints prevented some individuals from farming and if either or both of these conditions existed in association with an extensive wetland habitat, a higher level of economic diversity than is present in "village" settings is a reasonable expectation.

These arguments are essentially hypotheses, subject to testing provided they can be falsified. To do so would necessitate ranking resources with respect to their economic and perhaps social currencies, taking into account their storage potential, scheduling requirements, and the effects of climatic fluctuation on return rates, considering as well the differences in male versus female strategies and how these may have impacted resource choice. With such data we may be able to model the conditions under which farming would be favored over foraging and test the predictions of the model against data sets such as the one reported here. For now, we merely report our findings and suggest possible explanations for the patterning that is evident.

CONCLUSION

The isotope record from Great Salt Lake burials indicates that from A.D. 400 to 1150 diets were diverse. Some individuals subsisted on high C_4 diets, while others consumed diets primarily comprised of wild C_3 foods. Male diets were more diverse than female intake and may have covaried with status. After A.D. 1150, economic options apparently narrowed; agriculture was abandoned and groups returned to foraging in conjunction with what appears to be deteriorating climatic conditions.

In contrast, the isotope record from individuals outside the Great Salt Lake region indicates that they were subsisting on relatively uniform diets, high in maize, even at sites near wetland habitats. Fremont individuals sampled from Smoking Pipe, upsteam from Utah Lake, and Backhoe Village, adjacent to the Sevier River wetlands, exhibit stable carbon isotope readings consistent with high maize diets, showing no evidence for significant reliance on wetland resources. If the "village" sample is representative, it appears that Fremont economic diversity was geographically constrained by the feasibility of various subsistence strategies and their relative payoffs over time. Around the Great Salt Lake, diversity appears tied to a wetland habitat rich enough to compete with risky agricultural strategies, perhaps in the face of social constraints on farming. These results support a growing recognition that the role of wetland habitats in prehistoric Great Basin economies covaried with the importance of other resource patches and access to them.

Acknowledgments

We extend our deep gratitude to the Northwestern Band of the Shoshoni Nation for their forbearance. We thank Steven R. Simms for the opportunity to work with the Great Salt Lake wetlands collection, James Ehleringer, Craig Cook, and John Southon for generous and indispensable lab support, Dennis O'Rourke for unfailing encouragement and, finally, James O'Connell for exceeding patience. We thank Doug Edwards and Steve Josephson for help with statistical analysis. We also thank two anonymous reviewers for their careful reading of the manuscript and helpful comments. Research was funded by the National Science Foundation DBS 9223227 and the U.S. Bureau of Reclamation.

NOTES

1. Estimates of C_4 intake in the Discussion section substitute –26.5 ‰, the mean for modern C_3 plants (Price, Schoeninger, and Armelagos 1985), in place of δ_3.

2. Estimates of C_4 intake in the Discussion section substitute –10.0 ‰ in place of δ_4. The mean for modern C_4 plants is –12.5 ‰; however, this value is more negative than isotope readings from plants grown before extensive use of fossil fuels (see Tieszen and Fagre 1993a) and, if used, overestimates the role of C_4 foods.

3. With the advent of above-ground nuclear testing in the early 1950s, atmospheric ^{14}C concentrations in the Northern Hemisphere doubled, providing researchers with the opportunity to monitor carbon turnover rates in various human tissues using elevated levels of ^{14}C as a biochemical tracer.

4. In the eastern Great Basin, rainfall is supplied either by the winter Pacific storm track or summer monsoon system (see Whitlock and Bartlein 1993). Early in the Christian era,

monsoonal rains, which provide the Southwest with growing-season moisture, apparently transgressed their customary boundary at the Great Basin/Colorado Plateau rim, extending summer rainfall to the eastern Great Basin. While this led to a decline in annual precipitation (D. E. Newman 1994; Whitlock and Bartlein 1993; see also Grayson 1993 for a review), growing-season moisture increased. Moreover, since summer precipitation is generally accompanied by warmer temperatures, sites across the eastern Great Basin probably experienced longer growing seasons and more favorable temperature regimes than today, encouraging Fremont expansion.

5. 42Wb324 is located at 4,208 feet (1,282 m) in elevation, on a natural levee between a fork in Third Salt Creek (see Figure 4.3). The site appears to be a prepared burial surface approximately 15 feet (4.5 m) in diameter. Eleven individuals with associated Fremont artifacts were recovered. The effects of erosion, particularly in the upper stratum, made it difficult to reconstruct the sequence of burial events; however, radiocarbon dates (Table 4.7) confirm that interments were episodic. A minimum of three and possibly more burial events took place. Although other wetland burials were interred singly in shallow pits without grave goods, Burials 48, 49, 53, and 55 to 58 were recovered resting on a prepared, ashy lens composed of charred bulrush seeds and stems. The burials showed no evidence of charring. Remaining individuals were interred immediately above them, partially exposed at or just below the ground surface. Numerous grave goods, rare with Fremont burials, were recovered from the same level of origin as the initial interments. These included one complete and one fragmentary projectile point, bifaces, scrapers, lithic debitage, ground stone, bison horn, and worked bone: awls, fishhooks, gaming pieces and a small piece of carved bone resembling a duck's head (Simms, Loveland, and Stuart 1991:44–52).

6. Among the Fremont, evidence for social ranking is rare. The most commonly cited example is that of an adult male (Fs1276.83; Table 4.1) interred below the floor of an Evans Mound pit structure with the remains of a great horned owl (*Bubo virginianus*), several magpies (*Pica pica*), and assorted lithic, bone, and ceramic artifacts (Pecotte 1982). Unlike 42Wb324 burials, his diet was not high in C_4 intake relative to other Evans Mounds samples or "village" populations as a whole (Table 4.2).

7. If a subset of Great Salt Lake Fremont males cultivated maize largely or even in part for its fermentation properties or ritual function, factors in addition to economic utility would influence the decision to invest in agriculture. The ability to dispense maize beer might represent a social currency as important as or more important than the crop's caloric value or economic currency, suggesting that individuals may have invested in maize agriculture even when higher caloric returns per unit time could be obtained by foraging.

5

Molecular Genetic Variation in Prehistoric Inhabitants of the Eastern Great Basin

Dennis H. O'Rourke, Ryan L. Parr, and Shawn W. Carlyle

The advent of molecular genetic characterizations of prehistoric populations was made possible by two discoveries in the mid-1980s. The first discovery was that nucleic acids were frequently preserved in ancient specimens, were recoverable, and could be manipulated and analyzed. The second, and perhaps technically most important, was the development of the polymerase chain reaction (PCR). This elegant method enzymatically amplifies low copy number DNA into millions of copies, which are then available for further genetic research. The ability to document genetic variation in specimens recovered from antiquity, subsequently dubbed molecular archaeology (Pääbo 1986, 1987), offers the potential to approach studies of the past with the resolution previously reserved for modern studies of population and individual diversity.

As introduced by Simms (this volume), the skeletal sample recovered from the eastern margin of the Great Salt Lake provides a temporally and geographically controlled archaeological sample that is most appropriate for molecular analysis. The samples were initially considered to present an ideal circumstance for testing the Numic expansion hypothesis and to provide direct evidence for the relationship between prehistoric biological variability and aboriginal population movements in the Great Basin using genetic methods and data. The temporal distribution of the samples available for molecular analysis, however, precludes a direct test of the Numic expansion, or replacement, hypothesis as traditionally articulated (e.g., Lamb 1958; D. B. Madsen 1975; Simms 1986; Young and Bettinger 1992). This chapter, then, will focus on the molecular characterization of the Great Salt Lake wetlands sample and place the molecular variation documented in this skeletal series in a broader context through comparison to a roughly contemporary Anasazi sample from Grand Gulch, Utah, a comparable ancient sample from the western Great Basin, as well as present-day North American Indians. In so doing, we hope to illuminate aspects of the population dynamics of the prehistoric Fremont in northern Utah.

Our approach to the molecular characterization of the Great Salt Lake wetlands sample has three components: (1) extract DNA from as many individual specimens as possible and characterize at least four mitochondrial (mt) DNA markers in each; (2) evaluate any temporal trends in the distribution of these markers; and (3) contrast the distribution of the markers in the Great Salt Lake wetlands samples with that seen in other American Indian populations, both ancient and modern. The samples employed here are a subset of those discussed by Simms, Bright and Loveland, and Coltrain and Stafford in other chapters in this volume. With only three exceptions, each sample has been individually dated by AMS ¹⁴C. The samples employed for molecular analyses span an age range from approximately 540 B.P. to 1630 B.P.

MATERIALS AND METHODS

The spatial, temporal, and archaeological contexts for the samples utilized in this study have been discussed elsewhere (e.g., Simms, Loveland, and Stuart 1991; Fawcett and Simms 1993; Coltrain 1993; Simms, Coltrain and Stafford, and Bright and Loveland, this volume). Details of the molecular methods employed may be found in O'Rourke, Carlyle, and Parr (1996) and Parr, Carlyle, and O'Rourke (1996). In the current study, 47 individually dated skeletons were sampled for molecular analyses. The samples are associated with the Great Salt Lake Fremont archaeological tradition (Morss 1931; Gunnerson 1969; Jennings 1978; D. B. Madsen 1989), and all are pre-Columbian in age. Hence, with respect to genetic inferences to be drawn from the molecular analyses, non–Native American admixture is not an issue.

Slightly over half the skeletal elements used in the present study were identified as potential candidates for molecular analysis and removed to plastic bags by gloved archaeologists directly from the excavation (Simms, Loveland, and Stuart 1991). This procedure served to minimize contamination of samples with modern nucleic acids through repeated handling. The additional samples were selected from the collection subsequent to excavation, and were carefully handled by masked and gloved researchers. It should be emphasized that the samples under study do not constitute a breeding population as generally conceived, spanning as they do a millennium. We believe, however, it is appropriate to view them as representative of a population that was continuous in time as a result of the comparatively short time frame encompassed by the samples, the single geographic locale from which all derive, and the relatively uniform, and well-known, material culture characterizing burial areas. While more extensive genetic analyses of much larger skeletal series will be necessary to adequately test the hypothesis that the current samples derive from a single population linear in time, we will assume that the Great Salt Lake wetlands sample represents individuals from a continuous, local population occupying the eastern Great Basin during a specific period of prehistory. As discussed below, we see no evidence in the distribution of molecular markers examined in these samples to seriously question this working assumption.

Molecular Markers Examined

The mtDNA markers assayed here were selected for several reasons. First, the DNA recovered from ancient specimens (aDNA) is routinely degraded in size, highly modified, and usually contaminated with a variety of unknown substances that inhibit manipulation and analysis. The high copy number of mtDNA genomes per cell increases the probability that at least one target sequence will be recovered and accessible to the PCR procedure. Second, a full sequence of the human mtDNA molecule has been available for over a decade (S. Anderson et al. 1981), facilitating the comparative study of this genetic system. Finally, a number of researchers have been busily generating considerable data on mtDNA variation in contemporary Native Americans. Recent analyses based on high resolution restriction mapping as well as mtDNA sequence data suggest that over 90 percent of modern American Indians's mtDNAs fall in to one of four primary lineages, termed founding lineages by Torroni et al. (1993a).

The four markers minimally defining the four major lineages, and employed in this study, include (1) a 9 bp deletion in the cytochrome II-tRNA^{lys} intergenic region of the circular mtDNA molecule, associated with haplogroup (lineage) B; (2) a *Hae*III restriction site at np 663, associated with haplogroup A; (3) an *Alu*I restriction site at np 5176, the absence of which is associated with haplogroup D; and (4) a *Hinc*II restriction site at np 13259, the absence of which is associated with haplogroup C. The relationship of these markers to haplogroups is given in Table 5.1.

Each of these haplogroups was originally defined by high resolution restriction mapping (e.g., Torroni et al. 1993a; Wallace and Torroni 1992), and is predicated on the joint occurance of several restriction site polymorphisms and the 9 bp deletion. Indeed, each of these haplogroups may be viewed as being composed of at least two subgroups, based on the distribution of markers and/or hypervariable DNA sequence data (Bailliet et al. 1994; Merriwether, Rothhammer, and Ferrell 1995). While the markers used here are the defining, or diagnostic, markers for each haplogroup, lineage assignments should be recognized as provisional pending further analyses with additional markers. In addition, a fifth haplogroup, termed "N" by Stone and Stoneking (1993), "E" by Bailliet et al. (1994), and "X6" or "X7" by Easton et al. (1996) is identified by a change in state of any of the markers which define the four primary matrilines such that a sample is not congruent with any of the defined haplogroups. Easton et al. (1996) provide an extended analysis of this haplogroup relative to the distribution of several other markers and argue that it should also be considered a founding haplogroup rather than simply a marker of historical admixture (e.g., Torroni et al. 1993a). Although we cannot identify the

TABLE 5.1.
Lineage Distribution of mtDNA Markers

| | mtDNA Lineages | | | | |
Markers	A	B	C	D	X
Hae III	+	−	−	−	−
Alu I	+	+	+	−	+
Hinc II	+	+	−	+	+
9 bp deletion	−	+	−	−	−

+ indicates presence of a marker; − indicates its absence

subtypes defined by Easton et al. due to the limited number of markers examined to date, we will follow their convention and refer to this haplogroup as "X." The distribution of markers that define this haplotype is also given in Table 5.1.

Extraction Protocol

Based on a modification of an aDNA extraction protocol (Hagelberg et al. 1991; Hagelberg and Clegg 1991; Hagelberg 1994; Parr, Carlyle, and O'Rourke 1996), bone was chelated in 0.5 molar EDTA for approximately 72 hours, with a fresh change of EDTA every 24 hours. Decalcified samples were subsequently incubated overnight in 2 ml of Proteinase K (ProK) digest buffer (50 mM Tris, 1 mM CaCl$_2$, 1 mM DTT, 0.5 percent Tween 20, and 1 mg/ml PK) at 55°C. ProK digestion was followed by standard three-stage phenol/chlorphorm/isoamyl alcohol extraction and concentration of the recovered aDNA on Amicon 30 columns. Recovered volumes were brought to 200 μl with sterile distilled water and etoh precipitated in the presence of 2.3 M ammonium acetate and 10 mM MgCl$_2$, rinsed with 80 percent ethanol, desiccated and redissolved in DNA buffer. In order to confirm preliminary PCR results, a second extraction of individual samples was conducted in which each sample was soaked in 5 percent sodium hypochlorite for several minutes after being cross-linked with UV light (254 nm) to further ensure elimination of contemporary nucleic acid contaminants. These samples were then subjected to the extraction protocol described above.

All extractions were performed using sterile, disposable lab ware, and dedicated, autoclaved reagents by masked and coated laboratory personnel wearing UV cross-linked gloves. Gloves were changed frequently while the samples were handled during the extraction procedure. All procedures were carried out in dedicated areas sterilized with bleach and/or were UV cross-linked to eliminate contamination with modern nucleic acids. Additionally, at least one negative extract control was included in each extraction procedure in order to facilitate detection of the introduction of modern contaminants.

PCR Amplification Protocol

Dedicated pipettors, sterile barrier tips, sterile reagents and cross-linked latex gloves were used in all PCR setups. Reactions were prepared in a Cleansphere (Safetech), with internal UV light exposure to work surface and instruments, and continuously flushed with filtered air. All postextraction and pre-PCR steps were completed in a separate room, removed from the thermal cycler. Both positive and negative controls were also employed with each amplification. Negative controls included both the blank extract control and PCR tubes to which no template was added in order to provide a constant check on the purity of the reagents. HeLa cell extracts and DNA samples derived from laboratory personnel served as positive controls. It is useful to note that the positive control samples were not introduced into the reaction tubes until immediately prior to the PCR run. Thus, the modern nucleic acid samples were not open in the pre-PCR environment so they would not be a possible source of contamination in the ancient samples.

Amplifications were performed in 25 μl volumes using Deep Vent polymerase (DVP⁻; New England Biolabs), in manufacturer supplied buffer, with 100 μg/ml bovine serum albumin, 200 nM dNTPs, 2 mM $MgSO_4$, 0.25 μm of each primer, and 5 μl ancient DNA template. To ensure elimination of spurious DNA contamination, reaction mixtures were UV cross-linked for 10 minutes (Sarker and Sommer 1990) prior to the addition of the polymerase and DNA sample. All manipulations were done on ice with tubes placed in a 95°C thermal cycler to achieve a "hot start" effect (Chou et al. 1992). Primers identifying the four American Indian mtDNA haplogroups (Stone and Stoneking 1993; Parr, Carlyle, and O'Rourke 1996; Table 5.2), with the exception of region V primers, were annealed at 55°C for one minute, extended at 72°C for 15 seconds, and denatured at 95°C for 35 seconds through 40 cycles. Amplifications of region V were annealed at 59°C. All amplifications were treated with an initial denaturing step at 95°C for five minutes prior to the first round of amplification.

PCR products were visualized on 3–4 percent, 3:1 NuSieve gels to determine results. Products bearing restriction sites were re-extracted from the PCR reaction mixture, precipitated, and redissolved in ddH_2O, and restricted according to manufacturer's recommendations (BRL), with tenfold enzyme excess. Restriction digests were again resolved on 3–4 percent, 3:1 NuSieve gels. The region V length polymorphism was scored directly on the ethidium-bromide–stained PCR product gels.

Contamination and Quality Control

The methodological challenges of obtaining and analyzing aDNA are well known (e.g., Handt et al. 1994). Lindahl reviewed the mechanisms of nucleic acid diagenesis and suggested that claims for extreme antiquity of aDNA should be viewed with skepticism, but that nucleic acids less than several tens of thousands of

TABLE 5.2.
Primers Used in Fremont aDNA Analysis

Marker	Primer Sites	Sequence (5'–3')
Hae III: 663	L611	ACCTCCTCAAAGCAATACACTG
	H743	GTGCTTGATGCTTGTTCCTTTTG
Alu I: 5176	L5120	TAACTACTACCGCATTCCTA
	H5230	AAAGCCGGTTAGCGGGGGCA
Hinc II: 13259	L13232	CGCCCTTACACAAAATGACATCAA
	H13393	TCCTATTTTTCGAATATCTTGTTC
Region V Del.	L8267	GGGCCCGTATTTACCCTAT
	H8332	GGTCTTGGTTCTCTTAATCTT

L and H refer to the light and heavy chains of the mtDNA molecule. Numbers are nucleotide position according to S. Anderson et al. (1981).

years old would be expected to survive in degraded form (1993:713). Earlier, Shearin, King, and O'Rourke (1989) showed that substantial amounts of low molecular-weight human DNA were preserved in naturally dessicated tissue samples in the American Southwest by fluorescent histological techniques and direct probing of raw extracts with whole human genome probes. It is worth emphasizing that the demonstration of the preservation of intact nucleic acids in these prehistoric human samples (Shearin, King, and O'Rourke 1989) was done without the use of enzymatic amplification. The likelihood of the preservation of aDNA in the Fremont series reported here is expected to be roughly equivalent to that observed in the Southwestern tissue samples since the source material is bone and, as Lindahl (1993) has observed, binding of DNA to the hydroxyapatite matrix of skeletal material retards the degradation of nucleic acids, thereby enhancing their preservation. Moreover, the comparatively recent ages of the samples (e.g., < 2,000 years) is certainly within the time period when nucleic acids would be expected to remain in the samples.

The real concern with sources of contamination in aDNA research derives from the sensitivity of the PCR technique. Under appropriate conditions the method will replicate even a single target sequence. Given the low copy number of aDNA per sample, even extremely low levels of contamination may result in an erroneous inference based on amplification of introduced modern nucleic acids. As outlined above, we adopted a rigorous series of protocols to prevent this occurance. Pre- and post-PCR activities were carried out in separate laboratories. All procedures were performed with dedicated instruments, all glass- and plasticware was autoclaved prior to use (as were many of the chemicals and reagents employed), reagents were aliquoted in small volumes so as to be used only once, and laboratory personnel were gloved, coated, and masked when working with ancient samples.

TABLE 5.3.

Distribution of Molecular Variation, Haplogroup Assignment, and Ages
of Great Salt Lake Wetlands Samples

Burial Number	Region V	*Hinc* II	*Hae* III	*Alu* I	Haplogroup	Calibrated Ages A.D.
3	D	+	−	+	B	888–1178
6	R		−			789–1029
8	R	+		+	A/X	1016–1293
11	D	+	−	+	B	1167–1296
12	R	+	−	+	X	
13	D	+	−	+	B	
14	D	+	−	+	B	547–678
15	D	+	−	+	B	560–773
16	R	+	−	−	D	1016–1245
17		+	−	+	B/X	653–990
20	R		−	+	C/X	1022–1257
21	R	+		+	A/X	778–1020
22	D	+	−	+	B	1013–1275
23	D	+	−	+	B	1011–1177
27	D	+	−	+	B	996–1230
28	D	+	−	+	B	1019–1277
29	D		−	+	(B)	1025–1283
32	R	−	−	+	C	1019–1279
33	R	+	−	+	X	898–1179
33	R	+	−	+	X	898–1179
35	R	+	−	+	X	900–1162
37		+	−	+	B/X	818–1020
40	D	+	−	+	B	1031–1279
41	D	+	−	+	B	1046–1303
42	D	+	−	+	B	
43	D			+	B	1314–1442
45	R	−		+	(C)	662–1156
47	R	+	−	−	D	880–1162
48	R	−	−	+	C	895–1168
49	D	+	−	+	B	1010–1257
51	D	+	−	+	B	662–956
52	D			+	B	547–956
53	D	+	−	+	B	659–945
56	D	+	−	+	B	885–1168
57	R			+		608–786
58	D	+	−	+	B	983–1180
61	D	+	−	+	B	819–1033
62	D		−		(B)	727–1014
64	D		−		(B)	252–602
65	R		−	+	C/X	1010–1257
68	D		−		(B)	900–1162

69	D			(B)	1165–1303
73	R		–		898–1179
76	R	–	–	(C)	726–990

D = deletion, R = repeat; + and – indicate presence or absence of a restriction site, respectively. See text for discussion.

Neither of the laboratories employed in this research is used for molecular analysis or screening of modern samples (other than the positive controls described above), but both are dedicated to aDNA research. Thus, cross-contamination from modern samples is minimized. Work areas are sterilized with sodium hypochlorite and/or cross-linked by UV light exposure, as are pipettors, tips, tubes, etc. Barrier tips are routinely used in all PCR procedures. The process is labor and time intensive, but it yields positive and replicable results.

Despite the rigorous care taken in laboratory procedures, contamination is a constant threat, and only replication of results can instill confidence in aDNA research and inferences (Taylor 1996). In the Fremont material, results from only four samples are based on a single extraction from a single skeletal element. The majority of the samples was extracted twice, and 12 were subjected to three or more extractions from different bone fragments (3 were extracted no less than five times!). Amplifications from separate, independent extracts could then be compared, and the results confirmed. Virtually all the deletion marker results were confirmed with this type of replication. Because the ancient origin of the extracts was demonstrated by this method, fewer of the other markers were subjected to universal replication. Nevertheless, depending on the marker, 30 to 40 percent of all individual restriction site determinations were confirmed by replication of the PCR product and/or by treatment with restriction enzyme.

Finally, sequence data is likely to be the most convincing demonstration of reliability of aDNA results and to lend confidence to the inferences based on them (Taylor 1996). It is worth noting that in initial experiments to amplify regions of the mtDNA hypervariable region for sequencing in these Fremont samples, success in obtaining PCR products was negatively correlated to fragment size. This result satisfies one of the criteria suggested by Handt et al. (1994) as indicating the manipulation of ancient nucleic acids. Moreover, all samples did not amplify with all primer sets, nor did every extract from a single individual always amplify with the same primer sets. This is consistent with the experience of others (e.g., Filon et al. 1995) and suggests that difficulty obtaining consistent results is a hallmark of aDNA research and is indicative of noncontaminated material.

RESULTS

Of the 47 skeletons sampled, 43 yielded ancient nucleic acid samples that permitted enzymatic amplification and molecular characterization. The distribution

TABLE 5.4.

Summary of Fremont Samples Failing to Yield DNA

Burial	% Collagen Yield	^{14}C Age	Calibrated Age Range	Site
26	16.9	730 ± 60	A.D. 1217–1393	42Wb269
36	6.6	1500 ± 80	A.D. 411–672	42Wb318
66	17.3	980 ± 50	A.D. 983–1180	42Bo580
70	14.9	1130 ± 60	A.D. 778–1020	42Bo599

Collagen yields after Coltrain (1993 and this volume); dates after Simms (this volume).

of the four molecular markers examined in these samples is given in Table 5.3. Haplogroup assignments found in column six follow the marker/haplotype designations given in Table 5.1, while the calibrated age of each specimen is from Simms (this volume). The four specimens that failed to yield amplifiable DNA (Table 5.4), range in age from approximately 730 years B.P. to nearly 1500 B.P. Indeed, two of these samples (burials 26 and 36, respectively), are the second youngest and second oldest specimens in the entire sample. The other two samples that did not yield aDNA (burials 66 and 70) are of intermediate ages in this range. Thus, it is not just the oldest samples that prove recalcitrant to molecular analysis and thereby do not contribute to a temporal bias in the data. Also, since each burial listed in Table 5.4 was recovered from a different archaeological site, there is no suggestion of a geographic cluster for those specimens failing to yield workable aDNA.

These observations are consistent with the hypothesis that localized conditions of interment and preservation determine accessibility of ancient nucleic acids. This seems a particularly attractive inference here since the collagen yield in at least three of the four samples in Table 5.4 appear to be sufficient to expect the presence of aDNA (Tuross 1994; Coltrain and Stafford this volume). It seems quite plausible, then, that in these four samples aDNA may be present but inaccessible to amplification and further molecular characterization as a result of coextracted contaminants acting as enzyme inhibitors in the PCR.

Of those samples that did provide useable aDNA (Table 5.3), it is clear that not all primer sets were equally successful on all samples. While some samples only provided molecular information for two or three markers, 25 successfully amplified with all four primer sets, for a complete molecular characterization of 58 percent (25/43). Successful amplification rates and observed marker frequencies are summarized in Table 5.5. The highest success rate was achieved for the 9 bp deletion marker in Region V of the mitochondrial molecule, where 41 of 43 samples could be scored for this length polymorphism. Twenty-five of the samples carried the deletion for a marker frequency of 61 percent.

TABLE 5.5.
Frequency of mtDNA Markers in Fremont Skeletal Samples

	Deletion	*Hae* III	*Alu* I	*Hinc* II
Successful Amplifications	41	36	36	31
Number with Marker	25	0	34	27
Frequency of Marker	61%	0%	94%	87%

The high amplification success rate for this marker is the result of two factors. First, a number of investigators (e.g., Lorenz and Smith 1994; Merriwether, Rothhammer, and Ferrell 1994, 1995; Kaestle, Lorenz, and Smith, this volume) have focused on the distribution of this marker in both prehistoric and contemporary Native American groups, so comparative frequencies are in greater supply than for the other markers. We therefore initially focused on the deletion marker by optimizing the PCR reaction for this primer set so that the number of samples we successfully screened would be increased. This permitted maximizing the number of comparisons of the frequency of occurance of this marker in the Fremont with other ancient and modern groups. Second, it appeared early in the screening process that a larger than expected number of samples possessed the deletion. Since none of the laboratory personnel carried this marker, its presence in ancient samples was additional evidence that the results were not the result of introduction of modern contaminants by laboratory workers. We tested and retested the ancient samples in order to confirm the absence of modern contaminants and to demonstrate our ability to replicate our aDNA results. More of this effort will be discussed below. Finally, it is interesting to note that both of the samples (burials 17 and 37) that failed to provide information on the deletion marker, were successfully typed for all three of the restriction site polymorphisms.

None of the 36 samples that amplified with the *Hae*III primer set possessed the restriction site. The frequency of this marker, then, is 0.0, and the haplogroup associated with the presence of this restriction marker (haplogroup A) is also absent from this ancient series. Of interest is that, on average, haplogroup A is the most common one observed in contemporary American Indian populations (e.g., Merriwether, Rothhammer, and Ferrell 1995), although it has been reported absent or at low frequency in contemporary South America (Torroni et al. 1993a) and some modern populations of the American Southwest (Lorenz and Smith 1996).

In marked contrast, both the *Alu*I and *Hinc*II restriction sites are present in a large majority of samples (94 percent and 87 percent, respectively; Table 5.5). Since it is the absence of these restriction sites that is associated with haplogroup C or D membership, these lineages are present in the Fremont skeletal series at low frequency, commensurate with their occurance in modern populations.

As indicated in Table 5.1, it is the joint distribution of the four markers under examination that is used to assign membership to one of the primary haplogroups defined for modern American Indian populations. In the ancient Fremont skeletal series, 33 samples provided sufficient molecular data to make provisional haplogroup assignments (Table 5.3). Twenty-five could be relatively unambiguously assigned to haplogroup B, three each to haplogroups C and X, and only two to haplogroup D. Determining the frequency of these lineages in this collection is complicated because not all samples amplified with all primer sets. Thus, the 25 samples considered haplogroup B, out of 33 assigned a lineage, suggests a frequency of 76 percent for this haplogroup. As an estimate of the frequency of this lineage, this figure is too high; of the samples that successfully amplified with the region V primers, only 61 percent possessed the deletion, the hallmark of haplogroup B (Table 5.5). Similar computational ambiguities obtain in estimating the other lineage frequencies as well. What is clear is that however haplogroup frequencies are obtained, lineage A is absent in this sample, haplogroup B is at a very high frequency (e.g., > 60 percent), and all the other lineages (C, D, and X) are present at comparatively low frequencies (e.g., < 15 percent).

It is also clear that for a number of samples, haplogroup membership may be narrowed to one of two lineages. These are indicated in Table 5.3. It is possible, therefore, that haplogroup A may ultimately be shown to be present in this collection, pending a fuller molecular characterization of burials 8 and 21. Even if its presence is ultimately proven to be the case, the frequency of this lineage will still be quite low. It is also possible, although unlikely, that all of the ambiguous haplogroup samples in Table 5.3 could be haplogroup X, dramatically increasing its frequency. However, as is clear from Table 5.2, this lineage has no defining marker, as do the other four, so any ambiguity will of necessity identify lineage X as a potential alternative until the remaining markers are identified. It is worth noting here that this haplotype also occurs in modern American Indian populations, but was attributed by Torroni et al. (1993a) to a non-Indian admixture. While this may frequently be the case, since it is a common haplotype in non-Indian groups, its presence in several pre-Columbian samples suggests there are additional explanations to account for its presence in Indian populations (cf. Bailliet et al. 1994; Easton et al. 1996).

Finally, the samples whose haplogroups appear in parentheses are cases where, even though one of the markers has failed to amplify, a marker considered diagnostic for a specific haplogroup is present (e.g., absence of the *Hind*II restriction site defining haplogroup C for burial 45 or presence of the deletion for several other samples). These provisional, and presumptive, lineage assignments appear reasonable, granting the assumption that the full number of possible haplogroups has been specified and that there are no back mutations.

DISCUSSION
Archaeological Context

The principal aim of this component of the Great Salt Lake wetlands bio-archaeological research project, is to characterize the molecular diversity of prehistoric populations so as to provide information regarding the population dynamics of these groups. With respect to either individual markers or haplogroups, there is no evidence of a temporal trend in the molecular diversity observed in the samples (see Table 5.3). Interestingly, both the oldest (#64, A.D. 252–602) and youngest (#43, A.D. 1313–1442) burials provided molecular data on only two of the markers employed. In both cases, the 9 bp intergenic deletion marker was amplified, and both samples were characterized by the deletion. Thus, the deletion, and haplogroup B which it defines, is present throughout the temporal range of these samples.

Markers defining the other lineages are also distributed throughout the time frame described by this skeletal series. Haplogroup C is observed in the relatively recent burial 32 (A.D. 1019–1279) as well as in the much older burial 76 (A.D. 726–990). Haplogroup D represents a rather smaller temporal range (approximately 920–1050 B.P.), but it is clear that, with only two representatives of this lineage, assessment of temporal distribution is not particularly meaningful. The three X haplotypes appear somewhat more clustered in time, with the two dated samples being of comparable age (~1000 B.P.). The third representative of this haplotype is unfortunately undated. However, the mean of three dates from the site from which this specimen comes (42Wb185) is approximately 800 years ago, with a potential age range from A.D. 789 to 1455 (see Simms, this volume). Such a large temporal range indicates that the undated sample of haplotype X could easily be substantially older, or younger, than the two dated specimens and, hence, cautions against inferring any temporal clustering.

The restricted geographic area from which samples were recovered, the large number of individual sites in the area, as well as the temporal distribution of a limited number of samples, preclude any formal test of geographic distribution of markers. In sum, the distribution of these markers in time among a presumably representative sample of northern Fremont individuals is quite consistent with the picture of a polymorphic and continuous population base occupying much of the eastern margin of the prehistoric Great Salt Lake. The scenario of adaptive diversity of a local Fremont population inhabiting the eastern margin of the Great Salt Lake in prehistoric times articulated by Simms (this volume and earlier) is certainly consistent with the observed variability in the molecular data—although with the limited number of molecular markers examined to date, the latter hardly constitutes a rigorous test of the former. Finally, it may be observed that, at least with respect to the molecular data accumulated to date, there is little evidence of any discontinuity in the biological population inhabiting the prehistoric eastern Great Basin region, and the archaeological horizon of northern Fremont that characterizes the Great Salt Lake wetlands burials is at least for now consistent with the notion of a biological population continuous in time.

A Broader Geographic Perspective

It is useful to contrast the molecular variation observed in the ancient northern Fremont with that found elsewhere in the Great Basin and western North America, both in prehistory and in contemporary populations. The Fremont samples reported here, while exhibiting some similarities with other regional populations, are in some ways distinctive. Another sample of comparable antiquity emphasizes the contrast. Kaestle, Lorenz, and Smith (this volume) have examined the 9 bp deletion polymorphism in skeletal material from the Stillwater Marsh locality in western Nevada, and it is clear from their analysis that the frequency of this length polymorphism is significantly lower than that observed in the Fremont of northern Utah. In fact, it is little different from that seen in the Anasazi of Grand Gulch in southern Utah (O'Rourke, Carlyle, and Parr 1996), where the frequency of this marker is but 20 percent in an initial screening of 17 individuals. The Anasazi sample is slightly older than the Fremont samples discussed here (Anasazi samples: 1010–2010 B.P.), but the temporal range overlaps the Fremont series, and the samples (and populations from which they are drawn) are just 300 miles apart, perhaps not a great distance even in antiquity. The difference in frequency of the deletion between the Fremont and Anasazi is significant (χ^2; p < 0.02) even when controlled for the small number of observations. The deletion is also present at a low frequency (10 percent) in a more recent skeletal series of Oneota origin from Illinois (Stone and Stoneking 1993) and in an Archaic burial (> 2000 B.P.) from central Utah (Shearin et al. 1996). However, it is absent from a 7,000-year-old specimen from Florida (Pääbo, Gifford, and Wilson 1988). Thus, with respect to this marker, there is considerable spatial/temporal heterogeneity among ancient samples.

Two recent reviews of the distribution of the region V deletion polymorphism (Lorenz and Smith 1994; Merriwether, Rothhammer, and Ferrell 1995) confirms the apparent heterogeneity. Both studies note a clear north-to-south cline of increasing frequencies for this polymorphism in Native American populations. With one exception (Old Harbor Eskimos; Merriwether, Rothhammer, and Ferrell 1995), the deletion is unknown in Eskimo populations, being essentially absent north of 55° north latitude in both the Americas and Asia (G. F. Shields et al. 1992, 1993; Torroni et al. 1993a, 1993b; Lorenz and Smith 1994; Merriwether, Rothhammer, and Ferrell 1995; Ward et al. 1991). Among contemporary populations of the American Southwest, frequencies for this marker range from 14.3 percent among the Paiute and Shoshoni to over 85 percent among the Pima and Paipai (Lorenz and Smith 1994) and reach fixation among the modern Hopi (Lorenz and Smith 1996). The average frequency among 14 Southwestern populations reported by Merriwether, Rothhammer, and Ferrell (1995) is 39.4 percent.

However, even among contemporary populations single-marker frequencies may be misleading. For example, the Pima have been characterized by different researchers as possessing the 9 bp deletion at a frequency of 85.7 percent (Lorenz and Smith 1994) as well as 45.2 percent (T. G. Schurr et al. 1990). Similarly, the Navajo have reported frequencies of 37.5 percent and 60 percent (Torroni et al. 1993a; Lorenz and Smith 1994). Such disparities emphasize the importance of defining the population of study and clearly demonstrate that sampling, even in large, modern populations is not a trivial exercise. It may also be the case that some variation in estimation of marker frequency is attributable to sample-size variation. In the examples cited above, the higher estimates are based on substantially smaller numbers than the lower estimates. In any event, these concerns emphasize the difficulty of defining "populations" in prehistory for genetic analyses and the dangers of relying on single estimates for inferences regarding population affinity or dynamics.

The number of samples available for comparison is diminished when we look to lineage frequencies. For the ancient samples, it is problematic simply to compute the frequency of a lineage, where lineages are defined by the joint distribution of markers within individual samples, since not all markers are available for each individual. If, however, we follow the convention of presuming that the diagnostic marker for a lineage may be taken as an analog for the full suite of markers for purposes of haplogroup assignment, we can obtain first approximations to haplogroup frequencies in the Fremont series. In this case, the four primary haplogroup frequencies are apparent in Table 5.5: Haplogroup A, 0 percent; haplogroup B, 61 percent; haplogroup C, 13 percent; and haplogroup D, 6 percent. These frequencies sum to 80 percent, leaving 20 percent of indeterminate lineage. This remainder is composed of individuals of haplotype X as well as those for whom a haplogroup could not be assigned. (Note that the marker and lineage frequencies given here differ slightly from those in an earlier report [Parr, Carlyle, and O'Rourke 1996] as a result of resolving the marker status of several samples in the intervening time span.)

Examination of Table 5.3 suggests that haplogroup X accounts for approximately 8 percent of the observations, with the rest being unresolvable. These values are not too radically different from those seen in the few ancient and modern samples available for comparison. In the Southwest, the most likely ancient source for comparison is the Anasazi. In the study noted earlier (O'Rourke, Carlyle, and Parr 1996), the following haplogroup frequencies were obtained for a small Anasazi sample: haplogroup A, 7 percent; haplogroup B, 20 percent; haplogroup C, 8 percent; and haplogroup D, 0 percent. Clearly, a majority of samples have yet

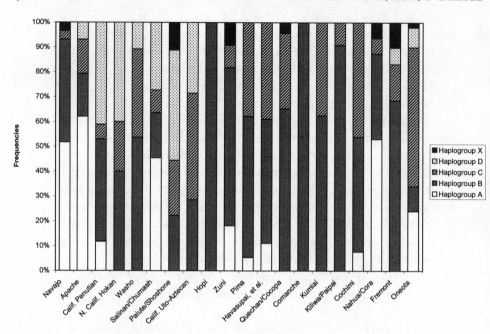

FIGURE 5.1. Comparison of haplogroup frequencies in two ancient American Indian samples and selected present-day populations of the western United States. Data from Lorenz and Smith (1996) are given in Table 5.6.

to be unambiguously assigned to a haplogroup, and these figures merely reflect the frequency of the diagnostic markers for each lineage among those samples that yielded successful, and replicated, amplification products. In addition, two individuals were unambiguously classified as haplogroup X. The Archaic burial reported by Shearin et al. (1996) was also successfully examined for the suite of four lineage markers and was found to represent lineage B. Despite the preliminary nature of these figures, they do suggest the same heterogeneity among ancient samples noted above.

Heterogeneity of lineage frequencies is also reflected in modern populations. While many groups have been screened for the presence or absence of the 9 bp deletion, few have been examined for the larger suite of markers. However, Lorenz and Smith (1996) recently analyzed mtDNA haplogroup diversity in North American Indian populations, and data for the western groups included in their study are given in Table 5.6 and displayed graphically in Figure 5.1. Also presented in Table 5.6 and Figure 5.1 are comparable data for the prehistoric northern Utah Fremont and Oneota of Illinois (Stone and Stoneking 1993).

The Navajo and Apache data illustrated in Figure 5.1 emphasize the origin of these populations outside the area of the American Southwest as well as their dis-

TABLE 5.6.

Lineage Distribution in Western U.S. American Indian Populations

Population	A	B	Haplogroup C	D	X
Navajo	0.517	0.414	0.034	0	0.034
Apache	0.621	0.172	0.138	0.069	0
Calif. Penutian	0.118	0.412	0.059	0.412	0
N. Calif. Hokan	0	0.4	0.2	0.4	0
Washo	0	0.536	0.357	0.107	0
Salinan/Chumash	0.455	0.182	0.091	0.273	0
Paiute/Shoshone	0	0.222	0.222	0.444	0.111
Calif. Uto-Aztecan	0	0.286	0.429	0.286	0
Hopi	0	1	0	0	0
Zuni	0.182	0.636	0.091	0	0.091
Pima	0.054	0.568	0.378	0	0
Havasupai, et al.	0.111	0.5	0.389	0	0
Quechan/Cocopa	0	0.652	0.304	0	0.043
Comanche	0	1	0	0	0
Kumiai	0	0.625	0.375	0	0
Kiliwa/Paipai	0	0.909	0.091	0	0
Cochimi	0.077	0.462	0.462	0	0
Nahua/Cora	0.531	0.344	0.063	0	0.063
Fremont	0	0.61	0.13	0.06	0.09
Oneota	0.24	0.1	0.56	0.08	0.02

Fremont data from Parr, Carlyle, and O'Rourke (1996); Oneota data from Stone and Stoneking (1993); remaining frequencies from Lorenz and Smith (1996).

tinctiveness from the remainder of the populations displayed. The Navajo and Apache are relatively recent Athapaskan-speaking migrants to the region and are characterized by relatively high frequencies of haplogroup A. The high frequency of this lineage in southern Athapaskans is hardly surprising since most northern Athapaskan groups are nearly fixed for this haplogroup. Indeed, the lowered frequencies among the Navajo and Apache are likely the result of admixture with non-Athapaskan groups as well as non-Indians. Haplogroup B is at a somewhat reduced frequency in these two groups. Haplogroups C and D appear to be absent in the Navajo data presented by Lorenz and Smith (1996), but present at frequencies among the Apache comparable to those reported for the ancient Fremont (see Table 5.6).

Alternatively, most populations from the Great Basin and California are characterized by an absence or low frequency of haplogroup A, relatively high and prominent frequencies of haplogroups C and D, and variable frequencies of haplogroup B, although the latter frequency is typically below 40 percent. In contrast, contemporary populations of the Southwest appear to be characterized by an absence or very low frequency of haplogroup A; a high, prominent frequency of haplogroup B; a low to moderate frequency of haplogroup C; and the effective absence of haplogroup D. It is, therefore, the relative absence of haplogroup A that distinguishes populations of the western United States from native populations of other regions of North and Middle America. Similarly, within the confines of the western U.S. region, it is the differing frequencies of haplogroups D, and to a lesser extent those of B, that reveal regional differentiation.

For example, the Pima of Arizona have an unusually low frequency of haplogroup A and a modest level of lineage B. This combination led to our noting a similarity between the modern Pima and the ancient northern Fremont (Parr, Carlyle, and O'Rourke 1996; O'Rourke, Carlyle, and Parr 1996). However, the Pima have a high frequency of haplogroup C and lack haplogroup D, which distinguishes them from our Fremont sample, but at least, with respect to the absence of the D lineage, is reminiscent of both the Anasazi and populations in central Mexico (O'Rourke, Carlyle, and Parr 1996; Torroni et al. 1994). Nevertheless, heterogeneity χ^2 (with Yates continuity correction) indicates that with respect to the frequency of the HindII morph, the defining character for haplogroup C, the modern Pima are significantly different from either of the two ancient samples (p < 0.025). It should be emphasized again that random deviations in marker or haplogroup frequencies are not unexpected in comparatively small populations (e.g., Avise, Neigel, and Arnold 1984; Heyer 1995), as those in the prehistoric Great Basin are likely to have been. It is therefore imperative to increase not only the number of individuals sampled in aDNA studies but also the number and variety of molecular markers used to infer population history and historical dynamics.

It is nonetheless instructive that the absence of haplogoup A and the high frequency of haplogroup B in the prehistoric sample is consistent with the general profile of extreme southwestern groups, but inconsistent with the typical profile of present-day Great Basin populations. This suggests that northern Fremont origins may be sought to the south and west of the eastern Great Basin, an inference not inconsistent with the Numic expansion hypothesis. Alternatively, the hypothesis is given little support in light of the disparity in haplogroup frequencies between the ancient northern Fremont and the single Paiute/Shoshone sample reported in Lorenz and Smith (1996). This ambiguity between the regional vs. sample specific comparisons emphasizes the current inadequacy of these data to directly and adequately test the Numic expansion hypothesis. It seems unlikely that the northern Utah sample discussed here completely characterizes the genetic diversity of the prehistoric Fremont peoples any more than a single, small sample adequately reflects the rich, genetic diversity that undoubtedly exists among modern peoples. However, it is clear that a larger suite of markers examined in both ancient samples and present-day populations will ultimately permit such a direct and adequate test of the Numic expansion hypothesis.

Finally, it is useful to note that the other ancient sample included in Table 5.6 and Figure 5.1, the Oneota, does not appear to have a genetic profile that is similar to any of the other populations surveyed. This is not surprising, and indeed is rather comforting, since the sample is from the eastern United States and would be expected to differ from western samples if the markers are at all useful in detecting any degree of population differentiation. The data presented appear to confirm the utility of the markers for assessing regional patterns of differentiation.

Handt et al. (1994) suggested that one benchmark for confirming that analyses reflect variation in aDNA rather than a modern contaminant is that the results make phylogenetic sense. The results presented here for the Fremont, in the context of regional patterns of variation in a large suite of western U.S. Native American populations, suggest that this criterion has been more than adequately met in the present analysis. Although the data presented for the northern Fremont do not constitute a formal, nor adequate, test of the Numic replacement hypothesis, they do extend our perspective of biological diversity into prehistory and demonstrate that with adequate samples and sufficient markers such hypotheses can and will be formally addressed with aDNA analyses.

SUMMARY AND CONCLUSIONS

Forty-seven northern Fremont burials recovered from the eastern Great Salt Lake wetlands were screened for four mtDNA markers. Of the 43 samples that provided aDNA, 61 percent carried a 9 bp deletion in the cytochrome oxidase II-tRNA^{lys} intergenic region associated with founding lineage B in American Indians (Torroni et al. 1993a; Merriwether, Rothhammer, and Ferrell 1995; Lorenz and Smith 1994). None of the individuals sampled possessed a *Hae*III restriction site at np 663, resulting in an absence of haplogroup A in this skeletal series. This marker and associated haplogroup are the most common morph among contemporary Indian populations, although not among western U.S. populations. Two additional lineages were present at a modest frequency.

Haplogroup B is present at a significantly higher frequency in these Fremont samples than in an ancient sample from the western Great Basin (Kaestle, Lorenz, and Smith, this volume) or in a small sample of Anasazi of slightly greater antiquity (O'Rourke, Carlyle, and Parr 1996). The absence of lineage A is similar to the low frequency reported for this haplogroup among the Pima (Torroni et al. 1993a; Lorenz and Smith 1996), although the high frequency of haplogroup C in this modern population distinquishes it from the ancient samples discussed here.

The results presented here and in Kaestle, Lorenz, and Smith (this volume) suggest a heterogeneous group of ancient populations inhabiting the Great Basin in antiquity. Frequency differences between ancient samples for specific markers may reflect both the diachronic nature of the samples and the well-known occurrence of lineage extinctions in small populations (Avise, Neigel, and Arnold 1984; Heyer 1995). Nevertheless, these results begin to define the biological characteristics of ancient populations in the Great Basin and to lay the foundation for future tests of archaeological hypotheses. They would seem to confirm the early optimism regarding the potential for aDNA studies to contribute to a fuller understanding of past populations and an appreciation of their diversity.

Acknowledgments

We gratefully acknowledge Steve Simms, Joan Coltrain, Geoffrey Hayes, Duncan Metcalfe, and James O'Connell for stimulating discussion, laboratory assistance, and archaeological guidance. The molecular analyses were supported by grants BNS 89-20463 (to D. H. O'Rourke) and DBS 92-23227 (to S. Simms) from the National Science Foundation, the Wenner-Gren Foundation (D. H. O'Rourke), and the University of Utah Research Committee (D. H. O'Rourke). Shawn Carlyle was supported by a Graduate Research Fellowship from the University of Utah and Ryan Parr was partially supported by a Utah State University Faculty Grant to S. Simms. We are especially pleased to extend our appreciation to the Northwestern Band of the Shoshoni Nation for permission to collect and analyze material from the Great Salt Lake wetlands burials.

6

A Biological Perspective on Prehistoric Human Adaptation in the Great Salt Lake Wetlands

Jason R. Bright and Carol J. Loveland

Anthropologists have increasingly focused on risk reduction as a goal of foragers, who alter their diets and subsistence strategies to meet changing resource potentials (Hayden 1981a, 1981b, as cited in Kelly 1995a:100). Breadth of diet models, however, suggest that the plasticity seen in a forager's diet is best explained as a function of the depletion of highly ranked resources, at which time foragers would include lower ranked, more costly resources to the diet. Decisions about diet breadth enable foragers to maximize the energy gained in relation to time spent foraging. Winterhalder (1986) has shown that rate-maximizing diets can closely resemble risk-minimizing diets. Thus, broadening diets can have the affect of minimizing risk. A model of adaptive diversity has been proposed for the Great Salt Lake wetlands that is consistent with several lines of archaeological and bioarchaeological evidence (Simms, this volume). Briefly, adaptive diversity refers to changes in a lifeway and to varying degrees of residential cycling over the life history of individuals. Since adaptive diversity is an outcome of diet-breadth choices and risk reduction (among other things), the pathologies present in the Great Salt Lake skeletal series provide another line of evidence to evaluate the relationship between adaptive diversity and risk reduction.

Since many of the pathologies we discuss below can result from nutritional inadequacies, food shortages, and infectious diseases, we cannot avoid broadening our treatment of "risk" to include "physiological stress." As Kelly states, "Usually, *risk* is taken to mean the chance of going without enough food, and *stress* refers to periods when this happens" (1995a:101; italics in original). Thus, behaviors that operate to reduce risk should reduce the frequency and severity of the physiological stresses incurred by an individual. We report on dental caries, enamel hypoplasia, transverse lines, periosteal lesions, and porotic hyperostosis as general indicators of phsyiological stress.

Since differences in the prevalence of pathologies in the Great Salt Lake series and other prehistoric groups could provide relative measures of stress, comparisons were made between the skeletal series from the Great Salt Lake wetlands and those from Stillwater and Malheur Lake (this volume), as well as with Andrews (1972), who provides comparable data from 28 individuals from 4 Great Salt Lake Fremont localities and 50 individuals from 10 more distant Fremont sites. This enabled comparison to frequencies in predominantly foraging and farming groups. Further comparison to summary data from other North American cases, and the rest of the world, provided a broad context. The Great Salt Lake skeletal series includes 85 individuals excavated from sites along the northeastern shore of the Great Salt Lake (Simms, Loveland, and Stuart 1991; Fawcett and Simms 1993). These skeletons form the basis of this study, which explores risk reduction as an outcome of adaptive diversity.

The Great Salt Lake series is well suited for addressing adaptive diversity in this way because it was exposed by natural processes occurring over a 64 km^2 area, exposing virtually all human remains interred there over the last 1,500 years. Thus, it avoids some of the common sample biases produced by selective excavation in cemeteries, which represents only a subset of the population, and by larger farming sites that have a strong archaeological pattern, which can overshadow the weak archaeological patterns of foragers (see Simms, this volume). The random nature of the sample may provide a more accurate reflection of the larger population than is commonly available.

MATERIALS, METHODS, AND RESULTS

For the physical anthropologist, skeletal remains provide the best evidence of stress. Although stress episodes affect soft tissue more clearly and severely than bone (McCance 1960; McCance et al. 1961, 1962), the physical anthropologist seldom has soft tissue to study. Unfortunately, only extreme or chronic insults leave evidence in the skeletal remains of past populations. In addition, most stress events cause general, rather than specific, changes. Thus, indicators of stress may be present, but the factors responsible for this stress must be treated broadly or remain unknown. Although a majority of the recovered bones from the Great Salt Lake wetlands are in fair or good condition, there is a tremendous range in the completeness of the specific individuals (Loveland 1993, 1991). Some skeletons are nearly complete, while others consist of a single or several bones. Therefore, when any particular element is considered, the effective sample size is much smaller than 85, the number of recovered individuals. All cranial and postcranial measurements were taken where possible according to methods provided by Bass (1964, 1987).

The sex of adult skeletons was determined according to established indicators, including pelvic morphology (Bass 1987; Phenice 1969; Suchey et al. 1979; Sutherland and Suchey 1987), cranial morphology (T. D. Stewart 1979), diameter

TABLE 6.1.

Age and Sex Distribution of the Great Salt Lake Skeletal Series

Age	Male	Female	Unknown Sex	Subadult
0.0–4.9				6
5.0–9.9				5
10.0–14.9				4
15.0–19.9	1	3		
20.0–24.9	2	1		
25.0–29.9	3		1	
30.0–34.9	1	2	1	
35.0–39.9	1	2		
40.0–44.9	1	1		
45+	5	3		
Adult	8	3	19	
Subadult				6
Unknown Age			6	
Total	22	15	27	21

of the femoral head (Krogman 1962), circumference of the femoral shaft (Black 1978), and diameter of the humeral head (Krogman 1962). In 37 of 85 cases, sex could be definitively assigned; the other cases are listed as indeterminate.

Subadult age-at-death was established by common methods following Schour and Massler (1941, 1944), Ubelaker (1989), Johnston (1961, 1962) McKern (1970), McKern and Stewart (1957), Maresh (1955) and Merchant and Ubelaker (1977). Observations were made on the pubic symphysis to ascertain adult age-at-death (Gilbert 1973; Gilbert and McKern 1973; Katz and Suchey 1986; McKern and Stewart 1957; Suchey, Brooks, and Katz 1988). Other, less reliable adult aging techniques were used when necessary (T. D. Stewart 1958; Ubelaker 1989; Krogman 1962). Where the fragmentary condition of the bones precluded more exact estimates of age, less specific categories of subadult (0–17 years) or adult (18+) were used.

Age-at-death could be ascertained for 43 of 85 individuals. Although this degree of incompleteness prevented ideal reconstruction of demographic parameters (Owsley and Bass 1979), several relevant observations may be noted. The skeletal collection contained 60 adults, 21 subadults, and 4 individuals whose remains were so fragmentary that neither age nor sex could be determined. Subadults represented 24.7 percent of the series, which is less than is documented in many prehistoric groups (Bass, Evans, and Jantz 1971; Loveland 1980), but higher than that documented in the western Great Basin. For instance, Galliher (1978) documented 8.6 percent subadult mortality in a small Nevada sample; C. Stark (1983) reported 20.5 percent of 260 skeletons from several sites in Nevada as subadults; and S. T. Brooks, Haldeman, and Brooks (1988) found 19.2 percent of the Still-water series younger than 20 at death. These differences in the frequency of subadult age-at-death across Great Basin samples are more likely a consequence of differential preservation and nonrepresentative samples rather than differences in the health status of children at different localities.

The adult sample is composed of 22 males and 15 females. Female age-at-death was highest in young adulthood (15–20 years) and old age (45+). The bias toward young adulthood may reflect hazards of pregnancy; however, there was no specific skeletal evidence of pregnancy-related complications. Peak age-at-death among males occurred between 25 and 30 years and during old age. A summary of age-at-death and sex of the 85 Great Salt Lake skeletons is presented in Table 6.1.

Forty of the skeletons had no obvious abnormalities (47 percent), although some skeletons were quite incomplete. Several osteological anomalies were analyzed as evidence of physiological stress. The following is a discussion of each one that provides our rationale for including it in the analysis, the sample available for observation, methods employed, and results.

Dental Caries

While dental caries are not evidence of "stress" per se, they are included in this analysis because diet is a central component of our proposed risk-reduction strategy (i.e., adaptive diversity). Carious lesions on teeth can be encouraged through consumption of carbohydrate-rich foods, as is commonly indicated in North America, where shifts to corn agriculture have been associated with increased caries rates in archaeological samples. Hillson discusses several cases (1996:282–84), demonstrating that hunter-gatherer populations often have low rates and that rates increase as the contribution of corn to diet increases. Stable carbon isotope data (Coltrain 1997; Coltrain and Stafford, this volume) indicate that evidence of corn consumption is apparent in the Great Salt Lake skeletal series, thus the rate of carious teeth in the series ought to be consistent with rates observed in other mixed-diet strategies.

All dentitions were examined for evidence of carious lesions. Conclusions concerning the dental characteristics of the sample are tentative because 59 skeletons contained fewer than 10 teeth each. Of the 519 permanent teeth available for observation, 21 were carious (4.0 percent). In this study, two individuals had four carious teeth and two others had two carious teeth. Seven of the skeletons with evidence of dental caries were over 35; only one was a subadult. Dental caries were observed in six males and four females.

Table 6.2 summarizes caries data (Turner 1979) on 64 populations with differing subsistence strategies and from other Fremont sites. The rate seen in the Great

TABLE 6.2.
Rate of Carious Teeth in Great Salt Lake Series and Others

	Number of Populations	Number of Teeth	% Carious	SD
Hunter-Gatherer[a]	19	>39,034	1.30[b]	1.46
Mixed Economy[a]	13	8,638	5.12[b]	3.40
Agricultural[a]	32	517,805	10.43[b]	6.47
Great Salt Lake Series		519	4.0	N/A

[a] From Turner 1979
[b] Mean percent carious
SD = Standard deviation

Salt Lake sample (4 percent) is consistent with results from populations combining agriculture with hunting and gathering. The rate of carious teeth reported here is higher than that reported in the western Great Basin, where Larsen, Russell, and Hutchinson (1995) report a rate of 2.8 percent in the Stillwater series, combining permanent and deciduous teeth. No caries were observed on 82 deciduous teeth in our sample, so, by combining deciduous and permanent teeth for comparison, the rate drops to 3.5 percent. This rate is higher than in the Stillwater series, but still falls within the range for mixed diets. The difference is consistent with the presence of corn agriculture in the eastern Great Basin.

Enamel Hypoplasia

Enamel hypoplasia is included in this analysis as a general indicator of stress. Both disease and nutritional inadequacies can slow down or stop proper enamel growth, resulting in pits, lines, or grooves of defective enamel (Larsen 1997:43–44). Thus, evaluation of enamel hypoplasia can provide a measure of stress. Several researchers (Cook 1971; Goodman et al. 1984) have suggested that a weaning diet, which is high in carbohydrate and low in protein, may be responsible for the development of hypoplasia in children between the ages of two and four. Skinner and Goodman (1992) and Blakey, Leslie, and Reidy (1994) present exceptions to this explanation. They found no correlation between weaning age and peak hypoplasia frequencies in a sample of African-American slaves, attributing hypoplasia instead to a trio of effects including "1) multiple environmental stresses, 2) differences in hypoplastic susceptibility in enamel, and 3) random factors" (Blakey, Leslie, and Reidy 1994:371).

It seems likely, nonetheless, that a two- to four-year-old child faces a variety of biological and psychological stresses that might contribute to enamel hypoplasia

Table 6.3.

Prevalence of Enamel Hypoplasia by Tooth Type—Permanent Dentition

MAXILLA

RIGHT								LEFT								
M3	M2	M1	PM4	PM3	C	LI	CI	CI	LI	C	PM3	PM4	M1	M2	M3	Total
2/6*	3/7	1/10	0/6	0/6	0/7	3/7	4/9	6/8	3/9	4/10	2/9	2/8	3/9	2/6	2/4	37/121

MANDIBLE

RIGHT								LEFT								
M3	M2	M1	PM4	PM3	C	LI	CI	CI	LI	C	PM3	PM4	M1	M2	M3	Total
3/5	2/7	1/10	3/6	2/7	1/9	1/8	1/8	1/8	3/9	1/9	2/8	2/6	0/9	0/8	0/5	23/122

* Number of teeth with hypoplasia/Number of teeth observed

formation. These can include possible nutritional shortages and disease, which would put a weaning child at high risk. We expect to find a low rate of enamel hypoplasia, if adaptive diversity minimizes the risk.

Measurement of enamel defects was limited to the 12 anterior teeth since a number of researchers (Goodman and Armelagos 1985a, 1985b; Hutchinson and Larsen 1988; Goodman and Rose 1990) have found that the permanent incisors and canines offer the greatest evidence for enamel hypoplasia. Scoring of these defects involved the "fingernail test." Regression equations found in Goodman and Rose (1990:98), based on the work of Swärdstedt (1966) and Massler, Schour, and Poncher (1941), were used to determine age at the time of defect formation. This approach involves dividing the crown into increments corresponding to half-year development intervals. Hypoplastic events can then be related to specific developmental ages.

The sample evaluated for evidence of enamel hypoplasia included 243 teeth from 14 individuals: three females, four males, and seven subadults. The numbers of maxillary and mandibular teeth observed were almost even: 121 of the former and 122 of the latter. Teeth exhibiting marked occlusal wear were not included in the enamel hypoplasia study. However, since the incisal/occlusal one-third of a tooth has the lowest frequency of defects (Goodman 1989; Hutchinson and Larsen 1988), teeth missing only this portion were included. In the anterior dentition, the majority of dental defects were horizontal grooves, referred to as type 4 enamel developmental defects (Fédération Dentaire International 1982). Pits (type 3 defects) were more common on molars.

Table 6.3 shows the prevalence of enamel hypoplasia by tooth type in permanent dentition as well as the number of each tooth type observed. Enamel hypoplasia occurred more frequently in the maxillary dentition (30.6 percent) than in the mandibular dentition (18.9 percent). Suga (1989) suggested that smaller teeth are less vulnerable to hypoplastic defects—a finding which certainly has relevance for explaining differences observed between maxillary and mandibular incisors.

The maxillary left central incisor exhibited the highest percentage of defects among permanent teeth observed (75 percent). Goodman and Armelagos (1985a, 1985b) found the greatest number of defects on maxillary central incisors and mandibular canines. Hutchinson and Larsen (1995) found that mandibular canines carried the highest percentage of defects in the Stillwater series, as did Nelson (this volume) in the Malheur Lake series. The number of defects in mandibular canines in this study, in contrast, is low—one on each canine.

Five of 14 individuals exhibited at least one hypoplastic defect (35.7 percent). Table 6.4 reports the number of hypoplastic events in the five affected individuals. Although sex has been determined for only three of the five individuals (two males, one female, two subadults), the one female exhibits a considerably higher number of hypoplasias per number of teeth observed than the males or subadults.

TABLE 6.4.
Number of Hypoplasias by Individual—Permanent Dentition

Burial Number	Age of Individual	Sex of Individual	Number of Hypoplasias/ Number of Teeth Observed
11	2–3	SA	8/11
17	25–30	M	4/12
52	12+	SA	6/23
55	19–24	M	3/17
64	18–23	F	39/29

SA = Subadult

Table 6.5 details the age of hypoplasia formation for the six left anterior teeth. The age of stress recorded in the six teeth ranges from 2.60 to 3.32 years, with the canines reflecting a higher age than the incisors. Age ranges for formation of enamel hypoplasia in this sample fall within the two- to four-year-old range discussed above.

The rate of affected individuals in the Great Salt Lake series is lower than that reported in the Malheur Lake series and Stillwater series (Hutchinson and Larsen 1995; Nelson, this volume), where nearly two-thirds of observed individuals had one or more hypoplastic event. However, hypoplastic defects in the Great Salt Lake sample were scored macroscopically, defects in the other series were scored microscopically. This difference in method surely accounts for at least some of the differences in reported rates of hypoplastic defects.

TABLE 6.5.
Age at Which Enamel Hypoplasia Developed by Tooth Type

	Number of Tooth Defects	Age Range	Mean Age
Maxilla			
Left Central Incisor	6	2.14–3.14	2.73
Left Lateral Incisor	3	3.07–3.29	3.15
Left Canine	4	2.84–3.97	3.32
Mandible			
Left Central Incisor	1	2.60	2.60
Left Lateral Incisor	3	2.29–3.02	2.63
Left Canine	1	3.15	3.15

TABLE 6.6.
Frequency of Enamel Hypoplasia in Great Salt Lake Skeletal Series and Others

Sample	No. of Teeth Observed	Frequency[a]
Great Salt Lake Series	243	24.7
Great Salt Lake Fremont*	298	46.9
Uinta Fremont*	150	26.7
Sevier Fremont*	131	23.7
San Rafael Fremont*	161	16.7
Parowan Fremont*	314	31.8

* Andrews 1972:47
[a] Number of defects/Number of teeth observed × 100

The prevalence of enamel hypoplasia is still low, however, when compared to other Fremont samples. Andrews (1972:47) computes the frequency as the number of pathologies observed divided by the number of teeth observed. By following a similar methodology, the rate in the Great Salt Lake series becomes 24.7 percent (60/243; see Tables 6.3 and 6.4), which is lower than that observed in three of five other Fremont samples reported (Table 6.6).

Transverse Lines

Transverse lines (or Harris lines) are formed following a slowdown or halt of epiphyseal cartilage growth (Clarke and Gindhart 1981:574). When growth resumes, a buildup of mineralized collagen matrix occurs, which appears as a line visible on radiographs. This interruption of growth may originate from a variety of systemic disturbances; however, in prehistoric populations, the most likely causes were childhood episodes of malnutrition or infection. Evaluation of transverse lines provides only a general, and often ambiguous, indicator of stress among members of a skeletal series. Lines frequently remodel away and do not persist into adulthood, so past episodes of childhood stress among the adult population may be underrepresented. Furthermore, Larsen (1997:43) cites cases where transverse line frequencies were contrary to children's known health history (i.e., healthy children had many lines, underweight children had few). The role of malnutrition and infection in development of transverse lines relates this analysis back to our issue of adaptive diversity. We suggest the adaptive diversity employed by the Great Salt Lake Fremont reduced the risk of malnutrition and infection, so we should see a low rate of transverse lines.

Clarke's methods (1982) were used to evaluate the radiographs of adults for the presence of transverse lines; Hummert's and Van Gerven's methods (1985) were

TABLE 6.7.
Transverse Lines in the Great Salt Lake Skeletal Series

Group	Number with Transverse Lines/ Number Observed	%
Males	7/15	46.6
Females	7/11	63.6
Adults	1/8	12.5
Subadults	5/11	45.5

used for subadults. Lines were counted if they were visible to the naked eye and if they extended at least halfway across the bone.

Radiographs of the long bones revealed transverse lines on 20 of 45 skeletons (44.4 percent). Table 6.7, which presents the occurrence of transverse lines on all long bones, shows that lines are more common in female skeletons than in any other group. However, a different picture emerges when only the tibia is evaluated (in order to utilize the methods of Clarke [1982] and Hummert and Van Gerven [1985]). Ten skeletons exhibited transverse lines on at least one tibia: four males, one female, one adult of undetermined sex, and four subadults. Table 6.8 documents the age of line formation in the 10 individuals. The age distribution is remarkably consistent, ranging from birth to four years, with most lines developing between one and two years of age.

Because of a small sample size and the potential resorption of lines in adult-

TABLE 6.8.
Age of Formation of Transverse Lines in Tibiae

Burial #	Age	Sex	Age at Line Formation
14	45+	M	1–2 years
53	35–40	M	1–2 years
55	19–24	M	0–1 year
73	adult	PM	1–2 years
3	30–35	F	1–2 years
20	30+	U	0–1 year
40	10–12.5	U	6 months–1 year
70	5.5–8.0	U	2–4 years
11	2–3	U	6 months–1 year
35	1.5–3.0	U	0–6 months

PM = Probable male, U = Undetermined, M = Male, F = Female

hood, it is difficult to reach conclusions about the impact of stress on this skeletal series through analysis of transverse lines. However, the high incidence of transverse lines, present in one or more long bones in 44.4 percent of the sample, attests to periods of disease and/or malnutrition early in life. This frequency is similar to the "elevated" frequency Larsen (1997:41) cites in some Arctic populations, as it also is in Fremont samples, where Andrews (1972:38) reports that "Harris's lines occurred at a high frequency."

Periosteal Lesions

Periosteal lesions develop on the surface of cortical bone when the periosteum becomes inflamed. Such inflammation is often caused by infectious disease and trauma in infants (T. D. White 1991:344; Mensforth et al. 1978; Larsen, Russell, and Hutchinson 1995). While periosteal lesions provide a nonspecific indicator of health, treponemal infections have frequently been discussed as a factor in New World cases (Larsen 1997:93–99).

Tibiae were analyzed for evidence of these lesions, as the tibia is almost always the element most frequently affected by periosteal reactions (Larsen 1997:85). Only tibiae that were 50 percent or more complete were included. In total, 38 tibiae were available for observation. Eighteen individuals provided two tibiae, and two individuals provided one each. No periosteal lesions were observed on any tibiae. This strikingly low value indicates that the major causes of periosteal lesions were absent in this sample.

Obviously, any comparisons made to a rate of 0 percent of individuals affected and 0 percent of observed bones affected will produce high prevalences, but comparisons to other Great Basin wetlands groups, as well as other Fremont samples, is interesting since they demonstrate the potentially high frequencies of these lesions in other prehistoric groups. Nelson (this volume) reports frequencies at Malheur Lake and Stillwater (42.6 percent and 16.4 percent, respectively) by individual. Furthermore, as Table 6.9 shows, the frequency of inflammations in observed bones in other Fremont groups ranges between 14.2 percent and 28.6 percent (Andrews [1972:Table 4] includes fibulae with tibiae).

Porotic Hyperostosis

Porotic hyperostosis involves expansion of the cranial diploe and thinning of cranial bone, leaving porous, coral-like lesions, often on parietal bones. Similar lesions found in eye orbits are referred to as "cribra orbitalia." Because both lesions share a common etiology, they are combined in this analysis. Iron deficiency anemia plays an important role in porotic hyperostosis (Stuart-Macadam 1992, 1987a, 1987b; Walker 1986; Larsen 1997:29–40). In North American archaeological samples, elevated prevalences of porotic hyperostosis have been attributed to ele-

TABLE 6.9.
Frequency of Periosteal Lesions in Great Salt Lake Skeletal Series and Others

Sample	No. of Tibiae Observed	Frequency[a]
Great Salt Lake Series	38	0.0
Great Salt Lake Fremont	24*	16.7
Uinta Fremont	16*	18.8
Sevier Fremont	14*	14.2
San Rafael	16*	25.0
Parowan	28*	28.6

* Andrews (1972); includes tibiae and fibulae
[a] Number of inflammations/Number of bones observed × 100

vated consumption of corn because corn provides very little absorbable iron (Holland and O'Brien 1997). While this makes porotic hyperostosis directly relevant to the problem at hand, other causes have been discussed, including parasitic infection, contaminated water, and generally poor sanitary conditions (Larsen 1997:35–39). Thus, porotic hyperostosis is treated as a general indicator of the status of overall health.

Twenty-five individuals were observed for porotic hyperostosis. Individuals were included in the sample if 50 percent or more of the cranial vault was present or if at least one complete eye orbit was present. Some skulls were complete, but others were represented by left, right, dorsal, or top (superior) halves.

There is little evidence of iron deficiency anemia in the Great Salt Lake skeletal series. Only two individuals exhibited these lesions (8.0 percent), and in each case they were slight cases occurring in eye orbits (cribra orbitalia). One individual was 1.5 to 3.0 years at death, the other was subadult. By comparison, Andrews (1972:38) reports approximately 25 percent of other Fremont skeletons exhibiting cribra orbitalia. Webb (1995) provides a table of frequencies of cribra orbitalia observed in populations across the world indicating that rates are often considerably higher than seen in the Great Salt Lake series, reaching as much as 93.3 percent in some subadults. Similarly, Larsen (1997:35) cites a particularly high prevalence of porotic hyperostosis in sites from the American Southwest.

DISCUSSION
The overall low frequencies of these pathologies in the Great Salt Lake series, compared to samples from Stillwater, Malheur Lake, and other Fremont sites, reflects a population less stressed than in either foraging or farming contexts. This finding is consistent with the expectation of risk reduction through a life history of

adaptive diversity. Changes in diet and settlement reduced susceptibility to food shortages and contributed to the overall health observed in the Great Salt Lake series by providing a wide resource base and lessening contact with various pathogens (Goodman et al. 1984).

By engaging in this sort of behavioral plasticity, the advantages of procuring wetland resources (i.e., a wider array of foods, with sometimes higher return rates [see Barlow 1997] through low population densities) could be traded off for the advantages of corn agriculture by producing a concentrated supply of storable and, hence, redistributable food during times of shortfall. Adjustments in group composition along age, kin, and band lines led to a residential cycling over the life history of individuals. This cycling produced a risk-reducing affect that left individuals less susceptible to physiological stress, as evidenced by the low rates of infection in the Great Salt Lake series when compared to foraging and predominatly farming groups.

As Kelly (1995a:100–101, 145) states, foragers are engaged in dietary choices on a day-to-day basis, yet the osteological anomalies discussed here are best considered evidence of more severe stress than may result from day-to-day variance. The relatively low prevalence of almost all pathologies discussed indicate that day-to-day risk management acted to decrease the frequency at which severe stress occurred over an individual's lifetime. If the low subadult mortality rate in the Great Salt Lake series accurately reflects that of the population as a whole, risk management of this sort also permitted more individuals to survive to maturity, providing an evolutionary potential.

CONCLUSIONS

The 85 Great Salt Lake skeletons contribute substantially to our understanding of Fremont adaptive diversity. They provide a large, essentially random skeletal sample which indicates relatively high levels of health compared to that of other skeletal series from foraging (Great Basin wetlands) and farming (other Fremont sites) groups. The rate of dental caries is consistent with a mixed diet, and the prevalence of enamel hypoplasia, periosteal lesions, and porotic hyperostosis is low. Only the frequency of transverse lines, which, as stated above, have been seen to offer evidence contrary to known levels of health, is high.

These data are consistent with our expectation that risk reduction was one outcome of a pattern of adaptive diversity in the Great Salt Lake wetlands during the Fremont period. Adaptive diversity operated to reduce risks related to subsistence and health, minimizing the physiological stresses incurred. The tendency to alternate among subsistence strategies over the course of an individual's life minimized the risks inherent in the practice of any single strategy, and seems to have produced a healthier population than some Fremont who lived their lives at residentially stable farming bases. What is needed is greater attention to the bias of existing Fremont skeletal series and care in interpreting the character of Fremont life in the absence of skeletal material from contexts outside large farming sites.

Acknowledgments

Carol Loveland conducted the initial osteological analyses of the Great Salt Lake skeletal series and produced an early draft of this paper prior to her death in December 1995. This manuscript is dedicated to the memory of Carol Loveland.

Thanks are extended to the Tribal Council (1989–1991) of the Northwestern Band of the Shoshoni Nation for their difficult but farsighted decision to pursue their heritage by permitting careful study of the Fremont remains. Funding was provided by the National Science Foundation (DBS 9223227 to S. R. Simms and D. H. O'Rourke), the State of Utah, the U.S. Bureau of Reclamation, and Utah State University (to S. R. Simms). The Eastman Kodak Company supplied radiographic film; radiographs were taken at the Western Surgery Center, Logan, Utah.

This chapter was greatly improved through the comments and criticisms from volume editors Brian Hemphill and Clark Larsen, as well as anonymous reviewers. Special thanks in this regard are owed to Steven Simms and Pat Lambert.

7

Theoretical and Archaeological Insights into Foraging Strategies among the Prehistoric Inhabitants of the Stillwater Wetlands

Robert L. Kelly

Hunter-gatherers have long been at the heart of anthropological theory, their ethnography and archaeology used as evidence of an allegedly common "primitive" society, the core of human nature (see Bettinger 1991b; Kelly 1995a). As a result, anthropologists long tried to sift through the many kinds of foraging economies in search of the essential foraging lifeway. In recent years, however, anthropologists have instead focused on variability in foraging lifeways as a means of understanding evolutionary processes rather than developing essentialist evolutionary categories or stages. This volume seeks to understand variation in lifeways of those prehistoric inhabitants of the Great Basin who made use of wetland environments.

Best known for vast stretches of sagebrush and arid mountain ranges, the Great Basin also contains several extensive wetlands. Past debate over how these were used focused on whether wetlands provided (a) high quality resources exploited by a sedentary population or (b) low quality resources used as secondary foods or in conjunction with other foods by nomadic foragers (Bettinger 1993; D. B. Madsen and Janetski 1990; Kelly 1988b, 1990, 1995b). A consensus has arisen that both positions are wrong. Wetlands contain many resources, some provide good returns and others not so good; and their use cannot be understood without considering the other options foragers had in the surrounding region.

In this chapter I employ a foraging model as background to the later Holocene prehistory of the Carson Desert and Stillwater Mountains in western Nevada. Coupled with postulated climatically induced changes in resource densities, the model suggests that residential mobility should have been lowest and that subsistence should have focused more on wetland resources from roughly 2000 or

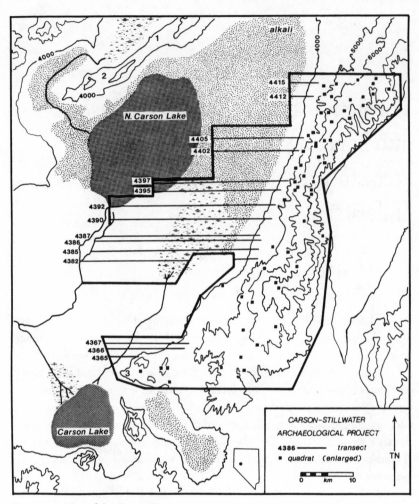

FIGURE 7.1. Map of the Carson Desert.

1500 B.P. until 500 B.P. At this time, the model suggests that women would have focused their activities on the wetlands, while men would have hunted bighorn sheep during long logistical forays. Piñon may not have been present in the region until 1600 B.P., but, even if present, the foraging model suggests it should not have figured prominently in the diet. Analyses of human skeletal remains from the Stillwater Marsh support these predictions (Larsen, Ruff, and Kelly 1995; Ruff, this volume; Schoeninger 1995a). The archaeological data come from a 1980–81 survey (Kelly 1985), from 1987–88 excavations in the marsh (Kelly 1995b, 1999; Larsen and Kelly 1995; Raven and Elston 1988, 1989; Raven 1990; Tuohy, Dansie, and Haldeman 1987), as well as from excavations at Hidden Cave (Thomas 1985), Lovelock Cave (Heizer and Napton 1970; Loud and Harrington 1929), and Humboldt Cave

(Heizer and Krieger 1956). The data suggest a prehistory that is not easily pigeon-holed into either a sedentary or a mobile lifeway.

THE CARSON DESERT ENVIRONMENT

The Carson Desert is a large basin filled with sand dunes, alkali flats, and slightly alkaline marshes. At 1,180 m above sea level (asl), it is one of the lowest points in the western Great Basin. The Carson River terminates here, as does the Humboldt River on occasion; the Walker River has also periodically flowed into the valley (Figure 7.1). Historically, the Carson Desert was the domain of the Toedökadö (Cattail-Eaters) Northern Paiute (see C. S. Fowler 1989, 1992).

After the drying of Pleistocene Lake Lahontan about 12,000 years ago, two lakes occasionally occupied the Carson Desert, one in the north, the Carson Sink, and one to the south, Carson Lake. These lakes today exist only in times of excep-tional runoffs. The southern half of the Carson Desert is covered by low, longitu-dinal and barchan dunes that are interspersed with small alkali flats. Vegetation is predominantly greasewood, four-wing saltbush, and shad scale. In the past, wetter areas of the desert probably had grassy meadows containing economically useful plants, such as Indian ricegrass, wild rye, and needle and thread.

In between the two lakes lies a 375 km² wetland, the Stillwater Marsh (Figure 7.2). The marsh contains a number of plants—such as bulrush, cattail, nut grass, and spike-grass—whose roots, tubers, seeds, shoots, and/or pollen were con-sumed. The marsh hosts some 160 waterbird species, such as mallard, pintail, cin-namon teal, redhead, canvasback, and coot. Most are migratory, and large num-bers can be found in the marsh in the early spring and fall. The marsh also supports three fish species: the Tahoe sucker, the Lahontan redside, and, most important, the tui chub. The tui chub is a small minnow, 30–35 cm long, and was probably taken with fine mesh nets or dip baskets. Fish remains recovered from human co-prolites and caches in nearby caves suggest that most fish consumed were 7–17 cm in length (Thomas 1985). Mussels are also found in the marsh, although they are not abundant in marsh sites and are rarely mentioned in ethnographic accounts. A variety of small mammals, such as jackrabbits and ground squirrels, inhabit the marsh and surrounding foothills and uplands (Wheat 1967).

To the east, the Carson Desert is bordered by the Stillwater Mountains, its highest point 2,650 m asl. There are few springs in the mountains and no signifi-cant creeks. In the north, the range contains a piñon-juniper forest above 1,830 m, while the rest of the range is blanketed with sagebrush. Grasses such as ricegrass and wild rye are present. Wood rats, ground squirrels, and other small game could be procured in the mountains, but the most important game resource was proba-bly bighorn sheep, whose butchered remains have been found in one excavated rock-shelter, Mustang Shelter in the northern Stillwater Mountains (Jung and Kelly 1996; Jung 1997).

FIGURE 7.2. Photograph of the Stillwater Marsh, taken in 1986.

Elsewhere in the Great Basin, piñon seeds were an important element of aboriginal diet. Gathered at a relatively high rate of return in late summer or early fall, they could be parched and stored for the winter. However, recent paleoecological data suggest that piñon may not have been present in the Stillwater Mountains until after 1600 B.P. (Wigand 1990).

Ethnographic sources provide some knowledge as to how these foods were procured (see C. S. Fowler 1989, 1992; Wheat 1967), and experiments point to the efficiency of harvesting methods (e.g., Simms 1987; Raymond and Sobel 1990).

Within the time period of interest, it is likely that a wetland has always existed in the Carson Desert (see Raven and Elston 1988). However, the particular topography of the Carson Desert, coupled with the vagaries of the Walker River (see Grayson 1993) and the variable precipitation of the western Great Basin, produces long- and short-term fluctuations in the water level of the marsh and, hence, in the kinds of resources present. Although it is possible that the marsh could have provided food for aboriginal inhabitants in all but the most extreme years, changes in marsh resource availability could have altered the efficiency of exploiting wetland resources relative to those in other areas (the mountains, other wetlands, or farther afield). This chapter provides an initial model that predicts the aboriginal response to long fluctuations in resource densities.

A SIMPLE MODEL OF MOBILITY

Low productivity and spatiotemporal variance in food resources have long been thought to be key factors in forager nomadism. Standing in contrast to the general Great Basin environment, wetlands appear to be highly productive and reliable sources of food. For some researchers, this meant, *ipso facto* that wetlands would have been used by a large, sedentary population (e.g., Heizer and Napton 1970; D. B. Madsen 1979). Indeed, the general character of wetland archaeology—large, dense sites with storage pits and houses—supports this notion (although there are few attempts to demonstrate either wetland productivity or sedentism [see Janetski 1986]). However, western Great Basin ethnographic data present an image that is not entirely consonant with the standard image of a sedentary society; for, although protohistoric inhabitants of this region may have been tethered to wetlands, residential movements within and outside the wetlands as well as lengthy logistical forays were a recurrent feature of their lives (Thomas 1985; Kelly 1995b, 1999).

To move beyond simple dichotomies of mobile and sedentary (Kelly 1992), of "good" or "bad" places to live (Bettinger 1993; D. B. Madsen and Janetski 1990), a model is needed that permits us to anticipate variability in how different prehistoric wetlands might have been used. Elsewhere, I have presented the initial framework of the model used below (Kelly 1990, 1995a). This framework employs Binford's concepts (1980) of residential mobility; movements of an entire residential unit, such as a family; and logistical movements, forays made by individual or small parties of men and/or women to and from a residential camp. The decision to move residentially is affected by the nature of individual foraging (Kelly 1995b). Foragers are expected to move before an area is depleted of resources, but how soon before is affected by many variables including the spatial distribution of food, variance in return rates, the terrain to be traversed in moving, regional population density, and the time it takes to break down and set up camp (Kelly 1995a). These variables all come down to weighing the cost of moving a family against the benefit of remaining in the current camp. Decisions to move are made with knowledge of the alternative resources of a region. To predict how a particular marsh might have been used prehistorically, we need to consider the benefit of remaining in the marsh, under a set of conditions, versus the cost of moving logistically or residentially to another area.

I am preceded in this effort by the late Christopher Raven (Raven and Elston 1989; Raven 1990; expanded by Zeanah et al. 1995). Using soil and hydrological information to reconstruct the prehistoric spatiotemporal distribution of food, Raven predicted (1) that, following D. B. Madsen and Jones (1988), sites would be placed centrally to women's foraging targets, with men foraging farther afield for large game; (2) that, contrary to my assertion (1985), the Stillwater Marsh would provide a diversity of high return-rate resources for most seasons of most years; and (3) that only in the fall, if wetland productivity was low, might it have been worthwhile to move into the mountains to gather piñon (Raven and Elston 1989:138–46).

To expand upon and verify Raven's conclusions, a model is needed that incorporates resources in the Stillwater Mountains as well as those of the marsh, which includes the cost of gathering and transporting those resources. The questions that such a model addresses are simple ones: Would foragers do best (maintain the highest mean daily foraging return rates) to remain in the marsh, to exploit distant resources alone while others remain in the marsh, to move the entire family to the distant resources, or to move the entire family to distant resources and send individuals back to gather in the marsh? The models are briefly reviewed here; a more complete discussion may be found in Kelly (1999).

Model 1: Foraging in the Marsh from a Residential Base

In this model, one forager is collecting food and the assumption is made that this individual seeks to maximize foraging efficiency. Other assumptions are that the forager walks at three km/hr at 300 kcal/hr (K. T. Jones and Madsen 1989), that the cost of walking increases by 30 percent when returning home with food, and that all traveling, foraging, and processing activities are conducted in eight hours.

Burden-basket size can limit the amount of food a forager can transport. I use an average basket size of 32 liters (Barlow, Henriksen, and Metcalfe 1993). Depending on the particular resource, a basket this size carries different amounts of food (measured in calories); I employ those amounts experimentally determined by Barlow, Henriksen, and Metcalfe (1993). The return rates (RR) used are from Simms (1987) and, for tui chub, from the experimental work of Raymond and Sobel (1990). Where possible, I use high and low return rates to model good and bad years. Initial return rates for small game and waterfowl were altered to include search and pursuit times as described in Model 2. The foraging distance (FD) is set at one-half the distance at which the return from collecting a resource is zero. The walking cost (WC) is figured as

$$WC = ((FD/3 \text{ km/hr}) \times 300 \text{ kcal/hr}) + ((FD/3 \text{ km/hr}) \times 390 \text{ kcal/hr})$$

and the walking time (WT) as

$$WT = 2(FD/3)$$

The time spent collecting (TC) is what remains of the eight-hour day less the amount of time devoted to walking. Since the return rates used here include some processing, I assume that the forager devotes some time to processing foods in the field or returns home to process them within the eight-hour limit. Thus,

$$TC = 8 - WT$$

Finally, the effective return rate (ER) to foraging for the eight-hour day (in kcal/hr) is

$$ER = ((TC \times RR) - WC)/8$$

Table 7.1 contains the results of this model for a range of wetland food resources. Note the returns from bulrush (in a good year), tui chub (especially in the summer and winter), and rodents (in a good year).

Model 2: Foraging in the Mountains
after a Residential Move from the Marsh

In this model, I had to alter return rates from those arrived at by Simms (1987) because his are postencounter return rates—the rate of return that can be expected once a resource has been located. The daily effective return rate, however, is affected by how hard a resource is to find. I did not include search costs in the valley-floor model because I assume that inhabitants have been there a while and do not spend time searching for a place to gather food. This might be true for a move to the mountains to gather plants—the location of piñon, for example, may have been acquired through reconnaissance trips. At any rate, the search costs for plants are often so low that including them does not dramatically alter the daily rate of return in most cases.

Large game, however, is another matter. People may know where the animals are likely to be found, but they will still have to spend some time seeking them out. Therefore, the return rate for game in this model is an overall rate of return from a day's activities, not just the postencounter return. Making this alteration substantially reduces the effective return from hunting bighorn sheep and small mammals.

Combining search and pursuit costs is a violation of the diet-breadth model that is the inspiration of the model used here. The diet-breadth model, however, assumes that resources are searched for simultaneously; this requires that search and pursuit costs be measured separately. But since the present model asks whether a forager would decide to stay on the valley floor or move to the mountains, we must include the overall returns from time spent in the mountains and not just the postencounter return rates. This permits us to balance the cost of going after a particular resource in the marsh as opposed to a particular resource in the uplands.

I altered the return rates for game using Simms's data (1987) as follows. The return is the number of calories acquired from procuring a single individual animal divided by the sum of the search time and the pursuit time. The search time (number of hours to procure one individual) is the edible weight of an individual animal divided by its intrapatch encounter rate (Simms 1987:Table 6), and the

TABLE 7.1.

Computations Used in Model 1,

Foraging from a Residential Base in the Stillwater Marsh

Resource	RR	FD	WC	WT	TC	ER
Bulrush Seeds	1700	4.0	920	2.7	5.3	1018
Bulrush Seeds	300	0.5	115	0.3	7.7	273
Cattail Roots	267	0.0	0	0.0	8.0	267
Cattail Pollen	9360	6.0	1380	4.0	4.0	4508
Cattail Pollen	2750	4.5	1035	3.0	5.0	1589
Waterfowl	1264	3.5	805	2.3	5.7	795
Waterfowl	219	0.0	0	0.0	8.0	219
Chub, winter	6625	5.5	1265	3.7	4.3	3430
Chub, winter	2194	4.5	1035	3.0	5.0	1242
Chub, spring	2473	4.5	1035	3.0	5.0	1416
Chub, spring	750	2.5	575	1.7	6.3	522
Chub, sum/fall	7514	5.5	1265	3.7	4.3	3912
Chub, sum/fall	1785	4.5	1035	3.0	5.0	986
Chub (storage)	2770	4.5	1035	3.0	5.0	1602
Chub (storage)	1043	3.0	690	2.0	6.0	696
Small Mammals	4052	4.5	1035	3.0	5.0	2403
Small Mammals	390	0.5	115	0.3	7.7	359
Indian Ricegrass	350	0.5	115	0.3	7.7	321
Tansy Mustard Seeds	1307	3.5	805	2.3	5.7	825
Sedge	202	0.0	0	0.0	8.0	202
Bulrush Roots	208	0.0	0	0.0	8.0	208
Rodent (snares)	928	3.0	690	2.0	6.0	610
Pickleweed Seeds	150	0.0	0	0.0	8.0	150
Salt Grass Seeds	160	0.0	0	0.0	8.0	160
Nuttal Shad Scale Seeds	1200	3.5	805	2.3	5.7	749
Squirreltail Seeds	91	0.0	0	0.0	8.0	91
Shad Scale Seeds	1033	3.0	690	2.0	6.0	689

pursuit time is taken from Simms (1987:Table 4). I have figured these using a variety of Simms's figures on search and pursuit times to produce a range of modified return rates to simulate good and bad years. As the "best" search time for bighorn seemed too high at 50 hours, I set it at 8 hours—a working day.

In this model, I also must predict how long a group of people remain in the mountains before moving back to the marsh or elsewhere. Although the length of stay depends on what resources the foragers could expect to exploit at the next location, I ignore this decision since the question is whether the foragers should move from the wetland and not whether they should move from the mountains. Once the model was set up, the length of stay was varied from 5 to 35 days. The effective daily return rate increases with increasing length of stay, but the marginal

TABLE 7.2.
Computations Used in Model 2, Foraging from a Camp in the Stillwater Mountains
after a Residential Move from the Stillwater Marsh

Resource	RR	D	WC	TD	TC	WT	ER
Piñon	841	30	4500	14	13	104	798
Piñon	1408	30	4500	14	13	104	1365
Bighorn Sheep	187	30	4500	14	13	104	144
Bighorn Sheep	4550	30	4500	14	13	104	4507
Small Mammals	390	30	4500	14	13	104	347
Small Mammals	4052	30	4500	14	13	104	4009
Bitteroot	1237	30	4500	14	13	104	1194
Indian Ricegrass	346	30	4500	14	13	104	303
Great Basin Wild Rye	369	30	4500	14	13	104	326

gain decreases and is minimal after a stay of 10 to 15 days. Therefore, the length of
stay is set at 13 days and 1 day is allotted for travel. The total working time (TW) is
the total number of collecting days times eight work-hours/day. The distance to
the mountains (D) is held constant at 30 km (but see below). The walking rate is
still 3 km/hr, but the caloric cost is increased to 450 kcal/hr since people will be carrying residential equipment and walking uphill. The walking cost therefore is

$$WC = 450(D/3)$$

I still assume an eight-hour workday, and, once again, I assume that all food collected can be returned to camp (i.e., it is not limited by burden-basket size). However, unlike the valley residential model, I assume that foragers would move quite
close to the foraging area for the particular resource being modeled and so the distance to the foraging area, which is an important element of Model 1, is zero here.
The effective return rate, then, is

$$ER = ((TW \times RR) - WC)/WT$$

Results from this exercise are given in Table 7.2.
    I also ran this model using the same equation as was used in Model 1 to pre-
dict ER—that is, a model that assumes resources are being collected at a distance
from camp (again, half the distance at which foraging returns are zero). The effective returns from this exercise are given in Table 7.3 as "corrected" return rates
(CRR). The corrected model may be more realistic for game, since the camp would
scare game away, thereby requiring some travel time, and the uncorrected model
more realistic for plants.

TABLE 7.3.

Computations Used in Model 2, Foraging from a Camp in the Stillwater Mountains
after a Residential Move from the Stillwater Marsh and after Correcting for the Effects of
Foraging Distances Greater than Zero

Resource	RR	FD	WC	WT	TC	CRR	D	WC	TD	ER
Piñon	841	4.0	920	2.7	5.3	446	30	4500	14	402
Piñon	1408	4.0	920	2.7	5.3	824	30	4500	14	780
Bighorn Sheep	187	2.0	460	1.3	6.7	98	30	4500	14	55
Bighorn Sheep	4550	5.5	1265	3.7	4.3	2306	30	4500	14	2263
Small Mammals	390	3.0	690	2.0	6.0	206	30	4500	14	163
Small Mammals	4052	5.5	1265	3.7	4.3	2037·	30	4500	14	1993
Bitteroot	1237	4.0	920	2.7	5.3	710	30	4500	14	666
Ricegrass	346	2.5	575	1.7	6.3	202	30	4500	14	159
Wild Rye	369	2.6	598	1.7	6.3	214	30	4500	14	171

*Model 3: Foraging in the Mountains Logistically
from a Base Camp in the Marsh*

In this model the amount of a food that can be carried in a burden basket is
critical. In-field processing determines how much fits in a basket; for piñon, I assume that the seeds are removed from the cone, but are not hulled (see Metcalfe
and Barlow 1992). Initially, I set a maximum load of 40 kg, but this is reached only
in the case of game. Basket loads (*BL*) of other foods—seeds and tubers—fall below 40 kg because load weight is limited by load volume (Barlow, Henriksen, and
Metcalfe 1993). Seeds and small roots or tubers require a basket for their transport,
but dried meat can be carried in bundles.

Given that meat weight is reduced by 60 percent through drying, a maximum
of 40 kg dried meat is equivalent to 100 kg fresh weight of edible meat, which requires about three bighorn sheep. Likewise, at an average fresh edible weight of .5
kg/animal for small game or rodents (averaged from Simms 1987:45), the number
of animals to be procured to make a full 40 kg load is 100/.5, equaling 200 animals.
This seems excessive. Small game was probably not fully butchered; we can imagine, in fact, that small game might have been simply skinned, gutted, and split
open to be dried. Admitting that it is a guess, I reduce the number of small game
to (a still high) 100 and make the dried weight equivalent to the fresh weight of .5
km (.5 kg fresh weight × .4 to account for drying = .2 kg plus .3 kg bone) for a maximum actual transport load of 24 kg.

I make some changes to accommodate the nature of piñon harvesting. The return rates used are for unprocessed seeds (Simms 1987:121–22)—that is, seeds removed from the cone, but not hulled, parched, winnowed, or ground. This raises
the return rate over that of Model 2. However, alterations must be made in the bas-

ket load since the seeds are transported with the hulls intact. Barlow and Metcalfe (1996) found that about 16 kg of seeds can be transported in a 32 lt basket, but only 57 percent of this weight is seed meat—the rest is hull. Therefore, although the basket load is 16 kg, the actual seed return is only 16 × .57 = 9.12 kg.

I assume that the walking cost increases by a factor that is related to the weight of the load up to a maximum of 50 percent when returning with a 40 kg load. Holding distance (D) constant at 30 km the total walking cost is

$$WC = ((D/3) \times 450) + ((D/3) \times ((((BL/40) \times .5) \times 450) + 450))$$

As in Model 2, the return rates are postencounter rates for plants, but those for game include search costs as well. And, assuming that logistical parties do not behave like central-place foragers, I have not included the effects of distance to foraging area on the returns. Thus, the time to collect (TC) a full basketload is

$$TC = (V \times BL)/RR$$

where V is the value of the resource in kcals/kg.

Assuming an eight-hour day, for every 8 hours of foraging, the forager spends another 16 hours sleeping, eating, etc. Adding two travel days, the total number of days (TD) in the mountains is

$$TD = ((TC + ((TC/8) \times 16))/24) + 2$$

(If TC < eight hours, then the total time is automatically one day and the minimum time for a logistical foray including travel time is three days.)

Taking the time spent traveling into account as well, the effective hourly return rate to logistical foraging in the mountains is

$$ER = ((BL \times V) - WC)/8TD$$

Results from this exercise are given in Table 7.4.

Model 4: Foraging in the Valley Logistically from a Base Camp in the Mountains

This model asks: what would the return be to a lone forager taking resources from the marsh and transporting them back to a camp in the mountains? It is the same as Model 3, but with some modifications. If the average edible weight of a duck is .6 kg and there is a 60 percent weight loss through drying, to obtain 40 kg of dried duck the hunter would need 100/.6 = 166 ducks. As with rodents above, this seems excessive. If ducks were plucked, split open, and dried before transport,

TABLE 7.4.

Computations Used in Model 3, Foraging Logistically in the Stillwater Mountains
from a Residential Base in the Stillwater Marsh

Resource	RR	V	BL	D	WC	TC	TD	ER
Piñon	2416	4880	9	30	9900	18.2	4.3	995
Piñon	9631	4880	9	30	9900	4.6	3.0	1418
Bighorn Sheep	187	1258	100	30	11250	672.7	86.1	166
Bighorn Sheep	4550	1258	100	30	11250	27.6	5.5	2624
Small Mammals	390	1078	50	30	10350	138.2	19.3	282
Small Mammals	4052	1078	50	30	10350	13.3	3.7	1486
Bitteroot	1237	3600	24	30	10350	69.8	10.7	886
Ricegrass	346	2740	11	30	9619	87.1	12.9	199
Wild Rye	369	2800	4	30	9225	30.4	5.8	43

TABLE 7.5.

Computations Used in Model 4, Foraging Logistically in the Stillwater Marsh
from a Residential Base in the Stillwater Mountains

Resource	RR	V	BL	D	WC	TC	TD	ER
Bulrush Seeds	1700	3050	20	30	10125	35.9	6.5	981
Bulrush Seeds	300	3050	20	30	10125	203.3	27.4	232
Waterfowl	1264	948	30	30	9675	23.7	5.0	473
Waterfowl	219	948	30	30	9675	142.2	19.8	119
Chub (storage)	2770	1250	38	30	9844	17.1	4.1	1136
Chub (storage)	1043	1250	38	30	9844	45.5	7.7	612
Small Mammals	4052	1078	50	30	10350	13.3	3.7	1468
Small Mammals	390	1078	50	30	10350	138.2	19.3	282
Tansy Mustard	1307	3600	24	30	10350	66.1	10.3	926
Pickleweed	120	2430	20	30	10125	405.0	52.6	91
Nuttal Shad Scale	1200	2790	11	30	9619	25.6	5.2	507
Shad Scale	1033	2790	11	30	9619	29.7	5.7	461

they could make a rather bulky load, so I lowered the number to (a still high) 50
ducks for an effective load of 30 kg of duck meat and an actual load of 12 kg of
dried duck. I suspect this is a maximum estimate.

For chub, I assume .37 kg weight/fish (which is perhaps at the high end). I do
not know by how much the weight is reduced when tui chub are dried, and will
continue to assume 60 percent. A load of 136 kilograms of fish (fresh weight) is
100/.37 = 270 fish. Raymond (Raymond and Sobel 1990) procured 15 to 112 fish
with net-set times of 6 to 24 hours, but this was in a low density, nonschooling set-

TABLE 7.6.

A Comparison of Effective Return Rates from the Four Models
in Good and Bad Years for Residential (Res), Logistical (Log), and
Modified Residential Mobility (Cor Res)

| Resource | Valley | | Mountains | | |
	Res	Log	Res	Cor Res	Log
Cattail Pollen	4508				
	1589				
Waterfowl	795				
	219				
Waterfowl (dried)		473			
		119			
Chub, winter	3430				
	1242				
Chub, spring	1416				
	522				
Chub, summer/fall	3912				
	986				
Chub (storage)	1602	1136			
	696	612			
Muskrat	3524	1774			
	2598	1585			
Small Mammals	2403	1486	4009	1993	1486
	359	282	347	163	282
Seeds and Roots*	1018	981	1194	666	886
	91	43	303	159	43
Piñon			1365	780	1418
			798	402	995
Bighorn			4507	2263	2624
			144	55	166
Sage Grouse			1757	863	569
			1157	642	456

* Not including winter cattail roots.

ting; I am, therefore, probably employing minimal return rates. It seems that 270 fish could be obtained within a reasonable amount of time on the valley floor. However, like seeds, tui chub probably have to be transported in some kind of container. And, since tui chub tend to curl as they dry, they may take up a large volume for their weight. We have no experimental figures to guide us; as a guess I offer a transport load of 15 kg for a fresh weight of 38 kilograms, or 102 fish. This is probably a low estimate.

Results from this exercise are given in Table 7.5. The data from all models are summarized in Table 7.6.

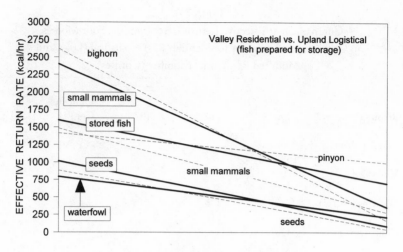

DECREASING INITIAL RETURN RATE

FIGURE 7.3. Returns from foraging from a residential camp in the marsh (Model 1) compared to returns from foraging logistically in the mountains (Model 3). Returns from processing fish for storage are used. Solid lines and boxed text = valley floor; dashed lines and unboxed text = uplands.

DISCUSSION

These models are very preliminary. We do not have sufficient information on return rate or transport load for many resources. I have held the distance to the mountains constant at 30 km, but forays were undoubtedly made into the low foothills of the Stillwater Mountains—a distance of some 10 km or so—for grass seeds and roots. In addition, I have made several assumptions about how prehistoric foragers behaved that raise many unanswerable questions (e.g., Is an eight-hour day realistic? Would foragers on a logistical foray spend more time foraging? Is a 32-liter burden basket the appropriate size for a logistical foray?)

Nonetheless, if the results are not read too closely, the models at least provide an illustration of gross patterns of resource use under different conditions. Figures 7.3 through 7.7 show the relationship between the different resources available through different strategies for good and bad years. In these figures, valley foods are noted by solid lines and boxed text, and upland foods by dashed lines and unboxed text.

Figure 7.3 shows the relationship between collecting food from a residential camp in the wetlands versus logistical use of upland resources. For the wetlands, I have used fishing returns that include the cost of preparing fish for storage. This figure suggests that the highest return would be secured by going after bighorn logistically in good years. In years of poorer bighorn harvests, the forager should seek

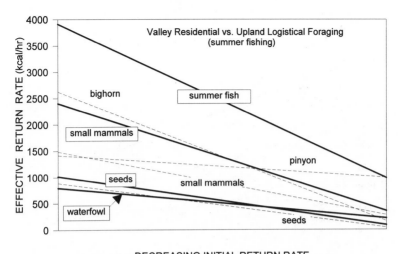

FIGURE 7.4. Returns from foraging from a residential camp in the marsh (Model 1) compared to returns from foraging logistically in the mountains (Model 3). Return from summer fishing used instead of that for fish processed for storage. Solid lines and boxed text = valley floor; dashed lines and unboxed text = uplands.

out waterfowl and fish instead. If fishing returns are *also* poor, then piñon (in the early fall) might be substituted for fish; in other words, I would expect to see piñon used only if several others resources are not present—and I presume this would be the case only rarely. While I could expect seeds and rodents to be taken in the wetlands, I would not expect to see foragers trading the opportunity to seek out wetland resources for seeds and rodents in the uplands. The state of bighorn hunting would probably control whether foraging trips were made into the mountains under these conditions. Given a sexual division of labor, I might expect to see men traveling to the mountains to hunt sheep while women remain in the wetlands to fish and gather.

Figure 7.4, however, employs the same data as Figure 7.3 except that summer/fall fishing is substituted for stored fish. Under these conditions, I expect men to forgo resources in the mountains in order to focus on wetland resources, especially fish. (The return from piñon, however, would be higher than bighorn and summer fishing in bad years for those two resources *if* longer logistical foraging days *and* a larger basket size was employed—even in bad years for piñon.) Looking only at this model, I suspect that, in most summers and falls, a group on the valley floor would probably opt to remain in the wetlands, perhaps moving short distances residentially on the valley floor, with individuals or groups (probably mostly men) making logistical forays to the mountains for bighorn and possibly

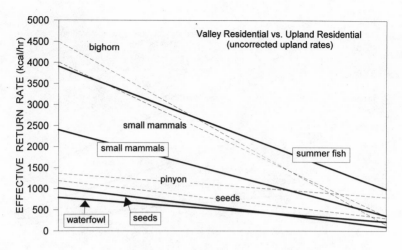

FIGURE 7.5. Returns from foraging from a residential base in the marsh (Model 1) compared to returns from a residential move to the mountains (uncorrected Model 2). Solid lines and boxed text = valley floor; dashed lines and unboxed text = uplands.

piñon (depending primarily on low returns from fishing). The use of dried large-game meat and piñon might become more important if winters required the use of more stored resources since hunting sheep outpaces the returns from processing fish for storage, as does piñon, especially under the conditions described above.

Figures 7.5 and 7.6 compare a residential occupation of the valley floor with residential moves to the mountains. Figure 7.5 uses the uncorrected return rates and Figure 7.6 uses the corrected return rates of Model 2; both employ the summer fish return rates. In the uncorrected version, bighorn hunting provides higher returns than fish in good years, although this difference is not great. In the corrected version, fish always provide the highest returns. Piñon is of little consequence in both. The primary resources of interest in Figure 7.5 are again bighorn and fish. Note, however, that sheep can be procured at a slightly higher return rate (compared to the corrected residential model) through logistical mobility.

What if a residential group is already living in the mountains? What would be the benefit of sending logistical parties to the valley floor? In this case (Figure 7.7), fish may play a much lesser role (assuming that they are transported after they are dried). Bighorn hunting provides the highest returns. However, if bighorn hunting was not especially profitable (and even if initially profitable it would rapidly decrease as the sheep were killed or scared away), then the returns from other foraging activities would rapidly approach those of logistical foraging on the valley

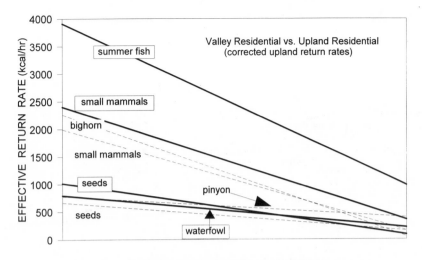

FIGURE 7.6. Returns from foraging from a residential base in the marsh compared to returns from a residential move to the mountains (corrected Model 2). Solid lines and boxed text = valley floor; dashed lines and unboxed text = uplands.

floor, making wetland resources, especially fish and rodents, look more attractive, especially in a good year for those foods.

Would I expect then to see foragers shift to or include logistical foraging to the valley floor from a camp in the mountains? With foraging as a simple average of all highest return rates, logistical foraging on the valley floor provides 1,019 kcal/hr (dried fish, rodents, seeds/roots, dried waterfowl), whereas residential foraging there can provide 2,032 kcal/hr (waterfowl, summer fish, rodents, seeds/roots). Residential foraging in the mountains (corrected) provides a mean of 1,425 kcal/hr (rodents, seeds/roots, piñon, bighorn), whereas logistical foraging in the mountains from a base in the marsh provides 1,603 kcal/hr. Given that foragers would wish to maximize their return rates and still gather sufficient stored resources for the winter, the best choice is perhaps to forage residentially in the marsh while opting for logistical forays to the mountains as return rates drop in response to local resource depletion or as the abundance of a particular resource (e.g., bulrush) decreases with the progression of its season of exploitation.

We do not have sufficient data on resource return rates from all resources to construct season-specific models. Given that fish can provide fairly high effective return rates in the winter, it is unlikely that mountain resources would provide an attractive alternative. The ethnographic Toedökadö occasionally wintered in the Stillwater Mountains (Wheat 1967; C. S. Fowler 1992), although the conditions of

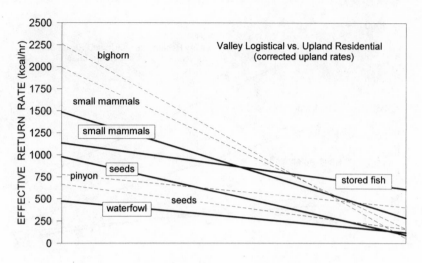

FIGURE 7.7. Returns from foraging from a residential base in the mountains (corrected Model 2) compared to returns from logistical foraging in the marsh (Model 4). Solid lines and boxed text = valley floor; dashed lines and unboxed text = uplands.

these occasions are not clear. The piñon harvest may have been critical. It is clear from the calculations presented here that logistical foraging in the wetlands from the mountains was not a productive enterprise compared to foraging from a residential base in the mountains—how much less so compared to the leisurely consumption of stored pine nuts.

In the spring, returns from root/seed collection and small mammal trapping may have enticed people away from the marshes, where roots and shoots would have been the only resources available. Roots do not provide high returns in the marsh, and shoots probably provided low returns as well. Nonetheless, logistical forays made from the wetlands in the spring would have been short, perhaps only a few kilometers into the foothills of the Stillwater Mountains.

In the models, I used 30 km as the standard distance to the mountains. Table 7.7 shows the expected return rates if the distance to the mountains is altered from 30 to 20, 10, and 5 km for Model 3 (logistical foraging). Spring fishing may provide low returns, similar to those of stored fish and waterfowl, and would provide low returns until large numbers began to gather as water levels rose with the melting of snow and ice in the Sierras. Bighorn sheep would have been in their most fat-depleted state in the spring, and their return rates should therefore be lower than those presented here. Returns from forays of 5 to 10 km for small game would be more profitable than foraging in the wetlands. Ethnographic data, in fact, point to the importance of small game hunting/trapping in the spring (Wheat 1967).

TABLE 7.7.
Expected Return Rates for Logistical Foraging in the Mountains
from a Camp in the Wetlands (Model 3) If the Distance to the Mountains
Is Altered from 30 to 20, 10, and 5 km (Good and Bad years Represented for
Piñon, Bighorn, and Small Mammals)

Resource	30 km	20 km	10 km	5 km
Piñon	1418	2333	2539	5284
	995	1426	1552	2325
Bighorn	2624	3314	3424	4482
	166	174	179	451
Small Mammals	1486	1604	1722	1781
	282	305	327	338
Bitterroot	886	1021	1066	1212
Ricegrass	199	249	283	328
Wild rye	43	132	212	318

Note: At 20 km, two days are still added for travel; at 10 km, one day is added (one-half day each way); and at 5 km, no days are added.

RELATION TO ENVIRONMENTAL CHANGE

For them to be truly relevant to archaeological and bioarchaeological data, we must consider the predictions of the above models in light of hypothesized temporal changes in the regional resource configuration of the Carson Desert (Figure 7.8). Evidence for environmental change in the western Great Basin is summarized elsewhere (see Kelly 1999; Grayson 1993; Wigand 1990). The following is a review of the model predictions in light of the resource changes to which climatic changes point.

From 5000 to about 4000 B.P., the local climate was quite arid and there was probably no piñon in the Stillwater Mountains (see Grayson 1993; Kelly 1997, 1999). Precipitation in the spring and early summer may have made grass seeds attractive, but this benefit may have been negated by the aridity of the Altithermal. The Walker River may have contributed water to the Carson Desert until 4700 B.P., but for the next 700 years or so the Carson Desert was probably dry, featuring a low and fluctuating marsh that would not have supported large numbers of tui chub, waterfowl, and marsh mammals. Nonetheless, alkali bulrush may have served as a continual late summer attraction since it does well in many climatic conditions. If present in low densities, only small fluctuations in the abundance of fish, waterbirds, and mammals would have made other foraging options more attractive, resulting in the Carson Desert being, in most years, only one point in a seasonal round during the height of the Altithermal.

From 4000 to 2000 B.P., annual temperatures decreased and precipitation be-

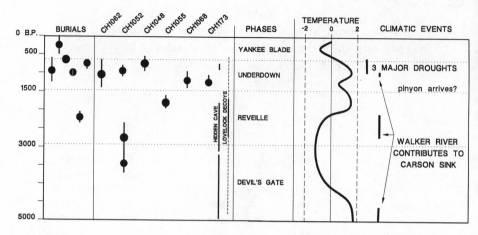

FIGURE 7.8. Correlation of archaeological phases, projectile point styles, archaeological occurrences, and climatic changes. Climatic data from Eddy and Bradley (1991, in Zeanah et al. (1995); Stine (1993, in Grayson 1993); Benson and Thompson (1987); Wigand (1990). All dates are from cultural features.

came winter dominant albeit in low to moderate amounts. Such conditions may have maintained more permanent wetlands in the Carson Desert, thereby increasing the abundance and reliability of fish, waterfowl, mammals, and plant life. If reconstructions of shifts in the Walker River channel are accurate, contributions from this river could have enhanced the expected form of settlement in the Carson Desert during the latter half of this period. The shift to winter precipitation might be expected to decrease grass seed and root production, but this deficit could have been offset by an increase in effective moisture with lower temperatures. As noted above, evidence suggests there was still no piñon in the Stillwater Mountains at this time (Wigand 1990).

During this time, I would expect to see greater use of wetlands than previously. However, the climatic data suggest a general increase in the productivity of the region surrounding the Carson Desert, including both the upland environments and other wetlands and lakes. Given that desert wetlands can be expected to fluctuate in productivity under any conditions, there were probably times when the balance of foraging efficiency fell toward the uplands or, perhaps more likely (although I cannot anticipate this option with the model used here), other wetlands in the western Great Basin. Such conditions may have created a scenario in which wetlands in the Carson Desert were used more intensively than previously, but which were, nonetheless, periodically abandoned when upland or more distant resources provided greater returns. The Walker River probably flowed into the Carson Sink from 2900 to 2100 B.P., which, by increasing march productivity relative to the surrounding region, could have played a role in conditioning decisions whether to reside near the marsh.

From 2000 to 1000 B.P., the local climate became increasingly arid (Grayson 1993; Kelly, 1999). The Walker River shifted back to Walker Lake, although it may have run into the Carson Desert for a while at 1000 B.P. There may have been precipitation in the spring and early summer, but decreasing amounts may have hampered the growth of desert vegetation. Lake levels were probably low, but radiocarbon dates indicate that wetlands were present from at least 3300 to 800 B.P. (Kelly 1999; Grayson 1993; Raven and Elston 1989). Piñon may have migrated into the Stillwater Mountains after 1600 B.P., but (even if piñon were present) with an arid climate, the wetlands probably provided higher return rates than almost any other kind of foraging (with the exception of logistical sheep hunting in the mountains in good years). During this time period (and especially when the Walker River ran into the Carson Sink), the general disparity between foraging in the wetlands versus other areas may have been at its greatest and, therefore, we could expect to see more intensive, less residentially mobile use of the wetlands at this time.

The nature of climatic change after 1000 B.P. is murky. Some data suggest that the climate became cooler with winter precipitation (Davis 1982), but other data suggest that the climate was extremely dry from 1000 to 500 B.P., with several significant droughts (Stine 1993). The Carson Desert wetlands may have experienced severe fluctuations at this time. Piñon was probably established in the Stillwater Mountains at a density that made it economically viable. Under such conditions, the wetlands may not have provided consistently higher returns than other foraging areas and, thus, I expect to see less intensive use of the marsh during this period and less tethering to the marsh as a source of storable winter foods (however, population growth and/or the migration of Numic-speaking peoples into the region after 1000 B.P. are potentially complicating factors in the model used here; see Kelly 1999).

After 500 years ago, during the Little Ice Age, precipitation increased and fell primarily in the winter, permitting a rejuvenation of wetlands. Large-game density may have decreased if increasing winter precipitation indicates an increase in winter severity (Kelly 1985). Such generally mesic conditions may have increased regional productivity, decreasing the difference between wetlands and uplands, producing the mix of resource use and mobility recorded by ethnographic data. Piñon, however, should not have been an important part of the diet unless the marsh was substantially reduced in quality. However, the wetlands may have taken on new significance as a source of storable food and as a location of winter foraging *even if piñon was available.*

In sum, then, the current foraging model, coupled with climatic data, suggests that the wetlands should have been used throughout the prehistoric sequence. However, it also suggests that the most intensive period of use should have been from 2000 to sometime after 1000 B.P. During this time, we should see evidence of decreased residential mobility in the wetlands and little use of upland resources, with the possible exception of bighorn sheep procured through logistical mobility. Sometime after 1000 to 500 B.P., we would expect to see a return to a settlement pattern that, although tethered to the wetlands, would still employ residential mobility in the exploitation of resources from the surrounding uplands and valleys. In other words, the prediction is a settlement pattern similar to that documented ethnographically.

Archaeological Expectations

A full discussion of the archaeological expectations of this model are presented in Kelly (1999), including derivation of a model that relates stone tool technology to mobility strategies. The following is a brief outline of some of the expectations. I would predict that any sites in the Stillwater Marsh manifesting evidence of a focus on wetland resources to the near exclusion of others would date to between 2000 and 500 B.P. I would also expect to see little evidence for the use of piñon prehistorically; this would mean few to no piñon macrofossils in sites and few to no grinding stones in the uplands, where piñon would have been collected and at least initially processed. Instead, the uplands should contain evidence of logistical hunting forays, including bifaces and expended projectile points (Kelly 1988b).

The way in which settlement forms on the valley floor might be reflected in lithic assemblages is based on the absence of lithic raw material on the valley floor—virtually all tool stone must be imported—and on the evidence that the closest tool stone sources, in the southern Stillwater Mountains, are poor quality basalts, rhyolites, and siltstones. It is hard to predict how prehistoric foragers might have organized their stone tool technology under these conditions. I suspect that short-term residential use would have entailed the initial importation of large nodules of material from the closest sources and that this material would have been used to produce simple flake tools until the supply was exhausted. Providing that foragers could time their length of stay and gauge the amount of raw material they needed, as the end of their stay approached and raw material dwindled in amount, they could either have made a special trip to replenish the raw material or, given that such trips are often the largest single cost in a stone tool technology, they might have settled for scavenging old (archaeological) tools or reusing current tools and cores, reducing them bipolarly.

As the time span of residential occupations lengthened, however, I would expect to see an increase in simple, flake tool production as a function of more frequent replenishing of tool-stone raw material stockpiles from the closest sources.

Seasonal occupations might not show evidence of tool manufacture and maintenance, but sites occupied year-round should show such evidence.

FITTING THE MODEL TO PREHISTORY

In this section, I briefly examine the archaeology of the Carson Desert and
Stillwater Mountains in light of these predictions. I employ the phase names used
by Thomas (1981) in central Nevada (Figure 7.8) because radiocarbon dates and
projectile point styles from sites in the region warrant borrowing this terminology
(Kelly 1985, 1999). I discuss the archaeology in terms of the region's cache caves, a
regional survey, and excavated sites within the Stillwater Marsh.

Cache Caves

The archaeology of this region was first known through artifacts recovered
from several caves, especially Lovelock, Humboldt, and Hidden Caves (Figure
7.1). Hidden Cave was used predominantly during the Devil's Gate and Reveille
phases. Lovelock Cave was used predominantly during the Reveille phase, although an apparent cessation of use may only be a function of historical guano
mining of the upper deposits; an alternative explanation posits that a roof collapse
about 1500 B.P. made the shelter less attractive to human occupation (Heizer and
Napton 1970). There are no radiocarbon dates from Humboldt Cave, but based
on projectile point styles, this cave appears to have been used during the Underdown phase, although one cache contained European goods indicating use during
the historic period.

Thousands of artifacts were recovered from Lovelock, Humboldt, and Hidden Caves, but no indicators of residential occupation, such as hearths, debitage,
and food remains, were found (Loud and Harrington 1929; Heizer and Krieger
1956:5; Heizer and Napton 1970:43; Thomas 1985). Two of the sites, Humboldt
and Hidden Caves, have very restricted openings and are dark and dusty places,
and therefore unsuited for long-term habitation (Thomas 1985). Over 40 cache
pits were recorded at Lovelock Cave, 31 in Humboldt Cave, and 22 in Hidden
Cave. Many artifacts recovered from these three sites were burial goods, and
people may have made some diurnal use of the shelters, but most of the objects
found were cached in the caves, stored for a future need (Thomas 1985; Kelly 1985).

Many of the artifacts cached within the caves (fishhooks, duck decoys, nets)
clearly indicate the use of wetland resources. Utilization of wetland resources is
also attested to by the contents of coprolites in Hidden and Lovelock Caves, which
contained bulrush seeds, the bones of tui chub, and cattail pollen (Kelly 1985;
Wigand and Mehringer 1985). In addition, analysis of the contents of these coprolites indicates use of the shelters during all but the winter season. The primary use
of these caves as caching facilities raises an important question: If people lived

sedentarily by the wetlands, why store materials in such caves? One interpretation is that the marshes were not used sedentarily, but were only one stop in a seasonal round (Kelly 1985). However, the opposite interpretation is also feasible, for the abundance of material in the caves is only a direct function of their excellent preservational environments. The caves *could* instead record a rare pattern—one that just happened to have been well preserved. Although I have argued for the former (Kelly 1985), it could just as easily have been the latter. In fact, if people had used the wetlands sporadically, we would not expect to see time-consuming technology, such as large fishing nets, lines, hooks, and duck decoys. So, on the one hand, the technology illustrated by caches recovered from these caves suggests a greater commitment to the use of wetland resources; but, on the other hand, because the material was cached points to periodic (but probably not regular seasonal) abandonment of the wetlands. This is precisely what the foraging models coupled with the environmental reconstruction for the late Devil's Gate and early Reveille phases predict.

Regional Survey

The second source of archaeological data is a 1980–1981 survey of the Carson Desert and Stillwater Mountains. This survey encompassed some 1,600 km^2 of the Carson Desert and Stillwater Mountains (Figure 7.1) and recorded 161 archaeological sites. Although I originally tried to sort sites into phases based upon projectile point frequencies for temporal analysis (Kelly 1985, 1988b, 1990), this procedure had no statistical validity (see Thomas 1988:400–401). Subsequent reanalysis focuses on geographic differences in stone tools and debitage taking differential exposure, amateur collection, raw material, and survey biases into account (Kelly 1999). The results are summarized below.

The analysis proceeded in terms of five geographic areas based on both the zones' economic potentials and the geomorphological characteristics that could bias surface collection. These geographic zones included (1) the Stillwater Marsh; (2) a dune region that lies between the marsh and the Carson River to the west; (3) the valley south of the marsh and immediately to the west of Hidden Cave; (4) the piñon-juniper zone of the Stillwater Mountains; and (5) the unwooded zone of the Stillwater Mountains above 4,000 feet asl.

The artifacts and debitage found within these five areas differ from one another in several significant ways (Table 7.8). In the dune area to the west of the marsh, there is significantly greater evidence of bipolar knapping and tool recycling or scavenging. There are also more ground stone tools here, and significantly fewer bifacial tools, scrapers, and utilized flakes. There is also considerable evidence of bipolar knapping in the southern part of the valley, but this is accompanied by evidence of simple, casual flake tool production and use.

In the marsh, where there are significantly higher amounts of imported ob-

TABLE 7.8.

Summary of Results of Analysis of Debitage and Stone Tools from
the Carson Desert and Stillwater Mountains

	Dune	Marsh	S. Valley	Piñon-Juniper	Upper Sagebrush
Artifacts[a]					
Biface Fragments	–		–	+	
Utilized Flake Fragments			+		
Utilized Bipolar Flakes	+	–		–	
"Smashed" Biface Fragments	+				
Mano	+	–	+	–	
Metates	+			–	
Bipolar Cores	+			–	
Ut. Lipped Platform Flakes				+	+
Ut. Single Platform Flakes	–	–		–	
Scrapers	–			–	+
Debitage[a]					
Core Reduction		+	+		
Single Platform Flakes	+	+	+		+
Bipolar Flakes	+		+		
Shatter	+		+		
Bipolar/Recycling	+				
Complete Flakes					+
Proximal Flake Fragments		+		+	+
Faceted Platform Flakes					+
Lipped Platform Flakes				+	
Biface Reduction				+	+
Distal Flake Fragments		+		+	
Raw Material	Chert	Obsidian and Other	Chert	Chert	Other

[a] + = Statistically significant higher frequency than expected; – = significantly lower frequency than expected.

sidian and poor quality tool stone (e.g., locally available siltstones, basalts, and rhyolites), there is evidence of simple flake production, rather than bipolar core reduction, and many utilized flake fragments. There is also a significantly higher frequency of ground stone tools on the valley floor than in the mountains (the reverse pattern of some other regions; e.g., Monitor Valley [Thomas 1988]).

In contrast to the valley floor, there is considerably more evidence for the use of bifacial tools and virtually no evidence of bipolar reduction in the Stillwater Mountains. In the unwooded area of these mountains, there is more evidence of simple flake tool production and use than in the piñon-juniper zone. There are higher numbers of bifacial tool fragments here than in the unwooded area, and there are significantly higher numbers of isolated projectile point fragments in the unwooded area.

Based on current arguments relating mobility to stone tool production and use (Kelly 1988, 1999), these patterns point to differences in the way the five geographic regions were used by native populations. The piñon-juniper zone may have been used through both residential and logistical mobility, although the high frequencies of bifacial tools suggest either logistical or high residential mobility, especially in light of the abundance of raw material in the mountains. In either case, the dearth of ground stone in this zone suggests that piñon and other seed harvesting was probably not the objective of these forays. The unwooded area of the mountains was probably used almost exclusively through short-term logistical mobility, possibly for hunting and seed collection, but, given the lack of grinding equipment here also, little processing of seeds likely took place, if seeds were taken at all.

On the valley floor, sites in the dune area to the west of the marsh contain the greatest evidence that inhabitants lived with strong constraints on their lithic resources. This could be because the dune area is the farthest removed from stone-tool raw materials. While a round trip from the dunes to the local stone-tool resource areas could easily be made within a day, the people apparently decided that such an investment was not worth the effort—they preferred instead to reduce small scraps of stone and scavenge old tools when pressed for raw material. This scenario suggests a shorter residential occupation than is indicated by the archaeological record in the Stillwater Marsh itself.

But even in the marsh, residential occupations may not have been year-round, sedentary ones. Although there are many biface fragments in the marsh sites, there is very little evidence of biface tool manufacture or repair. Bifacial tools were being heavily used, but not replenished; there is little evidence for biface knapping, which would probably not be the case for sites that were occupied year-round.

Stillwater Marsh Sites

Our third source of data is sites exposed in 1986 as floodwaters receded. These sites contained pit houses, storage pits, postholes, and a plethora of artifactual and biological remains (Figures 7.9 and 7.10), along with numerous human skeletal elements (see S. T. Brooks and Brooks 1990; S. T. Brooks, Haldeman, and Brooks 1988; Larsen and Kelly 1995; Raven and Elston 1988, 1989; Raven 1990; Tuohy, Dansie, and Haldeman 1987). Some of the pit houses were very shallow; the only two that were fully excavated (at 26Ch1062) were only 15 to 20 cm deep and may be the remnants of open-sided windbreaks (Kelly 1999) or originally deeper pit houses that were heavily eroded. Deeper houses were found elsewhere in the marsh

TABLE 7.9.
Summary of Stone Tool and Debitage Characteristics
at Several Stillwater Marsh Sites

	26Ch1048[a]	26Ch1068[a]	26Ch1052[a]	26Ch1173[a]	26Ch1062[b]
Tool Count	87	27	17	3	83[c]
Debitage Count	917	266	131	11	6243
M^3 Excavated	2.85	1.45	2.05	1.35	4.2
Tools/m^3	30.53	18.62	8.29	2.22	19.7
Debitage/m^3	321.40	183.40	63.90	8.10	1486.4
Tool/Debitage	.09	.10	.13	.27	.01[c]
Biface/Flake Tool Ratio	1.02	.56	1.42	2.00	6.11[d]

[a] Based on Raven and Elston (1988:Table 11)

[b] Data from Kelly (1998)

[c] Not including 13 projectile points, 29 bifacial tools, 10 unifacial tools, and 7 cores recovered from the surface; other assemblages all from subsurface context.

[d] All tools (projectile points, bifaces, and unifaces) including those from the surface.

(Raven and Elston 1988), but none so far were found to contain evidence of the internal features commonly found in year-round habitations (although few have been adequately tested). The sites also contained surprisingly few retouched stone tools, yet had high retouched-tool/flake-tool ratios (Table 7.9). Flakes and tools tend to be very small, utilized intensively, often derived from bipolar knapping, and fashioned predominantly from poor quality materials available in the nearby foothills (Raven and Elston 1988; Kelly 1999). Biface fragments were present, but there was little evidence of biface knapping, and many of these tools were clearly scavenged from old archaeological deposits. These traits of the lithic assemblage point to long-term residential occupations, but ones that were still not long enough to warrant consistent raw material replenishing, extensive tool production, or high investments in house construction. At present, we have no comparative data for these sites from later or earlier time periods.

The exposed sites provide some information on subsistence practices in the region. Muskrats and other aquatic mammals were hunted for food. A few remains of bighorn sheep indicate their exploitation as well. Carnivores, such as dogs and mink, were apparently used as food and for their pelts. The remains of tui chub are abundant, as are the remains of many species of waterbirds, especially coots and shallow-water ducks. Carbonized plant remains include the seeds of bulrush and lesser amounts of cattail seeds. Mussel shell is abundant at only one site (26Ch 1052); rare also are the bones of lagomorphs, and absent are remains of ricegrass and, importantly, piñon.

It is difficult to ascertain the season(s) during which these marsh sites were oc-

FIGURE 7.9. Photograph of feature 7, probably a house, at 26Ch1062, facing southwest, 1987. Trench is 0.5 m wide, excavated to base of feature and shows several pits crosscutting the midden filling the house feature.

cupied. The presence of eggshell indicates a spring/early summer occupation, while the use of cattail and bulrush seeds suggests a late summer/early fall occupation. David Rhode (in Kelly 1999) shows that the macrofossil remains from 26CH1062 point to an occupation somewhere between summer and early winter.

Projectile points and radiocarbon dates suggest that the majority of the occupation in the marsh dates to the Underdown phase. Table 7.10 contains radiocarbon ages from several sites and burials in the marsh. Four of the burials and four of the sites fall within the Underdown phase; one site has a late Reveille phase occupation and a sixth contains a late Devil's Gate/early Reveille as well as an Underdown phase occupation. Survey data collected by Kelly (1985, 1999) and Raven (1990) suggest that Desert Series points, indicative of a Yankee Blade phase occupation, are relatively rare in the marsh and more common in the dunes west of the marsh. Too few points were recovered from marsh sites to permit sorting of the sites in time (*contra* Raymond and Parks 1989), and Reveille phase points on many sites may have been scavenged from earlier deposits. To date, the wetland sites uncovered by flooding point to a predominantly late Reveille/Underdown phase occupation. Coupled with climatic data, the model predicted a more intensive use of wetland resources during this time period, although the model does anticipate a somewhat earlier onset of the more intensive marsh resource use suggested by the Stillwater Marsh sites.

FIGURE 7.10. Photograph of feature 2 at 26Ch1062. The upper part of this feature was truncated by wave action during the flood of 1983–86.

The archaeology suggests that different mobility strategies may have been used over time by the prehistoric inhabitants of the region. The evidence from the cave sites may suggest that prior to the late Reveille and Underdown phases, the Stillwater Marsh may have served as a hub of residential movements. That caches do not appear to be common during the Underdown and Yankee Blade phases may point to selective destruction of the caves' upper deposits, but it may also point to a significant shift in the settlement system between the Underdown and Yankee Blade Phases.

Archaeological data suggest that during the late Reveille/Underdown phases (from 1500? B.P. until 650 B.P.) the Stillwater wetlands may have frequently served as the hub of logistical movements for large game, but that subsistence largely focused on the wetlands when camps there were occupied. Residential mobility was lower than previously, perhaps resulting from use of the marsh as a source of stored food, but the lack of such features as prepared hearths in houses points to a system that was still residentially mobile. People were by no means living year-round in sedentary settlements. Relative to other Great Basin valley and range systems, the Stillwater Mountains may have been used more frequently through logistical mobility, and piñon, even after its apparently late appearance, may have been less intensively exploited than in other valleys.

The nature of the Yankee Blade occupation in the Carson Desert is harder to

TABLE 7.10.

Radiocarbon Dates from Stillwater Marsh Sites and Burials (All Dates on Burials Are AMS Dates on Bone)

Lab #	Location	Date[a]	Date[b]	Date Range[c]	Context
UCR 2336	Ch1044-2	1140 ± 80	A.D. 893	A.D. 688–1029	human bone[d]
UCR 2337	Ch1050-3	290 ± 80	A.D. 1644	A.D. 1443–1954	human bone
UCR 2338	Ch1070-4	660 ± 30	A.D. 1302	A.D. 1287–1396	human bone
UCR 2339	Ch1159-4	1080 ± 50	A.D. 984	A.D. 883–1029	human bone
Beta 33554	Ch1159-200	2265 ± 70	270 B.C.	409–130 B.C.	human bone
Beta 33555	L72-200	820 ± 70	A.D. 1229	A.D. 1036–1298	human bone
Beta 33255	Ch1052	2150 ± 90	181 B.C.	394 B.C.–A.D. 60	scattered carbon, feature 3
Beta 33003	Ch1062	1390 ± 80	A.D. 657	A.D. 541–786	scattered carbon, feature 7
Beta 23853	Ch1062	1100 ± 120	A.D. 973	A.D. 671–1214	single carbon piece, feature 4
Beta 25041	Ch1062	830 ± 80	A.D. 1225	A.D. 1025–1300	scattered carbon, feature 23
Beta 24884	Ch1062	2940 ± 70	1125 B.C.	1382–920 B.C.	buried soil horizon[f]
Beta 25140	Ch1052	3190 ± 70	1436 B.C.	1614–1270 B.C.	charcoal, IMR #105, stratum 2[e]
Beta 25141	Ch1052	2680 ± 160	818 B.C.	1257–399 B.C.	charcoal, IMR #307C, feature 6[e]
Beta 25142	Ch1052	2690 ± 70	822 B.C.	989–776 B.C.	shell, IMR #307S, feature 6[e]
Beta 24791	Ch1048	870 ± 70	A.D. 1195	A.D. 1019–1287	IMR #214, feature 16[e]
Beta 24792	Ch1048	800 ± 90	A.D. 1253	A.D. 1028–1391	IMR #215, feature 12[e]
Beta 24793	Ch1052	3290 ± 90	1525 B.C.	1749–1395 B.C.	IMR #102/103, feature 8, stratum 8[e]
Beta 24794	Ch1052	1040 ± 60	A.D. 1011	A.D. 888–1159	IMR #107/108, organic layer w[e,f]
Beta 24795	Ch1055	1860 ± 70	A.D. 141	A.D. 11–342	IMR #61/64, stratum 7, marsh layer[e,f]
Beta 24796	Ch1068	1320 ± 100	A.D. 680	A.D. 551–962	IMR #407, feature 19[e]
Beta 24797	Ch1173	1350 ± 70	A.D. 668	A.D. 599–862	IMR #157, feature 6[e]

[a] Dates are from either University of California Riverside or Beta Analytic, Inc; uncorrected B.P.

[b] Dates calibrated using the University of Washington CALIB program (Release 3.03, Method A; Stuiver and Reimer 1993).

[c] Corrected range (2 standard deviations)

[d] All dates on human bone are AMS dates; UCR dates submitted by Sheilagh Brooks under contract with the U.S. Fish and Wildlife Service (S. T. Brooks and Brooks 1990).

[e] Submitted by Intermountain Research under contract with the U.S. Fish and Wildlife Service (Raven and Elston 1989).

[f] Not associated with cultural material

describe. The Underdown pattern may have continued after 650 B.P., with perhaps only a change in marsh location by shifting the locus of a settlement on the valley floor, or the lifeway may have undergone an as yet undocumented transition. But caution is in order here. The geomorphology and hydrology of the desert is such that the wetlands could very well have been located in different places over the last several thousand years, and people could have lived someplace other than the current marsh. Alternatively, later occupations could have been obliterated by erosion, and the presence of an earlier marsh layer 2 m below the surface of 26Ch1062 suggests that earlier occupations may be buried deeper in the marsh (Kelly 1999). Our sample of radiocarbon dates is also woefully inadequate.

CONCLUSIONS

One of the difficulties in drawing conclusions from archaeological and bioarchaeological data is that such data are conglomerates of events, often the products of years if not decades or centuries of occupation. Food resources in Great Basin wetlands undoubtedly oscillated on a number of temporal scales. Although marshes may have provided sufficient resources each year, these resources would have changed in their kind and abundance from year to year, or on longer time scales. Thus, we can expect variation from year to year in diet and mobility. Archaeological data—and especially archaeological data with poor temporal controls, as is the case for much of the Great Basin—will only be able to recover the coarsest, most macroscale temporal and spatial patterns in human behavior. Nonetheless, archaeological remains are the product of the activities and decisions of individuals, and we need to model those decisions. Thus, archaeology must continually move between fine-grained models on the one hand and coarse-grained data and interpretations on the other.

In light of the foraging model, combined with climatic and archaeological data, the Stillwater Marsh may have served as a hub of settlement systems for the last 5,000 years, although settlement may have been more tightly tied to the marsh than at other times, perhaps especially during the Underdown period. This post-1500 B.P. transition may be related to the migration of Numic speakers into the Great Basin, postulated by some to have occurred about 1,000 years ago, or to population growth, but at this time we do not know (see Kelly 1999). From both the model and the archaeology, it does appear that residential and especially logistical mobility beyond the foraging patch of the marsh were employed to gather food resources, although possibly in different mixes at different times.

The question that initiated this research was: Did prehistoric foragers in the Great Basin live sedentarily by wetlands or not? As is so often the case, the primary conclusion is that the question needs to be recast. Not all wetlands are the same. Some are small with deep water, others are shallow with expanses of aquatic plants;

some have piñon and other resources nearby, others do not (Rhode 1990a). While the marshes may have afforded people the opportunity to become completely sedentary in some years, perhaps more so during some climatic periods than others, theoretical argument and archaeological data suggest that the aboriginal occupants of the Stillwater Marsh may not have availed themselves of this opportunity. People probably continued to move as groups, *and* as individuals, with men expected to have been more mobile than women, especially during the Underdown phase (see Ruff, this volume). This is a function of foragers calculating the trade-off between remaining in one camp or foraging patch versus moving to another. The decisions made can be expected to be different for wetlands of different characteristics and for wetlands situated in regions of different characteristics. Raven and Elston (1992), for example, argue that the resource distribution around Malheur Lake in the northern Great Basin, which differs substantially from that around the Stillwater Marsh, might have produced a settlement system that focused less on the wetlands than that which we see in the Carson Desert. The approach taken here should assist the systematic analysis and interpretation of the archaeology of different wetlands in the Great Basin.

The conclusions reported here are in substantial agreement with those recently reported by others (Zeanah et al. 1995). Using an extension of Raven's model (1990), Zeanah calculated the distribution of resource productivity of the Toedökadö territory. Shifting the values of key variables, he predicts both seasonal and long-term changes in regional productivity. Based on a diet-breadth model that separates male and female resources, Zeanah argues that wetlands would have always been the foraging choice of women and that residences would always be located near the wetlands.

More specifically, Zeanah et al. (1995) propose that during mesic intervals, women would forage in the marsh, while men hunted sheep logistically in the mountains. Springtime may have seen people move from the wetlands into nearby dune habitats and the uplands. During dry intervals, when the wetlands would have been reduced in size, women would have continued to forage in the marshes; the arrival of piñon, however, may have shifted women's foraging and residential bases to the uplands in the fall.

There are some differences in the predictions of the two approaches, but the major features are in agreement: (1) the wetlands were the focus of women's foraging; (2) the mountains would only rarely have witnessed residential occupations; and (3) men would have devoted time to logistical hunting of large game in the mountains. Where we differ, it is a difference in degree, not kind: The present model denotes a greater potential for fish to direct male activity (if we assume that fishing was an exclusively male activity, which it probably was not) and a lesser role for piñon. It also has occupation as more focused on the wetlands (when they were present) during hot/dry than during cool/wet intervals largely because of the increased productivity of the uplands and other regions in some seasons during the latter periods.

One final note: Based on analysis of survey data only, I concluded in 1985 that "there is no evidence of sedentism, semi-sedentism or focal use of the Carson Desert" (Kelly 1985:293). This chapter reveals that my earlier conclusion is incorrect.

8

Prehistoric Subsistence Strategies in the Stillwater Marsh Region of the Carson Desert

Margaret J. Schoeninger

The Great Basin of the western United States is marked by environmental variability across space and time, and archaeological data suggest that human subsistence strategies varied concomitantly. The first significant immigration into the area occurred around 5,000 years ago, was relatively intensive prior to 1,300 years ago, but declined over the last 500 years (Raven and Elston 1989). Prior to the Late Holocene, human density in the Basin, as a whole, and within the western Great Basin, in particular, was sparse and limited to valley bottoms near lakes or springs (Grayson 1993). Faunal remains recovered from these sites are largely wetland adapted species, which indicate that the ecological setting included marshes and shallow lakes. In contrast, Late Holocene sites are more numerous and are situated in a larger range of environments including the Stillwater Marsh area of the Carson Desert (Raven and Elston 1989). Grayson (1993) has suggested that the increase in human population during the Late Holocene may be associated with the spread of piñon into the Basin, although he acknowledges that it may not have been important in all localities. The Stillwater Marsh region may be one of these exceptions (Kelly 1985, 1995b). The region coincides with today's northernmost limit of piñon, which appears to have reached the area relatively recently, perhaps within the last 400 years (Wigand 1987). Kelly (1985, 1995b, this volume) has emphasized the importance of marsh resources for the human inhabitants of the area and, according to his models, the major ecological influence on human habitation was water, not piñon.

Although it is generally accepted that the prehistoric inhabitants of Stillwater Marsh followed a basic subsistence strategy of hunting and gathering (Raven and Elston 1989) similar to the historic Paiute (C. S. Fowler 1990a, 1990b), the extent of dependence on marsh resources continues to be a matter of debate (see Thomas 1985; Kelly 1985, Larsen and Kelly 1995, Kelly this volume). The goal of the present

TABLE 8.1.
Seasonality, Ecological Context, and Stable Isotope Signatures of Human Food Resources in the Prehistoric Carson Desert

Rank[a]	Resource[a] (Species)	Season of Availability[a]	Locale[a]	$\delta^{13}C$	Ref	$\delta^{15}N$
1	Rabbit (*Lepus* sp.)	Sp, S, F, W	various	C_4 −12.7	1	5.7
2	Cattail pollen (*Typha latefolia*)	Sp (S)	marsh	C_3 −26.2[b]	1	12.1
3	Rodents (various)	Sp, S, F, W	various	C_3/C_4		—
4	Birds	Sp, S, F, W	marsh	C_3/C_4	1	
	Coot (*Fulica* sp.)			−22.9	1	7.2
	Duck (*Anas* sp.)			−18.8	1	6.6
	(*Aythya* sp.)			−20.8	1	5.4
	Goose (genus ?)			−11.2	1	6.1
				−19.5	1	5.6
5	Fish (*Gila bicolor*)	Sp, S, F, W	marsh	C_3 −22.1	1	5.5
6	Shad scale (*Atriplex confertifolia*)	S, F	uplands & islands	C_4[c]	5	—
7	4-wing saltbush (*Atriplex canesens*)	S, F	uplands	C_4[c]	5	—
8	Bulrush seeds (*Scirpus acutus*)	S, F	marsh	C_3 −25.8	1	6.3
9	Nut grass (*Scirpus paludosis*)	S, F	marsh	C_3 −25.6	1	4.3
10	Seepweed (*Suaeda depressa*)	S, F	uplands & probably islands	C_4[d]	3	—
11	Torrey quail bush (*Atriplex torreyi*)	S, F	uplands	C_4[c]	5	—
12	Bluegrass (*Poa* spp.)	Sp	uplands	C_3	2	—
13	Basin wild rye (*Elymus cinereus* & *Elymus condensatus*)	S, F	uplands & floodplain	C_3	2	—
14	Indian rice grass (*Oryzopsis hymenoides*)	Sp	uplands	C_3 −23.3	1	2.6
15	Creeping wild rye (*Elymus triticoides*)	S, F	uplands	C_3 −23.4	1	6.4
16	Western wheatgrass (*Agropyron smithii*)	S, F	uplands	C_3	2	—

17	Slender wheatgrass (*Agropyron trachycaulum*)	S ,F	uplands	C_3	2	—
18	Cattail seeds (*Typha latefolia*)	S, F	marsh	C_3	1	—
19	Sand dropseed (*Sporobolus cruptandrus*)	S	uplands	$C_4{}^e$	2	—
20	Alkali sacaton (*Sporobolus airoides*)	Sp (S)	uplands	$C_4{}^e$	2	—
21	Forbs (*Mentzelia dispersa, Sophia sonnei, & Descurainia californica*)	Sp (S)	various	C_3		—
22	Spike rush (*Eleocharis sp.*)	S, F	marsh	C_3	4	—
23	Cattail roots (*Typha latefolia*)	S, F	marsh	C_3	1	—
24	Bulrush roots (*Scirpus acutus*)	S, F	marsh	C_3	1	—
25	Salt grass (*Distichlis stricta*)	S	uplands	C_4	4	—
—	Piñon (*Pinus monophyla*)	F	uplands	C_3 −21.2	1	1.0
—	Sheep (*Ovis canadensis*)		uplands	C_3 −18.6 −19.1	1 1	8.4 7.8
—	Artiodactyl (unidentified)		uplands	C_3 −18.1	1	10.2
—	Canid (genus ?)	Sp, S, F, W	various	C_3/C_4 −17.4 −17.5	1 1	9.1 12.0
—	Mustelid	—	—	C_3/C_4 −20.9 −17.1	1 1	8.8 9.3
—	Badger		—	C_3/C_4 −17.3	1	13.5

[a] The rank of species, season of availability, and locale are based on information presented in Raven and Elston (1989); some are unranked because they were not considered by Raven and Elston.

[b] The sample analyzed in this study was chafe.

[c] This genus includes both C_3 and C_4 species; these species display Kranz-type leaf anatomy associated with C_4 photosynthesis.

[d] The *Suaeda* sp. analyzed in this study is C_3; (δ^{13} C = −27.3); *Suaeda torreyana*, desert blite, is reported to be C_4 (Troughton, Card, and Hendy 1974).

[e] Of 138 species studied in this species' subfamily, all are C_4 with one exception.

References: 1. This study; 2. Waller and Lewis 1979; 3. Troughton, Card, and Hendy 1974; 4. Bender 1971; 5. Downton 1975 project, therefore, was to establish a baseline on human diet in the region by using stable isotope analysis of human bone to assess the possibility that human populations could have subsisted on marsh resources alone. The human data were compared to isotopic results on archaeological animal bone and modern plants, which represent resources thought to be important to humans in the marsh.

FOOD RESOURCES IN THE PREHISTORIC STILLWATER MARSH

Although floral remains have been sparse in the recovered archaeological record, a general picture of human diet emerges from ethnographic accounts of similar regions of the Great Basin in California (Balls 1962), of the Northern Paiute of western Nevada (C. S. Fowler 1990a, 1990b), and from optimal foraging assessments of the resources found in the Basin today (Simms 1987; Raven and Elston 1989). The focus appears to have been "small mammals, roots, and seeds... with large game being rare in the diet" (Simms 1987:88). Several small-seeded grasses (e.g., Indian ricegrass and wild rye), sedges (e.g., cattail and bulrush), and shrubs (e.g., shad scale and seepweed) found in the Stillwater Marsh are mentioned as foods in the ethnographic record of the area (C. S. Fowler 1990a, 1990b; see Table 8.1). In terms of immediate energy return relative to energy investment, such plants appear to have little value compared with deer, bighorn sheep, piñon, and acorn (Simms 1987), but the latter four resouces do not occur in the marsh. Furthermore, oak and piñon yields vary markedly year to year (Simms 1987; Grayson 1993), whereas a broad resource base composed of multiple small-seeded plants could offset annual productivity variations in any individual plant species (Simms 1987). Taking the period of availability into account and eliminating non-marsh food items from consideration raises the value rank of many small-seeded plants (see Table 8.1; Raven and Elston 1989). The seeds of shad scale, four-wing saltbush, bulrush, nut grass, and seepweed fall within the top 10 food items; cattail pollen ranks second because of its extraordinarily high caloric yield. In other words, plant resources fill 6 of the top 10 food items. Adding the ability to store the seeds over long periods should raise the value of plant foods even higher. Other portions of these plants were used as well even though these additional portions may have been of low rank. Archaeological reports state that the majority of identifiable quids found near the marsh are bulrush and cattail (Thomas 1985). Such use reflects ethnographic observations where, during the spring, stalks of these two plants are chewed like celery (C. S. Fowler 1990a, 1990b). Although the roots and stalks of these plants rank 23 and 24 overall, they could have been critical for short periods of time at the end of the winter.

A plant staple used by the California Indians was made from ground, leached acorns or pine nuts. Oaks are found in the eastern part of the Great Basin, but not near the Stillwater Marsh. Use of piñon by the marsh inhabitants would have required seasonal movements of a distance that would have depended on the timing of piñon immigration into the Stillwater Mountains (Grayson 1993).

> [R]esults suggest that pinyon was an extremely late arrival in this area. In Slinkard Valley, on the eastern flank of the Sierra Nevada and some 65 miles south of Reno, Wigand's middens first detect pinyon at about 1,400 years ago. In the southern Virginia Range, near Silver City and some 20 miles south and east of Reno, pinyon first shows up about 1,200 years ago. In the Hidden Valley area just east of Reno, pinyon does not appear until about 400 years ago. (Grayson 1993:221)

Remains of various types of fauna have been recovered from archaeological sites in the region. Although not locally available in the marsh, bighorn sheep have been identified and are highly ranked as potential resources in the eastern Great Basin (Simms 1987). Utilization would have required energy investments to travel to the area where the animals lived and to remain to hunt, on a seasonal or a short-term basis. Alternatively, there would have been additional energy costs of transporting the meat back to the marsh for consumption. Significantly, marsh faunal resources, including rabbits, various rodents, birds, and fish would have been available throughout the year (see Table 8.1; Raven and Elston 1989). Use of nets, snares, or drives would have increased the rate of return as well as the chances of a successful outcome (Simms 1987). Thus, large mammals were probably taken when available, but in the absence of scheduled movements out of the marsh, they could not have been a major part of human diet.

STABLE ISOTOPE ANALYSIS

The distribution of carbon stable isotope ratios (represented as $\delta^{13}C$ values[1] in per mil notation: ‰) across all plant species is bimodal. The majority of plants (referred to as C_3), including herbaceous vegetation, trees, and some high latitude grasses, display $\delta^{13}C$ values with ranges between −31 and −23 ‰ (O'Leary 1988). In

---

[1]A δ value is defined as

$$\delta = [R_{sample} / R_{std} - 1] \times 1000 ‰$$

where R is the isotope ratio (e.g., $^{13}C/^{12}C$ and $^{15}N/^{14}N$) and the standard is the internationally recognized standard. A negative δ value indicates a sample that is depleted in the heavier isotope relative to the internationally recognized standard and a positive δ value indicates a sample that is enriched relative to the standard. Due to historical accident, the international standard for carbon, PDB (Pee Dee Belemnite marine carbonate), has more ^{13}C relative to ^{12}C than is true for the vast majority of biological samples; thus, biological samples have carbon δ values that are negative. The opposite is true for nitrogen, where the majority of biological samples contain relatively more ^{15}N than is true of the standard (AIR, which is atmospheric nitrogen, formally referred to as Ambient Inhalable Reservoir). Thus, most biological samples have nitrogen δ values that are positive.

contrast, a significant number of plant species (referred to as C_4), including certain desert-adapted shrubs and grasses, have $\delta^{13}C$ values between -15 and -11 ‰ (O'Leary 1988). The C_3 and C_4 designations refer to the number of carbon atoms in the first metabolites formed during photosynthesis.

In C_3 photosynthesis, several variables can affect plant $\delta^{13}C$ values. Light affects the rate of carbon fixation and stomatal opening such that increased light levels associate with less negative leaf $\delta^{13}C$ values (Yakir and Israeli 1995). Additionally, the $\delta^{13}C$ values in plant leaves vary in negative association with water availability and humidity and during drought years in which those growing in dryer areas are less negative than those of the same species growing in better watered areas (Garten and Taylor 1992). The plants from the Stillwater Marsh today derive from a wide range of combinations of these variables and $\delta^{13}C$ values in C_3 plants from the region can be expected likewise to display a wide range of values. The values in C_4 plants in the area should display the normal range of values since plants using this photosynthetic pathway are less affected by light levels, humidity, and water availability (Farquhar 1983).

Animal tissues reflect the C_3/C_4 bimodality seen in plants (Vogel 1978). Proteins (i.e., bone collagen and hair) from experimental animals (DeNiro and Epstein 1978; R. J. Jones et al. 1981; Tieszen et al. 1983) and naturally occurring populations of animals (Minson, Ludlow, and Troughton 1975) and humans (Nakamura et al. 1982; C. White and Schwarcz 1994) reflect monotonous C_3 or C_4 diets, intermediate mixes of C_3 and C_4, and monitor changes in the diet. Thus, the $\delta^{13}C$ values in the humans and fauna from Stillwater Marsh should reflect their dependence on such plants. Because the C_3 plant range may be larger due to the reasons stated above, it is expected that the human values may be less negative than previously reported for those dependent on C_3 plants.

The stable isotope ratios of nitrogen ($^{15}N/^{14}N$) vary throughout the biosphere, but the distribution is determined in a different manner from that for carbon stable isotope ratios. The ratio (represented as $\delta^{15}N$ in per mil notation: ‰) in plants varies according to the amount of nitrogen in the soil and the $\delta^{15}N$ value of the nitrogen containing compounds taken up by plants (Shearer and Kohl 1994), although the interrelation of these two variables is incompletely understood. Certain plants, like legumes, grow in association with microorganisms that fix atmospheric nitrogen directly in a process which produces no alteration in the $^{15}N/^{14}N$ ratio from the ratio in air. When such nitrogen is the main source for the plant, the plant's tissues have a stable isotope ratio very close to that in air. Because air nitrogen is the defined standard for nitrogen isotope ratios, these plants have $\delta^{15}N$ values close to zero. This process of nitrogen fixation is energetically costly, however. Thus, under conditions where soil nitrogen is available, legumes fix nitrogen from soil. Significant for the present study, *Pinus* (the genus which includes piñon) has been reported as having stable nitrogen isotope ratios similar to that in atmospheric nitrogen (Virginia and Delwiche 1982). Thus, it was expected that piñon would have a $\delta^{15}N$ value close to zero.

The majority of plants lack the association with microorganisms capable of fixing atmospheric nitrogen and so are limited to fixing soil nitrogen. Nitrogen bound in soil compounds (e.g., nitrates, nitrites, and ammonium) is largely the result of biomass degradation. During degradation, elemental bonds are broken and relatively more ^{14}N than ^{15}N is removed from soil in the form of nitrogen gas and ammonia due to the faster reaction rate of ^{14}N compared with ^{15}N. This results in soil nitrogen that generally has more positive $\delta^{15}N$ values (i.e., has more ^{15}N) than air. Because of this, plants that utilize soil nitrogen tend to have $\delta^{15}N$ values more positive than air and more positive than legumes using fixed atmospheric nitrogen. The majority of terrestrial plants have $\delta^{15}N$ values around +3 to +5 ‰, but some annual herbaceous plants have been reported with elevated $^{15}N/^{14}N$ ratios (Virginia and Delwiche 1982; Vogel et al. 1990). For example, *Suaeda torreyana* (a genus of plant used in the marsh) varied from +5.9 ‰ to +13.0 ‰ (Shearer et al. 1983). One mechanism that could produce values at the high end of the range is biomass burning. During this process, up to 50 percent of organically bound nitrogen is lost as nitrogen gas (Kuhlbusch et al. 1991). If the fire temperature is relatively low (700°C or below), significant fractionation will occur and the remaining nitrogen would be enriched in the heavier isotope because the lighter isotope would be lost first. Fire, followed by plant uptake of soil with enriched organically bound nitrogen, could account for the very positive nitrogen isotope values. Herbaceous annuals would be expected to be most affected because all of their above-ground tissues would be synthesized using the nitrogen remaining after the burn. The Stillwater Marsh region undoubtedly experienced dry years following wet ones and would have been subject to fires similar to those experienced in southern California chaparrel regions today.

The $\delta^{15}N$ value in animal tissues, such as hair (DeNiro and Epstein 1981; Schwarcz and Schoeninger 1991), depends on diet (DeNiro and Epstein 1981) and various metabolic factors (Ambrose and DeNiro 1986). In concert, these variables result in an increase in $\delta^{15}N$ values between trophic levels (Schoeninger and DeNiro 1984). Plants, on average, have less positive $\delta^{15}N$ values than the herbivores feeding on them, which, in turn, have less positive values than the omnivores and carnivores (Schoeninger 1985). Nevertheless, there is variation in the range of $\delta^{15}N$ values within trophic systems that is not related to trophic level (Schoeninger, Iwaniec, and Glander 1997). Certain desert systems reportedly have elevated $\delta^{15}N$ values, and the explanation for this phenomenon probably includes water stress, food stress, elevated plant levels, or some combination of these variables (Heaton et al. 1986; Schoeninger 1989; Ambrose 1991).

TABLE 8.2.
Human Stable Isotope Data

Cat. #	Site	Sample	Age	Sex	$\delta^{13}C$ (‰)	$\delta^{15}N$ (‰)
1-2[a]	1044	rib	25–30	F	−16.3	13.6
12-11[a]	1058	rib	20–25	F	−16.5	11.6
3-5[a]	1050	rib	40+	M	−18.6	9.8
7-16[a]	1159	rib	16–19	M	−16.8	12.6
4-1[a]	1159	rib	30–40	M	−17.1	10.3
5-2-b[a]	1043	rib	40+	M	−16.0	12.0
2-3[a]	1044	rib	40+	M	−16.5	11.2
1/8-2[a]	910	rib	40+	F	−18.2	10.6
4-3[a]	1070	rib	40+	F	−18.0	10.2
3-3[a]	1070	rib	40+	F	−18.7	10.3
1-1[a]	L53	rib	35+	F	−18.1	9.7
1-2[a]	1062	rib	40+	M	−16.9	11.2
61-1[a]	1043	rib	30+	F	−16.5	10.6
1-1[a]	1158	rib	35–45	M	−18.9	9.5
1-4[a]	1055	rib	25–30	M	−18.5	10.4
1-3[a]	1054	rib	25–30	M	−17.8	11.2
9-11[a]	1046	rib	35–40	M	−16.1	12.6
222	1046	rib	adult	?	−16.5	11.6
200	L72	rib	35–40	F	−16.8	9.6
200	L108	rib	.5–1	?	−17.9	14.2
200	1159	rib	45+	F	−16.8	11.7
207	1173	rib	adult	?	−14.4	14.4
208	910	rib	2	?	−17.8	12.8
211	1058	rib	7.5	?	−17.7	16.7
200	1064	rib	10–15	?	−16.0	11.7
20-1	1065	rib	13–17	?	−18.2	11.9
201A	1064	rib	adult	?	−15.1	13.4
211	910	rib	1.5	?	−17.8	8.7
1-1	1163	rib	18–25	M	−16.6	11.2
200	1173	rib	25–30	F	−16.4	10.9
1-1-5a	1047	vertebra	18–25	M	−16.7	10.8
1-15[a]	1056	rib	30–40	F	−15.9	11.2
1-2-15[b]	1045	rib	30–40	F	−18.5	10.5
1-4a	1060	radius	adult	F?	−17.3	12.1
16-1	910	rib	35–40	F	−16.7	11.1
20-2-16(b)	1063	rib	40+	M	−18.9	10.8
6-1-29(b)	1159	rib	25–30	M	−16.7	10.9
1-2-14(c)	1064	femur	25–35	F	−16.8	11.3
13-1-4a	1047	humerus	40+	F?	−16.8	10.4

MATERIALS AND METHODS

Samples were taken from 39 human skeletons, seven plants, and 20 animal skeletons for carbon and nitrogen stable isotope analysis (Tables 8.1 and 8.2). As indicated in Table 8.2, the human skeletons were usually recovered as individual burials scattered throughout the marsh region. All of the faunal samples were recovered from archaeological sites and presumably are food remains. The plant samples are modern representatives collected by Robert Kelly and Elizabeth Budy. With the exception of *Suaeda,* all have been identified to species. In those cases where samples were not available, the photosynthetic pathway was determined from the literature whenever possible (see Table 8.1). Nitrogen isotope data were not available for plants not analyzed by the author.

The samples were prepared in laboratories at Harvard University or the University of Wisconsin. Handling of the samples was determined by their composition. Bone samples were cleaned mechanically in double-distilled water, broken into pieces approximately 1 mm², and placed in 1 percent hydrochloric acid (HCl) for approximately 10 days or until they were completely demineralized (K. Moore, Murray, and Schoeninger 1989; Schoeninger et al. 1989). Following demineralization, they were rinsed to neutrality in double-distilled water, soaked in 0.125 M sodium hydroxide (NaOH) for 10 hours to remove humic acid contamination, and again rinsed to neutrality. The samples were freeze-dried and then weighed to determine the amount of organic material (largely bone collagen) remaining in the bone as a means of screening skeletons acceptable for analysis.

Previous studies have demonstrated that significant shifts occur in nitrogen and carbon stable isotope ratios as a result of kinetic isotope effects when proteins have been markedly degraded (DeNiro, Schoeninger, and Hastorf 1985; Bada, Schoeninger, and Schimmelmann 1989). Carbon is less affected, but nitrogen ratios can increase by a factor of three when less than 1 percent of the original organic material is retained in bone. In the present study, all samples with less organic material than 3 percent of the original sample weight were discarded. Only the organic component of the human and faunal samples was analyzed. For the acceptable samples, approximately 3 mg were loaded into quartz tubes in preparation for combustion.

Plant samples were rinsed in double-distilled water, dried in a warm oven, and ground to ensure homogeneity. Approximately 7 mg were loaded into quartz tubes in preparation for combustion for analyses of carbon isotope ratios. Diatomaceous earth was added to the plant samples to provide excess silica during the combustion phase, thereby enhancing stability of the quartz sample tubes. A separate portion of each plant sample was prepared via the Kjeldahl method (Bradstreet 1965) for nitrogen stable isotope analysis. Whenever possible, the portion of the plant sample analyzed was limited to the part thought to have been eaten by humans.

All samples for combustion were treated identically. Excess elemental copper

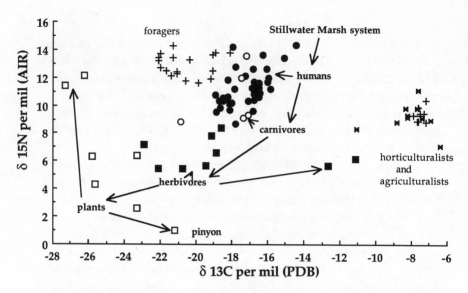

FIGURE 8.1. $\delta^{13}C$ values plotted against the $\delta^{15}N$ values for all the samples analyzed in this study. Each point represents an individual sample. These data indicate that two plants have very positive $\delta^{15}N$ values and that all plants analyzed are C_3. Two of the herbivorous animals have $\delta^{13}C$ values, indicating that they fed on C_4 plants and suggesting either that the animals came from outside the marsh region or, more likely, that C_4 plants existed in the region (see text and Table 8.1). The carnivorous animals are 3 to 4 ‰ more positive in $\delta^{15}N$ values than the herbivorous animals upon which they feed, as expected based on previous studies (Schoeninger and DeNiro 1984). The distribution of human values falls within that of the carnivorous animals, suggesting that the majority of the nitrogen incorporated into human bone collagen came from the herbivorous fauna or from plants with elevated $\delta^{15}N$ values. Further, some of the humans have less negative $\delta^{13}C$ values, indicating that they ate C_4 plants or animals with a C_4 isotopic signature; several of the plants used by prehistoric people in the region have been reported to be C_4 (see Table 8.1). When compared with other archaeological human populations, the Stillwater Marsh inhabitants are more similar to the Ontario foragers (data replotted from Schwarcz et al. 1985) than to part-time and full-time maize agriculturalists from the southwestern portion of North America (data replotted from Spielmann, Schoeninger, and Moore 1990; Habicht-Mauche, Levendosky, and Schoeninger 1994)

(Cu), cupric oxide (CuO), and silver (Ag) were added to each quartz tube along with the sample. The quartz tubes were sealed under vacuum, placed in a muffle furnace at 900°C for two hours, and permitted to cool to room temperature. The combustion products were purified and distilled cryogenically. The purified carbon dioxide (CO_2) was analyzed using a Finnegan MAT Delta E gas isotope ratio mass spectrometer in Hayes's laboratory at Indiana University or on the same type of mass spectrometer in my laboratory at the University of Wisconsin. The purified nitrogen gas (N_2) was analyzed using a VG Isogas 602E isotope ratio mass spectrometer in McCarthy's laboratory at Harvard University or a Finnegan MAT 251 isotope ratio mass spectrometer at the University of Wisconsin.

A homogenized proline sample and a homogenized glycine sample were analyzed as internal laboratory combustion standards. Repeated analyses of these standards yielded a replicability of less than ±0.2 ‰ in $\delta^{13}C$ and of ±0.3 ‰ in $\delta^{15}N$. As a check on interlaboratory and intralaboratory precision, 11 samples (including bone and plant samples) were analyzed in duplicate for carbon. These samples had $\delta^{13}C$ values within 0.6 ‰ of each other with an average difference of 0.2 ‰. Seven samples (including bone and plant samples) were analyzed in duplicate for nitrogen; these samples had $\delta^{15}N$ values within 0.5 ‰ of each other, with an average difference of 0.3 ‰. In cases of replicate analyses of samples, the average is reported.

RESULTS AND DISCUSSION

The results of isotopic analyses are presented in Tables 8.1 and 8.2 and in Figure 8.1. All plant samples analyzed in this study have $\delta^{13}C$ values indicative of C_3 photosynthesis, although the piñon is less negative than the range previously reported (O'Leary 1988). These results probably reflect the effects of water limitations, low humidity, and high light levels in the region. Other plants highly ranked by Raven and Elston (1989) are reported to be C_4 (Table 8.1) and are expected to fall around −12 ‰. The prehistoric representatives of these plants would have had $\delta^{13}C$ values approximately 1 ‰ less negative than today's plants, since atmospheric carbon dioxide would have been around 1 ‰ less negative than today (Keeling 1961; Bada et al. 1990; Wahlen 1994).

Among the faunal samples, the $\delta^{13}C$ values fall into two clusters. The *Lepus* and a duck (*Aythya*) exhibit values indicating a major dependence upon C_4 plants. As such, they would have contributed to a C_4 isotope signal in humans feeding on them. The remainder of the fauna have $\delta^{13}C$ values that indicate a dependence on C_3 plants (in the case of *Ovis,* the remaining birds, and the unidentified artiodactyl), C_3 plant detritus (in the case of the fish, *Gila bicolor*), or fauna feeding on C_3 plants.

The $\delta^{15}N$ values in the plant samples fall between 1.0 ‰ (piñon) and 12.1 ‰ (cattail). The former is close to zero, as expected in nitrogen fixing plants, and confirms previously reported observations of the genus *Pinus* (Virginia and Delwiche 1982). The cattail value is at the high end of nitrogen values reported in terrestrial plants (Wada, Kadonaga, and Matsuo 1975; Wada 1980). The sample of *Suaeda* sp. also has a very positive value (+11.4 ‰; average of two separate preparations [+11.5 ‰ and +11.3 ‰]). The species contrasts with other plants which have more normal values around +6 ‰. The relatively positive values may reflect high $\delta^{15}N$ values in soil resulting from biomass burning, although this possibility cannot be confirmed in the absence of analyses on soil nitrogen.

The $\delta^{15}N$ values in the fauna range from +5.4 ‰ (a duck) to +12.0 ‰ (a canid) and fall within two clusters as well. Those animals which are mainly herbivorous (duck, rabbit, and sheep) cluster between +5.4 ‰ and +8.4 ‰ with one outlier, an unidentified artiodactyl, at +10.5 ‰. Those animals which are omnivorous or carnivorous (canids and mustelids) cluster between 8.8 ‰ and 12.0 ‰, reflecting a trophic level effect (Schoeninger and DeNiro 1984).

Among the human samples, the absolute number for any single skeletal element is small (see Table 8.2), but there is no patterning of isotope values by bone. This supports findings reported previously of minimal variation (less than 0.5 ‰) in both carbon and nitrogen across skeletal elements (DeNiro and Schoeninger 1983). Similarly, there appears to be no age-associated variation in $\delta^{13}C$ values. Three samples from individuals two years old and less fall within the range of the remainder, which is similar to that observed previously in another foraging population (Lovell, Nelson, and Schwarcz 1986) and contrasts with that observed in a maize-based agricultural population (Katzenberg, Saunders, and Fitzgerald 1993). The nitrogen isotope picture is less certain. Two of the three young individuals have $\delta^{15}N$ values that fall at the high end of the overall range, which may represent a nursing signal. In a set of nursing infants, $\delta^{15}N$ values were elevated in comparison with weaned infants; and, among prehistoric foragers, young infants had higher values than did older infants (Fogel, Tuross, and Owsley 1989; Tuross and Fogel 1994; but see M. R. Schurr 1997). Thus, the values in the Stillwater Marsh infants may reflect the effect of nursing, although this interpretation is not conclusive. One infant has a $\delta^{15}N$ value that is at the low end of the range of variation, and one juvenile (7.5 years old) from site 26Ch1058 has the highest $\delta^{15}N$ value (+16.7 ‰). No alternative explanation can be given for this particular sample value. The sample was not included in any of the graphs presented here; its removal does not alter the average or the standard deviation.

The sample sizes for identifiable males and females are large, yet there is no difference in average values or in ranges for males and females. This indicates that there is no difference between the sexes in the isotopic ratios or in the general categories of foods eaten. In the comparison of 16 females and 14 males, the averages of both the $\delta^{15}N$ and the $\delta^{13}C$ values fall within 0.1 ‰ of each other (+11.0 ‰ versus +11.0 ‰, and −17.2 ‰ versus −17.1 ‰, respectively), and the ranges are virtually identical. The nitrogen isotopic values within the set of female samples show a range of +9.6 ‰ to 13.6 ‰ (with one outlier; the second most positive value is +12.1 ‰); within the males, it is +9.5 ‰ to 12.6 ‰. The carbon isotopic values show the same similarity in ranges: the female samples are −18.7 ‰ to −15.9 ‰, and the male samples are −18.9 ‰ to −16.0 ‰. The same finding has been reported in several other studies (reviewed in Schwarcz and Schoeninger 1991).

The overall range of variation within the human samples from the Stillwater Marsh is very large in both $\delta^{13}C$ and $\delta^{15}N$ values. Among animals on monotonous diets, the range was less than 2 ‰ in both carbon and nitrogen (DeNiro and Schoeninger 1983); whereas in this study, the range among the human samples is 4.5 ‰ in carbon and 5.7 ‰ in nitrogen. Compared with other foragers (data replotted from Schwarcz et al. 1985), maize agriculturalists, and part-time horticulturalists from the North American continental interior (data replotted from Spielmann, Schoeninger, and Moore 1990; Habicht-Mauche, Levendosky, and Schoeninger 1994), the range in $\delta^{13}C$ values among the Stillwater Marsh inhabitants is more similar to that among the other foragers, although it exceeds it (see Figure 8.1). The range of variation in $\delta^{15}N$ values is larger than that reported in the other human groups, but it is similar to horticulturalists from the Texas panhandle. These isotopic ranges within the marsh population indicate that there was a wide variety of diets being eaten. Some of the people could have eaten only plants and animals which had a C_3 signature; others must have eaten a significant amount of food with a C_4 signature. A similar variety of foods is suggested by the nitrogen data.

Indirect evidence suggests that people had distinctly different diets at various times throughout the occupation of the area. Raven and Elston (1989) discuss temporal cycles in fish abundance and viral diseases among ducks and rabbits that would have affected the availability of these animals. If these occurred on 5- or 10-year cycles, there would be people with distinctly different bone collagen isotope ratios such as those observed in this study. For example, an individual who ate a substantial number of rabbits ($\delta^{13}C$ value of −11 ‰) during childhood and adolescence, when most bone collagen is formed, would have a bone collagen $\delta^{13}C$ value distinctly different from her/his offspring if fish (−22 ‰) were substituted for rabbit in the offspring's diet. Similarly, individuals eating plants growing within several years of a major fire could have bone collagen $\delta^{15}N$ values that are more positive than others.

On average, the people from Stillwater Marsh are more similar to other foraging people (see Figure 8.1) than they are to agriculturalists and horticulturalists. In terms of carbon, the average difference in $\delta^{13}C$ values between the two foraging groups is explained by the use of wild C_4 plants in the Stillwater Marsh. This pattern is similar to that described by Coltrain and Stafford (this volume) in the eastern portion of the Great Basin where populations varied in their dependence on foraging throughout prehistory. In terms of nitrogen, the people from the Stillwater Marsh are also more similar, on average, to the fisher/foragers in Ontario. In this case, however, the similarity of values does not indicate a similarity of subsistence strategy. The positive values among the Ontario samples are due to ingestion of fish with high $\delta^{15}N$ values around 9 ‰ and 10 ‰ (Katzenberg 1989). In contrast, the fish samples from the Carson Desert had a $\delta^{15}N$ value of 5.5 ‰, which suggests that fish were not the major protein source for the individuals with positive nitrogen isotope values.

The Stillwater people display the same relative $\delta^{15}N$ values when compared with local carnivores and herbivores, as has been observed in several other trophic systems (Schoeninger 1995b). If the majority of the nitrogen which was used in the synthesis of their tissue proteins came from the animals that they ate rather than from plants, then the human values reflect a trophic level increase in $\delta^{15}N$ similar to that previously noted in animals (Figure 8.1; Schoeninger and DeNiro 1984). Because it seems likely that plants provided significant amounts of protein and nitrogen, the possibility of consumption of plants with high $\delta^{15}N$ values must also be considered.

The more general question addressed by this study, however, is whether the resources in the Stillwater Marsh region could have supported the human population or if supplementation with foods from outside the area was necessary. The foods inside the marsh display such a wide variety of stable isotope values that virtually all of the human values can be accounted for by dependence on marsh products. Although all of the plants analyzed in this study are C_3, several of the plants listed by Raven and Elston (1989) are C_4 (see references in Table 8.1). Three of these (i.e., shad scale, desert blite substituting for seepweed, and four-wing saltbush) are in the family Chenopodiaceae, which includes both C_3 and C_4 species; shad scale and four-wing saltbush have been identified as C_4 based on leaf anatomy (Downton 1975).

The season of availability is also important when considering whether people had to move out of the marsh region to obtain food. Several of the important plants produce seeds in the fall and/or summer (shad scale, four-wing saltbush, Torrey quail bush, sand dropseed, and salt grass). These plants have been identified as C_4 (see Table 8.1), but others (bulrush and nut grass) are C_3. A reasonable combination would provide the mix of C_3 and C_4 signals measured in the majority of the human samples. All of the higher ranked spring plants are C_3 (bluegrass and Indian ricegrass), although one lower ranked plant (alkali sacaton) is probably C_4. Bone collagen (human and fauna) records a dietary average, however. Thus, a lower amount of C_4 plants in spring could still result in the isotope signatures observed here. In addition, since many of the seeds would be stored for use throughout the winter (Simms 1987), the people may have eaten a mix of plants throughout the year. Meat from small mammals, birds, and fish also shows the mix of carbon isotope signals and would have been available year round.

Most significantly, the relatively positive $\delta^{15}N$ values in human bone collagen indicate that piñon was not an important component of diet. The nuts from the species available in the Carson Desert region (*Pinus monophylla* or single-leaf piñon) are high in fat (23 percent) and carbohydrates (54 percent), but also contain a significant amount of protein (10 percent) relative to other plants (Lanner 1981). The piñon $\delta^{15}N$ value is close to zero, and if it had provided a significant portion of the diet, its nitrogen isotope signal would have been recorded in human bone collagen. If this had been the case, the human bone collagen $\delta^{15}N$ values would have been lower than those actually measured.

CONCLUSIONS

As mentioned in the introduction, the goal of this study was to provide baseline information about the foods used by the people of the Stillwater Marsh region in order to provide data that could serve in evaluating two proposed explanations for increased human presence in the region between 5,000 and 1,300 years ago. One proposal is that people followed piñon; the other is that they followed water (see Grayson 1993). The former proposal requires use of nonmarsh resources, while the latter implies that marsh resources provided adequate food (Kelly 1985).

Within the set of human samples analyzed, there is no partitioning according to site, sex, or age group. Nevertheless, the range of isotope values (almost 6 ‰ in nitrogen and over 4 ‰ in carbon) indicates that a variety of foods were eaten. Such a generalized subsistence strategy has previously been suggested based on archaeological evidence (Kelly 1985), ethnographic analogy (Balls 1962; C. S. Fowler 1990a, 1990b), and foraging models (Simms 1987; Raven and Elston 1989; Kelly 1995b). The general lack of temporal associations between individuals used in this study does not permit direct assessment of the proposal that over time human diet changed to include greater amounts of marsh resources (Kelly 1985). Even so, the isotopic data indicate that the diet of these people depended on plants and animals similar to those living within the marsh since the beginning of the Late Holocene.

These data, therefore, do not refute a model suggesting that people remained year round in the vicinity of the marsh (see Kelly, this volume, for a similar result). Archaeological recovery of sheep bone argues that movement out of the marsh either occurred at some time during human habitation in the region, occurred on a regular seasonal basis, or occurred opportunistically throughout the year. Evidence of articular joint pathologies suggests that men, in particular, were moving long distances in difficult terrain, such as that which occurs in the uplands surrounding the marsh (Larsen, Ruff, and Kelly 1995). These possibilities cannot be evaluated using isotopic data. The human $\delta^{13}C$ values can be accounted for by a combination of plants and animals from the immediate marsh region. The very positive $\delta^{15}N$ values may be the result of ingesting local plants with high $\delta^{15}N$ values similar to those analysed in the present study. The high $\delta^{15}N$ values in the modern plants may be the result of landscape burning, although this suggestion requires further testing.

The human $\delta^{15}N$ values also indicate that piñon was not a very important food source. As such, these results suggest that, within the Stillwater Marsh region, water was more important than a specific food source in encouraging human habitation. Furthermore, taken as a whole, the data support previous suggestions that human diets and overall subsistence strategies in the Carson Desert would have varied in response to seasonal and annual fluctuations in availability (Simms 1987; Kelly 1995b).

Acknowledgements

Several individuals helped in preparing samples for analysis and in the mass spectrometry: Renee Robinson, Matthew Murray, John Blitz, Mark Schurr, Isabel Treichel, Al Hengge, and Urszula Iwaniec. Robert Kelly provided the plant samples and many useful discussions and e-mails. My thanks to Brian Hemphill and Clark Larsen for their invitation to participate in the symposium which led to this book, to Joan Coltrain who generously sent copies of unpublished manuscripts, and to Pat Lubinsky for discussions of many of the issues addressed here. I extend special thanks to Urszula Iwaniec who put an enormous effort into determining replicable methods for analyzing plant samples for nitrogen isotope analysis and to Pam Fitzer and Jim Stoltman for reading earlier versions of the manuscript. Funding for this project was provided by a National Science Foundation grant (BNS-8704094) to Robert Kelly and by the University of Wisconsin Alumni Research Foundation.

9

Molecular Genetics and the Numic Expansion

A Molecular Investigation of the Prehistoric Inhabitants of Stillwater Marsh

Frederika A. Kaestle, Joseph G. Lorenz, and David G. Smith

Hypotheses of prehistoric population movements in the Americas have long inspired debate among archaeologists and linguists. Although the practice of associating a unique technology, style, or language with a specific population is controversial (Bateman et al. 1990; Boas 1911; Elston 1994; Hughes 1994; K. T. Jones 1994), the diffusion pattern or sudden appearance of specific artifacts and the modern distribution of Native American languages have been interpreted as evidence for the past movement of people. One much debated controversy concerns the prehistoric movement of Native Americans into and within the Great Basin region of the Desert West.

Currently, Numic-speaking Native Americans inhabit most of the Great Basin (W. R. Miller 1986). Following Steward (1940), Lamb (1958) suggested that the Numic speakers expanded into this region from a homeland in the southwestern Great Basin. Lamb used glottochronological evidence to estimate the minimum age of the divergence of the Numic branch of the Uto-Aztecan language family, thus providing a minimum date for the appearance of Numic peoples in the Great Basin of 1000 B.P. Some linguists believe the distribution of modern Numic languages, patterns of linguistic borrowing, lexical analysis of floral and faunal vocabulary, and an analysis of place-names also provide evidence of an expansion of the Numic-speaking peoples northeast into the area at about that time (C. S. Fowler 1972; W. R. Miller 1986; W. R. Miller, Tanner, and Foley 1971; M. Nichols 1981). Many archaeologists believe that shifts in technology and residence patterns, accompanied by a change in subsistence strategy, occurred in the Great Basin at about the same time and that these changes also reflect the intrusion of Numic speakers (Adovasio and Pedler 1994; Bettinger 1994; Bettinger and Baumhoff 1982; Grosscup 1960; Janetski 1994; Sutton 1991; Young and Bettinger 1992). The ethnic affiliation of the earlier, presumably non-Numic, inhabitants of the Great Basin is unknown, but all of the major Native American groups of the area have at various times been suggested as descendants of these pre-Numic inhabitants (e.g., d'Azevedo et al. 1966; D. D. Fowler 1977; Hopkins 1965; Jorgensen 1980).

Some archaeologists see little evidence in the prehistoric record of a cultural discontinuity representing a population replacement at any time in the past several thousand years, or they interpret evidence for culture change as an in situ adaptation to increasing population density (Aikens and Witherspoon 1986; Elston 1982; Raven 1994; Swanson 1962). Some linguists also believe that the modern distribution of Numic languages is consistent with a long history of Numic speakers in the Great Basin (Crapo and Spykerman 1979; Goss 1977). Lamb himself has emphasized that 1000 B.P. is a minimum estimate of the date of the Numic expansion, with the Numic languages probably diverging earlier (Thomas 1994).

The study of protein and genetic material extracted from ancient tissues, including human bone from archaeological settings, made possible by recent advances in knowledge and technology, has contributed to our understanding of past population biology and history in ways completely unenvisioned just a decade ago (e.g., see Kaestle 1995, 1997; O'Rourke, Parr, and Carlyle, this volume; D. G. Smith, Bettinger, and Rolfs 1995; Stone and Stoneking 1993, 1998). Using automated polymerase chain reaction (PCR) technology, it is now possible to amplify millions of copies of specific fragments of deoxyribonucleic acid (DNA) from minute quantities of template DNA (either modern or ancient) (see Herrmann and Hummel 1993). This technological breakthrough opens a range of methodologies for addressing long-standing issues in anthropology and other fields. The frequencies of variant (mutational) forms of protein-coding loci and mitochondrial (mt) DNA lineages in ancient groups can be compared with those in modern groups to confirm or reject hypotheses about ancestor-descendant relationships and to test hypotheses about the occurrence and timing of prehistoric population movements.

The very limited distributions of some rare mutations do suggest common ancestry among some tribal groups (Szathmary and Ossenberg 1978; Torroni et al. 1992; R. C. Williams et al. 1985). For example, in addition to Al^A, the most common albumin allele in all human populations, several albumin locus mutations of probable New World origin are present in Native North American populations. Two of these mutations, albumin Naskapi (Al^{Na}) and albumin Mexico (Al^{Me}), exhibit allele frequencies between 0.01 and 0.13 in some Native American groups (Schell and Blumberg 1988). Al^{Na} is found in most Algonkian-speaking and Athabascan-speaking Native American groups (including the Navajo and Apache in the American Southwest), but is absent in other Native American groups with the exception of several cases resulting from admixture. In North America, Al^{Me} has been found only in some Uto-Aztecan and Yuman speakers, ranging in frequency between .01 and .05, except, again, in rare cases of admixture (Schell and Blumberg 1988).

Recent studies have shown that certain mtDNA mutations characterize at least four distinct founding mtDNA matrilines (haplogroups A, B, C, and D) to which most modern Native Americans belong (Horai et al. 1993; T. G. Schurr et al. 1990; Torroni et al. 1992, 1993a). The frequencies of these matrilines vary significantly among both modern (Lorenz and Smith 1994, 1996; Merriwether, Rothhammer, and Ferrell 1995; Torroni et al. 1993a) and prehistoric (Kaestle 1997; O'Rourke, Carlyle, and Parr 1996, this volume; Parr, Carlyle, and O'Rourke 1996; Stone and Stoneking 1993) Native American populations. This variability in the presence and frequency of Al^{Me}, Al^{Na}, and the mitochondrial haplogroups should be useful for identifying ancestor-descendant relationships (e.g., Hagelberg and Clegg 1993; Kaestle 1997; O'Rourke, Carlyle, and Parr 1996; Parr, Carlyle, and O'Rourke 1996).

Although genetic analyses have been completed on relatively few samples from populations that inhabited the western Great Basin and adjacent regions during historic times (e.g., Kaestle 1997; Lorenz and Smith 1994, 1996; D. G. Smith et al. 1999), a much larger number of such samples are available. The frequencies of Al^{Me}, Al^{Na}, and the mitochondrial haplogroups in ancient samples of bone from western Nevada that predate the time period of the proposed Numic expansion can be compared with those in modern Native American groups to assess the plausibility that the former are direct ancestors of the latter. It is possible that genetic bottlenecks and resulting drastic changes in gene frequencies accompanied population declines associated with European contact with some North American tribes. Evidence of additional matrilines (other than A, B, C, and D) in more remote modern Native American populations has been reported (Easton et al. 1996; Scozzari et al. 1997; Stone and Stoneking 1998), suggesting that some matrilines that are now rare or even extinct might have occurred with higher frequencies during prehistoric times. Nevertheless, there is some evidence that the geographic distribution of frequencies of the haplogroups did not change significantly in some areas of North America (see Kaestle 1995, 1997; Lorenz and Smith 1996). Because of this, it seems unlikely that the pre-Numic population in western Nevada is ancestral to any modern population from which its frequencies of Al^{Me}, Al^{Na}, and the mitochondrial haplogroups differ significantly. If the frequencies of the mtDNA haplogroups and albumin phenotypes in modern tribal groups in the Great Basin are similar to those of the ancient inhabitants, then no genetic evidence of a Numic expansion survives. If they differ, those frequencies might provide confirmation of the Numic expansion and evidence for the identity of the pre-Numic inhabitants of the Great Basin.

FIGURE 9.1. Geographic location at European contact of tribes sampled. 1 Costanoan (Ohlone), 2 Miwok, 3 Wintun, 4 Yokuts, 5 Zuni, 6 Karok, 7 Achumawi, 8 Pomo, 9 Walapai, 10 Havasupai, 11 Yavapai, 12 Paipai, 13 Quechan, 14 Mojave, 15 Kumia, 16 Cocopa, 17 Kiliwa, 18 Maricopa, 19 Cochimi, 20 Washo, 21 Salinan, 22 Chumash, 23 Northern Paiute/Shoshone, 24 Ute, 25 Kawaiisu, 26 Tubatulabal, 27 Chemehuevi (Southern Paiute), 28 Kitanemuk, 29 Gabrielino, 30 Luiseño, 31 Fernandeno, 32 Cahuilla, 33 Hopi, 34 Pima, 35 Papago (Tohono O'odham), 36 Apache, 37 Navajo (Dene)

MATERIAL AND METHODS

We have analyzed DNA extracted from bone samples of 27 Native Americans buried at Stillwater Marsh (see Figure 9.1). The sites from which the samples were obtained (site numbers 26Ch1043–1047, 26Ch1050, 26Ch1054, 26Ch1055, 26Ch1058, 26Ch1062–1064, 26Ch1070, 26Ch1158–1160; see Tuohy, Dansie, and Haldeman 1987), as well as other burial sites from Stillwater Marsh, are believed to date to between 3250 and 650 B.P. based on the projectile points recovered (Kelly 1995b; Larsen 1995). This age is also supported by radiocarbon dates from skeletal remains, charcoal, and other organic remains associated with the burials (Kelly 1995b; Larsen 1995; Raven and Elston 1988). Therefore, the individuals sampled for this study date to a time period that almost completely precedes the hypothesized date of the Numic expansion. In addition, homogeneity in morphology among

TABLE 9.1.
Modern Native Americans Sampled for Albumin Analyzed by
Language Group and Geographic Region

Group	Subgroup	Sub-subgroup	Number Tribal Members Sampled*	Geographic Group
Penutian	California Penutian		1 Costanoan (Ohlone)	California
			1 Miwok	California
			2 Wintun	California
	Zuni		655 Zuni	Southwest
Hokan	Northern Hokan		2 Karok	California
			1 Achumawi	California
			5 Pomo	California
	Yuman		222 Walapai	Southwest
			96 Havasupai	Southwest
			118 Yavapai	Southwest
			14 Paipai	Baja Cal.
			143 Quechan	Southwest
			19 Mojave	Southwest
			24 Kumia	Baja Cal.
			164 Cocopa	Baja Cal.
			8 Kiliwa	Baja Cal.
			1110 Maricopa	Southwest
			13 Cochimi	Baja Cal.
	Washo		133 Washo	Great Basin
Uto-Aztecan	Northern Uto-Aztecan	Numic	150 N. Paiute/Shoshone	Great Basin
			17 Ute	Great Basin
			2 Chemehueve (Southern Paiute)	Great Basin
		Hopi	82 Hopi	Southwest
	Central Uto-Aztecan		1641 Pima	Southwest
			840 Papago (Tohono O'odham)	Southwest
Athabascan	Southern		417 Apache	Southwest
			292 Navajo (Dene)	Southwest

*Samples were reported in Johnston et al. (1969), Schell and Blumberg (1988), and D. G. Smith et al. 1999).

these individuals (S. T. Brooks, Haldeman, and Brooks 1988) suggests that these individuals "can be regarded as a cohesive skeletal sample that is amenable to broadscale comparisons" (Kelly 1995b:38). Most of the bone fragments (between 4.1 and 11.5 g) had been stored at room temperature at the Nevada State Museum in Carson City for up to three years.

Because the data for most of the modern samples with which the albumin

Table 9.2.
Modern Native Americans Sampled for Mitochondrial Haplogroup Analyzed by Language Group and Geographic Region

Group	Subgroup	Sub-subgroup	Number Tribal Members Sampled*	Geographic Group
Penutian	California Penutian		5 Costanoan (Ohlone)	California
			1 Miwok	California
			1 Maidu	California
			1 Wintun	California
	Zuni		9 Yokuts	California
			20 Zuni	Southwest
Hokan	Northern Hokan		1 Karok	California
			1 Achumawi	California
			3 Pomo	California
	Yuman		5 Walapai	Southwest
			5 Havasupai	Southwest
			5 Yavapai	Southwest
			8 Paipai	Baja Cal.
			19 Quechan	Southwest
			3 Mojave	Southwest
			16 Kumia	Baja Cal.
			3 Cocopa	Baja Cal.
			3 Kiliwa	Baja Cal.
			13 Cochimi	Baja Cal.
	Washo		28 Washo	Great Basin
	Central Coast Hokan		2 Salinan	California
			9 Chumash	California
Uto-Aztecan	Northern Uto-Aztecan	Numic	98 N. Paiute/Shoshone	Great Basin
			1 Kawaiisu	Great Basin
			4 Tubatulabal	California
		Takic	4 Kitanemuk	not included
			1 Gabrielino	not included
			1 Luiseno	not included
			1 Fernandeno	not included
			1 Cahuilla	not included
		Hopi	4 Hopi	Southwest
	Central Uto-Aztecan		37 Pima	Southwest
Athabascan	Southern		29 Apache	Southwest
			56 Navajo (Dene)	Southwest

*Most of the samples were reported in Lorenz and Smith (1994); Pima samples were reported in T. G Schurr et al. (1990) and Torroni et al. (1992). To provide for comprehensive comparisons additional sample that were available were also analyzed and included in this table.

phenotypes of the 27 ancient samples from Stillwater Marsh were compared were gathered from the literature (Johnston et al. 1969; Lorenz and Smith 1994; Schell and Blumberg 1988; T. G. Schurr et al. 1990; D. G. Smith et al. 1999; D. G. Smith, Bettinger, and Rolfs 1995; Torroni et al. 1992, 1993a), it was impossible to sample the same tribes and individuals for the albumin phenotype analysis as were sampled for the mitochondrial haplogroup analysis. Additional samples from Northern Paiute, Shoshone, and Washo tribes were analyzed by F. Kaestle to increase the size of particularly important samples compared in this study. Most modern DNA samples were extracted from sera collected for various clinical studies, although some of the California and Baja samples were extracted from hair follicles and blood leukocytes, respectively. When available, genealogical records or interviews were used to eliminate samples that were not full-blooded members of the tribe they represent. The approximate geographic locations of the sampled tribes at the time of European contact are noted in Figure 9.1.

The modern samples were sorted into both language and geographic groups for estimating the frequencies of the mitochondrial haplogroups and albumin phenotypes. This was done because the correlation between shared language and common genetic ancestry is problematic (Campbell 1986; Ruvolo 1987; Lorenz and Smith 1994, 1996; Weiss and Woolford 1986). There is evidence that the language of one group is sometimes adopted *in toto* by another unrelated group (Ammerman and Cavalli-Sforza 1984; Fromkin and Rodman 1993; J. Nichols 1990) and that considerable gene flow has occurred among unrelated language groups in North America (Lorenz and Smith 1994, 1996). The language groups compared (see Tables 9.1 and 9.2) were those hypothesized by Greenberg (1987) and Campbell (1997) based on comparative linguistic analysis. The geographic groups are based on culture groups defined by Driver (1961), although some Takic-speaking groups located in southern California were excluded from the analysis because it is unclear in which group they should be included (see Tables 9.1 and 9.2). Moreover, including the Takic groups in any geographic group does not change the statistical inferences made. Unavoidably, boundaries between different geographic regions occasionally separated groups, such as the Cocopa of the lower Colorado River, from others with whom they share close cultural, economic, or genealogical ties. Similarly, as for the Apache and Navajo, groups that are known immigrants are sometimes included within a geographic region occupied solely by tribes to which they are unrelated (or only remotely related).

Deproteinization
The bone samples were pulverized to a powder consistency using a ceramic mortar and pestle, and the powder was deproteinized overnight while magnetically stirred in a 5 percent (weight/volume) Tris-buffered saline solution (TBS: .147 M NaCl, .01 M Tris), pH 7.4 (Gurtler et al. 1981), then centrifuged, and the

supernatant was removed and reserved. The bone residue was deproteinized a second time with a 20 percent (weight/volume) TBS solution, and the supernatants from both deproteinizing washes were combined, desalted, and concentrated to a volume of approximately .5 ml by reverse dialysis against PVP K30 at room temperature. Both the powdered bone residues and the concentrated supernatant were frozen at −20C.

Albumin Phenotype Identification

After thin layer polyacrylamide isoelectric focusing (IEF) (using pH 5–6 ampholytes), ancient protein separations were immobilized on a sheet of TBS-saturated (.45 micron) nitrocellulose paper (NCP) following the method of Kamboh and Ferrell (1986). The NCP was blocked for 1.5 hours with a 5 percent (weight/ volume) solution of nonfat dry milk in TBS, rinsed, then incubated successively with a .1 percent solution (in TBS) of goat antihuman serum albumin and a .02 percent solution (in TBS) of rabbit antigoat immunoglobulin conjugated with alkaline phosphatase. After a two- to four-hour rinse in TBS, the NCP was stained for alkaline phosphatase activity (Boyer 1961) to reveal the albumin bands. Modern samples were analyzed using electrophoretic procedures previously described (D. G. Smith et al. 1999).

DNA Extraction

Approximately .25 g of thawed bone residue was decalcified by incubation with slight agitation for 72 to 96 hours at 4°C in .5 M EDTA, pH 8.0; the EDTA solution was changed every 24 hours. One hundred μl of serum, or one to three hair follicles, or the decalcified bone residue were incubated overnight at 37°C with a proteinase K buffer (50 mM Tris pH 8.0, 1 mM CaCl$_2$, 1 mM DTT, .5 percent Tween 20, and 1 mg/ml proteinase K). Samples were successively extracted with phenol, phenol-chloroform (1:1), and chisam (chloroform:isoamyl alcohol 24:1). Modern samples were ethanol-precipitated and resuspended in autoclaved ddH$_2$O, whereas ancient samples were concentrated with Centricon® 100 microconcentrators to about 50 μl, washed twice with autoclaved, UV irradiated Tris-EDTA, pH 8.0 (TE), then reconcentrated to 50 μl. Contamination controls were as described in Kaestle (1995, 1998), and are comparable to those of O'Rourke, Parr, and Carlyle (this volume). Because results must be confirmed by testing at least two successful extracts from each sample, multiple extracts were performed from total samples of three to five grams of bone material.

PCR Amplification

The fragments of the mtDNA containing the sites defining the mitochondrial haplogroups were amplified using the polymerase chain reaction (PCR) (for primer coordinates see Handt et al. 1996; Parr, Carlyle, and O'Rourke 1996). Re-

TABLE 9.3.

Distribution of the Mitochondrial Haplogroups and Albumin Phenotypes among Modern and Ancient Native Americans

Super-Group	Group	Subgroup	DNA No.*	Freq. A	Freq. B	Freq. C	Freq. D	Albumin No.*	# A/Na Hetero.	Freq. A/Na Heterozyg.	#A/Me Hetero.	Freq. A/Me Heterozyg.
Penutian	California Penutian		17	0.118	0.412	0.059	0.412	4	0	0	0	0
	Zuni		20	0.2	0.7	0.1	0	655	0	0	16	0.024
Hokan	Northern Hokan		5	0	0.4	0.2	0.4	8	0	—	0	—
	Yuman		80	0.038	0.625	0.338	0	931	2	0.002	47	0.05
	Washo		28	0	0.536	0.357	0.107	133	0	0	0	0
	Central Coast Hokan		11	0.455	0.182	0.091	0.273	—	—	—	—	—
Uro-Aztecan	Northern		116	0	0.422	0.147	0.431	251	1	0.004	2	0.008
		Numic	103	0	0.417	0.117	0.466	169	0	0	2	0.012
		Hopi	4	0	1	0	0	82	1	0.012	0	0
		Takic	9	0	0.222	0.556	0.222	—	—	—	—	—
	Central		37	0.054	0.568	0.378	0.378	2481	0	0	135	0.054
Athabascan	Southern		85	0.565	0.341	0.071	0.024	709	34	0.048	38	0.054
Ancient	Stillwater		19	0.053	0.368	0	0.579	27	0	0	4	0.148
	Fremont		30	0	0.833	0.1	0.067	—	—	—	—	—
Geog. Groups	California		37	0.189	0.351	0.108	0.351	12	0	—	0	—
	Baja		43	0.023	0.674	0.302	0	223	0	0	16	0.072
	Great Basin		127	0	0.441	0.165	0.394	302	0	0	2	0.007
	Southwest		98	0.082	0.612	0.306	0	4635	37	0.008	220	0.047

* No. = Number of individuals sampled

TABLE 9.4.

Statistical Test for Homogeneity of Albumin Mexico Frequencies between
Members of Modern Groups and 27 Individuals from Stillwater Marsh

Group	No.	Chi-Square w/ CC*	df	p w/ CC	Fisher's exact p
Northern Hokan	8	0.27474	1	0.6	0.553
Cal. Penutian	4	0.00066	1	0.98	1
Zuni	655	9.93631	1	0.002	0.006
Yuman	931	3.21698	1	0.073	0.069
Washo	133	14.58804	1	0.000	0.000
Numic	169	10.34578	1	0.001	0.004
Hopi	82	8.76828	1	0.003	0.003
All Northern Uto-Az	251	16.53413	1	0.000	0.000
Central Uto-Aztec	2481	2.87097	1	0.09	0.059
Southern Athabascan	709	2.74277	1	0.098	0.062
California	12	0.69836	1	0.403	0.292
Baja	223	1.01299	1	0.314	0.247
Great Basin	302	20.38464	1	0.000	0.000
Southwest	4635	3.95166	1	0.047	0.038

*CC = correction for continuity

actions were performed in 25 μl volumes with 3 μl of DNA extract. Bovine serum albumin (BSA), in a final concentration of 1 mg/ml, was added to all ancient DNA sample reactions. Reactions were subjected to 45 cycles of 45 seconds at 94°C, 45 seconds at 45–59°C, and 45 seconds at 72°C, with an initial denaturing of four minutes at 94°C and a terminal extension of three minutes at 72°C. The equivalent of a hot start was achieved using Platinum Taq (Gibco BRL). Five to 10 μl of the amplification product containing the restriction site gains that characterize haplogroups A and C and the restriction site loss that characterizes haplogroup D were digested overnight at 37°C with HaeIII or AluI according to manufacturers' recommendations. Restriction fragments and the presence/absence of the 9 bp (base pair) deletion defining haplogroup B were resolved on 6 percent polyacrylamide gels, stained with ethidium bromide and visualized, then photographed on a UV transilluminator using an IS2000 imaging system (Alpha Innotech). Contamination controls were as described in Kaestle (1995, 1998) and are comparable to those of O'Rourke, Parr, and Carlyle (this volume). It became apparent that some of the Stillwater bone residues had become contaminated with one of the authors' DNA (DGS) while the albumin extraction procedures were performed. Our earlier failure to recognize this is responsible for the difference between the frequency of haplogroup B in the Stillwater population reported in this study and that previ-

TABLE 9.5.
Statistical Test for Homogeneity of Mitochondrial Haplogroup Frequencies
between Members of Modern Groups and 19 Ancient Individuals
from Stillwater Marsh

Group	No.	Chi-Square	df	p
Northern Hokan	5	4.308	3	0.23
Cal. Penutian	17	2.118	3	0.548
Zuni	19	17.119	3	0.001
Yuman	80	54.571	3	0.000
Washo	28	17.395	3	0.001
Central Coast Hokan	11	9.563	3	0.023
Numic	103	8.152	3	0.043
Takic	9	13.109	3	0.004
Hopi	4	5.282	2	0.071
All Northern Uto-Az	116	9.795	3	0.020
Central Uto-Aztec	37	29.606	3	0.000
Southern Athabascan	85	48.341	3	0.000
Fremont	30	18.836	3	0.000
California	37	5.2203	3	0.156
Baja Cal.	43	33.116	3	0.000
Great Basin	127	11.385	3	0.009
Southwest	98	64.379	3	0.000

ously reported by Kaestle (1995). However, because none of the authors belongs to haplogroups A, B, C, or D, it was still possible to resolve the haplogroup status of the contaminated Stillwater remains.

Statistical Analysis

Chi-square values, corrected for continuity (Siegel 1956), were calculated to assess the probability that the observed frequencies of Al^{Me}, Al^{Na}, and the mitochondrial haplogroups in the ancient Stillwater samples differ from those representing each of several specific modern language or geographic groups (see Tables 9.4 and 9.5). For this purpose, the distributions of the numbers of ancient samples with each of the mitochondrial haplogroups and with and without Al^{Me} (or Al^{Na}) were compared with those in the modern samples. In cases of extremely small numbers of albumin samples, Fisher's exact probability was also calculated using the SPSS® 6.1 software (Norusis 1995; SPSS, Inc. 1995). Although the two tests provided numerically different p values, in no case did they yield contradictory statistical inferences. Unless noted, in all cases alpha levels for statistical rejection were set at the .025 level of probability (p < .025). This probability level was chosen to minimize errors in inference resulting from sampling error and the uncertainty regarding the effect of prehistoric evolutionary forces, such as genetic drift, on gene frequencies which might, in some cases, be substantial due to the small size of demes.

RESULTS

The frequencies of heterozygous albumin phenotypes and the mitochondrial haplogroups in modern geographic and language groups are given in Table 9.3. Frequencies of albumin phenotypes rather than alleles are provided, so the data are concordant with those for the mitochondrial haplogroups. Al^{Me} is absent in California, most common in Baja California, and of intermediate frequency in the Southwest. Although present in the Great Basin, the frequency of Al^{Me} there is low, and was not found among the Northern Paiute, who now occupy the Stillwater Marsh region (D. G. Smith et al. 1999). Al^{Me} is present in at least one of the groups representing each of the four language groups sampled, with the highest frequencies occurring in Central Uto-Aztecans, Southern Athabascans, and Yumans. The marker is either absent or low in frequency (< 1 percent), and its presence probably results from admixture in all other groups except Zuni. Al^{Na} was absent in all modern Native American groups (*sensu* Greenberg 1987) that were sampled except the Hopi and two different Yuman groups (the Mohave and the Maricopa) in each of which only a single heterozygote has been reported. Since Al^{Na} is found in almost all Northern and Southern Athabascan groups in which it has been studied, and is almost completely absent elsewhere, its presence in the Hopi and Yuman groups probably results from admixture with nearby Southern Athabascan groups (Navajo, Apache).

The frequencies of the four mitochondrial haplogroups vary significantly among modern groups, but small samples sizes in some cases (e.g., Hopi, Northern Hokan) might have biased these results. The Northern Hokan, Washo, and Northern Uto-Aztecan language groups and the Great Basin geographic group lack haplogroup A, which, of the groups compared in the present study, is found at its highest frequency (0.565) in the Southern Athabascan speakers. Haplogroup B is found in all modern groups, but its frequency is especially high in the Southwest and Baja geographic groups and among the language groups spoken in those regions (e.g., Zuni, Yuman, Central Uto-Aztecan). Haplogroup C is present in all modern groups with reasonable sample sizes and varies in frequency between 0.06 in the California Penutian and 0.56 in the Takic language groups. Haplogroup D is absent in the Southwest and Baja geographic groups and among the language groups spoken in those regions. It is found at its highest frequency among the California Penutian and Northern Uto-Aztecan speakers.

The albumin phenotypes were resolvable in all of the 27 ancient samples, and mitochondrial haplogroup fragments amplified reliably in 19. Twenty-three of the

27 samples were monomorphic for Al^A, while 4 were heterozygous Al^A/Al^{Me} for a total heterozygote frequency of .148 for Al^{Me}. Al^{Na} was not present among the 27 Stillwater individuals. Of the 19 samples that amplified reliably, 1 possessed the marker for haplogroup A (for a frequency of 0.053), 7 possessed the marker for haplogroup B (0.368), none possessed the marker for haplogroup C (0), and 11 possessed the marker for haplogroup D (0.579).

DISCUSSION AND CONCLUSIONS

Among the ancient Stillwater samples, the frequencies of Al^{Me} and haplogroup D are very high and both Al^{Na} and haplogroup C are absent. It seems unlikely that the Stillwater population is ancestral to any modern language or geographic group in which Al^{Me} or haplogroup D is absent or where Al^{Na} or haplogroup C is common. The assumption that major changes in the distribution of the frequency of mitochondrial haplogroups have not occurred recently (e.g., were not caused by European contact) has been supported by Stone and Stoneking's study (1993) of the Norris Farms archaeological population from Illinois. Specifically, the frequencies of the mitochondrial haplogroups in this 700-year-old skeletal population were not statistically significantly different from those of modern populations in that area, but *were* different from most *other* modern populations (see Kaestle 1995). The ancient Fremont population exhibits frequencies of the mitochondrial haplogroups that are typical of the modern inhabitants of the Southwestern United States (O'Rourke, Parr, and Carlyle, this volume) and very atypical of populations living outside the region. However, it is possible that the frequencies of the mitochondrial haplogroups (and Al^{Me} and Al^{Na}) were less stable in some geographic regions and time periods than in others.

Because Al^{Na} has been found in most Athabascan- (both Northern and Southern) and Algonkian-speaking groups that have been studied, it seems unlikely that the ancient Stillwater population is ancestral to either group. Although populations ancestral to Southern Athabascans probably had very low frequencies of Al^{Me}, like the ancient Stillwater population, they should also exhibit Al^{Na}, which the ancient Stillwater population lacks. Unless sampling error or stochastic evolutionary changes have profoundly influenced the results of this study, the Zuni, Washo, and all Northern (but not Central) Uto-Aztecan language groups, including Numics, and the Great Basin geographic group can also be eliminated from consideration as probable descendants; the frequency of Al^{Me} in these groups is statistically significantly lower than in the ancient Stillwater population. The modern Native American groups with the highest frequencies of Al^{Me} and, therefore, those most similar in this regard to the ancient Stillwater population, are the delta and river Yumans (e.g., Cocopa, Mohave, Maricopa, and Quechan) and the Central Uto-Aztecans (Pima and Papago). No samples were available to determine albumin phenotypes in the Central Coast Hokan and Takic language groups or in the Fremont ancient population, and the sizes of our samples from California Penutian and Northern Hokan language groups and the California geographic groups were very small. If Al^{Me} were not discovered in larger samples of these groups, they too would be eliminated as likely descendants of the ancient Stillwater population.

The Zuni, Yuman, Washo, Takic, Northern Uto-Aztecan, Central Uto-Aztecan, and Southern Athabascan language groups and all of the geographic groups except California can be eliminated from consideration as probable descendants; the frequencies of the mitochondrial haplogroups in these groups are statistically significantly different ($p < 0.025$) from that of the ancient Stillwater population. Of interest is that the frequency distribution of the mitochondrial haplogroups in the other nearby ancient population, the Fremont (Parr, Carlyle, and O'Rourke 1996; O'Rourke, Parr, and Carlyle, this volume), is statistically significantly different from that of the Stillwater population. Groups eliminated by the frequencies of both the mitochondrial haplogroups and Al^{Me} are the Zuni, Washo, and Northern Uto-Aztecan speakers and the Great Basin geographic group. Of the groups tested for both Al^{Me} and the mitochondrial haplogroups, all groups are rejected at the .025 level of probability as descendants of the ancient Stillwater group by one or both tests. The Northern Hokan and California Penutian language groups and the California geographic group were not eliminated as descendants of the ancient Stillwater group based on the distribution of their mitochondrial haplogroups, but they have not been tested for Al^{Me}.

Consideration of the frequencies of Al^{Me} and the mitochondrial haplogroups leads to at least one of four alternative conclusions. First, the Stillwater skeletal population might be ancestral to the historical Numic-speaking people of the western Great Basin, the latter now inhabiting territory previously occupied by the former. This contradicts the hypothesis that the Numic-speaking people are relatively recent colonizers of the Great Basin (Adovasio and Pedler 1994; Bettinger and Baumhoff 1982; Janetski 1994; D. B. Madsen 1994; Reed 1994; Young and Bettinger 1992). According to this first hypothesis, the changes that have been interpreted as a Numic expansion might not have resulted from the replacement of any indigenous population at all (see Goss 1977; W. R. Miller 1986; Swanson 1962). However, both the Great Basin geographic group and the Northern Uto-Aztecan language group are eliminated as likely descendants of the ancient Stillwater group by both the Al^{Me} and the mitochondrial haplogroup frequencies (see Tables 9.4 and 9.5). Therefore, this hypothesis requires that haplogroup A and Al^{Me} were lost and that haplogroup C increased significantly in frequency among the inhabitants of the Great Basin over the last two millennia. We regard this as the least likely of the four hypotheses.

A second alternative is that the ancient Stillwater population might be unmixed Yuman, with whom they share high frequencies of both Al^{Me} and haplogroup B. This scenario requires that the frequencies of mitochondrial haplogroups in the descendants of the ancient Stillwater peoples have changed significantly (i.e., C has been gained, while D has been lost). This hypothesis presupposes that lineage attrition (whose effects are far more severe on mitochondrial DNA than on nuclear DNA [Harrison 1989; Wilson et al. 1985]) rather than a founder (or even bottleneck) effect (Wallace, Garrison, and Knowler 1985) is responsible for the paucity of mitochondrial DNA haplogroups (of Asian descent) in modern Native Americans. The discovery of high frequencies of mtDNA haplogroups in some ancient samples that are not members of one of the four haplogroups most common in most living populations of Native Americans (Easton et al. 1996) would be consistent with this hypothesis. However, preliminary studies suggest that haplogroups other than the four common ones in modern groups were rare in ancient populations in the western Great Basin (Kaestle 1997). Moreover, the lack of haplogroup D is so uniformly characteristic of modern Yuman tribes (far more characteristic than is the presence of Al^{Me} in Uto-Aztecan tribes) that it seems unlikely an ancestral proto-Yuman population exhibited a frequency of haplogroup D as high as that in the ancient Stillwater population. Therefore, we regard the second alternative hypothesis as relatively unlikely.

Third, it is possible that speakers of Northern Hokan and/or California Penutian languages, or members of the California geographic group in general, are descended from the ancient Stillwater population since these modern groups share similar frequencies of mitochondrial haplogroups with the Stillwater samples and cannot be rejected statistically as possible descendants (see Table 9.5). It is significant that historical narratives of the Northern Paiute, who currently inhabit the Stillwater area, identify the Achumawi/Atsugewi, members of the Northern Hokan language group, as the descendants of the pre-Numic inhabitants of the Great Basin (Heizer 1970; O. C. Stewart 1939). Sample sizes of albumin phenotypes in these groups were extremely small (see Table 9.4), making it difficult to assess this hypothesis using albumin phenotype frequencies. However, efforts are underway to increase the sample size for California groups so that Al^{Me}, if present, can be identified.

A fourth possibility is that the direct descendants of the Stillwater population are extinct, in which case the ancient group's resemblance to any modern group of Native Americans would be due to chance. If this explanation for the outcome of this study is correct, it should be possible to demonstrate that the frequencies of other genetic markers in modern Native American groups not rejected in this study differ from those of the ancient Stillwater population.

A related alternative is that modern Numic people are a hybrid population and their phenotype frequencies reflect admixture between pre-Numic inhabitants, like those at Stillwater, who left no unmixed living descendants, and Uto-Aztecan (proto-Numic) invaders. Because the gene coding for albumin is a nuclear gene, it is inherited from both parents and thus traces the biological ancestry of both males and females. However, mtDNA is maternally inherited and therefore represents only the history of the female line. For example, Merriwether, Roth-hammer, and Ferrell (1995) report that the tendency for Hispanic males to mate with American Indian females (but rarely the converse) in certain regions resulted in a contribution of American Indian mtDNA to Hispanic mtDNA that was nearly twice what it was to Hispanic nuclear DNA. If a population replacement took place in the Great Basin during which the females of the pre-Numic group were assimilated into the Numic groups, but the males were not, the mtDNA of the pre-Numic group would comprise a greater component of the modern Numic population than would the nuclear DNA of the pre-Numic group (Harrison 1989; Moritz, Dowling, and Brown 1987). This is not an unreasonable scenario, given Bettinger and Baumhoff's hypothesized difference (1982) in subsistence strategies between the pre-Numic and Numic inhabitants of the Great Basin, in which the pre-Numic inhabitants utilized a low-cost, male-biased 'traveler' strategy, while the Numic immigrants utilized a high-cost, female-biased 'processor' strategy in which females may have been more valued members of the group. If the invading Numics had relatively high frequencies of haplogroups B and C, but lacked hap-logroups A and D and had a low frequency of Al^{Me}, like the modern Papago tribe (authors' unpublished data), and the pre-Numic group had relatively high fre-quencies of haplogroups B and D and Al^{Me}, but low frequencies of haplogroups A and C, like the ancient Stillwater population, admixture between Numic males and females and pre-Numic females might have produced the pattern seen today among modern Numic peoples.

The third hypothesis, or possibly a version of the third hypothesis allowing for some admixture between Numic and pre-Numic peoples, is more parsimo-nious with the existing evidence than are the other hypotheses. However, in the absence of a clear, most likely descendant of the ancient Stillwater population, none of the four hypotheses outlined above can be discounted. The collection of albumin phenotypes and other highly polymorphic genetic markers, such as those at microsatellite DNA (SSR) loci (Morin and Smith 1995) from other modern Na-tive American groups, should provide an assessment of the Northern Hokan and the California Penutian as possible descendants of the ancient Stillwater popula-tion. In addition, analysis of the four common mitochondrial haplogroups of Na-tive Americans (and detection of others that might since have become extinct) in skeletal samples from other archaeological sites in western Nevada and analysis of sequence data from a hypervariable region of the mitochondrial DNA, which is now underway (Kaestle 1997; Kaestle and Smith, n.d.), should provide a more conclusive inference.

Acknowledgments

This study was supported by NSF predoctoral grant GER9255683 and by grants RR00169 and RR05090 from the NIH. We are indebted to Ms. Amy Dansie, Dr. John Johnson, and numerous personnel (cited in Lorenz and Smith 1994, 1996) for providing specimens for analysis and to Drs. Robert Bettinger and Victor Golla for their advice on the archaeological and comparative linguistic perspectives on the demographic history of the Great Basin and surrounding areas. The cooperation of the Fallon Paiute-Shoshone Tribe was also greatly appreciated.

10

Osteopathology of Carson Desert Foragers

Reconstructing Prehistoric Lifeways in the Western Great Basin

Clark Spencer Larsen and Dale L. Hutchinson

Since the founding of anthropology, a great deal of attention has been focused on hunter-gatherers. Much of this attention has been devoted to characterizing the adaptive "efficiency" or "affluence" of human populations whose sole means of acquiring sustenance is by foraging (Kelly 1995a). The Hobbesian portrayal of hunter-gatherer existence as "nasty, brutish, and short" has dominated popular and scholarly perceptions of foraging societies, with regard to both past and living groups. This perspective is perhaps best captured in Braidwood's statement that prior to the domestication of plants and animals "most men must have spent their waking moments seeking their next meal, except when they could gorge following a great kill" (1960:10). In the 1960s, this perspective took an about face in response to a growing body of data suggesting that past hunter-gatherers may have been well off in a variety of settings. Especially following the now-famous "Man the Hunter" conference in 1966 (Lee and DeVore 1968), the view was held by many that far from being downtrodden and deprived, foragers enjoyed negligible work loads, their food supply was plentiful and nutritious, and leisure was rife (Sahlins 1972).

Over the course of the last couple of decades, a diverse and rich body of data has been generated by anthropologists of all manner, including archaeologists, testing hypotheses relating to adaptation in living and past foragers. Based on a series of ecologically oriented field projects, the picture that has emerged in recent years is one of a high degree of variability in foraging groups. Far from presenting a picture of uniformity, these studies have shown that by virtually any measure—food selection, food preference, nutritional quality, work load, mobility, and so forth—foraging populations do not seem to fit any single pattern.

Importantly, we have also learned that the investigation of patterns in the context of well-defined regional studies helps us to understand the circumstances surrounding early and present-day foragers. Owing to the availability of a rich archaeological record, coupled with ethnographic and historical documentation, the American Great Basin has revealed key aspects of foraging behavior and adaptation in highly challenging circumstances (Bettinger 1989; Heizer and Krieger 1956; Jennings 1957; Simms 1987; Thomas 1988; Zeier and Elston 1992).

Bioarchaeology—the study of the human skeletal record in archaeological context—has provided an essential component to the study of adaptive processes and biological history in a wide variety of settings (Cohen and Armelagos 1984; Grauer 1995; Huss-Ashmore, Goodman, and Armelagos 1982; Iscan and Kennedy 1989; Larsen 1997; Larsen and Milner 1994; Saunders and Katzenberg 1992). Skeletal and dental tissues are remarkably sensitive to the environment, including dietary practices, subsistence technology, nutritional quality, chronic disease, physical activity, and life-style in general, thus serving as a retrospective "memory" of an individual's biological history.

Until the recent recovery and study of human remains from flooded wetlands in the mid- to late-1980s, the human biological record for much of the Great Basin was virtually nonexistent. Except for isolated skeletons and parts of skeletons from caves, rock crevices, shelters, and other contexts collected since the late nineteenth century (e.g., Larsen 1985a, 1985b; summarized in Kobori 1981; Pendleton, McLane, and Thomas 1982), the Carson Desert and its environs were devoid of a meaningful osteological sample from which to base biological interpretations of earlier populations. With the sudden availability of a significant sample of human remains following the retreat of floodwaters in the Stillwater Marsh, a picture of human adaptation of this setting based on the study of hundreds of bones and teeth has emerged (S. T. Brooks, Haldeman, and Brooks 1988; Larsen and Kelly 1995). In this chapter, we draw upon the archaeological skeletal and dental record from the Carson Desert in order to characterize health and life-style. By doing so, we provide an independent means of understanding behavioral patterns and land use in this area of the west-central Great Basin. Our purpose is twofold: First, we examine work load and activity based on the study of osteoarthritis. These findings will then be used to assess currently competing hypotheses of pre-Euroamerican use of wetlands resources. Second, we assess quality of life and physiological stress via study of growth arrest in teeth, infection experience in skeletal tissues, and cranial pathology reflecting iron status.

THE CULTURAL AND ECOLOGICAL SETTING

The native peoples of the Carson Desert observed by ethnographers and others in the nineteenth and twentieth centuries were a Northern Paiute group locally known as the Toedökadö or "Cattail-Eaters." The Toedökadö utilized a wide range of resources acquired by hunting and collecting activities. Ethnographic and archaeological data indicate that the Stillwater Marsh—the dominant feature of the

Carson Desert encompassing some 375 km^2 of the region—may have served as a "hub" of settlement systems for the last five millennia (Kelly 1995a, this volume). During some periods, human settlement was likely more tightly linked with the marsh than at other times because of the relative abundance of important plant and animal resources (C. S. Fowler 1989, 1990a, 1992; Kelly 1995a; Wheat 1967). Some 160 species of water birds, including mallards (*Anas platyrhynchos*), cinnamon teal (*Anas cyanoptera*), and coots (*Fulica americana*), were hunted with nets and decoys. Fishing focused on several species, including tui chub (*Gila bicolor obesus*). The marshes contain a number of economically important plants, such as bulrush (*Scirpus* sp.) and cattail (*Typha* sp.), which provided essential nutrients from their seeds and roots. Away from the marsh, the Carson Desert is exceedingly dry with relatively fewer plants and animals. However, areas near the wetlands likely had grassy meadows supplying various economically important plants, such as Indian grass (*Oryzopsis hymenoides*) and wild rye (*Elymus* sp.). The relative abundance of these resources fluctuated both seasonally and annually depending on water availability. Because of the orographic effect of the Sierra Nevadas located 100 km to the west, very little precipitation in the form of rain or snow falls on the Carson Desert. Therefore, most water is derived from the Carson and Humboldt Rivers fed by snowmelt during the spring and summer months. Due to variable water availability, the wetlands have fluctuated in size and productivity during the past.

In contrast to the wetlands and valley floors, the surrounding uplands, such as the Stillwater Mountains bordering the Carson Desert to the east, have an extremely rugged topography. The uplands provided important resources to native populations, such as ricegrass and wild rye. Ethnographic and archaeological data point to the importance of seeds from piñon pine (*Pinus monophylla*) in a number of regions of the Great Basin (see Bettinger 1989; Kelly, 1995a; Thomas 1988). These highly nutritious seeds, high in fat, carbohyrates, and protein, were gathered on a seasonal basis and could be stored for use over the year. However, piñon may have been only recently introduced to the Stillwater Mountains and, therefore, may not have been consumed to an appreciable degree in this region (Kelly 1995a; also see Schoeninger, this volume). Game animals, including bighorn sheep (*Ovis canadensis nelsoni*) in the upper elevations and antelope (*Antilocapra americana*) in the lower elevations, as well as a variety of small mammals (e.g., rodents) were hunted and trapped.

Although the marshes at times provided important resources, ethnographic and historical information indicates that movement of residences and long forays to other regions were commonplace in the late nineteenth century (Kelly 1995a). This information suggests that the native populations of this area led highly demanding, active lifeways. The aforementioned roster of plant and animal foods obtained from various ecological settings—marshes, surrounding lowlands, and upland areas—would indicate an adequate diet, but this general adequacy may have been punctuated by periods of shortages related in large part to decreased water availability (Larsen 1995). The skeletal and dental data based on the study of human remains from the Stillwater Marsh will be used in this paper to address the adequacy of diet and health status generally.

THE CARSON DESERT SKELETAL SAMPLE

The archaeological survey and testing of the Carson Desert in the region of the Stillwater Marsh revealed a distribution of human remains across a 16 km^2 landscape (S. T. Brooks, Haldeman, and Brooks 1988; Larsen and Kelly 1995; Tuohy, Dansie, and Haldeman 1987). Field collection of a larger initial sample by Tuohy and coworkers and a smaller sample by Kelly and Larsen resulted in the availability for study of 400 or more individuals of varying completeness (S. T. Brooks, Haldeman, and Brooks 1988; Larsen and Kelly 1995). Of these remains, about 50 or so juvenile and adult skeletons from this region are complete or nearly so. The Stillwater Marsh remains are not from formal disposal areas archaeologists would identify as cemeteries. Rather, they are mostly from isolated graves dispersed throughout the wetland area. Some burial sites appeared to have contained more individuals than others. For example, S. T. Brooks and coworkers (1988) list 58 individuals from a single site (26CH1043).

Like the Malheur and Salt Lake wetlands, the temporal use of this region for burial of deceased is imprecisely understood. Only a handful of Stillwater Marsh skeletons (n = 6) have been radiometrically dated, and these dates span a 2,000-year period (corrected radiocarbon years of 270 B.C. to A.D. 1644; see S. T. Brooks and Brooks 1990; Larsen and Kelly 1995). Few graves contained associated temporally diagnostic artifacts (e.g., projectile points), but other classes of archaeological evidence (e.g., middens) and projectile points indicate most intensive use during the Reveille phase (1300 B.C.–A.D. 700) and the following Underdown phase (A.D. 700–1300) (Kelly 1995a; Raymond and Parks 1990). Occupation of the region was apparently less intensive during the last prehistoric period, the Yankee Blade phase (A.D. 1300–1850).

In summary, the prehistoric utilization of the region is temporally expansive, but primarily focused on a 2,600-year period. Because the human remains are from sites encompassing hundreds or even thousands of years of occupation, these remains should not be considered a population of necessarily related individuals but rather a collection that may or may not represent a biological succession of human groups. Preliminary assessment of skeletal measurements and discrete traits by S. T. Brooks and co-workers (1988) suggests homogeneity in the series. And, such homogeneity suggests that the Stillwater series may be treated as a cohesive unit amenable to statistical analysis and comparison with other assemblages. Therefore, despite the wide temporal dispersion, the series is treated as a single unit of study in order to draw inferences about life-style and health. The lack of adequate temporal control prohibits, however, delineation of patterns of diachronic variation.

METHODS OF STUDY

Osteoarthritis

Osteoarthritis is a disorder involving degenerative changes along the margins and surfaces of articular joints, including proliferative lipping along joint margins, porosity, and polishing (eburnation) of joint surfaces due to direct bone-on-bone contact subsequent to cartilage destruction. A number of predisposing factors are included in its etiology, such as nutrition, age, sex, heredity, and endocrine status (McCarty and Koopman 1993). However, cumulative mechanical factors—the physical wear and tear on the joints over the course of an individual's lifetime—figure most prominently in its explanation (Hough and Sokoloff 1989). The linkage between physical demands and osteoarthritis are well illustrated in the higher prevalences observed in human populations engaged in high or excessive levels of activity or in occupations placing mechanical loads on specific joints or on the body generally (K. A. R. Kennedy 1989; Larsen 1997). For the present investigation, lipping and erosional changes (porosity, eburnation) were observed on all major weight-bearing and nonweight-bearing adult joints, including intervertebral (cervical, thoracic, lumbar, sacral), shoulder, elbow, wrist, hand, hip, knee, ankle, and foot (Figure 10.1). The skeletal manifestations of the disorder in intervertebral (disk) joints are not arthritic per se because, unlike the other joints discussed in this chapter, they are not diarthroidial joints. However, given the similarity in degenerative pathology seen in vertebral bodies, we have included them in the study of osteoarthritis prevalence in the Stillwater skeletal series.

Enamel Defects

Defects in the tooth enamel—the outer covering of the crown—arise from physiological perturbations occurring either during the production of enamel matrix or during its mineralization (approximately five months in utero to 12 years). Disturbances during enamel matrix deposition result in the most common defect in human populations, hypoplasia. Enamel mineralization disruption results in hypocalcification. Hypoplasias are quantitative defects involving deficiencies in the amount or thickness of enamel, varying in appearance from small pits or furrows to large, deep grooves, or missing enamel (Goodman and Rose 1990; Suckling 1989). Typically, these defects are horizontal grooves called linear enamel hypoplasias. Hypocalcifications are enamel defects involving color or texture differences.

Hypoplasias are nonspecific indicators of physiological perturbation since numerous causes have been linked with them in epidemiologic, clinical, and ex-

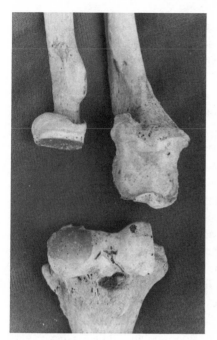

FIGURE 10.1. Pathology associated with osteoarthritis. *Left:* marginal lipping in components of elbow joint (humerus, radius, ulna) and eburnation on humerus capitulum (site 26CH1047, no. 13). *Right:* marginal lipping on two lumbar vertebral bodies (site 26CH1050, no. 3).

perimental investigations. In this regard, associations with systemic diseases, neonatal disturbances, and nutritional deficiencies have been documented (Hillson 1986; Pindborg 1982). Hypoplasias arise at some point during the process of growth and development of the tooth crown commencing at the incisal/occlusal surface and terminating at the base of the crown. Some investigators have suggested, therefore, that given the well-known age along each stage of development for each tooth type, the chronology of stress can be accurately depicted in human populations (e.g., Goodman and Armelagos 1985b; Swärdstedt 1966). Moreover, some investigators have suggested that the widths of hypoplasias measured from the superior to inferior margins represent a quantification of duration (e.g., Blakey and Armelagos 1985; Hutchinson and Larsen 1988, 1990) or severity (Suckling, Elliot, and Thurley 1986) of stress events. Thus, hypoplasia widths may reflect either duration or severity or, perhaps, both.

For the present investigation, we report on hypoplasia data collected from permanent incisors and canines, the teeth that best represent enamel defect prevalence in humans (Goodman and Rose 1990). Hypoplasias were identified on the labial surfaces of teeth with the use of a dissecting binocular microscope at low power magnification (10x). The hypoplasia was identified and recorded on a data processing sheet showing the position of the defect and its approximate age of oc-currence. Defect age was based on dental development standards (Massler, Schour, and Poncher 1941) adapted for use in bioarchaeological research by Swärdstedt (1966) and Goodman and Rose (1990). The superior and inferior margins of hy-poplastic events were measured relative to the cementoenamel junction at the crown base along the midsagittal plane of each tooth. Measurement was accom-plished with a fixed 0.1 mm measurement reticle mounted into the eyepiece of the microscope. Our experience suggests that this procedure is a more reliable means of location and measurement of hypoplasia width than use of sliding calipers (Hutchinson and Larsen 1988, 1990). Other researchers have reported a low mea-surement error and high replicability of hypoplasia width determined in this man-ner (Danforth, Herndon, and Propst 1993). In addition to prevalence, two vari-ables are reported, including hypoplasia "area" and hypoplasia "event." "Area" represents the sum total of hypoplastic enamel widths within half-year intervals. For example, if two bands of hypoplastic enamel are recorded within a half-year period, the widths of the two bands are summed. "Event" refers to the measure-ment of width of continuous hypoplastic enamel regardless of age. Teeth from the left side were examined. If the tooth was missing, the antimere was substituted if available. Because of the apparent differential susceptibility of tooth types—ante-rior teeth are more affected than posterior teeth (Goodman and Armelagos 1985b)—data are reported by tooth type.

Periosteal Reactions

Commonly observed skeletal lesions involving the outer surface of cortical bone—the subperiosteum—are periosteal reactions (or periostitis). Typically, this is a mild form of nonspecific inflammatory response to skin infection, systemic bacterial invasion, other soft tissue infections (e.g., affecting a muscle), or trauma (Ortner and Putschar 1985). Lesions are typically osseous plaques or irregular ele-vations of bone surfaces. The documentation of prevalence in archaeological samples has provided an important index of community health, especially in tracking temporal changes in response to major shifts in subsistence economy (e.g., Goodman et al. 1984; Lambert 1993). In general, these studies show a positive correlation with population density. Population aggregation appears to promote periosteal reactions due to heightened interpersonal contact, poor sanitation, and related factors promoting infection and disease.

The tibia is the most commonly affected bone in archaeological series (Larsen and Harn 1994; Powell 1988; Webb 1995; and many others). Specific reasons for the penchant for the lower leg are unclear, but the tibia has the largest and most vascu-larly and physiologically inactive periosteal surface, thus possibly lending itself to bacterial colonization, which may also be exacerbated by the slow circulatory flow in the lower legs (Cotran, Kumar, and Robbins 1994; D. L. Martin et al. 1991;

Steinbock 1976). For this study, we report on prevalence of Stillwater tibiae with periosteal reactions.

Porotic Hyperostosis

Skeletal changes associated with iron deficiency anemia are part of a generalized syndrome called "porotic hyperostosis," represented as an expansion (hyperostosis) of the cranial diploë and thinning of ectocranial (and sometimes endocranial) cortical bone. Due to this expansion and cortical thinning, the bone surface shows numerous small, sievelike perforations across the major flat bones, especially the parietals and occipital squamous. The syndrome also includes similar changes in the roof areas of the eye orbits, called "cribra orbitalia." Due to their common etiology, we include vault and orbital lesions under porotic hyperostosis. These pathological changes have been definitively linked with iron deficiency anemia; the skeletal modifications result from the hypertrophy of the blood-forming tissues in order to increase the output of red blood cells in response to the anemia. Other factors have been linked with this pathological condition, including scurvy, rickets, and infection (e.g., Schultz, 1993).

In archaeological skeletons, porotic hyperostosis has been found in all ages and both sexes. However, the preponderance of cases—especially in active forms—are in young juveniles, indicating that the condition represents childhood anemia (Stuart-Macadam 1985). Factors leading to iron deficiency anemia in past populations are variable and include iron-poor diets, parasitism, infantile diarrhea, infection, poor living conditions, or a combination of these circumstances that might influence iron status in the growing child (D. S. Carlson, Armelagos, and Van Gerven 1974; Kent 1986; D. L. Martin et al. 1991; D. M. Mittler and Van Gerven 1994; Ubelaker 1992b; Webb 1995).

CHARACTERIZING BEHAVIOR AND HEALTH IN THE CARSON DESERT

Osteoarthritis

The majority of Stillwater adults were affected to one degree or another by osteoarthritis (77 percent), including all individuals greater than 30 years of age. Adult males tended to be affected more often than adult females (79 percent vs. 72 percent). Distribution of osteoarthritis in the skeleton indicated a tendency for low prevalence in the hand and high prevalence in the spine, especially lumbar vertebrae (Table 10.1). For example, male prevalences ranged from a low of 18 percent in the hand to 62 percent for the cervical, shoulder, and elbow joints. Not surprisingly, older adults (> 35 years) had higher osteoarthritis prevalences than younger adults (Table 10.2).

Most of the osteoarthritis observed in the Stillwater remains is proliferative lipping along joint margins. However, a number of osteoarthritic adults also dis-

TABLE 10.1.

Osteoarthritis Summary Statistics: Total (Males, Females,
Indeterminate Sex Combined), Males, and Females

	Total		Males		Females	
Joint[a]	No.[b]	%[c]	No.[b]	%[c]	No.[b]	%[c]
Cervical	25	52.0	13	61.5	10	40.0
Thoracic	27	33.3	13	46.2	13	23.1
Lumbar	24	66.7	11	54.5	12	75.0
Sacrum	21	42.9	11	45.5	10	40.0
Shoulder	26	42.3	13	61.5	13	23.1
Elbow	28	50.0	13	61.5	15	40.0
Wrist	25	32.0	12	41.7	13	23.1
Hand	23	13.0	11	18.2	11	9.1
Hip	26	19.2	10	40.0	16	6.3
Knee	27	29.6	12	33.3	15	26.7
Ankle	26	19.2	11	45.5	14	0.0
Foot	18	16.7	10	20.0	8	12.5

[a] Two male/female comparisons were significant (chi-square): hip ($p \leq 0.03$); ankle ($p \leq$ 0.02). One male/female comparison approached significance: shoulder ($p = 0.11$).

[b] Number of articular joints observed for presence/absence of osteoarthritis.

[c] Percent of articular joints affected by osteoarthritis.

played marked eburnation or polishing of articular surfaces due to cartilage degeneration. Of the 34 relatively complete adult skeletons, 4 displayed one or more joints with eburnation (see also S. T. Brooks, Haldeman, and Brooks 1988). All adults with eburnation exceeded 40 years of age (two females, two males).

Enamel Defects

Some two-thirds (64 percent) of the 39 permanent dentitions possessed at least one hypoplastic defect. By way of illustrating the pattern of hypoplasia across age categories, the chronological distribution of hypoplasias are shown in Figure 10.2 for the mandibular canine and maxillary first incisor. The patterning of hypoplastic defects shows a peak in the regions of tooth crowns representing ages between about three and four years. The frequency, areas, and event widths are presented in Table 10.3. These data reveal that the mandibular canine exhibits the highest prevalence of hypoplasias (52 percent) and the mandibular first incisor the lowest prevalence (13 percent). Measurement of hypoplasias reveals that the mandibular first incisor has the smallest area (.23 mm) and the mandibular second incisor the highest area (.43 mm). In parallel fashion, the event width is smallest in the mandibular first incisor (.23 mm) and is highest in the mandibular second incisor (.60 mm).

TABLE 10.2.

Sex Comparisons of Osteoarthritis Prevalence in Young Adults (20.1–35 Years) and Old Adults (> 35 Years)

Joint/Age Group[a]	Males		Females	
	No.[b]	%[c]	No.[b]	%[c]
Cervical				
20.1–35	7	42.9	5	0.0
35.1+	6	83.3	5	80.0
Thoracic				
20.1–35	7	14.3	8	0.0
35.1+	6	83.3	5	60.0
Lumbar				
20.1–35	6	16.7	7	57.1
35.1+	5	100.0	5	100.0
Sacrum				
20.1–35	6	16.7	5	20.0
35.1+	5	80.0	5	60.0
Shoulder				
20.1–35	7	28.6	8	12.5
35.1+	6	100.0	5	40.0
Elbow				
20.1–35	7	42.9	9	22.2
35.1+	6	83.3	6	66.7
Wrist				
20.1–35	6	0.0	8	0.0
35.1+	6	83.3	5	60.0
Hand				
20.1–35	5	0.0	6	0.0
35.1+	6	33.3	5	20.0
Hip				
20.1–35	5	20.0	10	0.0
35.1+	5	60.0	6	16.7
Knee				
20.1–35	7	0.0	9	11.1
35.1+	5	80.0	6	50.0
Ankle				
20.1–35	5	20.0	10	0.0
35.1+	6	66.7	4	0.0
Foot				
20.1–35	5	0.0	4	0.0
35.1+	5	40.0	4	25.0

[a] No comparisons were significant (chi-square: p > 0.05); four comparisons (cervical, 20.1–35; shoulder, 35.1+; hip, 35.1+; ankle, 35.1+) approached significant levels (p ≤ 0.25).

[b] Number of articular joints observed for presence/absence of osteoarthritis.

[c] Percent of articular joints affected by osteoarthritis.

TABLE 10.3.
Prevalence (Percent), Area (in mm), and Event Width (in mm) of
Enamel Hypoplasias in Stillwater Dentitions

Tooth type	No.*	Prevalence	Area	Width
Mandible				
I1	12	17	.23	.23
I2	15	33	.43	.60
C	21	62	.31	.44
Maxilla				
I1	25	44	.36	.40
I2	21	48	.26	.28
C	29	38	.30	.42

* Number of teeth examined per tooth type.

Periosteal Reactions

Study of 61 juveniles and adults with either the left or right tibiae or both bones present indicates that only 16 percent (n = 10) displayed periosteal reactions on at least one element. For all tibiae available for study, 16 percent (13/84) were affected in some manner by periosteal reactions (l. tibia = 11.9 percent; r. tibia = 19.1 percent). With the exception of one adult male who displayed proliferative widespread lesions on virtually all major long bones, all lesions were localized and largely limited to single skeletal elements, usually a single tibia.

Porotic Hyperostosis

Four juveniles in the Stillwater sample displayed clear indications of porotic hyperostosis. Three of the cases were cribrotic lesions, and the fourth involved the vault. In addition, a fifth individual—an adult female—had unusually porous vault bones, which may or may not represent porotic hyperostosis. The porosity, however, does not present the classic symptomatology of porotic hyperostosis. Excluding this individual, the prevalence for the series is 7 percent (4/54).

INTERPRETING BEHAVIOR AND HEALTH FROM OSTEOPATHOLOGY

Physical Activity and Behavioral Implications

Our analysis of patterning of osteoarthritis indicates the primacy of mechanical factors in the Stillwater series. Few skeletal elements of the hand were affected, especially with regard to metacarpal-phalangeal articulations, indicating that systemic factors do not enter into the etiology of osteoarthritis here. In clinical settings, the hand joints are usually involved in nonmechanical, systemic arthritises, such as rheumatoid arthritis (Cockburn, Duncan, and Riddle 1979; Merbs 1983).

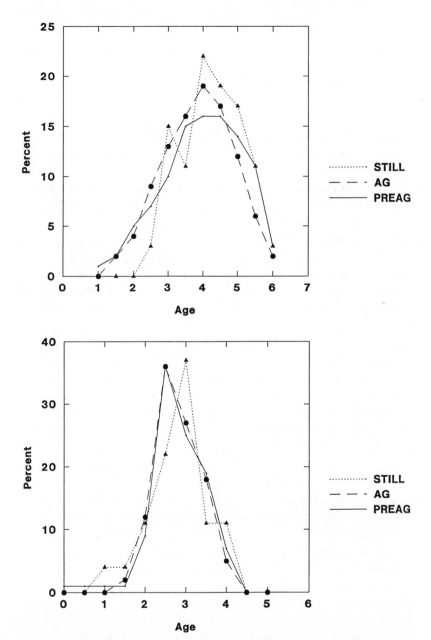

FIGURE 10.2. Chronological distribution of linear enamel hypoplasias for the mandibular canine (top) and maxillary first incisor (bottom). For comparison, prehistoric samples from coastal Georgia, pre-A.D. 1150 (PREAG) and A.D. 1150–1500 (AG), are included to show the pattern of three- to four-year peak in physiological stress (Georgia coastal data from Hutchinson and Larsen 1988, 1990)

These findings indicate that the Stillwater groups led a rigorous and demanding life-style. In particular, the vertebral column was highly arthritic, suggesting pronounced mechanical loading of the back. A number of individuals exhibited various manifestations of osteoarthritis, including pronounced marginal lipping of the vertebral bodies, anterior compression fractures, and surface depressions arising from the herniation of intervertebral discs (Schmorl's nodes).

There is a tremendous range of variation in sexual dimorphism in osteoarthritis in archaeological skeletal series, although males generally display higher prevalences than females (see Bridges 1992). Most affected joints in the Stillwater sample show a higher prevalence among males; three differences are statistically significant, including the shoulder, hip, and ankle (chi-square: $p \leq 0.05$). Women did hunt in many foraging societies. However, among most foragers, men were responsible for hunting and women were responsible for gathering (see Kelly 1995a). The pattern of greater osteoarthritic involvement in male shoulders, hips, and ankles in comparison with females at Stillwater indicates sex differences in mechanical demands that may be related to resource procurement generally and hunting activities specifically. We speculate that excessive use of the shoulder might have arisen from thrusting activities, perhaps involving the use of the atlatl and spear throwing. This may explain the unilateral involvement of the upper limb for several individuals who showed more advanced osteoarthritis in the right upper limb than in the left. However, if atlatl use was a primary factor in explaining upper limb osteoarthritis, then most cases should be unilateral. However, with the exception of three individuals, upper limb osteoarthritis was bilateral. Thus, this behavioral reconstruction only applies to part of the adult male population. Also the great involvement of the hip and ankle in males may represent the rigors of running and walking in difficult terrain and over long distances. The relatively higher frequencies of osteoarthritis in males than in females for these joints suggest that the pathology was acquired over the course of a lifetime of physically demanding activities.

In addition to mechanical factors, Brooks and coworkers suggest that the ingestion of *Fusarium* mycotoxins derived from contaminated stored seeds and resultant destruction of articular (hyaline) cartilage may have exacerbated osteoarthritis and "could easily be the causative factor involved in the unusual frequencies of eburnation in the Stillwater skeletal series" (S. T. Brooks, Haldeman, and Brooks 1990:105). We regard this interpretation as a potential explanation. However, a mechanical explanation seems more likely given what is known about the physically challenging life-styles of Great Basin Native Americans. A mechanical-behavioral interpretation is also more in line with findings based on cross-sectional geometric analysis of femora (Ruff, this volume; see Larsen, Ruff, and Kelly 1995) showing high levels of physical activity in Stillwater adults, especially males.

Osteoarthritis prevalence is very high in the Stillwater skeletal remains in comparison with other archaeological samples from North America (cf. Jurmain 1977, 1980; Merbs 1983). This may represent simply a difference in data collection methods (see Bridges 1992). However, comparison with other skeletal series from the American Southeast studied by us using the same methods (Larsen 1982; Larsen and Ruff 1994) also indicates a marked elevation in the Stillwater series. Thus, the ubiquitous nature of osteoarthritis in Stillwater remains and the very high frequencies in comparison with other North American populations argues that, indeed, osteoarthritis was a common pathological condition in the west-central Great Basin.

S. T. Brooks and co-workers (1988) review the range of potential activities that could account for osteoarthritis in Great Basin native populations. Among other behaviors, they report on lifting and carrying of excessively heavy loads, preparation and cutting of animal hides, seed grinding and pounding using stone implements, stone tool production, and hunting with the use of the bow and arrow and spear thrower. Each of these activities places heavy mechanical demands on different parts of the body in obvious ways. Because these behaviors cannot be documented and tied to osteoarthritis in living populations, it is not possible at present to link specific behaviors to patterns of osteoarthritis in the Stillwater series.

In summary, the high prevalence of osteoarthritis in the Stillwater series provides a compelling picture of a population or populations that were involved in heavy, repetitive physical activities resulting in an elevated prevalence of the disorder and severe manifestations for older individuals. In our view, the high prevalence is not consistent with a sedentary population that was tied to the wetlands on a year-round basis. Unfortunately, the documentation of osteoarthritis does not inform our reconstruction of time spent in the marsh relative to other settings. We speculate, however, that although the populations were likely drawn to the wetlands for important dietary resources, they expended appreciable amounts of energy and time walking in difficult terrain, such as the nearby uplands. The lower prevalence in adult women suggests perhaps relatively greater sedentary behavior, probably in the marsh. However, the high frequency of lumbar osteoarthritis in females may point to a range of behaviors involving heavy mechanical loading of the back, such as carrying children and other burdens (e.g., firewood, food, collecting equipment) while foraging, or the demanding nature of food processing, such as seed grinding with stone implements.

Quality of Life and Health Status

The study of physiological stress in human populations, past and present, has taken on increasing importance in the reconstruction of adaptation and the assessment of the history of the human condition in recent years (Goodman et al. 1988; Huss-Ashmore, Goodman, and Armelagos 1982; Larsen 1997). As such, stress has become central to understanding well-being and health in earlier societies. A wide range of studies of dental defects in teeth from archaeological settings and in living populations has demonstrated the sensitivity of enamel to exposure to environmental insults (Goodman and Rose 1990; various authors in Goodman and Capasso 1992).

Comparisons of the prevalence of linear enamel hypoplasias between the Stillwater series and other archaeological samples indicate that physiological stress was neither rampant (cf. Blakey, Leslie, and Reidy 1994; Hutchinson and Larsen 1988, 1990; M. E. Mack and Coppa 1992; D. J. Martin et al. 1991) nor infrequent (cf. Schulz and McHenry 1975; Ubelaker 1992a). In relation to a simple prevalence of individuals affected (64 percent), the Stillwater series is moderately high in comparison with other populations. Thus, while physiological stress was not extreme, it was clearly present. Because comparisons of widths of hypoplasias, areas and events, have been studied in only a limited number of skeletal samples, we are unable to draw comparative-based conclusions regarding the Stillwater sample and other populations. However, hypoplasias are certainly narrower than in other series studied from eastern North America, both with respect to prehistoric foragers and prehistoric and contact-period agriculturalists (see Hutchinson and Larsen 1988, 1990).

Direct associations have been made between hypoplastic defects and nutritional disorders, disease, or other factors, such as low birthweight and low socioeconomic status (see Goodman and Rose 1990; Hillson 1986; Pindborg 1982; papers in Goodman and Capasso 1992). Commonly observed in many disadvantaged settings (e.g., underdeveloped or developing nations) is the presence of malnutrition and infection/infectious disease. Both factors have deleterious effects on growth and development, and the two operating concurrently have a synergistic relationship. That is, poor nutrition, especially protein deficiency, will lower an individual's resistance to infection; whereas, infectious disease interferes with nutrition by simultaneously suppressing absorption and increasing the need for nutrients, especially protein. Researchers speculate that nutrition, or disease, or some combination thereof was responsible for the high prevalence of hypoplasias in past societies (e.g., various studies in Cohen and Armelagos 1984). What factors might explain the presence of moderate levels of relatively narrow hypoplasias in the Stillwater population living in the Carson Desert?

Our study of Great Basin periosteal reactions indicates that infectious disease or infection generally was probably not a major health risk in the west-central Great Basin. That is, 16 percent of individuals and tibiae affected by periosteal reactions is low in comparison with other samples studied by bioarchaeologists. The prevalence of periosteal reactions in the Stillwater sample is either lower than, or similar to, other hunter-gatherer archaeological skeletal series in North America (e.g., Cassidy 1984; Cook 1984; Lambert 1993; Rose et al. 1984; Ubelaker 1984), in

Australia (Webb 1995), or in Japan (Suzuki 1991). Moreover, the prevalence is well under values documented in late prehistoric agriculturalists in North America (e.g., Cook 1984; Lallo, Armelagos, and Rose 1978; Milner and Smith 1990; Stodder 1994), albeit with some exceptions (e.g., Larsen 1982). We regard the relatively low prevalence of skeletal infection as a general indication, in this setting, of low population density and high degree of mobility, which appear to be critical variables in explaining elevated prevalence of periosteal reactions in archaeological samples (Larsen 1997). It is conceivable that trauma may have contributed to some of the periosteal inflammations observed in the Carson Desert population. Minor injuries involving blows to the shins can cause inflammatory responses in the periosteum. In the kinds of rugged terrain that these individuals traversed, it is possible that some periosteal reactions were caused by this type of injury. Thus, the circumstances causing periosteal reactions, as well as the low prevalence of the pathology, suggest that infection or infectious disease contributed only minimally to systemic physiological insult.

It is possible that other diseases, such as parasitic infection, may have caused developmental insults in the Carson Desert. Experimental studies involving induced parasitism in laboratory animals have shown an increase in physiological perturbation and enamel defects (Suckling, Elliot, and Thurley 1986). Indeed, parasites have been identified in human coprolites from Lovelock Cave in the nearby Humboldt Sink as well as from other areas of the Great Basin and Desert West (Fry 1970; Reinhard 1990, 1992). Some of these parasites have lethal consequences for the host (e.g., thorny-headed worm, Acanthocephala; J. G. Moore, Fry, and Englert 1969), but others are relatively harmless (e.g., pinworm, *Enterobius vermicularis;* Fry 1970). The link between parasites and enamel defects is uncertain, since at least one parasitic infection (helminthiasis) was uncommon in the western Great Basin, in contrast to the eastern Great Basin (Reinhard 1990).

Porotic hyperostosis occurred with very low prevalence among individuals in the Stillwater sample. Such low prevalence suggests that iron status was normal during the years of growth and development. Alternatively, it suggests that other conditions that cause porotic hyperostosis—for example, scurvy, rickets, and infection—were not operating in this region. Stillwater porotic hyperostosis prevalence is low in relation to other populations studied worldwide, foragers and farmers alike (cf. various studies in Cohen and Armelagos 1984; Goodman et al. 1984; Walker 1986; Webb 1995); therefore, low iron bioavailability cannot be invoked as an argument for dental defects in this setting.

A number of epidemiological studies have found a causal link between enamel hypoplasias and protein-calorie malnutrition. For example, Goodman and coworkers (Dobney and Goodman 1991; Goodman, Martinez, and Chavez 1991; May, Goodman, and Meindl 1993) have documented prevalences of enamel defects in rural Mexico and Guatemala. In these settings, children receiving dietary supplements have fewer hypoplasias than their nonsupplemented peers. These investigations demonstrate that adequate nutrition is critical for normal growth and development of the body generally, as well as its component hard tissues such as tooth enamel.

In the absence of an infectious agent or agents as primary causal factors in explaining physiological perturbations and growth arrest, we argue that nutritional deficiencies were potentially the most likely source of growth disruption leading to enamel defects in this Great Basin setting. In the Carson Desert, the availability of economically important plants and animals is very much tied to the fluctuations in water availability deriving from snowpack melt in the Sierra Nevadas. In recorded history since the late nineteenth century, water availability has varied tremendously in this region (Kelly and Hattori 1985). In years with low snowfall in the Sierras, the Stillwater Marsh is excessively dry, resulting in marked reductions in dietary resources, such as water birds, fish, other fauna, and plants. The impact of limited water is underscored by ethnographer Margaret Wheat's remark that "In the Great Basin the marshes . . . were intermittent affairs, always at the mercy of dry cycles and shifting dunes and channels. In a half a dozen years a marsh could change into a dust bowl" (1967:3; cited in Thomas 1985:20). Conversely, heavy winter snowfall ensures the availability of adequate water supplies and, hence, economically important plants and animals. Therefore, we suggest that periodic food shortfalls engendered by limited water availability may have caused growth arrest in hunter-gatherers occupying the Carson Desert. Based on the measurement of widths of hypoplasias, we regard these stress episodes as short-term affairs or at least not severe. Thus, stress was relatively acute and not the kind of chronic disruption observed in some other settings, especially in sedentary agriculturalists (e.g., Hutchinson and Larsen, 1990).

A nutritional interpretation for growth arrest in the Stillwater group is consistent with measurement of bone mass, especially percent cortical area (percent CA) in humeri and femora. Analyses of bone mass indicate that percent CA is relatively low in comparison with other North American skeletal samples (Ruff, this volume; Larsen, Ruff, and Kelly 1995). As with living populations (e.g., Garn et al. 1964), suboptimal cortical bone mass may reflect general systemic stress, such as nutritional deprivation, in the Carson Desert. Although thin cortical bone may reflect relatively high mean age-at-death in the Stillwater series (see Ruff, this volume), that younger adults (< 35 years) had generally low values of percent CA (Ruff, this volume; Larsen, Ruff, and Kelly 1995) suggests that age can be ruled out as a factor in explaining lower values of percent CA in this setting.

The chronological distribution of hypoplasias is similar to other archaeological populations reported in a large and growing literature (e.g., Corruccini, Handler, and Jacobi 1985; Goodman, Armelagos, and Rose 1980; Hillson 1979; Hodges 1989; Powell 1988; Storey 1992; and others). That is, many archaeological series show peaks during the two- to four-year period of development. The relatively higher frequency of hypoplasias during this period is due not only to the susceptibility of the midcrown region of the tooth to growth disruption (Goodman and Armelagos 1985b) but also to extrinsic factors (Goodman and Rose 1990). A major trauma that occurs during the early years of childhood is weaning, which involves the shift from maternal dependence to postweaning diet and adult foods. Nonmaternal sources of foods may be less sanitary and potentially of poorer nutritional quality, thus leading to diarrhea, reduction in host resistance to infection, and increased incidence of metabolic and growth disruption (Acheson 1960; Eveleth and Tanner 1990; Lowrey 1986). This period of juvenile growth also involves a reduced availability of nutrients and immunities transferred from the mother to the nursing infant (Popkin et al. 1986). Thus, weaning is a potentially dangerous period for infants and young children. Weaning likely contributes to physiological disruption, but when applied to archaeological samples, it is difficult to establish a specific causative link with hypoplasias. Although it is often assumed that weaning and hypoplasia concentration are related, it is clear that in at least one case, weaning appears to have preceded chronological peaks in hypoplastic activity (see Blakey, Leslie, and Reidy 1994; Corruccini, Handler, and Jacobi 1985). Regardless of the role of weaning, however, we regard the moderate levels of hypoplasias to be tied to dietary factors and not disease in this setting.

CONCLUSIONS

The recovery of human remains and their subsequent study by physical anthropologists (S. T. Brooks, Haldeman, and Brooks 1988; Larsen and Kelly 1995) have facilitated a vastly improved understanding of the biological history and adaptation of prehistoric native populations in the Carson Desert. The conclusions of our analyses are threefold. First, the Stillwater adults show a remarkably high prevalence of osteoarthritis with some individuals displaying extreme forms of articular degeneration. This prevalence reflects a very physically demanding life-style. The presence of high levels of osteoarthritis also indicates activities that involved carrying heavy loads and, perhaps, travel over long distances and in difficult terrain. These findings provide little support for models that characterize these populations as sedentary foragers. However, females may have been relatively more sedentary than males in this setting.

Second, analysis of dental hypoplasias reveals moderate levels of metabolic insult. We found only minimal evidence of infectious disease in the Stillwater series. This finding, combined with low population density, suggests that disease or infection played a minor—if any—role in growth arrest. Rather, growth arrest likely resulted from periodic food shortages and occasional nutritional deficiencies. Negative factors associated with weaning may have contributed to metabolic stress in young children.

Third, documentation of porotic hyperostosis indicates that these groups did not suffer from iron deficiency anemia or other factors linked with the pathological condition. Therefore, we conclude that iron deficiency anemia (or scurvy, rickets, or infection) was of minimal importance and certainly did not contribute to growth disruption.

Taken as a whole, we regard the Carson Desert native populations as having been subjected to a highly demanding life-style, but their health as being relatively robust. Although dental and skeletal indicators are suggestive of periodic stress from nutritional deficits, diet generally was varied, an assessment that is supported by the ethnographic record and by analysis of stable isotopes from archaeological human bone samples (Schoeninger, this volume). The characterizations of forager lifeways as marginal at one extreme or affluent at the other do not fit the results of this investigation. Rather, we see a highly mixed pattern that reflects neither the deprivation nor the affluent models. We conclude from this assessment that it is not important to say whether the Hobbesian or affluent models best characterize foraging societies in the Carson Desert or elsewhere, but, rather, that what is more impressive is the variability seen in these populations. The discussion presented in this chapter informs our understanding of the sources of this variation rather than a debate over which model best portrays hunter-gatherers. In the study of the human remains from the Stillwater Marsh, a number of areas remain conjectural or otherwise unclear, but arguably, bioarchaeological investigation has brought us closer to comprehending prehistoric human ecology in this region.

Acknowledgments

Funding for fieldwork and laboratory analysis was provided by a grant from the National Science Foundation to R. L. Kelly and C. S. Larsen (award BNS-8704094). We thank the staff of the Stillwater Wildlife Management Area (U.S. Department of the Interior, U.S. Fish and Wildlife Service), Ron Anglin, Delvan Lee, Ernie Lantto, and Eugene Duffney, and especially former staff archaeologist Anan Raymond, for their assistance in fieldwork and follow-up analysis. Support of the research by the Fallon Paiute-Shoshone Tribe and then Tribal Chairman Richard Hicks is gratefully acknowledged. Data collection was facilitated by the efforts of Michelle Haldeman, Sheilagh Brooks, Amy Dansie, and Donald Tuohy at the Nevada State Museum, Carson City. Christine E. Larsen provided invaluable assistance in data collection. Katherine Russell's participation in the project as field director, osteologist, and consultant extraordinaire is appreciated. Thanks are extended to Patricia Lambert for her comments on an earlier draft of the manuscript.

II

An Examination of Wetland Adaptive Strategies in Harney Basin

Comparing Ethnographic Paradigms and the Archaeological Record

Albert C. Oetting

Harney Basin is the largest internally draining basin in Oregon and the northernmost in the Great Basin. Although the basin is semiarid in climate, it contains a complex hydrologic system of streams, rivers, marshes, and lakes maintained by precipitation to the surrounding watershed (Figure 11.1). The central lakes—Malheur, Harney, and Mud—flooded in the 1980s, inundating over 180,000 acres before they receded. Water and wave action along the changing shorelines of the central lake system eroded and exposed dozens of archaeological sites, artifacts, cultural features, and human burials (Oetting 1990a, 1990b, 1992). With the consent of the Burns Paiute Tribe, 54 burials were exhumed, specific analyses were conducted, and all of the remains were then reinterred (Hemphill 1992a,b,c). These burials form the bioarchaeological sample analyzed by Hemphill, Nelson, and Ruff in this volume.

This paper summarizes pertinent aspects of the Harney Basin archaeological record and presents some inferences regarding regional chronology and land use to provide a context for the bioarchaeological studies. The rich archaeological record of the Harney Basin wetlands provides indications that two settlement-subsistence systems, involving differing residential mobility strategies, may have operated at different periods during the last 5,000 years. The mobility strategies and settlement-subsistence patterns of the Wadatika Northern Paiute, the ethnographic inhabitants of Harney Basin, are used to model the later prehistory of the region. The Klamath-Modoc, ethnographic inhabitants of the Klamath lakes and marshes on the western periphery of the northern Great Basin, are used as analogues to model settlement and subsistence practices before 500 or 1000 B.P.

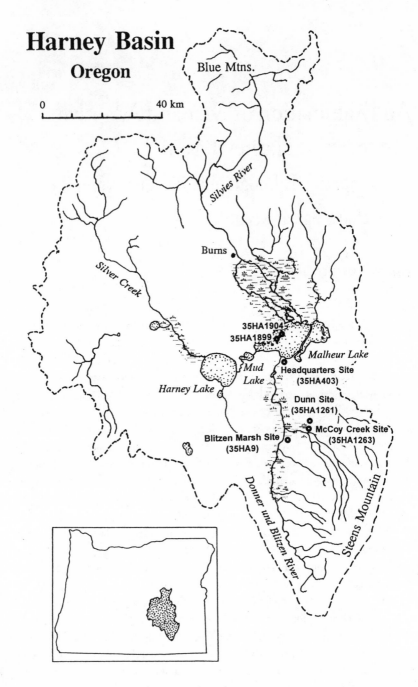

Harney Basin
Oregon

Blue Mtns.

0   40 km

Silvies River

Silver Creek

Burns

35HA1904
35HA1899

Malheur Lake

Mud Lake

Headquarters Site
(35HA403)

Harney Lake

Dunn Site
(35HA1261)

McCoy Creek Site
(35HA1263)

Blitzen Marsh Site
(35HA9)

Donner und Blitzen River

Steens Mountain

FIGURE 11.1. The hydrologic system of Harney Basin, when the lakes are full, and the location of sites mentioned in the text.

THE NATURAL SETTING

Malheur, Mud, and Harney Lakes occupy the lowest elevations of the basin. Runoff from the Blue Mountains flows into the basin from the north through the Silvies River and other small streams, while runoff from Steens Mountain provides water to the southern part of the basin through several streams and the Donner und Blitzen River. Water levels in the basin fluctuate seasonally in response to inflow from the rivers, direct precipitation, and evapotranspiration.

Periodic fluctuations in water levels are beneficial to and necessary for the maintenance of marsh water chemistry and biotic productivity (Duebbert 1969:20), but, in general, wetlands operate within a balance of moisture conditions. Extended periods of either wet or dry climatic episodes may deleteriously affect wetlands—wet periods flooding the marshes and surrounding terrestrial areas; dry intervals constricting and possibly eliminating the wetlands. Duebbert (1969:5) believes that marshes similar to the modern system have been present in Harney Basin throughout the Holocene, and although there have been frequent fluctuations between wet and dry conditions, the regional ecology and its biota are well-adapted to tolerate these extremes.

Harney Basin contains one of the richest primary biotic systems in the northern Great Basin (see Figure 11.1). In times of low to moderate water levels, the central lakes area forms a complex series of freshwater- to alkaline-marsh habitats, with open water present only in the deepest areas (Duebbert 1969). This marsh and lake complex covers as much as 500 km². The tributary rivers also support extensive freshwater marshes along their lower courses. The lower Donner und Blitzen River flows through a riverine marsh 30 km long and 3 to 8 km wide. The lower courses of the Silvies River and tributary streams from the north probably also supported similar marshes prior to historical irrigation and water control efforts. The location and composition of these riverine marshes and meadows have probably been more constant through time than the wetlands bordering the central lakes since water depth (and therefore marsh type) varies more widely in these lakes, which have no outlet. The wetlands along the rivers and around the central lakes comprise a mosaic of thousands of acres of grasslands, wet meadows, shallow to deep emergent marshes, and areas of open water, supporting a wide variety of plant and animal life.

THE ARCHAEOLOGICAL RECORD IN HARNEY BASIN

Hundreds of archaeological sites have been recorded in Harney Basin, most of them in or near Malheur National Wildlife Refuge (T. M. Newman et al. 1974), but much of the recent archaeological information comes from surveys on the shores of Malheur Lake conducted for the refuge in 1988–89 after this enclosed basin lake had flooded and the water was beginning to recede (Oetting 1990a, 1990b, 1992). Since that time, further surveys by the U.S. Fish and Wildlife Service

have documented additional sites around the lakes (Burnside 1991; Raymond
1994).

The post-flood surveys inspected numerous islands as they were reemerging
from the lake and large sections of the changing shorelines. In all, nearly 100 archaeological sites have been recorded at Malheur Lake, ranging in size from less
than 200 m² to as much as 80,000 m². Very few of these localities had been previously recorded. Several of the moderate-to-large sites had very dense artifact scatters with peak densities in excess of 100 items/m², and spectacular arrays of hundreds to thousands of tools from a wide range of artifact classes. Over 2,000 tools
and other formed objects were collected during the 1988–89 surveys and many
more were observed in the field (Oetting 1990a, 1990b). This total included hundreds of projectile points, many finely finished large biface blades, numerous other
bifacial and unifacial flaked stone tools, hundreds of well-made ground stone tools
(including very large and heavy implements), over 100 notched or girdled net
weights, and numerous ornaments.

The stratigraphy and cultural features of some of these sites have been damaged or destroyed by the flooding and erosion cycles, leaving carpets of artifacts on
erosional beach platforms. However, some cultural features remain, including
three possible house floors profiled in a cutbank on one of the northwest-shore
islands and a possible house depression at a nearby site (see below). House depressions were recorded in the 1970s at a third site in this area. A number of artifact features have been found, including several clusters of notched net weights (Burnside
1991; Oetting 1990b; Raymond 1994) and a cache of bone tools and finely flaked
projectile points, possibly the bundled contents of a flint knapper's kit (Oetting
1990b). Twenty-seven partially exposed burials were located during the surveys,
and 27 more were subsequently found by the U.S. Fish and Wildlife Service.

Test excavations conducted at the Headquarters site on the south shore of
Malheur Lake (Aikens and Greenspan 1988; Carter and Dugas 1994) and at three
sites in the extensive marshes south of the lake (Fagan 1974; Musil 1995), as well as
limited explorations at flood-damaged sites along the margins of Malheur Lake
(Elston and Dugas 1993; Raven and Elston 1992) have also contributed significant
data.

Small test excavations have been conducted intermittently at the Headquarters site (35HA403), located at a spring on the south shore of Malheur Lake now
occupied by the headquarters of the wildlife refuge (Minor and Greenspan 1985;
Aikens and Greenspan 1986; Carter and Dugas 1994). The various archaeological
projects demonstrate that the site was intensively used over a long period. The
density and variety of cultural materials, a diverse faunal assemblage dominated by
small mammals and fish, the presence of human burials, and the exposure of a
house pit profile with an associated uncalibrated radiocarbon age of 4760 B.P.

(Carter and Dugas 1994) indicate that the site was used as a residential base—possibly as a winter village—for extended periods.

Three saucer-shaped dark lenses of fill, possibly house floors, were observed in the cutbank profile of a dune remnant at site 35HA1904 during the 1988–89 surveys (Oetting 1990b). One of these features was tested during geoarchaeological investigations at flood-damaged sites (Elston and Dugas 1993). The function of this feature could not be determined, but there was a fire hearth below this that produced a radiocarbon age of 1050 B.P. (Elston et al. 1993b). At site 35HA1899, a small oval depression was tentatively identified as a residential rather than a storage feature (Elston et al. 1993a).

Three stratified components were identified at the Dunn site (35HA1261), above the eastern edge of Diamond Swamp, in the riverine marsh system 25 km south of the lake (Musil 1995). The middle component yielded the remains of a semisubterranean pit house, a diverse artifact assemblage with heavy ground-stone site furniture, and an array of terrestrial and aquatic plant and animal resources. The house contained a central fire hearth, a storage pit, and postholes along the pit wall. A radiocarbon age of 3255 B.P. was obtained from the house floor and is congruent with the broad-necked projectile points associated with this feature.

Several circular depressions were observed on the surface of the Blitzen Marsh site (35HA9), located on the eastern edge of Blitzen Marsh south of the central lakes. Excavations revealed a rich, stratified cultural deposit (Fagan 1974). Portions of three living floors and two house pits were exposed, and nine radiocarbon ages (from 170 B.P. to 2350 B.P.) were obtained. One of the house pits had a steep-sided rim and several associated floors, one of which had been lined with clay. This floor yielded ages of 930 B.P. and 1110 B.P.

Three cultural components were identified at the McCoy Creek site (35HA1263) on the southeast edge of Diamond Swamp (Musil 1995; Toepel, Minor, and Greenspan 1984). The middle component contained a large, dense artifact assemblage and numerous cultural features similar to those found at the Blitzen Marsh site, including two house floors with storage pits, large ground stone implements, and hearths. The floors had been reused several times and one was clay-lined. A wide variety of wetland and terrestrial plants and animals were identified. Three radiocarbon ages, ranging between 990 B.P. and 1270 B.P. were associated with the floors, and two-thirds of the recovered projectile points were narrow-necked Rosegate series specimens. The houses, storage features, heavy ground stone tools, diverse food resources, and dense artifact assemblage indicate long-term and repeated residential occupations focused on the Diamond Swamp wetlands and nearby grasslands.

The upper cultural component at the McCoy Creek site suggests a more mobile adaptation (Musil 1995). A shallow house depression, interpreted as a wickiup, was excavated and produced a radiocarbon age of 480 B.P. Storage facilities were much smaller than those in the house floors of the earlier component, and the artifact assemblage was quite different, consisting of small, portable ground stone tools, Desert Side-notched as well as Rosegate series projectile points, and smaller and less diverse faunal and botanical assemblages. These features and artifacts suggest a less permanent, shorter-term use of the site during this period.

CHRONOLOGY

Chronology in Harney Basin has been based primarily on the analysis of time-sensitive projectile point types, but radiocarbon ages are available from the recovered burials and from the excavations just described. Archaeological and paleoenvironmental research in the basin suggests that human populations have utilized the region throughout the Holocene, but this use appears to have increased significantly about 5,000 years ago, possibly correlated with the reexpansion or reestablishment of the basin wetland systems at the beginning of the Medithermal (Oetting 1992; Wigand 1985, 1987). This intensification is inferred from the increased frequency and wide distribution of Elko series points, which were most commonly used between 5,000 and 1,000 years ago in the northern Great Basin (Oetting 1994). However, the most intensive period of human activity appears to have occurred in the Late Archaic of the last 2,000 years, indicated by the presence and numerical dominance of narrow-necked Rosegate series points at many sites. Rosegate series points are common in the northern Great Basin from about 2000 B.P. to historical contact. Small, triangular Desert Side-notched points, present in the region only in the last 500 to 1,000 years, are found at several sites.

The impression of greater human activity in the last 2,000 years is reinforced by numerous radiocarbon ages (Aikens and Greenspan 1988; Oetting 1992). The nine radiocarbon ages from the Blitzen Marsh site are all less than 2400 B.P. (Fagan 1974), and the seven ages from the McCoy Creek site range from 1900 B.P. to 480 B.P. (Musil 1995). The hearth feature at site 35HA1904 produced an age of 1050 B.P. (Elston and Dugas 1993). The Dunn site is somewhat older, with an age of 3255 B.P., and an age of 4760 B.P. is associated with a buried house floor at the Headquarters site (Carter and Dugas 1994). Nine of 10 radiocarbon ages from the lakeside burials are less than 1100 B.P., ranging from 160 B.P. to 1070 B.P. The tenth burial dates to 1830 B.P. (Burnside 1992; Hemphill 1992a,b,c).

ETHNOGRAPHIC MODELS AND WETLAND USE IN THE NORTHERN GREAT BASIN

There has been much debate in Great Basin anthropology over the role of wetlands in subsistence and settlement strategies (Janetski and Madsen 1990), focusing on the economic value of wetland resources and the mobility strategies employed by people using these resources. Most researchers now agree that wetlands are biotic magnets. Marshes, springs, lakes, and rivers not only provide water in a regionally arid landscape but also attract and sustain a diverse array of wetland and terrestrial plants and animals (Kelly 1990; D. B. Madsen 1988; Oetting 1989; Raven and Elston 1989; Simms 1984, 1985, 1988). Of course, it is also recognized that wetland systems in different regions provide different kinds and relative proportions of resources (Raven 1992; Rhode 1990b); thus, the ways in which wetlands were used by people may vary from area to area.

Debate persists, however, over the role Great Basin wetlands can play in settlement and mobility strategies, especially as to whether wetland resources fostered the development of semisedentary or possibly sedentary settlement adaptations. Anthropologists traditionally assumed that hunter-gatherers moved about because they had to and that, given sufficient nearby resources, people would settle down and become sedentary (Beardsley et al. 1956). This has been termed the "Pull" hypothesis since it is argued that resource abundance would encourage, or pull, people to settle down (Brown 1985:203). Recent theorists (Binford 1980, 1983; Hitchcock 1982; Kelly 1985; J. E. Rafferty 1985), however, relying on analogies with modern hunter-gatherers, argue that mobility is an integral part of the hunter-gatherer life-style and not something to be avoided if possible. Even if foodstuffs are abundantly available, these groups prefer to move about—to gather information on resources and conditions, share information with others, maintain social and trading ties, and avoid conflict. Thus, mobility serves as a means of risk management (Binford 1983:204). Hunter-gatherers settled down only under duress because of demographic, environmental, or resource stresses that forced people to restrict or eliminate their mobile life-style. This is termed the "Push" hypothesis, where stresses push people toward settlement-subsistence strategies involving reduced mobility (Brown 1985:202).

Researchers have recognized that there are actually several kinds of mobility (Binford 1980, 1982; Kelly 1992), which individuals and groups may employ in a variety of different combinations. For hunter-gatherers, the primary forms of movement are *residential mobility*, when groups move their residential base from one place to another; *logistic mobility*, round trips to and from residential bases by individuals and groups for specific purposes; *long-term mobility*, which describes the cyclical movements of groups through a set of territories; and *permanent migration*, where groups move permanently to a new territory. The following discussion of wetland settlement-subsistence systems highlights archaeological evidence for residential settlements; thus, the focus is on differences in the residential mobility of individuals and groups. It should be remembered, however, that while the process of sedentism involves the reduction and ultimate elimination of residential mobility (Hitchcock 1987; Kelly 1992; Oetting 1989), it does not entail the elimination or even restriction of logistical mobility or other kinds of mobility for individuals or task groups.

The existence of a stable settlement-subsistence adaptation to wetlands in western Nevada, termed the *limnosedentary* (or Great Basin Lacustrine Pattern), was proposed by Heizer (1967) and his students (Cowan 1967; Heizer and Napton 1970; Napton 1969; Rozaire 1963). This model promoted the Pull hypothesis, suggesting the development of a sedentary or semisedentary pattern of settlement based on intensive use of abundant river, marsh, spring, and lake resources. Similar wetland-adapted, residentially stable patterns were subsequently identified elsewhere in the northern and eastern Great Basin (Bettinger 1978; Elston 1982) in Surprise Valley (O'Connell 1975), Warner Valley (Weide 1968), Harney Basin (Aikens 1985; Minor and Toepel 1988; Oetting 1992), Lake Abert–Chewaucan Marsh Basin (Pettigrew 1985; Oetting 1989), and for some Sevier/Fremont and other Late Holocene groups in the eastern Great Basin (D. B. Madsen 1979, 1982; D. B. Madsen and Lindsey 1977).

The validity of the limnosedentary pattern for western Nevada, and for abundance-based approaches in general, has been challenged by proponents of the stress-based Push approaches. The initial conclusions of studies in western Nevada found little evidence to suggest either sedentism or a wetland subsistence focus (Kelly 1985, 1988a; Thomas 1985). Subsequent research at Stillwater Marsh in western Nevada (Raven and Elston 1989; Raven 1992) has demonstrated that wetland resources do provide sufficient resources for most of any given year, but that, while people could and did stay in the marshes throughout the year, residential mobility within the marshes remained relatively high with little evidence for sedentary or semisedentary adaptations. This model reflected the mobility patterns of the ethnographic Toedökadö Northern Paiute inhabitants of the Stillwater region.

Wada'tika Northern Paiute: Mobile Foragers in Harney Basin

Recently, similar arguments have been applied to Harney Basin. Raven (1992) noted that the rich biotic landscape of the basin and its surrounding hinterlands invited greater rather than reduced residential mobility and suggested that the mobility patterns of the ethnographic inhabitants, the Wada'tika Northern Paiute, supported this proposition.

The settlement and subsistence patterns of the Wada'tika (Whiting 1950; Couture 1978; Couture, Ricks, and Housely 1986) reflect the fusion-fission systems of most Numic-speaking people in the Intermountain West. Harney Basin families left their winter camps in early May and journeyed northeast to spring root-gathering camps in the Stinkingwater Mountains, where they were joined by other Northern Paiute families and other ethnic groups. While the women dug a wide variety of roots, the men visited fishery sites on the Middle Fork of the Malheur River for the spring salmon run. As the root gathering was completed, the women journeyed to the Malheur River to assist in drying the salmon. Wada'tika families then spent the summer hunting and moving independently from place to place within their foraging range as specific seed, root, and insect resources became available. Summer structures were temporary, often a roofless brush enclosure or windbreak, reflecting the transient nature of the people during these months.

In late August the family clusters, often with other ethnic groups, reunited on the northeast shore of Malheur Lake to gather the ripening waada seeds (seep-weed, *Suaeda depressa*). This was typically the largest gathering of the year, and many festivities took place at this time. Other fall-ripening seeds were harvested around the lake by parties from this encampment, and communal rabbit and antelope hunts were conducted. By November, families were setting up winter camps in lowland areas near the springs and lakes. These winter camps contained 3 to 10 houses dispersed in favored nearby camping spots rather than clustered as a village. Winter houses were usually small conical structures with unexcavated circular floors, a central pole, and a covering of bark, brush, grass, earth, or woven mats. The members of these camps varied annually because people did not always return to the same place from year to year.

Using this reconstruction of Wadaʼtika lifeways, Raven (1992) suggested that wetland resources were used selectively and only during certain portions of the year, thus emphasizing the residentially mobile aspects of this fusion-fission settlement pattern over the residentially stable period of winter camps since much of the seasonal round was spent foraging and traveling away from the wetlands.

Klamath-Modoc: Semisedentary Wetland Adaptations

However, other researchers in the northern Great Basin (Aikens 1985; Cressman 1942; Oetting 1989; Pettigrew 1985; Weide 1968) have consistently found archaeological evidence suggesting that different prehistoric settlement and subsistence strategies may have been practiced during some periods in the past. Sites with the remnants of semisubterranean house pits situated in or adjacent to wetlands are found in Harney Basin and the other regions cited above. Discussions of residential and economic stability in virtually all of these regions have focused around this archaeological evidence—the presence of pit house villages positioned near areas of substantial wetlands. Several of these studies incorporate supporting botanical and faunal evidence, but spatial patterning and the presence of pit houses have been significant factors. The ethnographic analogy used for the limnosedentary model of Heizer and Napton (Napton 1969:57–58) and for virtually every other archaeological reconstruction of residentially stable, wetland-oriented societies has been the Klamath-Modoc (D. B. Madsen and Lindsey 1977:88; O'Connell 1975:50; Oetting 1989:232; Rozaire 1963:75; Weide 1968:301–4).

The Klamath and Modoc are closely related Penutian-speaking groups who inhabit the wetlands and forests of the Klamath Lake and Marsh region, 150 km southwest of Harney Basin. Situated on the western margin of the arid basin-and-range country and at the base of the Cascades Mountains, this forested volcanic upland region receives slightly higher annual precipitation than the high desert basins to the east and supports extensive marsh systems along rivers and lakes.

Prior to disruption by Euroamericans, Klamath families generally pursued a semisedentary life-style focused on fixed winter villages and mobile subsistence activities during the summer (Barrett 1910; Spier 1930; Stern 1966). The largest cohesive sociopolitical unit among the Klamath was the winter village or community, with some large villages having multiple leaders and very small villages following the leadership of nearby larger communities. These villages were permanent sites that were returned to every year by the same families and groups. The elderly and sick sometimes stayed in these villages during seasons when most families were moving about. Villages in very favorable locations were sometimes occupied throughout the year. Winter houses were large semisubterranean earth-covered lodges, dismantled in the spring but rebuilt over the same circular house pits each winter. Smaller dome-shaped pole-and-mat houses were used during the summer and as winter outbuildings. When constructed over shallow pits, these smaller houses were also used as winter dwellings for the poor and elderly.

Families moved independently during the summer, taking advantage of seasonally available resources, but the moves were often between established fishing or gathering sites in the marshes, and families often camped with other family groups. Klamath economy focused on fish and wokas (pond lily seeds, *Nuphar polysepalum*). Fishing and drying the catch during runs was a communal enterprise that often drew other ethnic groups. Major fish runs occurred in spring, fall, and midwinter, and fishing was an occasional activity year round. Roots from meadows and marshes (camas, wapato, tule, cattail, etc.) were gathered in early summer. The major wokas harvest occurred in midsummer in the region's many marshes. Berries, wokas seeds, and other edible seeds were gathered in higher elevations as they ripened. Much of this produce was stored for winter use. Although hunting was not emphasized, people hunted a variety of game as diet supplements.

The preceding ethnographic sketches indicate that, although the Klamath have been used to model a wetland-oriented, sedentary life-style, they were not sedentary in the strict sense defined by J. E. Rafferty (1985:115) and others (Hitchcock 1987:374; Kelly 1985:10)—full-time year-round occupation of a site by a portion of the population. This may have been true in certain situations, when the sick and elderly (with children caretakers) might remain in villages and when villages in particularly favorable locations might be occupied throughout the year (Stern 1966:11). Klamath settlement patterns, however, are more appropriately described as being semisedentary—most families occupied fixed, winter village locations, but they spent some portion of each year away from these sites.

The Klamath settlement pattern was recorded as seminomadic in the *Ethnographic Atlas* (Murdock 1967:107), as were the settlement patterns of several Paiute groups. This parallel was clearly grasped by Weide (1968:302), who pointed out that the differences between the Klamath and ethnographic Great Basin Numic groups are ones in degree rather than in kind. The differences rest primarily with the greater association of families with specific winter villages among the Klamath and the greater year-to-year stability of those villages. The use of the semisedentary Klamath as an analogue for the limnosedentary hypothesis actually serves to point out that, as an examination of wetland settlement and subsistence strategies, the investigation is really one of identifying adaptational variations along a continuum rather than trying to dichotomize between nonsedentary and sedentary systems.

SETTLEMENT AND SUBSISTENCE IN HARNEY BASIN

While it is doubtful that the subsistence and settlement strategies of the prehistoric inhabitants of Harney Basin followed either of these ethnographic examples exactly, they do serve as useful general analogies for comparison and model development. The archaeological and chronological evidence presented above indicates that, although people have frequented Harney Basin throughout the Holocene, widespread use and occupation of the basin and its wetlands increased only after 5,000 years ago. Sites with semisubterranean house features situated in or near the marshes and other wetlands suggest that the Klamath-Modoc model may be the more appropriate comparison for much of the period between about 5000 B.P. and 1000 or 500 B.P., with the Wada'tika model providing a better analogue after this time.

The Dunn, McCoy Creek, Blitzen Marsh, and Headquarters sites seem to have functioned as annually reoccupied, semisedentary villages with substantial pit houses during certain periods. It has been suggested that these periods are correlated with moist climatic intervals (Musil 1995), but perhaps they reflect a somewhat broader moderate climatic range. As noted above, wetlands are most productive in a fluctuating balance of moisture conditions. Moderately dry to moderately moist periods with seasonal water-level fluctuations should produce greater biotic productivity in wetlands than very dry or very wet periods. Thus, rather than simply equate reduced residential mobility with increased moisture and greater mobility with aridity, mobility is more directly linked with wetland productivity, which in turn may vary with numerous interlinked environmental factors.

These sites were situated on high dry ground directly adjacent to the marshes, and contain evidence that the diverse and nearby resources of both the wetlands and surrounding grasslands were employed. The construction and maintenance of pit houses at these sites represent considerable investments in labor, energy, and time. The large and heavy ground stone implements also suggest some permanence for these structures, as do the storage facilities. Evidence for multiple occupations indicates that the houses were reused and occasionally refurbished. The features at the Headquarters site and the Dunn site are dated to 4760 B.P. and 3255 B.P., respectively. The McCoy Creek and Blitzen Marsh floors yielded ages be-

tween 930 B.P. and 1270 B.P. In contrast, the McCoy Creek wickiup floor with its
more portable associated artifacts is dated to 480 B.P., and may reflect a more mobile adaptation that coincides with a distinct drought which occurred between 800
and 400 B.P. (Musil 1995).

Several of the large, artifact-dense sites recorded around Malheur Lake during
the postflood surface surveys may also be villages. Site locations in or near wetlands and the artifact assemblages are very similar to the excavated village sites.
Possible house features have been found at some of these sites. Numerous burials
were encountered. Many of the sites have large quantities and varieties of flaked
stone tools, well-made ground stone tools, and net weights, as well as tools and ornaments made of bone, antler, and shell. In addition to the diversity of finished
tools, the large cores, tool blanks, preforms, and impressive quantities of debitage
provide further evidence that some of these sites were well-used locations rather
than temporary camps or task locations. The quantity of lithic raw materials and
the size of many unused waste flakes reflect plentiful local sources for these materials and little need to economize on use or transport.

Wetland resources in the form of marsh/meadow plants, waterfowl, fish, and
aquatic mammals, as well as terrestrial mammals drawn to the local water and forage, appear to have been central to the subsistence practices of Harney Basin populations, and these resources may have fostered this relatively stable semisedentary
existence during the later Holocene. Many sites are located on high dry ground adjacent to permanent freshwater springs and varied nearby wetland and terrestrial
resources. Faunal and botanical remains from the excavated marsh-edge village
sites also indicate that a variety of terrestrial and wetland resources were used. Although the postflood surface surveys did not recover any direct faunal or botanical
evidence, the abundance of ground stone tools and net weights suggests a lakemarsh wetland subsistence orientation for many of these sites. Of course, hunting
equipment in the form of projectile points was also abundant.

The presence of pit house habitation sites, or villages, positioned near areas of
substantial wetlands is incongruous with arguments citing high residential mobility (within wetlands or between wetlands and uplands) or with considering wetland resources as secondary foods. It is unlikely that people foraging in the marshes
and moving as local resources were depleted would build labor-intensive semisubterranean pithouses. Likewise, if a group were forced to make more intensive use
of marsh resources in a time of stress and became sedentary by attempting to minimize energy expenditures (Kelly 1985), it is again unlikely that the group would
expend their energy by building pit houses. The well-finished nature and occasional decoration of ground stone implements also reflect substantial labor and
energy invested in manufacture and maintenance. It is doubtful that such investment would be made in implements to process occasionally used secondary resources. The presence of pit houses and well-finished ground stone tools in this

and other Great Basin wetland settings suggest that many factors should be considered when exploring hunter-gatherer mobility and sedentism.

Wetlands, while perhaps not consistently providing the highest-ranked resources, nonetheless have abundant, concentrated, diverse, and reliable resources in comparison with drier basins and uplands (Oetting 1989:272–74). Such resources, however, also require some processing time and equipment, transportation time, as well as bulk storage space and storage facilities. The relative reliability, abundance, and diversity of foods all found within a limited geographic area, coupled with the processing, movement, and storage requirements of these products would foster reduced residential mobility. Logistical mobility for obtaining and transporting certain resources would probably increase with reduced residential mobility, but the establishment of residential sites near wetland procurement areas would minimize overall transportation requirements. Stored resources would also contribute to the residential stability of sites by providing buffers against short-term and seasonal resource shortages. Even in times of resource stress, the most reliable food sources would probably be in wetland areas (Kelly 1985:307).

A semisedentary and, eventually, a sedentary settlement pattern could develop in this situation, where people would continue the basic fusion-fission strategy, but where the same winter villages were returned to every year and length of residence increased. This stability would encourage greater labor investments in buildings, tools, and processing equipment. These villages would be a long-term, stable adaptation to wetland resources that should leave traces in the archaeological record and, in Harney Basin and elsewhere, have left such traces in the form of marsh-edge pit house villages.

ANALOGY OR CULTURAL AFFILIATION?

The differences observed in the artifact assemblages and adaptive strategies between the earlier pit house structures and the later wickiup at the McCoy Creek site may reflect in situ adaptive transitions made by the local inhabitants as environmental conditions changed (Musil 1995), with pit house villages and a wetland subsistence focus during moderately wet to moderately dry climatic periods and more mobile strategies during intervals of climatic extremes. However, these differences may instead, or *also*, reflect cultural or ethnic differences. Beyond the use of the Paiute and Klamath as ethnographic analogues, they may also represent actual cultural or ethnic affiliations for certain periods of Harney Basin prehistory. As discussed above, the plateau-related, Penutian-speaking Klamath-Modoc are analogous to the archaeological residential patterns, but these patterns may be the result of actual prehistoric Penutian populations residing in Harney Basin (Cressman 1942; Minor and Toepel 1988). The more residentially mobile, later prehistoric strategies may reflect the advent of the local ethnographic inhabitants, the Wada'tika Northern Paiute.

The presence of large biface blades; decorated ground stone and bone tools; well-shaped manos, metates, and pestle/mauls; as well as the semisubterranean pit houses suggest cultural contacts outside of the Great Basin (Oetting 1992). Large bipointed and sometimes waisted obsidian blades, similar to the Malheur Lake specimens, have been found in ethnographic contexts in northwestern California (Rust 1905; Kroeber 1925) and in archaeological contexts in southwestern Oregon (Cressman 1933; Hughes 1990), the Klamath-Modoc region (Sampson 1985), and on the Columbia River (E. Strong 1960), but have rarely been found in the Great Basin. One decorated pestle/maul and a decorated bone "head scratcher" or "sweat scraper" were collected during the surveys (Oetting 1990b). The decoration of utilitarian stone tools is rare among traditional ethnographic or prehistoric Great Basin groups, but has been documented for the Klamath (Barrett 1910; R. L. Carlson 1959) and is relatively common along the Columbia River (W. Strong, Schenck, and Steward 1930; E. Strong 1960). Similarly, the decorated bone head scratcher is comparable to Klamath specimens, and the decorations distinguish it from ethnographic Paiute examples. The variety of well-finished and shaped manos, metates, and pestle/mauls is reminiscent of both Klamath and Columbia River ground stone tools (Cressman 1956; Trygg 1971; W. Strong et al. 1930).

The presence of houses and types of artifacts with similarities to plateau and Klamath material culture is suggestive of some sort of prehistoric cultural affiliation, but is by no means conclusive (Aikens 1985; Oetting 1989; Weide 1968). Likewise, the relatively stable residential sites and the wetland-oriented subsistence practices, while similar to the Klamath, are certainly not exclusive to them. Extensive and detailed research will be necessary to evaluate these potential associations and their extent and to determine the prehistoric periods during which these connections, influences, or parallels were manifest.

THE RELEVANCE OF BIOARCHAEOLOGICAL INVESTIGATIONS
Bioarchaeological analyses of the human burials recovered during the Malheur Lake flood provide a promising avenue of inquiry for examining some of the models and issues discussed above since these analyses can provide relatively direct reflections of the health, lifeways, and even genetic affiliations of prehistoric individuals and groups (e.g., Larsen and Kelly 1995). In particular, such topics as prehistoric mobility strategies and settlement-subsistence practices can be approached through a variety of bioarchaeological analyses, including osteoarthritis incidence (Hemphill, this volume), long-bone structural morphology (Ruff, this volume), and dental development (Nelson, this volume). No genetic studies were conducted on the Malheur Lake burials.

However, using bioarchaeological data to examine the settlement models presented for Harney Basin may be a difficult task. As discussed above, the differences distinguishing these two ethnographically derived settlement-subsistence models are ones of degree, not of kind. Thus, the physical differences in bone structure and pathologies that might reflect these two models may be relatively subtle differences in degree of wear or structural development. Individuals in semisedentary groups using annually reoccupied winter villages analogous to the Klamath-Modoc may have led lives that were just as vigorous and rigorous as individuals in groups with greater residential mobility analogous to the Wada'tika Northern Paiute since both groups spent a portion of the year moving about. Although the Klamath model reflects reduced residential mobility, the logistical mobility of individuals and task groups may have been quite high.

In addition, since the models discussed in this paper are thought to have operated at different times, it is crucial to control the temporal aspect of any bioarchaeological studies. Differences between individuals and populations from different eras may be masked or missed without such controls. Only nine of the analyzed Malheur burials have radiocarbon ages and eight of these are less than 1,100 years old, with five less than 500 years old. Only one time-sensitive projectile point, a narrow-necked Rosegate specimen, was directly associated with a burial (Hemphill 1992a,b,c). Thus, the majority of the sample may correspond to the ethnographic Wada'tika Northern Paiute and reflect their highly mobile seasonal round (as modeled by Raven 1992). Such findings would not negate the possibility that a different settlement-subsistence system was operating prior to the last 500 or 1,000 years.

It should also be remembered that while osteoarthritis is generally inferred to reflect the activity levels of and, hence, mobility of the individual, the development of this disorder is also age- and sex-related. Thus, osteoarthritis in elderly individuals may reflect degenerative changes associated with advancing age rather than high activity levels. Indeed, mortuary populations containing significant numbers of elderly individuals with osteoarthritis and other infirmities may result from semisedentary residential patterns rather than mobility-related activities by affording elderly people greater opportunities to survive to an older age by not having to always move with the family group. As noted above, ill and elderly Klamath, with children acting as caretakers, stayed in the winter villages while the rest of the family moved on the seasonal round (Stern 1966:11).

SUMMARY AND CONCLUSIONS

This brief review of archaeological research in Harney Basin demonstrates that the basin has a long and rich archaeological record. Sites of all sizes and functions are known, including task-specific activity sites such as quarries, lithic reduction/knapping locales, hunting stations, and plant procurement and processing sites, along with larger multiple activity sites that are interpreted as long-term seasonal camps and villages. Bioarchaeological analyses have been conducted on 54 human burials recovered in the area (presented in this volume). House pits have been tested at four sites and similar features have been observed at several other localities. Assemblage density and diversity at some of the sites have, at present, few parallels in the northern Great Basin. Artifacts such as the large biface blades and the well-finished ground stone implements have rarely been found in the region and never in the numbers seen at these Harney Basin sites.

These village sites are preferentially located near the extensive marshes around Malheur Lake and along the marshy shores of the lake itself. A wetland subsistence focus can be inferred for many of the recorded sites, based on the location of sites, the presence of particular tool types, and recovered faunal and botanical data. The variety and density of artifacts, along with the presence of semisubterranean pit house features at several sites in the marshes, suggest that some of the sites were semisedentary winter villages. These data contrast with the residentially mobile lifeways of the ethnographic Wada'tika Northern Paiute and suggest that different patterns of settlement and subsistence may have been operating in the region prior to 500 or 1000 B.P.. Sites with semisubterranean house features situated in or near the wetlands suggest that the semisedentary residential patterns and wetland subsistence focus of the ethnographic Klamath-Modoc may be the more appropriate analogue for much of the period between about 5000 B.P. and 1000 or 500 B.P.

12

Environmental Fluctuation and Physiological Stress in the Northern Great Basin

Greg C. Nelson

Although periodically abundant, Great Basin wetlands are susceptible to fluctuations in climate and can at times dry up completely (Duebbert 1969; Grayson 1993). How prehistoric inhabitants reacted, both culturally and physically, to these fluctuations can be investigated through the study of subsistence strategies and physiological stress. By combining the study of human remains from Malheur Lake, Oregon, with models of subsistence strategy and data concerning environmental fluctuation, this chapter will explore the relationship between physiologic stress and environmental change. In the Malheur Lake area the prevalence and severity of linear enamel hypoplasia and periosteal reactions among prehistoric inhabitants show considerable increase during the last 1,800 years. Climatically, this period is considered to be much like that of today (Aikens 1993; Grayson 1993), characterized by alternating wet and dry periods of varying durations. In marginal environments, this type of climatic fluctuation can have tremendous effects on the availability of resources. Unlike more mesic environments, a drop in effective moisture of only one or two years duration can lead to shrinking lakes and desiccated marshes which, in turn, result in diminished resource availability (Hutchinson and Larsen 1995) and altered adaptive strategies (Kelly 1990). If drought conditions continue for more than a few years, then lakes may dry completely, resulting in marked population reductions owing to declining fertility and out-migration.

STRESS AND PHYSIOLOGY

Stress, as defined by Selye (1973:692) "is the nonspecific response of the body to any demand made upon it." In these terms, nonspecific relates to the fact that the body can react in the same way to different stressors. Although the causative agent may be specific—that is, nutritional deficit, disease, or infection—the body's response to these different stressors can be the same. In general, linear enamel hypoplasia and periosteal reactions are consistent with a nonspecific model in that both pathological conditions can have many causes. However, both conditions provide a useful record of population health and well-being.

Hypoplasia

Numerous studies have shown dental enamel hypoplasia to be a good indicator of nonspecific physiological stress (e.g., Corruccini, Handler, and Jacobi 1985; Powell 1988; Lanphear 1990; Van Gerven, Beck, and Hummert 1990; Goodman and Rose 1990). Several characteristics make the study of hypoplasia important in determining levels of stress during childhood in prehistoric skeletal series. First, while the tooth is forming, it is very sensitive to developmental disruptions brought on by poor diet or disease. These disruptions can cause enamel development to either slow down or stop, resulting in areas of decreased enamel thickness. Generally, this decrease in enamel thickness manifests itself as either pits or bands of deficient enamel. Second, enamel is laid down in a systematic way and at a known rate. This means that the age of disturbance can be determined with some accuracy (Goodman and Rose 1990). And finally, unlike bone, enamel does not undergo remodeling. Therefore, except in cases of extreme tooth wear, hypoplasia provides a permanent record of growth disturbance.

Periosteal Reactions

Periosteal reactions occur when the contact between the periosteum, the thin sheath that covers the outer bone surface, and the underlying bone is disturbed through either direct trauma or infection. Infection may originate either through the circulatory system or from surrounding soft tissue (Ortner and Putschar 1985). Characteristic lesions consist of new bone growth on the surface of the existing bone and range in size from small patches to involvement of an entire bone diaphysis. Prevalence of periosteal reactions, particularly when combined with other stress markers, is a good indicator of overall community health (Rose and Hartnady 1991).

Environment and Dietary Context

The northern Great Basin (Figure 12.1) is a high desert environment of hot summers and cold winters lying in the rain shadow of the Cascade Mountains. Precipitation comes as fall and spring rains and winter snows, with little falling between May and October. Because this area experiences relatively high, dry-season evaporation, it does not take many years of decreased precipitation to affect lake levels and flora dependant on wetter conditions.

Over the last 7,500 years, there have been two major climatic episodes in which either generally wet or dry conditions prevailed (Aikens 1993; Grayson

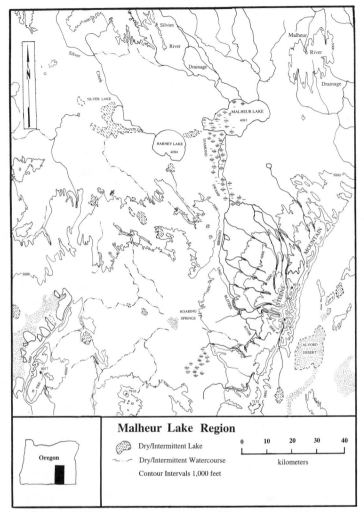

FIGURE 12.1. Malheur Lake area, including Donner und Blitzen River and Steens Mountain, Oregon.

1993). From approximately 7500 to 4500 B.P. the northern Great Basin (as well as much of western North America) experienced conditions dryer than today. Defined by Antevs (1948, 1955) as the Altithermal, this was a period in which many wetland areas dried up and several parts of the Great Basin appear to have been abandoned by the human inhabitants (see Grayson 1993 for discussion on the validity of the Altithermal). Beginning around 4500 B.P., wetter conditions, similar to those of today, returned with an expansion of the pluvial lakes and rehabitation by humans. As important as these large-scale environmental trends are, it is the yearly to decades-long fluctuations in rainfall that truly characterize the climate of

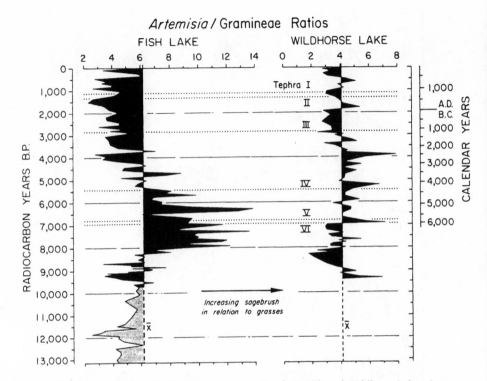

FIGURE 12.2. Ratios of sagebrush and grass pollen from Fish and Wildhorse Lakes, Steens Mountain, Oregon (Mehringer 1985:181). An increase in sagebrush pollen and concomitant decrease in grass pollen indicates relatively dry conditions. Note the increase in sagebrush pollen at approximately 500 B.P. in the Fish Lake sample after many years of high grass-pollen levels. A spike indicating high sagebrush levels at Wildhorse Lake near this time period is also visible.

the northern Great Basin and are of importance in understanding human adaptation. Mehringer (1985), in a study of sagebrush and grass pollen from lake sediment cores collected from Fish and Wildhorse Lakes in the Steens Mountain area of southeastern Oregon, details many episodes of increased and decreased moisture (Figure 12.2). On an even smaller time scale, Antevs's study (1938) of tree rings is indicative of the fluctuations that can occur from year to year and from decade to decade (Figure 12.3). Considerable climate fluctuation for southeastern Oregon is also indicated by pack-rat midden analysis from Diamond Craters (Mehringer and Wigand 1990) and pollen analysis from Diamond Pond (Wigand 1987). Both Diamond Craters and Diamond Pond are located only 20 km south of Malheur Lake, while Fish and Wildhorse Lakes are approximately 60 km distant, also to the south.

The climatic record for the last 2,000 years, the time frame of interest for this

TABLE 12.1.
Radiocarbon Dates for Malheur Lake (Burnside 1992)

Specimen	^{14}C Date	Lab. No.
1899.1	460 ± 120	BETA-49698
1899.3	1830 ± 120	BETA-49691
1905.1	1050 ± 140	BETA-49692
1906.1	310 ± 120	BETA-49693
1906.3	700 ± 120	BETA-49694
1911.1	1070 ± 140	BETA-49699
2095.1	160 ± 100	BETA-49697
2095.9	310 ± 100	BETA-49695
2095.2	300 ± 100	BETA-49696

study, indicates essentially modern levels of precipitation (Grayson 1993). However, beginning about 500 B.P. there seems to have been a noticeable decrease in effective moisture that lasted approximately 200 years (see Figure 12.3). It is during this time period that site 35HA2095, comprising the majority of individuals assigned to the Late Malheur component, seems to have been occupied (Table 12.1). That 35HA2095 was inhabited during a dry episode is further supported in that it is from a low lake-level context.

Subsistence

The ethnographic record concerning aboriginal subsistence in the Malheur Lake area is derived from reports of the Wada'tika Paiute (Whiting 1950; Couture 1978; Couture, Ricks, and Housley 1986; Aikens and Greenspan 1988; Aikens 1993). The Wada'tika Paiute were highly mobile. During their annual seasonal round, they exploited several different areas and associated resources. Winter was spent in base camps located near the lake and the river marshes. During the winter, subsistence consisted of stored foods, fish from the lake, and the occasional waterfowl. In late April or early May, large numbers of people would congregate in the hills to the north and east in order to collect root crops for winter storage. During late May and early June, salmon were taken from the upper portions of the Malheur River (just over the divide into the Snake/Columbia River drainage area), camas bulbs were collected, and marmots were hunted. For the hot part of the summer, July and August, people dispersed into small bands that hunted and gathered throughout the uplands. In the fall, berries were collected, rabbit drives commenced, and large game (e.g., elk, deer, and antelope) were hunted. In November, the winter camps were reestablished.

For the Malheur area and environment, this seasonally oriented strategy was highly efficient, involving the exploitation of nearly all available resources. In the

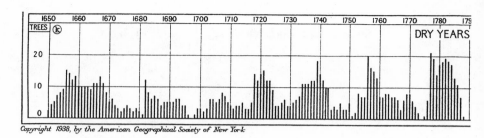

FIGURE 12.3. Tree-ring analysis of precipitation in the northern Great Basin (Antevs 1938:Plate I). Zero equals wet conditions, whereas 20 equals drought.

Harney Basin, mobility appears to have been an important factor, with winters spent in the lowlands in large camps and late spring through fall spent in the uplands exploiting both animal and plant food sources.

In contrast to subsistence models suggested by Kelly (1985, 1990, 1995b) and Raven and Elston (1989) for the Stillwater Marsh of western Nevada and Jenkins (1994) for the Fort Rock Basin of Oregon, the ethnographically based model for the Harney Basin includes much higher levels of residential mobility. In several respects, the subsistence pattern seen in the Harney Basin is similar to that discussed by Simms (1987) for the Great Salt Lake area, in which temporal and spatial variability in resource base implies a highly mobile, exploitative strategy.

With Raven and Elston (1989) and Kelly (1985, 1990, 1995b) focusing on the Stillwater Marsh area, it is informative to note their differing views. Both place a heavy emphasis on marsh resources, but disagree on the amount of residential mobility and the extent of upland resource exploitation. Raven and Elston argue that everything centers around relatively permanent residences near the marsh, with use of the uplands limited to large game hunting and seasonal piñon nut collecting. Because Raven and Elston were primarily concerned with "identify[ing] where, within our area of interest, [people] are most likely to have spent their time and left an archaeological record" (1989:152), they give only cursory notice to upland resources in their model.

Kelly (1985, 1990, 1995b) includes mobility in his model, but focuses on logistical mobility for men, hunting forays to the mountains and small animal hunting on the valley floor, while women—and residences—moved around the marsh. This model downplays the importance of piñon pine for two reasons. First, piñon only occurs in the northern portion of the Stillwater Mountains and, second, there is evidence that piñon is a relatively recent (later than 1500 B.P.) migrant into the area (Kelly 1995b). Kelly (1990) also ties the increase in marsh-based subsistence after 1500 B.P. with a decrease in precipitation, which would make the already dry Stillwater Mountains even less productive.

Jenkins's model (1994) for Fort Rock is upland based and centers around the

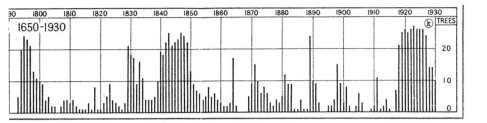

collection of root crops and hunting. Interestingly, this upland-based economy appears to have intensified after 1500 B.P., with the largest number of village sites dating to around 500 B.P. The intensification of upland exploitation coincides with the drop in effective moisture seen elsewhere in the northern Great Basin. Unlike the Harney Basin, the lowland lake and marsh resources of the Fort Rock Basin are more ephemeral (Freidel 1994) and, therefore, are more susceptible to virtually complete desiccation during dry periods. With adequate water sources near the upland root-collecting region, it is easy to envision abandonment of the lowlands very shortly after the establishment of arid conditions.

The subsistence model described for the Malheur Lake area lies between the models for Stillwater Marsh (Raven and Elston 1989; Kelly 1985, 1990, 1995b) and the Fort Rock Basin (Jenkins 1994). The differences between the various models are all directly related to differences in the physiography and hydrology of the basins to which they apply. In particular, the contrast between Stillwater Marsh and the Malheur Lake/Harney Basin area seems to be in the nature of the upland resources. First, water is more abundant in the uplands to the north, east, and south of Malheur Lake than is apparently the case for the Stillwater Mountains (Cressman 1986; Raven and Elston 1989; Kelly 1995b). Second, although piñon is absent, root crops, such as camas and bitterroot, are abundant in the hills. Third, the upper reaches of the Malheur River, with its yearly runs of anadromous fish, is only about 10 miles east of Malheur Lake. In nutritionally marginal environments, such as the Great Basin, the inhabitants would, by necessity, maximally exploit available resources wherever and whenever they might occur. In the Malheur Lake area, upland resources are relatively abundant, have generally stable water sources, and are close enough that residential movement to the resource would not have been overly taxing. Such features illustrate why subsistence models constructed for aboriginal use of Great Basin wetlands cannot be all-encompassing, for each basin has unique characteristics that effect the subsistence strategy employed by the inhabitants (see Hemphill, this volume). Under normal conditions in the Malheur region, good upland resources meant that people would not have to be residentially tethered to the marshes year-round as is proposed for Stillwater Marsh (Raven 1992).

It is important to understand the subsistence strategies used in the Great Basin if one is to explore how environmental fluctuation affects human populations residing in the Malheur Lake wetlands. According to Aikens (1993:56), archaeological evidence indicates that the subsistence pattern described for the contact-period Wadatika Paiute "existed in the region for at least the last 4,000 years." If so, fluctuating moisture levels would have effected many aspects of this subsistence base by leading to increased or decreased availability of resources. During periods of less effective moisture, the lake and riverine marsh areas could undergo drastic changes. The lakes would shrink, the river marshes would desiccate and both would become less productive in both plant resources and waterfowl availability. If a few dry years stretched into several years of drought, then the waters could recede to the point where the marshes became unproductive (Piper, Robinson, and Park 1939; Wigand 1987) and Malheur Lake could become nothing more than a series of intermittently flooded playas (McDowell 1992).

Persistent drought would force the inhabitants to migrate out of the Malheur Lake area, most probably to the north toward the Blue Mountains and the John Day Basin or southwest toward Chewaucan Marsh and Lake Abert (Oetting 1989; Aikens 1993, Jenkins 1994). But, a return to wetter conditions and more abundant resources would result in rehabitation of the river marshes.

However, early in a dry period, as the river marshes desiccated and the lake shrank, the marshes that encircled the lake could become larger and more productive in plant resources as the area of open water decreased and the emergent vegetation-rich shallows expanded. In the uplands, the consequences of drying would be less obvious. As effective moisture decreased, the length of the season of availability of plant resources could shorten and the area in which they were available could shrink or move upslope (Cressman 1986). Large game would retreat to higher elevations and, in times of extreme drought, might decrease in population size or migrate out of the area entirely. Any of these occurrences would decrease the availability of specific resources and increase the time involved in procuring them. The combination of diminishing upland resources and readily accessible marshes could create a situation in which more people spent a longer time near the lake. Although the Malheur lake margins were usually occupied to some degree, they now would become an area of population concentrations, resulting in increased stress on both the resource base and the inhabitants.

Archaeological evidence supports population movements during times of reduced moisture. Although the Harney Basin was probably never completely abandoned, due to perennial springs on the valley floor and in the uplands (Fagan 1974), population reduction is evident. At Diamond Swamp, part of the Donner und Blitzen riverine marsh system, Musil (1995) found decreases in site number and occupation intensity corresponding to the dry period that began around

500 B.P. At this same time period, population increases are noted in the upper John Day Basin (Connolly, Jenkins, and Benjamin 1993) and in the uplands near the Fort Rock Basin (Jenkins 1994).

MATERIALS AND METHODS

Malheur Lake is located in the extreme northwestern corner of the Great Basin within the Harney Basin (Figure 12.1). It is a fluvial lake fed by streams originating in the highlands to the north, west, and south. Under normal to wet conditions, there are marshes throughout the body of the lake and around the margins. According to Duebbert (1969) the whole of Malheur Lake is, in reality, classified as an Inland Deep Fresh Marsh. An extensive marsh system also borders the Donner und Blitzen River, which empties into the lake from the south. Ethnographic reports of the Wada'tika Paiute indicate that the lake margins and river marshes were the sites of large winter camps of long duration (Aikens and Greenspan 1988; Aikens 1993).

Human skeletal remains recovered from the shore and islands were examined for this study. Exposed during an extreme high-water event of 1985–1986, they were collected between 1988 and 1991 and represent 54 individuals. The remains have since been reinterred under an agreement between the U.S. Department of Interior, Fish and Wildlife Service, and the Burns Paiute Tribe (Hemphill 1992a, 1992b, 1992c).

Radiocarbon dates obtained from nine of these individuals range from 160 to 1830 years B.P. Five of the dates cluster around 300 B.P., and three are older than 1000 years B.P. One site, 35HA2095, has dates of 160, 300, and 310 years B.P. (see Table 12.1).

The sample consists of 17 males, 24 females, and 13 individuals of unknown sex. Thirty-four individuals are adults, and 20 are juveniles. Sex was determined through morphologic (limited to the cranium, mandible, sacrum, and innominate) and metric (univariate and/or multivariate analyses of the femur, tibia, humerus, sacrum, scapula, cranial base, and the talus and calcaneus) analyses. Age was assessed via dental development and wear, epiphyseal union, pubic symphyseal and auricular surface changes, cranial suture closure, and rib phase analysis. Utilized age and sex determination methods are described in depth by Hemphill (1992a).

Linear enamel hypoplasias (LEH) were recorded by Hemphill (1992a, 1992b, 1992c). The number of defects per tooth and the distance from the center of each line to the cementoenamel junction was recorded. For each defect, the age at formation was estimated using the regression formulae provided by Goodman and Rose (1990). For this study, frequencies of occurrence by individual and tooth type, number of lines per individual, number of teeth affected per individual,

TABLE 12.2.
Incisor and Canine Tooth Data from Malheur Lake Used for
Comparison with Stillwater Marsh

Specimen	Tooth[a]	Events[b]	Age[c]	Specimen	Tooth[a]	Events[b]	Age[c]
403-D2*	C^1	0	0	1906-1	$_1C$	3	3.6
403-D2	^1C	0	0	1906-1	I^2	0	0
403-2	C_1	0	0	1906-1	C^1	0	0
403-2	$_1C$	0	0	1906-1	^1C	0	0
403-3	I_1	0	0	1906-3	I_2	0	0
403-3	I_2	2	1.9	1906-3	$_2I$	0	0
403-3	C_1	4	3.0	1906-3	$_1C$	0	0
403-3	$_1I$	0	0	1906-3**	^2I	1	2.8
403-3	$_2I$	3	1.1	1906-3	^1C	0	0
403-3	$_1C$	4	2.9	1907-1	I_1	0	0
403-3	I^1	0	0	1907-1	I_2	0	0
403-3	I^2	2	1.9	1907-1	C_1	0	0
403-3	C^1	0	0	1907-1	$_2I$	0	0
403-3	^1I	0	0	1907-1	$_1C$	0	0
403-3	^1C	0	0	1911-3	I_1	0	0
1032a-1a	I_1	0	0	1911-3	I_2	0	0
1032a-1a	I_2	0	0	1911-3	C_1	1	4.7
1032a-1a	C_1	2	4.5	1911-3	$_1I$	0	0
1032a-1a	$_2I$	0	0	1911-3	$_2I$	0	0
1032a-1a	$_1C$	2	4.5	1911-3	$_1C$	0	0
1899-1a	C_1	4	3.4	1911-1.69	I^1	0	0
1899-1a	$_2I$	1	2.7	1911-1.69	C^1	0	0
1899-1a	$_1C$	4	3.0	1911-1.69	^2I	0	0
1899-1a	I^2	0	0	1911-1.69	^1C	0	0
1899-1a	C^1	3	2.2	1911-1.98	I_2	1	2.1
1899-1a	^1C	3	2.2	1911-1.98	C_1	1	3.7
1899-3	I_1	3	2.2	1911-1.98	$_2I$	0	0
1899-3	I_2	0	0	1911-1.98	$_1C$	1	3.7
1899-3	C_1	3	1.7	1911-1.98	C^1	1	3.2
1899-3	$_1I$	2	2.7	1949-8b***	$_2I$	0	0
1899-3	$_2I$	0	0	1949-8b	$_1C$	0	0
1899-3	$_1C$	0	0	1949-HB1	$_1C$	3	3.03
1899-3	I^1	2	2.2	1949-HB5	C^1	2	3.5
1899-3	C^1	4	2.4	1977-1	I_1	0	0
1899-3	^1I	3	1.7	1977-1	I_2	0	0
1899-3	^2I	3	1.6	1977-1	C_1	4	2.9
1899-3	^1C	4	2.7	1977-1	$_1I$	0	0
1906-1	I_1	1	2.5	1977-1	$_2I$	0	0
1906-1	I_2	0	0	1977-1	$_1C$	4	2.9
1906-1	C_1	3	3.6	1991-2	I_1	0	0
1906-1	$_1I$	1	2.2	1991-2	I_2	0	0
1906-1	$_2I$	0	0	1991-2	$_1I$	0	0

Specimen	Tooth[a]	Events[b]	Age[c]	Specimen	Tooth[a]	Events[b]	Age[c]
1991-2	$_2$I	0	0	2095-9	I$_2$	0	0
1991-4	I$_1$	0	0	2095-9	C$_1$	1	5.6
1991-4	C$_1$	0	0	2095-9	$_1$I	0	0
1991-4	$_1$I	0	0	2095-9	$_2$I	0	0
1991-4	$_1$C	0	0	2095-9	$_1$C	0	0
1991-4	I^2	0	0	2095-9	I^1	1	2.7
1991-4	^{1}C	0	0	2095-9	I^2	0	0
2095-1	I$_1$	0	0	2095-9	C^1	0	0
2095-1	I$_2$	0	0	2095-9	^{1}I	0	0
2095-1	C$_1$	5	2.1	2095-9	^{2}I	0	0
2095-1	$_1$I	0	0	2095-9	^{1}C	0	0
2095-1	$_2$I	2	2.1	2095-12a	I$_1$	1	2.5
2095-1	$_1$C	4	2.9	2095-12a	I$_2$	2	2.2
2095-1	C^1	4	2.2	2095-12a	C$_1$	4	2.5
2095-1	^{1}I	0	0	2095-12a	$_1$I	2	2.5
2095-1	^{2}I	0	0	2095-12a	$_2$I	2	2.1
2095-1	^{1}C	0	0	2095-12a	$_1$C	3	3.6
2095-3	I$_1$	0	0	2095-12a	I^1	0	0
2095-3	I$_2$	0	0	2095-12a	I^2	5	1.3
2095-3	C$_1$	1	4.7	2095-12a	C^1	3	2.0
2095-3	$_1$I	0	0	2095-12a	^{1}C	4	1.6
2095-3	$_2$I	0	0	2095-12b	I$_1$	0	0
2095-3	$_1$C	1	4.4	2095-12b	I$_2$	0	0
2095-3	I^1	2	2.8	2095-12b	C$_1$	1	5.3
2095-3	I^2	2	2.8	2095-12b	$_1$I	0	0
2095-3	C^1	1	4.4	2095-12b	$_2$I	2	2.9
2095-3	^{1}I	3	3.5	2095-12b	$_1$C	4	4.1
2095-3	^{2}I	1	3.6	2095-12b	I^1	3	1.7
2095-3	^{1}C	1	4.1	2095-12b	I^2	3	2.6
2095-4	I$_2$	1	2.7	2095-12b	C^1	4	3.6
2095-4	C$_1$	3	4.4	2095-12b	^{1}C	1	4.9
2095-4	$_1$I	0	0	2095-14	I$_1$	1	2.6
2095-4	$_2$I	0	0	2095-14	I$_2$	2	2.3
2095-4	$_1$C	3	4.2	2095-14	C$_1$	4	2.3
2095-4	I^1	0	0	2095-14	$_1$I	1	2.5
2095-4	I^2	1	3.6	2095-14	$_2$I	2	2.7
2095-4	C^1	2	4.1	2095-14	I^1	3	1.8
2095-4	^{1}I	1	3.6	2095-14	I^2	1	2.4
2095-4	^{2}I	1	3.3	2095-14	C^1	0	0
2095-4	^{1}C	2	3.8	2095-14	^{1}I	2	1.8
2095-5a	I^1	0	0	2095-14	^{2}I	2	2.1
2095-5a	I^2	0	0	2095-14	^{1}C	0	0
2095-5a	^{1}I	0	0	2095-15	I$_1$	1	2.6
2095-5a	^{2}I	0	0	2095-15	I$_2$	2	1.9
2095-9	I$_1$	0	0	2095-15	C$_1$	6	1.4

Specimen	Tooth[a]	Events[b]	Age[c]	Specimen	Tooth[a]	Events[b]	Age[c]
2095-15	$_1$I	2	2.2	2095-A672	I$_2$	0	0
2095-15	$_2$I	0	0	2095-A672	C$_1$	0	0
2095-15	$_1$C	5	2.9	2095-A672	$_2$I	0	0
2095-15	I^1	4	1.7	2095-A672	$_1$C	0	0
2095-15	I^2	4	2.1	2095-A682	I$_1$	0	0
2095-15	C^1	6	0.9	2095-A682	I$_2$	0	0
2095-15	^{1}I	4	1.7	2095-A682	C$_1$	0	0
2095-15	^{2}I	3	2.9	2095-A682	$_1$C	0	0
2095-15	^{1}C	5	0.4	2095-A682	I^2	0	0
2095-20	I$_1$	0	0	2095-A682	C^1	0	0
2095-20	I$_2$	2	1.9	2095-A682	^{1}I	0	0
2095-20	C$_1$	6	1.2	2095-A682	^{2}I	0	0
2095-20	$_1$I	0	0	2095-A682	^{1}C	0	0
2095-20	$_2$I	2	2.3	2095-B48	I$_1$	0	0
2095-20	$_1$C	5	1.1	2095-B48	I$_2$	0	0
2095-20	I^1	3	1.3	2095-B48	C$_1$	2	4.1
2095-20	I^2	3	1.6	2095-B48	$_2$I	0	0
2095-20	C^1	4	0.4	2095-B48	$_1$C	4	3.5
2095-20	^{2}I	1	3.2	2095-B146	^{2}I	2	2.0
2095-20	^{1}C	3	0.2	2095-B146	^{1}C	2	2.6

[a] I$_1$ = lower right central incisor; I$_2$ = lower right lateral incisor; C$_1$ = lower right canine; $_1$I = lower left central incisor; $_2$I = lower left lateral incisor; $_1$C = lower left canine; I^1 = upper right central incisor; I^2 = upper right lateral incisor; C^1 = upper right canine; ^{1}I = upper left central incisor; ^{2}I = upper left lateral incisor; ^{1}C = upper left canine.

[b] Number of linear enamel hypoplasia events per tooth.

[c] Age of occurrence of first hypoplasia event.

* 403-D2 has a band of hypoplastic pitting on the upper left third molar.

** 1906-3 has a circular hypoplastic defect on the upper left lateral incisor.

*** 1949-8B has one hypoplastic line on the lower left third premolar.

number of events per individual, interval between events, and age at time of disruption were calculated. This was done for the group as a whole as well as by sex and age.

Of the 54 individuals from Malheur Lake, 32 were included in the hypoplasia analysis. Research concerning the study of hypoplasia indicates that the permanent incisors and canines are the most useful in recording this pathology (Goodman and Armelagos 1985b; Goodman and Rose 1990; Hutchinson and Larsen 1990, 1995). Therefore, only those individuals who retained permanent incisors and/or canines were considered for study (Table 12.2). Secondarily, individuals in which attrition was extreme (more than two-thirds of tooth crown worn away) were excluded. However, analysis was not limited solely to these teeth. Linear enamel hypoplasias appearing on the premolars and molars were included in the analyses of number of events and age of occurrence. As these teeth tend to record disturbances that happen later in childhood (Goodman and Armelagos 1985b) their inclusion in this portion of the study increases the amount of information attainable and, therefore, improves our insight into the effects of stress as recorded in the dentition.

All skeletal elements were examined for proliferative lesions that characterize periosteal reactions. Lesion size was recorded and location described. Data were analyzed by age, sex, lesion location, and remodeling status (active or healed).

For both hypoplasias and periosteal reactions, the data set was split between Early (n = 31) and Late (n = 23) components. Twenty of the 23 individuals included in the Late group come from one site (35HA2095), with the remaining three from two other sites, 35HA1899 (n = 2) and 35HA1906 (n = 1). All radiocarbon dates obtained from these individuals indicate a late occupation of this wetland environment. Additionally, in an effort to place the findings from Malheur into the context of this volume, comparisons with material from Stillwater Marsh (Hutchinson and Larsen 1995) were done for the Malheur Lake area as a whole as well as the subsets.

RESULTS

Linear Enamel Hypoplasia

Nearly two-thirds (65.6 percent) of individuals exhibit at least one linear enamel hypoplastic defect on their incisors or canines (Table 12.3). More females are affected than males (81.8 percent vs. 57.1 percent) but, due to the relatively small numbers of individuals represented, it is difficult to accurately predict if this difference is significant.

Number of hypoplastic events per individual and age at first occurrence reveal some interesting trends. For the adult females, the average age of occurrence of the initial disruption is 2.9 years, and the average age for males is 2.5 years. Among the small sample (n = 4) of individuals of unknown sex, initial disruption is 1.3 years. Small sample size, combined with early age at death are possible confounding factors in this low rate.

The difference between females and males in number of events is negligible (4.2 vs. 4.1 events), and the average of the unknown sex segment is slightly higher (5.0 events).

Some differences in prevalence emerge when the Malheur skeletal series is split into Early and Late groups (Table 12.4). Statistically significant differences occur in average number of disruptive events and in age at first occurrence. For number of events, individuals from the Late period average significantly (t = 2.57; p <

TABLE 12.3.

Frequencies of Linear Enamel Hypoplasia, Number of Hypoplasia Events, and
Age of First Occurrence for the Combined Sample from Malheur Lake,
Separated by Sex

Sex	Linear Enamel Hypoplasia			Events Mean	Age Mean
	Present	Number	Percent		
Male	8	14	57.1	4.10	2.45
Female	9	11	81.8	4.20	2.93
Unkn.	4	7	57.1	5.00	1.30
Total	21	32	65.6	4.32	2.43

.05) more episodes of stress with an average of 5.15 lines per individual compared to
3.11 for the Early group. Likewise, for age at first occurrence, the difference between the samples is significant ($t = 2.28$; $p < .05$). First occurrence averages 1.92
years for the Late group, a full year earlier than the 3.09 years recorded for the Early
sample. Age at death may be a confounding factor in interpreting the age of first
occurrence. That is, the younger the individual, the less wear is likely to be present,
and, therefore, a higher number of hypoplastic lines are likely to be preserved.
However, age at death by itself does not explain the pattern because the two groups
show very similar age-at-death profiles (i.e., nine adults and four subadult/juve-
niles from the Late sample and seven adults, one subadult/juveniles, and one child
from the Early sample).

Figures 12.4 and 12.5 illustrate the hypoplasia profiles of the two groups. For
the number of events per individual (Figure 12.4), the Late group has a lower percentage of individuals with one through three lines, but higher frequencies of
those with four through eleven lines. With the interval between events (Figure
12.5), it is apparent that the stresses which cause hypoplasia occurred more frequently in the Late sample since nearly 50 percent of the intervals between lines are

TABLE 12.4.
Number of Hypoplasia Events and Age at First Occurrence for Malheur Lake

Site	Number of Events			Age of 1st Event	
	No.	Mean	SD	Mean	SD
Early	9	3.11	1.96	3.09	1.34
Late Malheur	13	5.15	1.63	1.92	0.89
Total	22	4.32	2.01	2.43	1.21

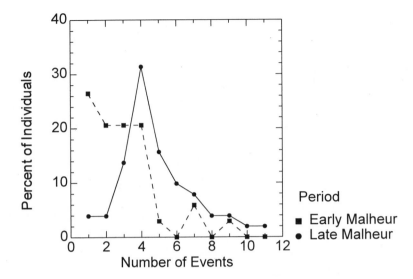

FIGURE 12.4. Average number of hypoplastic events.

six months apart, whereas the intervals found in the Early sample are more spread out and show no peak. This profile also indicates that stress was prevalent for both groups throughout the early childhood years although more severe among individuals recovered from the Late period.

Periosteal Reactions
Of the Malheur Lake series, 42.6 percent have at least one skeletal element that displays periosteal reactions. Prevalence among adult males (35.3 percent) is lower than among either females (45.8 percent) or among those of unknown sex (46.2 percent). Periosteal reactions occur with highest frequency among children (45.5 percent), slightly less often among adults (44.1 percent), and most infrequently among subadults (33.3 percent). In neither case are the differences statistically significant. Of the 23 individuals affected by periosteal reactions, 12 (52.2 percent) have at least one tibia involved (see Table 12.5). After the tibia, the most frequently affected elements are the humerus (39.1 percent), fibula (30.4 percent), and femur (26.1 percent). The scapula, clavicle, and innominate are affected in two individuals, and the ulna and radius are periostitic in only one individual each.

Differences in periostitis prevalence between the Early and Late samples are statistically significant (χ^2 = 11.92; p < .001). Seventy-five percent of individuals from the Late group exhibit periosteal reactions in at least one skeletal element, while only 22.6 percent of those from the Early group do.

Other characteristics of the sample suggest more severe and more widespread

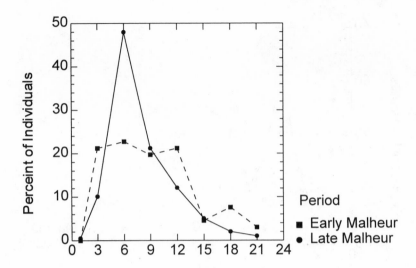

FIGURE 12.5. Interval between hypoplastic events in months.

infection in the Late group. This is illustrated by the fact that 87.5 percent of the Late series with periosteal reactions manifest these reactions in more than one skeletal element. In contrast, only 71.4 percent of individuals of the Early series exhibit multiple-bone involvement. Because there are no cases in which cranial bones were affected and only two examples of lower arm bone infection, the pattern of involvement does not fit the etiological pattern associated with treponemal disease (Powell 1988; Bogdan and Weaver 1992).

Malheur Lake vs. Stillwater Marsh

When taken in its entirety, the skeletal sample from Malheur Lake records higher frequencies of both hypoplasia and periosteal reactions than seen at Still-water Marsh. This is the case not only for rates by individual (65.6 percent vs. 64.1 percent for hypoplasia; 42.6 percent vs. 16.4 percent for periostitis) but also when the samples are analyzed by individual tooth (hypoplasia) or bone (periostitis). However, when the Malheur Lake material is split into its two components, the Early sample groups fairly closely with that from Stillwater while the Late subset becomes an outlier to the other two groups.

Table 12.6 and Figure 12.6 report the hypoplasia frequencies for the mandibular and maxillary anterior teeth. In all cases, rates for the Late Malheur group exceed those from Stillwater, while rates for the Early Malheur group are lower for three teeth (I_2, I^1, and I^2), higher for two (C_1, and C^1), and equal for one (I_1). The number of tibiae exhibiting periosteal reactions (Figure 12.7) indicates that the Early subset from Malheur (10.8 percent, 4/37) is similar in prevalence to Stillwater

TABLE 12.5.
Skeletal Elements Affected by Periosteal Reactions;
Number and Percent Afflicted for Each Bone

Element	Early (n = 7)		Late (n = 16)		Total (n = 23)	
	Number	Percent	Number	Percent	Number	Percent
Tibia	3	42.9	9	56.3	12	52.2
Humerus	2	28.6	7	43.8	9	39.1
Fibula	3	42.9	4	25.0	7	30.4
Femur	1	14.3	5	31.3	6	26.1
Scapula	—	—	2	12.5	2	8.7
Clavicle	—	—	2	12.5	2	8.7
Innominate	2	28.6	—	—	2	8.7
Ulna	—	—	1	6.3	1	4.4
Radius	1	14.3	—	—	1	4.4

TABLE 12.6.
Comparative Enamel Hypoplasia Rates for Malheur Lake and Stillwater Marsh,
by Percent of Teeth Affected

Tooth	Malheur Lake			Stillwater Marsh
	Early	Late	Total	Total
I_1	12.5 (1/8)	33.3 (4/12)	25.0 (5/20)	12.5 (2/16)
I_2	20.0 (2/10)	57.1 (8/14)	41.7 (10/24)	26.3 (5/19)
C_1	58.3 (7/12)	85.7 (12/14)	73.1 (19/26)	52.2 (12/23)
I^1	33.3 (1/3)	63.6 (7/11)	57.1 (8/14)	42.3 (11/26)
I^2	20.0 (1/5)	57.1 (8/14)	47.4 (9/19)	43.5 (10/23)
C^1	33.3 (3/9)	75.0 (9/12)	57.1 (12/21)	29.0 (11/38)

(15.5 percent, 13/84), whereas over half (53.8 percent, 14/26) of tibiae from the Late group are periostitic.

DISCUSSION

Hypoplasia and Periosteal Reactions

A comparison of hypoplasia frequencies for Malheur Lake with other North American skeletal series (Table 12.7) suggests that physiological stress at Malheur was moderate to severe. Although the rate for the combined sample (65.6 percent) is relatively high, it is skewed upward by the extremely high rate for the Late component (81.3 percent), a rate higher than for all of those included in the compara-

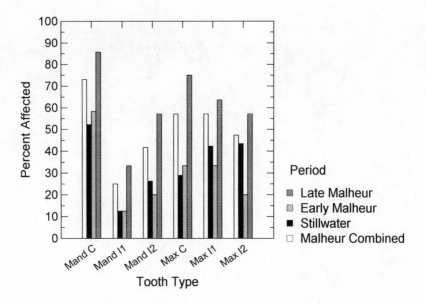

FIGURE 12.6. Hypoplasia frequency for Malheur Lake compared to Stillwater Marsh by tooth.

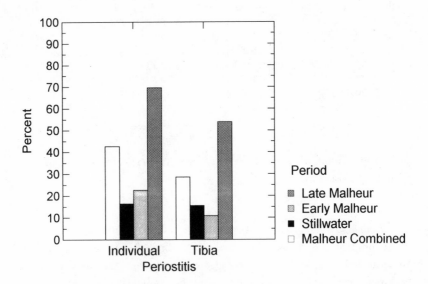

FIGURE 12.7. Periosteal reaction frequency for Malheur Lake compared to Stillwater Marsh.

TABLE 12.7.
Individual Hypoplasia Frequencies of Comparative Archaeological Samples from
North America

Group/Site	Period/ Subsistence	Hypoplasia Prevalence (%)	Reference
Malheur Combined	Hunter-Gatherer	65.6	This study
Early Malheur	Hunter-Gatherer	55.5	This study
Late Malheur	Hunter-Gatherer	81.3	This study
Stillwater	Hunter-Gatherer	64.1	Hutchinson and Larsen 1995
Dickson Mounds	Late Woodland	45.0	Goodman et al. 1980
Dickson Mounds	Mississippian Acculturated Late Woodland	60.0	Goodman et al. 1980
Dickson Mounds	Middle Mississippian	80.0	Goodman et al. 1980
Moundville	Mississippian	54.0	Powell 1988
Adena	Mixed economy	30.0	Sciulli 1978
Hopewell	Mixed economy	27.3	Sciulli 1978
Glacial Kame	Mixed economy	33.3	Sciulli 1978
Cole	Agricultural	70.0	Sciulli 1978
Ft. Ancient	Agricultural	42.9	Sciulli 1978
Erie	Agricultural	44.4	Sciulli 1978
California Early	Hunter-Gatherer	14.0	Dickel et al. 1984
California Middle	Hunter-Gatherer	11.0	Dickel et al. 1984
California Precontact	Hunter-Gatherer	14.0	Dickel et al. 1984
California Postcontact	Mission-acculturated	20.5	Dickel et al. 1984
Oaxaca Early Formative	Agricultural	68.2	Hodges 1987
Oaxaca Late Formative	Intensive agriculture	72.7	Hodges 1987
Mexico Children	Modern	35.7	Goodman et al. 1987
18th-Century Slaves	Historic	56.0	Kelley and Angel 1987
19th-Century Slaves	Historic	26.0	Kelley and Angel 1987
South Carolina Slaves	Historic	77.4	Rathbun 1987
Barbados Slaves	Historic	54.5	Corruccini et al. 1985
19th-Century U.S. Poorhouse	Historic	73.0	Lanphear 1990

tive sample—including the agricultural Middle Mississippian occupation at Dickson Mounds (Goodman, Armelagos, and Rose 1980). This pattern is also seen in a comparison of periosteal reaction prevalence. The Late sample exhibits a much higher incidence of periostitis than those representing other areas of the Desert West (Table 12.8), and is generally comparable to those samples derived from agriculturally based peoples.

TABLE 12.8.

Individual Periostitis Frequencies of Comparative Archaeological Samples from
North America

Group/Site	Period/ Subsistence	Periostitis Prevalence (%)	Reference
Malheur Combined	Hunter-Gatherer	42.6	This study
Early Malheur	Hunter-Gatherer	22.6	This study
Late Malheur	Hunter-Gatherer	69.6	This study
Stillwater	Hunter-Gatherer	16.4	Hutchinson and Larsen 1995
Dickson Mounds	Late Woodland + Miss. Acculturated LW	31.0	Goodman et al. 1984
Dickson Mounds	Middle Mississippian	67.0	Goodman et al. 1984
Klunk	Late Archaic	25.0	Cook 1984
Anderson Village (Ft. Ancient assoc.)	Agriculture	81.8	Lallo 1979
Eiden (N. Ohio)	Agriculture	70.0	Lallo and Blank 1977
Norris Farms	Oneota	61.0	Milner 1992
Northern Plains	Archaic + Woodland	5.7	J. A. Williams 1994
Southwest	Seventeen sites	all <37	Stodder and Martin 1992
Fourche Maline	Late preagriculture	11.5	Rose et al. 1984
Caddo I & II	Agriculture	19.5	Rose et al. 1984

As can be seen by the differing hypoplasia and periostitis occurrence rates between the Early and Late Malheur occupations, the amount of stress affecting the prehistoric inhabitants of Malheur Lake was quite variable. If Stillwater Marsh and the Early group from Malheur Lake are taken as a benchmark for physiological stress in the northern and western Great Basin, then stress levels at the time 35HA2095 was occupied were aberrantly high.

Why were the people who lived at 35HA2095 so stressed? In other words, what factors could lead to conditions in which these high levels of hypoplasia and periosteal reactions were reached? To understand how this happens it is necessary to comprehend how environment and subsistence interact and how fluctuating environmental conditions affect health. Once this is accomplished, then it is relatively easy to see how physiological stress could fluctuate and why at times stress levels would be extremely high.

Implications for Health

The effects of wetland reduction on human population are quite varied. If a dry period follows several wet years (as is often the case; see Figure 12.3), then population pressure becomes a problem. During times of resource abundance, population growth due to increasing fertility would occur. However, with the onset of drying, this large population would be forced to congregate near the lake due to desiccation of the river marshes. The decline in resources that accompanies drying increases stress due to nutritional deprivation, and the concentration of people increases the potential for transmission and maintenance of infectious disease brought on by relatively large populations confined to a small area (McGrath 1988). Due to decreases in the availability of upland resources, there is less food for storage, which can cause famine conditions in late winter.

It is apparent, based on hypoplasia and periosteal reactions, that later inhabitants of the Malheur Lake area were exposed to more frequent, severe, long lasting, and widespread episodes of stress than either the Early Malheur skeletal series or that from Stillwater Marsh. The change in prevalence of these pathological conditions at Malheur suggests that individuals recovered from site 35HA2095 experienced relatively elevated levels of physiological stress, possibly as a result of the combined effects of high population and reduced resource availability brought on by a period of low effective moisture. In this area, environmental fluctuation is the driving force behind fluctuating levels of stress. During wet periods, population increases with an attendant resource increase resulted in lower levels of physiological perturbation. With the arrival of the inevitable dry episodes, this population may have been forced to congregate in a smaller area due to desiccated marshes, a situation that exacerbated the shortage of stored foods. Resulting from this change in settlement, late winter famine may have contributed to growth stress, and the potential for disease transmission may have increased through high population density and a populous weakened by malnutrition.

As discussed by Scrimshaw (1964, 1975) and Scrimshaw and Young (1976), the synergistic relationship between nutrition and disease plays an important role in changing levels of physiologic stress such as those seen at Malheur Lake. Populations weakened by malnutrition, and in this case doubly vexed by high population density during sparse times, are more susceptible to disease. Infection, in turn, can result in the need for more dietary protein because of reduced nutrient uptake through the gastrointestinal tract (Scrimshaw and Young 1976). This produces a vicious cycle in which nutritionally stressed individuals require higher intakes of, most probably unavailable, food, which stresses them further.

CONCLUSION

Nonspecific indicators of physiological stress, such as dental enamel hypoplasia and periosteal reactions, are useful in estimating levels of community health of past peoples. In the Malheur Lake wetlands, human skeletal remains from different occupation periods suggest that environmental fluctuation may have played an influential role in the occurrence and severity of pathological conditions. Later residents, represented by site 35HA2095, experienced both more frequent and severe instances of periosteal reaction and more episodes of hypoplastic disturbance. Because site 35HA2095 may have represented a relatively dry period, these findings seem to be indicative of the negative impact more xeric conditions had on the health of the prehistoric inhabitants.

In a wider context, comparisons between the Late Malheur occupation, in particular site 35HA2095, and other North American skeletal series further support the proposition that peoples occupying this site were experiencing relatively elevated levels of stress. First, the frequency of affliction for both hypoplasia and periosteal reactions is much higher than that for both Stillwater Marsh and the Early Malheur group. And second, the rates for the Late group are so high that they are most comparable to such agricultural groups as those belonging to sites associated with the Mississippian period.

The relationship between environmental fluctuation, subsistence strategy, and health is strong. The Harney Basin area of the northern Great Basin is characterized by alternating periods of wet and dry that vary in duration from years to decades. The model of resource exploitation discussed in this chapter could result in increased fertility and population growth during wet times due to increased food availability and less rampant physiologic stress. When the climate eventually shifted to a dryer period, an inflated human population would tax the resource base and encounter elevated levels of physiologic stress.

Thus, it appears that the precontact inhabitants of the Malheur Lake wetlands were living on the edge of nutritional adequacy. Compared to the whole spectrum of nutritional environments around the world, the northern Great Basin is relatively poor. In such an environment, it would not take much deterioration in resource availability to greatly affect the health of its inhabitants. Increased prevalence of hypoplasia and periosteal reactions among the precontact peoples living about the margins of Malheur Lake is an indication of this environmental change as well as an indication of what can happen to the overall health of populations living in a nutritionally marginal area subject to pronounced environmental fluctuations.

Acknowledgments
Thanks go to Brian Hemphill for encouraging this analysis of the Malheur Lake human remains and to both him and Clark Larsen for inviting me to contribute to this volume.

13

Wear and Tear

Osteoarthritis as an indicator of Mobility among Great Basin Hunter-Gatherers

Brian E. Hemphill

Anthropological inquiry into levels of mobility practiced by hunter-gatherer societies has a long history, and in no region of the world is this issue debated with greater fervor than in the Great Basin. After years of research, students of Great Basin archaeology are divided into two camps—those who maintain that the wetlands of this region of the Desert West supported highly sedentary populations and those who maintain that the precontact inhabitants of the Great Basin participated in a highly mobile seasonal round in which wetland resources represented an important but by no means primary component of the aboriginal lifeway.

Recent studies of modern hunter-gatherers have recast the mobility/sedentism issue from a monolithic, population-based entity to an individual phenomenon. Such studies suggest not only that there are different kinds of mobility but also that various members of hunter-gatherer populations may practice widely different intensities of mobility which engender disparate levels of physical demand. When coupled with ethnographic evidence for sex-based differences in activity among the hunter-gatherer populations of the northern and western Great Basin wetlands at the time of European contact, the issue has been raised whether aboriginal males may have been more mobile and thus suffered more physical stress than aboriginal females.

Studies of modern hunter-gatherers have also sparked the realization among anthropologists that myriad foraging strategies are employed to achieve successful adaptation. Optimum foraging models indicate that various strategies are utilized to meet differences in the distribution, quality, and seasonal availability of usable resources (c.f. Raven 1992). In light of such advances, the issue has arisen over whether local variations in resources available in individual Great Basin wetlands may have led to the development of different foraging strategies and, hence, different levels of activity among Great Basin hunter-gatherer populations.

Yet, although archaeological study of the aboriginal inhabitants of the Great Basin has a long history, systematic osteological analyses of the precontact occupants of this area have been virtually nonexistent. Until recently, human remains recovered from the Great Basin have been either too few, too fragmentary, or too poorly documented to help illuminate the life histories of early Great Basin inhabitants (see Larsen 1995). This is unfortunate, for osteological analyses can provide important information about the lifeways and subsistence patterns of ancient peoples.

However, during the last decade, three important skeletal series have been discovered and analyzed. The first was obtained from the Stillwater Marsh, located near Fallon, Nevada, in the western Great Basin (S.T. Brooks, Haldeman, and Brooks 1988; Larsen and Kelly 1995). The second was recovered from the margins of the Great Salt Lake in the eastern Great Basin (Loveland 1991), and the third was recovered from the Malheur Lake wetlands of the Harney Basin near Burns, Oregon, in the northern Great Basin (Hemphill 1990, 1992a, 1992b, 1992c).

An analysis of osteoarthritis provides a valuable means to address issues raised by decades of anthropological research. And, presence of osteoarthritis provides a measurable record of the levels of mechanical stress experienced by individuals throughout adulthood (Bridges 1991; Jurmain and Kilgore 1995; Larsen, Ruff, and Kelly 1995). Individuals who have been subjected to repeated bouts of mechanical stress tend to be more often affected by osteoarthritis. In addition, as levels of repetitive mechanical stress increase, the velocity of degenerative changes increases and spreads to a greater number of the major joint regions of the body.

A comparison of frequencies of osteoarthritis in northern (Malheur Lake) and western (Stillwater Marsh) Great Basin hunter-gatherers with preagricultural and agricultural populations from the southeastern United States provides a means to assess whether the aboriginal occupants of Great Basin wetlands were highly sedentary or highly mobile. If Great Basin hunter-gatherers were highly mobile, it is likely that such mobility could have produced high levels of repetitive physical demands that would be reflected by higher frequencies of osteoarthritis throughout the body than manifested by more sedentary populations from the southeastern United States.

Sex-based differences in activity levels are addressed by comparing osteoarthritic affectation between precontact Great Basin males and females. Males and females are contrasted for differences in osteoarthritis frequency by individual and by joint region. The rate of osteoarthritic degeneration is assessed by comparing the percentage of individuals experiencing initial onset of osteoarthritis by age group and by contrasting the proliferation velocity of degenerative changes throughout the body with increasing age at death.

Comparison of osteoarthritic affliction between Malheur Lake and Stillwater Marsh skeletal series provides the basis for evaluating the impact of local distinctions in the distribution, quality, and seasonality of resources upon the patterns and intensities of physical demand experienced by the aboriginal occupants of different Great Basin wetlands. This contrast will examine overall levels of osteoarthritic affliction and whether males and females of each skeletal series were exposed to similar levels of repetitive mechanical stress.

AN OVERVIEW OF THE ISSUES
Osteoarthritis as an Indicator of Mobility
Osteoarthritis represents one of the most frequently documented pathological conditions in humans. Because this disorder is so commonly found in skeletal remains, biological anthropologists have given osteoarthritis considerable attention (e.g., Jurmain 1977, 1990; Merbs 1983; Larsen 1987; Bridges 1992). Nevertheless, the exact causes of this disorder remain unresolved (Pugh 1982). The age of the individual appears to be the most obvious systemic factor influencing the prevalence of osteoarthritis, for degenerative changes within synovial joints represent a normal aspect of the aging process. Thus, all things being equal, the older the individual, the more likely degenerative changes will be manifested as a pathological state (for a review see Jurmain 1978, 1980). Yet, while age certainly represents a predisposing factor in the overall development of osteoarthritis, advancing age does not completely explain the distribution of osteoarthritis. Other systemic factors that appear to play a role in the development of osteoarthritis include sex of the individual (Kellgren and Moore 1952; Kellgren and Lawrence 1958; Moskowitz 1972; Radin, Parker, and Paul 1971; Roberts and Burch 1966), occupation (Engel and Burch 1966), body build (Engel 1968; Seltzer 1943), trauma (Pinals 1972; Hettinga 1980; Sokoloff 1969), metabolic factors (Kellgren and Moore 1952), endocrine factors, and heredity (Jurmain 1977).

Osteoarthritis, however, is often not manifested as a systemic affliction. Quite frequently, osteoarthritis affects some joints, while others remain completely free of any degeneration. Even among those joints affected, the progression of this disorder may be much more advanced in some joints than in others or on one side more than the other. These findings have led many researchers to support a "stress hypothesis" (Cobb 1971; Engel and Burch 1966; Radin, Paul, and Rose 1972) in which excessive and repetitive loading of articular joints contributes the foremost etiological factor for the frequency and patterning of nonsystemic, idiopathic osteoarthritis in human populations (Jurmain 1977, 1990; Duncan 1979; Larsen 1982; Merbs 1983; Radin 1983; Moskowitz 1987; Hough and Sokoloff 1989; Miles 1989; Pascale and Grana 1989; Walker and Holliman 1989).

Despite such widespread support, recent studies of long-bone biomechanical data and osteoarthritis prevalence across the transition from a hunting-gathering lifeway to agricultural subsistence have led Bridges (1991, 1992) to reject the "stress hypothesis" for osteoarthritis prevalence. Attempts to draw relationships between biomechanical strengthening, osteoarthritis prevalence, and subsistence economy have yielded discordant results. In some areas (northwestern Alabama: Bridges 1989b), biomechanical parameters indicate increased strengthening of long bones with the transition to agricultural subsistence; but in other areas (Georgia coast: Ruff and Larsen 1990), this change in lifeway was accompanied by a decrease in long-bone strengthening. Comparisons of osteoarthritis prevalence also yield varying results. In some areas, osteoarthritis prevalence is unchanged (northwestern Alabama: Bridges 1991) or decreases (Georgia coast: Larsen 1982), while in other areas osteoarthritis prevalence increases with the transition to agriculture (Caddoan area of the Central Mississippi Valley: Rose et al. 1984; Lower Illinois Valley: Pickering 1984; Dickson Mounds: Goodman et al. 1984; Lallo 1973).

Bridges (1991) suggests such disparities may be due to different etiological pathways involved in the development of long-bone biomechanical strengthening and osteoarthritis. While the relationship between biomechanical parameters and habitual activities appears well established (for a review see Ruff, this volume), Bridges proposes that the lack of correlation between osteoarthritis prevalence and subsistence economy indicates that osteoarthritis prevalence may not be reflective of habitual activities. Rather, noting studies which document that osteoarthritis may be caused by subclinical microtrauma (Hettinga 1980; Sokoloff 1969) and studies which fail to find a correlation between running and osteoarthritis prevalence (Eichner 1989; Lane et al. 1986; Panush et al. 1986), Bridges concludes that osteoarthritis may be more an indicator of intensive but infrequent activities.

Although Bridges (1991) prefers to explain conflicting results obtained from analyses of long-bone strengthening and osteoarthritis prevalence as a product of different etiological pathways, a more parsimonious explanation is that such discordant results reflect the impact of conflating changes in overall mobility with changes in economic-specific task activities. Support for this possibility is provided by an examination of the nature of changes in osteoarthritis prevalence found to accompany the transition to agriculture. Although attempts to correlate osteoarthritis of particular joint regions with specific behaviors have proved frustrating (Angel 1966, 1971; Angel et al. 1987; Bridges 1989b, 1990, 1991, 1992; Edynak 1976; Jurmain 1991; Jurmain and Kilgore 1995; Kelley and Angel 1987; Merbs 1980, 1983; R. J. Miller 1985; Ortner 1968; Pickering 1984), studies which document an increase in osteoarthritis prevalence among agriculturalists relative to earlier hunter-gatherer populations reveal that these increases are not equally manifested throughout the major joint regions of the body or by sex (Goodman et al. 1984; Lallo 1973; Pickering 1984; Rose et al. 1984). By contrast, those studies which find osteoarthritis prevalence to decrease with the transition to agriculture, see these decreases expressed in nearly all joint regions and equally by both sexes (Larson 1984).

Because of the compounded effects of the degree of mobility practiced by hunter-gatherer groups prior to the transition to agriculture with changes in work load engendered by adoption of an agricultural lifeway, the increase in biomechanical strengthening documented by Bridges (1991) among northwest Alabamians may be more a reflection of low-level mobility practiced by the Archaic hunter-gatherers of this area than an increase in overall work load among agriculturalists. This may explain why opposite results were obtained from Georgia coast populations, in which the decrease in both osteoarthritis prevalence and long-bone strengthening may be more indicative of the greater degree of mobility of hunter-gatherers in this latter region than a reduction in overall work load among agriculturalists.

Although certain studies have demonstrated that there is no correlation between running and osteoarthritis, they fail to take into account travel over rough, uneven terrain or the effects caused by mobility while carrying loads. One such study suggests that running may worsen arthritis in a previously injured joint (Pascale and Grana 1989). Given an increased likelihood of trauma, or even subclinal microtrauma, to joints throughout the body caused by movement by an individual through rough, uneven terrain while carrying loads, it is likely that as overall mobility increases, initial onset of osteoarthritis will occur earlier in life, subsequent proliferation of degenerative changes will accelerate, and elevated levels of osteoarthritis prevalence will occur throughout the major joint regions of the body.

Thus, the initial onset, distribution, and overall prevalence of osteoarthritic affliction may provide an excellent indicator of the degree of overall mobility incurred as a part of the lifeway practiced by precontact populations. Such an approach may be especially appropriate when the effects of mobility are not compounded by a major change in economic-specific, habitual task activities. The precontact record of the aboriginal inhabitants of Great Basin wetlands document no such changes in habitual task activities. Therefore, I expect that if Great Basin hunter-gatherers were highly mobile, the repetitive physical demands incurred by such a life-style will be reflected by an early onset of osteoarthritis, by a rapid proliferation of degenerative changes, and by elevated frequencies of osteoarthritis throughout all of the major joint regions of the body in both males and females.

Were Great Basin Dwellers Highly Sedentary or Highly Mobile?

Factors contributing to the nature and intensity of mobility practiced by hunter-gatherers represent a topic of recent theoretical interest among anthropologists (Binford 1979, 1980, 1982, 1986; Kelly 1983; Bettinger 1987), and some of these discussions have focused on whether the aboriginal occupants of Great Basin wetlands were sedentary or not (D. B. Madsen 1979; Binford 1983; Thomas 1985; Kelly 1985). For many years, the dominant view of aboriginal life in the Great Basin envisioned populations of precontact inhabitants constantly on the move in a search for food (Steward [1938] 1999; Jennings 1957; Aikens 1970, 1978). This view was challenged by Robert Heizer and his students, who maintained that the wetland environment of several western Nevada basins provided abundant, diverse, and reliable resources that permitted a sedentary, or nearly sedentary, lifestyle (Heizer 1967; Napton 1969; Heizer and Napton 1970). Subsequent investigations have led other researchers to extend this distinctive residentially stable pattern to wetlands in other regions of the Great Basin (Weide 1968, 1974, 1978; O'Connell and Hayward 1972; O'Connell 1971; Aikens and Greenspan 1988; Pettigrew 1980, 1985; Oetting 1989, this volume; D. B. Madsen 1979; D. B. Madsen and Lindsay 1977). A number of these investigations emphasized the abundance and diversity of wetland resources as a primary factor in promoting such a sedentary or semisedentary subsistence strategy (D. B. Madsen and Lindsay 1977; D. B. Madsen 1979; Pettigrew 1985; Aikens and Greenspan 1988; Oetting 1989, 1992, this volume).

Recent investigations in the Stillwater Marsh and at Hidden Cave by Kelly (1985, 1990) and Thomas (1985) have criticized cultural reconstructions that call for residentially stable occupations of Great Basin wetlands. These researchers conclude that marsh resources are of relatively poor quality and, therefore, would not have served as the primary focus of a group's subsistence strategy. Rather, Kelly and Thomas propose that the precontact inhabitants of the Carson Sink participated in a highly mobile lifeway in which wetland resources of the Stillwater Marsh merely provided a secondary food source—a source that was only exploited to any significant degree when shortages of higher ranked resources in the surrounding uplands occurred. Because they consider wetlands to be repositories of lower ranked resources, Kelly and Thomas express severe reservations about any model which suggests that these wetlands were occupied by highly sedentary communities.

In a microcosm, differences of opinion over the degree of mobility practiced by precontact inhabitants of Great Basin wetlands reflect a larger division among scholars over the general nature of the transition from nomadism to sedentism worldwide. Price and Brown (1985) summarize this division as the product of fundamentally opposing views over the attractiveness of sedentism for human populations. They designate these opposing views as the "pull" and "push" hypotheses.

Pull models are based on the belief that sedentism has a greater survival value than a nomadic lifeway and, because of this, human populations will become sedentary wherever sufficient localized resources will support such a transition (Beardsley et al. 1956). Sedentism, it is asserted, is inherently more energy efficient because residential stability saves the expense of moving from one location to another—costs that could be particularly high for children, the elderly, and the infirm (J. E. Rafferty 1985; B. L. Stark 1981). Consequently, models for the transition to sedentism founded on the pull hypothesis predict that hunter-gatherers will become residentially stable when resources are abundant (Aikens 1981; Brown 1985; Harris 1978; Musil 1995; Price and Brown 1985; J. E. Rafferty 1985; B. L. Stark 1986).

Models for the transition to sedentism based on the push hypothesis differ radically because they assert that hunter-gatherers often do not exploit the opportunity to become sedentary, even when sufficient resources are available (Binford 1980, 1983). Rather, push model proponents argue that hunter-gatherers will often remain mobile because mobility allows local groups to maintain knowledge of their greater surroundings. Such knowledge serves to enhance opportunities for individual groups to move in the event of local resource failure. Thus, hunter-gatherers will choose to remain mobile if at all possible. Only as a last resort will hunter-gatherers adopt sedentism under such stresses as population pressure, environmental deterioration, or territorial circumscription (Kelly 1990). As a result, Kelly (1995b) proposes that residential stability among hunter-gatherers should be marked by use of nonlocal resources, a marginal diet, and evidence of periodic resource failure.

Mobility as an Individual Phenomenon: Unpacking the Concept of Mobility

Some of the polarization of debate surrounding the degree of mobility practiced by precontact inhabitants of Great Basin wetlands may be due more to a confusion over the concept of mobility itself than to the data per se. Early discussions (e.g., Beardsley et al. 1956) regarded mobility as a monolithic, population-based entity. The problems with such views are twofold. First, mobility is an individual rather than a group phenomenon, for individuals may move at different times, in differing degrees, and in various aggregations. Second, individuals may move in different ways (Kelly 1992). Recognizing this, Binford (1980, 1982, 1983) attempted to unpack the general concept of mobility into three primary forms. These include *residential mobility*, the intra- or interseasonal movement from one residential domicile to another, *logistical mobility*, the movement of some individuals from a residential domicile on specific foraging forays, and *long-term mobility*, the movement of a group's range or primary aggregation site to another location.

Ethnographic information about the protocontact inhabitants of northern and western Great Basin wetlands highlights the problems with a monolithic, population-based conception of mobility. At the time of European contact, the Malheur Lake wetlands of the Harney Basin and adjacent areas were inhabited by the Wada'tika Northern Paiute (O. C. Stewart 1939; C. S. Fowler 1982a; C. S. Fowler and Liljeblad 1986), while the Carson Sink region was inhabited by the

Toedökadö Paiute (DeQuille 1963; C. S. Fowler and Bath 1981; Loud and Harrington 1929; Lowie 1924; Speth 1969; O. C. Stewart 1941; Wheat 1967). The seasonal
round of both groups featured temporary residential sedentism in winter camps,
coupled with high residential mobility of independently moving foraging bands
throughout the rest of the year. Population aggregates varied greatly both in composition and in absolute numbers during the course of a given year. This fluidity in
levels of mobility, types of mobility, and combinations of individuals led Thomas
(1983) to designate this form of social organization as a "fission-fusion" system. Although originally applied to the Toedökadö, the strong similarities in ethnographic descriptions indicate that this term is equally applicable to the Wada'tika
as well (Aikens and Greenspan, 1988).

Ethnographic accounts not only emphasize that the protocontact inhabitants
of both areas practiced varying levels of residential mobility, logistical mobility,
and population aggregations but also describe a sex-based division of activities. For
example, large-game hunting appears to have been an almost exclusively male occupation—an occupation that most often took place in the surrounding uplands
rather than in the lowlands. Females appear to have been the chief root and seed
collectors in both groups, and these activities occurred not only in the lowlands in
general but also in the wetlands in particular.

Thus, ethnographic accounts of the occupants of northern and western Great
Basin wetlands at the time of European contact reveal that levels and types of mobility varied greatly among individuals. Importantly, males and females were often
engaged in different activities, activities that may have led to strong differences in
the nature and severity of repetitive mechanical stresses experienced throughout
adulthood. If accurate, a record of the impact of these sex-based differences may be
reflected by the prevalence and patterning of osteoarthritis found in skeletal remains of these aboriginal inhabitants of Great Basin wetlands.

Different Marshes, Different Resources, Different Patterns of Mobility?
Optimum foraging strategy represents another avenue used by anthropologists to address patterns of mobility practiced by hunter-gatherer populations.
Optimal foraging studies focus on foraging time, location, group size, and diet
breadth (Charnov 1976; D. B. Madsen 1988; Stephens and Krebs 1986). Basically,
optimal foraging models are predicated on the premise that as foragers consume
food around their camp, they reach a point of diminishing returns. At this point,
foragers may only remain residentially sedentary by either increasing the costs involved in procuring more distant, high-quality resources or shifting to subsistence
on locally available, low-quality resources. Either way, once the point of diminishing returns is reached, foragers can only remain residentially sedentary at the expense of an increase in procurement costs or a decrease in foraging returns. Optimal foraging theory holds that it is likely foragers will choose residential

movement when the returns of logistical forays from the current residence fall below those expected from moving to another residence, after allowing for the cost of relocation to a new residential site (Kelly 1990).

The first step in applying optimal foraging strategy models to real situations is a quantification of the costs and returns incurred in obtaining and processing a number of food resources in a given area. In the Great Basin, such research has been vigorously pursued by the experimental studies of Simms (1984, 1985, 1987). While the ethnographic record suggests that the protocontact occupants of northern and western Great Basin wetlands exhibit a number of similarities in their seasonal round, the environments in which they lived were not identical. As pointed out by Rhode (1990b), some wetlands are small but contain deep water, while others feature rather shallow bodies of water. Some wetlands contain rather large marshes fractured into a mosaic of microenvironments and highly diverse biotic communities, while others are composed of narrow, annular stands of nearly monomorphic vegetation. The topography and resources available in the surrounding uplands also differ markedly, for some wetlands, such as the Stillwater Marsh have stands of piñon in the vicinity, while others, such as the Malheur Lake wetlands, do not.

Because of such factors, it would be extremely hazardous to assume that patterns of mobility observed in one area, such as the Carson Sink/Stillwater wetlands, can be legitimately extended to other Great Basin wetlands. After all, the patterns of mobility developed by the aboriginal occupants of the Carson Sink represent an adaptive response to specific environmental, even microenvironmental, conditions in a particular locality. As Kelly (this volume) notes, there is no single "forager mobility" strategy, but rather a whole series of strategies, and each is attuned to local circumstances and exigencies. The intensity and patterning of osteoarthritic affliction among Malheur Lake and Stillwater Marsh individuals are compared to test for possible disparities in physical stress—disparities that may have been incurred as a by-product of locally attuned mobility strategies in response to local environmental offerings provided by northern and western Great Basin wetlands.

MATERIALS AND METHODS

A higher than normal precipitation during the winters of 1982 to 1984 and the subsequent spring runoff led to a flooding of the Harney Basin floor that served to inundate the Malheur Lake wetlands and coalesce Malheur, Harney, and Mud Lakes into one large lake. The flooding peaked in 1985 and slowly receded through 1991. Subsequent erosion from wind and rain removed vegetation and topsoil, exposing over 35 archaeological sites and 54 human burials on the lake shore and islands of Malheur Lake (Burnside 1990; Oetting 1990a, 1990b). Faced with imminent danger from looters, the Burns Northern Paiute permitted the U.S. Fish and

Wildlife Service and Heritage Research Associates to remove the burials for further analysis. I analyzed these remains at the Oregon State Museum of Natural History and returned them to the Burns Northern Paiute for reburial.

Bioarchaeological analysis of these remains is beset by two problems that also plague the other two large skeletal series from the Great Basin (Stillwater Marsh and Great Salt Lake). First, the remains were not recovered from a formal cemetery. Rather, with the exception of burials recovered from site 35HA2095, most individuals were from isolated interments of one to three individuals. Consequently, there is no reason to assume that these human remains provide a representative sample of the aboriginal population of this area. Second, the remains encompass an unknown range in antiquity. Artifacts recovered from the surfaces of these sites represent nearly every time period of the known prehistory of this region (Oetting 1990a, 1990b). However, frequencies of diagnostic projectile points suggest an increase in occupation of the Malheur Lake wetlands after 5000 B.P., with most intensive use postdating 2000 B.P. (Oetting 1992, this volume). The nine radiocarbon dates obtained from human remains are broadly consistent with the temporal pattern revealed by diagnostic projectile points. None of the radiocarbon dates exceed 1830 B.P., and over half fall within the last 500 years (Hemphill 1992a, 1992b, 1992c). Since the human remains from the Malheur Lake wetlands were obtained from a number of sites and since these sites may represent hundreds or thousands of years of occupation, they should not be viewed as representative of a single aboriginal Malheur Lake population at any specific point in time. Nevertheless, these remains provide the first opportunity to utilize osteological techniques to illuminate the patterns of lifeway experienced by precontact inhabitants of the northern Great Basin.

The skeletal remains of 35 individuals from the Malheur Lake skeletal series provide the sample of articular joints employed in this analysis (Table 13.1). Nineteen additional individuals are either too young (less than 20 years old) at the time of death (n = 16) or too fragmentary (n = 3) to be of utility in this assessment of osteoarthritis. The Malheur Lake skeletal series also includes 296 isolated elements, many of which had preserved intact articular surfaces. However, given the difficulty of sex identification, individuation, and accurate estimation of age at death, these isolated elements are not included in this analysis. An element by element description of the preservation and pathological status of these isolated elements may be found elsewhere (Hemphill 1992a, 1992b, 1992c).

This report follows DeRousseau's definition (1988:7) of osteoarthritis as including all degenerative articular joint changes. All articular surfaces and margins of all major weight-bearing and non–weight-bearing regions were examined macroscopically for degenerative changes. Articular regions assessed include the intervertebral joints (cervical, thoracic, lumbar, sacral), shoulder, elbow, wrist, hand, hip, knee, ankle, and foot. Specific articular surfaces and margins examined

TABLE 13.1.

Inventory of Malheur Burials (Number of Individuals = 54)

Specimen	Sex	Age	Arthritis Sample*	Specimen	Sex	Age	Arthritis Sample*
403.2	M	37	X	1949.8a	F	40	X
403.3	U	9		1949.8b	F	28	
1032A.1a	M	23		1949.9	F	30	X
1032A.1b	F	30	X	1977.1	F	33	X
1032B.1a	F	34	X	1991.2	U	8	
1032B.1b	U	35		1991.4	M	37	X
1899.1a	F	11		1991.5	F	40	X
1899.1b	U	6		2095.1	M	41	X
1899.2a	M	34	X	2095.2a	F	32	X
1899.2b	M	15		2095.2b	U	7	
1899.3	F	35	X	2095.3	F	37	X
1905.1	F	34	X	2095.4	F	31	X
1906.1	M	47	X	2095.5a	U	6	
1906.2	M	30	X	2095.5b	U	1	
1906.3	M	35	X	2095.6	F	47	X
1907.1	M	18		2095.7	U	6	
1911.1	F	60+	X	2095.9	F	56	X
1911.2	M	27	X	2095.12a	F	23	X
1911.3	F	40	X	2095.12b	M	37	X
1911.4	F	44	X	2095.12c	U	1	
1949.1	F	60+	X	2095.14	U	10	
1949.2	M	47	X	2095.15	U	14	
1949.3	F	22	X	2095.17	F	45	X
1949.4	F	37	X	2095.18	F	40	X
1949.5	M	30	X	2095.19	U	6	
1949.6	M	30	X	2095.20	M	19	
1949.7	M	22	X	2095.21	U	3	

* Only individuals in excess of 20 years of age at the time of death were included in the arthritis sample (n = 35). Specimen 1032A.1a not included because skeletal remains observed are limited to the cranium and mandible. Specimens 1032B.1b and 1949.8b not included because the highly fragmentary preservation of skeletal elements precluded assessment of osteoarthritis.

for each joint region are presented in Table 13.2. Although degenerative changes involving the intervertebral disks are not osteoarthritic in the strict sense of the term, numerous studies have concluded that inclusion of such degenerative osteophytotic changes in intervertebral amphiarthrotic joints in a general analysis of diarthrotic osteoarthritis is entirely appropriate (Bridges 1991; Pickering 1984; Larsen 1982; Griffin and Larsen 1989; Larsen, Ruff, and Kelly 1995; Jurmain 1990; Jurmain and Kilgore 1995; Merbs 1983; Walker and Hollimon 1989; Kilgore 1984).

TABLE 13.2.
Articular Surfaces and Margins of Major Adult Joints Observed for
Presence or Absence of Osteoarthritis (Adapted from Larsen [1982];
Larsen, Ruff, and Kelly [1995])

Articular Joint	Skeletal Components
Cervical	Intervertebral body; superior and inferior articular processes
Thoracic	Intervertebral body; superior and inferior articular processes
Lumbar	Intervertebral body; superior and inferior articular processes
Sacrum	Superior intervertebral body
Shoulder	Proximal humerus; glenoid fossa and acromio-clavicular facet of scapula
Elbow	Distal humerus (trochlea, capitulum); proximal radius (head, radial tuberosity); proximal ulna (semilunar notch, radial notch, coronoid process)
Wrist	Distal ulna (head, styloid process); distal radius (lunate and scaphoid articular surfaces); carpals; metacarpals (proximal)
Hand	Metacarpals (heads); proximal, intermediate and distal phalanges
Hip	Femur (head); innominate (auricular, acetabulum)
Knee	Femur (lateral and medial condyles); patella (condylar surfaces); tibia (lateral and medial condyles)
Ankle	Tibia (talar articular surfaces); tarsals; metatarsals (proximal)
Foot	Metatarsals (heads); proximal, intermediate and distal phalanges

Manifestation of osteoarthritis within the Malheur Lake skeletal series ranges from slight to severe. Osteoarthritis was recorded as present if any one or a combination of the following modifications was observed: proliferation of excess bone along joint margins, loss of bone on articular surfaces due to resorption, or polishing (eburnation) of joint surfaces caused by direct bone-on-bone contact due to degeneration of articular cartilage. In this study, all degrees of osteoarthritic affliction have been collapsed into presence/absence for the 12 articular regions. Following the procedure of Larsen, Ruff, and Kelly (1995), a joint region was scored as positive for osteoarthritis if any articular surfaces encompassed within that joint region exhibited any degree of osteoarthritis.

Numerous researchers have found significant differences in the prevalence and patterning of osteoarthritis that appear to be associated with a sexual division of labor in habitual activities (e.g., J. E. Anderson 1976; Pickering 1979; Fahlstrom 1981; Pfeiffer 1977; Larsen 1982, 1987; Larsen, Ruff, and Kelly 1995; Larsen and Hutchinson, this volume; Griffin and Larsen 1989; Merbs 1983; Webb 1989, 1995; McCafferty et al. 1992; Waldron 1992; Goodman et al. 1984; Lallo 1973; Pierce 1987; Jurmain 1977; Walker and Hollimon 1989; but see Pickering 1984; Bridges 1991; Kilgore 1984). Due to these findings, the Malheur Lake skeletal series was di-

vided by sex, and osteoarthritic affliction was compared between males and females. Determination of sex was accomplished with standardized morphological,
univariate metric, bivariate metric, and multivariate metric techniques (see
Hemphill 1992a, 1992b, 1992c).

To provide a general perspective of the prevalence and patterning of osteoarthritic affliction within the Malheur Lake skeletal series, these data are compared with data collected by Larsen, Ruff, and Kelly (1995) for the Stillwater Marsh
skeletal series and by Larsen (1982) for Georgia coast samples. As discussed in the
chapters in this volume by Kelly; Schoeninger; Kaestle, Lorenz, and Smith; and
Larsen and Hutchinson, the Stillwater Marsh skeletal series represents the remains
of hunter-gatherers from the western Great Basin. The Georgia coast samples are
representative of hunter-gatherers (pre-A.D. 1150) and later agriculturalists (A.D.
1150–1450) who occupied the Georgia coast prior to European contact (Larsen
1982, 1990; Griffin and Larsen 1989). These comparative samples were selected to
provide greatest comparability in the scoring of osteoarthritis. Differences in the
frequency of joint regions affected by osteoarthritis by sex are evaluated by means
of chi-square. Yates's correction for small samples is used when more than half of
cell values fall below five.

Analysis of sex-differences in osteoarthritic affliction among Malheur Lake
individuals included assessments of overall prevalence, age at initial onset, and the
velocity of polyarticular involvement. Sex-differences in prevalence of osteoarthritis by joint region were tested for statistical significance by means of chi-square according to the procedures described above for general comparisons. Because osteoarthritis is also known to be an age-progressive disorder, the prevalence of
osteoarthritis was examined in five-year age categories. Age at death for adult individuals was estimated according to a number of standardized techniques (see
Hemphill 1992a, 1992b, 1992c). These methods provided a range in age at death for
each individual. The specific ages at death utilized in this analysis were obtained by
taking the midpoint of the narrowest range in age at death for each individual. Significant difference in age at death by sex was tested with an independent samples
t-test. Differences in the initial onset of osteoarthritis by sex and by five-year age
group were evaluated by means of chi-square.

Since osteoarthritic affliction provides a cumulative and age-progressive picture of habitual activities, a deeper understanding of the intensity of physical demands placed upon individuals may be obtained through regression analysis. Each
individual within the Malheur Lake skeletal series was assessed for the percentage
of joint regions affected by osteoarthritis. Percentages were used to control for
differential preservation of joint regions by individual. The percentage of joints
affected by osteoarthritis was correlated with age at death by linear regression
analysis to determine the velocity of polyarticular involvement. Significance of the

TABLE 13.3.

Articular Joints Affected by Osteoarthritis among Malheur Lake Individuals

Individual	C	T	L	S	Sho	Elb	Wri	Han	Hip	Kne	Ank	Foot
403.2	1	1	1	—	1	1	1	1	1	0	1	1
1032A.1b	0	—	—	—	0	0	0	0	0	0	0	0
1032B.1a	—	—	1	—	—	—	—	—	—	0	0	—
1899.2a	—	—	—	—	0	0	0	—	0	0	0	—
1899.3	—	—	1	0	—	0	0	—	0	0	—	—
1905.1	1	1	1	—	—	0	0	0	1	0	1	—
1906.1	1	1	0	0	1	1	1	—	0	1	1	1
1906.2	—	0	1	0	—	—	—	0	0	0	1	—
1906.3	0	1	1	1	0	1	0	0	0	0	0	1
1911.1	1	1	—	—	0	1	1	1	0	1	1	—
1911.2	—	—	1	—	—	—	—	—	—	0	0	—
1911.3	0	1	—	—	0	0	1	0	0	—	—	0
1911.4	—	—	1	0	0	—	—	—	1	0	0	—
1949.1	1	1	1	1	0	0	1	1	0	1	1	0
1949.2	1	1	1	0	1	1	1	0	1	0	0	—
1949.3	0	0	0	0	0	0	0	0	0	0	0	0
1949.4	—	—	—	—	1	0	—	—	0	1	0	—
1949.5	—	—	—	—	0	—	—	—	0	0	0	—
1949.6	—	—	—	—	—	—	—	—	0	0	0	—
1949.7	0	—	—	—	0	0	—	—	0	0	—	—
1949.8a	—	—	1	—	—	—	—	—	0	0	0	—

TABLE 13.3. (continued)
Articular Joints Affected by Osteoarthritis among Malheur Lake Individuals

Individual	Joint*											
	C	T	L	S	Sho	Elb	Wri	Han	Hip	Kne	Ank	Foot
1949.9	—	—	—	—	0	0	0	1	—	0	—	—
1977.1	0	0	0	0	0	0	0	0	0	0	0	0
1991.4	0	0	0	0	0	0	0	0	0	0	0	—
1991.5	0	0	1	0	0	0	0	—	0	0	0	—
2095.1	1	1	1	1	0	1	0	0	1	0	0	—
2095.2a	—	1	1	1	0	0	—	1	1	1	0	—
2095.3	1	1	1	1	1	1	1	—	0	0	0	—
2095.4	1	—	1	0	0	0	—	1	0	1	0	0
2095.6	1	1	1	1	1	1	0	1	1	1	0	—
2095.9	1	1	1	0	1	1	1	—	1	1	0	0
2095.12a	0	0	0	0	0	0	0	0	0	0	0	0
2095.12b	1	1	1	1	1	1	1	1	1	1	1	1
2095.17	—	—	—	1	0	1	0	—	1	0	—	—
2095.18	—	—	—	0	0	0	—	—	0	0	0	—

* C = cervical, T = thoracic, L = lumbar, S = sacrum, Sho = shoulder, Elb = elbow, Wri = wrist, Han = hand, Hip = hip, Kne = knee, Ank = ankle, Foot = foot; 0 = osteoarthritis absent, 1 = osteoarthritis present, — = missing data (joint not present for assessment of osteoarthritis presence/absence).

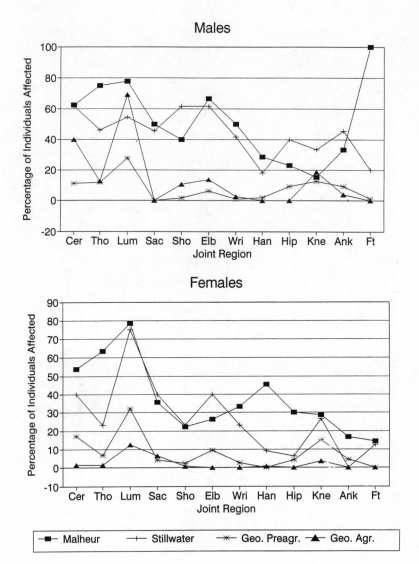

FIGURE 13.1. Osteoarthritis affectation by joint region among Great Basin and Georgia coast samples.

association between the percentage of joints affected and age at death was tested with Pearson's correlation coefficient and analysis of variance. The resulting regression slopes provided an assessment of the velocity of polyarticular osteoarthritic acquisition such that the greater the slope the more rapidly multiple joints were affected by osteoarthritis at a given age at death.

TABLE 13.4.

Comparison of Osteoarthritis Frequency by Sex among
Great Basin and Georgia Coast Samples

Joint	Malheur Lake No.[b]	Malheur Lake %[c]	Stillwater[a] No.[b]	Stillwater[a] %[c]	Geo.-Preagr. No.[b]	Geo.-Preagr. %[c]	Geo.-Agr. No.[b]	Geo.-Agr. %[c]
Males								
Cervical	8	62.5	13	61.5	20	40.0	53	11.3
Thoracic	8	75.0	13	46.2	16	12.5	51	11.8
Lumbar	9	77.8	11	54.5	13	69.2	47	27.7
Sacrum	6	50.0	11	45.5	10	0.0	33	0.0
Shoulder	10	40.0	13	61.5	38	10.5	120	1.7
Elbow	9	66.7	13	61.5	51	13.7	114	6.1
Wrist	8	50.0	12	41.7	39	2.6	106	0.9
Hand	7	28.6	11	18.2	28	0.0	100	2.0
Hip	13	23.1	10	40.0	51	0.0	110	9.1
Knee	13	15.4	12	33.3	59	18.6	111	12.6
Ankle	12	33.3	11	45.5	49	4.1	109	9.2
Foot	3	100.0	10	20.0	26	0.0	93	1.1
Females								
Cervical	13	53.9	10	40.0	29	17.2	73	1.4
Thoracic	11	63.6	13	23.1	30	6.7	72	1.4
Lumbar	14	78.6	12	75.0	28	32.1	64	12.5
Sacrum	14	35.7	10	40.0	23	4.3	47	6.4
Shoulder	18	22.2	13	23.1	83	2.4	144	0.7
Elbow	19	26.3	15	40.0	94	9.6	167	0.0
Wrist	15	33.3	13	23.1	77	2.6	140	0.0
Hand	11	45.5	11	9.1	50	0.0	129	0.8
Hip	20	30.0	16	6.3	93	4.3	148	0.0
Knee	21	28.6	15	26.7	94	15.0	147	3.4
Ankle	18	16.7	14	0.0	88	4.5	139	0.0
Foot	7	14.3	8	12.5	48	0.0	120	0.0

[a] Stillwater (from Larsen, Ruff, and Kelly 1995); Geo.-Preagr. = Georgia coast, preagricultural (from Larsen 1982; Griffin and Larsen 1989); Geo.-Agr. = Georgia coast, agricultural (from Larsen 1990; Griffin and Larsen 1989).

[b] Number of articular joints observed for presence or absence of osteoarthritis.

[c] Percentage of articular joints affected by osteoarthritis.

Osteoarthritis prevalence within Malheur Lake and Stillwater Marsh samples
was compared to provide a more detailed assessment of physical stresses incurred
by Great Basin hunter-gatherers. Differences in age at death by sex across the two
samples were tested for statistical significance by means of independent samples
t-tests. Intersite differences in initial onset of osteoarthritis by sex and by five-year
age groups were evaluated by means of chi-square. Regression analysis was per-

TABLE 13.5.
Chi-Square Analysis of Osteoarthritis Frequencies by Sex among Great Basin and Georgia Coast Samples

Joint	Mal-Still* X^2	p	Mal-GeoP* X^2	p	Mal-GeoA* X^2	p	Still-GeoP* X^2	p	Still-GeoA* X^2	p	GeoP-GeoA* X^2	p
MALES												
Cervical	0.000	1.00	0.434	0.510	9.098	0.003	1.463	0.226	12.891	0.000	7.705	0.006
Thoracic	0.711	0.399	6.773	0.009	13.387	0.000	2.556	0.110	5.943	0.015	0.000	1.000
Lumbar	0.375	0.540	0.000	1.000	6.225	0.013	0.101	0.751	2.925	0.087	5.894	0.015
Sacrum	0.000	1.000	3.309	0.069	11.527	0.001	3.723	0.054	12.711	0.000	0.000	1.000
Shoulder	0.365	0.546	3.057	0.080	22.719	0.000	11.317	0.001	52.163	0.000	4.013	0.045
Elbow	0.000	1.000	9.706	0.002	26.244	0.000	13.198	0.000	29.269	0.000	2.611	0.106
Wrist	0.000	1.000	11.119	0.002	31.791	0.000	10.012	0.002	29.084	0.000	0.000	1.000
Hand	0.000	1.000	4.010	0.045	6.514	0.011	2.280	0.131	3.538	0.060	0.000	1.000
Hip	0.174	0.676	7.723	0.005	1.154	0.283	15.792	0.000	5.763	0.016	3.506	0.061
Knee	0.338	0.561	0.000	1.000	0.000	1.000	0.560	0.454	2.248	0.134	1.117	0.291
Ankle	0.028	0.867	6.294	0.012	4.031	0.045	11.176	0.001	8.936	0.003	0.629	0.428
Foot	3.318	0.069	19.220	0.000	48.606	0.000	2.354	0.125	5.722	0.017	0.000	1.000
FEMALES												
Cervical	0.057	0.812	4.236	0.040	30.066	0.000	1.077	0.299	16.862	0.000	6.794	0.009
Thoracic	2.537	0.111	12.103	0.001	35.606	0.000	1.048	0.306	7.220	0.007	0.631	0.427
Lumbar	0.000	1.000	6.312	0.012	23.748	0.000	4.622	0.032	19.275	0.000	4.989	0.026
Sacrum	0.000	1.000	4.205	0.040	5.774	0.016	4.397	0.036	5.811	0.016	0.000	1.000
Shoulder	0.000	1.000	7.148	0.008	18.115	0.000	5.988	0.014	15.888	0.000	0.237	0.627
Elbow	0.717	0.397	2.684	0.101	35.662	0.000	10.090	0.001	57.100	0.000	13.809	0.000
Wrist	0.032	0.857	12.782	0.000	38.136	0.000	5.416	0.020	22.043	0.000	1.377	0.241

Table 13.5. (continued)

Chi-Square Analysis of Osteoarthritis Frequencies by Sex among Great Basin and Georgia Coast Samples

Joint	Mal-Still*		Mal-GeoP*		Mal-GeoA*		Still-GeoP*		Still-GeoA*		GeoP-GeoA*	
	χ^2	p	χ^2	p	χ^2	p	χ^2	p	χ^2	p	χ^2	p
Hand	2.063	0.151	19.084	0.000	39.034	0.000	0.703	0.402	0.824	0.364	0.000	1.000
Hip	1.864	0.172	10.479	0.001	37.745	0.000	0.000	1.000	1.851	0.174	4.106	0.043
Knee	0.000	1.000	1.385	0.239	15.134	0.000	0.587	0.444	9.957	0.002	10.427	0.001
Ankle	0.987	0.321	1.866	0.172	15.563	0.000	0.005	0.942	0.000	1.000	4.074	0.044
Foot	0.000	1.000	1.274	0.259	3.830	0.050	1.061	0.303	3.292	0.070	0.000	1.000

* Mal = Malheur Lake; Still = Stillwater Marsh; GeoP = Georgia coast, preagricultural; GeoA = Georgia coast, agricultural.

formed among Stillwater Marsh individuals in the same fashion described for
Malheur Lake individuals, and velocities of polyarticular involvement across the
two skeletal series were compared by sex.

RESULTS

A General Assessment of Great Basin Osteoarthritic Affliction

Frequencies of osteoarthritis by joint region exhibited by Malheur Lake individuals were compared with frequencies obtained from other skeletal series to address whether Great Basin hunter-gatherers were highly mobile or highly sedentary. Comparative skeletal series include the Stillwater Marsh skeletal series from
the western Great Basin (Larsen, Ruff, and Kelly 1995) and preagricultural and
agricultural samples from the Georgia coast (Larsen 1982, 1990; Griffin and Larsen
1989).

The most common manifestation of osteoarthritis within the Malheur Lake
sample is proliferative bone development; 73.5 percent (108/147) of joint regions
affected by this disorder manifest this condition as marginal lipping. Resorption
represents the second most common manifestation of osteoarthritis, with 25.2 percent (37/147) of joint regions affected by bone loss. Eburnation is extremely uncommon; only 1.4 percent (2/147) of joint regions exhibit this severe symptom of
osteoarthritis. Evaluation by individual yields a similar trend. Of the 23 individuals affected by osteoarthritis, 95.7 percent (22/23) exhibit proliferative lipping,
60.9 percent (14/23) suffer resorptive bone loss, and only 8.7 percent (2/23) manifest this disorder as eburnation.

A total of 47 bilateral joint regions (e.g., shoulder, elbow, hip) were assessed
on both right and left sides in the Malheur Lake skeletal series. Twenty-one (44.7
percent) exhibit osteoarthritis on one side, while 26 (55.3 percent) are bilaterally
affected. Unilateral affectation is more common in the lower limb (13/24 = 54.2
percent) than in the upper limb (9/23 = 39.1 percent), but there is no marked
predilection for osteoarthritis to occur more often on the right side than on the left
for either the upper (right: 5/9 = 55.6 percent; left: 4/9 = 44.4 percent) or the lower
(right: 7/13 = 53.8 percent; left: 6/13 = 46.2 percent) limb. Since there were no
marked disparities by side among bilateral joints in either the upper or lower limb,
right and left sides were combined for analysis (i.e., if one or both sides of nonver-
tebral joints exhibit degenerative changes, the articular joint is scored as positive
for osteoarthritis). The total distribution of arthritic and nonarthritic joints in the
Malheur Lake skeletal series is provided in Table 13.3.

A comparison of osteoarthritis prevalence by joint region among samples by
sex reveals a close correspondence between Malheur Lake and Stillwater Marsh
samples and a strong separation of these two Great Basin samples from those obtained from the Georgia coast (Figure 13.1, Table 13.4). Malheur males exceed
Georgia coast preagricultural males in osteoarthritic prevalence for 11 of 12 joint re-

gions. The sole exception is the knee, where affectation among Georgia coast pre-agricultural males (18.6 percent) slightly exceeds that found at Malheur Lake (15.4 percent). Osteoarthritis frequencies are higher among Malheur Lake males than among Georgia coast agricultural males for all 12 joint regions. The results of chi-square analyses are provided in Table 13.5. These tests reveal that of 12 possible contrasts between Malheur Lake males and preagricultural males from the Georgia coast, Malheur Lake males exhibit significantly higher frequencies for nine joint regions. Similarly, Malheur Lake males show significantly greater prevalence than Georgia coast agricultural males for 10 of 12 joint regions. Differences in osteoarthritis frequency between Malheur Lake and Georgia coast males are especially marked for the spine (with the sole exception of lumbar vertebrae among preagricultural males) and the joints of the upper limb. Differences in the lower limb, however, are less dramatic, especially for the knee.

Contrasts among females reveal a pattern broadly similar to that described for males. The two Great Basin samples exhibit similarities to one another, but are strongly divergent from the two Georgia coast samples. Differences in affliction between Malheur Lake and Georgia coast females are most conspicuous for the spine and upper limb, while disparities in the lower limb are less distinctive. Of the 24 possible comparisons by joint region between Malheur Lake females and Georgia coast females, 8 of 12 joint regions significantly separate Malheur Lake females from preagricultural Georgia coast females, while all 12 joint regions are significantly more often affected by osteoarthritis in Malheur Lake females than in Georgia coast agricultural females.

Sex Differences in Osteoarthritic Affliction at Malheur Lake

A graphic depiction of osteoarthritis frequencies among Malheur Lake males and females by joint region is provided in Figure 13.2. Among males (n = 13), highest prevalence occurs for the foot (100.0 percent), but this high affectation is likely a product of sampling error (n = 3). Once the foot is removed from consideration, osteoarthritis prevalence among males ranges from a high of 77.8 percent for lumbar vertebrae to a low of 15.4 percent for the knee. Other joint regions affecting 50 percent or more of Malheur Lake males include thoracic vertebrae (75.0 percent), elbow (66.7 percent), cervical vertebrae (62.5 percent), wrist (50.0 percent), and sacrum (50.0 percent). Among females (n = 22), osteoarthritis prevalence ranges from a high of 78.6 percent for lumbar vertebrae to a low of 14.3 percent for the foot. Other joint regions exhibiting frequencies greater than or equal to 50 percent among Malheur Lake females are limited to thoracic (63.6 percent) and cervical (53.9 percent) vertebrae.

Neither sex is uniformly more affected by osteoarthritis than the other. Overall, males tend to be affected by osteoarthritis in the spine and upper limb slightly more often than females. The only two exceptions are the hand, where females are

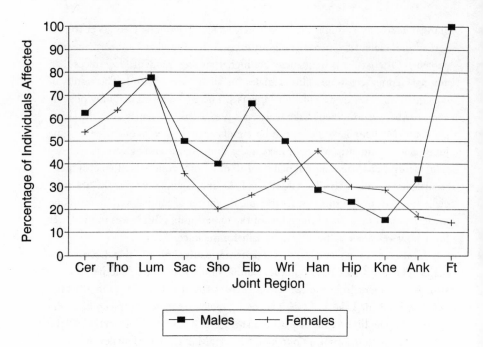

FIGURE 13.2. Osteoarthritis affectation by joint region among Malheur Lake individuals by sex.

more affected (males = 28.6 percent; females = 45.5 percent), and the lumbar vertebrae, where frequencies are virtually identical (males = 77.8 percent; females = 78.6
percent). This pattern is partially reversed for the lower limb. Females suffer higher
prevalence for the hip and knee, but males exhibit higher frequencies for the ankle.
Given the small sample size for the foot region in males, the markedly higher frequencies of affectation among males (100.0 percent) relative to females (14.3 percent) is of questionable statistical validity, and may be of no value for behavioral
interpretation.

    Although such a mixed pattern of osteoarthritis may appear discouraging for
assessment of differential mobility among males and females, it must be remembered that osteoarthritis is an age-progressive disorder. In the Malheur Lake skeletal series, mean age at death among females (38.6 years) exceeds that of males (34.9
years) by 3.7 years. While this difference is not statistically significant (t = 1.152, p =
0.258), it is apparent that when the sample is divided into five-year age groups, a
greater proportion of males are found in the younger groups, while females out-
number males in each of the older groups (Figure 13.3). Thus, the mixed pattern of
osteoarthritis frequencies by sex depicted in Figure 13.2 may reflect the compounded effects of both age and behavior.

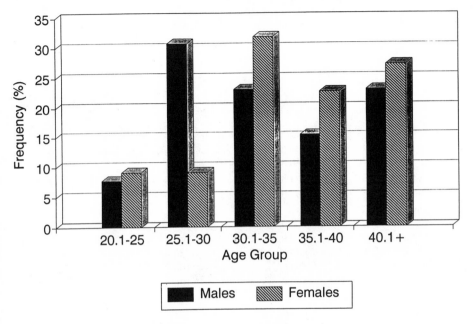

FIGURE 13.3. Age profile of the Malheur Lake osteoarthritis sample by sex.

A contrast of osteoarthritis frequencies by joint region for males and females of each five-year age group is presented in Table 13.6. This comparison reveals that in most cases, osteoarthritis is more common among males than among females for each joint region and each cohort. Although none of these comparisons yields a statistically significant difference, the lack of significance is likely a consequence of the extremely small sample sizes for each joint by sex when the sample is divided into five-year age groups.

To circumvent the problem of small sample sizes, the influence of age at death upon osteoarthritis prevalence is reconsidered by collapsing five-year age cohorts into two broad categories designated as "young adults" (20.1–35 years) and "old adults" (35.1+ years). This comparison yields two important results (Table 13.7). First, no comparisons between young adult males and females or between old adult males and females result in any significant differences by joint region. Second, the age-progressive nature of this disorder is strongly confirmed by the Malheur Lake skeletal series. Comparisons of osteoarthritis frequencies between young and old females and between young and old adult males result in four significant differences among females (thoracic vertebrae, elbow, wrist, knee) and two nearly significant differences among males (shoulder: p = 0.053; elbow: p = 0.097). Most importantly, every single joint region (except the foot for males) is

Table 13.6.

Osteoarthritis Summary Statistics among Malheur Lake Individuals
by Five-Year Age Groups

Age Group	Total No.	%	Males No.	%	Females No.	%
Cervical						
20.1–25	3	0.0	1	0.0	2	0.0
25.1–30	1	0.0	—	—	1	0.0
30.1–35	6	50.0	2	50.0	4	50.0
35.1–40	4	75.0	2	100.0	2	50.0
40.1+	7	100.0	3	100.0	4	100.0
Thoracic						
20.1–25	2	0.0	—	—	2	0.0
25.1–30	1	0.0	1	0.0	—	—
30.1–35	5	40.0	2	50.0	3	33.3
35.1–40	4	100.0	2	100.0	2	100.0
40.1+	7	100.0	3	100.0	4	100.0
Lumbar						
20.1–25	2	0.0	—	—	2	0.0
25.1–30	1	0.0	1	0.0	—	—
30.1–35	8	75.0	3	66.7	3	80.0
35.1–40	4	100.0	2	100.0	2	100.0
40.1+	8	100.0	3	100.0	4	100.0
Sacrum						
20.1–25	2	0.0	—	—	2	0.0
25.1–30	1	0.0	1	0.0	—	—
30.1–35	7	14.3	2	0.0	5	20.0
35.1–40	3	66.7	1	100.0	2	50.0
40.1+	7	71.4	2	100.0	5	60.0
Shoulder						
20.1–25	3	0.0	1	0.0	2	0.0
25.1–30	3	0.0	1	0.0	2	0.0
30.1–35	7	0.0	3	0.0	4	0.0
35.1–40	6	66.7	2	100.0	4	50.0
40.1+	9	44.4	3	66.7	6	33.3
Elbow						
20.1–25	3	0.0	1	0.0	2	0.0
25.1–30	2	0.0	—	—	2	0.0
30.1–35	9	11.1	3	33.3	6	0.0
35.1–40	6	50.0	2	100.0	4	25.0
40.1+	8	87.5	3	100.0	5	80.0

TABLE 13.6 (continued)

Age Group	Total No.	%	Males No.	%	Females No.	%
Wrist						
20.1–25	2	0.0	—	—	2	0.0
25.1–30	2	0.0	—	—	2	0.0
30.1–35	7	0.0	3	0.0	4	0.0
35.1–40	4	100.0	2	100.0	2	100.0
40.1+	8	62.5	3	66.7	5	60.0
Hand						
20.1–25	2	0.0	—	—	2	0.0
25.1–30	3	33.3	1	0.0	2	50.0
30.1–35	4	0.0	2	0.0	2	0.0
35.1–40	4	75.0	2	100.0	2	50.0
40.1+	5	60.0	2	0.0	3	100.0
Hip						
20.1–25	4	0.0	1	0.0	3	0.0
25.1–30	5	0.0	4	0.0	1	0.0
30.1–35	8	25.0	2	0.0	6	33.3
35.1–40	7	28.6	3	66.7	4	0.0
40.1+	9	55.6	3	33.3	6	66.7
Knee						
20.1–25	3	0.0	1	0.0	2	0.0
25.1–30	6	0.0	4	0.0	2	0.0
30.1–35	10	0.0	3	0.0	7	0.0
35.1–40	6	50.0	2	50.0	4	50.0
40.1+	9	55.5	3	33.3	6	66.7
Ankle						
20.1–25	2	0.0	—	—	2	0.0
25.1–30	5	20.0	4	25.0	1	0.0
30.1–35	10	10.0	3	0.0	7	14.3
35.1–40	5	40.0	2	100.0	3	0.0
40.1+	8	37.5	3	33.3	5	40.0
Foot						
20.1–25	2	0.0	—	—	2	0.0
25.1–30	2	50.0	1	100.0	1	0.0
30.1–35	1	0.0	—	—	1	0.0
35.1–40	2	100.0	2	100.0	—	—
40.1+	3	33.3	—	—	3	33.3

marked by an increase in osteoarthritis prevalence among old adults relative to young adults (Figure 13.4).

A closer inspection of Figure 13.4 suggests that the patterning of osteoarthritis prevalence differs by age for males and females. Young adult females appear more often affected by this disorder, for young females exceed their male counterparts in four joint regions: lumbar vertebrae, sacrum, hand, and hip. This difference is especially well marked for the latter two joint areas. Young adult males also exceed their female counterparts in osteoarthritis for four joint regions (discounting the anomalous foot), but only for the elbow does this difference reach the magnitude of overrepresentation seen among females for the hand and hip.

The patterning of osteoarthritis prevalence by joint region is markedly different among old adult males and females. Old adult males exhibit higher frequencies than old adult females for seven joint regions (once again discounting the foot), and these differences are especially striking for the sacrum, shoulder, elbow, and ankle. Affectation among old females exceeds old males for only two joint regions, the hand and the knee. Only for the hand does this difference approach the magnitude of overrepresentation seen for males in the sacrum, shoulder, elbow, and ankle.

Frequencies of initial onset of osteoarthritis by individual for each five-year cohort among Malheur Lake individuals are presented in Table 13.8 and illustrated in Figure 13.5. Although both males and females of the youngest cohort are entirely free of osteoarthritis, females in the second cohort are more frequently affected than males (50.0 percent vs. 25.0 percent). By the 30.1–35 years cohort, the prevalence of initial onset of osteoarthritis by an individual increases dramatically among males (41.7 percent), while females exhibit only a mild increase (7.1 percent). As a result, males of this cohort are more often affected by osteoarthritis than their female counterparts (66.7 percent vs. 57.1 percent). This sharp increase in the frequency of initial onset of osteoarthritis by an individual among males continues to the next cohort. All males in this 35.1–40 years age group are affected by osteoarthritis, an increase in initial onset of 33.3 percent over the previous cohort. Females of this cohort, however, feature a weaker increase in the initial onset of osteoarthritis (12.9 percent) than males; and, as a result, females of the fourth cohort are much less often affected by this disorder than their male counterparts (80.0 percent vs. 100.0 percent). All members of the Malheur Lake skeletal series in excess of 40 years of age at the time of death are affected by osteoarthritis.

The relationship between age at death and the percentage of joint regions affected by osteoarthritis is particularly useful for assessment of potential differences in the velocity of polyarticular involvement. The number of joint regions observed, the number of regions affected by osteoarthritis, the percentage of joint regions affected, and individual ages at death for each member of Malheur Lake and Stillwater Marsh osteoarthritis samples are provided in Table 13.9. Regression

Table 13.7.

Comparisons of Osteoarthritis Prevalence among Young and Old Adults from Malheur Lake

Age Group[a]	Total No.[b]	%[c]	Males No.[b]	%[c]	χ^2	p	Females No.[b]	%[c]	χ^2	p
Cervical										
20.1–35	10	30.0	3	33.3	1.600	0.206	7	28.6	2.006	0.157
35.1+	11	90.9	5	100.0			6	83.3		
Thoracic										
20.1–35	8	25.0	3	33.3	1.600	0.206	5	20.0	4.482	0.034
35.1+	11	100.0	5	100.0			6	100.0		
Lumbar										
20.1–35	11	54.5	4	50.0	0.972	0.324	7	57.1	1.697	0.193
35.1+	12	100.0	5	100.0			7	100.0		
Sacrum										
20.1–35	10	10.0	3	0.0	2.667	0.102	7	14.3	1.244	0.265
35.1+	10	70.0	3	100.0			7	57.1		
Shoulder										
20.1–35	13	0.0	5	0.0	3.750	0.053	8	0.0	2.125	0.145
35.1+	15	53.3	5	80.0			10	40.0		
Elbow										
20.1–35	14	7.1	4	25.0	2.756	0.097	10	0.0	4.947	0.026
35.1+	14	71.4	5	100.0			9	55.6		
Wrist										
20.1–35	11	0.0	3	0.0	2.133	0.144	8	0.0	5.658	0.017
35.1+	12	75.0	5	80.0			7	71.4		
Hand										
20.1–35	9	11.1	3	0.0	0.365	0.546	6	16.7	2.228	0.136
35.1+	9	66.7	4	50.0			5	80.0		
Hip										
20.1–35	17	11.8	7	0.0	2.169	0.141	10	20.0	0.238	0.626
35.1+	16	43.8	6	50.0			10	40.0		
Knee										
20.1–35	19	0.0	8	0.0	1.333	0.248	11	0.0	6.534	0.011
35.1+	15	53.3	5	40.0			10	60.0		
Ankle										
20.1–35	17	11.8	7	14.3	1.071	0.301	10	10.0	0.045	0.832
35.1+	13	46.2	5	60.0			8	25.0		
Foot										
20.1–35	5	20.0	1	100.0	0.000	1.000	4	0.0	0.024	0.876
35.1+	5	60.0	2	100.0			3	33.3		

[a] Young adults = 20.1–35 years; old adults = 35.1+ years. No comparisons between young males versus young females, or old males versus old females were significant (chi-square: p < 0.05).

[b] Number of articular joints observed for presence or absence of osteoarthritis.

[c] Percentage of articular joints affected by osteoarthritis.

analysis of polyarticular acquisition of osteoarthritis among the members of the Malheur Lake skeletal series is presented in Figure 13.6.

This analysis reveals that while both males and females show a significant association between the percentage of joint regions affected by osteoarthritis and age at death (females: r = 0.655, F = 15.045, p = 0.001; males: r = 0.762, F = 15.222, p = 0.002), the progression of this disorder throughout adulthood differs markedly. The smaller y-intercept for males (y = −112.520 + 4.319x) than for females (y = −73.454 + 2.901x) indicates that polyarticular involvement among young adult females exceeds that of young adult males. However, the steeper regression slope for males relative to females indicates that the velocity of polyarticular involvement increases more rapidly with advancing age among males, thereby resulting in the greater frequencies of osteoarthritis involvement in old adult males than in old females. These results strongly suggest that the nature of habitual physical stresses encountered by Malheur Lake males exeeded those experienced by Malheur Lake females.

A Comparison of Osteoarthritis among Great Basin Samples

Malheur Lake and Stillwater Marsh males exhibit marked correspondence in osteoarthritic affliction by joint region (Figure 13.1, Table 13.4). Although Malheur Lake males display somewhat higher frequencies of osteoarthritis in the spine (especially thoracic and lumbar regions) and upper limb (except the shoulder), Stillwater Marsh males feature slightly higher frequencies in the lower limb (except for the foot). Malheur Lake and Stillwater Marsh females also exhibit similar trends in osteoarthritic frequency by joint region. This correspondence is especially apparent for lumber vertebrae, sacrum, shoulder, knee, and foot. Malheur Lake females stand apart from their Stillwater Marsh counterparts by possessing higher frequencies of osteoarthritis in cervical vertebrae, thoracic vertebrae, wrist, hand, hip, and ankle, while Stillwater Marsh females only exceed Malheur females for the elbow. Chi-square analysis by sex, however, reveals that no joint regions differ significantly in osteoarthritis prevalence between these two samples of Great Basin hunter-gatherers (Table 13.5).

Despite these overall similarities, assessment of osteoarthritis by individual (Table 13.8) reveals that a greater percentage of Stillwater individuals are affected in at least one joint region than are Malheur Lake individuals (76.5 percent vs. 65.7 percent). This pattern holds true for both sexes, although the difference between the two samples is greater for males (Stillwater = 78.6 percent; Malheur = 61.5 percent; difference = 17.1 percent) than for females (Stillwater = 72.2 percent; Malheur = 68.2 percent; difference = 4.0 percent). These results are intriguing given that the mean age at death for the Stillwater Marsh sample as a whole (33.4 years) and by sex (males = 32.5 years; females = 34.1 years) is less than that of the Malheur Lake sample (entire sample = 37.3 years; males = 34.9 years; females = 38.6 years).

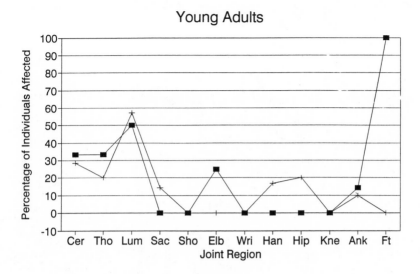

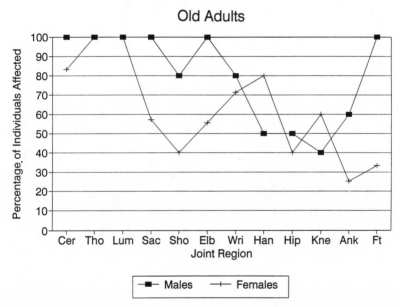

Figure 13.4. Osteoarthritis affectation by joint region among young adult and old adult Malheur Lake individuals by sex.

TABLE 13.8.

Age Comparison of Initial Onset of Osteoarthritis among Malheur Lake and Stillwater Marsh Individuals

	Malheur Lake[a]						Stillwater Marsh[b]					
	Total (37.3)[c]		Males (34.9)		Females (38.6)		Total (33.4)[c]		Males (32.5)		Females (34.1)	
Age Group	No.[d]	%[e]	No.[d]	%[e]	No.[d]	%[e]	No.[d]	%[e]	No.[d]	%[e]	No.[d]	%[e]
20.1–25	3	0.0	1	0.0	2	0.0	5	20.0	3	33.3	2	0.0
25.1–30	6	33.3	4	25.0	2	50.0	8	50.0	3	66.7	5	40.0
30.1–35	10	60.0	3	66.7	7	57.1	8	100.0	2	100.0	4	100.0
35.1–40	7	85.7	2	100.0	5	80.0	11	100.0	6	100.0	5	100.0
40.1+	9	100.0	3	100.0	6	100.0	2	100.0	0	—	2	100.0
Total	35	65.7	13	61.5	22	68.2	24	76.5	14	78.6	18	72.2

[a] No significant differences between Malheur Lake males and females, either by age-group (chi-square: p < 0.05 for each age class) or overall (t = 1.152, p = 0.258).

[b] Values for Stillwater individuals are from Larsen, Ruff, and Kelly (1995:Table 8-4).

[c] No significant differences in age at death between Malheur Lake and Stillwater Marsh individuals, either overall (t = 1.941, p = 0.057) or by sex (males: t = 0.873, p = 0.391; females: t = 1.617, p = 0.114).

[d] Number of individuals observed for presence/absence of osteoarthritis; presence of pathology denoted by at least one articular joint affected.

[e] Percentage of individuals affected by osteoarthritis.

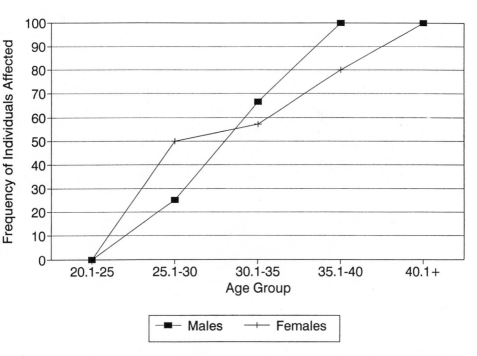

FIGURE 13.5. Initial onset of osteoarthritis among Malheur Lake individuals by sex.

A plot of individual initial onset of osteoarthritis by five-year age categories is presented in Figure 13.7. Stillwater males of the first three age cohorts are more often affected by osteoarthritis than are Malheur males. For both groups, all males in excess of 35 years of age are affected by this disorder. The pattern of initial acquisition of osteoarthritis among females is more complex. While females of the first age cohort from both Great Basin series are entirely free of osteoarthritis, half of Malheur females of the second cohort exhibit osteoarthritis compared to only 40 percent of their Stillwater counterparts. This relationship is dramatically reversed for the third cohort. All Stillwater females between 30.1 and 35 years of age are affected by osteoarthritis, a 60 percent increase in the prevalence of initial onset over the previous age group. By contrast, Malheur females show only a 9 percent increase (57 percent) over the previous cohort. This trend continues in the fourth cohort, where Stillwater females exhibit 100 percent affectation, while Malheur females continue to remain less affected (80 percent). By the fifth cohort, all females from Malheur Lake and Stillwater Marsh are affected by osteoarthritis.

A comparison of young and old adult females from Malheur Lake and Stillwater Marsh (Figure 13.8) indicates that young adult females from Malheur Lake exhibit higher frequencies of osteoarthritis in the upper spine (cervical, thoracic), hand, and hip, while young adult females from Stillwater Marsh feature higher

TABLE 13.9.

Frequency of Arthritis by Joint Region among Malheur Lake and Stillwater Marsh Individuals

		Malheur Lake						Stillwater Marsh			
Specimen	Sex	Age[a]	Aff[b]	Tot[c]	Pct[d]	Specimen	Sex	Age[a]	Aff[b]	Tot[c]	Pct[d]
403.2	M	37	10	11	90.9	1043-5	M	40+	5	8	62.5
1032A.1b	F	30	0	9	0.0	1043-8	U	33	1	3	33.3
1032B.1a	F	34	0	2	0.0	1043-ind. 4	F	40	2	4	50.0
1899.2a	M	34	1	7	14.3	1043-61	F	30+	1	8	12.5
1899.3	F	35	0	4	0.0	1044-1	F	27	0	12	0.0
1905.1	F	34	4	9	44.4	1044-2	M	40+	12	12	100.0
1906.1	M	47	8	9	88.9	1044-ind. 2	M	35+	4	9	44.4
1906.2	M	30	2	8	25.0	1045-1	F	35	2	12	16.7
1906.3	M	35	3	11	27.3	1046-9	M	37	2	12	16.7
1911.1	F	60+	10	12	83.3	1047-1	M	21	0	9	0.0
1911.2	M	27	0	3	0.0	1047-13	F	40+	2	4	50.0
1911.3	F	40	2	6	33.3	1050-3	M	40+	11	12	91.7
1911.4	F	44	1	5	20.0	1051-ind. 6	F	25	0	6	0.0
1949.1	F	60+	8	12	66.7	1054-1	M	27	0	12	0.0
1949.2	M	47	7	11	63.6	1055-1	M	27	1	9	11.1
1949.3	F	22	0	12	0.0	1056-1	F	35	1	6	16.7
1949.4	F	37	2	5	40.0	1057-1	U	33	1	3	33.3
1949.5	M	30	0	4	0.0	1058-1	M	25	0	1	0.0
1949.6	M	30	0	3	0.0	1058-12A	F	22	0	8	0.0
1949.7	M	22	0	5	0.0	1060-1	F	33	2	6	33.3
1949.8a	F	40	1	4	25.0	910-ind. 3	F	27	0	7	0.0
1949.9	F	30	1	5	20.0	1062-1	M	40+	10	12	83.3
1977.1	F	33	0	12	0.0	1063-19,20	M	40+	10	11	90.1
1991.4	M	37	0	11	0.0	1063-1,18	F	30	1	10	10.0
1991.5	F	35	1	10	10.0	1070-3	F	40+	6	12	50.0
2095.1	M	42	6	11	54.5	1070-4	F	40+	10	12	83.3
2095.2a	F	32	4	8	50.0	1159-4	M	35	4	12	33.3
2095.3	F	37	9	11	81.8	1159-6	M	27	3	12	25.0
2095.4	F	31	2	8	25.0	1159-200	F	45+	6	12	50.0
2095.6	F	47	9	12	75.0	L53-B-1	F	35+	2	7	28.6
2095.9	F	56	8	10	80.0	1160-2	F	45	2	5	40.0
2095.12a	F	24	0	12	0.0	1249-1	M	21	1	9	11.1
2095.12b	M	37	12	12	100.0	L72-200	F	37	2	12	16.7
2095.17	F	45	3	6	50.0	1173-200	F	27	0	7	0.0
2095.18	F	40	0	6	0.0						

[a] In order to maximize comparability between samples, all Malheur individuals assigned an age at death in excess of 45 years were set at 45.0 for statistical analysis.

[b] Aff = Number of joint regions scored positive for the presence of osteoarthritis.

[c] Tot = Number of joint regions possible to assess for the presence/absence of osteoarthritis.

[d] Pct = Number of joints affected by osteoarthritis divided by the number of joints available for assessment of osteoarthritis presence/absence.

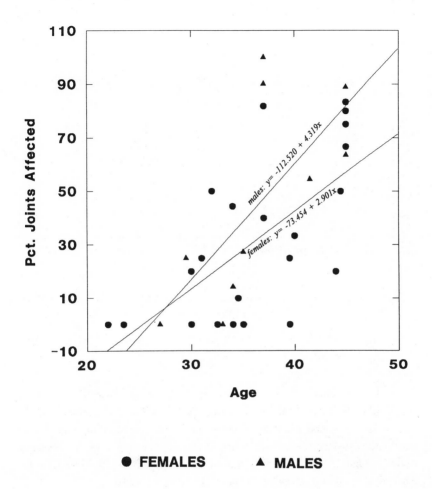

FIGURE 13.6. Regression of polyarticular osteoarthritis among Malheur Lake individuals by sex.

prevalence in the sacrum, shoulder, elbow, and knee. Some of these trends continue among old adult females of both series, but perhaps the most interesting trend is that old adult females from Malheur Lake show higher frequencies of osteoarthritis for all joints of the lower limb including the hip.

A contrast between young and old adult males from Malheur Lake and Stillwater Marsh is provided in Figure 13.9. Young adult males from Malheur Lake fea-

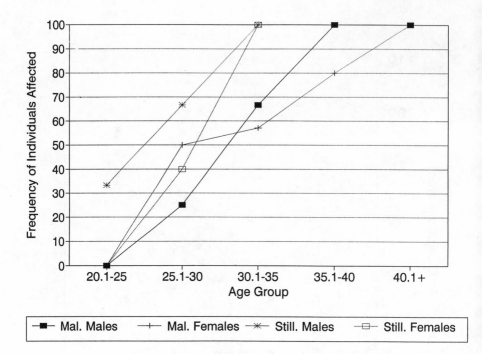

FIGURE 13.7. Initial onset of osteoarthritis among Malheur Lake and Stillwater Marsh individuals by sex.

ture higher frequencies of osteoarthritis in the midspine (thoracic, lumbar), while young adult Stillwater males exceed their Malheur Lake counterparts in the sacrum, shoulder, elbow, hip, and ankle. A contrast among old adult males reveals that Malheur Lake males exhibit higher frequencies of osteoarthritis in the spine, elbow, and hand, while all joint regions of the lower limb and hip (except for the foot) are affected more often among old adult Stillwater males.

Regression analysis of the association between the percentage of joint regions affected by osteoarthritis and age at death for Stillwater individuals is provided in Figure 13.10. This comparison reveals a general correspondence between these two Great Basin samples, but illustrates differences as well. Like Malheur Lake individuals, males and females from Stillwater Marsh exhibit different regression slopes, with males possessing a steeper regression slope (y = −100.461 + 4.342x) than females (y = −74.372 + 2.931x). However, unlike the Malheur Lake series, there is no intersection of Stillwater male and female regression slopes. This indicates that throughout all phases of adulthood, Stillwater males are marked by greater polyarticular involvement than their female counterparts and confirm the pattern of initial onset of osteoarthritis by individuals presented in Figure 13.9. A second difference reflected by the plot of regression slopes for Stillwater individuals from

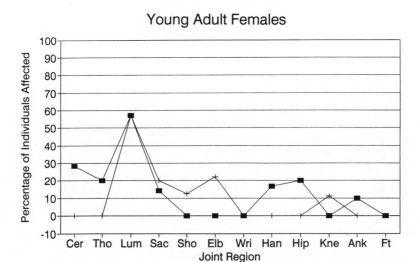

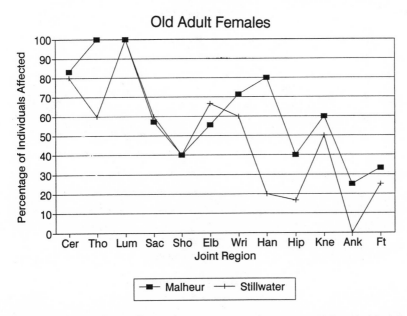

FIGURE 13.8. Osteoarthritis affliction by joint region among young adult and old adult females from Malheur Lake and Stillwater Marsh.

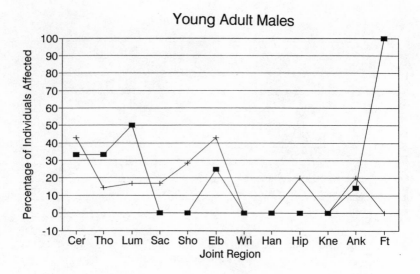

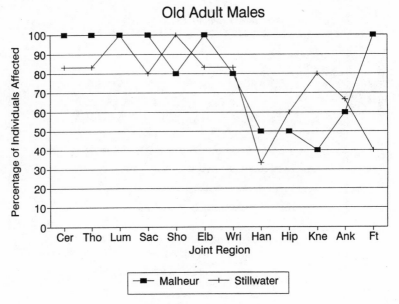

FIGURE 13.9. Osteoarthritis affliction by joint region among young adult and old adult males from Malheur Lake and Stillwater Marsh.

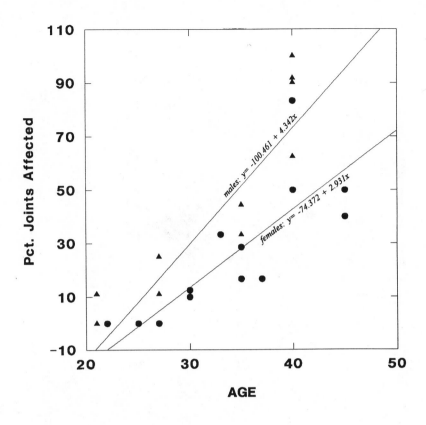

FIGURE 13.10. Regression analysis of polyarticular osteoarthritis among Stillwater Marsh individuals by sex.

those seen at Malheur Lake is a greater disparity in the percentage of joints affected by osteoarthritis among old adult males and females. Comparison of Figures 13.6 and 13.10 reveals that a greater percentage of joints are affected among Stillwater old adult males relative to old adult females than shown by their counterparts from Malheur Lake.

A comparison of the relationship between the percentage of joint regions affected by osteoarthritis and age at death between Malheur Lake and Stillwater Marsh skeletal series with sexes pooled is presented in Figure 13.11. While both groups exhibit a significant correlation between the percentage of joint regions affected and age at death (Malheur Lake: r = 0.678, F = 28.143, p = 0.000; Stillwater Marsh: r = 0.778, F = 48.914, p = 0.000), the higher y-intercept for Stillwater indi-

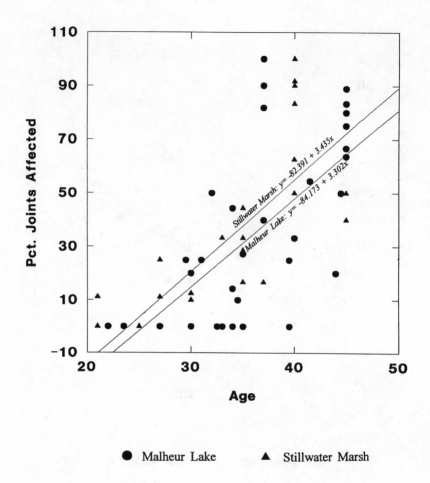

FIGURE 13.11. Regression analysis of polyarticular osteoarthritis across sex-pooled Great Basin samples.

viduals (y = −82.391 + 3.435x) indicates that these individuals suffered a greater percentage of joint regions affected by osteoarthritis throughout adulthood than did individuals from Malheur Lake (y = −84.173 + 3.302x). Nevertheless, the close similarity in regression slopes for sex-pooled samples from Stillwater Marsh and Malheur Lake indicate that the rate of osteoarthritic progression was the same.

Figure 13.12 provides a comparison of the relationship between polyarticular involvement and advancing age at death for females and males of the two skeletal series. A comparison of Malheur Lake and Stillwater females shows a remarkably similar relationship between the percentage of joints affected by osteoarthritis and age at death. By contrast, a comparison of males shows that, while the velocity of polyarticular involvement with increasing age is the same for males from the two

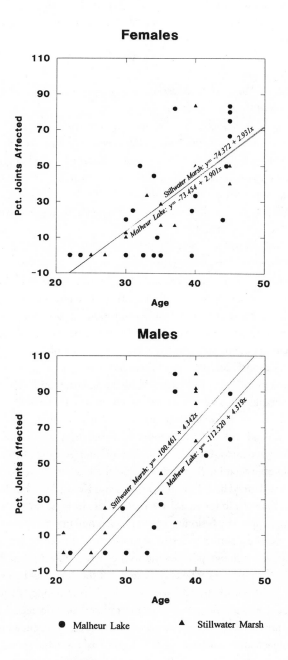

FIGURE 13.12. Regression analysis of polyarticular osteoarthritis across Great Basin samples by sex.

sites (i.e., the regression slopes are nearly identical), Stillwater males exhibit a greater percentage of joint regions affected by osteoarthritis throughout all stages of adulthood (greater y-intercept).

DISCUSSION
To Move or Not to Move: Sedentism and Mobility among Great Basin Wetland Dwellers

Although archaeologists have historically been polarized over the issue of whether precontact occupants of Great Basin wetlands were sedentary or mobile (limnosedentary vs. limnomobility), reexamination of the ethnographic model employed by limnosedentary proponents, recent research on the nature of mobility strategies employed by hunter-gatherer populations, and application of optimum foraging models to the Stillwater Marsh wetlands suggest that neither extreme position may be accurate.

As pointed out by Oetting (1989, this volume), there has been a semantic confusion over the term "limnosedentary." Thomas (1985) discounted a residentially stable wetland-based subsistence strategy for the inhabitants of Hidden Cave because he equated such a strategy with sedentism. The problem is that, except in a few cases (D. B. Madsen 1979; possibly Napton 1969), the term "sedentism" has not been used by limnosedentary proponents in the strict sense of year-round residential occupation, but rather in a relative sense to describe increased residential stability as a seasonal reoccupation of preferred sites.

In almost every case, proponents of the limnosedentism invoke the Klamath as an ethnographic analogy for modeling precontact residentially stable subsistence adaptations in the wetlands of the Great Basin (Jennings and Norbeck 1955; Rozaire 1963; Weide 1968; Napton 1969; O'Connell 1975; D. B. Madsen and Lindsay 1977; Pettigrew 1980; Oetting 1989, this volume). As noted by Oetting (1989, this volume) ethnographic data indicate that the Klamath were not sedentary in the strict sense defined by J. E. Rafferty (1985) and Kelly (1985), but *semi*sedentary. That is, the Klamath followed a pattern of repeated, but seasonal, occupation of fixed sites interrupted by fissioning of the social group into smaller foraging bands during the rest of the annual round. The similarity of this semisedentary lifeway of the Klamath with ethnographic descriptions of several Great Basin Paiute groups was noted by Weide (1968), who emphasized that the difference between the "limnosedentary" pattern of the Klamath and the "limnomobile" pattern of Great Basin groups represents differences in degree rather than differences in kind. Thus, use of the semisedentary Klamath as a model for the limnosedentary hypothesis to assess precontact subsistence strategies in Great Basin wetlands reveals that the issue is really one of identifying subsistence differences along a continuum rather than attempting to assign precontact subsistence patterns to a dichotomy between sedentary and nonsedentary lifeways.

Recent research of mobility strategies employed by modern hunter-gatherers emphasize that different kinds of mobility are utilized by individuals and groups in various combinations to comprise myriad effective subsistence adaptations (Binford 1980, 1982; Kelly 1983, 1992). Resource abundance-based limnosedentary models based on analogy with the Klamath, as well as stress-based limnomobile models based on Great Basin groups, admit seasonal sedentary occupation of preferred sites. Hence, the main difference between these models is the *relative* proportion of the annual round spent in seasonally stable residential aggregations versus that spent in residentially mobile foraging bands. While the traditional focus of discussions of precontact utilization of Great Basin wetlands has centered on residential mobility, a reduction in residential mobility need not entail a reduction in the amount of overall mobility during an average annual round. Logically, the greater the amount of time spent in residentially stable localities, the greater the degree of logistical foraging required to maintain an effective subsistence strategy. Conversely, as the amount of time spent in residentially mobile foraging bands increases, the lesser the demand for logistical foraging. Either way, the level of *overall mobility* incurred by group members during the annual round may be the same so long as the distribution of resources remains unchanged.

Refinements in optimum-foraging strategy theory permit anthropologists to simulate mobility patterns among hunter-gatherer populations as they respond to the costs and benefits incurred in obtaining and processing vital resources. In the Great Basin, these efforts have been spearheaded by Simms (1985, 1987, 1988), and a recent application of these values by Raven (1990) in a stratified survey in the Carson Sink led to a different interpretation of mobility than the extreme limnosedentism of Napton (1969) or the highly limnomobile interpretation of Kelly (1983, 1985, 1990).

Raven's survey (1990) demonstrates that, although resources within the Stillwater Marsh were volatile and subject to both annual and periodic shortages, the sheer richness, diversity, and predictability of wetland resources encouraged virtually continuous reliance on the marsh by a fairly stable population of aboriginal hunter-gatherers. However, he is careful to point out that this reliance did not lead to year-round sedentary occupation of individual residential sites within the marsh. Rather, small-scale adjustments in residence location would have been made frequently throughout a given year due to the patchy distribution, seasonal availability, and limited benefits of transporting collected resources over local storage. Raven's data suggest that upland resources represented a secondary food source. He predicts that foraging parties would only have left the valley floor when the marsh simply could not provide a necessary resource or when the uplands offered seasonal opportunities for high-quality items (piñon, fish, large game) energetically more profitable than resources locally available in the marsh. Consequently, utilization of upland resources was likely accomplished through short-term and resource-specific logistical forays from the lowlands rather than through residential movement. Because of these factors, Raven's reconstruction stakes out a middle ground between expectations of extreme limnosedentary and limnomobility models. Given a wetland-focused residential stability in the marsh, the small-scale adjustments in residential location and logistical forays into the surrounding uplands would have resulted in a subsistence strategy in which both residential and logistical mobility likely remained high.

Recent research by Kelly (1995b, this volume) is largely in agreement with Raven's model of precontact mobility in the Carson Sink. Kelly emphasizes that, while wetlands appear to be highly productive and reliable sources for food compared to general Great Basin habitats, the low productivity and spatiotemporal variance in availability of these resources influenced the mobility patterns of aboriginal hunter-gatherers. Kelly hypothesizes that although tethered to the wetlands, Stillwater Marsh hunter-gatherers likely utilized foraging strategies marked by residential movements within and outside the marsh coupled with frequent and lengthy logistical forays for more widely dispersed resources. Thus, while not emphasizing residential stability within the marsh to the degree stressed by Raven (1990), Kelly also provides a reconstruction based on optimum foraging strategy that would permit some degree of residential stability in wetland-focused localities as part of a more wide-ranging subsistence strategy that likely involved high levels of both residential and logistical mobility.

If the reconstructions offered by Raven and Kelly are accurate, analysis of human skeletal remains from Stillwater Marsh should show that these individuals suffered high levels of osteoarthritis caused by the heavy and repetitive physical demands incurred by such a mobile lifeway. A recent comparison of osteoarthritis prevalence in the Stillwater Marsh skeletal series with Georgia coast preagricultural and agricultural samples by Larsen, Ruff, and Kelly (1995) reveals markedly higher osteoarthritis frequencies for nearly all joint regions of Stillwater males and females. These results likely expose two interrelated differences in behavior between Great Basin hunter-gatherers and the precontact inhabitants of the Georgia coast. The higher frequencies of osteoarthritis at Stillwater Marsh relative to preagricultural Georgia may reflect greater stresses and strains placed on the joints of individuals frequently engaged in traversing and exploiting upland resources adjacent to Great Basin wetlands (see also Ruff, this volume). By contrast, analysis of food remains from a large number of sites indicates that preagricultural Georgia coast hunter-gatherers placed a primary emphasis on acquisition of marine resources and only a secondary emphasis on securing terrestrial resources from topographically mild, inland regions (Larsen 1990). Hence, differences in osteoarthritis frequencies between Great Basin and Georgia coast hunter-gatherers are likely a function of topographical severity as well as the degree of general mobility. Differences in osteoarthritis frequencies between Stillwater Marsh hunter-gatherers and

Georgia coast agriculturalists likely indicate that the inhabitants of Stillwater Marsh suffered prolonged exposure to very heavy, repetitive physical activities not experienced by sedentary Georgia coast agricultural populations, whose rates of osteoarthritis prevalence are markedly and consistently low.

A comparison of osteoarthritis prevalence by joint region indicates that Malheur Lake individuals also suffered from high frequencies of this disorder. The frequency and patterning of osteoarthritis prevalence in the Malheur Lake skeletal series strongly separates individuals from Georgia coast preagricultural and agricultural samples. By contrast, Malheur Lake and Stillwater Marsh individuals show very similar frequencies and patterns of osteoarthritis. These results suggest that the people of the Malheur Lake wetlands experienced not only prolonged levels of intense physical activity unexpected of a sedentary way of life but also habitual activities involving frequent forays into the surrounding rugged uplands.

While these data could be used to call into question archaeological evidence offered by some researchers in support of residentially stable wetland occupations (Oetting 1989, 1992, this volume; O'Connell 1971; Pettigrew 1985; Weide 1968), there are three possible alternative explanations to account for this apparent incongruity between archaeological and biological interpretations. First, precontact utilization of Great Basin wetlands may have varied greatly in the past, and these variations could have resulted in greater or lesser residential sedentism at different times depending on seasonal and annual fluctuations in precipitation (Kelly 1995b, this volume; Musil 1995). It is possible that the aboriginal inhabitants of Great Basin wetlands altered their foraging strategies throughout different periods in prehistory in the face of such environmental variations. Unfortunately, the uncertain time depth encompassed by the osteological evidence currently in hand is inadequate to provide a definitive test of this proposal.

Second, it may be that, although the precontact inhabitants of the Harney Basin practiced a highly sedentary seasonal round, they engaged in occupational activities which resulted in high levels of physical stress. The data from osteoarthritis analysis, however, provide no support for such an interpretation. The nearly universal higher prevalence and bilateral affectation among Malheur Lake individuals compared to preagricultural and agricultural populations of the Georgia coast strongly suggest that these demands were not occupation-specific, but involved the entire body. Such universally high levels of osteoarthritis, present not only among individuals from the Malheur Lake wetlands in the northern Great Basin but also among those from the Stillwater Marsh wetlands of the western Great Basin, indicate that these aboriginal peoples participated in a lifeway that exposed them to very excessive and repetitive physical demands. Such levels of osteoarthritis imply not only a more vigorous lifeway but also a lifeway that likely entailed an high degree of mobility.

Third, it may be that the biological evidence simply does not stand in opposition to archaeological reconstructions which call for semisedentary, residentially stable wetlands occupations. Evidence obtained from osteoarthritis analysis merely indicates that occcupants of northern (Malheur Lake) and western (Still-water Marsh) Great Basin wetlands participated in a lifeway that led to repeated and heavy physical demands. Given that these demands affected all major joint regions of the body and that prevalence was universally high among both males and females, it follows that the magnitude of mobility *of one form or another* was very high. However, this need not mean that they did not spend some portion of the year in wetland-focused, residentially stable localities, for high mobility alone does not allow assessment of the degree of residential stability. This is because a subsistence strategy that permitted residentially stable wetland occupations may only have been possible if this strategy also entailed a high degree of logistical mobility to provide a sufficient and regular resupply of these stable residences. Since differences between linomobile and limnosedentary models are but ones of degree, rather than of kind, the key issue is over what *proportion* of this mobility was the product of residential movement in small foraging bands relative to that due to logistical foraging by residentially stable aggregations. To address this issue, differences in osteoarthritis prevalence by sex must be evaluated.

Differential Mobility: The Sex Factor?
     The recognition that mobility is an individual, rather than a group, phenomenon has raised the possibility that various members of aboriginal Great Basin hunter-gatherer populations may have participated in widely differing levels and types of mobility. While some of these differences may be idiosyncratic, or environmentally induced (Kelly, this volume; Musil 1995), others may be inherent of a foraging lifeway. Numerous studies of modern hunter-gatherers have documented differences in habitual task activities and mobility between males and females (Kelly 1983, 1992). Such sex-based behaviors are clearly documented by ethnographic studies of the occupants of northern and western Great Basin wetlands at the time of European contact. In both areas, females were the predominant collectors and processors of plant commodities such as roots and seeds. Most often, a strategy of residential mobility was employed, whereby the whole community moved to areas with an abundance of vegetative resources. Large-game hunting, however, was an exclusively male activity governed by logistical foraging. Parties of males would depart residential base camps for the uplands, crossing over rough terrain for days before returning to camp (Whiting 1950; Couture 1978; Couture, Ricks, and Housley 1986; Wheat 1967; Speth 1969; C. S. Fowler and Bath 1981).
     If such sex-based differences in habitual activities among the protocontact inhabitants of the Harney Basin and Carson Sink also hold true for the earlier occupants of these areas, these differences should be reflected in the skeleton. If pre-

contact females were largely engaged in obtaining and processing vegetative foods, while males tended to traverse rough upland terrain in search of big game, females should be less afflicted by arthritis overall, show a later initial onset of this disorder, and exhibit a slower progression of degenerative changes throughout the major joint regions of the body.

Results from osteoarthritis analysis provide strong evidence of differential behavior among Great Basin males and females. In both Malheur Lake and Stillwater Marsh skeletal series, sex-based disparities in osteoarthritis by joint region increase from young adults to old adults, and this difference is due to a greater preponderance of affectation among old adult males. Likewise, with the exception of the first two five-year cohorts of Malheur individuals, initial onset of osteoarthritis occurs earlier in adulthood among Great Basin males than females. Regression analysis indicates that males of both skeletal series exhibit a more rapid progression of osteoarthritis throughout the body than do females.

These results confirm two important aspects of analogous behavior among the precontact and protohistoric inhabitants of Great Basin wetlands. First, males and females were not identically affected by osteoarthritis, and these differences indicate that Great Basin males and females were exposed to different levels of physical stress throughout adulthood. Such disparities were likely the product of variations in work load and mobility produced by sex-based distinctions in subsistence activities. Second, the levels of long-term physical stress incurred during subsistence activities was greater for males than for females. This is reflected by the fact that males and females acquired polyarticular arthritic affliction at different rates, and in both skeletal series the velocity of degenerative changes was greater among males than among females. The greater biomechanical stresses incurred by males during bouts of logistical foraging for big game in the rugged topography of the surrounding uplands likely represent a primary factor contributing to this difference in osteoarthritis affectation among Great Basin males and females.

Of Marshes, Resources, and Patterns of Mobility

Kelly (this volume) has taken an important step to demonstrate how environmental changes in a wetlands area, such as the Carson Sink, can have profound impact on the relative costs and benefits of procurement and storage of resources— impacts that would have had profound influences on the choices made by early foragers in adjusting their patterns of annual mobility to dynamic exigencies imposed by their environment. If such factors can wreak influences on foraging strategy in a single area, it is even more likely that the differences in resources offered by another wetland system could result in a local pattern of annual mobility different from that proposed for the precontact inhabitants of the Carson Sink.

Raven (1992) maintains that, although the Harney Basin superficially resembles the Carson Sink, the two basins exhibit significant differences in overall water budget, marsh composition, and distribution of secondary resources that likely affected utilization by aboriginal populations. The overall water budget of the Carson Sink is less than that of the Harney Basin. While this leads to an increased potential for periodic failure of the lake system, such fluctuations also serve to fragment the marsh into a rich diversity of biotic habitats. These deep and diverse marshes render the "central place" strategy of site location (Orians and Pearson 1979) in the marsh highly effective. However, away from the wetlands, sources of food and water are scarce. Because of these factors, Raven (1992) proposes that the Stillwater Marsh may have been a hub for a fundamentally *centripetal* foraging strategy. This strategy favors primary emphasis on exploitation of local marsh resources and secondary exploitation of upland resources. In this scenario, the precontact inhabitants of the Stillwater Marsh may have developed a seasonal round that featured a pattern of high residential mobility within the marsh, coupled with frequent logistical forays for targeted exploitation of specific upland resources.

In marked contrast to the Carson Sink, Raven (1992) asserts that the greater overall water budget of the Harney Basin has led to the formation of large, and less intermittent, lakes. Although an increased water budget confers the benefit of a regular water supply, such large bodies of water only support narrow, annular marshes featuring nearly monomorphic vegetation. Away from the Malheur Lake wetlands, the remainder of the Harney Basin supports a far richer biosphere. Raven proposes that the combined effects of a less diverse, annular marsh in conjunction with a greater abundance of diverse resources in surrounding regions, may have favored a *centrifugal* foraging strategy among the precontact inhabitants of the Harney Basin. Because of less disparity in resource availability between the marsh and the surrounding countryside, the precontact inhabitants of the Harney Basin may have practiced a seasonal round marked by high levels of residential mobility both within and outside the wetlands, coupled with lower levels of logistical mobility than practiced by the more highly tethered inhabitants of the Carson Sink.

If these interpretations are correct, the skeletal remains of precontact inhabitants of the Malheur Lake and Stillwater Marsh wetlands should exhibit evidence of differences in physical stresses incurred as a result of these two foraging strategies. If the aboriginal occupants of the Carson Desert were more highly tethered to the Stillwater Marsh wetlands, and therefore utilized a greater amount of logistical foraging to obtain upland resources, there should be a greater disparity in osteoarthritis between Stillwater males and females than among their more transient counterparts from Malheur Lake.

These differences should occur for two reasons. First, logistical foraging in the uplands surrounding the Carson Sink was largely restricted to males. This is because hunting for big game, an activity participated in exclusively by males, represents the only upland resource obtained through logistical foraging. Other upland resources, such as piñon and fish, were either little used (piñon: see Schoeninger, this volume) or obtained through residential mobility (fish: O. C. Stewart 1941; Wheat 1967; Speth 1969; C. S. Fowler and Bath 1981). Second, Raven's model suggests that the precontact inhabitants of the Harney Basin would have practiced a high level of residential mobility both within and outside the wetlands. Such greater residential mobility permits logistical foraging to decrease. Since both males and female participate equally in residential mobility, the degree of sex difference in osteoarthritis should be less among the inhabitants of the Malheur Lake wetlands.

A general contrast of osteoarthritis by joint region produced mixed results and no significant differences between the two samples. A comparison by individual indicates that a greater percentage of Stillwater individuals were affected in at least one joint region than were Malheur Lake individuals and that differences between the two samples are greater for males than females. These results are intriguing given that the mean age at death for the Stillwater Marsh sample as a whole and by sex is less than that of the Malheur Lake sample. If age were the sole explanation for intersite differences in osteoarthritis, then the higher mean age at death for the Malheur Lake sample should result in a higher prevalence of this disorder. Since Malheur Lake individuals do not exhibit higher rates of osteoarthritis than Stillwater Marsh individuals do, these intersite differences cannot be attributed to differences in age at death. This suggests that acquisition of osteoarthritis occurred earlier in life among Stillwater Marsh individuals than among Malheur Lake individuals.

This disparity in the rate of osteoarthritis acquisition by individual raises the possibility that Stillwater individuals may have participated in a more vigorous lifeway than Malheur Lake individuals. Regression analysis of the association between the percentage of joint regions affected by osteoarthritis and advancing age at death for sex-pooled samples from Malheur Lake and Stillwater Marsh confirms that greater affectation by individual among Stillwater occupants holds true for the progression of polyarticular involvement as well.

While such results could be interpreted as evidence that Stillwater individuals as a whole were more active than their counterparts from Malheur Lake, a comparison of regression slopes by sex and affectation by joint region among old adult females reveals that this is not the case. Regression analysis indicates that the differences in affectation between northern and western Great Basin hunter-gatherers are largely confined to males. Stillwater males suffered from a greater percentage of osteoarthritic joint regions throughout adulthood than did Malheur males. A similar comparison among females reveals no differences between the occupants of these two Great Basin wetlands, but comparison of affectation by joint region among old females indicates that females from Malheur Lake suffered higher prevalence of osteoarthritis in all joints of the lower limb.

A better explanation of these dissimilarities in osteoarthritis affliction between Malheur Lake and Stillwater Marsh individuals is that these disparities reflect variations in physical stresses incurred through distinctive foraging strategies employed by the aboriginal occupants of these two Great Basin wetlands. Raven's proposal that the aboriginal occupants of the Carson Sink utilized a centripetal foraging strategy centered on the Stillwater Marsh contends that such a foraging strategy not only would lead to a greater divergence in mobility between Stillwater males and females but also would lead Stillwater Marsh males to participate in lengthier logistical forays in the uplands relative to Malheur Lake males. These predictions are confirmed by a greater sex-disparity in osteoarthritis between Stillwater individuals and Malheur Lake individuals, as well as by a greater number of osteoarthritic joint regions suffered by Stillwater Lake males throughout adulthood than by Malheur Lake males. Raven's proposal that the environmental offerings of the Harney Basin favored a more widely transient centrifugal strategy by the aboriginal occupants of the Malheur Lake wetlands is also confirmed. Not only do the precontact inhabitants of the Malheur Lake wetlands exhibit less marked sex-disparity in osteoarthritis—and, hence, sex-based differences in uplands foraging—but also the greater range of area and topography encompassed by residential mobility in the Harney Basin is attested by higher frequencies of osteoarthritis for all joints of the lower limb among old adult Malheur females relative to old adult females from Stillwater Marsh.

CONCLUSIONS

Analysis of osteoarthritis affliction among precontact hunter-gatherers from northern and western Great Basin wetlands provides no support for either extreme limnosedentary or limnomobile models of aboriginal subsistence. If extreme limnosedentary models are correct, the high degree of sedentism and limited logistical foraging of females in the lowlands should be reflected by low levels and late initial onset of osteoarthritis. This is not the case, for both Malheur Lake and Stillwater Marsh females exhibit early initial onset of osteoarthritis and uniformly higher prevalence of this disorder than do preagricultural and agricultural females from the Georgia coast. If extreme limnomobility models are correct, joint participation of males and females in high levels of residential mobility should have led to virtually identical patterns and prevalence of osteoarthritis. This is not the case, either, for contrasts of initial onset and prevalence of osteoarthritis reveal that Malheur Lake and Stillwater Marsh males experienced greater osteoarthritis than their female counterparts. Rather, these results provide support for reconstructions which envision precontact inhabitants of Great Basin wetlands participating in a variety of semisedentary lifeways supplemented by local variations in foraging strategy. In particular, the results obtained in this study lend support to Raven's proposal (1992) that the precontact inhabitants of the Carson Sink participated in a somewhat more collector-based centripetal subsistence strategy than the slightly greater forager-based centrifugal subsistence strategy utilized by the aboriginal occupants of the Harney Basin.

14

Skeletal Structure and Behavioral Patterns of Prehistoric Great Basin Populations

Christopher B. Ruff

It is well known that mechanical forces influence skeletal structure (Wolff 1892; Pauwels 1976; Jaworski, Liskova-Kiar, and Uhthoff 1980; Woo et al. 1981) although this relationship is probably complex and variable, depending in part on the type of structural feature considered (Ruff, Scott, and Liu 1991; Ruff and Runestad 1992; Ruff et al. 1993; Ruff, Walker, and Trinkaus 1994; Trinkaus, Churchill, and Ruff 1994; K. L. Rafferty and Ruff 1994). Long bone diaphyses are particularly developmentally plastic, altering their relative thickness (robusticity) and shape in response to changes in their mechanical environment (Trinkaus, Churchill, and Ruff 1994), thereby preserving a record of the magnitude and types of mechanical loadings placed on them during life. Because differences in mechanical loadings often imply differences in behavior, this in turn can be used to help reconstruct behavioral patterns of past populations from their skeletal remains (Ruff 1992; Bridges 1996).

In order to more fully understand the mechanical and thus behavioral significance of variation in long-bone diaphyseal morphology, it is useful to employ an analogy to an engineering model, namely a *beam* model (Timoshenko and Gere 1972). Huiskes (1982) demonstrated that a beam model is appropriate for long bone diaphyses, accurately predicting the stresses in diaphyses under mechnical loadings of the bone. In a beam model, certain cross-sectional geometric properties of the structure are used to estimate its rigidity and strength to resist particular types of applied mechanical forces. These properties are the cross-sectional area of cortical bone, abbreviated CA, and the second moments of area, or cross-sectional moments of inertia, abbreviated I or J. CA is proportional to the axial, or end-on rigidity of the structure, while I is proportional to bending rigidity and J to torsional (twisting) rigidity. All of this assumes that the intrinsic material properties of the bone are relatively constant so that rigidity and strength are reflected primarily in geometry, an assumption justified on the basis of many comparative and experimental studies (see Ruff 1989).

Cross-sectional geometric analysis of long bone diaphyses has been applied to human archaeological and paleontological samples with increasing frequency over the past 25 years (Endo and Kimura 1970; Lovejoy, Burstein, and Heiple 1976; Lovejoy and Trinkaus 1980; Lovejoy 1982; Kimura and Takahashi 1982; Ruff and Hayes 1983a, 1983b; Kimura and Takahashi 1984; Ruff, Larsen, and Hayes 1984; Sumner 1984; R. B. Martin, Burr, and Schaffler 1985; Van Gerven, Hummert, and Burr 1985; Ruff 1987; Ben-Itzhak, Smith, and Bloom 1988; Brock and Ruff 1988; Bridges 1989a, 1989b; Trinkaus and Ruff 1989; Fresia, Ruff, and Larsen 1990; Ruff and Larsen 1990; Trinkaus et al. 1991; Larsen et al. 1992; Ruff et al. 1993; Churchill 1994; Larsen and Ruff 1994; Ruff 1994; Ruff, Walker, and Trinkaus 1994; Trinkaus, Churchill, and Ruff 1994; Grine et al. 1995; Larsen, Ruff, and Kelly 1995; Larsen, Ruff, and Griffin 1996; Trinkaus and Ruff 1996; for recent reviews see Ruff 1992; Bridges 1996). Of particular relevance to the present investigation are several studies of prehistoric North American skeletal samples from New Mexico (Ruff and Hayes 1983a, 1983b; Brock and Ruff 1988), the Georgia coast (Ruff, Larsen, and Hayes 1984; Ruff and Larsen 1990), the northern Great Plains (Ruff 1994), and the Tennessee River valley (Bridges 1989a, 1989b).

The purpose of this study is to describe the skeletal structural data available for three Great Basin samples—Stillwater Marsh, Nevada, Malheur Lake, Oregon, and the eastern shore of the Great Salt Lake, Utah—and to situate them in a broader context within North American prehistoric populations. Through comparative analyses of these populations, the potential influence of several factors, including geographical terrain, subsistence strategy, and sex, on limb-bone structural properties is assessed. For example, the previous observation that sexual dimorphism in lower-limb-bone cross-sectional diaphyseal properties is greater in hunter-gatherers than in agriculturalists (Ruff 1987) is further tested using these samples. The effects of geographical terrain on mechanical loading of the limbs, and thus long bone structure, are investigated here for the first time to my knowledge. In addition, the relationship between mechanical loading (bone structural properties) and diet (stable isotope data) is explored in one Great Basin sample (eastern margin of Great Salt Lake). Again, this represents the first attempt to compare directly these two types of data in the same sample. Results of these comparisons have several important implications regarding the interpretation of long bone structure in human archaeological samples and, in particular, the behavior and life-style of pre- and protohistoric Great Basin populations.

SAMPLES
Great Basin Samples
General descriptions of the skeletal samples from which the present study sample was derived and their provenience have been given elsewhere (Oetting 1990b; Simms, Loveland, and Stuart 1991; Hemphill 1992a, 1992b; Fawcett and

Simms 1993; Larsen and Kelly 1995). The samples were recovered between 1985 and 1992, virtually all as surface finds exposed following the increased precipitation, high-water levels, and subsequent erosion near Great Basin lakes and marshes in the early to mid-1980s.

The Stillwater sample was recovered from the Stillwater Marsh area in western Nevada (Kelly, this volume). Because most of the burials lacked contexts, dating is difficult, but the sample probably derives from about 1000 B.C. to A.D. 1300, with the majority from about A.D. 500 to 1300 (Larsen and Kelly 1995). A seasonally oriented hunting-fishing-gathering subsistence economy has been inferred (see also Kelly, this voume).

The Malheur sample was collected from the Harney Basin near Malheur Lake in southwestern Oregon. The sample derives from about 3000 B.C. to the protohistoric period, but most burials probably date to after A.D. 1000 (B. Hemphill, personal communication). A hunting-fishing-gathering subsistence strategy has again been inferred for this sample, with a particular emphasis on exploitation of lacustrine resources (Oetting 1990b).

The Great Salt Lake sample was collected from exposures (in one case, a shallow excavation) in the area immediately east of the lake in Utah. Radiocarbon dates were obtained for 18 of the 20 individual burials included in the study (Simms, this volume). Using the mean of the calibrated age range for each determination, all but one range in age between A.D. 600 and 1150; one burial had a mean determination of A.D. 1380. A mixed economy of hunting-fishing-gathering together with some corn horticulture has been suggested, with considerable geographic and temporal diversity (Simms and Stuart 1993; Simms, this volume; also see Discussion, this chapter).

From among the skeletal material recovered during these field projects, complete or nearly complete and well-preserved long bones were made available for the present study. The samples from Stillwater, Malheur, and Great Salt Lake regions included in this study are listed in Table 14.1. Femora, humeri, or both were available for an average of about 20 individuals per region, fairly equally divided by sex. In the majority of cases (46 individuals), femora and humeri were matched from the same individual. A relatively small sample of tibiae was also included from the Great Salt Lake region; all but one of these were matched with a femur. All individuals in the sample were adults, with fused long bone epiphyses. Determination of sex was carried out using standard methods (see references given with individual samples above for details).

In the case of femora and tibiae, left and right sides were chosen randomly, when both were available, and about equal numbers of each side are represented in each regional sample. For humeri, both sides were analyzed when available. A total of 29 bilateral humeral pairs were included (see Table 14.1; a breakdown by region and sex is given later with analyses of humeral asymmetry). For most comparisons,

TABLE 14.1.

Numbers of Individuals in the Great Basin Samples

Region	Femora			Humeri			Tibiae		
	Male	Female	Total	Male	Female	Total	Male	Female	Total
Gr. Salt Lake	8	7	15	10(14)[a]	8(11)	18(25)	6	6	12
Malheur	9	14	23	8(13)	11(21)	19(34)	—	—	—
Stillwater[b]	11	13	24	11(14)	9(13)	20(27)	—	—	—
Total	28	34	62	29(41)	28(45)	57(86)	6	6	12

[a] Numbers in parentheses refer to total number of bones, including bilateral pairs.

[b] One female femur in the Stillwater sample was previously misclassified as male; thus, sex-specific numbers here differ slightly from those in a previous publication (Larsen, Ruff, and Kelly 1995). Results of the previous study are not significantly affected by this error.

values for right and left humeri were averaged; levels of bilateral asymmetry were also examined and used to adjust values for individuals with only one side represented, as described in Methods, below.

Comparative Samples

In order to provide the analysis of Great Basin populations a wider context, additional previously analyzed American Indian samples were also included in this study. Samples used in comparative analyses are listed in Table 14.2. Femoral structural data were available for skeletal samples from the Southwest (Pecos Pueblo, New Mexico), the northern Great Plains (Middle Missouri, South Dakota), and the Southeast (Georgia coast) (Ruff and Hayes 1983a; Ruff, Larsen, and Hayes 1984; Ruff 1994). A total of 206 adult femora, about equally divided between males and females, is included here. Two comparative samples are considered to be pre-agricultural in subsistence economy: a pre-Coalescent period sample from the Great Plains (about A.D. 400–1600, but almost all A.D. 900–1250), and a sample from the Georgia coast (about 2000 B.C.–A.D. 1150, but almost all A.D. 500–1150). Three samples are considered to be agricultural: A Coalescent period sample from the Great Plains (about A.D. 1600–1850), a Georgia coast sample (about A.D. 1150–1550), and the Pecos Pueblo sample (about A.D. 1300–1650). (See references above in this paragraph for more information on subsistence classifications and dating.) These samples, and the Stillwater Great Basin sample, were also included in a broader study of temporal trends in femoral robusticity within *Homo* (Ruff et al. 1993). (Numbers here vary in some cases from this previous comparative study: three additional individuals are included in the Great Plains pre-Coalescent period sample, and only 60 individuals from Pecos Pueblo are included—those who are part of another ongoing study that includes the upper as well as lower limb bones.)

TABLE 14.2.

Comparative Samples

		Femora			Humeri		
Region/Site	Subsistence	Male	Female	Total	Male	Female	Total
Georgia coast	Preagricultural	8	12	20	15	15	27
Georgia coast	Agricultural	11	9	20	15	14	29
Great Plains	Preagricultural	27	21	48	—	—	—
Great Plains	Agricultural	33	25	58	—	—	—
Pecos Pueblo	Agricultural	30	30	60	—	—	—
Total		109	97	206	30	26	56

Only femoral midshaft data are available for the Great Plains samples; therefore, comparative analyses of the femur concentrated on that section (see below).

Structural data for 56 humeri from the Georgia coast are also available for comparative analyses (Table 14.2) (Ruff and Larsen 1990). Of these, 27 are from preagricultural contexts and 29 are from agricultural contexts; males and females are about equally represented. Right and left side values, when available, were averaged, or unilateral specimens were adjusted for bilateral asymmetry as described below for Great Basin samples. Because the comparative database for humeri is much more limited than that for femora, only a few preliminary comparisons for this bone were carried out. The same is even more true for the small sample of tibiae from the Great Salt Lake region (Table 14.1). The only available comparative data here are from Pecos Pueblo (n = 60); these are briefly compared in the text.

Stable Carbon Isotope Data

$\delta^{13}C$ values were obtained (Coltrain and Stafford, this volume) for bone samples from 18 of the 20 individuals in the Great Salt Lake sample. Of these, 17 had humeri and 14 had femora. The precise interpretation of stable carbon isotope data is complex, with values influenced not only by the amount of cultivated crops (i.e., maize) consumed but also by the direct consumption of native C_4 plants as well as by indirect means from eating bison, which graze on native C_4 plants (Coltrain and Stafford, this volume). However, it is still most probable that individuals with more positive $\delta^{13}C$ values consumed more maize than those with lower values. Tentatively, then, for this study, $\delta^{13}C$ values of greater than about −13 percent will be taken to indicate a diet including a significant proportion of maize, values of about −13 percent to −18 percent to indicate a diet including a small amount of maize, and values under −18 percent to indicate a diet without any significant maize contribution (Coltrain and Stafford, this volume). Radiocarbon absolute dates (calibrated) were also available for these same 18 individuals. These data are relevant to issues involving the nature of the "Fremont" archaeological culture and the transition to the "Late Prehistoric" culture in this area about A.D. 1300–1350 (Simms and Stuart 1993; Simms, this volume). Direct comparisons of skeletal structural properties and $\delta^{13}C$ data for the same individuals were carried out for this study in order to assess the potential relationship between diet and skeletal robusticity.

METHODS

Derivation of Cross-Sectional Properties

Prior to cross-sectional analyses, all bones were oriented and measured for length following previously described protocols (Ruff and Hayes 1983a; Ruff and Larsen 1990). Length', the bone length used to locate cross sections, was taken on all specimens (see table footnotes for definition of length' for each bone).

Prior to obtaining sections, each bone was "leveled" so that the diaphysis was approximately in a horizontal position (see Ruff and Hayes 1983a; Ruff and Larsen 1990). In the femur, sections were taken perpendicular to the longitudinal axis of the diaphysis at 50 percent ("midshaft") and 80 percent ("subtrochanteric") of bone length', measured from the distal end. In the humerus, a section was taken at 35 percent of bone length' from the distal end ("mid-distal" location). In the tibia, a 50 percent (midshaft) section was taken.

Cross-sectional images of the Great Basin samples were obtained by computed tomographic (CT) scanning. Scanning was carried out for the Stillwater sample at the VA Hospital in Reno, Nevada, for the Malheur sample at the Sacred Heart Hospital in Eugene, Oregon, and for the Great Salt Lake sample at Francis Scott Key Hospital in Baltimore, Maryland. Hard copies of each section image were made, photographed, and developed as slides. CT display window settings for images varied from 500 to 800 H at center, with window widths from 500 to 850 H (i.e., ± 250–425 H [Hounsfield units] from the centers), appropriate for distinguishing compact cortical bone boundaries in archaeological material (Ruff and Leo 1986). For each sample, a CT slice that was taken next to a natural transverse break in at least one specimen and the transverse break surface were photographed. These slides were used to empirically verify bone dimensions under the CT display settings, as recommended for materials of uncertain chemical composition and density and when using different scanners (Ruff and Leo 1986).

Except for the Malheur sample, all prescanning measurements and the scans themselves were taken by me or under my supervision in Carson City, Nevada (Stillwater sample), and Baltimore (Great Salt Lake Sample). The Malheur sample was premeasured and scanned by Brian Hemphill in Oregon, and the section slides were sent to Baltimore for analysis.

Cross-section slides were back-projected onto a large transparent digitizer screen and periosteal and endosteal contours manually traced (for illustrations, see

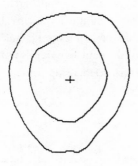

```
GB10FR50

Cortical Properties

TA    :      527.11
CA    :      319.19
Xbar  :       17.08
Ybar  :       32.16
Ix    :    21960.20
Iy    :    16168.20
Theta:        73.09
Imax  :    22550.40
Imin  :    15578.00
J     :    38128.50
```

User scale points @ (10 , 10) (30 , 10)

FIGURE 14.1. Computer output from program SLICE of a Great Basin femoral midshaft digitized tracing, with section properties listed at right. Xbar and Ybar are section centroid coordinates (in mm); Theta is the angular orientation of greatest bending rigidity, measured in degrees from the M-L axis. See text for explanation of other section property abbreviations. Other units in mm² (TA, CA) or mm⁴ (all others).

Ruff 1989 or 1992). X, y point coordinates at 1 mm intervals were sent to a microcomputer (DEC), where the program SLICE (Nagurka and Hayes 1980) was used to automatically calculate section properties. An example of a SLICE printout of a femoral midshaft section from the Stillwater sample is shown in Figure 14.1.

As mentioned earlier, the properties of a long bone cross section of most interest in a mechanical anlysis are its cross-sectional area (CA) and second moments of area (I, J), which are proportional to axial, bending, and torsional rigidities, respectively. Bending rigidity, I, can be evaluated about any axis through the cross section, usually indicated through a subscript. In this study, as in past investigations (Ruff and Hayes 1983a; Ruff, Larsen, and Hayes 1984; Ruff 1987, 1994), I_x will refer to bending rigidity in the anteroposterior (A-P) plane and I_y to bending rigidity in the mediolateral (M-L) plane. In addition, I_{max} will refer to the maximum bending rigidity and I_{min} to the minimum rigidity (the two can be oriented at any angle, but are always perpendicular to each other). J is calculated as the sum of I_{max} and I_{min} (Ruff and Hayes 1983a). Thus, J represents not only torsional rigidity but also an average bending rigidity about all planes through the section. As such, it is a useful measure of overall bending/torsional rigidity.

In this study, CA and J are taken as the principal indicators of bone rigidity or strength, while other second moments of area, considered as ratios, are used to examine cross-sectional shape differences or relative strengths in different planes. Thus, I_x/I_y is used as a measure of relative A-P/M-L bending rigidity, while

I_{max}/I_{min} is a measure of relative maximum to minimum bending rigidity. Because of the respective morphologies of the femoral midshaft and mid-distal humerus, I_x/I_y is most useful as a shape index, whereas I_{max}/I_{min} is most useful in the femoral subtrochanteric section.

In addition to these properties, the total area within the periosteal surface (TA) and the medullary area (MA) was also calculated. This calculation is useful in determining whether variation in CA and second moments of area is due primarily to changes in the endosteal or periosteal surfaces. For example, an increase in CA or J can be caused by endosteal contraction, periosteal expansion, or both. The percent cortical area (percent CA), calculated as (CA/TA) • 100, is also listed as another cross-sectional "shape" characteristic, although its significance in a mechanical functional context is limited (see Ruff 1992).

Because bilateral asymmetry in human upper-limb-bone structural properties can be considerable (Ruff 1992; Trinkaus, Churchill, and Ruff 1994), it is important to compensate for unequal numbers of right and left sides in comparative analyses of these properties. In the present study, about half of all Great Basin individuals with humeri were represented by either a right or left side. Using the average levels of asymmetry present within the bilateral pairs available for each region (Table 14.1), properties for the nonpaired bones were adjusted upwards or downwards by the appropriate percentages to achieve "side averaged" values—that is, values that would have been obtained had both sides been available and the sides had been averaged (as was actually done for the bilateral pairs). The same general procedure was used for the comparative humeral samples from the Georgia coast (Ruff and Larsen 1990).

Statistical Analysis

Standard descriptive statistics (means, standard errors) for the various structural properties and bone lengths are given for each Great Basin sample by sex. Two-way analysis of variance (ANOVA), with sex and sample (i.e., the three regions) as factors, followed by Tukey multiple comparison tests, was used to investigate differences within and among the Great Basin samples. Results were also compared to data available for other American Indian samples, again using ANOVA (see below). Probability levels of .05 or less were considered statistically significant and levels between .05 and .10 as near-significant. The multivariate general linear model (MGLH) procedure in SYSTAT (1992) was used for these analyses.

In order to examine skeletal robusticity, or relative strength, some "size" measure against which to evaluate cross-sectional properties was necessary. It has been argued that skeletal robusticity is best defined as the "strength or rigidity of a structure relative to the mechanically relevant measure of body size" and that the "mechanically relevant measure of body size" for the lower limb bones is body mass

(Ruff et al. 1993:25). In the same study, it was found that if body shape (body breadth to height) remains fairly constant, the theoretically expected and empirically observed relationships between cross-sectional properties and femoral length, with body mass factored out, are: CA α Length$^{3.0}$; J α Length$^{5.33}$. Although there is some variation in body breadth to height among Native American groups, the differences are relatively small, especially compared to the major differences observed between tropical and higher latitude populations (Ruff et al. 1993); thus, these relationships should hold true among the present study samples. (In fact, many of the groups in the present study were included in the earlier study used to test these scaling factors.) Therefore, to derive robusticity indices here, CA was divided by Length^3 (and multiplied by 10^8), and J was divided by Length$^{5.33}$ (and multiplied by 10^{12}). (Note that these scaling factors differ slightly from those used in some previous studies: e.g., Ruff, Larsen, and Hayes 1984; Ruff and Larsen 1990; Ruff 1994; Larsen, Ruff, and Kelly 1995.) "Length" here refers to length', as defined above. This procedure effectively allows comparisons between groups of different overall body size. Both raw and size-standardized data are given for the Great Basin samples.

It should be noted that these particular size scaling factors are not as well established for the upper limb as for the lower limb, in part because of the relative independence of upper limb bone dimensions from body mass per se (Ruff et al. 1993; Churchill 1994; Trinkaus, Churchill, and Ruff 1994). To further test the applicability of these scaling factors to the humerus, log-log reduced major axis (RMA) regressions of CA and J against humeral length' were carried out (Ruff et al. 1993) within the pooled Great Basin sample (n = 57), within the Great Basin plus Georgia coast sample of humeri (n = 113), and for both pooled sex and males and females separately. RMA slopes for CA ranged between 2.63 and 3.45 (all correlations were significant or near-significant); the 95 percent confidence intervals for all slopes included 3.0. Thus, this supports the use of length'^{3} as a size scaling factor for CA in the humerus. Similar analyses for J showed somewhat more variability, with slopes ranging from 3.38 to 5.34 (all r's significant). The two lower slopes (under 4.76) that did not include the theoretically predicted value of 5.33 in the 95 percent CI's were both for females. Thus, while combined sex and male samples supported the use of length'$^{5.33}$ as a size scaling factor for J in the humerus, the analyses of females suggested a somewhat lower scaling factor. It is not clear why there should be a within-sex difference in scaling for this particular property. In any event, for consistency with the femoral analyses, and to follow the majority of the humeral results, the 5.33 power of bone length was used to standardize humeral J. In most comparisons, use of the lower power of humeral length (length'^{4}) for size standardizing had no effect on the statistical significance of results, but where results do differ it is pointed out in the text.

TABLE 14.3.

Raw Data, Femoral Midshaft Section and Length

Property*	Gr. Salt Lake Mean	SE	Malheur Mean	SE	Stillwater Mean	SE
			MALES			
Length'	407.5	12.1	403.9	5.6	423.4	9.0
CA	379.5	17.4	383.8	14.8	396.2	15.4
MA	139.9	11.2	146.3	19.7	185.4	12.8
TA	519.4	20.9	530.0	26.0	581.6	21.0
I_x	24344	2341	21823	1938	27910	2092
I_y	17609	1071	20824	1811	22403	1734
J	41953	3208	42647	3583	50313	3588
			FEMALES			
Length'	365.9	3.3	388.4	4.5	393.2	4.0
CA	279.4	3.3	310.8	13.1	299.4	11.4
MA	123.4	7.6	138.2	7.2	180.6	12.5
TA	402.8	12.4	449.0	12.4	480.0	11.4
I_x	12411	922	13852	846	15597	742
I_y	11397	596	16034	1050	16140	882
J	23808	1457	29886	1814	31737	1464

* Length': The distance from the average of the distal-most projecting points of the femoral condyles to the superior surface of the femoral neck, just medial to the greater trochanter, measured parallel to the diaphyseal long axis; CA: cortical area; MA: medullary area; TA: total subperiosteal area; I_x: second moment of area about M-L axis (A-P bending rigidity); I_y: second moment of area about A-P axis (M-L bending rigidity); J: polar second moment of area. Length' in mm, areas in mm^2, second moments of area in mm^4.

Because of the characteristics of the comparative samples (Table 14.2), in these broader comparisons it was possible to test for the effects of several factors on variation in cross-sectional properties. These factors included (a) subsistence strategy: preagricultural or agricultural; (b) geographic terrain: mountains (Great Basin and Pecos samples), plains (Great Plains samples), or coastal (Georgia coast samples); and (c) sex: male or female. The Great Basin samples were included as part of these larger comparative analyses. Three-way ANOVA was used, with subsistence, terrain, and sex as independent factors and cross-sectional properties as dependent variables. Interactions between factors were also examined. Size-standardized properties were used in all analyses (except cross-sectional shape properties) to eliminate body size as a factor. Because of the much more limited comparative data available for the humerus (Table 14.2), these analyses of variance were only carried

CHRISTOPHER B. RUFF

TABLE 14.4.
Raw Data, Femoral Subtrochanteric Section

Property*	Gr. Salt Lake		Malheur		Stillwater	
	Mean	SE	Mean	SE	Mean	SE
MALES						
CA	371.1	13.4	389.7	17.6	401.4	11.7
MA	223.7	23.5	212.4	24.1	248.3	16.5
TA	594.8	29.0	602.1	25.6	649.7	20.7
I_{max}	32329	2524	34104	2615	39187	3045
I_{min}	18694	1609	20143	1897	21507	1134
J	51023	4024	54247	4056	60694	3931
FEMALES						
CA	300.5	12.5	337.5	12.4	305.7	9.4
MA	189.0	13.2	178.5	10.7	247.8	17.7
TA	489.4	13.1	516.0	9.9	553.5	16.5
I_{max}	23741	1222	17342	1437	27456	1301
I_{min}	11142	724	13005	711	13743	680
J	34883	1742	40347	1760	41199	1917

* CA: cortical area; MA: medullary area; TA: total subperiosteal area; I_{max}: maximum second moment of area; I_{min}: minimum second moment of area; J: polar second moment of area. Areas in mm^2, second moments of area in mm^4.

out for the femur, specifically the femoral midshaft section. For the humerus, t-tests were used to compare the pooled Great Basin samples with Georgia coast preagriculturalists and agriculturalists.

RESULTS
Comparisons within the Great Basin

The raw (non–size-standardized) data for bone lengths and cross-sectional properties in the three Great Basin samples, by sex, are given in Tables 14.3–14.5 for the femoral midshaft, subtrochanteric, and humeral mid-distal sections, respectively. Size-standardized data and cross-sectional shape indices for the same sections are listed in Tables 14.6–14.8. Results of 2-way ANOVA of the effects of region and sex on bone length, size-standardized CA and J, and cross-sectional shape properties within the Great Basin are given in Table 14.9.

In many respects, the three Great Basin regional samples are fairly homogeneous in terms of femoral and humeral size and structure. In particular, there are no significant differences between regions in relative overall bending/torsional

TABLE 14.5.
Raw Data, Humeral Mid-Distal Section and Length

Property*	Gr. Salt Lake		Malheur		Stillwater	
	Mean	SE	Mean	SE	Mean	SE
			MALES			
Length'	319.1	3.4	300.6	2.8	317.3	5.8
CA	178.6	4.2	183.2	11.4	187.8	11.6
MA	88.4	8.3	91.0	10.5	110.0	10.9
TA	267.0	8.9	274.1	15.4	297.8	7.0
I_x	5198	302	5415	525	6444	364
I_y	5106	303	5550	652	5902	365
J	10304	568	10965	1162	12347	684
			FEMALES			
Length'	275.4	3.5	298.2	3.8	294.1	4.2
CA	131.4	4.7	144.0	6.6	138.6	8.2
MA	72.5	5.0	72.9	6.3	84.5	8.0
TA	203.9	6.3	217.0	4.5	223.1	7.9
I_x	2899	174	3511	198	3668	279
I_y	3097	209	3249	144	3315	268
J	5996	369	6760	316	6984	533

* Length': The distance between the lateral lip of the trochlea and the proximal-most point on the humeral head, measured parallel to the diaphyseal long axis; CA: cortical area; MA: medullary area; TA: total subperiosteal area; I_x: second moment of area about M-L axis (A-P bending rigidity); I_y: second moment of area about A-P axis (M-L bending rigidity); J: polar second moment of area. Length' in mm, areas in mm^2, second moments of area in mm^4.

strength (J-standardized) of the humerus or femur (Table 14.9). There are a few differences between regions, however, with most of these involving the Stillwater sample relative to the other two samples. (Note that the 2-way ANOVA and Tukey tests take into account sex-related differences, thus compensating for any inequalities in sex composition of the samples [Table 14.1]). The Stillwater sample is slightly greater in femoral length, reaching significance relative to the Great Salt Lake sample (Tables 14.3 and 14.9). Stillwater also tends to have lower percent CA and size-standardized CA in both femoral sections relative to the other two regions (Tables 14.6, 14.7, and 14.9). Comparisons of size-standardized MA and TA, not shown here, demonstrate that the reduction in percent CA and CA-standardized in Stillwater femora is due to a larger medullary cavity, with the periosteal area equivalent in the three samples. Finally, Malheur has a lower I_x/I_y index in the femoral midshaft than either of the other samples, and the Great Salt Lake sample

TABLE 14.6.

Size-Standardized and Shape Data, Femoral Midshaft Section

Property*	Gr. Salt Lake		Malheur		Stillwater	
	Mean	SE	Mean	SE	Mean	SE
			MALES			
CASTD	569.4	35.9	586.7	30.1	527.3	26.2
JSTD	527.6	52.8	551.0	51.1	511.2	40.3
% CA	73.1	1.8	73.1	2.7	68.2	1.7
I_x/I_y	1.37	.11	1.06	.06	1.26	.06
			FEMALES			
CASTD	574.1	33.9	533.8	24.2	491.7	16.5
JSTD	524.8	45.0	479.2	31.1	470.0	19.8
% CA	69.3	1.7	69.0	1.6	62.5	2.2
I_x/I_y	1.08	.05	.88	.04	.98	.05

* CASTD: (cortical area/length$^{'3}$) $\times$ 10^8; JSTD: (polar second moment of area/length$^{'5.33}$) $\times$ 10^{12}; % CA: (cortical area/total subperiosteal area) $\times$ 100; I_x/I_y: A-P/M-L bending rigidity.

TABLE 14.7.

Size-Standardized and Shape Data, Femoral Subtrochanteric Section

Property*	Gr. Salt Lake		Malheur		Stillwater	
	Mean	SE	Mean	SE	Mean	SE
			MALES			
CASTD	564.2	48.0	597.3	37.2	533.6	29.2
JSTD	651.4	78.7	703.2	64.0	635.5	51.9
% CA	63.1	2.6	65.2	3.0	60.5	2.1
I_{max}/I_{min}	1.75	.08	1.75	.10	1.85	.10
			FEMALES			
CASTD	615.0	28.4	580.7	25.7	503.6	11.7
JSTD	762.8	47.3	652.5	41.0	596.4	22.8
% CA	61.4	2.2	65.4	2.0	56.7	2.1
I_{max}/I_{min}	2.16	.11	2.16	.12	2.00	.06

* CASTD: (cortical area/length$^{'3}$) $\times$ 10^8; JSTD: (polar second moment of area/length$^{'5.33}$) $\times$ 10^{12}; % CA: (cortical area/total subperiosteal area) $\times$ 100; I_{max}/I_{min}: maximum/minimum bending rigidity.

TABLE 14.8.

Size-Standardized and Shape Data, Humeral Mid-Distal Section

	Gr. Salt Lake		Malheur		Stillwater	
Property*	Mean	SE	Mean	SE	Mean	SE
			MALES			
CASTD	551.4	17.5	674.1	39.6	590.5	37.5
JSTD	465.9	26.2	677.8	72.2	586.1	42.9
% CA	67.4	2.3	67.1	3.0	63.0	3.5
I_x/I_y	1.02	.04	1.00	.04	1.10	.06
			FEMALES			
CASTD	634.5	36.9	543.8	22.9	541.1	20.3
JSTD	612.3	74.9	442.3	26.0	483.6	27.5
% CA	64.6	1.9	66.4	2.7	62.3	3.6
I_x/I_y	.94	.03	1.08	.04	1.11	1.04

* CASTD: (cortical area/length^{3}) × 10^8; JSTD: (polar second moment of area/length$^{5.33}$) × 10^{12}; % CA: (cortical area/total subperiosteal area) × 100; I_x/I_y: A-P/M-L bending rigidity.

has a lower I_x/I_y index in the mid-distal humerus than Stillwater (Tables 14.6, 14.8, and 14.9).

Significant sex differences within the Great Basin samples, aside from the expected greater absolute size of males, are limited to femoral cross-sectional shape variables. In particular, males have significantly larger I_x/I_y ratios in the femoral midshaft, and smaller I_{max}/I_{min} ratios in the subtrochanteric section than females (Table 14.9), a pattern that holds across every regional sample (Tables 14.6 and 14.7). Males also have larger percent CA in the femoral midshaft, although not in the subtrochanteric section. Interestingly, size-standardized CA and J do not differ between the sexes in any section. However, if length^{4} rather than length$^{5.33}$ is used as a scaling factor for humeral J, males are significantly greater than females in J-standardized.

Comparisons with Other American Indians

Table 14.10 compares the pooled Great Basin sample with other American Indian samples (Table 14.2) for bone lengths and size-standardized and shape properties of the femoral midshaft and mid-distal humerus. The comparative sample was analyzed both across pooled subsistence categories and as preagricultural hunter-gatherers only. Sexes were combined in all comparisons. Although there is evidence that some of the Great Salt Lake sample incorporated maize agriculture

TABLE 14.9.
Effects of Region and Sex within the Great Basin

Property[a]	Region[b]	Sex[b]	Paired Group Differences[c]
		FEMUR	
Length'	*	***	M>F; Stillwater > G.S.L.
Midshaft CASTD	†	n.s.	(Stillwater < G.S.L.)
Midshaft JSTD	n.s.	n.s.	
Midshaft % CA	**	**	M>F; Stillwater < both other
Midshaft I_x/I_y	***	***	M>F; Malheur < both other
Subtroch. CASTD	*	n.s.	Stillwater < Malheur, (G.S.L.)
Subtroch. JSTD	n.s.	n.s.	
Subtroch. % CA	**	n.s.	Stillwater < Malheur
Subtroch. I_{max}/I_{min}	n.s.	***	M < F
		HUMERUS	
Length'	n.s.	**	M > F
Mid-Distal CASTD	n.s.	n.s.	
Mid-Distal JSTD	n.s.	n.s.	
Mid-Distal % CA	n.s.	n.s.	
Mid-Distal I_x/I_y	*	n.s.	G.S.L. < Stillwater

[a] See Tables 14.3 to 14.8 for definitions.

[b] Results of 2-way ANOVA with sex and region as factors; n.s.: nonsignificant; † $.10 > p > .05$; * $p < .05$; ** $p < .01$; *** $p < .001$.

[c] Results of Tukey multiple comparison tests: significant or near-significant (in parentheses) differences between males and females and between three regions.

in the subsistence base, this sample is included here as hunter-gatherers for simplicity and because the majority of the sample was primarily nonagricultural (see stable carbon isotope data results below).

The Great Salt Lake sample as a whole tends to be somewhat shorter in bone lengths than other Native Americans, especially other hunter-gatherers. In the femur, size-standardized CA and J are increased in the Great Basin sample relative to either of the comparative samples, although this is only significant for J-standardized. However, in contrast, Great Basin humeri are not more robust than other Native Americans; in fact, in CA-standardized at least they tend to be less robust. Percent CA is significantly lower in both the femur and humerus in the Great Basin sample relative to either of the comparative groups. Ratios of A-P/M-L bending rigidities (I_x/I_y) do not differ between groups in any comparison.

Because the different compositions of the comparative samples available for

TABLE 14.10.

Comparisons of Great Basin with other American Indians (Combined Sex)

Property[c]	Great Basin		Other Amer.[a]		Other H.-G.[b]	
	Mean	SE	Mean	SE	Mean	SE
FEMUR						
Length'	397.8	3.4	407.0*	1.9	416.4***	3.0
Midshaft CASTD	540.6	11.2	521.0	6.0	510.9†	12.9
Midshaft JSTD	504.8	15.4	449.1**	9.1	439.2*	22.1
Midshaft % CA	68.7	.9	71.5**	.5	71.8*	1.0
Midshaft I_x/I_y	1.08	.03	1.11	.01	1.10	.02
HUMERUS						
Length'	302.0	2.5	307.0	2.7	312.7*	4.5
Mid-Distal CASTD	584.8	13.3	636.0*	18.7	644.5†	32.3
Mid-Distal % CA	65.1	1.2	73.2***	1.3	73.3***	1.9
Mid-Distal I_x/I_y	1.05	.02	1.04	.02	1.05	.03

[a] Other American Indians: For femur, includes Georgia coast, Great Plains, and Pecos (n = 206); for humerus, includes Georgia coast only (n = 56). See Tables 14.1 and 14.2.

[b] Other American Indian hunter-gatherers: For femur, includes Georgia coast and Great Plains (n = 68); for humerus, includes Georgia coast only (n = 27). See Tables 14.1 and 14.2.

[c] † .10 > p > .05; * p < .05; ** p < .01; *** p < .001; t-test between group and Great Basin.

the femur and humerus (Table 14.2) may have affected these results, comparisons of femoral properties were also carried out against the Georgia coast sample alone (which provided the only comparative humeri). Results were virtually identical for both pooled-subsistence and preagricultural-only comparisons. The only exceptions were for midshaft femoral percent CA and I_x/I_y when compared to Georgia coast hunter-gatherers, where percent CA showed no significant difference between groups and I_x/I_y was larger in the Georgia coast sample.

Table 14.11 shows the results of the 3-way ANOVA of terrain, subsistence strategy, and sex on size-standardized and shape characteristics of the femoral midshaft section, pooling all Great Basin and other comparative samples. Variation in terrain has a significant effect on both CA- and J-standardized. In both cases, samples from mountainous regions (Great Basin and Pecos) show relatively greater robusticity than those from the plains and coastal regions. This is illustrated graphically in Figure 14.2, which plots the least squares adjusted means and standard errors (i.e., adjusted for any effects of sex and subsistence) for CA and J in the three terrain categories. The much greater values for J-standardized in the moun-

TABLE 14.11.

Effects of Terrain, Subsistence, and Sex on Femoral Midshaft Properties in
Combined American Indian Sample (n = 268)

Property[a]	Terrain[b]	Subsistence[b]	Sex[b]	Paired Group Differences[c]
CASTD	**	n.s.	*	M>F; mtns.>plains
JSTD	**	n.s.	**	M>F; mtns.>plains & coast
PCCA	†	n.s.	**	M>F; (coast>mtns.)
I_x/I_y	n.s.	n.s.	***	M>F

[a] See Tables 14.6 to 14.8 for definitions.

[b] Results of 3-way ANOVA with terrain, subsistence, and sex as factors; n.s.: nonsignificant; † $.10 > p > .05$; * $p < .05$; ** $p < .01$; *** $p < .001$.

[c] Results of Tukey multiple comparison tests: significant or near-significant (in parentheses) differences between terrains (mountains, plains, and coast), subsistence strategies (agricultural or preagricultural), and sexes.

tainous terrain samples are particularly striking. Samples from the plains and coast show no significant differences from each other in these or any other parameters.

There is also a near-significant effect of terrain on percent CA (Table 14.11), with mountainous regions showing lower values than coastal regions. Terrain has no effect on I_x/I_y. Variation in subsistence strategy has no significant effect on any of the properties examined.

Sex has a significant effect on all properties, with males showing greater values than females. The difference between the sexes in A-P/M-L bending rigidity (I_x/I_y) of the femoral midshaft is particularly large. There is also a highly significant sex/subsistence interaction for this property (p < .001) as well as for CA- and J-standardized (p < .01). In each case preagricultural samples show more sexual dimorphism than the agricultural samples; in fact, sexual dimorphism in these properties is not significant in agricultural samples (Tukey tests on least square adjusted means). This is illustrated graphically for I_x/I_y in Figure 14.3. Sex/terrain and subsistence/terrain interactions are generally not significant.

Because of the much more limited comparative sample available for the humerus, no similar analyses were carried out for this bone. However, comparisons between Great Basin and Georgia coast samples, summarized in Table 14.10 and in the text above, suggest that terrain has a much less marked effect on the humerus than on the femur. This was further investigated by calculating ratios of femoral to humeral CA and J in those individuals for whom both bones were available (n = 46 from the Great Basin; n = 32 from the Georgia coast). Because bivariate plots showed evidence of significant heteroscedasticity (inequality of variances), data were logged prior to calculating ratios. When compared with the

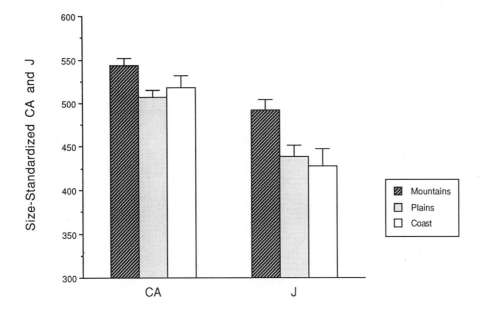

FIGURE 14.2. Effects of geographical terrain on robusticity of the femoral midshaft. Bars show means + 1 SE, least squares adjusted for any sex or subsistence-related effects. See Table 14.11 for statistics.

entire Georgia coast sample, the pooled Great Basin samples showed significantly greater femoral to humeral CA and J. When compared with Georgia coast hunter-gatherers only, the Great Basin samples were still significantly greater in femoral to humeral CA, although not J. Thus, the preferential increase in femoral strength in the Great Basin samples is largely borne out by interlimb comparisons.

Humeral Bilateral Asymmetry

Percent differences in CA and J between paired right and left humeri in the Great Basin and two comparative samples are given in Table 14.12. Average asymmetry values were calculated (see Trinkaus, Churchill, and Ruff 1994) as the median of the larger minus the smaller over the smaller side, which accommodates potential left- as well as right-handers. The two comparative American Indian samples are a historical sample from the Georgia coast and a prehistoric sample from northern California. The first can be considered "agricultural," since it derives from a Spanish mission, while the second is preagricultural (see above reference for details). Data summaries are given both for pooled samples and by sex.

On the whole, the Great Basin samples exhibit about average levels of

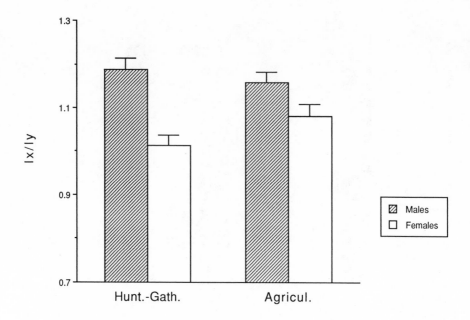

FIGURE 14.3. Sex differences in anteroposterior to mediolateral bending rigidity of the femoral midshaft in hunter-gatherers and agriculturalists. Bars show means + 1 SE, least squares adjusted for any terrain or subsistence-related effects. Sex difference is significant for hunter-gatherers (p < .001), but not for agriculturalists (p = .11), *post-hoc* Tukey tests.

TABLE 14.12.
Humeral Bilateral Asymmetry

Sample	Total			Males			Females		
	No.	CA	J	No.	CA	J	No.	CA	J
Gr. Salt Lake	7	4.8	8.3	4	8.6	14.3	3	1.4	2.6
Malheur	15	7.0	6.8	5	6.3	9.5	10	7.4	6.7
Stillwater	7	4.1	8.7	3	11.2	11.3	4	4.0	7.1
Pooled Great Basin	29	6.7	8.3	12	7.7	10.9	17	4.8	6.6
Georgia coasta	37	4.9	8.7	19	4.9	9.9	18	5.0	4.9
Californiaa	71	6.2	11.2	31	8.3	19.5	40	5.8	8.4

Note: Asymmetry calculated as median of [(maximum-minimum)/minimum] × 100. See Tables 14.3 to 14.5 for definitions of CA and J.

a Comparative American Indian samples from a historical Spanish mission cemetery on Amelia Island, Georgia, and a prehistoric "Late Horizon" sample from the San Francisco Bay area (see Trinkaus, Churchill, and Ruff 1994 for details).

TABLE 14.13.

Raw Data, Tibial Midshaft Section and Length, Great Salt Lake Sample

	Males		Females		Pooled Sex	
Property*	Mean	SE	Mean	SE	Mean	SE
Length'	347.7	9.2	296.5	4.8	322.1	9.2
CA	308.2	8.9	221.7	16.9	265.0	15.9
MA	136.6	6.7	122.8	13.4	129.7	7.4
TA	444.8	11.2	344.5	16.0	394.7	17.8
% CA	69.3	1.2	64.3	3.8	66.8	2.0
J	32976	1732	18670	1883	25823	2477
I_{max}/I_{min}	2.69	.21	2.50	.27	2.60	.17

* Length': The distance between the center of the talar articular surface and the average position of the centers of the tibial plateaus; CA: cortical area; MA: medullary area; TA: total subperiosteal area; % CA: (cortical area/total subperiosteal area) × 100; J: polar second moment of area; I_{max}/I_{min}: maximum/minimum bending rigidity. Length' in mm, areas in mm^2, second moments of area in mm^4.

humeral asymmetry when compared to other American Indians. Some of the variation between Great Basin samples, particularly in the within-sex comparisons, probably reflects sampling error, due to the small sample sizes available. Great Basin males show more asymmetry than females in almost every comparison, a pattern that matches the preagricultural California sample. Overall, though, while levels of asymmetry in CA are fairly high in the Great Basin pooled sex and male samples, asymmetry in J is fairly low in the same samples.

Tibiae

Summary statistics for the small number of 12 tibiae (six males, six females) from the Great Salt Lake sample are shown in Table 14.13. In almost all respects, pooled and by sex, the sample characteristics are remarkably similar to those reported for Pecos Pueblo tibiae (Ruff and Hayes 1983a, 1983b). The only discernible difference is that the Great Salt Lake sample tends to have somewhat lower I_{max}/I_{min} values (mean 2.60) than the Pecos sample (mean 2.93), indicating a slightly more circular cross section, although still much more "platycnemic" (mediolaterally flattened) than modern Euramerican tibiae (I_{max}/I_{min} means ranging from 2.09 to 2.40; see Ruff and Hayes 1983b).

Scaling of tibial cross-sectional properties to body size (and bone length) has not been as extensively investigated as in the femur, although preliminary analyses of several samples (my unpublished data) suggest that length scaling factors similar to those used for the femur may apply to the tibia. If this is done for the Great Salt Lake and Pecos samples, J-standarized is not significantly different in the two

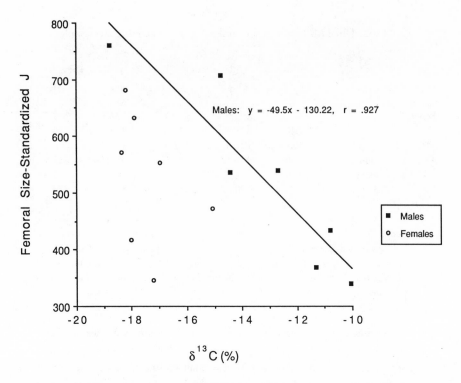

FIGURE 14.4. Femoral midshaft robusticity (J-standardized) against relative maize consumption ($\delta^{13}C$) in the Great Salt Lake sample. $\delta^{13}C$ values above about −13 percent indicate a substantial proportion of maize in the diet, while values below about −18 percent indicate little or no maize. Least squares regression line is drawn through males. The negative correlation in males is highly significant (p < .005); females show no significant or near-significant relationship.

samples, while CA-standardized is larger in the Great Salt Lake sample (p < .05; pooled sex comparison).

Stable Carbon Isotope Data
Plots of femoral midshaft and mid-distal humeral J-standardized against $\delta^{13}C$ values for the Great Salt Lake sample are shown in Figures 14.4 and 14.5, respectively. There is a significant negative correlation between J-standardized and $\delta^{13}C$ for both bones. However, when broken down by sex, only males show significant correlations (Figures 14.4 and 14.5). Although there is a suggestion of a negative relationship among females, r's do not reach significance or near-significance (p > .40; all comparisons). In part, this may be due to the more limited range of $\delta^{13}C$ values for females, with no individuals falling above −15 percent, while males range

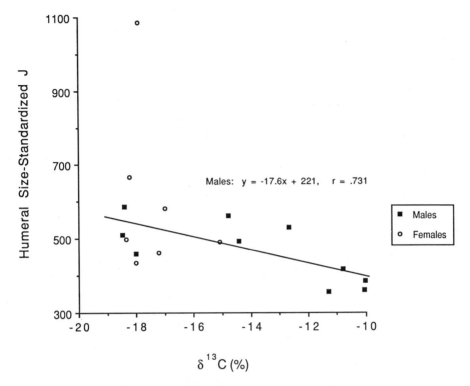

FIGURE 14.5. Humeral mid-distal shaft robusticity (J-standardized) against relative maize consumption (δ¹³C percent) in the Great Salt Lake sample. Least squares regression line through males; correlation significant at p < .02.

from nearly –19 percent to –10 percent (Figures 14.4 and 14.5). CA-standardized also shows a significant negative correlation with δ¹³C for the femur, again limited to males, but not for the humerus.

Together these results indicate that increasing amounts of maize in the diet are associated with *decreasing* femoral and humeral robusticity, at least in males. The association is stronger in the femur (higher correlation, larger slope), although the high female outlier in Figure 14.5 partly obscures the true difference between bones. In fact, for the humerus only the four highest δ¹³C values in males— between –10 percent and –12 percent—demonstrate a reduction in J-standardized (Figure 14.5), whereas in the femur a more continuous trend is evident (Figure 14.4). Interestingly, it is in precisely this uppermost range of δ¹³C values that maize would most likely constitute a large fraction of the diet (Coltrain and Stafford, this volume).

δ¹³C values are also strongly correlated with bone length for both humerus and femur, although for only the femur in males (p < .001). However, in this case the correlation is *positive;* that is, males who consumed more maize had longer femora. Again, the lack of females with high $\delta^{13}C$ values may have precluded the finding of a significant correlation with length.

If the males in the Great Salt Lake sample are broken down into those with $\delta^{13}C$ values above and below –12 percent, the group with high $\delta^{13}C$ values has significantly longer but less robust femora and humeri (p < .05, t-tests, length', and J-standardized). The decline in robusticity is brought about by a relative reduction in both periosteal and endosteal dimensions, with significantly smaller TA- and MA-standardized in both the femur and humerus in the maize-consuming group. Percent CA shows no significant difference between these groups.

DISCUSSION

When compared to other Native American groups, the Great Basin samples, as a whole, are notable for having relatively robust femora, but not humeri, and for having relatively thin cortices, or low percent CA, in both the humerus and femur. A breakdown of comparative samples by terrain, subsistence strategy, and sex indicates that the increase in femoral robusticity in the Great Basin is most likely related to the ruggedness of the terrain in this region. A mountainous environment would be expected to impose significantly larger mechanical loadings on the lower limb bones than the flatter environments of the plains or coastal regions of North America, given similar activity levels. Hunter-gatherers from other regions, who presumably shared broadly similar patterns of behavior, have significantly less robust femora than those from the Great Basin, which supports this interpretation. Also, the equivalence or even decrease in humeral robusticity in the Great Basin samples relative to other Native American groups argues for a specifically localized increase in mechanical loadings of the lower limb, as would be expected in such an environment. Another possible explanation is that the Great Basin inhabitants (and other populations living in mountainous terrains; e.g., Pecos Pueblo) had to travel farther during foraging than most other American Indian groups, thereby imposing more prolonged mechanical loading of the lower limbs. It may be that a combination of the two factors is responsible for the increased femoral robusticity observed for these samples.

These results are in part corroborated by studies of osteoarthritis (OA) occurrence among Great Basin samples (Larsen, Ruff, and Kelly 1995; Hemphill, this volume). Both the Stillwater and Malheur samples have high frequencies of OA compared to other American Indians, supporting the interpretation of a very active life-style with pronounced mechanical loading of the limbs. However, unlike diaphyseal robusticity, increased OA in Great Basin samples characterizes *both* the upper and lower limbs. The precise etiology of OA is uncertain, but in most cases is thought to result from heavy, repetitive joint loading (Larsen et al. 1995). It may be that the kinds of activities that can increase joint loadings in the upper limb (e.g., during food preparation) do not necessarily also increase bending and torsional loadings of the upper limb diaphyses. Interestingly, Bridges (1991) also found some noncorrespondence between OA and diaphyseal robusticity in Native American samples from the Tennessee River valley. She hypothesized that OA may be a response to "intensive or infrequent activities" that could potentially cause joint injury, while diaphyseal robusticity better reflects "normal" activities. Obviously, more work is needed to disentangle these various relationships, but it would not be surprising if different types of mechanical loadings had contrasting effects on different skeletal structural features, particularly since these features appear to vary in their developmental sensitivity to mechanical factors (Trinkaus, Churchill, and Ruff 1994).

The low percent CA in the Great Basin samples indicates a relatively thin cortex in both the femur and humerus. Further analyses show that this is a result of combined medullary and periosteal expansion of the cortex, particularly in the femur. (Both MA- and TA-standardized are highly significantly larger [p < .001] in Great Basin femora than in the pooled American Indian or hunter-gatherer comparative samples.) This outward distribution of bone leads to an increase in second moments of area (e.g., J) of the femur, since second moments of area are strongly dependent on the distance from the cortex to the center of the section or an axis running through it. Thus, despite a decline in percent CA, relative femoral strength increases (see Ruff 1992 for an illustration). In some ways this is analogous to the cortical bone remodeling observed with aging, most prominently in active populations such as that at Pecos Pueblo, where systemic hormonal changes lead to loss of bone from the endosteal surface, while the periosteal surface expands and thus helps to maintain bone strength (Ruff and Hayes 1982, 1983b; Ruff 1992; also see Lazenby 1990a, 1990b).

A plausible interpretation of these findings is that Great Basin populations were under general systemic, possibly nutritional stress that not only adversely affected the growth of bone but also promoted its optimal distribution in order to best resist the high mechanical loadings placed on the lower limbs (also see Larsen, Ruff, and Kelly 1995). Another possible explanation is that the Great Basin samples were, on average, significantly older at death than the other comparative samples utilized here. Precise ages at death were available for portions of the Stillwater sample (18 of 24 individuals) and the eastern Great Basin sample (15 of 23 individuals) and did include a number of individuals of advanced age (40 years or over). The mean age at death of known-aged individuals from these two samples was 34.6 years. If only individuals over 35 years of age are considered, the mean percent CA of the femoral midshaft is 66.8 percent, very close to the mean percent CA for the entire two samples of 67.5 percent. The age effect on humeral percent CA is somewhat larger: mean percent CA for individuals over 35 years of age is 60.6 percent, compared to 64.3 percent for the total combined Stillwater–eastern Great Basin sample. (It is interesting to note that aging appears to have had more of an effect on cortical thinning in the humerus than in the femur, which is in agreement with the argument above that localized mechanical influences were more important in the femoral diaphyses than in the humeral diaphyses among Great Basin populations.) However, even if older individuals are eliminated, humeral percent CA for the pooled Great Basin samples (67.5 ± 1.2 SE) is still significantly lower than that for other American Indians (Table 14.10). Thus, variation in age at death is unlikely to explain the majority of the differences in relative cortical thickness between populations in the Great Basin and those in other regions.

The particularly low values of percent CA for the Stillwater sample suggest that this sample may have been under higher systemic stress than the other two Great Basin samples. If this stress was dietary, then it may indicate significant variation in food types and availability in the three regions of the Great Basin. However, the frequency of dental hypoplasia occurrence (per individual) is about the same in the Stillwater and Malheur samples (Hutchinson and Larsen 1995; Nelson, this volume), which does not support the suggestion of greater general systemic stress at Stillwater. Also, the Stillwater sample is not short in bone length compared to the other two samples, which may argue against dietary insufficiency in this sample. It should also be noted that despite some variability in percent CA, none of the Great Basin samples differ significantly from each other in relative bending and torsional strength (i.e., J-standardized). This again shows how misleading the use of percent CA or relative cortical thickness can be in evaluating the *mechanical* characteristics of a long bone and, thus, the behaviorial factors leading to such a morphology (Ruff 1992; Ruff et al. 1993).

The shorter femora and humeri of Great Basin samples relative to the groups living in other areas, particularly other hunter-gatherers, may also argue for a reduction in dietary quantity or quality relative to the groups living in other areas. A relatively low stature is also characteristic of the Pecos Pueblo comparative sample along with other Puebloan populations (Hrdlička 1935). This may be, in part, a response (or adaptation) to similar dietary restrictions, although other factors, such as genetic history, must obviously also be considered in evaluating the general morphological patterns. (For example, not every Southwestern U.S. American Indian group is short in stature [Hrdlička 1935; Johnston and Schell 1979].)

The lack of any significant effects of subsistence strategy on femoral robusticity in the broad comparative analyses is interesting in light of previous studies that have documented such effects in specific regions of the United States (Ruff, Larsen, and Hayes 1984; Bridges 1989b). The present results support the view that behavioral changes occurring with the shift from hunting-gathering to food producing were heterogeneous and varied from region to region (Ruff and Larsen 1990; Bridges 1996). Thus, no general, consistent trend can be discerned that cuts across all regions. The same also holds for the cross-sectional "shape" indices of the femur, percent CA, and I_x/I_y. Although comparative data for the humerus are much more limited, they support the same general conclusion: humeri from the Great Basin are actually *less* similar in robusticity to Georgia coast hunter-gatherers than they are to Georgia coast agriculturalists.

There is one way, however, in which subsistence strategy appears to have a strong and consistent effect on structural properties: the degree of sexual dimorphism in lower limb bone structure present within populations. Hunter-gatherers consistently have greater sexual dimorphism in robusticity and A-P/M-L bending rigidity of the femoral midshaft than the agriculturalists. The difference for A-P/M-L bending rigidity is particularly striking and is illustrated for a number of population samples in Figure 14.6 that were gathered from the literature (Ruff 1987, 1994; Robbins, Rosenberg, and Ruff 1989; data from this study). As shown there, sexual dimorphism in midshaft femoral I_x/I_y for the three Great Basin samples is the highest of any yet reported for Native American groups, ranging between 21 and 26 percent.

The greater difference between the sexes in femoral midshaft A-P/M-L bending rigidity among hunter-gatherers than among agriculturalists has been attributed to changes in activity patterns related to sexual division of labor (Ruff 1987). Specifically, in preagricultural societies, males tend to be assigned subsistence-related tasks that require a high degree of mobility (such as hunting), while females, largely because of the demands of child care, are more restricted to local areas. In food-producing societies, male and female economic activities tend to become more similar (e.g., soil preparation for planting perhaps is shared), thereby imposing more similar mechanical loads on the skeleton. Because of the anatomy of the lower limb and the mechanics of bipedal locomotion, a high degree of mobility implies a relative increase in A-P bending loads on the lower limb bones, particularly in the region about the knee. Thus, preagricultural males and females show greatly different bone cross-sectional morphologies from the midfemur through the midtibia, while in agricultural societies this difference is reduced. (The trend continues throughout industrial societies, which show virtually no sexual dimorphism in femoral midshaft I_x/I_y.)

In this respect, then, the Great Basin samples fit the predicted pattern for hunter-gatherers perfectly; they are also remarkably similar to each other (Figure 14.6). Their very large values of sexual dimorphism in femoral midshaft I_x/I_y are consistent with very different degrees of mobility in males and females. (Comparisons of osteoarthritis incidence in Great Basin males and females also support this interpretation [Larsen, Ruff, and Kelly 1995; Hemphill, this volume].) In addition, there is the possibility that the ruggedness of the terrain helped push sexual dimorphism in this feature to such high levels, since this might be expected to add to the mechanical loading of the lower limbs of long-distance travelers. In this regard

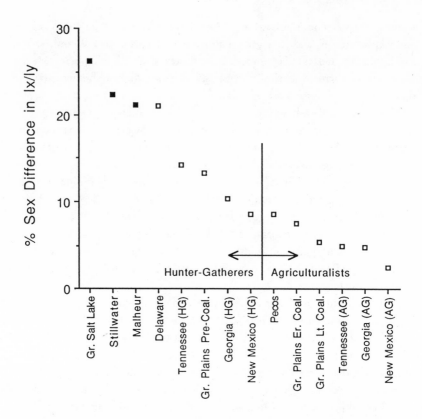

FIGURE 14.6. Percent sex difference ([(male–female)/female] • 100) in anteroposterior to mediolateral bending rigidity of the femoral midshaft in American Indian samples arranged in descending order. Great Basin samples indicated by filled squares. See text for sources of other sample data. HG: hunter-gatherers; AG: agriculturalists (used only for paired regional data presented in the same original source)

it is noteworthy that the Pecos Pueblo sample has the highest level of sexual dimorphism of any of the agricultural samples shown in Figure 14.6. However, another New Mexico agricultural sample has a low level of sexual dimorphism, and one of the highest levels of dimorphism among preagriculturalists is found in a coastal sample from Delaware. Also, no significant sex/terrain or sex/subsistence/terrain effects were found in the 3-way ANOVA's of the pooled comparative sample. Thus, while subsistence strategy has a consistent effect on this feature, terrain apparently does not, perhaps reflecting subtle regional differences in environmental utilization.

Based on the same line of reasoning, the lower A-P/M-L bending rigidity (I_x/I_y) of the femoral midshaft in the Malheur sample, particularly among males, could indicate a somewhat more sedentary life-style when compared to the Stillwater and eastern Great Basin samples. This index in isolation must be interpreted cautiously, however, since population differences in other factors, such as general body build, can also influence femoral diaphyseal shape (Ruff 1995). That the Malheur sample does *not* exhibit reduced overall femoral robusticity compared to other Great Basin samples also argues against a generally "easy" life-style, as does the continued marked sexual dimorphism in femoral shape. It is possible that this sample as a whole had an overall physically demanding yet more geographically limited life-style than the other two Great Basin samples, with males remaining more mobile than females, which would be consistent with the particularly heavy dependence of the Malheur sample on lacustrine resources, as documented by archaeological evidence (Oetting 1990b). It is also possible that the somewhat less rugged environment of the Harney Basin relative to that of the other two Great Basin samples accounts for the relatively reduced A-P bending strength of the femur in the Malheur sample (B. Hemphill, personal communication). It is noteworthy that the reduction in relative A-P bending strength of the midshaft femur in Malheur compared to Stillwater is more marked among males than among females (Table 14.6). This is consistent with osteoarthritis data for these samples (Hemphill, this volume), which indicate a greater difference in OA occurrence between males from the two sites (with Malheur lower) than between females. Because males were usually more mobile than females in hunter-gatherer societies (Ruff 1987), a reduction in long-range mobility for the society as a whole should have had more effect on males, which seems to have been the case at Malheur.

Besides changes in femoral midshaft cross-sectional shape, another population characteristic that has been associated with the adoption and intensification of agriculture is a decline in humeral cross-sectional asymmetry, suggesting more equal use of the right and left arms, perhaps in part associated with bilateral activities, such as corn grinding (Bridges 1989b, 1996; Fresia, Ruff, and Larsen 1990; Ruff 1992). Some recent studies, however, suggest a more complex pattern, with no consistent, straightforward association between subsistence strategy and upper-limb bilateral asymmetry (Trinkaus, Churchill, and Ruff 1994; Bridges 1995). The present results for the Great Basin samples appear to confirm this impression, with only moderate levels of humeral bilateral asymmetry present. Males show greater levels of asymmetry than females, which is consistent with most (but not all) earlier studies of hunter-gatherers (Bridges 1989b; Fresia, Ruff, and Larsen 1990; Ruff 1992; Trinkaus, Churchill, and Ruff 1994). While extreme cases of upper-limb-bone bilateral asymmetry are readily explained in mechanical/behavioral terms (Trinkaus, Churchill, and Ruff 1994), more comparative structural data are needed to fully evaluate the significance of more subtle patterns of variation in this characteristic.

One sex-related difference in femoral structure that seems to be unaffected by terrain or subsistence strategy is the degree of circularity of the proximal femoral shaft (I_{max}/I_{min}). Females are consistently less circular and more M-L buttressed than males, an apparent adaptation to increased M-L bending of the proximal femoral shaft resulting from sex differences in pelvic morphology (Ruff 1987, 1995). The present study's results are no exception, with high levels of sexual dimorphism in this feature found in every Great Basin sample. Because this is related to biological factors that have no direct relationship to subsistence or environment, the results have no direct bearing on these other influences, although the high values of femoral subtrochanteric I_{max}/I_y for Great Basin females, at least, in comparison with some other American Indian groups (Ruff 1987), are consistent with generally high activity levels (Ruff and Larsen 1990).

The results of comparisons between bone structural properties and the stable carbon isotope data for the Great Salt Lake sample not only support and extend the above interpretation but also have implications for this specific region. As described earlier, the Great Salt Lake region during the time period from which these burials derive (in all but one case dating to A.D. 600–1150) is thought to have exhibited considerable diversity in subsistence strategy, with a basically hunting-gathering-fishing economy overlain by varying degrees of maize cultivation (Simms and Stuart 1993; Simms, this volume). Due probably to sampling error (Simms, this volume and personal communication), only males in the present sample exhibited $\delta^{13}C$ values consistent with a significant maize component in the diet ($\delta^{13}C$ of over –13). When compared with males having smaller or no amounts of maize in their diets, the male maize consumers were found to be not only significantly taller but also relatively less robust.

These results are consistent with the previously proposed hypothesis that as the importance of agriculture increases, males become more sedentary (Ruff 1987, also see discussion above). The effect in the Great Salt Lake sample seems to be more continuous for the femur, where declines in relative mobility with increasing importance of maize agriculture might be expected to be fairly gradual, and more abrupt for the humerus, where only the intensified use of maize seems to have led to differential use of the upper limb among males, perhaps due to more wholesale participation in food production activities.

A similar decline in relative mechanical loading of the limbs with the adoption of agriculture was found in Georgia coast samples (Ruff, Larsen, and Hayes 1984; Ruff and Larsen 1990). However, in Georgia this was accompanied by a decrease in bone lengths, unlike the increase in bone lengths found in the Great Basin. It is possible that the incorporation of maize in a Great Basin subsistence economy led to an improvement in diet, and thus an increase in stature, while the same subsistence change on the Georgia coast led to a decline in dietary quality, at least, and thus a decline in body size (Larsen 1981, 1982). Given the probable differences in natural resources available in the two regions (Great Basin relatively sparse, Georgia coast relatively rich), this hypothesis appears plausible. It also reemphasizes the fact that nutritional and mechanical effects on the skeleton are not necessarily directly linked (Ruff, Larsen, and Hayes 1984; Ruff and Larsen 1990). In Tennessee River valley archaeological samples, Bridges (1985) documented yet another pattern: the shift to food production there was associated with a general increase in both bone lengths and femoral robusticity, although the latter was significant only in males. Regional context must obviously be considered in any attempt to interpret variation in body size and skeletal structural properties associated with changes in subsistence strategy.

The results for the Great Salt Lake sample do little to resolve issues involving the "Fremont" to "Late Prehistoric" transition in this region (Simms and Stuart 1993; Simms, this volume) since all but one of the individuals predates A.D. 1200, the beginning of the transitional period. The one individual who postdates this period, a female, has a $\delta^{13}C$ value of −17.1, indicating very little or no reliance on maize in the diet, as predicted for "Late Prehistoric" populations. However, several individuals from earlier times have $\delta^{13}C$ values even lower (as well as much higher) than this; also, there is no significant correlation between $\delta^{13}C$ values and burial age, within sex or pooled sex, in this sample. This supports the view of the "Great Salt Lake Fremont" culture as highly diversified with regard to subsistence strategy, incorporating some maize agriculture when and if it became advantageous to do so (Simms and Stuart 1993; Simms, this volume). This diversity in subsistence activities apparently had direct effects on variation in both body size and skeletal structure through alterations of diet and activity patterns, respectively.

These results also have implications regarding interpretations of sex-related differences within the Great Salt Lake sample and others in the Great Basin. It was noted in the broader American Indian comparisons that size-standardized CA and J of the femoral midshaft were larger in males than in females in preagricultural samples. Yet in the Great Basin samples, no significant effect of sex on these properties was observed. Comparison of the data in Table 14.6 with those shown in Figure 14.4 suggests an explanation for this apparent paradox. In both the Malheur and Stillwater samples, males are larger in these properties than the females; but in the Great Salt Lake sample, the two sexes are virtually identical (Table 14.6). However, when only males with $\delta^{13}C$ values in the range of females are considered (about −19 to −15; i.e., individuals without a significant maize dietary component), Great Salt Lake males have greater J-standardized values than do females (Figure 14.4). The same general effect can be discerned in comparisons of size-standardized humeral properties (compare Table 14.8 with Figure 14.5). Thus, the partial deviation of the Great Salt Lake sample from the other two Great Basin samples in sexual dimorphism may very well be a result of including some agriculturalist males in the former sample and not in the others. This factor did not affect sexual dimorphism in femoral midshaft I_x/I_y, though, where the Great Basin samples have the largest male-female difference of any Native American sample yet analyzed (Figure 14.6). In this regard, it would be extremely interesting to examine skeletal material from maize-consuming females from this region to compare femoral shape variables with those of males.

CONCLUSIONS

Great Basin long bones are relatively short, with very robust femora (but not humeri) and relatively thin cortices. Analysis of variation in a broad sampling of American Indians indicates that geographical terrain is the most critical factor in determining relative structural strength of the lower limb. Thus, the marked robusticity of the femur in Great Basin samples is very likely due to the ruggedness of the physical environment, coupled with a vigorous and mobile life-style. The shorter stature and thinner bone cortices may be a result of lower dietary quality or quantity compared to other regions. Sexual dimorphism in femoral midshaft morphology is very high, consistent with the marked sexual division of labor and consequent greater mobility of males characteristic of hunter-gatherers. These interpretations are supported by stable carbon isotope data for the Great Salt Lake sample, in which an increased reliance on maize found in some males is associated with greater stature but reduced skeletal robusticity. On the whole, the three Great Basin samples—Stillwater, Malheur, and Great Salt Lake—are very similar in morphology, as they are in inferred behavioral patterns, although there is some evidence for either a more geographically limited or perhaps slightly less physically demanding life-style in the Malheur Lake sample.

Acknowledgments

I would like to thank Clark Larsen and Brian Hemphill for inviting me to participate in the symposium that led to the creation of this volume and, with Steven Simms, for generously providing the skeletal material as well as partial funding to carry out these analyses. I also want to thank the Northwestern Band of the Shoshoni Nation for permission to study some of the remains. The comparative analyses carried out for this study were also supported in part by grants from the National Science Foundation.

15

Faces in Prehistory
Great Basin Wetlands Skeletal Populations

Robert L. Bettinger

It is no secret that North American archaeologists and biological anthropologists operate in a social, legal, and political environment that has increasingly limited access to and use of Native American skeletal materials for research. The reasons for this are many and often beyond our control, but some are of our own doing. In particular, it would seem we have not established to the satisfaction of many that the study of skeletal remains is important enough to warrant disturbing Native American grave sites and removing the remains for study in our laboratories. In one sense, this is how we should measure the contributions in this volume: Do they contribute enough to our understanding of Great Basin prehistory, that of Great Basin wetlands specifically, to justify the effort and, on some sides, hardfeelings? Did we learn enough this time to merit the opportunity to do the same thing in the future? More optimistically, did we learn enough here to lobby for greater future opportunities, perhaps for maintaining, in tandem with Native Americans, skeletal remains for study in perpetuity? I am biased in this matter, naturally. Nevertheless, it stands that what has been learned in the course of the research presented here fundamentally changes our understanding of Great Basin wetlands prehistory. This change could not have come about in the absence of direct, intensive, sometimes destructive, analysis of skeletal remains. My summary of these findings and their implications is divided into three sections, centering on (1) ancient DNA evidence for genetic affiliation, population movement, and modern relationships (Who Were They?); (2) isotopic evidence pertaining to ancient wetland diet and dietary variability (What Did They Eat?); and (3) skeletal evidence for wetland mobility, land use, and health as it bears on archaeological interpretation of these patterns (Do Marshes Bring Happiness?). A concluding section (Implications) argues that these data will change not only what we think about Great Basin wetlands adaptation but also how we think about the archaeological record and the importance of the individuals who generated it.

WHO WERE THEY?

To paraphrase someone else, the genetic evidence is intensely exciting, but strangely unsatisfying. Until just recently, archaeologists had largely abandoned the idea of being able to relate Holocene skeletal populations one to another except on the basis of morphometrical evidence, which generally lacks the precision needed to sort out the details of prehistoric population movements. Ancient DNA (aDNA) changed that. It is now possible to assign many, if not most, individual prehistoric North American skeletons to one of just five mitochondrial DNA (mtDNA) clades that dominate this continent and to identify in these same individuals the presence of albumin polymorphisms whose distributions are highly restricted either geographically or ethnolinguistically. There are problems with both systems.

Albumin is the less well studied, presumably because, as summarized by Kaestle et al. (this volume), most ancient and modern Native North Americans are monomorphic for the common allele Al^A, lacking either Al^{Me}, which is most common in the Southwest and Baja California, or Al^{Na}, which is largely restricted to Algonkian and Athabascan speakers. Owing to this and to the eclectic distribution and frequently limited sizes of the samples that have been studied, it is exceedingly difficult to interpret albumin variant frequencies obtained from single sites or local site complexes in other than a very gross way. In the present case, for instance, we lack albumin data for the Great Salt Lake sample. The same is true for mtDNA, in this case because most Native American populations are characterized by mixtures of the four most common matriclades A, B, C, and D, the distributions of which are only coarsely resolved by the ancient and modern samples presently available and because, as discussed by O'Rourke et al. (this volume), archaeological samples frequently do not amplify for all four markers required to assign an individual unambiguously to a given matriclade. Despite all this, some important patterns emerge from the analysis of the Great Salt Lake Fremont sample studied by O'Rourke et al. and the Stillwater Marsh sample studied by Kaestle et al.

It is clear that these samples, if they are to be trusted, likely draw from different populations. The Great Salt Lake sample is characterized by very high frequencies (ca. 83 percent) of matriclade B, identified by the nine base pair (9 bp) deletion, and very low frequences of matriclade D (< 1 percent). In contrast, the Stillwater Marsh sample shows much lower frequencies (37 percent) of matriclade B and much higher frequencies of matriclade D (58 percent). The difference between the two confirms the understanding of archaeologists, who have long recognized fundamental distinctions in the culture histories of the eastern and western Great Basin. That this separation remained as recently as 650 B.P. is also consistent with the widely held archaeological (and linguistic) view that Numic-speaking groups arrived in the eastern Great Basin later than that—after 650 B.P.—which would presumably have erased major differences in clade distribution between the two. Beyond this, the picture grows more cloudy.

That the Stillwater Marsh sample represents an ancient population ancestral to the Numic-speaking groups who occupied the Great Basin at contact seems fairly unlikely. The albumin allele Al^{Me} occurs in very high frequency (15 percent) in the Stillwater series, but not in the modern Numic (1 percent), while clade C is moderately common in modern Numic (12 percent), but not in the Stillwater sample (0 percent). It is conceivable, of course, that the Stillwater Marsh population is ancestral to Numic speakers, but the odds are against it. The more likely possibility places the Stillwater Marsh population ancestral to either modern Northern Hokan (i.e., Northern California Hokan) or modern California Penutian, although in neither case is the match particularly close given the sample sizes that are available. As it turns out, the same situation obtains when it comes to finding matches for the Great Salt Lake sample. While it fits most comfortably within the larger Southwest, where clade B is most common, it differs in overall clade composition from any known ancient or modern sample inside or outside the Southwest. That neither the Great Salt Lake nor the Stillwater Marsh samples have any other known ancient or modern close match, then, makes it altogether less surprising that they do not match each other. The problem, in short, is either that the Stillwater Marsh and Great Salt Lake samples both represent extinct populations or that aDNA frequencies are too variable and our current samples of them too small to be of much help in sorting out the relationships between ancient populations or between ancient and modern populations. It is difficult to know what to make of this.

The problem is surely at least part statistical in that the tests used to ascertain differences between groups (e.g., chi-square) assume samples consisting of individuals selected randomly from a larger population. The assumption is not met, of course, because the Stillwater Marsh and Great Salt Lake (and Malheur Lake) samples come from sites that frequently contain more than one individual. That is, we have what are called cluster samples, not simple random samples—hence, more individual skeletons than independent cases. Ignoring this by treating each skeleton as though it had been selected independently inflates true sample size and makes it easier to reject the null hypothesis that two groups were drawn from the same parent population. That skeletons from the same cluster (site) are more likely to be genetically related than skeletons from different sites compounds the problem. Because of this, it is likely that relationships between the Great Salt Lake and Stillwater Marsh skeletal collections and some ancient and modern assemblages (which suffer the same problem) are closer than they seem. There is no easy way around this dilemma because the sizes of samples with which we are dealing are already perilously low. More than anything else, this suggests that we should remain open-minded about the possibilities of relationships between groups that outwardly seem quite different in aDNA composition—that is to say, remain very conservative in rejecting the null hypothesis that two samples derive from the same population. In the long run, of course, the only way to improve the situation is to obtain more and larger samples. In the meantime, it would certainly be worthwhile to explore the relationships between existing samples using statistics designed specifically for cluster samples with multivariate techniques to search for the broader patterns of relationship obscured in pairwise comparisons. In the worst case, it might turn out that mtDNA clade frequencies do, in fact, fluctuate so wildly in archaeological samples as to be of little use in sorting out ancient population movements. This need not be the case, however, as data cited by Kaestle et al. suggest long-term stability in clade distribution in many parts of North America. Nevertheless, it is certainly possible—indeed, virtually inevitable—that local population enclaves are going to vary substantially from larger regional norms, both temporally and spatially.

WHAT DID THEY EAT?

Should there remain any lingering doubt on the matter, the studies of Coltrain and Stafford for Great Salt Lake and Schoeninger for Stillwater Marsh (both studies, this volume) provide concrete evidence that adaptations in the Great Basin wetlands were not all the same. There are striking contrasts between the two samples with respect to mean and standard deviation of $\delta^{13}C$ values, suggesting basic differences in diet. This, of course, is partly due to the rise and fall of corn agriculture in areas adjacent to the Great Salt Lake wetlands. Because the Great Salt Lake samples are individually dated by radiocarbon, it is possible to trace this phenomenon with precision through time, given the assumption that it is being driven primarily by corn consumption. Excluding two outliers, the record covers the interval from A.D. 600 to A.D. 1300 and shows a dramatic increase in $\delta^{13}C$ between A.D. 600 and 900 and an even more dramatic fall in $\delta^{13}C$ after A.D. 1000. It is interesting to compare these data to the pattern of Fremont variability discussed by Simms in this volume and elsewhere (Simms 1990), who sees three adaptive forms: full-time horticulture, mixed horticulture and foraging, and full-time foraging. His scenario starts with the spread of corn to full-time foragers, some of whom ignore it, others of whom adopt its production in degrees varying to essentially full-time horticulture. Climate then makes corn horticulture untenable and farmers gradually shift back to full-time foraging. Again, if $\delta^{13}C$ variability is assumed to be driven mainly by the presence of corn, and not buffalo meat, the record after A.D. 1150 corresponds to Simms's postagricultural interval characterized almost entirely by foragers—presumably wetland oriented—with $\delta^{13}C$ levels of less that −17 (mean = −18.2, std = 0.62). Assuming this ($\delta^{13}C \leq −17$) is the wetland-based, full-time forager signature, then the period immediately prior (from about A.D. 850 to A.D. 1150) displays a range of $\delta^{13}C$ values (mean = −15.69, std = 3.1) consistent with the adaptive diversity Simms postulates during the height of Great Salt Lake corn agriculture, with about half of the population (56 percent) following full-time wetland foraging and the other half engaged in mixtures of wetland foraging and horticulture ranging all the way to essentially full-time horticulture. It would appear, however, that this diversity did not emerge from an earlier full-time Great Salt Lake forager base, as Simms envisions, because the full-time forager signal is very poorly represented between A.D. 600 and A.D. 850. Rather, this period is most distinctive for a proportion (82 percent) of individuals relying to some degree on corn ($\delta^{13}C$ > −17) that is greater than anytime after that (mean = −14.9, std = 2.3). Against this, the following interval, A.D. 850 to A.D. 1150, is distinctive mainly for the developing emphasis on full-time wetland foraging, although full-time agriculture also becomes prominent. This produces a weak but nonetheless significant correlation between $\delta^{13}C$ value and age—declining toward the present—in the Great Salt Lake skeletal series (r = −.32, $p_{r=0}$ < .02, n = 57, for the sample overall; r = −.37, $p_{r=0}$ < .01, n = 55, for individuals dating A.D. 600 to A.D. 1300). What this suggests is that the system responsible for the Great Salt Lake skeletal sample began mainly as one of mixed farmer-foragers and that full-time wetland foraging and full-time horticulture *both* developed as later specializations, perhaps facilitated by extensive symbiotic trade relations between the two, as Simms speculates. It is thinkable, in any event, that horticulture may have been instrumental in the development of intensive wetland foraging in the Great Salt Lake region. This may have implications for the "Fremont collapse," attributed by many to climatic change that diminished corn productivity after A.D. 1050. It is clear from the Great Salt Lake sample, however, that, in this region at any rate, some individuals and groups had begun to move away from mixed horticulture-foraging toward full-time foraging by at least A.D. 900, which raises the possibility that the demise of Fremont corn agriculture was not due solely to climate, but in some instances to the presence of cheaper foraging alternatives, in this case, wetlands.

The late Great Salt Lake wetlands pattern, as represented by the range of $\delta^{13}C$ values for the period A.D. 1150 to A.D. 1300, is remarkable in its uniformly low $\delta^{13}C$ values (mean = −18.2, std = .62)—especially in comparison to the Stillwater Marsh sample, where $\delta^{13}C$ is higher and more variable (mean = −17.1, std = 1.05). This presumably reflects differences of environment, Great Salt Lake groups perhaps having less access to high-quality C_4 resources or more access to high-quality C_3 resources than Stillwater Marsh groups. Either way, as noted above, the differences are a concrete demonstration that Great Basin wetlands adaptations are not all the same.

The Stillwater Marsh sample is less amenable to the kind of detailed analysis laid out by Coltrain and Stafford (this volume) because there is less chronological control. The bulk of the sample is probably concentrated in roughly the same interval, A.D. 600 to A.D. 1300, although parts of it may extend as far back in time as 1200 B.C. In any case, it is not possible to relate individual $\delta^{13}C$ values to points within this span. As I have just observed, the mean and range of $\delta^{13}C$ values are greater than for the A.D. 1150–A.D. 1300 Great Salt Lake sample, presumably reflecting the greater availability of high-quality C_4 resources relative to high-quality C_3 resources. Since plants with more positive $\delta^{13}C$ values are especially abundant in stressful, and especially xeric, environments (Tieszen 1991; B. Smith and Epstein 1971), it is tempting to attribute this to the greater use of C_4 plants (e.g., *Atriplex, Chenopodium, Panicum, Distichilis*) available in the more arid tracts surrounding the marsh rather than in the marsh itself. Unfortunately, there are enough C_4 species in the marsh (e.g., *Zostera, Carex*) and C_3 species in the uplands (e.g., *Oryzopsis*) to generate the observed distribution of $\delta^{13}C$ values by combinations ranging from complete reliance on marsh resources to complete reliance on upland resources. Although Schoeninger (this volume) does not comment on it, one clue that may help to discern among these possibilities is the fairly strong positive correlation between $\delta^{13}C$ and $\delta^{15}N$ (r = .54, $p_{r=0}$ < .001, n = 38, discounting one extreme $\delta^{15}N$ value that Schoeninger suggests should be ignored). Since the similarity between humans and carnivores in the Stillwater Marsh sample suggests that $\delta^{15}N$ varies directly with animal consumption, it follows that animal consumption is positively correlated with C_4 resource consumption. Furthermore, that most marsh fish, birds, and omnivores registered low $\delta^{13}C$ values, whereas the single upland animal tested (*Lepus*) registered high $\delta^{13}C$ values, suggests that values of $\delta^{13}C$ and $\delta^{15}N$ are measuring variation along an adaptive spectrum ranging from a more plant-dependent marsh pattern to a more animal-dependent upland one. This argument is strongly supported by differences between the sexes in the strength of this effect (i.e., the correlation between $\delta^{13}C$ and $\delta^{15}N$), which is greater for males (r = .73, $p_{r=0}$ < .01, n = 14), who used the uplands more frequently than females (r = .54, $p_{r=0}$ < .05, n = 14). It is further the case that in females (but not males) the values of $\delta^{13}C$ and $\delta^{15}N$ both vary inversely with age (r_{13C} = −.71, $p_{r=0}$ < .05; r_{15N} < .1; n = 10) and the severity of osteoarthritis as measured by percent of joints affected (r_{13C} = −.65, $p_{r=0}$ < .05; r_{15N} = −.56, $p_{r=0}$ < .1; n = 10). It would appear, in short, that younger females less affected by osteoarthritis consumed greater quantities of upland game. The sample sizes are small to be sure—and many scenarios are possible—but it is tempting to argue that younger, more mobile females enjoyed greater access to game because they traveled into the uplands with males and that older, less mobile females more residentially tethered to the Stillwater Marsh had lesser access. This would suggest that, while the purpose of male logistical hunting was partly to provision the occupants of marsh residential camps, those who depended on provisioning consumed less animal protein than those actually present at the upland locations where it was obtained. This parallels the findings of Larsen (1982:253) in coastal Georgia, who sees female nutrition declining following the introduction of corn agriculture, which restricted female movement and consequently their access to wild game as a source of animal protein.

DO MARSHES BRING HAPPINESS? HEALTH AND MOBILITY

Ethnographers and archaeologists have traditionally emphasized the challenges the harsh and unpredictable Great Basin environment posed for hunter-gatherers equipped with relatively simple technologies. Indeed, for many, including Julian Steward ([1938] 1999), the food quest was the overriding preoccupation of humans in this area. Against this backdrop of environmental austerity, wetlands are surely in some sense exceptional, offering a range of reliable resources that set them apart from the less well watered expanses that characterize much of the Great Basin. As noted in many of the papers here, the debate continues regarding the productivity of these Great Basin wetlands and their inherent attraction to human populations. A large fraction of this debate centers on patterns of mobility, under the assumption that productive wetlands should result in restricted movement, perhaps approximating that of the Klamath-Modoc of the Klamath Lake basin. As Oetting (this volume) makes clear, however, the Klamath-Modoc pattern is not one of full-time sedentism, but rather one of marsh-tethered semisedentism that involved seasonal movements to high-quality resource patches some distance away. As Hemphill (following Raven 1992) notes, Stillwater groups may have been more marsh-tethered simply as a consequence of the more limited range of alternatives outside that marsh. I think this view is shared, at least in general, by many of the contributors to this volume. The answer to the question "Do marshes bring happiness?" then, is clearly "No." Marshes by themselves do not provide a sufficiently reliable set of high-quality resources to attract full-time sedentism, which is why the Klamath-Modoc—living on one of the world's most productive wetlands—were not sedentary. Again, if Stillwater groups were more residentially tethered to their less favored marsh than the Klamath-Modoc were to theirs, that is likely only because the Stillwater Marsh was the best of a very bad lot—as a glance at a Nevada vegetation map will show.

It is relevant in this regard that the skeletal samples from all three of these wetland localities are highly restricted in time, concentrated mainly between A.D. 600 and A.D. 1300, an interval of subsistence intensification throughout much of the Great Basin. It was at this time, for example, that residential bases were first consistently established in the resource-poor alpine zone of the White Mountains (e.g., Bettinger 1991a). It is possible, then, to view the wetland skeletal series reviewed here as reflecting a similar case of expanding use of a marginal environment that was for some reason abandoned in most places after A.D. 1300. The problem with this argument, as with most of the wetland debate, is that it centers around a second-order phenomenon—subsistence-settlement pattern—when what we are really trying to measure is quality of life: how did people in Great Basin wetlands fare in comparison to other Great Basin hunter-gatherers and to hunter-gatherers and agriculturalists elsewhere? The osteopathology and skeletal structure of the Great Salt Lake, Stillwater Marsh, and Malheur Lake burial complexes provide firsthand evidence of this.

Great Basin archaeologists have always cast their constructions of ancient lifeways as strategies for survival—in modern parlance, for enhancing fitness. Skeletal studies provide direct measures of the success of these various strategies. It is important to understand, however, that while these studies measure various indices of fitness and overall health quite directly—surely more directly than settlement and subsistence patterns—their interpretation is inherently elusive because fitness and health themselves are composite, multidimensional phenomena. Behaviors that enhance individual or population fitness/health in one respect frequently compromise it in another. Residential mobility, for instance, almost certainly works more to the advantage of males than females (because it reduces logistical travel) and more to the advantage of healthy adults than the young, the old, and the infirm, who are less capable walkers. Similarly, logistical hunting probably increases access to high-quality resources for males, improving their nutritional status but, at the same time, increasing their rate of skeletal deterioration and affecting their ability later in life to keep up with others during residential moves. Accordingly, the studies in this volume provide general impressions, rather than definitive findings, about the overall fitness status in the Great Salt Lake, Stillwater Marsh, and Malheur Lake wetlands. Because of this, and because the data presented by Larsen and Hutchinson, Ruff, Nelson, and Hemphill are too many and complex to review in detail, I confine my discussion to a few key points.

It is easiest to compare the Stillwater Marsh and Malheur Lake samples because both are comparatively large, are measured in comparable ways, and lack the adaptive complication added by horticulture in the Great Salt Lake case. On balance, these data indicate substantially higher rates of periostitis equally distributed by age and sex and slightly higher rates of hypoplasia, suggesting both lower overall quality of health for the Malheur Lake sample and higher overall rates of osteoarthritis, indicating greater work-induced hardship, for the Stillwater Marsh sample. As Nelson (this volume) shows, however, this coarse comparison glosses substantial temporal variation in the Malheur sample. In particular, it hides an unusually high frequency of hypoplasia and periostitis at one site, 35HA2095, that is evidently younger than the rest of the Malheur Lake sample, dating between A.D. 1640 and 1790. Data presented by Hemphill (this volume, Table 13.4) indicate that the incidence of osteoarthritis, too, is significantly higher for this site than the rest of the Malheur Lake series.[1] Adjusting for this, the older portion of the Malheur

---

[1] This is partly due to the greater age at death for the 35HA2095 sample. When this is adjusted for, the difference is less dramatic, but nevertheless present.

Lake sample shows a markedly lower incidence of osteoarthritis and about the same incidence of hypoplasia and periostitis as does the Stillwater Marsh sample, with which it is essentially contemporaneous. The younger Malheur Lake sample appears uniformly more "stressed" in all these respects than either of the two older samples (i.e., Stillwater and older Malheur Lake).

These patterns broadly correspond to mobility-related differences in non-pathological skeletal sculpturing (i.e., other than osteoarthritis) summarized by Ruff, who argues for lower mobility in the Malheur Lake sample than in the Stillwater Marsh sample. Ruff does not segregate the older and younger Malheur Lake samples, but a reasonable assumption is that the lower mobility indicated for the Malheur Lake sample overall is due to the older material, which constitutes approximately 70 percent of the entire collection, and that sculpturing in the younger sample is characterized by values that equal or exceed those observed at Stillwater Marsh.

Taken at face value, then, the data from these three wetland samples (i.e., counting the younger and older Malheur Lake samples separately) suggest that mobility is inversely related to quality of life—just as intuited by original proponents of limnosedentism. Mobility responds to nutritional stress (hypoplasia, periostitis) and results in greater wear and tear on the human body (osteoarthritis), as shown by the younger Malheur Lake sample. By similar logic, osteoarthritis is higher in the Stillwater Marsh than in the older Malheur Lake sample, despite similar rates of hypoplasia and periostitis, because the less productive Stillwater Marsh setting required more hard work to achieve the same nutritional result. This basic trend is evident on a larger scale in a comparison of the Great Salt Lake, Malheur Lake, and Stillwater Marsh samples with other North American hunter-gatherers. The mobility being measured, however, need not be residential, as the limnosedentists would have. Indeed, the aberrant level of sexual dimorphism in skeletal robusticity reported by Ruff for the Malheur Lake, Stillwater Marsh, and Great Salt Lake samples suggests that logistical mobility, or simply foraging mobility, is the more critical variable. This is consistent with the argument of Larsen and Hutchinson, who attribute the unusually high incidence of osteoarthritis in Stillwater Marsh males to logistical hunting, and with Hemphill's contention that the lower levels of osteoarthritis more equally distributed among males and females suggest a Malheur Lake life-style that was more residentially mobile, hence less logistically demanding, than the one at Stillwater Marsh. What emerges from both discussions is that osteoarthritis is caused not so much by mobility per se, but rather by mobility under stressful conditions (perhaps when carrying heavy loads) that exacerbates otherwise minor injuries—by "playing hurt" in modern parlance. In other words, what we may be monitoring here is varying intensities of what Chayanov (1986:6) would term "drudgery"—you're moving camp or foraging far from camp, or in difficult terrain, when you'd rather not. As Hemphill and Oetting both point out, the Klamath pattern of spring-summer movement is highly instructive in this regard, since it was mobilized to take advantage of very high quality resources—fish and roots—that pulled people away from marshes, presumably when conditions made this attractive. Klamath winter reliance on *wocas* (*Nuphar*) obtained in the fall near the winter villages reduced the need to acquire and transport spring-summer resources in bulk and thereby reduced the drudgery of spring-summer mobility.

The opposite situation is the one in which an individual moves in response to resource depletion whether it is convenient or not or is constantly acquiring resources in bulk to set aside for later (winter) use. This scenario would seem more accurately to characterize the Stillwater situation as envisioned by Raven (1992) and Kelly (this volume), with males constantly traveling distances away from camp to hunt, and camps being consistently moved around the marsh to permit maximum access to resources that had to be carried back and stored for winter. As Hemphill notes, the Stillwater situation may have been more residentially tethered and concentrated in space, but, as the pathological data indicate, the quality of life was relatively low in comparison to other North American groups for which data are available.

Conditions were even more extreme for the peoples of 35HA2095 (the late Malheur Lake sample), which strikes me as the very picture of extreme hunter-gatherer drudgery. It is difficult—given my predilections (e.g., Bettinger and Baumhoff 1982)—to resist connecting this group to the spread of Numic peoples into southern Oregon, which occurred at roughly the time indicated for 35HA2095 (ca. A.D. 1640–1790). It is thinkable, for instance, that 35HA2095 represents a pre-Numic population stressed to the limit by environmental deterioration, as Nelson suggests, that ultimately gave way to Numic-speaking groups better adapted to xeric environments. It is also possible, however, to see the 35HA2095 series as a Numic group that had just entered an unfamiliar environment and was having difficulty coping with its resources and their distribution. It is of relevance in regard to the latter hypothesis that at least one of the 35HA2095 individuals— 2095.3, a 27-year-old female—evidently died from wounds inflicted by arrows, one tipped with a Rosegate projectile point (Hemphill 1992c:69), and that at least two other individuals from the same site—2095.1 (a male; Hemphill 1992b:19) and 2095.12a (a female; Hemphill 1992c:159)—show evidence of nonfatal cutting or penetrating wounds. On the basis of the Rosegate point embedded in 2095.3, it is tempting to speculate that 35HA2096 represents hostilities directed against spreading Numic speakers by long-time Malheur Lake occupants. Of course, such violence might as easily be the result of disputes within or among groups that had traditionally resided in the region. It is a pity, indeed, that the Malheur Lake series was not—and now can never be—studied for aDNA, for that would be the simplest and most direct test of these possibilities.

IMPLICATIONS

In the final analysis, the Stillwater, Great Salt Lake, and Malheur Lake skeletal samples are important because they put a face on the wetland archaeological record that is otherwise lacking. Archaeological interpretations of artifact assemblages, faunal remains, and settlement patterns are necessarily cast in very coarse terms. At best, we model at the level of regional subsistence-settlement systems that were followed by groups of unspecified size over broad intervals of time. It is sometimes possible to argue for differences in behavior by sex, but in truth we cannot distinguish sex in the archaeological record at this level, but merely activities, such as hunting or gathering, that we assume were allocated by sex in the past in essentially the same way as described in ethnographic accounts. It is different with skeletons.

Skeletons are individuals whose age and sex we often know. Skeletal data do not tell us everything, of course, but they do record in aDNA, in isotopic composition, in stature and structure, in pathologies, and in a host of other details what happened to specific individuals in the past, thus capturing a level of actualistic behavioral detail that is available nowhere else. This is especially critical in light of the current attention being paid to evolutionary theory both in archaeology and social anthropology, because individuals are always important in evolutionary explanation. Skeletal data provide a critical link between these theories and the scenarios of prehistoric human behavior we can develop from more coarse-grained archaeological data. It is possible, given skeletal data, to discern differences between male and female, young and old, and on this basis to generate testable hypotheses about critical limiting factors and the life history strategies that would optimize individual fitness within these limits. Hypoplasias suggesting that weaning was a particularly risky period, for instance, provide a basis for speculating about the subsistence and settlement strategies that might diminish this risk or about the reproductive strategies (e.g., birth spacing intervals) that might compensate for it. Too, the strikingly high level of sexual dimorphism in skeletal robusticity and osteoarthritis which characterizes Great Basin wetlands skeletons provides a solid foundation for arguing that men and women acted differently in ways directly affecting their health and that, as a consequence, must have pursued rather different life history strategies to maximize individual fitness. Differences between localities in the onset and velocity of osteoarthritis further suggest these strategies may have varied locally to suit specific subsistence-settlement types or larger adaptive strategies.

The observed variability in $\delta^{13}C$ and $\delta^{15}N$ values suggest much the same thing. It is certainly clear, for instance, there were profound differences in the adaptive behaviors pursued by individuals in the Great Salt Lake region between A.D. 850 and 1150. The variability is less dramatic in the Stillwater Marsh series, but important nevertheless, although its meaning is easily missed. The intuitive interpretation of the Stillwater variability relates it to local variations in subsistence patterns from year to year, which are well known to both Great Basin archaeologists and ethnographers. One year the ricegrass is good, another year it is bad, and people accommodate this variation. This is imagined, generally, from the perspective of a prototypical individual who, through his/her lifetime, experiences the full range of this variation. It is clear from these samples, however, that all individuals did not experience the same range of variation or behave the same way when confronting it, for, if they had, they would display virtually identical $\delta^{13}C$ values. The observed isotopic variation, then, is reflecting differences in individual experience and behavior that do not seem to end up "averaging out." Some individuals ate more animals and C_4 resources than did others—and did so often enough over extended periods for this behavior to be reflected in the record. In the Great Salt Lake case, Simms sees this and other kinds of evidence as implying greater than imagined adaptive variability (i.e., from individual to individual) for the Great Salt Lake Fremont as a whole. Viewed from the perspective of the individual, however, both this variability and that observed at Stillwater imply just the opposite: that the practices of individuals were more specialized (i.e., less flexible and generalized) than is envisioned in our archaeological models, which treat this variability as though it were due to a range of behavior alternatives employed by all individuals in much the same way. That is, when trying to explain a range of behavioral variability observed in a group or culture, we cannot argue for greater variability between individuals without in some sense implying less behavior variability for individuals themselves. Our problem, then, is not only one of establishing the range of behavioral variability for a group or culture but also one of determining whether the variability we observe archaeologically is a group-level phenomenon, expressed by all individuals in essentially the same way, or an individual-level phenomenon, expressing differences between less variable individuals. These are not theoretical, but rather empirical, questions of profound importance in resolving such debatable issues as the rise and fall of the Fremont and the spread of Numic speakers across the Great Basin and beyond. Because they place individuals squarely in the forefront, the papers in this volume open the door to this sort in inquiry. It remains to be seen whether bioarchaeologists and archaeogeneticists will be permitted (legally and practically) to pursue these questions further in the future—and whether archaeologists will accept the challenge this research poses for rethinking an archaeological record generated by the complex interactions between groups and individuals.

References

Acheson, R. M.

1960   Effect of nutrition and disease on human growth. In *Human growth,* edited by J. M. Tanner, 73–92. New York: Pergamon Press.

Adovasio, J. M., and D. R. Pedler

1994   A tisket, a tasket: Looking at the Numic speakers through the "lens" of a basket. In *Across the West: Human population movement and the expansion of the Numa,* edited by D. B. Madsen and D. Rhode, 114–23. Salt Lake City: University of Utah Press.

Aikens, C. M.

1966   *Fremont-Promontory-Plains relationships, including a report of excavations at the Injun Creek and Bear River No. 1 sites, northern Utah.* University of Utah Anthropological Papers no. 82. Salt Lake City: University of Utah Press.

1967   *Excavations at Snake Rock Village and the Bear River No. 2 site.* University of Utah Anthropological Papers no. 87. Salt Lake City: University of Utah Press.

1970   *Hogup Cave.* University of Utah Anthropological Papers no. 93. Salt Lake City: University of Utah Press. (Reprinted by the University of Utah Press, 1999.)

1978   Archaeology of the Great Basin. *Annual Review of Anthropology* 7:71–87.

1981   The last 10,000 years in Japan and eastern North America: Parallels in environment, economic adaptation, growth of social complexity and the adoption of agriculture. In *Affluent foragers: Pacific coasts east and west,* edited by S. Koyama and D. H. Thomas. Senri Ethnological Studies no. 9:261–74. Osaka, Japan.

1985   The Nightfire Island lakemarsh adaptation in the broader context of Desert West prehistory. In *Nightfire Island: Later Holocene lakemarsh adaptation on the west edge of the Great Basin,* edited by C. Garth Sampson, 519–28. University of Oregon Anthropological Papers no. 33. Eugene.

1993   *Archaeology of Oregon.* Portland, Oregon: U.S. Department of the Interior, Bureau of Land Management.

1994   Adaptive strategies and environmental change in the Great Basin and its peripheries as determinants in the migrations of Numic-speaking peoples. In *Across the West: Human population movement and the expansion of the Numa,* edited by D. B. Madsen and D. Rhode, 35–43. Salt Lake City: University of Utah Press.

Aikens, C. M., and R. L. Greenspan

1986   Archaeological investigations at the Headquarters site, Malheur National Wildlife Refuge, Harney County, Oregon. Submitted to U.S. Fish and Wildlife Service. Report on file, Malheur National Wildlife Refuge, Princeton, Oregon.

1988   Ancient lakeside culture in the northern Great Basin: Malheur Lake, Oregon. *Journal of California and Great Basin Anthropology* 10(1):32–61.

Aikens, C. M., and Y. T. Witherspoon

1986   Great Basin prehistory: Linguistics, archaeology and environment. In *Anthropology of the Desert West: Papers in honor of Jesse D. Jennings,* edited by C. J. Condie and D. D. Fowler, 7–20. University of Utah Anthropological Papers no. 110. Salt Lake City: University of Utah Press.

Ambler, J. R.

1966   *Caldwell Village.* University of Utah Anthropological Papers no. 84. Salt Lake City: University of Utah Press.

Ambrose, S. H.

1990   Preparation and characterization of bone and tooth collagen for isotopic analysis. *Journal of Archaeological Science* 17:431–51.

1991   Effects of diet, climate and physiology on nitrogen isotope abundances in terrestrial foodwebs. *Journal of Archaeological Science* 18:293–317.

Ambrose, S. H., and M. J. DeNiro

1986   The isotopic ecology of East African mammals. *Oecologia* 69:395–406.

Ambrose, S. H., and L. Norr

1993   Experimental evidence for the relationship of the carbon isotope ratios of whole diet and dietary protein to those of bone collagen and carbonate. In *Prehistoric human bone: Archaeology at the molecular level,* edited by J. B. Lambert and G. Grupe, 1–37. New York: Springer-Verlag.

Ammerman, A. J., and L. L. Cavalli-Sforza

1984   The wave of advance model. In *The Neolithic transition and the genetics of populations in Europe,* edited by A. J. Ammerman and L. L. Cavalli-Sforza, 63–84. Princeton: Princeton University Press.

Anderson, J. E.

1976   The human skeletons. In *Ancient people of Port au Choix: The excavation of an Archaic Indian cemetery in Newfoundland,* edited by J. A. Tuck, 124–31. Social Economic Studies no. 17. St. John's, Newfoundland.

Anderson, S., A. T. Bankier, B. G. Barrell, M. H. L. de Bruijn, A. R. Coulson, J. Drouin, I. C. Eperon, D. P. Nierlich, B. A. Roe, F. Sanger, P. H. Schreier, A. J. H. Smith, R. Staden, and I. G. Young

1981   Sequence and organization of the human mitochondrial genome. *Nature* 290: 457–65.

Andrews, J.

1972   The paleopathology of the eastern Great Basin Fremont population. M.A. thesis, University of Utah, Salt Lake City.

Angel, J. L.

1966   *Early skeletons from Tranquillity, California.* Smithsonian Institution Contributions to Anthropology no. 2:1–19. Washington, D.C.

1971   *The people of Lerna.* Washington, D.C.: Smithsonian Institution Press.

Angel, J. L., J. O. Kelley, M. Parrington, and S. Pinter

1987   Life stresses of the free Black community as represented by the First African Baptist Church, Philadelphia, 1823–1841. *American Journal of Physical Anthropology* 74:213–29.

Antevs, E.

1938   *Rainfall and tree growth in the Great Basin.* Washington, D.C. and New York: Carnegie Institution of Washington and American Geographical Society of New York.

1948   Climatic changes and pre-White man. In *The Great Basin with emphasis on glacial and post-glacial times.* Biological Series 10(7). University of Utah Bulletin, vol. 38(20):168–91. Salt Lake City.

1955   Geologic-climatic dating in the West. *American Antiquity* 20:317–35.

Atwood, G.

1994   Geomorphology applied to flooding problems of closed-basin lakes . . . specifi-cally Great Salt Lake, Utah. *Geomorphology* 10:197–219.

Avise, J. C., J. E. Neigel, and J. Arnold

1984   Demographic influences on mitochondrial DNA lineage survivorship in animal populations. *Journal of Molecular Evolution* 20:99–105.

Bada, J. L., R. O. Peterson, A. Schimmelmann, and R. E. M. Hedges

1990   Moose teeth as monitors of environmental isotopic parameters. *Oecologia* 82: 102–6.

Bada, J. L., M. J. Schoeninger, and A. Schimmelmann

1989   Isotopic fractionation during peptide bond hydrolysis. *Geochemica et Cosmo-chimica Acta* 53:3337–41.

Bailey, R. C.

1991   *The behavioral ecology of the Efe Pygmy men in the Ituri forest, Zaire.* Anthro-pological Papers no. 86. Ann Arbor: Museum of Anthropology, University of Michigan.

Bailliet, G., F. Rothhammer, F. R. Carnese, C. M. Bravi, and N. O. Bianchi

1994   Founder mitochondrial haplotypes in Amerindian populations. *American Jour-nal of Human Genetics* 54:27–33.

Baker, S., S. E. Billat, L. D. Richens, and R. K. Talbot

1992   *An archaeological survey of Bureau of Reclamation lands around Willard Bay Reser-voir, northern Utah.* Brigham Young University Museum of Peoples and Cultures Technical Series no. 92-2. Provo, Utah.

Baldwin, G. C.

1945   Notes on ceramic types in southern Nevada. *American Antiquity* 10:389–90.

Balls, E. K.

1962   *Early uses of California Plants.* Berkeley: University of California Press.

Barlow, K. R.

1997   Foragers that farm: A behavioral ecology approach to the economics of corn farming for the Fremont case. Ph.D. diss., Department of Anthropology, Uni-versity of Utah, Salt Lake City.

Barlow, K. R., P. R. Henriksen, and D. Metcalfe

1993   Estimating load size in the Great Basin: Data from conical burden baskets. *Utah Archaeology 1993,* 6:27–38.

Barlow, K. R., and D. Metcalfe

1996   Plant utility indices: Two Great Basin examples. *Journal of Archaeological Science* 23:351–71.

Barrett, S. A.

1910   *The material culture of the Klamath Lake and Modoc Indians of northeastern Cali-fornia and southern Oregon.* University of California Publications in American Archaeology and Ethnology no. 5(4). Berkeley.

Bass, W. M.

1964   The variation in physical types of the prehistoric Plains Indians. Memoir no. 1. *Plains Anthropologist* 9:65–145.

1987   *Human osteology.* Special Publication no. 2. Columbia: Missouri Archaeological Society.

Bass, W. M., D. R. Evans, and R. L. Jantz
  1971   *The Leavenworth site cemetery: Archaeology and physical anthropology.* University of Kansas Publications in Anthropology no. 2. Lawrence.
Bateman, R., I. Goddard, R. O'Grady, V. A. Funk, R. Mooi, W. J. Kress, and P. Cannell
  1990   Speaking of forked tongues: The feasibility of reconciling human phylogeny and the history of language. *Current Anthropology* 31:1–24.
Beardsley, R. K., P. Holder, A. D. Krieger, B. J. Meggars, J. B. Rinaldo, P. Kutsche
  1956   Functional and evolutionary implications of community patterning. In *Seminars in archaeology 1955,* edited by R. Wauchope, 129–57. Society for American Archaeology Memoir no. 11. Washington, D.C.
Ben-Itzhak, S., P. Smith, and R. A. Bloom
  1988   Radiographic study of the humerus in Neandertals and *Homo sapiens sapiens. American Journal of Physical Anthropology* 77:231–42.
Bender, M. M.
  1971   Variations in the ^{13}C and ^{12}C ratios of plants in relation to the pathway of photosynthetic carbon dioxide fixation. *Phytochemistry* 10:1239–44.
Benson, L. V., and R. S. Thompson
  1987   Lake level variation in the Lahontan Basin for the past 50,000 years. *Quaternary Research* 28:69–85.
Berry, M. S.
  1974   The Evans Mound: Cultural adaptation in southwestern Utah. M.A. thesis, Department of Anthropology, University of Utah, Salt Lake City.
Bettinger, R. L.
  1978   Alternative adaptive strategies in the prehistoric Great Basin. *Journal of Anthropological Research* 34(1):27–46.
  1987   Archaeological approaches to hunter-gatherers. *Annual Review of Anthropology* 16:121–42.
  1989   *The archeology of Pinyon House, Two Eagles, and Crater Middens: Three residential sites in Owens Valley, eastern California.* American Museum of Natural History Anthropoplogical Papers no. 67. New York.
  1991a Aboriginal occupation at high-altitude: Alpine villages in the White Mountains of eastern California. *American Anthropologist* 93:656–79.
  1991b *Hunter-gatherers: Anthropological and archeological theory.* New York: Plenum Press.
  1993   Doing Great Basin archaeology recently: Coping with variability. *Journal of Archaeological Research* 1:43–66.
  1994   How, when and why Numic spread. In *Across the West: Human population movement and the expansion of the Numa,* edited by D. B. Madsen and D. Rhode, 44–55. Salt Lake City: University of Utah Press.
Bettinger, R. L., and M. A. Baumhoff
  1982   The Numic spread: Great Basin cultures in competition. *American Antiquity* 47:485–503.
Billat, L. B., and S. E. Billat
  1988   *The Salina Sisters burial sites: Archaeological investigations along the Mountain Fuel Supply Pipeline in central and southwestern Utah.* Brigham Young University Museum of Peoples and Cultures Technical Series no. 88. Provo, Utah.
Binford, L. R.
  1979   Organization and formation processes: Looking at curated technologies. *Journal of Anthropological Research* 35:255–73.

1980   Willow smoke and dogs' tails: Hunter-gatherer settlement systems and archaeo-
        logical site formation. *American Antiquity* 45:4–20.
1982   The archaeology of place. *Journal of Anthropological Archaeology* 1(1):5–31.
1983   *In pursuit of the past: Decoding the archaeological record.* London: Thames and
        Hudson.
1986   In pursuit of the future. In *American archaeology past and future: A celebration of
        the Society for American Archaeology, 1935–1985,* edited by D. J. Meltzer, D. D.
        Fowler, and J. A. Sabloff, 459–79. Washington, D.C.: Smithsonian Institution
        Press.

Black, T. K.
1978   A new method of assessing the sex of fragmentary skeletal remains: Femoral shaft
        circumference. *American Journal of Anatomy* 4:19–31.

Blakey, M. L., and G. J. Armelagos
1985   Deciduous enamel defects in prehistoric Americans from Dickson Mounds:
        Prenatal and postnatal stress. *American Journal of Physical Anthropology* 66:
        371–80.

Blakey, M. L., T. E. Leslie, and J. P. Reidy
1994   Frequency and chronological distribution of dental enamel hypoplasia in en-
        slaved African Americans: A test of the weaning hypothesis. *American Journal of
        Physical Anthropology* 95:371–83.

Boas, F.
1911   Introduction. In *Handbook of American Indian languages,* edited by F. Boas, 1–84.
        Washington, D.C.: Smithsonian Institution.

Bogdan, G., and D. S. Weaver
1992   Pre-Columbian treponematosis in coastal North Carolina. In *Disease and demog-
        raphy in the Americas,* edited by J. W. Verano and D. H. Ubelaker, 155–63. Wash-
        ington, D.C.: Smithsonian Institution Press.

Boyer, S. H.
1961   Alkaline phosphatase in human sera and placentae. *Science* 134:1002.

Bradstreet, R. B.
1965   *The Kjeldahl method for organic nitrogen.* Orlando, Florida: Academic Press.

Braidwood, R. J.
1960   The agricultural revolution. *Scientific American* 203:130–48.

Bridges, P. S.
1985   Changes in long bone structure with the transition to agriculture: Implications
        for prehistoric activities. Ph.D. diss., University of Michigan, Ann Arbor.
1989a   Bone cortical area in the evaluation of nutrition and activity levels. *American
        Journal of Human Biology* 1:785–92.
1989b   Changes in activities with the shift to agriculture in the southeastern United
        States. *Current Anthropology* 30:385–94.
1990   Osteological correlates of weapon use. In *A life in science: Papers in honor of
        J. Lawrence Angel,* edited by J. E. Buikstra, 87–98. Center for American Archae-
        ology Scientific Paper no. 6. Kampsville, Illinois.
1991   Degenerative joint disease in hunter-gatherers and agriculturalists from the
        southeastern United States. *American Journal of Physical Anthropology* 85:397–91.
1992   Prehistoric arthritis in the Americas. *Annual Review of Anthropology* 21:67–91.
1995   Biomechanical changes in long bone diaphyses with the intensification of agri-
        culture in the lower Illinois valley. *American Journal of Physical Anthropology*
        Suppl. 20:68.

1996   Skeletal biology and behavior in ancient humans. *Evolutionary Anthropology* 4:112–20.

Bright, J., M. Memmott, S. Simms, and A. Ugan
1998   Plain Gray ceramics and residential mobility in Utah's west. Paper presented at the 26th Great Basin Anthropological Conference, Bend, Oregon.

Brock, S. L., and C. B. Ruff
1988   Diachronic patterns of change in structural properties of the femur in the prehistoric American Southwest. *American Journal of Physical Anthropology* 75:113–27.

Brooks, R. H., and S. T. Brooks
1990   An interpretation of forager burial patterns in the Great Basin, suggested from analysis of human remains in two Nevada cave sites. Paper presented at the 22nd Great Basin Anthropological Conference, Reno, Nevada.

Brooks, S. T., and R. H. Brooks
1990   Who were the Stillwater Marsh people? *Halcyon* 12:63–74.

Brooks, S. T., M. B. Haldeman, and R. H. Brooks
1988   *Osteological analyses of the Stillwater skeletal series, Stillwater Marsh, Churchill County, Nevada.* U.S. Department of the Interior Fish and Wildlife Service, Region 1, Cultural Resource Series no. 2. Portland, Oregon.

1990   Unusual eburnation frequencies in a skeletal series from the Stillwater Marsh area, Nevada. In *Wetland adaptations in the Great Basin,* edited by J. C. Janetski and D. B. Madsen, 97–105. Brigham Young University Museum of Peoples and Cultures Occasional Papers no. 1. Provo, Utah.

Brown, J. A.
1985   Long-term trends to sedentism and the emergence of complexity in the American Midwest. In *Prehistoric hunter-gatherers: The emergence of cultural complexity,* edited by T. D. Price and J. A. Brown, 201–23. New York: Academic Press.

Burnside, C. D.
1990   Preliminary investigation at FY90 Mal 3, Tern Island, Malheur National Wildlife Refuge, Harney County, Oregon. Paper presented at the annual meeting of the Association of Oregon Archaeologists, Portland State University, Portland, Oregon.

1991   Surface artifacts reveal activity areas at a site on Malheur Lake, northern Great Basin. Paper presented at the 44th Northwest Anthropological Conference, Missoula, Montana.

1992   The reburial of human remains at Malheur National Wildlife Refuge. *Current archaeological happenings in Oregon (CAHO)* 17(2):3–5. Eugene: Association of Oregon Archaeologists, State Museum of Anthropology.

Campbell, L. R.
1986   Comments. *Current Anthropology* 27:488.

1997   *American Indian languages: The historical linguistics of Native America.* New York: Oxford University Press.

Carlson, D. S., G. J. Armelagos, and D. P. Van Gerven
1974   Factors influencing the etiology of cribra orbitalia in prehistoric Nubia. *Journal of Human Evolution* 3:405–10.

Carlson, R. L.
1959   Klamath henwas and other stone sculpture. *American Anthropologist* 61:88–96.

Carter, J., and D. Dugas
1994   Holocene occupation at Sodhouse Spring: Results of the 1993 field season. Paper presented at the 24th Great Basin Anthropological Conference, Elko, Nevada.

Cassidy, C. M.
  1984   Skeletal evidence for prehistoric subsistence adaptation in the central Ohio River
         valley. In *Paleopathology at the origins of agriculture,* edited by M. N. Cohen and
         G. J. Armelagos, 307–45. Orlando, Florida: Academic Press.

Cerling, T. E.
  n.d.   Plant delta ^{13}C sort. Ms. in possession of author.

Chamberlin, R. V.
  1911   *The ethnobotany of the Gosiute Indians.* Proceedings of the Academy of Natural
         Science of Philadelphia, vol. 63:24–99. Philadelphia.

Charnov, E. L.
  1976   Optimal foraging: The marginal value theorem. *Theoretical Population Biology*
         9:129–36.

Chayanov, A. V.
  1986   *A theory of peasant economy.* Oxford: Manchester University Press.

Chisholm, B. S., D. E. Nelson, and H. P. Schwarcz
  1982   Stable-carbon isotope ratios as a measure of marine versus terrestrial protein in
         ancient diets. *Science* 216:1131–32.

Chou, Q., R. Marion, D. E. Birch, J. Raymond, and W. Bloch
  1992   Prevention of pre-PCR mis-priming and primer dimerization improves low-
         copy-number amplifications. *Nucleic Acids Research* 20(7):1717–23.

Churchill, S. E.
  1994   Human upper body evolution in the Eurasian later Pleistocene. Ph.D. diss., Uni-
         versity of New Mexico, Albuquerque.

Clarke, S. K.
  1982   The association of early childhood enamel hypoplasias and radiopaque transverse
         lines in a culturally diverse prehistoric skeletal sample. *Human Biology* 54(1):77–84.

Clarke, S. K., and P. Gindhart
  1981   Commonality in peak age of early-childhood morbidity across cultures and over
         time. *Current Anthropology* 22(5):574–75.

Cobb, S.
  1971   *The frequency of rheumatic diseases.* Cambridge, Harvard University Press.

Cockburn, A., H. Duncan, and J. M. Riddle
  1979   Arthritis, ancient and modern: Guidelines for field workers. *Henry Ford Hospital
         Medical Journal* 27:74–79.

Cohen, M. N., and G. J. Armelagos, eds.
  1984   *Paleopathology at the origins of agriculture.* Orlando, Florida: Academic Press.

Coltrain, J. B.
  1993   Fremont corn agriculture in the eastern Great Basin: A pilot stable carbon iso-
         tope study. *Utah Archaeology 1993* 6(1):49–55.
  1997   Fremont economic diversity: A stable carbon isotope study of Formative subsis-
         tence practices in the eastern Great Basin. Ph.D. diss., Department of Anthro-
         pology, University of Utah, Salt Lake City.

Connolly, T. J., D. L. Jenkins, and J. Benjamin
  1993   *Archaeology of Mitchell Cave (35WH122): A late period hunting camp in the Ochoco
         Mountains, Wheeler County, Oregon.* University of Oregon Anthropological Pa-
         pers no. 46. Eugene.

Cook, D. C.
  1971   Patterns of nutritional stress in some Illinois Woodland populations. M.A. the-
         sis, University of Chicago, Chicago.

1984   Subsistence and health in the lower Illinois valley: Osteological evidence. In *Paleopathology at the origins of agriculture*, edited by M. N. Cohen and G. J. Armelagos, 235–69. Orlando, Florida: Academic Press.

Cornell, A., M. E. Stuart, and S. R. Simms
1992   An obsidian cache from the Great Salt Lake wetlands, Weber County, Utah. *Utah Archaeology* 5:154–59.

Corruccini, R. S., J. S. Handler, and K. P. Jacobi
1985   Chronological distribution of enamel hypoplasias and weaning in a Caribbean slave population. *Human Biology* 57:699–711.

Cotran, R. S., V. Kumar, and S. L. Robbins
1944   *Robbins pathologic basis of disease.* 5th ed. Philadelphia: W. B. Saunders.

Couture, M. D.
1978   Recent and contemporary foraging practices of the Harney Valley Paiute. M.A. thesis, Department of Anthropology, Portland State University, Portland, Oregon.

Couture, M. D., M. F. Ricks, and L. Housley
1986   Foraging behavior of a contemporary northern Great Basin population. *Journal of California and Great Basin Anthropology* 8(2):150–60.

Cowan, R. A.
1967   *Lake-margin ecologic exploitation in the Great Basin as demonstrated by an analysis of coprolites from Lovelock Cave, Nevada.* University of California Archaeological Survey Reports no. 70:21–35. Berkeley.

Craig, H.
1957   Isotopic standards for carbon and oxygen and correction factors for mass-spectrometric analysis of carbon dioxide. *Geochemica et Cosmochimica Acta* 12: 133–49.

Crapo, R. H., and B. R. Spykerman
1979   Social variation in Shoshoni phonology: An ecological interpretation. *Human Ecology* 7:317–32.

Cressman, L. S.
1933   *Contributions to the archaeology of Oregon: Final report on the Gold Hill burial site.* University of Oregon Studies in Anthropology no. 1(1). Eugene.
1942   *Archaeological researches in the northern Great Basin.* Carnegie Institution of Washington Publication no. 538. Washington, D.C.
1956   *Klamath prehistory.* Transactions of the American Philosophical Society 46(4). Philadelphia.
1986   Prehistory of the northern area. In *Handbook of North American Indians*, vol. 11: *Great Basin*, edited by W. L. d'Azevedo, 120–26. Washington, D.C.: Smithsonian Institution Press.

Danforth, M. E., K. S. Herndon, and K. B. Propst
1993   A preliminary study of patterns of replication in scoring linear enamel hypoplasias. *International Journal of Osteoarchaeology* 3:297–302.

Davis, J. O.
1982   Bits and pieces: The last 35,000 years in the Lahontan area, Nevada and California. In *Man and environment in the Great Basin*, edited by D. B. Madsen and J. F. O'Connell, 53–75. Society for American Archaeology Selected Paper no. 2. Washington, D.C.

d'Azevedo, W. L., W. Davis, D. D. Fowler, and W. Suttles, eds.
1966   *The current status of anthropological research in the Great Basin: 1964.* Desert

Research Institute Publications in the Social Sciences no. 1. Reno and Las Vegas, Nevada.

Dean, P. A.
1992   Prehistoric pottery in the northeastern Great Basin: Problems in the classification and archaeological interpretation of undecorated Fremont and Shoshoni wares. Ph.D. diss., Department of Anthropology, University of Oregon, Eugene.

Decker, K. W., and L. L. Teiszen
1989   Isotopic reconstruction of Mesa Verde diet from Basketmaker III to Pueblo III. *Kiva* 55:33–44.

DeNiro, M. J., and S. Epstein
1978   Influence of diet on the distribution of carbon isotopes in animals. *Geochimica et Cosmochimica Acta* 42:495–506.
1981   Influence of diet on the distribution of nitrogen isotopes in animals. *Geochimica et Cosmochimica Acta* 45:341–51.

De Niro, M. J., and M. J. Schoeninger
1983   Stable carbon and nitrogen isotope ratios of bone collagen: Variations within individuals, between sexes, and within populations raised on monotonous diets. *Journal of Archaeological Science* 10:199–203.

DeNiro, M. J., M. J. Schoeninger, and C. A. Hastorf
1985   Effect of heating on the stable carbon and nitrogen isotope ratios of bone collagen. *Journal of Archaeological Science* 12:1–7.

DeQuille, D. (W. Wright)
1963   *Washoe rambles.* Los Angeles: Westernlore Press.

DeRousseau, D. J.
1988   *Osteoarthritis in rhesus monkeys and gibbons: A locomotor model of joint degeneration.* Contributions to Primatology no. 25. Basel: Karger.

Dickel, D. N., P. D. Schulz, and H. M. McHenry
1984   Central California: Prehistoric subsistence change and health. In *Paleopathology at the origins of agriculture,* edited by M. N. Cohen and G. J. Armelagos, 439–62. New York: Academic Press.

Dobney, K., and A. H. Goodman
1991   Epidemiological studies of dental enamel hypoplasias in Mexico and Bradford: Their relevance to archaeological skeletal studies. In *Health in past societies: Biocultural interpretations of human skeletal remains in archaeological contexts,* edited by H. Bush and M. Zvelebil, 81–100. BAR International Series no. 567. Oxford, England: British Archaeological Reports.

Dodd, W. A., Jr.
1982   *Final year excavations at the Evans Mound site.* University of Utah Anthropological Papers no. 106. Salt Lake City: University of Utah Press.

Don, R. H., P. T. Cox, B. J. Wainwright, K. Baker, and J. S. Mattick
1992   "Touchdown" PCR to circumvent spurious priming during gene amplification. *Nucleic Acids Research* 19(14):4008.

Dongoske, K. E.
1996   The Native American Graves Protection and Repatriation Act: A new beginning, not the end, for osteological analysis—a Hopi perspective. *American Indian Quarterly* 20:287–98.

Downton, W. J. S.
1975   The occurrence of C_4 photosynthesis among plants. *Photosynthetica* 9:96–105.

Driver, H. E.

   1961   *Indians of North America.* Chicago: University of Chicago Press.

Duebbert, H. F.

   1969   *The ecology of Malheur Lake and management implications.* Princeton, Oregon:
          U.S. Fish and Wildlife Service, Malheur National Wildlife Refuge.

Duncan, H.

   1979   Osteoarthritis. *In* Arthritis: Modern concepts and ancient evidence, edited by
          A. H. Cockburn, 6–9. *Henry Ford Hospital Medical Journal* 27.

Easton, R. D., D. A. Merriwether, D. E. Crews, and R. E. Ferrell

   1996   Mitochondrial DNA variation in the Yanomami: Evidence for additional New
          World founding lineages. *American Journal of Human Genetics* 59(1):213–25.

Eddy, J. A., and R. S. Bradley

   1991   Changes in time in the temperature of the earth. In *Global changes of the past,*
          edited by R. S. Bradley, 61–81. Boulder, Colorado: OIES.

Edynak, G. J.

   1976   Life-styles from skeletal material: A medieval Yugoslov example. In *The measures
          of man,* edited by E. Giles and J. S. Friedlaender, 408–32. Cambridge, Massachu-
          setts: Peabody Museum Press.

Eichner, E. R.

   1989   Does running cause osteoarthritis? *Physical Sports Medicine* 17:147–54.

Elston, R. G.

   1982   Good times, hard times: Prehistoric culture change in the western Great Basin.
          In *Man and environment in the Great Basin,* edited by D. B. Madsen and J. F.
          O'Connell, 186–206. Society for American Archaeology Papers no. 2. Washing-
          ton, D.C.

   1988   Flaked stone tools. In *Preliminary investigations in Stillwater Marsh: Human his-
          tory and geoarchaeology,* vol. 1, 155–83. U.S. Fish and Wildlife Service Cultural
          Resource Series no. 1. Portland, Oregon.

   1994   How will I know you? Archaeological visibility of the Numic spread in the west-
          ern Great Basin. In *Across the West: Human population movement and the expan-
          sion of the Numa* edited by D. B. Madsen and D. Rhode, 150–51. Salt Lake City:
          University of Utah Press.

Elston, R. G., and D. P. Dugas, eds.

   1993   *Dune Islands and the archaeological record in Malheur Lake.* U.S. Department of
          the Interior Fish and Wildlife service, Region 1, Cultural Resource Series no. 7.
          Portland, Oregon.

Elston, R. G., D. P. Dugas, K. Ataman, E. Ingbar, and M. Bullock

   1993a The archaeology of 35HA1899. In *Dune Islands and the archaeological record in
          Malheur Lake,* edited by R. G. Elston and D. P. Dugas, 39–62. U.S. Department
          of the Interior Fish and Wildlife Service, Region 1, Cultural Resource Series no.
          7. Portland, Oregon.

   1993b The archaeology of 35HA1904. In *Dune Islands and the archaeological record in
          Malheur Lake,* edited by R. G. Elston and D. P. Dugas, 63–86. U.S. Department
          of the Interior Fish and Wildlife Service, Region 1, Cultural Resource Series no.
          7. Portland, Oregon.

Endo, B., and T. Kimura

   1970   Postcranial skeleton of the Amud man. In *The Amud man and his cave site,* edited
          by H. Suzuki and F. Takai, 231–406. Tokyo: Academic Press.

Engel, A.
1968 *Osteoarthritis and body measurements.* National Center for Health Statistics Series, vol. II, no. 29. Washington, D.C.

Engel, A., and T. A. Burch
1966 *Osteoarthritis in adults by selected demographic characteristics.* National Center for Health Statistics Series, vol. II, no. 20. Washington, D.C.

Enger, W. D., and W. Blair
1947 Crania from the Warren Mounds and their possible significance to Northern Periphery archaeology. *American Antiquity* 13:142–46.

Eveleth, P. B., and J. M. Tanner
1990 *Worldwide variation in human growth.* 2d ed. Cambridge, England: Cambridge University Press.

Ezzo, J. A.
1993 *Human adaptation at Grasshopper Pueblo, Arizona.* International Monographs in Prehistory, Archaeological Series 4. Ann Arbor, Michigan.

Fagan, J. L.
1974 *Altithermal occupation of spring sites in the northern Great Basin.* University of Oregon Anthropological Papers no. 6. Eugene.

Falhström, G.
1981 The glenohumeral joint in man: An anatomic-experimental and archaeo-osteological study on joint function. *Ossa* 8 (Suppl. 1):1–154.

Farquhar, G. D.
1983 On the nature of carbon isotope discrimination in C_4 species. *Australian Journal of Plant Physiology* 9:121–37.

Fawcett, W. B., and S. R. Simms, eds.
1993 *Archaeological test excavations in the Great Salt Lake wetlands and associated analyses, Weber and Box Elder Counties, Utah.* Utah State University Contributions to Anthropology no. 14. Logan.

Fédération Dentaire International
1982 An epidemiological index of developmental defects of dental enamel (DDE index). *International Dental Journal* 32:159–67.

Filon D., M. Faerman, P. Smith, and A. Oppenheim
1995 Sequence analysis reveals a β-thalassaemia mutation in the DNA of skeletal remains from the archaeological site of Akhziv, Israel. *Nature Genetics* 9:365–68.

Fogel, M. L., N. Tuross, and D. W. Owsley
1989 *Nitrogen isotope tracers of human lactation in modern and archaeological populations.* Annual Report of the Director, Geophysical Laboratory of the Carnegie Institution of Washington, vol 89:111–17. Washington, D.C.

Forsyth, D. W.
1984 *Preliminary report of archaeological investigations at the Smoking Pipe site (42Ut150), Utah Valley, Utah: The 1983 and 1984 seasons.* Brigham Young University Museum of Peoples and Cultures Technical Series no. 84–92. Provo, Utah.

Fowler, C. S.
1972 Some ecological clues to proto-Numic homelands. In *Great Basin cultural ecology: A symposium,* edited by D. D. Fowler, 105–22. Desert Research Institute Publications in the Social Sciences no. 8. Reno and Las Vegas, Nevada.

1982a Food-named groups among Northern Paiute in North America's Great Basin: An ecological interpretation. In *Resource managers: North American and Australian hunter-gatherers,* edited by N. M. Williams and E. S. Hunn, 113–29. American Association for the Advancement of Science Selected Symposium no. 67. Boulder, Colorado.

1982b   Settlement patterns and subsistence systems in the Great Basin: The ethnographic record. In *Man and environment in the Great Basin,* edited by D. B. Madsen and J. F. O'Connell, 121–38. Society for American Archaeology Papers no. 2. Washington, D.C.

1990a   Ethnographic perspectives on marsh-based cultures in western Nevada. In *Wetland adaptations in the Great Basin,* edited by J. C. Janetski and D. B. Madsen, 17–32. Brigham Young University Museum of Peoples and Cultures Occasional Papers no. 1. Provo, Utah.

1990b   *Tule technology: Northern Paiute uses of marsh resources in western Nevada.* Washington, D.C.: Smithsonian Institution Press.

1992   *In the shadow of Fox Peak: An ethnography of the Cattail-Eater Northern Paiute people of Stillwater Marsh.* U.S. Department of the Interior Fish and Wildlife Service, Region 1, Cultural Resource Series no. 5. Portland Oregon.

_____, comp. and ed.

1989   *Willard Z. Park's ethnographic notes on the Northern Paiute of western Nevada, 1933–1944,* vol. 1. University of Utah Anthropological Papers no. 114. Salt Lake City: University of Utah Press.

Fowler, C. S., and J. Bath

1981   Pyramid Lake Northern Paiute fishing: The ethnographic record. *Journal of California and Great Basin Anthropology* 3:176–86.

Fowler, C. S., and D. D. Fowler

1990   A history of wetlands anthropology in the Great Basin. In *Wetlands adaptations in the Great Basin,* edited by J. C. Janetski and D. B. Madsen, 5–16. Brigham Young University Museum of Peoples and Cultures Occasional Papers no. 1. Provo, Utah.

Fowler, C. S., and S. Liljeblad

1986   Northern Paiute. In *Handbook of North American Indians,* vol. 11: *Great Basin,* edited by W. L. d'Azevedo, 435–65. Washington, D.C.: Smithsonian Institution Press.

Fowler, D. D., ed.

1977   *Models and Great Basin prehistory: A symposium.* Desert Research Institute Publications in the Social Sciences no. 12. Reno and Las Vegas, Nevada.

Freidel, D. E.

1994   Paleolake shorelines and lake level chronology of the Fort Rock Basin, Oregon. In *Archaeological researches in the northern Great Basin: Fort Rock archaeology since Cressman,* edited by C. M. Aikens and D. L. Jenkins, 21–40. University of Oregon Anthropological Papers no. 50. Eugene.

Frémont, J. C.

[1845] 1988   *The exploring expedition to the Rocky Mountains.* Reprint. Washington, D.C.: Smithsonian Institution Press.

Fresia, A., C. B. Ruff, and C. S. Larsen

1990   *Temporal decline in bilateral asymmetry of the upper limb on the Georgia coast.* American Museum of Natural History Anthropological Papers no. 68:121–32. New York.

Fromkin, V., and R. Rodman

    1993   Language in society. In *An introduction to language,* edited by V. Fromkin and R. Rodman, 273–321. New York: Harcourt Brace Jovanovich.

Fry, G. F.

    1970   Appendix III: Preliminary analysis of the Hogup Cave coprolites. In *Hogup Cave,* by C. M. Aikens, 247–50. University of Utah Anthropological Papers no. 93. Salt Lake City: University of Utah Press.

Fry, G. F., and G. F. Dalley

    1979   *The Levee site and the Knoll site.* University of Utah Anthropological Papers no. 100. Salt Lake City: University of Utah Press.

Galliher, M.

    1978   Anthropometry and paleodemography of selected Great Basin sites. M.A. thesis, University of Nevada, Las Vegas.

Garn, S. M., C. G. Rohmann, F. Behar, F. Viteri, and M. A. Guzman

    1964   Compact bone deficiency in protein-calorie malnutrition. *Science* 145:1444–45.

Garten, C. T. J., and G. E. J. Taylor

    1992   Foliar $\delta^{13}C$ within a temperate deciduous forest: Spatial, temporal, and species sources of variation. *Oecologia* 90:1–7.

Giesen, M., and L. M. Gagne

    1996   NAGPRA: A review of 1995 regulations and current case law. Paper posted on the Internet and presented at the Flint Hills Archaeological Conference in St. Joseph, Missouri, March 1996.

Gilbert, B. M.

    1973   Misapplication to females of the standard for aging the male *os pubis. American Journal of Physical Anthropology* 38:39–40.

Gilbert, B. M., and T. W. McKern

    1973   A method for aging the female *os pubis. American Journal of Physical Anthropology* 38:31–38.

Gilman, P. A.

    1987   Architecture as artifact: Pit structures and pueblos in the American Southwest. *American Antiquity* 52:538–64.

Goodman, A. H.

    1989   Dental enamel hypoplasias in prehistoric populations. *Advances in Dental Research* 3:264–71.

Goodman, A. H., L. H. Allen, G. P. Hernandez, A. Amador, L. V. Arriola, A. Chavez, and G. H. Pelto

    1987   Prevalence and age at development of enamel hypoplasia in Mexican children. *American Journal of Physical Anthropology* 72:7–19.

Goodman, A. H., and G. J. Armelagos

    1985a   The chronological distribution of enamel hypoplasia in human permanent incisor and canine teeth. *Archives of Oral Biology* 30:503–7.

    1985b   Factors affecting the distribution of enamel hypoplasias within the human permanent dentition. *American Journal of Physical Anthropology* 68:479–93.

Goodman, A. H., G. J. Armelagos, and J. C. Rose

    1980   Enamel hypoplasias as indicators of stress in three prehistoric populations from Illinois. *Human Biology* 52:515–28.

Goodman, A. H., and L. L. Capasso, eds.

1992 *Recent contributions to the study of enamel development defects.* Journal of Paleo-pathology Monographic Publications no. 2. Chieti, Italy: Associazione Antropologica Abruzzese.

Goodman, A. H., J. Lallo, G. J. Armelagos, and J. C. Rose

1984 Health changes at Dickson Mounds, Illinois (A.D. 950–1300). In *Paleopathology at the origins of agriculture,* edited by M. N. Cohen and G. J. Armelagos, 271–305. Orlando, Florida: Academic Press.

Goodman, A. H., D. L. Martin, G. J. Armelagos, and G. Clark

1984 Indications of stress from bone and teeth. In *Paleopathology at the origins of agriculture,* edited by M. N. Cohen and G. J. Armelagos, 13–44. Orlando, Florida: Academic Press.

Goodman, A. H., C. Martinez, and A. Chavez

1991 Nutritional supplementation and the development of linear enamel hypoplasias in children from Tezonteopan, Mexico. *American Journal of Clinical Nutrition* 53:773–81.

Goodman, A. H., and J. C. Rose

1990 Assessment of systemic physiological perturbations from dental enamel hypoplasias and associated histological structures. *Yearbook of Physical Anthropology* 33:59–110.

Goodman A. H., R. B. Thomas, A. C. Swedlung, and G. J. Armelagos

1988 Biocultural perspectives on stress in prehistoric, historical, and contemporary population research. *Yearbook of Physical Anthropology* 31:169–202.

Goss, J. A.

1977 Linguistic tools for the Great Basin prehistorian. In *Models and Great Basin prehistory: A symposium,* edited by D. D. Fowler, 48–70. Desert Research Institute Publications in the Social Sciences no. 12. Reno and Las Vegas, Nevada.

Grauer, A. L., ed.

1995 *Bodies of evidence: Reconstructing history through skeletal analysis.* New York: Wiley-Liss.

Grayson, D. K.

1984 *Quantitative zooarchaeology.* New York: Academic Press.

1993 *The desert's past: A natural prehistory of the Great Basin.* Washington, D.C.: Smithsonian Institution Press.

Greenberg, J.

1987 *Language in the Americas.* Palo Alto, California: Stanford University Press.

Griffin, M. C., and C. S. Larsen

1989 Patterns in osteoarthritis: A case study from the prehistoric and historic southeastern U.S. Atlantic Coast. *American Journal of Physical Anthropology* 78:232.

Griffiths, H.

1992 Carbon isotope discrimination and the integration of carbon assimilation pathways in terrestrial CAM plants. *Plant, Cell and Environment* 15:1051–62.

Grine, F. E., W. L. Jungers, P. V. Tobias, and O. M. Pearson

1995 Fossil *Homo* femur from Berg Aukas, northern Namibia. *American Journal of Physical Anthropology* 97:151–85.

Griset, S., ed.

1986 *Pottery of the Great Basin and adjacent areas.* University of Utah Anthropological Papers no. 111. Salt Lake City: University of Utah Press.

Grosscup, G. L.

1960   *The culture history of Lovelock Cave, Nevada.* University of California Archaeological Survey Reports no. 52:1–72. Berkeley.

Gunnerson, J. H.

1969   *The Fremont culture: A study in cultural dynamics on the northern Anasazi frontier.* Papers of the Peabody Museum of Archaeology and Ethnology, vol. 59, no. 2. Cambridge, Massachusetts: Harvard University.

Gurtler, L. G., V. Jager, W. Gruber, I. Hillmar, R. Schoblock, P. K. Muller, and G. Ziegelmayer

1981   Presence of proteins in human bones 200, 1200 and 1500 years of age. *Human Biology* 53:137–50.

Habicht-Mauche, J. A., A. A. Levendosky, and M. J. Schoeninger

1994   Antelope Creek phase subsistence: The bone chemistry evidence. In *Skeletal biology in the Great Plains: Migration, warfare, health, and subsistence,* edited by D. W. Owsley and R. L. Jantz, 291–304. Washington, D.C.: Smithsonian Institution Press.

Hagelberg, E.

1994   Mitochondrial DNA from ancient bones. In *Ancient DNA,* edited by B. Herrmann and S. Hummel, 195–204. New York: Springer-Verlag.

Hagelberg, E., L. S. Bell, T. Allen, A. Boyde, S. Jones, and J. B. Clegg

1991   *Analysis of ancient bone DNA: Techniques and applications.* Philosophical Transactions of the Royal Society of London, Series B, vol. 333:399–407. London, England.

Hagelberg, E., and J. B. Clegg

1991   *Isolation and characterization of DNA from archeological bone.* Proceedings of the Royal Society of London, Series B, vol. 244:45–50. London, England.

1993   *Genetic polymorphisms in prehistoric Pacific islanders determined by analysis of ancient bone DNA.* Proceedings of the Royal Society of London, Series B, vol. 252:163–70. London, England.

Handt, O., M. Höss, M. Krings, and S. Pääbo

1994   Ancient DNA: Methodological challenges. *Experientia* 50:524–29

Handt, O., M. Krings, R. M. Ward, and S. Pääbo

1996   The retrieval of ancient human DNA sequences. *American Journal of Human Genetics* 59:368–76.

Harkness, D. D., and A. Walton

1972   Further investigations of the transfer of bomb ^{14}C to man. *Nature* 240:302–3.

Harper, K. T.

1967   Appendix: The vegetational environment of the Bear River No. 2 archaeological site. In *Excavations at Snake Rock Village and the Bear River No. 2 site,* by C. M. Aikens, 62–65. University of Utah Anthropological Papers no. 87. Salt Lake City: University of Utah Press.

Harris, D. R.

1978   Settling down: An evolutionary model for the transition of mobile bands into sedentary communities. In *The evolution of social systems,* edited by J. Friedrich and M. S. Rowlands, 401–17. London: Duckworth.

Harrison, R. G.

1989   Animal mitochondrial DNA as a genetic marker in population and evolutionary biology. *Trends in Ecology and Evolution* 4:6–11.

Hassel, F. K.

1961   An open site near Plain City, Utah. *Utah Archaeologist 1961* 7(2).

Hastorf, C. A.

1991   Gender, space, and food in prehistory. In *Engendering archaeology,* edited by J. M.
        Gero and M. W. Conkey, 132–59. Cambridge, England: Blackwell.

Hastorf, C. A., and S. Johannessen

1993   Pre-Hispanic political change and the role of maize in the central Andes of Peru.
        American Anthropologist 95:115–38.

Heaton, T. H. E., J. C. Vogel, G. von la Chevallerie, and G. Gollett

1986   Climatic influence on the isotopic composition of bone nitrogen. *Nature*
        322:822–23.

Heizer, R. F.

1967   *Analysis of human coprolites from a dry Nevada cave.* University of California Ar-
        chaeological Survey Reports no. 70. Papers on Great Basin Archaeology nos.
        1–20. Berkeley.

1970   Ethnographic notes on the Northern Paiute of the Humboldt Sink, west-central
        Nevada. In *Languages and cultures of western North America: Essays in honor of
        Sven S. Liljeblad,* edited by E. H. Swanson, Jr., 232–45. Pocatello: Idaho State
        University Press.

Heizer, R. F., and A. D. Krieger

1956   *The archaeology of Humboldt Cave, Churchill County, Nevada.* University of Cali-
        fornia Publications in American Archaeology and Ethnology no. 47(1). Berkeley.

Heizer, R. F., and L. K. Napton

1970   *Archaeology and the prehistoric Great Basin lacustrine subsistence regime as seen from
        Lovelock Cave, Nevada.* Contributions of the University of California Archaeo-
        logical Research Facility no. 10. Berkeley.

Hemphill, B. E.

1990   Human remains. In *An archaeological survey of the recently flooded shores of Mal-
        heur Lake, Harney County, Oregon,* edited by A. C. Oetting, 95–117. Heritage Re-
        search Associates Report no. 97. Eugene, Oregon. Submitted to the Oregon State
        Historic Preservation Office. (Report on file, State Historic Preservation Office,
        Salem, Oregon)

1992a   *An osteological analysis of the human remains from Malheur Lake, Oregon,* vol. 1:
        HRA field seasons, 1988–1990. U.S. Department of the Interior Fish and Wildlife
        Service, Region 1, Cultural Resource Series no. 6. Heritage Research Associates
        Report no. 118. Portland, Oregon. (Report on file, Malheur National Wildlife
        Refuge, Princeton, Oregon)

1992b   *An osteological analysis of the human remains from Malheur Lake, Oregon,* vol. 2:
        Refuge field season, 1990. U.S. Department of the Interior Fish and Wildlife Ser-
        vice, Region 1, Cultural Resource Series no. 6. Heritage Research Associates
        Report no. 118. Portland, Oregon. (Report on file, Malheur National Wildlife
        Refuge, Princeton, Oregon)

1992c   *An osteological analysis of the human remains from Malheur Lake, Oregon,* vol. 3:
        Refuge field season, 1991. U.S. Department of the Interior Fish and Wildlife Ser-
        vice, Region 1, Cultural Resource Series no. 6. Heritage Research Associates
        Report no. 118. Portland, Oregon. (Report on file, Malheur National Wildlife
        Refuge, Princeton, Oregon)

Herrmann, B., and S. Hummel

1993   *Ancient DNA: Recovery and analysis of genetic material from paleontological, archaeological, museum, medical, and forensic specimens.* New York: Springer-Verlag.

Hettinga, D. L.

1980   Normal joint structures and their reactions to injury. *Journal of Orthopedics of Sports and Physical Therapy* 1:178–85

Heyer, E.

1995   Mitochondrial and nuclear genetic contribution of female founders to a contemporary population in northeast Quebec. *American Journal of Human Genetics* 56:1450–55.

Hillson, S.

1979   Diet and dental disease. *World Archaeology* 11:147–62.

1986   *Teeth.* Cambridge, England: Cambridge University Press.

1996   *Dental anthropology.* Cambridge, England: Cambridge University Press.

Hitchcock, R. K.

1982   Patterns of sedentism among the Basarwa of eastern Botswana. In *Politics and history in band societies,* edited by E. Leacock and R. Lee, 223–67. Cambridge, England: Cambridge University Press.

1987   Sedentism and site structure: Organizational change in Kalahari Basarwa residential locations. In *Method and theory for activity area research,* edited by S. Kent, 374–423. New York: Columbia University Press.

Hodges, D. C.

1987   Health and agricultural intensification in the prehistoric valley of Oaxaca, Mexico. *American Journal of Physical Anthropology* 73:323–32.

1989   *Agricultural intensification and prehistoric health in the valley of Oaxaca, Mexico.* University of Michigan Museum of Anthropology Memoir no. 22. Ann Arbor.

Holland, T.D., and M. J. O'Brien

1997   Parasites, porotic hyperostosis, and the implications of changing perspectives. *American Antiquity* 62:183–93.

Holmer, R. N.

1994   In search of the ancestral Northern Shoshoni. In *Across the West: Human population movement and the expansion of the Numa,* edited by D. B. Madsen and D. Rhode, 179–87. Salt Lake City: University of Utah Press.

Holmer, R. N., and D. G. Weder

1980   Common post-Archaic projectile points of the Fremont area. In *Fremont perspectives,* edited by D. B. Madsen, 55–68. Antiquities Section Selected Papers no. 16. Salt Lake City: Utah State Historical Society.

Hopkins, N. A.

1965   Great Basin prehistory and Uto-Aztecan. *American Antiquity* 31:48–60.

Horai, S., R. Kondo, Y. Nakagawa-Hattori, S. Hayashi, S. Sonoda, and K. Tajima

1993   Peopling of the Americas, founded by four major lineages of the mitochondrial DNA. *Molecular Biology and Evolution* 10:23–47.

Hough, A. J., and L. Sokoloff

1989   Pathology of osteoarthritis. In *Arthritis and allied conditions,* edited by D. J. McCarty, 1571–94. 11th ed. Philadelphia: Lea & Febiger.

Hrdlička, A.

1935   The pueblos. *American Journal of Physical Anthropology* 20(o.s.):235–460.

Hughes, R. E.

1990   The Gold Hill site: Evidence for a prehistoric socioceremonial system in south-
       western Oregon. In *Living with the land: The Indians of southwest Oregon*, edited
       by N. Hannon and R. K. Olmo, 48–55. Medford: Southern Oregon Historical
       Society.

1994   Methodological observations on Great Basin prehistory. In *Across the West: Hu-
       man population movement and the expansion of the Numa*, edited by D. B. Mad-
       sen and D. Rhode, 67–70. Salt Lake City: University of Utah Press.

Huiskes, R.

1982   On the modelling of long bones in structural analyses. *Journal of Biomechanics*
       15:65–69.

Hummert, J. R., and D. P. Van Gerven

1985   Observations on the formation and persistence of radiopaque transverse lines.
       American Journal of Physical Anthropology 66:297–306.

Hunt, A.

1953   *Archaeological survey of the La Sal Mountain area, Utah.* University of Utah An-
       thropological Papers no. 14. Salt Lake City: University of Utah Press.

Huss-Ashmore, R., A. H. Goodman, and G. J. Armelagos

1982   Nutritional inference from paleopathology. In *Advances in archaeological method
       and theory,* vol. 5, edited by M. B. Schiffer, 393–474. New York: Academic Press.

Hutchinson, D. L., and C. S. Larsen

1988   Determination of stress episode duration from linear enamel hypoplasias: A case
       study from St. Catherines Island, Georgia. *Human Biology* 60:93–110.

1990   Stress and lifeway change: The evidence from enamel hypoplasias. In *The archae-
       ology of Mission Santa Catalina de Guale,* pt. 2: *Biocultural interpretations of a pop-
       ulation in transition,* edited by C. S. Larsen, 50–65. American Museum of Nat-
       ural History Anthropological Papers no. 68. New York.

1995   Physiological stress in the prehistoric Stillwater Marsh: Evidence of enamel de-
       fects. In *Bioarchaeology of the Stillwater Marsh: Prehistoric human adaptation in
       the western Great Basin,* edited by C. S. Larsen and R. L. Kelly, 81–95. American
       Museum of Natural History Anthropological Papers no. 77. New York.

Iscan, M. Y., and K. A. R. Kennedy, eds.

1989   *Reconstruction of life from the skeleton.* New York: Alan R. Liss.

Janetski, J. C.

1986   The Great Basin lacustrine subsistence pattern: Insights from Utah Lake. In *An-
       thropology of the Desert West: Essays in honor of Jesse D. Jennings,* edited by Carol
       Condie and D. D. Fowler, 145–68. University of Utah Anthropological Papers
       no. 110. Salt Lake City: University of Utah Press.

1990   Wetlands in Utah Valley prehistory. In *Wetland adaptations in the Great Basin,*
       edited by J. C. Janetski and D. B. Madsen, 233–58. Brigham Young University
       Museum of Peoples and Cultures Occasional Papers no. 1. Provo, Utah.

1994   Recent transitions in the eastern Great Basin: The archaeological record. In
       Across the West: Human population movement and the expansion of the Numa,
       edited by D. B. Madsen and D. Rhode, 157–78. Salt Lake City: University of
       Utah Press.

1997   Fremont hunting and resource intensification in the eastern Great Basin. *Journal
       of Archaeological Science* 24:1075–88.

Janetski, J. C., and D. B. Madsen, eds.

1990   *Wetland adaptations in the Great Basin.* Brigham Young University Museum of Peoples and Cultures Occasional papers no. 1. Provo, Utah.

Janetski, J. C., and R. K. Talbot

1997   Social and community organization. In *Clear Creek Canyon archaeological project,* vol. 5, *Results and synthesis,* by J. C. Janetski, R. K. Talbot, D. E. Newman, L. D. Richens, J. D. Wilde, S. B. Baker, and S. E. Billat, 309–28. Brigham Young University Museum of Peoples and Cultures Technical Series 95–9. Provo, Utah.

Jaworski, Z. F. G., M. Liskova-Kiar, and H. K. Uhthoff

1980   Effect of long-term immobilisation on the pattern of bone loss in older dogs. *Journal of Bone and Joint Surgery* 62B:104–10.

Jenkins, D. L.

1994   Settlement-subsistence patterns in the Fort Rock Basin: A cultural-ecological perspective on human responses to fluctuating wetlands resources of the last 5000 years. In *Archaeological researches in the northern Great Basin: Fort Rock archaeology since Cressman,* edited by C. M. Aikens and D. L. Jenkins, 599–618. University of Oregon Anthropological Papers no. 50. Eugene.

Jennings, J. D.

1957   *Danger Cave.* University of Utah Anthropological Papers no. 27. Salt Lake City: University of Utah Press. (Reprinted by the University of Utah Press, 1999.)

1978   *Prehistory of Utah and the eastern Great Basin.* University of Utah Anthropological Papers no. 98. Salt Lake City: University of Utah Press.

Jennings, J. D., and E. Norbeck

1955   Great Basin prehistory: A review. *American Antiquity* 21:1–11.

Johnston, F. E.

1961   Sequence of epiphyseal union in a prehistoric Kentucky population from Indian Knoll. *Human Biology* 33:66–81.

1962   Growth of the long bones of infants and young children at Indian Knoll. *American Journal of Physical Anthropology* 20:249–54.

Johnston, F. E., B. S. Blumberg, S. S. Agarwal, L. Melartin, and T. A. Burch

1969   Alloalbuminemia in Southwestern U.S. Indians: Polymorphisms of albumin Naskapi and albumin Mexico. *Human Biology* 41:263–70.

Johnston, F. E., and L. M. Schell

1979   Anthropometric variation of Native American children and adults. In *The first Americans: Origins, affinities and adaptations,* edited by W. S. Laughlin and A. B. Harper, 275–91. New York: Gustav Fischer.

Jones, K. T.

1994   Can the rocks talk? Archaeology and Numic languages. In *Across the West: Human population movement and the expansion of the Numa,* edited by D. B. Madsen and D. Rhode, 71–75. Salt Lake City: University of Utah Press.

Jones, K. T., and D. B. Madsen

1989   Calculating the cost of resource transportation: A Great Basin example. *Current Anthropology* 30:529–34.

Jones, R. J., M. M. Ludlow, J. H. Troughton, and C. G. Blunt

1981   Changes in the natural carbon isotope ratios of the hair from steers fed diets of C_4, C_3, and C_4 species in sequence. *Search* 12:85–87.

Jorgensen, J.

1980   *Western Indians: Comparative environments, languages, and cultures of 172 western American Indian tribes.* San Francisco: W. H. Freeman.

Judd, N. M.

1917   *Notes on certain prehistoric habitations in Utah.* Proceedings of the 19th International Congress of Americanists, December 1915, 119–24. Washington, D.C.

1919   *Archeological investigations at Paragonah, Utah.* Smithsonian Miscellaneous Collections, vol. 70(3):1–22. Washington, D.C.

1926   *Archaeological observations north of the Rio Colorado.* Bureau of American Ethnology Bulletin no. 82. Washington, D.C.

Jung, S.

1997   An examination of methods for determining small mammal depositional origin. M.A. thesis, Department of Anthropology, Chico State University, Chico, California.

Jung, S., and R. L. Kelly

1996   The Mustang Shelter (26CH1082) archaeofaunal assemblage: The view from above the Carson Sink. Paper presented at the 25th Great Basin Anthropological Conference, Lake Tahoe, California.

Jurmain, R. D.

1977   Stress and etiology of osteoarthritis. *American Journal of Physical Anthropology* 46:353–66.

1978   Paleoepidemiology of degenerative joint disease. *Medical College of Virginia Quarterly* 14:45–56.

1980   The pattern of involvement of appendicular degenerative joint disease. *American Journal of Physical Anthropology* 53:143–50.

1990   Paleoepidemiology of a central California prehistoric population from CA-ALA-329, pt. 2: Degenerative disease. *American Journal of Physical Anthropology* 83: 83–94.

1991   Degenerative changes in peripheral joints as indicators of mechanical stress: Opportunities and limitations. *International Journal of Osteoarchaeology* 1:247–52.

Jurmain, R. D., and L. Kilgore

1995   Skeletal evidence of osteoarthritis: A palaeopathological perspective. *Annals of the Rheumatic Diseases* 54:443–50.

Kaestle, F. A.

1995   Mitochondrial DNA evidence for the identity of the descendants of the prehistoric Stillwater Marsh population. In *Bioarchaeology of the Stillwater Marsh: Prehistoric human adaptation in the western Great Basin,* edited by C. S. Larsen and R. L. Kelly, 73–80. American Museum of Natural History Anthropological Papers no. 77. New York.

1997   Molecular analysis of ancient Native American DNA from western Nevada. *Nevada Historical Society Quarterly* 40(1):85–96.

1998   *Site CA-SCL-755: Implications of ancient Native American DNA.* Research Manuscript Series on the Cultural and Natural History of Santa Clara no. 9. (In press)

Kaestle, F. A., and D. G. Smith

n.d.   Mitochondrial D-loop sequence in ancient Native Americans: Implications for prehistoric population movement. (To be submitted to the *American Journal of Human Genetics*)

Kamboh, M. I., and R. E. Ferrell
  1986 A sensitive immunoblotting technique to identify thyroxine-binding globulin protein heterogeneity after isoelectric focusing. *Biochemical Genetics* 24:273–80.
Katz, D., and J. M. Suchey
  1986 Age determination of the male *os pubis*. *American Journal of Physical Anthropology* 69:427–35.
Katzenberg, M. A.
  1989 Stable isotope analysis of archaeological faunal remains from southern Ontario. *Journal of Archaeological Science* 16:319–29.
Katzenberg, M. A., S. R. Saunders, and W. R. Fitzgerald
  1993 Age differences in stable carbon and nitrogen isotope ratios in a population of prehistoric maize horticulturalists. *American Journal of Physical Anthropology* 90:267–81.
Keeling, C. D.
  1961 A mechanism for cyclic enrichment of carbon-12 by terrestrial plants. *Geochimica et Cosmochimica Acta* 24:299–313.
Kelley, J. O., and J. L. Angel
  1987 Life stresses of slavery. *American Journal of Physical Anthropology* 74:199–211.
Kellgren, J. H., and J. S. Lawrence
  1958 Osteoarthritis and disk degeneration in an urban population. *Annals of the Rheumatic Diseases* 17:388–97.
Kellgren, J. H., and R. Moore
  1952 Generalized osteoarthritis and Heberden's nodes. *British Medical Journal* 1:181–87.
Kelly, R. L.
  1983 Hunter-gatherer mobility strategies. *Journal of Anthropological Research* 39:277–306.
  1985 Hunter-gatherer mobility and sedentism: A Great Basin study. Ph.D. diss., Department of Anthropology, University of Michigan, Ann Arbor. Ann Arbor: University Microfilms.
  1988a Archaeological context. In *Preliminary investigations in Stillwater Marsh: Human prehistory and geoarchaeology,* edited by C. Raven and R. G. Elston, 5–20. U.S. Department of the Interior Fish and Wildlife Service, Region 1, Cultural Resource Series no. 1. Portland, Oregon.
  1988b The three sides of a biface. *American Antiquity* 53:717–34.
  1990 Marshes and mobility in the western Great Basin. In *Wetland adaptations in the Great Basin,* edited by J. C. Janetski and D. B. Madsen, 259–76. Brigham Young University Museum of Peoples and Cultures Occasional Papers no. 1. Provo, Utah.
  1992 Mobility/sedentism: Concepts, archaeological measures, and effects. *Annual Review of Anthropology* 21:43–66.
  1995a *The foraging spectrum: Diversity in hunter-gatherer lifeways.* Washington, D.C.: Smithsonian Institution Press.
  1995b Hunter-gatherer lifeways in the Carson Desert: A context for bioarchaeology. In *Bioarchaeology of the Stillwater Marsh: Prehistoric human adaptation in the western Great Basin,* edited by C. S. Larsen and R. L. Kelly, 12–32. American Museum of Natural History Anthropological Papers no. 77. New York.

1997   Late Holocene Great Basin prehistory. *Journal of World Prehistory* 11:1–49.

2000   *Archaeological survey and excavations in the Carson Desert and Stillwater Mountains, Nevada.* University of Utah Anthropological Papers no. 123. Salt Lake City: University of Utah Press.

Kelly, R. L., and E. Hattori

1985   Present environment and history. In *The archaeology of Hidden Cave,* edited by D. H. Thomas, 39–46. American Museum of Natural History Anthropological Papers no. 61(1). New York.

Kennedy, K. A. R.

1989   Skeletal markers of occupational stress. In *Reconstruction of life from the skeleton,* edited by M. Y. Iscan and K. A. R. Kennedy, 129–60. New York: Alan R. Liss.

Kennedy, O. A.

1930   "Old Indian relics of Willard puzzle." *Salt Lake Tribune.* Filed in box 8, file 7, Charles Kelly Collection, scrapbook on archaeology. Utah State Historical Society, Salt Lake City.

Kent, S.

1986   The influence of sedentism and aggregation on porotic hyperostosis and anaemia: A case study. *Man* 21:605–36.

Kilgore, L.

1984   Degenerative joint disease in a medieval Nubian population. Ph.D. diss., University of Colorado, Boulder. Ann Arbor: University Microfilms.

Kimura, T., and H. Takahashi

1982   Mechanical properties of cross section of lower limb long bones in Jomon man. *Journal of Anthropological Society of Nippon* 90:105–17.

1984   Mechanical properties of cross section of lower limb long bones in Jomon man. *Journal of Anthropological Society of Nippon* 90 Suppl.:105–18.

Kobori, L. S.

1981   Human skeletal remains from the Carson-Humboldt Sinks, In *A cultural resources overview of the Carson & Humboldt Sinks, Nevada,* edited by J. C. Bard, C. I. Busby, and J. M. Findlay, 188–95. U.S. Department of the Interior Bureau of Land Management Cultural Resource Series no. 2. Berkeley: Basin Research Associates.

Kroeber, A. L.

1925   *Handbook of the Indians of California.* Bureau of American Ethnology Bulletin no. 78. Washington, D.C.

Krogman, W. M.

1962   *The human skeleton in forensic medicine.* Springfield: Charles C. Thomas.

Kuhlbusch, T. A., J. M. Lobert, P. J. Crutzen, and P. Warneck

1991   Molecular nitrogen emissions from denitrification during biomass burning. *Nature* 351:135–37.

Lallo, J. W.

1973   The skeletal biology of three prehistoric American Indian societies from Dickson Mounds. Ph.D. diss., University of Massachusetts, Amherst. Ann Arbor: University Microfilms.

1979   Disease and mortality at the Anderson Village site. *Ohio Journal of Science* 79:256–61.

Lallo, J. W., G. J. Armelagos, and J. C. Rose

1978   Paleoepidemiology of infectious disease in the Dickson Mounds population. *Medical College of Virginia Quarterly* 14:17–23.

Lallo, J. W., and J. E. Blank
    1977   Ancient diseases in Ohio: The Eiden population. *Ohio Journal of Science* 77: 55–62.

Lamb, S. M.
    1958   Linguistic prehistory in the Great Basin. *International Journal of American Linguistics* 24:95–100.

Lambert, P. M.
    1993   Health in prehistoric populations of the Santa Barbara Channel Islands. *American Antiquity* 58:509–22.

Lane, N. E., D. A. Bloch, H. H. Jones, W. H. Marshall, Jr., P. D. Wood, and J. F. Fries
    1986   Long-distance running, bone density, and osteoarthritis. *Journal of the American Medical Association* 255:1147–51.

Lanner, R. M.
    1981   *The piñon pine: A natural and cultural history.* Reno: University of Nevada Press.

Lanphear, K. N.
    1990   Frequency and distribution of enamel hypoplasia in a historic skeletal sample. *American Journal of Physical Anthropology* 81:35–43.

Larsen, C. S.
    1981   Functional implications of postcranial size reduction on the prehistoric Georgia coast, U.S.A. *Journal of Human Evolution* 10:489–502.

    1982   *The anthropology of St. Catherines Island,* pt. 3: *Prehistoric human adaptation.* American Museum of Natural History Anthropological Papers 57(3). New York.

    1984   Health and disease in prehistoric Georgia: The transition to agriculture. In *Paleopathology at the origins of agriculture,* edited by M. N. Cohen and G. J. Armelagos, 367–92. Orlando, Florida: Academic Press.

    1985a Human remains from Hidden Cave. In *The archaeology of Hidden Cave, Nevada,* edited by D. H. Thomas, 179–82. American Museum of Natural History Anthropological Papers 61(1). New York.

    1985b Human remains from the Carson Sink. In *The archaeology of Hidden Cave, Nevada,* edited by D. H. Thomas, 395–404. American Museum of Natural History Anthropological Papers 61(1). New York.

    1987   Bioarchaeological interpretations of subsistence economy and behavior from human skeletal remains. In *Advances in Archaeological Method and Theory,* vol. 10, edited by M. B. Schiffer, 39–45. San Diego: Academic Press.

    1990   *The archaeology of Mission Santa Catalina de Guale,* pt.2: *Biocultural interpretation of a population in transition.* American Museum of Natural History Anthropological Papers no. 68. New York. .

    1995   Prehistoric human biology of the Carson Desert: A bioarchaeological investigation of a hunter-gatherer lifeway. In *Bioarchaeology of the Stillwater Marsh: Prehistoric human adaptation in the western Great Basin,* edited by C. S. Larsen and R. L. Kelly, 33–40. American Museum of Natural History Anthropological Papers no. 77. New York.

    1997   *Bioarchaeology: Interpreting behavior from the human skeleton.* Cambridge, England: Cambridge University Press.

Larsen, C. S., and D. E. Harn
    1994   Health in transition: Disease and nutrition in the Georgia Bight. In *Paleonutrition: The diet and health of prehistoric Americans,* edited by K. D. Sobolik, 222–34. Center for Archaeological Investigations Occasional Paper no. 22. Carbondale: Southern Illinois University.

Larsen, C. S., and R. L. Kelly, eds.

1995   *Bioarchaeology of the Stillwater Marsh: Prehistoric human adaptation in the western Great Basin.* American Museum of Natural History Anthropological Papers no. 77. New York.

Larsen, C. S., and G. R. Milner, eds.

1994   *In the wake of contact: Biological responses to conquest.* New York: Wiley-Liss.

Larsen, C. S., and C. B. Ruff

1994   The stresses of conquest in Spanish Florida: Structural adaptation and change before and after contact. In *In the wake of contact: Biological responses to conquest,* edited by C. S. Larsen and G. R. Milner, 21–34. New York: Wiley-Liss.

Larsen, C. S., C. B. Ruff, and M. C. Griffin

1996   Implications of changing biomechanical and nutritional environments for activity and lifeway in the eastern Spanish Borderlands. In *Bioarchaeology of Native American adaptation in the Spanish Borderlands,* edited by B. J. Baker and L. L. Kealhofer, 95–125. Gainesville: University of Florida Press.

Larsen, C. S., C. B. Ruff, and R. L. Kelly

1995   Structural analysis of the Stillwater postcranial human remains: Behavioral implications of articular joint pathology and long bone diaphyseal morphology. In *Bioarchaeology of the Stillwater Marsh: Prehistoric human adaptation in the western Great Basin,* edited by C. S. Larsen and R. L. Kelly, 107–33. American Museum of Natural History Anthropological Papers no. 77. New York.

Larsen, C. S., C. B. Ruff, M. J. Schoeninger, and D. L. Hutchinson

1992   Population decline and extinction in La Florida. In *Disease and demography in the Americas: Changing patterns before and after 1492,* edited by D. H. Ubelaker and J. W. Verano, 25–39. Washington, D.C.: Smithsonian Institution Press.

Larsen, C. S., K. F. Russell, and D. L. Hutchinson

1995   The human skeletal field survey. In *Bioarchaeology of the Stillwater Marsh: Prehistoric human adaptation in the western Great Basin,* edited by C. S. Larsen and R. L. Kelly, 41–67. Anthropological Papers of the American Museum of Natural History no. 77. New York.

Lazenby, R. A.

1990a Continuing periosteal apposition, I: Documentation, hypotheses, and interpretation. *American Journal of Physical Anthropology* 82:451–72.

1990b Continuing periosteal apposition, II: The significance of peak bone mass, strain equilibrium, and age-related activity differentials for mechanical compensation in human tubular bone. *American Journal of Physical Anthropology* 82:473–84.

Lee, R. B., and I. DeVore, eds.

1968   *Man the hunter.* Chicago: Aldine.

Libby, W. F., R. Berger, J. F. Mead, G. V. Alexander, and J. F. Ross

1964   Replacement rates for human tissue from atmospheric radiocarbon. *Science* 146:1170–72.

Lindahl, T.

1993   Instability and decay of the primary structure of DNA. *Nature* 362:709–15.

Lindsay, L. W.

1986   Fremont fragmentation. In *Anthropology of the Desert West,* edited by C. J. Condie and D. D. Fowler, 229–52. University of Utah Anthropological Papers no. 110. Salt Lake City: University of Utah Press.

Lockett, C. L., and L. C. Pippin

1990 Re-examining Brownware ceramics in the central and southern Great Basin. In *Hunter-gatherer pottery from the Far West,* edited by J. M. Mack, 67–82. Nevada State Museum Anthropological Papers no. 23. Carson City.

Lorenz, J. G., and D. G. Smith

1994 Distribution of the 9 bp mitochondrial DNA region V deletion among North American Indians. *Human Biology* 66:777–88.

1996 Distribution of four founding mtDNA haplogroups among Native North Americans. *American Journal of Physical Anthropology* 101(3):307–23.

Loud, L. L., and M. R. Harrington

1929 *Lovelock Cave.* University of California Publications in American Archaeology and Ethnology no. 25:1–183. Berkeley.

Lovejoy, C. O.

1982 Diaphyseal biomechanics of the locomotor skeleton of Tautevel man with comments on the evolution of skeletal changes in Late Pleistocene man. In *L'Homo erectus et la place de l'homme de Tautevel parmi les hominid's fossiles,* edited by H. de Lumley, 447–70. Paris: Centre National de la Recherche Scientifique.

Lovejoy, C. O., A. H. Burstein, and K. G. Heiple

1976 The biomechanical analysis of bone strength: A method and its application to platycemia. *American Journal of Physical Anthropology* 44:489–506.

Lovejoy, C. O., and E. Trinkaus

1980 Strength and robusticity of the Neandertal tibia. *American Journal of Physical Anthropology* 53:465–70.

Loveland, C. J.

1980 The skeletal biology of the Caddo Indians of the Kaufman-Williams site, Red River County, Texas. Ph.D. diss., University of Tennessee, Knoxville.

1991 Osteological analysis of Great Salt Lake skeletons. In *Prehistoric human skeletal remains and the prehistory of the Great Salt Lake wetlands,* edited by S. R. Simms, C. J. Loveland, and M. E. Stuart, 62–80. Utah State University Contributions to Anthropology no. 6. Logan.

1993 Osteological analysis of human remains from the Willard Bay area. In *Archaeological test excavations in the Great Salt Lake wetlands and associated analyses, Weber and Box Elder Counties, Utah,* edited by W. B. Fawcett and S. R. Simms, 185–96. Utah State Contributions to Anthropology no. 14. Logan.

Lovell, N. C., D. E. Nelson, and H. P. Schwarcz

1986 Carbon isotope ratios in palaeodiet: Lack of age or sex effect. *Archaeometry* 28:51–55.

Lowery, G. H.

1986 *Growth and development of children.* 8th ed. Chicago: Yearbook Medical Publishers.

Lowie, R. H.

1924 *Notes on Shoshonean ethnology.* American Museum of Natural History Anthropological Papers 20(3):183–314. New York.

Lupo, K. D., and D. N. Schmitt

1997 On Late Holocene variability in bison populations and human subsistence strategies in the northeastern Great Basin. *Journal of California and Great Basin Anthropology* 19:50–69.

Lyneis, M. M.

    1982   Prehistory in the southern Great Basin. In *Man and environment in the Great Basin,* edited by D. B. Madsen and J. F. O'Connell, 172–85. Society for American Archaeology Papers no. 2. Washington, D.C.

    1994   East and onto the plateaus? An archaeological examination of the Numic expansion in southern Nevada, northern Arizona, and southern Utah. In *Across the West: Human population movement and the expansion of the Numa,* edited by D. B. Madsen and D. Rhode, 141–49. Salt Lake City: University of Utah Press.

Mabey, D. R.

    1986   Notes on the historic high level of Great Salt Lake. *Utah Geological and Mineralogical Survey Notes* 20:13–15.

McCafferty, K. E., D. M. Mittler, D. P. Van Gerven, and S. G. Sheridan

    1992   Vertebral osteophytosis in a prehistoric Hohokam population from Pueblo Grande. *American Journal of Physical Anthropology* Suppl. 14:119.

McCance, R. A.

    1960   Severe undernutrition in growing and adult animals. *British Journal of Nutrition* 14:59–73.

McCance, R. A., J. W. T. Dickerson, G. Bell, and O. Dunbar

    1962   Severe undernutrition in growing and adult animals, 9: The effects of undernutrition and its relief on the mechanical properties of bone. *British Journal of Nutrition* 16:1–12.

McCance, R. A., E. H. R. Ford, and W. A. B. Brown

    1961   Severe undernutrition in growing and adult animals, 7: Development of the skull, jaws and teeth in pigs. *British Journal of Nutrition* 15:213–24.

McCarty, D. J., and W. J. Koopman, eds.

    1993   *Arthritis and allied conditions.* 12th ed. Philadelphia: Lea & Febiger.

McDowell, P. F.

    1992   An overview of Harney Basin geomorphic history, climate, and hydrology. In *Land and life at Malheur Lake: Preliminary geomorphological and archaeological investigations,* edited by C. Raven and R. G. Elston, 13–34. U.S. Department of the Interior Fish and Wildlife Service, Region 1, Cultural Resource Series no. 8. Portland, Oregon.

McGovern-Wilson, R., and C. Quinn

    1996   Stable isotope analysis of ten individuals from Afetna, Saipan, northern Mariana Islands. *Journal of Archaeological Science* 23:59–65.

McGrath, J. W.

    1988   Multiple stable states of disease occurrence: A note on the implications for the anthropological study of human disease. *American Anthropologist* 90:323–34.

Mack, J. M., ed.

    1990   *Hunter-gatherer pottery from the Far West,* Nevada State Museum Anthropological Papers no. 23. Carson City.

Mack, M. E., and A. Coppa

    1992   Frequency and chronological distribution of enamel hypoplasias from the Ra's al-Hamra-5 (RH5) skeletal collection (Oman). In *Recent contributions to the study of enamel developmental defects,* edited by A. H. Goodman and L. L. Capasso, 131–41. Journal of Paleopathology Monographic Publications no. 2. Chieti, Italy: Associazione Antropologica Abruzzese.

McKern, T.
 1970   Estimation of skeletal age: From puberty to about 30 years of age. In *Personal identification in mass disasters,* edited by T. D. Stewart. Washington, D.C.: Smithsonian Institution Press.

McKern, T., and T. D. Stewart
 1957   *Skeletal age changes in young American males, analyzed from the standpoint of identification.* Technical Report EP-45. Natick, Massachusetts: Headquarters, Quartermaster Research and Development Command.

Madsen, B. D.
 1986   *Chief Pocatello: The white plume.* Salt Lake City: University of Utah Press.

Madsen, D. B.
 1975   Dating Paiute-Shoshoni expansion in the Great Basin. *American Antiquity* 40: 82–97.
 1979   The Fremont and the Sevier: Defining prehistoric agriculturalists north of the Anasazi. *American Antiquity* 44:711–22.
 1982   Get it where the gettin's good: A variable model of Great Basin subsistence and settlement based on data from the eastern Great Basin. In *Man and environment in the Great Basin,* edited by D. B. Madsen and J. F. O'Connell, 207–26. Society for American Archaeology Papers no. 2. Washington, D.C.
 1988   The prehistoric use of Great Basin marshes. In *Preliminary investigations in Stillwater Marsh: Human prehistory and geoarchaeology,* edited by C. Raven and R. G. Elston, 414–18. U.S. Department of the Interior Fish and Wildlife Service, Region 1, Cultural Resource Series no. 1. Portland, Oregon.
 1989   *Exploring the Fremont.* Utah Museum of Natural History Occasional Publication no. 8. University of Utah, Salt Lake City.
 1994   Mesa Verde and Sleeping Ute Mountain: The geographical and chronological dimensions of the Numic expansion. In *Across the West: human population movement and the expansion of the Numa,* edited by D. B. Madsen and D. Rhode, 24–34. Salt Lake City: University of Utah Press.

Madsen, D. B., and J. C. Janetski
 1990   Introduction. In *Wetland adaptations in the Great Basin,* edited by J. C. Janetski and D. B. Madsen, 1–4. Brigham Young University Museum of Peoples and Cultures Occasional Papers no. 1. Provo Utah.

Madsen, D. B., and K. T. Jones
 1988   Transportation, seasonality and storage among mid-latitude hunter-gatherers. Paper presented at the 21st Great Basin Anthropological Conference, Park City, Utah.

Madsen, D. B., and L. W. Lindsay
 1977   *Backhoe Village.* Utah State Historical Society Antiquities Section Selected Papers no. 4(12). Salt Lake City.

Madsen, D. B., and S. R. Simms
 1998   The Fremont complex: A behavior perspective. *Journal of World Prehistory* (in press).

Maguire, D.
 1892   Report of the Department of Ethnology, Utah World's Fair Commission in Utah at the World's Columbian Exposition, 105–10. Washington, D.C.

Manful, E.
 1938   George East: A pioneer personal history. Ms. on file, Utah State Historical Society, Salt Lake City.

Maresh, M. M.

1955   Linear growth of long bones of extremities from infancy through adolescence. *American Journal of Diseases of Children* 89:725–43.

Martin, D. L., A. H. Goodman, G. J. Armelagos, and A. L. Magennis

1991   *Black Mesa Anasazi health: Reconstructing life from patterns of death and disease.* Center for Archaeological Investigations Occasional Paper no. 14. Carbondale: Southern Illinois University.

Martin, R. B., D. B. Burr, and M. B. Schaffler

1985   Effects of age and sex on the amount and distribution of mineral in Eskimo tibiae. *American Journal of Physical Anthropology* 67:371–80.

Marwitt, J. P.

1970   *Median Village and Fremont culture regional variation.* University of Utah Anthropological Papers no. 95. Salt Lake City: University of Utah Press.

Massler, M., I. Schour, and H. G. Poncher

1941   Developmental pattern of the child as reflected in the calcification pattern of the teeth. *American Journal of Diseases of Children* 62:33–67.

Matson, R. G., and B. Chisholm

1991   Basketmaker II subsistence: Carbon isotopes and other dietary indicators from Cedar Mesa, Utah. *American Antiquity* 56:444–59.

May, R. L., A. H. Goodman, and R. S. Meindl

1993   Response of bone and enamel formation to nutritional supplementation and morbidity among malnourished Guatemalan children. *American Journal of Physical Anthropology* 92:37–51.

Mehringer, P. J., Jr.

1985   Late-Quaternary pollen records from the interior Pacific Northwest and northern Great Basin of the United States. In *Pollen record of late-Quaternary North American sediments,* edited by V. M. Bryant, Jr., and R. G. Holloway, 167–89. Dallas, Texas: American Association of Stratigraphic Palynologists Foundation.

Mehringer, P. J., Jr., and P. E. Wigand

1990   Comparison of Late Holocene environments from woodrat middens and pollen: Diamond Craters, Oregon. In *Packrat Middens: The last 40,000 years of biotic change,* edited by J. L. Betancourt, T. R. Van Devender, and P. S. Martin, 294–325. Tucson: University of Arizona Press.

Mensforth, R. P., C. O. Lovejoy, J. W. Lallo, and G. J. Armelagos

1978   The role of constitutional factors, diet, and infectious disease in the etiology of porotic hyperostosis and periosteal reactions in prehistoric infants and children. *Medical Anthropology* 2(1):1–59.

Merbs, C. F.

1980   The pathology of a La Jollan skeleton from Punta Minitas, Baja California. *Pacific Coast Archaeological Society Quarterly* 16:37–43.

1983   *Pattern of activity-induced pathology in a Canadian Inuit population.* Archaeological Survey of Canada Mercury Series Paper no. 119. Ottawa, Ontario: National Museum of Man.

Merchant, V., and D. Ubelaker

1977   Skeletal growth of the protohistoric Arikara. *American Journal of Physical Anthropology* 46:61–72.

Merriwether, D. A., F. Rothhammer, and R. E. Ferrell

1994   Genetic variation in the New World: Ancient teeth, bone, and tissue as sources of DNA. *Experientia* 50:592–601.

1995 Distribution of the four founding lineage haplotypes in Native Americans suggests a single wave of migration for the New World. *American Journal of Physical Anthropology* 98:411–30.

Metcalfe, D. B.
1984 *Gooseberry archeological project: 1983.* University of Utah Archaeological Center Reports of Investigations no. 83-1. Salt Lake City.

Metcalfe, D. B., and R. K. Barlow
1992 A model for exploring the optimal tradeoff between field processing and transport. *American Anthropologist* 94:340–56.

Metcalfe, D. B., and N. Shearin
1989 *Jordan River marsh survey.* University of Utah Archaeological Center Reports of Investigations no. 89-1. Salt Lake City.

Miles, A. E. W.
1989 *An early Christian chapel and burial ground on the Isle of Ensay, Outer Hebrides, Scotland, with a study of the skeletal remains.* BAR International Series no. 212. Oxford, England: British Anthropological Reports.

Miller, R. J.
1985 Lateral epicondylitis in a prehistoric central Arizona Indian population from Nuvakwewtaqa. In *Health and disease in the prehistoric Southwest,* edited by C. F. Merbs and R. J. Miller, 391–400. Arizona State University Anthropological Research Paper no. 34. Tempe.

Miller, W. R.
1986 Numic languages. In *Handbook of North American Indians,* vol. 11: *Great Basin,* edited by W. L. d'Azevedo, 98–106. Washington, D.C.: Smithsonian Institution.

Miller, W. R., J. Tanner, and L. Foley
1971 A lexicostatistic study of Shoshoni dialects. *Anthropological Linguistics* 13(4): 142–64.

Milner, G. R.
1992 Disease and sociopolitical systems in late prehistoric Illinois. In *Disease and demography in the Americas,* edited by J. W. Verano and D. H. Ubelaker, 103–16. Washington, D.C.: Smithsonian Institution Press.

Milner, G. R., and V. G. Smith
1990 Oneota human skeletal remains. In *Archaeological investigations at the Morton Village and Norris Farms 36 cemetery,* edited by S. K. Santure, A. D. Harn, and D. Esarey, 111–48. Illinois State Museum Reports of Investigations no. 45. Springfield.

Minor, R., and R. L. Greenspan
1985 *Archaeological testing in the southeast area of the Headquarters site, Malheur National Wildlife Refuge, Harney County, Oregon.* Heritage Research Associates Report no. 36. Submitted to U.S. Fish and Wildlife Service. Report on file, Malheur National Wildlife Refuge, Princeton, Oregon.

Minor, R., and L. A. Toepel
1988 *Surface investigations in the northwest area of the Headquarters site (35HA403), Malheur National Wildlife Refuge, Harney County, Oregon.* Heritage Research Associates Report no. 72. Submitted to the U.S. Fish and Wildlife Service. (Report on file, Malheur National Wildlife Refuge, Princeton, Oregon)

Minson, D. J., M. M. Ludlow, and J. H. Troughton
1975 Differences in natural carbon isotope ratios of milk and hair from cattle grazing tropical and temperate pastures. *Nature* 256:602.

Mittler, D. M., and D. P. Van Gerven

1994   Developmental, diachronic, and demographic analysis of cribra orbitalia in the medieval Christian populations of Kulubnarti. *American Journal of Physical Anthropology* 93:287–97.

Momaday, S.

1996   "Disturbing the spirits: Indian bones must stay in the ground." *New York Times,* November 2.

Moore, J. G., G. F. Fry, and E. Englert, Jr.

1996   Thory-headed worm infection in North American Prehistoric man. *Science* 163:563–68.

Moore, K., M. Murray, and M. J. Schoeninger

1989   Effects of preservatives on trace element and stable isotope analysis of bone. *Journal of Archaeological Science* 16:437–46.

Morin, P. A., and D. G. Smith

1995   Nonradioactive detection of hypervariable simple sequence repeats in short polyacrylamide gels. *Biotechniques* 19:223–27.

Moritz, C., T. E. Dowling, and W. M. Brown

1987   Evolution of animal mitochondrial DNA: Relevance for population biology and systematics. *Annual Review of Ecology and Systematics* 18:269–92.

Morss, N. M.

1931   *The ancient culture of the Fremont River in Utah: Report on the explorations under the Claflin-Emerson Fund, 1928–29.* Papers of the Peabody Museum of American Archaeology and Ethnology, vol. 12, no. 3. Cambridge, Massachusetts: Harvard University.

Moskowitz, R. W.

1972   Clinical and laboratory findings in osteoarthritis. In *Arthritis and allied conditions,* edited by J. L. Hollander and D. J. McCarty, 1032–53. Philadelphia: Lea and Febiger

1987   Primary osteoarthritis: Epidemiology, clinical aspects, and general management. *American Medical Journal* 83(Suppl. 5A):5–10.

Murchison, S. B.

1989   *Fluctuation history of Great Salt Lake, Utah, during the last 13,000 years.* Department of Geography Limneotectonics Laboratory Technical Report 89-2. Salt Lake City: University of Utah.

Murdock, G. P.

1967   *Ethnographic atlas.* Pittsburgh: University of Pittsburgh Press.

Musil, R. R.

1995   *Adaptive transitions and environmental change in the northern Great Basin: A view from Diamond Swamp.* University of Oregon Anthropological Papers no. 51. Eugene.

Nagurka, M. L., and W. C. Hayes

1980   An interactive graphics package for calculating cross-sectional properties of complex shapes. *Journal of Biomechanics* 13:59–64.

Nakamura, K., D. A. Schoeller, F. J. Winkler, and H. L. Schmidt

1982   Geographical variations in the carbon isotope composition of the diet and hair in contemporary man. *Biomedical Mass Spectrometry* 9:390–94.

Napton, L. K.

1969   *Archaeological and paleobiological investigations in Lovelock Cave, Nevada.* Kroeber Anthropological Society Special Publication no. 2. Berkeley: University of California.

Newman, D. E.

1988 Paleoenvironments of the Late Archaic and Formative periods in central Utah. Paper presented at the 21st Great Basin Anthropological Conference, Park City, Utah.

1994 Pollen analysis of sediments from Steinaker Dam site. In *Steinaker Gap: An early Fremont agriculture farmstead,* edited by R. L. Talbot and L. D. Richens, 149–76. Brigham Young University Museum of Peoples and Cultures Technical Series no. 94-18. Provo, Utah.

Newman, T. M., R. Bogue, C. D. Carley, R. D. McGilvra, and D. Moretty

1974 Archaeological reconnaissance of the Malheur National Wildlife Refuge, Harney County, Oregon: 1974. Ms. on file, Oregon State Museum of Anthropology, University of Oregon, Eugene.

Nichols, J.

1990 Linguistic diversity and the first settlement of the New World. *Language* 66:475–521.

Nichols, M.

1981 *Old Californian Uto-Aztecan.* Reports from the Survey of California and Other Indian Languages no. 1:5–41. Berkeley.

Norusis, M.

1995 *SPSS® 6.1 guide to data analysis.* Englewood Cliffs, New Jersey: Prentice Hall.

O'Connell, J. F.

1971 The archaeology and cultural ecology of Surprise Valley, northeast California. Ph.D. diss., University of California, Berkeley. Ann Arbor: University Microfilms.

1975 *The prehistory of Surprise Valley.* Ballena Press Anthropological Papers no. 4. Ramona, California.

O'Connell, J. F., and P. S. Hayward

1972 Altithermal and Medithermal human adaptations in Surprise Valley, northeast California. In *Great Basin cultural ecology: A symposium,* edited by D. D. Fowler, 25–42. Desert Research Institute Publications in the Social Sciences no. 8. Reno, Nevada.

Oetting, A. C.

1989 *Villages and wetlands adaptations in the northern Great Basin: Chronology and land use in the Lake Abert–Chewaucan Marsh basin, Lake County, Oregon.* University of Oregon Anthropological Papers no. 41. Eugene.

1990a *An archaeological survey on the recently flooded shores of Malheur Lake, Harney County, Oregon.* Heritage Research Associates Report no. 97. Submitted to the Oregon State Historic Preservation Office. (Report on file, State Historic Preservation Office, Salem, Oregon)

1990b *The Malheur Lake survey: Lacustrine archaeology in the Harney Basin, central Oregon.* Heritage Research Associates Report no. 96. Submitted to the U.S. Fish and Wildlife Service. (Report on file, Malheur National Wildlife Refuge, Princeton, Oregon)

1992 Lake and marsh-edge settlements on Malheur Lake, Harney County, Oregon. *Journal of California and Great Basin Anthropology* 14(1):110–29.

1994 Another look at projectile points as temporal indicators. In *Contributions to the archaeology of Oregon, 1990–1944,* edited by P. W. Baxter, 65–79. Association of Oregon Archaeologists Occasional Papers no. 5. Eugene.

O'Leary, M. H.
1988   Carbon isotopes in photosynthesis. *Bioscience* 38:328–36.

O'Leary, M. H., S. Madhavan, and P. Paneth
1992   Physical and chemical basis of carbon isotope fractionation in plants. *Plant, Cell and Environment* 15:1099–1104.

Orians, G. H., and N. E. Pearson
1979   On the theory of central place foraging. In *Analysis of ecological systems,* edited by D. G. Horn, R. D. Mitchell, and G. R. Stairs, 154–77. Columbus: Ohio State University Press.

O'Rourke, D. H., S. W. Carlyle, and R. L. Parr
1996   Ancient DNA: A review of methods, progress, and perspectives. *American Journal of Human Biology* 8(5):557–71.

Ortner, D. J.
1968   Description and classification of degenerative bone changes in the distal joint surfaces of the humerus. *American Journal of Physical Anthropology* 28:139–56.

Ortner, D. J., and W. G. J. Putschar
1985   *Identification of pathological conditions in human skeletal remains.* Washington, D.C.: Smithsonian Institution Press.

Owsley, D., and W. M. Bass
1979   A demographic analysis of skeletons from the Larson site (30WW2) Walworth County, South Dakota: Vital statistics. *American Journal of Physical Anthropology* 51:145–54.

Pääbo, S.
1986   *Molecular genetic investigations of ancient human remains.* Cold Spring Harbor Symposia on Quantitative Biology, vol. 51:441–46. Plainview, New York.
1987   Molecular genetic methods in archaeology: A prospect. *Anthropologischer Anzeiger* 45:9–17.

Pääbo, S., J. A. Gifford, and A. C. Wilson
1988   Mitochondrial DNA sequences from a 7,000-year-old brain. *Nucleic Acids Research* 16(2):9775–87.

Palmer, E.
1878   Plants used by Indians of the United States. *American Naturalist* 12:593–653.

Panush, R. S., C. Schmidt, J. R. Caldwell, N. L. Edwards, S. Longely, R. Yonker, E. Webster, J. Nauman, J. Stork, and H. Petterson
1986   Is running associated with degenerative joint disease? *Journal of the American Medical Association* 255:1152–54.

Parr, R. L., S. W. Carlyle, and D. H. O'Rourke
1996   Ancient DNA analysis of Fremont Amerindians of the Great Salt Lake wetlands. *American Journal of Physical Anthropology* 99:507–18.

Pascale, M., and W. A. Grana
1989   An orthopedic perspective: Does running cause osteoarthritis? *Physical Sports Medicine* 17:156–66.

Pauwels, F.
1976   *Biomechanics of the normal and diseased hip.* Berlin: Springer-Verlag.

Pecotte, J. K.
1982   Appendix: Human skeletal remains. In *Final year excavations at the Evans Mound*

site, by W. A. Dodd, Jr., 117–28. University of Utah Anthropological Papers no. 106. Salt Lake City: University of Utah Press.

Peisker, M., and S. A. Henderson

1992 Carbon: Terrestrial C_4 plants. *Plant, Cell and Environment* 15:987–1004.

Pendergast, D.

1961 Excavations at the Bear River site, Box Elder County, Utah. *Utah Archeology* 7(2).

Pendleton, L. S. A., A. R. McLane, and D. H. Thomas

1982 *Cultural resource overview, Carson City District, west central Nevada.* U. S. Department of the Interior Bureau of Land Management Cultural Resource Series no. 5(1). Reno, Nevada.

Pettigrew, R. M.

1980 *The ancient Chewaucanians: More on the prehistoric lake dwellers of Lake Abert, southeastern Oregon.* Association of Oregon Archaeologists Occasional Papers no. 1:49–67. Portland.

1985 *Archaeological investigations on the east shore of Lake Abert, Lake County, Oregon,* vol. 1. University of Oregon Anthropological Papers no. 32. Eugene.

Pfeiffer, S.

1977 *The skeletal biology of Archaic populations of the Great Lakes region.* Archaeological Survey of Canada Papers no. 64. Ottawa.

Phenice, T. W.

1969 A newly developed visual method of sexing the *os pubis. American Journal of Physical Anthropology* 30:297–302.

Pickering, R. B.

1979 Hunter-gatherer/agriculturalist arthritis patterns: A preliminary investigation. *Henry Ford Hospital Medical Journal* 27:50–53.

1984 Patterns of degenerative joint disease in Middle Woodland, Late Woodland, and Mississippian skeletal series from the lower Illinois valley. Ph.D. diss., Northwestern University, Evanston, Illinois. Ann Arbor: University Microfilms.

Pierce, L. C.

1987 A comparison of the pattern of degenerative joint disease between agricultural and non-agricultural skeletal series. Ph.D. diss., University of Tennessee, Knoxville. Ann Arbor: University Microfilms.

Pinals, R. S.

1972 Traumatic arthritis and allied conditions. In *Arthritis and allied conditions,* edited by J. L. Hollander and D. J. McCarty, 1391–1410. Philadelphia: Lea and Febiger.

Pindborg, J. J.

1982 Aetiology of developmental defects not related to fluorosis. *International Dental Journal* 32:123–34.

Piper, A. M., T. W. Robinson, and C. F. Park, Jr.

1939 *Geology and ground-water resources of the Harney Basin, Oregon.* U.S. Geological Survey Water-Supply Paper no. 841. Washington, D.C.

Plog, F.

1984 Exchange, tribes, and alliances: The northern Southwest. *American Archaeology* 4:217–23.

Popkin, B. M., T. Lasky, J. Litvin, D. Spicer, and M. E. Yamamoto

1986 *The infant-feeding triad: Infant, mother and household.* New York: Gordon and Breach.

Powell, M. L.
   1988   *Status and health in prehistory: A case study of the Moundville chiefdom.* Washington, D.C.: Smithsonian Institution Press.
Price, T. D., and J. A. Brown
   1985   Aspects of hunter-gatherer complexity. In *Prehistoric hunter-gatherers: The emergence of cultural complexity,* edited by T. D. Price and J. A. Brown, 3–20. New York: Academic Press.
Price, T. D., C. M. Johnson, J. A. Ezzo, J. Ericson, J. H. Burton
   1994   Residential mobility in the prehistoric Southwest United States: A preliminary study using strontium isotope analysis. *Journal of Archaeological Science* 21:315–30.
Price, T. D., M. J. Schoeninger, and G. J. Armelagos
   1985   Bone chemistry and past behavior: An overview. *Journal of Human Evolution* 14:419–47.
Pugh, J.
   1982   Biomechanical aspects of osteoarthritic joints: Mechanisms and noninvasive detection. In *Osteoarthromechanics,* edited by D. N. Ghista, 161–91. New York: McGraw-Hill.
Radin, E. L.
   1983   The relationship between biological and mechanical factors in the etiology of osteoarthritis. *Journal of Rheumatology* 10(Suppl. 9):20–21.
Radin, E. L., H. G. Parker, and I. L. Paul
   1971   Pattern of degenerative osteoarthritis: Preferential involvement of distal finger-joints. *Lancet* 1:377–79.
Radin, E. L., I. L. Paul, and R. M. Rose
   1972   Role of mechanical factors in pathogenesis of primary osteoarthritis. *Lancet* 1:519–22.
Rafferty, J. E.
   1985   The archaeological record on sedentariness: Recognition, development, and implications. In *Advances in archaeological method and theory,* vol. 8, edited by M. B. Schiffer, 113–56. Orlando, Florida: Academic Press.
Rafferty, K. L., and C. B. Ruff
   1994   Articular structure and function in *Hylobates, Colobus,* and *Papio. American Journal of Physical Anthropology* 94:395–408.
Raghavendra, A. S., and V. S. R. Das
   1978   The occurrence of C_4 photosynthesis: A supplementary list of C_4 plants reported during late 1974–mid 1977. *Photosynthetica* 12:200–208.
Rathbun, T. A.
   1987   Health and disease at a South Carolina plantation. *American Journal of Physical Anthropology* 74:239–53.
Raven, C.
   1990   *Prehistoric human geography in the Carson Desert, pt. 2: Archaeological field tests of model predictions.* U.S. Department of the Interior Fish and Wildlife Service, Region 1, Cultural Resource Series no. 4. Portland, Oregon.
   1992   Prehistoric wetland adaptations in the Great Basin and the special case of Malheur Lake. In *Land and life at Malheur Lake: Preliminary geomorphological and archaeological investigations,* edited by C. Raven and R. G. Elston, 5–12. U.S. Department of the Interior Fish and Wildlife Service, Region 1, Cultural Resource Series no. 8. Portland, Oregon.

1994   Invisible from the West: Numic expansion from the perspective of the Carson Desert. In *Across the West: Human population movement and the expansion of the Numa*, edited by D. B. Madsen and D. Rhode, 152–56. Salt Lake City: University of Utah Press.

Raven, C., and R. G. Elston

1989   *Prehistoric human geography in the Carson Desert*, pt. 1: *A predictive model of land use in the Stillwater wildlife management area.* U.S. Department of the Interior Fish and Wildlife Service, Region 1, Cultural Resource Series no. 3. Portland, Oregon.

_____, eds.

1988   *Preliminary investigations in Stillwater Marsh: Human prehistory and geoarchaeology.* U.S. Department of the Interior Fish and Wildlife Service, Region 1, Cultural Resource Series no. 1. Portland, Oregon.

1992   *Land and life at Malheur Lake: Preliminary geomorphological and archaeological investigations.* U.S. Department of the Interior Fish and Wildlife Service, Region l, Cultural Resource Series no. 8. Portland, Oregon.

Raymond, A. W.

1994   *The surface archaeology of Harney Dune (35HA718), Malheur National Wildlife Refuge, Oregon.* U.S. Department of the Interior Fish and Wildlife Service, Region 1, Cultural Resource Series no. 9. Portland, Oregon.

Raymond, A. W., and V. M. Parks

1989   *Surface archaeology of Stillwater Marsh, Churchill County, Nevada.* Fallon, Nevada: U.S. Fish and Wildlife Service.

1990   Archaeological sites exposed by recent flooding of Stillwater Marsh, Carson Desert, Nevada. In *Wetland adaptations in the Great Basin,* edited by J. C. Janetski and D. B. Madsen, 33–61. Brigham Young University Museum of Peoples and Cultures Occasional Papers no. 1. Provo, Utah.

Raymond, A. W., and E. Sobel

1990   The use of tui chub as food by Indians of the western Great Basin. *Journal of California and Great Basin Anthropology* 12:2–18.

Reed, A. D.

1994   The Numic occupation of western Colorado and eastern Utah during the prehistoric and protohistoric periods. In *Across the West: Human population movement and the expansion of the Numa,* edited by D. B. Madsen and D. Rhode, 188–99. Salt Lake City, University of Utah Press.

Reinhard, K. J.

1990   Archaeoparasitology in North America. *American Journal of Physical Anthropology* 82:145–63.

1992   Patterns of diet, parasitism, and anemia in prehistoric west North America. In *Diet, demography, and disease: Changing perspectives on anemia,* edited by P. Stuart-Macadam and S. Kent, 219–58. Hawthorne: Aldine de Gruyter.

Rhode, D.

1990a   Settlement patterning and residential stability at Walker Lake, Nevada: The view from above. In *Wetland adaptations in the Great Basin,* edited by J. C. Janetski and D. B. Madsen, 107–20. Brigham Young University Museum of Peoples and Cultures Occasional Papers no. 1. Provo, Utah.

1990b   On transportation costs of Great Basin resources: An assessment of the Jones-Madsen model. *Current Anthropology* 31:413–19.

1994   Thermoluminescence dating of Brownware ceramics from the Great Basin. In

Across the West: Human population movement and the expansion of the Numa, edited by D. B. Madsen and D. Rhode, 124–30. Salt Lake City: University of Utah Press.

Richens, L. D.

    1997   Ceramics. In *Clear Creek Canyon archaeological project,* vol. 5, *Results and synthesis,* by J. C. Janetski, R. K. Talbot, D. E. Newman, L. D. Richens, J. D. Wilde, S. B. Baker, and S. E. Billat, 67–90. Brigham Young University Museum of Peoples and Cultures Technical Series 95–9. Provo, Utah.

Ringe, B. L.

    1986   Stone tools. In *Shoshone-Bannock culture history,* edited by R. N. Holmer, 72–141. Pocatallo: Swanson/Crabtree Anthropological Research Laboratory, Idaho State University.

Robbins, D. R., K. R. Rosenberg, and C. B. Ruff

    1989   Activity patterns in Late Middle Woodland, Delaware. *American Journal of Physical Anthropology* 78:290–91.

Roberts, J., and T. A. Burch

    1966   *Prevalence of osteoarthritis in adults by age, sex, race, and geographic area, United States 1960–1962.* National Center for Health Statistics Series no. 11. Washington, D.C.

Rose, J. C., B. A. Burnett, M. W. Blaeuer, and M. S. Nassaney

    1984   Paleopathology and the origins of maize agriculture in the lower Mississippi Valley and Caddoan culture areas. In *Paleopathology at the origins of agriculture,* edited by M. N. Cohen and G. J. Armelagos, 393–424. Orlando, Florida: Academic Press.

Rose, J. C., and P. Hartnady

    1991   Interpretation of infectious skeletal lesions from a historic Afro-American cemetery. In *Human paleopathology: Current syntheses and future options,* edited by D. J. Ortner and A. C. Aufderheide, 119–27. Washington, D.C.: Smithsonian Institution Press.

Rozaire, C. E.

    1963   *Lake-side cultural specializations in the Great Basin.* Nevada State Museum Anthropological Papers no. 9:72–77. Carson City.

Ruff, C. B.

    1987   Sexual dimorphism in human lower limb bone structure: Relationship to subsistence strategy and sexual division of labor. *Journal of Human Evolution* 16:391–416.

    1989   New approaches to structural evolution of limb bones in primates. *Folia Primatologica* 53:142–59.

    1992   Biomechanical analyses of archaeological human material. In *The skeletal biology of past peoples,* edited by S. R. Saunders and A. Katzenburg, 41–62. New York: Alan R. Liss.

    1994   Biomechanical analysis of northern and southern Plains femora: Behavioral implications. In *Skeletal biology in the Great Plains: A multidisciplinary view,* edited by D. W. Owsley and R. L. Jantz, 235–45. Washington, D.C.: Smithsonian Institute Press.

    1995   Biomechanics of the hip and birth in early *Homo. American Journal of Physical Anthropology* 98:527–74.

Ruff, C. B., and W. C. Hayes

1982   Subperiosteal expansion and cortical remodeling of the human femur and tibia with aging. *Science* 217:945–48.

1983a   Cross-sectional geometry of Pecos Pueblo femora and tibiae: A biomechanical investigation, I: Method and general patterns of variation. *American Journal of Physical Anthropology* 60:359–81.

1983b   Cross-sectional geometry of Pecos Pueblo femor and tibiae: A biomechanical investigation, II: Sex, age, and side differences. *American Journal of Physical Anthropology* 60:383–400.

Ruff, C. B., and C.S. Larsen

1990   Postcranial biomechanical adaptations to subsistence strategy changes on the Georgia coast. In *The archaeology of Mission Santa Catalina de Guale,* vol. 2: *Biocultural interpretation of a population in transition,* edited by C. S. Larsen, 94–120. American Museum of Natural History Anthropological Papers no 68. New York.

Ruff, C. B., C. S. Larsen, and W. C. Hayes

1984   Structural changes in the femur with the transition to agriculture on the Georgia coast. *American Journal of Physical Anthropology* 64:125–36.

Ruff, C. B., and F. P. Leo

1986   Use of computed tomography in skeletal structural research. *Yearbook of Physical Anthropology* 29:181–95.

Ruff, C. B., and J. A. Runestad

1992   Primate limb bone structural adaptations. *Annual Review of Anthropology* 21:407–33.

Ruff, C. B., W. W. Scott, and A. Y.-C. Liu

1991   Articular and diaphyseal remodeling of the proximal femur with changes in body mass in adults. *American Journal of Physical Anthropology* 86:397–413.

Ruff, C. B., E. Trinkaus, A. Walker, and C. S. Larsen

1993   Postcranial robusticity in *Homo,* I: Temporal trends and mechanical interpretation. *American Journal of Physical Anthropology* 91:21–53.

Ruff, C. B., A. Walker, and E. Trinkaus

1994   Postcranial robusticity in *Homo,* III: Ontogeny. *American Journal of Physical Anthropology* 93:35–54.

Russell, K. W., M. E. Stuart, J. A. Brannan, and H. M. Weymouth

1989   *Archaeological reconnaissance in the Ogden/Weber River marshes.* Weber State College Reports of Investigation no. 89–1. Ogden, Utah.

Rust, H. N.

1905   The obsidian blades of California. *American Anthropologist* 7:688–95.

Ruvolo, M.

1987   Reconstructing genetic and linguistic trees: Phenetic and cladistic approaches. In *Biological metaphor and cladistic classification: An interdisciplinary perspective,* edited by H. M. Hoenigswald and L. F. Wiener, 193–216. Philadelphia: University of Pennsylvania Press.

Sahlins, M.

1972   *Stone Age economics.* Chicago: Aldine.

Sampson, C. G.

1985   *Nightfire Island: Later Holocene lakemarsh adaptations on the western edge of the Great Basin.* University of Oregon Anthropological Papers no. 33. Eugene.

Sarker, G., S. Sommer
  1990   Shedding light on PCR contamination. *Nature* 343:27.
Saunders, S. R., and M. A. Katzenberg, eds.
  1992   *The skeletal biology of past peoples: Advances in research methods.* New York: Wiley-
            Liss.
Schell, L. M., and B.S. Blumberg
  1988   Alloalbuminemia and the migrations of Native Americans. *Yearbook of Physical
            Anthropology* 31:1–13.
Schmitt, D. N., S. R. Simms, and G. P. Woodbury
  1994   Archaeological salvage investigations at a Fremont site in the Jordan River delta.
            Utah Archaeology 7:69–80.
Schoeninger, M. J.
  1985   Trophic level effects on $^{15}N/^{14}N$ and $^{13}C/^{12}C$ ratios in bone collagen and stron-
            tium levels in bone mineral. *Journal of Human Evolution* 14:515–25.
  1989   Prehistoric human diet. In *Chemistry of prehistoric human bone,* edited by T. D.
            Price, 38–67. Cambridge, England: Cambridge University Press.
  1995a   Dietary reconstruction in the prehistoric Carson Desert: Stable carbon and ni-
            trogen isotopes analysis. In *Bioarchaeology of the Stillwater Marsh: Prehistoric hu-
            man adaptation in the western Great Basin,* edited by C. S. Larsen and R. L. Kelly,
            96–106. American Museum of Natural History Anthropological Papers no. 77.
            New York.
  1995b   Stable isotope studies in human evolution. *Evolutionary Anthropology* 4:83–98.
Schoeninger, M. J., and M. J. DeNiro
  1984   Nitrogen and carbon isotopic composition of bone collagen from marine and
            terrestrial animals. *Geochimica et Cosmochimica Acta* 48:625–39.
Schoeninger, M. J., U. T. Iwaniec, and K. E. Glander
  1997   Stable isotope ratios monitor diet and habitat use in New World monkeys. *Amer-
            ican Journal of Physical Anthropology* 103:69–83.
Schoeninger, M. J., K. M. Moore, M. L. Murray, and J. C. Kingston
  1989   Detection of bone preservation in archaeological and fossil samples. *Applied Geo-
            chemistry* 4:281–92.
Schour, I., and M. Massler
  1941   The development of the human dentition. *Journal of the American Dental Associ-
            ation* 28:1153–60.
  1944   *Chart: Development of the human dentition.* 2d ed. Chicago: American Dental As-
            sociation.
Schultz, M.
  1993   Initial stages of systematic bone disease. In *Histology of ancient human bone:
            Methods and diagnosis,* edited by G. Grupe and A. N. Garland, 185–203. Berlin:
            Springer-Verlag.
Schulz, P. D., and H. M. McHenry
  1975   Age distribution of enamel hypoplasias in prehistoric California Indians. *Journal
            of Dental Research* 54:913–20.
Schurr, M. R.
  1992   Isotopic and mortuary variability in a Middle Mississippian population. *Ameri-
            can Antiquity* 57:300–320.
  1997   Stable nitrogen isotopes as evidence for the age of weaning at the Angel site:

A comparison of isotopic and demographic measures of weaning age. *Journal of Archaeological Science* 24:919–27.

Schurr, T. G., S. W. Ballinger, Y. Gan, J. A. Hodge, D. A. Merriwether, D. N. Lawrence, W. C. Knowler, K. M. Weiss, and D. C. Wallace

    1990   Amerindian mitochondrial DNAs have rare Asian mutations at high frequencies, suggesting they derived from four primary maternal lineages. *American Journal of Human Genetics* 46:613–23.

Schwarcz, H. P., J. Melbye, M. A. Katzenburg, and M. Knyf

    1985   Stable isotopes in human skeletons of southern Ontario: Reconstructing paleodiet. *Journal of Archaeological Science* 12:187–206.

Schwarcz, H. P., and M. J. Schoeninger

    1991   Stable isotope analyses in human nutritional ecology. *Yearbook of Physical Anthropology* 34:283–321.

Sciulli, P. W.

    1978   Developmental abnormalities of the permanent dentition in prehistoric Ohio Valley Amerindians. *American Journal of Physical Anthropology* 48:193–98.

Scozzari, R., F. Cruciani, P. Santolamazza, D. Sellitto, D. E. C. Cole, L. A. Rubin, D. Labuda, E. Marini, V. Succa, G. Vona, and A. Torroni

    1997   MtDNA and Y chromosome-specific polymorphisms in modern Ojibwa: Implications about the origin of their gene pool. *American Journal of Human Genetics* 60:241–44.

Scrimshaw, N. S.

    1964   Ecological factors in nutritional disease. *American Journal of Clinical Nutrition* 14:112–22.

    1975   Interactions of malnutrition and infection: Advances in understanding. In *Protein-calorie malnutrition,* edited by R. E. Olson, 353–67. New York: Academic Press.

Scrimshaw, N. S., and V. R. Young

    1976   The requirements of human nutrition. *Scientific American* 235:51–64.

Seltzer, C. C.

    1943   Anthropometry and arthritis. *Medicine* 22:163–203.

Selye, H.

    1973   The evolution of the stress concept. *American Scientist* 61:692–99.

Sharp, N. D.

    1989   Redefining Fremont subsistence. *Utah Archaeology 1989* 2:19–31.

Shearer, G. B., and D. H. Kohl

    1994   Information derived from variation in the natural abundance of ^{15}N in complex biological systems. In *Isotopes in organic chemistry: Heavy atom isotope effects,* edited by E. Buncel and W. H. J. Saunders, 191–237. Amsterdam: Elsevier Science.

Shearer, G. B., D. H. Kohl, R. A. Virginia, B. A. Bryan, J. L. Skeeters, E. T. Nilsen, M. R. Sharifi, and P. W. Rundel

    1983   Estimates of N2-fixation from variation in the natural abundance of ^{15}N in Sonoran Desert ecosystem. *Oecologia* 56:365–73.

Shearin, N. L., E. J. King, and D. H. O'Rourke

    1989   DNA preservation in pre-Columbian remains from the American Southwest. *Human Evolution* 4:263–70.

Shearin, N. L., C. J. Loveland, R. L. Parr, and D. Sack
  1996   A Late Archaic burial from the Thursday site, Utah. *Journal of California and Great Basin Anthropology* 18:155–68.
Shields, G. F., K. Hecker, M. I. Voevoda, and J. K. Reed
  1992   Absence of the Asian-specific Region V mitochondrial marker in native Beringians. *American Journal of Human Genetics* 50:758–65.
Shields, G. F., A. M. Schmiechen, B. L. Frazier, A. Redd, M. I. Voevoda, J. K. Reed, and R. H. Ward
  1993   MtDNA sequences suggest a recent evolutionary divergence for Beringian and northern North American populations. *American Journal of Human Genetics* 53:5449–562.
Shields, W. F., and G. F. Dalley
  1978   *The Bear River No. 3 site.* Miscellaneous Collected Paper no. 22. University of Utah Anthropological Papers no. 99:55–104. Salt Lake City: University of Utah Press.
Shuey, R. T.
  1979   Appendix I: Archeomagnetic dating at the Levee site. In *The Levee site and the Knoll site,* by G. F. Fry and G. F. Dalley, 103–6. University of Utah Anthropological Papers no. 100. Salt Lake City: University of Utah Press.
Siegel, S.
  1956.   *Nonparametric statistics for the behavioral sciences.* New York: McGraw-Hill.
Simms, S. R.
  1984   Aboriginal Great Basin foraging strategies: An evolutionary analysis. Ph.D. diss., Department of Anthropology, University of Utah, Salt Lake City. Ann Arbor: University Microfilms.
  1985   Acquisition cost and nutritional data on Great Basin resources. *Journal of California and Great Basin Anthropology* 7(1):117–26.
  1986   New evidence for Fremont adaptive diversity. *Journal of California and Great Basin Anthropology* 8:204–16.
  1987   *Behavioral ecology and hunter-gatherer foraging: An example from the Great Basin.* BAR International Series no. 381. Oxford, England: British Archaeological Reports.
  1988   Some theoretical bases for archaeological research at Stillwater Marsh. In *Preliminary investigations in Stillwater Marsh: Human prehistory and geoarchaeology,* edited by C. Raven and R. G. Elston, 413–19. U.S. Department of the Interior Fish and Wildlife Service, Region 1, Cultural Resource Series no. 1. Portland, Oregon.
  1990   Fremont transitions. *Utah Archaeology 1990* 3:1–18.
  1993   The past as commodity: Consultation and the Great Salt Lake skeletons. *Utah Archaeology 1993* 6:1–5.
  1994   Unpacking the Numic spread. In *Across the West: Human population movement and the expansion of the Numa,* edited by D. B. Madsen and D. Rhode, 76–83. Salt Lake City: University of Utah Press.
Simms, S. R., and K. Heath
  1990   Site structure of the Orbit Inn: An application of ethnoarchaeology. *American Antiquity* 55:797–812.
Simms, S. R., C. J. Loveland, and M. E. Stuart
  1991   *Prehistoric human skeletal remains and the prehistory of the Great Salt Lake wetlands.* Utah State University Contributions to Anthropology no. 6. Logan.

Simms, S. R., and M. E. Stuart

1993 Prehistory and past environments of the Great Salt Lake wetlands. In *Archaeological test excavations in the Great Salt Lake wetlands and associated sites,* edited by W. B. Fawcett and S. R. Simms, 5–31. Utah State University Contributions to Anthropology no. 14. Logan.

1999 Prehistory of the Great Salt Lake wetlands. In *Great Salt Lake, Utah, 1980–1998,* edited by J. W. Gwynn (update). Salt Lake City: Utah Geological Survey.

Simms, S. R., M. E. Stuart, S. Beckstead, E. Jensen, and S. Sarver

1990 *Archaeological reconnaissance in the lower Bear River marshes, Utah.* Utah State University Contributions to Anthropology no. 13. Logan.

Simms, S. R., A. Ugan, and J. Bright

1997 Plain-ware ceramics and residential mobility: A case study from the Great Basin. *Journal of Archaeological Science* 24:779–92.

Simms, S. R., A. Ugan, S. Jackson, and J. Bright

1993 Ceramics and behavior. In *Archaeological text excavations in the Great Salt Lake wetlands and associated sites,* edited by W. B. Fawcett and S. R. Simms, 139–69. Utah State University Contributions to Anthropology no. 14. Logan.

Simms, S. R., and S. N. Whitesides

1993 Lithics and behavior. In *Archaeological test excavations in the Great Salt Lake wetlands and associated sites,* edited by W. B. Fawcett and S. R. Simms, 170–84. Utah State University Contributions to Anthropology no. 14. Logan.

Skinner, M., and A. H. Goodman

1992 Anthropological uses of developmental defects of enamel. In *Skeletal biology of past peoples: Research methods,* edited by S. R. Saunders and M. A. Katzenberg. New York: Wiley-Liss.

Smith, B., and S. Epstein

1971 Two categories of $^{13}C/^{12}C$ ratios for higher plants. *Plant Physiology* 47:380–84.

Smith, D. G., R. L. Bettinger, and B. K. Rolfs

1995 Serum albumin phenotypes at Stillwater: Implications for population history in the Great Basin. In *Bioarchaeology of the Stillwater Marsh: Prehistoric human adaptation in the western Great Basin,* edited by C. S. Larsen and R. L. Kelly, 68–72. American Museum of Natural History Anthropological Papers no. 77. New York.

Smith, D. G., J. G. Lorenz, S. Kanthaswamy, and R. L. Bettinger

1999 Ethnohistorical implications of the distributions of albumin Naskapi and albumin Mexico in Native Americans. *American Journal of Physical Anthropology.* (In press)

Smith, S. J.

1994 Fremont settlement and subsistence practices in Skull Valley, northern Utah. *Utah Archaeology 1994* 7:51–69.

Sokoloff, L.

1969 *The biology of degenerative disease.* Chicago: University of Chicago Press.

Speth, L. K.

1969 Possible fishing cliques among the Northern Paiutes of the Walker River reservation, Nevada. *Ethnohistory* 16:225–44.

Spielmann, K. A., M. J. Schoeninger, K. Moore

1990 Plains-Pueblo interdependence and human diet at Pecos Pueblo, New Mexico. *American Antiquity* 55:745–65.

Spier, L.
   1930   *Klamath ethnography.* University of California Publications in American Archaeology and Ethnology no. 30. Berkeley.
SPSS, Inc.
   1995   *Statistical package for the social sciences (SPSS®), 6.1 for the Macintosh™.* Chicago, Illinois.
Stafford, T. W., Jr., P. E. Hare, L. Currie, A. J. T. Jull, and D. Donahue
   1990   Accuracy of North-American human skeleton ages. *Quaternary Research* 34:111–20.
Stark, B. L.
   1981   The rise of sedentary life. In *Supplement to the Handbook of Middle American Indians,* vol. 1: *Archaeology,* edited by J. Sabloff, 345–72. Austin: University of Texas Press.
   1986   Origins of food production in the New World. In *American archaeology past and future: A celebration of the Society for American Archaeology, 1935–1985,* edited by D. J. Meltzer, D. D. Fowler, and J.A. Sabloff, 277–321. Washington D.C.: Smithsonian Institution.
Stark, C.
   1983   The determination of variation in skeletal remains in Nevada through the use of discrete morphological traits and anthropometry. M.A. thesis, University of Nevada, Las Vegas.
Steinbock, R. T.
   1976   *Paleopathological diagnosis and interpretation.* Springfield: Charles C. Thomas.
Stenhouse, M. J., and M. S. Baxter
   1977   Bomb ^{14}C as a biological tracer. *Nature* 245:828–32.
   1979   The uptake of bomb ^{14}C in humans. In *Radiocardon dating,* edited by R. Berger and H. E. Suess, 324–41. Proceedings of the Ninth International Radiocarbon Dating Conference. Berkeley: University of California Press.
Stephens, D. W., and J. R. Krebs
   1986   *Foraging theory.* Princeton: Princeton University Press.
Stern, T.
   1966   *The Klamath tribe: A people and their reservation.* American Ethnological Society Monograph no. 41. Seattle: University of Washington Press.
Steward, J. H.
   1933   *Early inhabitants of western Utah.* Bulletin of the University of Utah 23(7):1–34. Salt Lake City.
   1936   *Pueblo material culture in western Utah.* University of New Mexico Bulletin no. 287, Anthropological Series, vol. 1, no. 3. Albuquerque.
   [1938] 1999 *Basin-Plateau aboriginal sociopolitical groups.* Bureau of American Ethnology Bulletin no. 120. Washington, D.C. Reprint. Salt Lake City: University of Utah Press.
   1940   Native cultures of the Intermountain (Great Basin) area. In *Essays in historical anthropology of North America, published in honor of John S. Swanton.* Smithsonian Miscellaneous Collections no. 100:445–502. Washington, D.C.: Smithsonian Institution.
Stewart, O. C.
   1939   *The Northern Paiute bands.* University of California Anthropological Records, no. 2(3):127–49. Berkeley.

1941   *Culture element distributions,* pt. 14: *Northern Paiute.* University of California Anthropological Records no. 4:361–446. Berkeley.

Stewart, T. D.

1958   The rate of development of osteoarthritis in identification. *The Leech* 28:144–51.

1979   *Essentials of forensic anthropology.* Springfield: Charles C. Thomas.

Stine, S.

1993   Extreme persistent drought in California and Patagonia during Mediaeval time. *Nature* 369:546–49.

Stodder, A. L. W.

1994   Bioarchaeological investigations of protohistoric pueblo health and demography. In *In the wake of contact: Biological responses to conquest,* edited by C. S. Larsen and G. R. Milner, 97–107. New York: Wiley-Liss.

Stodder, A. L. W., and D. L. Martin

1992   Health and disease in the Southwest before and after Spanish contact. In *Disease and demography in the Americas,* edited by J. W. Verano and D. H. Ubelaker, 55–73. Washington, D.C.: Smithsonian Institution Press.

Stone, A. C., and M. Stoneking

1993   Ancient DNA from a pre-Columbian Amerindian population. *American Journal of Physical Anthropology* 92:463–71.

1998   MtDNA analysis of a prehistoric Oneota population: Implications for the peopling of the New World. *American Journal of Human Genetics* 62:1153–70.

Storey, R.

1992   *Life and death in the ancient city of Teotihuacan.* Tuscaloosa: University of Alabama Press.

Strong, E.

1960   *Stone age on the Columbia River.* Portland, Oregon: Binfords and Mort.

Strong, W. D., W. E. Schenck, and J. H. Steward

1930   *Archaeology of The Dalles-Deschutes region.* University of California Publications in American Archaeology and ethnology no. 29(1). Berkeley.

Stuart-Macadam, P.

1985   Porotic hyperostosis: Representative of a childhood condition. *American Journal of Physical Anthropology* 66:391–98.

1987a   Porotic hyperostosis: New evidence to support the anemia theory. *American Journal of Physical Anthropology* 74:521–26.

1987b   A radiographic study of porotic hyperostosis. *American Journal of Physical Anthropology* 74:511–20.

1992   Porotic hyperostosis: A new perspective. *American Journal of Anthropology* 87:39–47.

Stuart-Macadam, P., and S. Kent, eds.

1992   *Diet, demography, and disease.* New York: Aldine de Gruyter.

Stuiver, M., and P. J. Reimer

1993   Extended ^{14}C data base and revised CALIB 3.0 ^{14}C age calibration program. *Radiocarbon* 35:215–30.

Suchey, J. M., S. T. Brooks, and D. Katz

1988   Instructional materials accompanying female pubic symphyseal models of Suchey-Brooks system. Distributed by France Casting (Diane France, 2190 West Drake Road, Suite 259, Ft. Collins, Colorado 80526).

Suchey, J. M., D. V. Wiseley, R. F. Green, and T. T. Noguichi
    1979   Analysis of dorsal pitting in the os pubis in an extensive sample of modern American females. *American Journal of Physical Anthropology* 51:517–40.

Suckling, G.
    1989   Developmental defects of enamel: Historical and present-day prespectives of their pathogenesis. *Advances in Dental Research* 3:87–94.

Suckling, G., D. C. Elliot, and D. C. Thurley
    1986   The macroscopic appearance and associated histological changes in the enamel organ of hypoplastic lesions of sheep incisor teeth resulting from induced parasitism. *Archives of Oral Biology* 31:427–39.

Suga, S.
    1989   Enamel hypomineralization viewed from the pattern of progressive mineralization of human and monkey developmental enamel. *Advances in Dental Research* 3:188–98.

Sumner, D. R.
    1984   Size, shape, and bone mineral content of the human femur in growth and aging. Ph.D. diss., University of Arizona, Tucson.

Sutherland, L. D., and J. M. Suchey
    1987   Use of the ventral arc in sex determination of the os pubis. Paper presented at the 39th annual meeting of the American Academy of Forensic Sciences, San Diego, California.

Sutton, M. Q.
    1991   Approaches to linguistic prehistory. *North American Archaeologist* 12:303–24.

Sutton, M. Q., and D. Rhode
    1994   Background to the Numic problem. In *Across the West: Human population movement and the expansion of the Numa,* edited by D. B. Madsen and D. Rhode, 6–15. Salt Lake City: University of Utah Press.

Suzuki, T.
    1991   Paleopathological study on infectious diseases in Japan. In *Human paleopathology: Current syntheses and future options,* edited by D. J. Ortner and A. C. Aufderheide, 128–39. Washington, D.C.: Smithsonian Institution Press.

Swanson, E. H.
    1962   Early cultures in northwestern America. *American Antiquity* 28:151–58.

Swärdstedt, T.
    1966   *Odontological aspects of a medieval population from the Province of Jämtland/mid-Sweden.* Translated by D. Burton. Stockholm: Tiden-Barnängen Tryckerier.

SYSTAT
    1992   *SYSTAT: Graphics.* Version 5.2 edition. Evanston, Illinois: SYSTAT, Inc.

Szathmáry, E. J. E., and N. S. Ossenberg
    1978   Are the biological differences between North American Indians and Eskimos truly profound? *Current Anthropology* 19:673–701.

Talbot, R. K.
    1997   Fremont architecture. In *Clear Creek Canyon archeological project,* vol. 5, *Results and synthesis,* by J. C. Janetski, R. K. Talbot, D. E. Newman, L. D. Richens, J. D. Wilde, S. B. Baker, and S. E. Billat, 177–328. Brigham Young University Museum of Peoples and Cultures Technical Series 95–9. Provo, Utah.

Talbot, R. K., and J. D. Wilde
    1989   Giving form to the Formative. *Utah Archaeology 1989* 2:3–18.

Taylor, P. G.
  1996   Reproducibility of ancient DNA sequences from extinct Pleistocene fauna. *Molecular Biology and Evolution* 13:283–85.
Thomas, D. H.
  1981   How to classify the projectile points from Monitor Valley, Nevada. *Journal of California and Great Basin Anthropology* 3:7–43.
  1983   *The archaeology of Monitor Valley*, pt. 1: *Epistemology.* American Museum of Natural History Anthropological Papers 58(1). New York.
  1988   *The archaeology of Monitor Valley*, pt. 3: *Survey and additional excavations.* American Museum of Natural History Anthropological Papers 66(2). New York.
  1994   Chronology and the Numic expansion. In *Across the West: Human population movement and the expansion of the Numa,* edited by D. B. Madsen and D. Rhode, 56–61. Salt Lake City: University of Utah Press.
———, ed.
  1985   *The archaeology of Hidden Cave, Nevada.* American Museum of Natural History Anthropological Papers 61(1). New York.
Tieszen, L. L.
  1991   Natural variations in the carbon isotope values of plants: Implications for archaeology, ecology, and paleoecology. *Journal of Archaeological Science* 18:227–48.
  1994   Stable isotopes on the Plains: Vegetation analyses and diet determinations. In *Skeletal biology in the Great Plains: Migration, warfare, health and subsistence,* edited by D. W. Owsley and R. L. Janz, 261–82. Washington, D.C.: Smithsonian Institution Press.
Tieszen, L. L., T. W. Boutton, K. G. Tesdahl, and N. A. Slade
  1983   Fractionation and turnover of stable carbon isotopes in animal tissues: Implications for ^{13}C analysis of diet. *Oecologia* 57:32–37.
Tieszen, L. L., and T. Fagre
  1993a   Carbon isotopic variability in modern and archaeological maize. *Journal of Archaeological Science* 20:25–40.
  1993b   Effect of diet quality and composition on the isotopic composition of respiratory CO_2, bone collagen, bioapatite, and soft tissue. In *Prehistoric human bone: Archaeology at the molecular level,* edited by J. B. Lambert and G. Grupe, 121–55. New York: Springer-Verlag.
Timoshenko, S. P., and J. M. Gere
  1972   *Mechanics of materials.* New York: Van Nostrand Reinhold.
Toepel, K. A., R. Minor, and R. L. Greenspan
  1984   *Archaeological testing in Diamond Valley, Malheur National Wildlife Refuge, Harney County, Oregon.* Heritage Researh Associates Report no. 30. Submitted to the U.S. Fish and Wildlife Service. (Report on file, Malheur National Wildlife Refuge, Princeton, Oregon)
Torroni, A., Y.-S. Chen, O. Semino, A. S. Santachiara-Beneceretti, C. R. Scott, M. T. Lott, M. Winter, and D. C. Wallace
  1994   MtDNA and Y-chromosome polymorphisms in four Native American populations from southern Mexico. *American Journal of Human Genetics* 54:303–18.
Torroni, A., T. G. Schurr, M. F. Campbell, M. D. Brown, J. V. Neel, M. Larsen, D. G. Smith, C. M. Vullo, and D. C. Wallace
  1993a   Asian affinities and continental radiation of the four founding Native American mtDNAs. *American Journal of Human Genetics* 53:563–90.

Torroni, A., R. I. Sukernik, T. G. Schurr, Y. B. Starikovskaya, M. F. Campbell, M. H. Craw-
ford, A. G. Comuzzie, and D. C. Wallace
  1993b MtDNA variation of aboriginal Siberians reveals distinct genetic affinities with
         Native Americans. *American Journal of Human Genetics* 53:591–608.
Torroni, A., T. G. Schurr, C. Yang, E. J. E. Szathmary, R. C. Williams, M. S. Schanfield,
G. A. Troup, W. C. Knowler, D. N. Lawrence, K. M. Weiss, and D. C. Wallace
  1992   Native American mitochondrial DNA analysis indicates that the Amerind and
         the Nadene populations were founded by two independent migrations. *Genetics*
         130:153–62.
Train, P., J. R. Henrichs, and W. A. Archer
  1957   *Medicinal uses of plants by Indian tribes of Nevada.* Lawrence, Massachusetts:
         Quarterman Publications.
Trinkaus, E., S. E. Churchill, and C. B. Ruff
  1994   Postcranial robusticity in *Homo,* II: Humeral bilateral asymmetry and bone plas-
         ticity. *American Journal of Physical Anthropology* 93:1–34.
Trinkaus, E., S. E. Churchill, I. Villemeur, K. G. Riley, J. A. Heller, and C. B. Ruff
  1991   Robusticity versus shape: The functional interpretation of Neandertal appendic-
         ular morphology. *Journal of Anthropological Society of Nippon* 99:257–78.
Trinkaus, E., and C. B. Ruff
  1989   Diaphyseal cross-sectional morphology and biomechanics of the Fond-de-Forêt
         1 femur and the Spy 2 femur and tibia. Bulletin de la Société royale belge d'An-
         thropologie et de Préhistoire. *PrJhist.* 100:33–42.
  1996   Early modern human remains from East Asia: The Yamashita-cho 1 immature
         postcrania. *Journal of Human Evolution* 30:299–314.
Troughton, J. H., K. A. Card, and C. H. Hendy
  1974   Photosynthetic pathways and carbon isotope discrimination by plants. *Carnegie
         Institution Year Book* 73:768–80.
Trygg, E. E.
  1971   A study of the McLeod artifact collection from south central Oregon. M.A. the-
         sis, Department of Anthropology, University of Oregon, Eugene.
Tuohy, D. R.
  1973   Nevada's non-ceramic culture sphere. *Tebiwa* 16:54–61.
Tuohy, D. R., A. J. Dansie, and M. B. Haldeman
  1987   *Final report on excavations in the Stillwater Marsh Archaeological District, Nevada.*
         Nevada State Museum Department of Anthropology Archaeological Service
         report to the regional office of the U.S. Fish and Wildlife Service, Portland, Ore-
         gon. (Copy on file at the Nevada State Museum, Carson City).
Turner, C.
  1979   Dental anthropological indications of agriculture among the Jomon people of
         central Japan. *American Journal of Physical Anthropology* 51:619–36.
Tuross, N.
  1994   The biochemistry of ancient DNA in bone. *Experientia* 50:530–35.
Tuross, N., and M. L. Fogel
  1994   Stable isotope analysis and subsistence patterns at the Sully site. In *Skeletal biol-
         ogy in the Great Plains: Migration, warfare, health and subsistence,* edited by D. W.
         Owsley and R. L. Jantz, 283–90. Washington, D.C.: Smithsonian Institution
         Press.

Ubelaker, D. H.

    1984   Prehistoric human biology of Ecuador: Possible temporal trends and cultural correlations. In *Paleopathology at the origins of agriculture,* edited by M. N. Cohen and G. J. Armelagos, 491–513. Orlando, Florida: Academic Press.

    1989   *Human skeletal remains: Excavation, analysis, interpretation.* Washington, D.C.: Taraxacum.

    1992a   Enamel hypoplasia in ancient Ecuador. In *Recent contributions to the study of enamel developmental defects,* edited by A. H. Goodman and L. L. Capasso, 207–17. Journal of Paleopathology Monographic Publications no. 2. Chieti, Italy: Associazione Anthropologica Abruzzese.

    1992b   Porotic hyperostosis in prehistoric Ecuador. In *Diet, demography, and disease: Changing perspectives on anemia,* edited by P. Stuart-Macadam and S. Kent, 201–17. Hawthorne: Aldine de Gruyter.

Ugan, A., and S. R. Simms

    1994   Ceramic investment and behavior. Paper presented at the 24th Great Basin Anthropological Conference, Elko, Nevada.

Upham, S.

    1988   Archaeological visibility and the underclass of prehistory. *American Antiquity* 53:245–61.

    1994   Nomads of the Desert West: A shifting continuum in prehistory. *Journal of World Prehistory* 8:113–67.

Van Gerven, D. P., R. Beck, and J. R. Hummert

    1990   Patterns of enamel hypoplasia in two medieval populations from Nubia's Batn El Hajar. *American Journal of Physical Anthropology* 82:413–20.

Van Gerven, D. P., J. R. Hummert, and D. B. Burr

    1985   Cortical bone maintenance and geometry of the tibia in prehistoric children from Nubia's Batn el Hajar. *American Journal of Physical Anthropology* 66:275–80.

Virginia, R. A., and C. C. Delwiche

    1982   Natural ^{15}N abundance of presumed N^2-fixing and non-N^2-fixing plants from selected ecosystems. *Oecologia* 54:317–25.

Vogel, J. C.

    1978   Isotopic assessment of the dietary habits of ungulates. *South African Journal of Science* 74:298–301.

Vogel, J. C., A. S. Talma, A. J. Hall-Martin, and P. J. Viljoen

    1990   Carbon and nitrogen isotopes in elephants. *South African Journal of Science* 86:147–50.

Wada, E. T.

    1980   Nitrogen isotope fractionation and its significance in biogeochemical processes occurring in marine environments. In *Isotope marine chemistry,* edited by E. D. Goldberg, Y. Horibe, and K. Saruhaski, 375–98. Tokyo, Japan: Uchida Rokakuho Publishing.

Wada, E. T., T. Kadonaga, and S. Matsuo

    1975 ^{15}N abundance in nitrogen of naturally occurring substances and global assessment of denitrification from isotopic viewpoint. *Geochemical Journal* 9:139–48.

Wahlen, M.

    1994   Carbon dioxide, carbon monoxide and methane in the atmosphere: Abundance and isotopic composition. In *Stable isotopes in ecology and environmental science,* edited by K. Lajtha and R. H. Mitchener, 93–113. Oxford, England: Blackwell Scientific Publications.

Waldron, T.

1992   Osteoarthritis in a Black Death cemetery in London. *International Journal of Osteoarchaeology* 2:235–40.

Walker, P. L.

1986   Porotic hyperostosis in a marine-dependant California Indian population. *American Journal of Physical Anthropology* 69:345–54.

Walker, P. L., and S. E. Hollimon

1989   Changes in osteoarthritis associated with the development of a maritime economy among southern California Indians. *International Journal of Anthropology* 4:171–83.

Wallace, D. C., K. Garrison, and W. C. Knowler

1985   Dramatic founder effects in Amerindian mitochondrial DNAs. *American Journal of Physical Anthropology* 68:149–55.

Wallace, D. C., and A. Torroni

1992   American Indian prehistory as written in the mitochondrial DNA: A review. *Human Biology* 64:403–16.

Waller, S. S., and J. K. Lewis

1979   Occurrence of C_3 and C_4 photosynthetic pathways in North American grasses. *Journal of Range Management* 32:12–28.

Ward, R. H., B. L. Frazier, K. Dew-Jager, and S. Pääbo

1991   Extensive mitochondrial diversity within a single Amerindian tribe. *Proceedings of the National Academy of Science* 88:8720–24.

Webb, S.

1989   *Prehistoric stress in Australian aborigines.* BAR International Series no. 490. Oxford, England: British Archaeological Reports.

1995   *Paleopathology of aboriginal Australians: Health and disease across a hunter-gatherer continent.* Cambridge, England: Cambridge University Press.

Weide, M. L.

1968   Cultural ecology of lakeside adaptation in the western Great Basin. Ph.D. diss., University of California, Los Angeles. Ann Arbor: University Microfilms.

1974   *North Warner subsistence network: A prehistoric band territory.* Nevada Archaeological Survey Research Papers no. 5:62–79. Reno.

1978   On the correspondence between villages and wetlands in the Great Basin. *Journal of California Anthropology* 5:289–92.

Weiss, K. M., and E. B. Woolford

1986   Comments. *Current Anthropology* 27:491–92.

Welkie, G. W., and M. Caldwell

1970   Leaf anatomy of species in some dicotyledon families as related to the C_3 and C_4 pathways of carbon fixation. *Canadian Journal of Botany* 48:2135–46.

Whalen, M. E.

1994   *Turquoise Ridge and Late Prehistoric residential mobility in the desert Mogollon region.* University of Utah Anthropological Papers no. 118. Salt Lake City: University of Utah Press.

Wheat, M. M.

1967   *Survival arts of the primitive Paiutes.* Reno: University of Nevada Press.

White, C., and H. Schwarcz
  1994   Temporal trends in stable isotopes for Nubian mummy tissues. *American Journal of Physical Anthropology* 93:165–88.
White, T. D.
  1991   *Human osteology.* San Diego: Academic Press.
Whiting, B. B.
  1950   *Paiute sorcery.* Viking Fund Publications in Anthropology no. 15. New York.
Whitlock, C., and P. J. Bartlein
  1993   Spatial variations of Holocene climate change in the Yellowstone region. *Quaternary Research* 39:231–38.
Wigand, P. E.
  1985   Diamond Pond, Harney County, Oregon: Man and marsh in the eastern Oregon desert. Ph.D. diss., Department of Anthropology, Washington State University, Pullman.
  1987   Diamond Pond, Harney County, Oregon: Vegetation history and water table in the eastern Oregon desert. *Great Basin Naturalist* 47:427–58.
  1990   The study of links between climate and human activities in the Lahontan Basin. In *Studies of climatic variations and their impact on the Great Basin,* compiled by J. Warburton, 64–117. Final report, contract #NA878A-D-CP114, National Climatic Center Program Office, National Oceanic and Atmospheric Administration. Rockville, Maryland.
Wigand, P. E., and P. J. Mehringer, Jr.
  1985   Pollen and seed analyses. In *The archaeology of Hidden Cave, Nevada,* edited by D. H. Thomas, 108–24. American Museum of Natural History Anthropological Papers 61(1). New York.
Williams, J. A.
  1994   Disease profiles of Archaic and Woodland populations in the northern Plains. In *Skeletal biology in the Great Plains: Migration, warfare, health, and subsistence,* edited by D. W. Owsley and R. L. Jantz, 91–108. Washington, D.C.: Smithsonian Institution Press.
Williams, R. C., A. G. Steinberg, H. Gershowitz, P. H. Bennett, W. C. Knowler, D. J. Pettitt, W. Butler, R. Baird, L. Dowda-Rea, T. A. Burch, H. G. Morse, and C. G. Smith
  1985   GM allotypes in Native Americans: Evidence for three distinct migrations across the Bering land bridge. *American Journal of Physical Anthropology* 66:1–19.
Wilson, A. C., R. L. Cann, S. M. Carr, M. George, U. B. Gyllensten, K. M. Helm-Bychowski, R. G. Higuchi, S. R. Palumbi, E. M. Prager, R. D. Sage, and M. Stoneking
  1985   Mitochondrial DNA and two perspectives on evolutionary genetics. *Biological Journal of the Linnean Society* 26:375–400.
Winterhalder, B.
  1986   Diet choice, risk and food sharing in a stochastic environment. *Journal of Anthropological Archaeology* 5:369–92.
Wolff, J.
  1892   *Das Gesetz der Transformation der Knochen,* Berlin: A. Hirchwild.
Wolley, A. M.
  1988   Prehistoric zinc nutrition: Archaeological, ethnographic, skeletal and chemical evidence. M.A. thesis, Department of Anthropology, University of Nebraska, Lincoln.

Woo, S. L. Y., S. C. Kuei, D. Amiel, M. A. Gomez, W. C. Hayes, F. C. White, and W. H. Akeson

    1981   The effect of prolonged physical training on the properties of long bones: A study of Wolff's law. *Journal of Bone and Joint Surgery* 63A:780–87.

Yakir, D., and Y. Israeli

    1995   Reduced solar irradiance effects on net primary productivitiy (NPP) and the $\delta^{13}C$ and $\delta^{18}O$ values in plantations of *Musa* sp., Musaceae. *Geochimica et Cosmochimica Acta* 59:2149–51.

Young, D. A., and R. L. Bettinger

    1992   The Numic spread: A computer simulation. *American Antiquity* 57:85–99.

Zeanah, D. W.

    1996   Predicting settlement patterns and mobility strategies: An optimal foraging analysis of hunter-gatherer use of mountain, desert, and wetland habitats in the Carson Desert. Ph.D. diss., University of Utah, Salt Lake City.

Zeanah, D. W., J. A. Carter, D. P. Dugas, R. G. Elston, and J. E. Hammett

    1995   *An optimal foraging model of hunter-gatherer land use in the Carson Desert.* Report in partial fulfillment of U.S. Fish and Wildlife Service Contract #14–48–0001–93015(DB), prepared for U.S. Fish and Wildlife Service and U.S. Department of the Navy. Copies available from Intermountain Research, Silver City, Nevada.

Zeanah, D. W., and S. R. Simms

    1999   Modeling the gastric: Great Basin subsistence studies since 1982 and the evolution of general theory in Great Basin archaeology. In *Models for the millennium,* edited by C. Beck. Salt Lake City: University of Utah Press.

Zeier, C. D., and R. G. Elston

    1992   *Changes in Washoe land use patterns: A study of three archaeological sites in Diamond Valley, Alpine County, California.* Madison: Prehistory Press.

Zeveloff, S. I., and F. R. Collett

    1988   *Mammals of the Intermountain West.* Salt Lake City: University of Utah Press.

Zimmerman, L

    1988   Human bones as symbols of power: Aboriginal American belief systems toward bones and "grave robbing" archaeologists. In *Conflict in the archaeology of living traditions,* edited by R. Layton, 211–16. One World Archaeology no. 8. Winchester, Maryland: Unwin Hyman.

Contributors

Robert L. Bettinger
University of California
Department of Anthropology
Davis, CA 95616

Jason R. Bright
Department of Anthropology
University of Utah
Salt Lake City, UT 84112

Shawn W. Carlyle
Department of Anthropology
University of Utah
Salt Lake City, UT 84112

Joan Brenner Coltrain
Department of Anthropology
University of Utah
Salt Lake City, UT 84112

Brian E. Hemphill
Department of Sociology and
    Anthropology
California State University, Bakersfield
Bakersfield, CA 93311

Dale L. Hutchinson
Department of Anthropology
East Carolina University
Greenville, NC 27858

Frederika A. Kaestle
Department of Anthropology
Yale University
New Haven, CT 06520

Robert L. Kelly
Department of Anthropology
University of Wyoming
Laramie, WY 82071

Clark Spencer Larsen
Department of Anthropology and Re-
    search Laboratories of Archaeology
University of North Carolina
Chapel Hill, NC 27599-3120

Joseph G. Lorenz
Analytical Genetic Testing Center
Cherry Creek South Drive, Suite 201
Denver, CO 80231

Carol J. Loveland (deceased)
Department of Sociology, Social Work,
    and Anthropology
Utah State University
Logan, UT 84322

Greg C. Nelson
Department of Anthropology
University of Oregon
Eugene, OR 97403

Albert C. Oetting
Heritage Research Associates, Inc.
1997 Garden Avenue
Eugene, OR 97403

Dennis H. O'Rourke
Department of Anthropology
University of Utah
Salt Lake City, UT 84112

Anan W. Raymond
U.S. Fish and Wildlife Service
c/o Tualatin River National Wildlife
    Refuge
20555 SW Gerda Lane
Sherwood, OR 97140

Christopher B. Ruff
Department of Cell Biology and
    Anatomy
Johns Hopkins School of Medicine
725 North Wolfe Street
Baltimore, MD 21205

Margaret J. Schoeninger
Department of Anthropology
University of Wisconsin
Madison, WI 53705

Steven R. Simms
Department of Sociology, Social Work,
    and Anthropology
Utah State University
Logan, UT 84322

David Glenn Smith
Department of Anthropology
University of California
Davis, CA 95616

Thomas W. Stafford, Jr.
Institute of Arctic and Alpine Research
University of Colorado
Boulder, CO 80309

David Hurst Thomas
Department of Anthropology
American Museum of Natural History
Central Park West at 79th Street
New York, NY 10024

Index

adaptive diversity: and ceramic use, 50–51; ethnographic comparisons and evidence for in Harney Basin, 203–18; and evidence from Great Salt Lakes Wetlands Project, 38–49; introduction to concept of, 21–23; and physiological stress in skeletal samples from Great Salt Lake wetlands, 115–16; population, peoples, and migrations in Great Salt Lake wetlands and, 51–54; Great Salt Lake skeletal series and risk reduction, 103; and variability in behavior, 49, 331–32

age: and dental hypoplasias in skeletal samples from Great Salt Lake wetlands, 109, 110; and dental hypoplasias in skeletal samples from Malheur Lake, 231; and dental hypoplasias in skeletal samples from Stillwater Marsh, 192; and formation of transverse lines, 112; and osteoarthritis in skeletal samples from Stillwater Marsh, *193*; and osteoarthritis in skeletal samples from Malheur Lake, 227, 253, *263*, 266, *267*, *270*; and prevalence of osteoarthritis, 243; and subadult mortality in skeletal samples from Great Salt Lake wetlands, 115. *See also* age at death

age at death: and diets of Great Salt Lake wetlands, 70–72, *73*; establishment of for subadult skeletons, 105–106; identification of in skeletal samples from Stillwater Marsh, 313; and osteoarthritis in skeletal sample from Malheur Lake, 232, 253, 262, 262, 266, 268, 274, 277–78, 280, 287. *See also* age

agriculture. *See* farming

Alabama, and study of biomechanical strengthening of long bones, 245

albumin phenotype identification, and molecular genetic analysis, 174

Algonkian language group, and molecular genetics, 168–69, 179

Anasazi: and carbon isotope analysis of diet, 72, *74*; diet of and farming, 30; and Fremont culture in Great Salt Lake wetlands, 53; and molecular genetic analysis of samples from Great Salt Lake wetlands, 96, 97, 100, 101

Andrews, J., 104, 111, 113, 114

anemia, iron-deficiency and porotic hyperostosis: in skeletal samples from Great Salt Lake wetlands, 113–14; in skeletal samples from Stillwater Marsh, 191, 202

animals. *See* bighorn sheep; bison; fauna and faunal assemblages; hunting

Antevs, E., 221, 222

Apache, 98–99

Archaeological Resources Protection Act (ARPA), 12–13

Armelagos, G. J., 109

Athabascan-speaking populations, and molecular genetic analysis, 52, 99, 168–69, *171–72*, 178, 179

Backhoe Village site (Utah), 72–73, 82

Baillert, G., 86

Barlow, K. R., 41, 122, 127

base camps, and foraging in Stillwater Marsh and Stillwater Mountains, 126–29. *See also* sedentarism; villages

Baumhoff, M. A., 182

beam model, of long-bone diaphyseal morphology, 290

Bear River sites (Great Salt Lake wetlands), 35, 36

behavior: adaptive diversity and variability in, 49; behavioral options and adaptive diversity of Fremont culture, 41; impact of stress on, xviii; osteopathology and analysis of skeletal samples from Stillwater Marsh, 191–94, 196–202; skeletal structure and patterns of in Great Basin populations, 290–320

Berry, M. S., 58–59

Bettinger, R. L., 6, 182

bighorn sheep: and environment of Stillwater Marsh, 119; and food procurement in Stillwater Mountains, 130, 132, 134, 155. *See also* fauna and faunal assemblages; hunting

Binford, L. R., 121, 247

bioarchaeology: Great Basin and insights offered by, 3–4; and interpretation of Harney Basin sites, 216–18; recent advances in, 185; use of term, xvii. *See also* biological anthropology

biological anthropology: contributions of to excavation team, xvii; and model of adaptive diversity in Great Salt Lake wetlands, 45–49; and osteoarthritis as indicator of mobility, 243; and reconstruction of past dietary patterns, 3. *See also* bioarchaeology